D1564019

MY CAMPAIGN IN IRELAND

THE WORKS OF

JOHN HENRY NEWMAN

BIRMINGHAM ORATORY

MILLENNIUM EDITION

VOLUME XVI

SERIES EDITOR

JAMES TOLHURST DD

ASSOCIATE EDITOR

ANDREW NASH MA PhD

MY CAMPAIGN IN IRELAND

PART I

BY

JOHNN HENRY CARDINAL NEWMAN

with an Introduction and Notes
by

PAUL SHRIMPTON

GRACEWING

Printed for private circulation only 1896

Published in the Birmingham Oratory Millennium Edition
in 2021
by
Gracewing
2 Southern Avenue
Leominster
Herefordshire HR6 0QF

www.gracewing.co.uk

Typography by Andrew Nash.

ISBN 978 0 85244 409 2

CONTENTS

SUPPLEMENT

APPENDIX

ABBREVIATIONS

AW	*John Henry Newman: Autobiographical Writings*, ed. H. Tristram (London: Sheed & Ward, 1956)
BOA	Birmingham Oratory archives
CUG	*Catholic University Gazette* 1–55 (1854–56)
DDA	Dublin diocesan archives
DIB	*Dictionary of Irish Biography*
HS	*Historical Sketches*, vol. iii (1872; London: Longmans, Green & Co., 1909)
Idea	*The Idea of a University: Defined and Illustrated 1. In Nine Discourses Delivered to the Catholics of Dublin, 2. In Occasional Lectures and Essays Addressed to the Members of the Catholic University* (1873; London: Longmans, Green & Co., 1907)
Idea, ed. Ker	*The Idea of a University*, ed. I. T. Ker (Oxford: Clarendon, 1976)
JHN	John Henry Newman
L&H	Literary and Historical Society

LD	*Letters and Diaries of John Henry Newman*, 32 vols, ed. C. S. Dessain *et al.* (London: T. Nelson, 1961–72; Oxford: Clarendon Press, 1973–2008)
MC	*My Campaign in Ireland, Part 1: Catholic University Reports and Other Papers*, ed. W. Neville (Aberdeen [Ireland]: A. King & Co., 1896)
MM	P. Shrimpton, *The 'making of men': the* Idea *and reality of Newman's university in Oxford and Dublin* (Leominster: Gracewing, 2014)
NU	F. McGrath, *Newman's University: Idea and Reality* (London: Longmans, Green & Co., 1951)
ODNB	*Oxford Dictionary of National Biography*
Royal Commission Endowed Schools (1858)	*Report of Her Majesty's Commissioners Appointed to Inquire into the Endowments, Funds, and Actual Condition of All Schools Endowed for the Purpose of Education in Ireland*, British Parliamentary Papers, 1858, vol. xxi
Royal Commission Queen's Colleges (1858)	*Report of Her Majesty's Commissioners Appointed to Inquire into the Progress and Condition of the Queen's Colleges at Belfast, Cork, and Galway: with minutes of evidence, Documents, and Tables and Returns*, British Parliamentary Papers, 1858, vol. xxi

Abbreviations

Royal Commission Trinity College (1853)	*Report of Her Majesty's Commissioners Appointed to Enquire into the State, Discipline, Studies and Revenues of the University of Dublin and of Trinity College, together with Appendices, containing Evidence, Suggestions, and Correspondence*, British Parliamentary Papers, 1853, vol. xlv
UCDA	University College Dublin archives
WPN	William Paine Neville

EDITOR'S INTRODUCTION

This volume of John Henry Newman's Dublin university papers, *My Campaign in Ireland, Part I*, was collected and arranged by William Neville, who acted as Newman's private secretary from 1875 until Newman's death in 1890. He had it printed for private circulation in 1896, and since then it has only been reproduced in facsimile; the printed original is vanishingly rare. This volume is the first critical edition of the work. The entire text has been re-set, and comprehensive editorial footnotes have been added to elucidate the significance of the volume's various documents by providing a historical context for Newman's endeavours in Dublin.

Posthumously published six years after Newman's death, *My Campaign in Ireland, Part I,* brings together the most important documents penned by Newman in the 1850s in his efforts to establish the first Catholic university in Ireland (what would later become University College Dublin). Newman became involved in the campaign for a university in 1851 at the request of the Irish Catholic bishops, who were seeking to provide an alternative to the non-denominational Queen's Colleges established by the British government in 1845. He agreed to be the founding Rector in 1851, but it was not until November 1854 that the university opened its doors; finding his dual roles of Provost of the Birmingham Oratory and Rector of the Catholic University to be incompatible, he resigned the post in 1858.

If 'all' this volume contained were Newman's university papers, it would already be a treasure, but there is an additional item that makes it very special: the 'missing discourse' from Newman's educational classic, *The Idea of a University* (1873). The first half of the *Idea* comprises nine of the ten discourses that Newman composed in 1852; after appearing separately as pamphlets, they were printed together as *Discourses on the Scope and Nature of University Education* (1852). However, Discourse V was omitted from the 1859 edition of the *Discourses* – and indeed from all nine editions of the *Idea*. Although Newman did not give any reason for the omission, it seems it was mainly because Discourse V did not fit in easily with the other discourses. Neither was it reprinted in Newman's collected works: other than the 1852 publications just mentioned (of which few copies survive), it can only be found in the critical edition of the *Idea* by the leading Newman scholar Ian Ker. There, Ker argues that Discourse V 'provides a devastating contrast between modern fragmented secularist education and an integrated liberal education in the Christian tradition, and is therefore one of the most eloquent parts of the Discourses'.[1]

My Campaign in Ireland, Part I also contains the original version of Discourse I, which was abridged and incorporated into Discourse II for the 1859 edition of the *Discourses*. When the discourses appeared in the *Idea* (1873), Discourse I was restored, but only the first section; this was because the second section had been written for a local, Dublin audience with the specific purpose of preparing for the foundation of the Catholic University, while the *Idea* was a treatise on university education for a universal audience. But given that *My Campaign in Ireland, Part I* is mainly about events contemporaneous with the discourses, the compiler of the volume, William Neville,

---

[1] *Idea*, ed. Ker, p. xxxvi.

(rightly) judged that Discourse I should be given in its entirety.

Newman's fame in education is almost entirely due to the discourses and lectures that went to form the *Idea*. Indeed, the *Idea* has had an immense influence on both secular and Christian universities. Described by a leading historian of university education as 'unquestionably the single most important treatise in the English language on the nature and meaning of higher education',[2] it is endlessly cited, especially by those who take a 'high' view of a university education and see Newman as the most inspiring advocate of a liberal education.

That Newman provides a much-needed educational vision for today is hardly contentious, because it is generally recognised that the *Idea* provides an attractive alternative to the shapeless, relativistic and uninspiring outlook of so many contemporary universities. The concept of a university as an institution of unique purpose has all but dissolved; modern universities increasingly function as performance-oriented, heavily bureaucratic organisations committed to a narrowly economic conception of human excellence. Just as Newman battled against destructive trends within education in his own day, so others fight in our own times against the lack of direction and loss of vision of the modern university. In attempting to recover a sense of purpose, several of these modern critiques use the *Idea* as a key point of reference,[3] and some use Newman as

---

[2] S. Rothblatt, 'An Oxonian "Idea" of a University: J. H. Newman and "Well-being"', *The History of the University of Oxford* vi, ed. M. G. Brock & M. C. Curthoys (Oxford: OUP, 1997), p. 287.

[3] Examples include: D. Maskell & I. Robinson, *The New Idea of a University* (2001); G. Graham, *Universities: The Recovery of an Idea* (2002); S. Collini, *What are Universities For?* (2012); M. Higton, *A Theology of Higher Education* (2012), as well as MacIntyre's *God, Philosophy, Universities* (2009).

the pivotal figure in their analysis.[4] It is unsurprising that his educational vision, with the pastoral idea at its root, is an ideal foil to the schemes of modern-day planners, since the bureaucratic is the rival of *caritas*, the engine of true education.

Yet the *Idea* is incomplete, and even those familiar with Newman's thinking are apt to overlook the fact that it was not intended to be a systematic or exhaustive treatment of a subject – and that indeed key elements of his thinking barely feature in it, or are missing altogether. It is easy to forget that the purpose of the discourses was *not* to inspire or guide future generations, but the much more immediate task of winning over his audience to the type of university he was trying to set up. The historical context is vital for understanding why Newman developed the arguments he did, as they were composed to deal with the particular problems he faced in 1852. In writing the discourses, he dwelt extensively on what he considered was the *essence* of the university, not its fully functioning state and pastoral well-being.

One of the 'problems' of the *Idea* lies in its idealism, for if it inspires some readers, it has the opposite effect on others. They may admire the high ideals, but they simultaneously dismiss them on account of their perceived impracticality. Thus Roy Jenkins, a former Chancellor of Oxford University, confessed that the *Idea* left him dazzled but intellectually unsatisfied; 'Newman had mostly held me spellbound in the grip of his prose, but he had convinced me neither that he had a practical plan for an Irish university in the 1850s or that he had left guidelines of great relevance

---

[4] Newman is the pivotal figure in Jaroslav Pelikan's *The Idea of the University: A Re-examination* (1992) and in Sheldon Rothblatt's *The Modern University and its Discontents: The Fate of Newman's Legacies in Britain and America* (1997).

for a university of any nationality or any or no faith today'.[5] Jenkins seems to have been unaware that Newman had taken a leading part in the reform of Oxford University while he was a Fellow at Oriel College (1822–45), which was leading that reform; or that Newman managed to bring the Catholic University into being almost singlehandedly.

The lecturers and professors at the Catholic University were well aware of the onerous task Newman had taken on; they knew from personal experience that virtually every aspect of life at the University came into being through his hands. Besides overseeing academic affairs, the financial administration, the launching of new faculties and schools, delivering lectures each term, preaching sermons and even editing the weekly *Catholic University Gazette*, Newman also acted as the academic and moral conscience of the University. Despite all the administrative pressures bearing down on him, he continued to give priority to his dealings with the academic staff. This emphasis resonated with his abiding concern for the pastoral well-being of the University. All this and more emerges from the university papers which comprise this volume, and they serve as an instructive 'corrective' to the *Idea*.

Unfortunately, few of those involved in institutions of higher education know about Newman's organisation and government of the Catholic University; and of these, fewer still even know of the existence of *My Campaign in Ireland, Part I* let alone have consulted it. Thanks to William Neville and to Gracewing's decision to include this volume in their Newman Millennium Edition, Newman's university papers will, I hope, become much better known. On the occasion of Newman's elevation to the cardinalate in 1879, Bartholomew Woodlock, his successor as Rector of the Catholic University, spoke about the value of these papers:

---

[5] 'Newman and the Idea of a university', *Newman: A Man for our Time*, ed. D. Brown (London: SPCK, 1990), p. 155.

'we feel assured that the plan for the higher education and the system of University government which you initiated and organized, will, centuries hence, be studied by all who may have to legislate for Catholic education, as among the most precious of the documents which they shall possess to inform and guide them.'[6] It is to be hoped this volume will enable that prophecy to come true.

It was no simple task for Newman to translate his vision into a living institution, for he faced a series of nearly insurmountable difficulties: an absence of a university tradition among Irish Catholics, and little appreciation of the purpose of a liberal education; a complete lack of experience in dealing with students *qua* students; serious financial constraints in the years following the Great Famine; a population which was dispirited and had little confidence in new ventures; deep divisions between the clergy and the educated laity, manifested in clerical high-handedness and lay anticlericalism; a British government which refused even to recognise the new foundation, let alone provide financial aid or grant it a charter; and a good dose of anti-English feeling within Ireland. Though these difficulties severely hampered Newman's plans and meant that the university which emerged bore only a limited likeness to his ideal, Newman's plans and deeds are instructive for everyone with a stake in higher education, because they illustrate how this great Christian humanist adapted his principles to the Irish situation of the mid-1850s.

One of the key principles which runs through all Newman's university papers was his concern that young students living away from home should find a 'home from home' at the crucial juncture in life between childhood and adulthood. This, like other working rules that guided

[6] From the 'Address from the Rector and Senate of the Catholic University of Ireland', which can be found in full on pp. [413–15].

Newman in setting up the Catholic University, is not easily deduced from any blow-by-blow account of life at the University during his rectorship: it emerges more clearly from his university papers and private correspondence as they record the way his plans evolved and thereby reveal what was of fundamental importance to him and what was marginal.

There are six key documents that effectively contain the essence of Newman's evolving plan and they were written in six successive years: the 'Report on the Organization of the Catholic University of Ireland' (October 1851),[7] which he co-wrote with two others; his first major memorandum about the university project, 'The Statement of August 14th 1852';[8] the memorandum written when 86 St Stephen's Green was acquired as the central University building (19 February 1853);[9] the memorandum composed (29 April 1854) for the episcopal synod of 1854;[10] the annual Report for 1854–55 (completed in October 1855);[11] and the 'Scheme of Rules and Regulations' (submitted to the University Council in April 1856).[12] All of these are foundational documents – and this includes the 1854–55 Report and the 'Rules and Regulations', because they distilled Newman's earlier thoughts about the University and gave them lasting literary expression.

The centrality of the lodging houses in Newman's scheme of education – missing from the *Idea* – is evident in all these documents and shows that Newman had a clear

---

[7] The Report and its Postscript can be found on pp. [77–87].

[8] The memorandum can be found on pp. [271–8].

[9] This, the 'Memorandum Relating to the Catholic University' (A 3.8, BOA), is not included in *My Campaign in Ireland, Part I.* A digest of its contents can be found in *MM*, pp. 86–9.

[10] The memorandum can be found on pp. [93–100]. The original uncorrected version can be found in *LD* xvi, pp. 557–61.

[11] This Report can be found on pp. [3–56].

[12] The 'Scheme of Rules and Regulations' can be found on pp. [101–45].

vision of his aims from the outset. Knowing he was operating under severe constraints in pioneering a Catholic university in a cultural environment that was foreign to him, in this matter as in others he adopted a flexible approach when translating his ideas into practical arrangements. After the first sketch of 1851, the details were gradually filled in, and occasionally some were erased or altered – but none of the modifications he was forced to make altered his overall conception.[13]

One idea running through these key documents is the notion of 'jurisdiction', to such an extent that it might seem that Newman was obsessed with it. Though it might seem that he was attempting to apply a legal concept to a setting where it was inappropriate, his preoccupation was more than a legal quibble. Legally, indeed, he was on strong ground, for most of the students were minors – the age of majority was then twenty-one years – and the University was therefore legally acting *in loco parentis*. But more importantly, Newman held strongly that the University undertook a grave responsibility of oversight for those who entered its doors; it acted on behalf of parents in its attentiveness to growth in virtue; it was 'an Alma Mater, knowing her children one by one, not a foundry, or a mint, or a treadmill'.[14] For someone with such an elevated understanding of the role of the university, it was not a matter of indifference whether jurisdiction could be exercised or not. This also explains why Newman had originally entertained the idea of the University and its collegiate houses being configured as a personal diocese.[15]

---

[13] The published 'Report for 1854–55' was, in fact, the first occasion the public were able to read about the system of lodging houses – and this included the bishops, since the memorandum of April 1854 did not descend to detail.

[14] *Idea*, pp. 144–5.

[15] For more about this scheme, see the relevant footnote on p. [23].

Newman felt strongly that those who put themselves under the University's jurisdiction were entitled to a deep intellectual and moral training, which would ideally include tutorial teaching. In the Report of October 1851 he wrote 'that the principal making of men must be by the Tutorial system'. What did he mean by this? As he explains elsewhere, he was convinced that personal influence is what gives any system its dynamism: the action of mind on mind, personality on personality, heart on heart. And if acquaintance became friendship, all the better, since friendship was the privileged way of doing good to someone; 'it requires one to be intimate with a person, to have a chance of doing him good', Newman once told his sister Jemima.[16] He was intent on giving a deep formation to students, a formation which operated at various levels: the intellectual, the moral, the spiritual. In particular, it operated on the human and the supernatural levels, according to an understanding that has a long tradition. Looking back from the twenty-first century, it seems overly ambitious to have attempted to introduce a modified version of the tutorial system into Ireland in the 1850s when the resources were pitiful and the demand non-existent. Yet it should be noted that Newman's aim was to adopt and adapt Oxbridge arrangements at a time when tutors were generally young academics who had not long graduated.[17]

All this – and more – is missing from the *Idea*.

Little else needs to be said by way of introduction to this volume, as William Neville undertook that task in his 64-page Advertisement: but some background detail about Neville himself and his intentions in printing this collection is called for.

---

[16] 8 February 1829, *LD* ii, p. 119.

[17] In 1828 the ages of the four tutors at Oriel were, respectively, thirty-four, twenty-seven (Newman), twenty-six and twenty-five.

William Paine Neville (1824–1905) was educated at Winchester College and Trinity College, Oxford. He was received into full communion with the Catholic Church in 1851, became a novice at the Birmingham Oratory the following year, and was ordained to the priesthood in 1861. While a novice, Neville stayed with Newman in Dublin for two months in 1854, where he assisted him during the first term of the Catholic University; he was, in fact, the only Oratorian who saw Newman at close quarters while he was Rector.[18] After the death of Ambrose St John in 1875, Neville became Newman's private secretary and, towards the end of his life, his carer. After Newman's death in 1890, he acted as his literary executor, seeing through to publication the documents that went to make up *Meditations and Devotions of the late Cardinal Newman* (1893), *My Campaign in Ireland, Part I* (1896), and *Addresses to Cardinal Newman and his Replies* (1905).[19]

My Campaign in Ireland, Part I was arranged and edited by Neville. Although the title indicates that this is only *Part I*, in fact no further parts were printed. However, one of the files in the Newman archive at the Birmingham Oratory is labelled 'My Campaign in Ireland Part II' (D 9.9); it consists of a cover note which reads, 'This must be *Part ii* of the "Irish Campaign"'. It is almost certain that this was the cover note for Newman's 'Memorandum about my Connection with the Catholic University' and its appendix. Quite probably the cover note got separated at the time when the memorandum was published as the last section of

[18] Neville stayed at 16 Harcourt Street, which was not only the Rector's house, but the collegiate house of St Mary's, which Newman presided over as dean. During his stay there (8 October to 8 December 1854) Neville wrote to the Birmingham Oratory with observations about how Newman dealt with the students and academics (Neville to St John, 21 November 1854, cited in *NU*, p. 344).

[19] *Addresses to Cardinal Newman and his Replies* was published shortly after Neville's death using the manuscript he had prepared.

Autobiographical writings (*AW*, 1956, pp. 277–333), edited by the Oratorian Henry Tristram. It seems clear, therefore, that the memorandum and its appendix were intended by Neville to form *My Campaign in Ireland, Part II*, to be printed or published at some later date. It is probable, too, that it was Neville's intention to append to this memorandum the collection of correspondence about the University which Newman had copied out and annotated.

There are two manuscripts of Newman's 'Memorandum about my connection with the Catholic University'. The first is a rough copy dated 25 November 1870, and it contains material that Newman later omitted, though some of it found a place in the appendix.[20] The second manuscript is the fair copy and consists of 172 pages, accompanied by an appendix (not included in *AW*) comprising a further 657 pages of letters or excerpts of letters – all but three of them in Newman's own hand – chosen to illustrate the story of the Catholic University.[21] The seventh section of the main text is dated 9 January 1873, and the four introductory pages which detail the contents of the papers record that they were put together on 31 May 1873. Thus the memorandum represents Newman's considered view of his 'Irish campaign' some fifteen years after standing down as the founding Rector.

In his introduction to this memorandum, the Oratorian and archivist C. Stephen Dessain remarks that Newman considered that the memorandum could be published at any time, as 'there was nothing compromising about it' (*AW*, p. 279). This is a bizarre statement, given the content of the memorandum – the detailed account of Newman's difficulties with Archbishop Paul Cullen and his doubts

---

[20] This rough draft can be found in the file B 4.1, BOA.

[21] The fair copy can be found in the file A 34.1, BOA, but without the appendix. The 657 pages of extracts can be found in files M3–M6, Dublin Papers (using the catalogue numbers of Teresa Iglesias), BOA.

about the 'perennial sagacity' of Pope Pius IX – and it is difficult to credit Newman with this observation. Newman's actual thoughts are recorded in a note dated 5 July 1876, where he says that 'it must be fully understood, that [...] I leave all my papers as *materials* and *documents* only, to be used simply at the discretion (for publication or not, in whole or in part) of the parties who after my death come into possession of my papers' (*AW*, p. x).[22]

As regards *My Campaign, Part I*, there are several peculiarities about this collection of documents that need to be addressed. Unlike the other volumes in the Newman Millennium Edition, the editorial decisions about *My Campaign, Part I* were carried out not by Newman but by Neville, and influenced, perhaps, by Ignatius Ryder, who succeeded Newman as provost of the Birmingham Oratory. The questions about these editorial decisions fall into three types.

The first questions concern publication. Why was *My Campaign in Ireland, Part I* 'printed for private circulation only' – with this wording printed prominently on the hard cover – and not published like the other two volumes that Neville edited? Why was it printed by Arthur King & Co., printers to the University of Aberdeen, and not by Longmans, Green and Co., who brought out the other two volumes? We do not know how many copies were run off, nor do we have a list of those to whom they were sent (although we do know some of the recipients, from the letters of thanks that Neville received).[23] In keeping with its status as a privately-printed volume, no reviews of *My*

[22] This note is missing from *LD* and has not been found. Shortly after writing it, Newman composed his 'Memorandum as to a Biography', 24 July 1876 (*LD* xxviii, pp. 93–4).

[23] 'Newman correspondence 1896', WPN papers, BOA. Recipients include the president of the Catholic University, the president of University College Dublin, and the president of the College of St Thomas Aquinas, Catholic University, Washington.

Campaign, Part I came out, though it was listed along with six other new books in a review article in 1898 on the 'Irish University Question' in the *Edinburgh Review*; the article refers to *My Campaign, Part I* only once, and then tangentially.[24]

The second set of questions concerns content. Why include 'Cathedra Sempiterna', a collection of extracts gathered by Newman in 1867 from Discourse I for the 1,800th anniversary of the martyrdom of the Apostles Peter and Paul, when it had no bearing on Newman's university, and was in any case followed by the full text of Discourse I? And why include the complete text of the *Biglietto* speech of 1879, which does not refer to the Catholic University or indeed *appear* to have any direct bearing on it?[25]

The third set of questions relates to why *My Campaign, Part II* was not published (or at least privately printed), when that would appear to have been Neville's original intention.

In addressing these questions it is useful to bear in mind

---

[24] *The Edinburgh Review* 187:383 (1 January 1898), pp. 101–29.

[25] In fact, the *Biglietto* speech was not out of place in *My Campaign, Part I*, as a letter from Newman to Catherine Froude makes clear. 'Curious it will be if Oxford is imported into Ireland, not in its members only, but in its principles, methods, ways and arguments. The battle there will be what it was in Oxford twenty years ago'. Newman goes on to spell out what this battle was: 'It is very wonderful,—Keble, Pusey, Maurice, Sewell, etc., who have been able to do so little against Liberalism in Oxford will be renewing the fight, although not in their persons, in Ireland' (14 October 1851, *LD* xiv, p. 389). In this sense, the foundation of the Catholic University can be seen as a new episode in Newman's life-long campaign against liberalism – though this was probably not obvious to most of the readers of *My Campaign, Part I*.

That said, in the Advertisement (p. [lii]) Neville does make this link. He quotes Newman to show that one reason for setting up the university was that of 'increasing the intellectual force of Ireland, to strengthen the defences, in a day of great danger, of the Christian religion'. Then Neville points out that this 'campaign against liberalism' was expressed years later in the *Biglietto* speech.

that the Birmingham Oratory was concerned about how best to safeguard Newman's legacy after his death. The correspondence of the Oratorians shows that they were all engaged in this task, above all William Neville, Newman's literary executor.[26] In order to make sense of Neville's decisions, it is therefore necessary to consult the detailed instructions Newman left him.

In his 'Memorandum on Future Biography', dated 15 November 1872, Newman explains why he did not want a biography written about him: in the *Apologia pro Vita Sua* (1864) he had 'virtually written my life up to 1845'; but if his life as a Catholic were 'attempted other men's toes will be trod upon, and the Life will be answered and a controversy ensue — or if nothing is said in the Life, *then again* there is a sure opening for controversy, for a reason must be given by the writer, *why* there is nothing to say — and this cannot be without throwing the blame on others, as bringing it about that there is nothing to say'. Newman realised that if friends did not write a life, strangers would take on the task, but he felt that the danger could be offset 'by publishing private papers, memoranda, letters of mine, in a volume or two, with a memoir of four pages or so, to introduce them'.[27]

In July 1876 Newman revisited this matter in his 'Memorandum As To a Biography'. There he concedes that an Anglican friend could write about his Anglican days, while stressing that he did not 'want a panegyric written of me, which would be sickening, but a real fair downright account of me according to the best ability and judgment of

---

[26] Besides the correspondence in the BOA, there is substantial collection about the writing of a biography of Newman and the publication of his letters in University of St Andrews Special Collections, RCMO, Papers of Wilfred Ward, 'Life of Cardinal Newman' (MSS 38347/VI-VII and 838348/B); and there are various other relevant items elsewhere in RCMO. Neville is the central figure in this correspondence.

[27] *LD* xxvi, pp. 200–1.

the writer'. As for his life as a Catholic, 'There is very little to say, unless at the risk of causing great scandal, controversy, partizanship. If my representatives in my behalf attacked others e.g. Barnabò or Manning, their friends would be sure to retort upon me, and this would not be edifying.' Newman made a note here that he had 'written with freedom about my dissatisfaction with the present state of Catholic affairs' to William Monsell (Lord Emly), Emily Bowles, the Earl of Dunraven (Lord Adare), T. W. Allies, 'perhaps to Sir John Acton', Robert Ornsby, W. G. Ward and Charlotte Wood[28] – all of whom were converts and three of whom had been heavily involved in the Catholic University.

In the 1872 memorandum Newman explains that, 'I have put into order several large collections of letters, or hope to do so, letters both my own and addressed to me, i.e. large collections of correspondence, which are *not* for publication — either because they are mainly the letters of others, or because they are so fragmentary; or because they relate to matters, which cannot be touched upon without getting into controversy.' The latter, important collections consist of his correspondence on four matters: *The Rambler* and the *Home and Foreign Review*; 'our quarrel with London House'; the Catholic University; and the translation of the Scriptures. 'These collections I make with the view of their being used, and only used, *in defence* — i.e. if enemies make misstatements or impute motives, these collections are authorities to refer to.'[29]

He spells out his meaning at length in an addition (dated 22 October 1876) to the memorandum of July 1876. Here he makes reference to the same four matters and writes, 'I wish all statements which reflect on others to be withheld from publication, unless and until reflections are published

[28] *LD* xxviii, p. 92n.
[29] *LD* xxvi, p. 201.

in any quarter against me'.[30] He goes on to say, 'But such publication is not to be determined on hastily, or without real necessity. [...] It is only on great provocation and grave reasons of expedience or propriety that one could consent to reopen the past.'[31]

In the absence of any particular need to defend Newman's educational work in Ireland, it seems that Neville felt that if he could not *publish* Newman's university papers, he could at least *print them for private circulation*. These papers excluded most of the correspondence about the Catholic University, so Neville would avoid going directly against Newman's clear stipulation that they should only be published to defend him. The long 'Memorandum about my Connection with Catholic University' and the collection of letters accompanying it appears to have been prepared by Newman for such an event, but it did not arise in his lifetime or, indeed, in the following years.

But there were other considerations affecting Neville's editorial decisions, and to understand these it is necessary to consider the wider background. It comes as a surprise to many people today to realise that during much of his life as a Catholic, Newman was mistrusted by influential members of the higher clergy, both in the United Kingdom and in Rome. After his article 'On Consulting the Faithful in Matters of Doctrine' (1859) was denounced to the Roman authorities for heresy and due to an administrative error in London not resolved – Rome waiting for an explanation and Newman offering one, but made to understand it was not necessary – Newman remained 'under a cloud' for many years. During the period 1859–64, Newman was on the

---

[30] On 7 August 1881 Newman added, 'I think my friends ought to do nothing; but, from the papers I leave, to correct misstatements, whether they are for me or against me' (*LD* xxviii, p. 93).

[31] *LD* xxviii, p. 93.

receiving end of gossip and slander: it was said that he had quarrelled with the Pope, that his school was out of control, that he was administratively impractical (as evidenced by difficulties at the Catholic University), that he was unable to manage others, that he was over-sensitive and difficult to work with, that he was thinking of returning to the Church of England, that he had preached in favour of Garibaldi and even sent him money, that the Birmingham Oratory was a failure for they had no vocations. Moreover, his theology was suspect, and it was spread about that he had never fully accepted Catholic teachings; he was a danger for the Catholic Church because he was attempting to introduce into it Protestant ideas and practices.

After 1862 the relationship between Newman and Henry Edward Manning became strained; this was to affect Newman considerably after 1865, when Manning became Archbishop of Westminster, not least because he was a leading Ultramontane. Various incidents contributed to the lack of understanding between them which are too complicated to summarise here. Suffice it to say that they were two very different characters, occupying different places in the public eye – living 'indoor and outdoor lives', as David Newsome puts it in his *Convert Cardinals* (1993). Manning was a man of action and practical intellect, who saw a single solution to a problem; Newman, who in his own way was also a man of action, had a speculative intellect, and saw all sides of a problem. At root, Manning was convinced that Newman lacked the Catholic spirit; and when he saw that Newman stood in his way, began to consider him an adversary of himself – and the Pope. Newman was aware of this, but was determined not to be pushed aside.[32]

---

[32] After telling a friend confidentially about the various ways in which Manning dealt with him and his schemes, Newman added: 'I don't impute to him any animosity to me – but I think he is of a nature to be

Newman used the last chapter of his *Apologia* to provide a general defence of Catholicism, arguing (against the extreme Ultramontanes) for elbow room in theology, where the interaction between the magisterium and theologians is depicted as creative for the life of the Church. The *Apologia* was a turning point for Newman both within and outside the Church, even though opposition to him in influential clerical quarters – other than from his own bishop – remained. In 1866, when the Pope's temporal power was under threat, a day of prayer for him was called. Newman obliged and preached a sermon on 'The Pope and the Revolution'. [33] It contained beautiful expressions of obedience and encouragement for his hearers to pray that the Papal States remain as they were; but it went on to say, that if God allowed them to be taken away, He would still care for his Church. For saying as much Newman was taken to be disloyal, and his sermon was submitted for inclusion on the Index.

Other events were used by Newman's detractors to tarnish his reputation and make him appear as a disloyal Catholic. The push for a strong definition of papal infallibility at the First Vatican Council in 1869–70 was led by Manning. Newman, by contrast was an 'inopportunist', as he considered that there was no special need calling for such a definition. He wrote privately to his bishop outlining his thoughts, expressing his fears and making reference to 'an aggressive and insolent faction'.[34] But the letter was made public, much to Newman's discomfort. When the 'moderate' definition was approved, Newman had no

determined to *crush* or to *melt* every person who stands in his way. He has his own views and is determined to carry them – and I must either go with him or be annihilated' (Newman to Charlotte Wood, 21 December 1866, *LD* xxii, p. 329).

[33] See the footnote on p. [416] for more about this sermon.

[34] Newman to Ullathorne, 28 November 1870, *LD* xxv, p. 19.

problem in accepting it fully.

In 1874 Gladstone issued a best-selling pamphlet on papal infallibility alleging that its definition deprived Catholics of their intellectual freedom and meant that their first allegiance was to a foreign power, that is, it called into question their civic loyalty. A response was needed and Newman provided one in the form of his *Letter to the Duke of Norfolk* (1875). In it he explains that interpretations by theologians were similar to the determination of the meaning of laws; definitions are of an abstract nature which needed to be applied to concrete situations and admitted of exceptions; theology had its own principles, which put a brake on the force and scope of the new teaching. The most quoted part of the letter was Newman's raising a toast, 'to the Pope if you please – still to Conscience first, and the Pope afterwards'.[35] Then, as now, this phrase is quoted out of context to justify dissent from the teaching of the Church's Magisterium.

In the years following Newman's death the allegations that Newman had not been loyal to Rome persisted. It was no doubt to undo the force of these allegations that Neville decided to include 'Cathedra Sempiterna' in the Supplement, even though its content was replicated in the (unrevised) Discourse I, which follows, and to give it prominence by making it the first piece in this section. The effect is to make Newman look like an ardent Ultramontanist, and on its own gives a misleading impression. The volume's contents clearly have a strategic purpose, and one might even say that its tactics are rather clumsy. Those in the know must have recognised that the Birmingham Oratory was doing more than merely providing some interesting information about Newman's work in Dublin.

---

[35] *Certain Difficulties felt by Anglicans* ii (Longman, Green and Co.: London, 1900), p. 261.

Discourse I, itself, contains the passage (omitted from the *Idea*) where Newman praises the perennial sagacity of papal decisions. Newman changed his mind about this precisely because he belatedly realised the Pope's ignorance of the true state of affairs in Ireland at that time. As he ruefully put it in the 1870s, 'I relied on the word of the Pope, but from the event I am led to think it not rash to say that I knew as much about Ireland as he did'.[36] Clearly, the publication of this memorandum in *Part II* would have supplied evidence for Ultramontane accusations about Newman's alleged disloyalty.

Newman did, however, hint at these changed views in his *Letter to the Duke of Norfolk*. There he gives the Pope having forbidden 'mixed' education in Ireland as an explicit example of papal teaching which is *not* infallible: 'orders which issue from him [the Pope] for the observance of particular countries, or political or religious classes, have no claim to be the utterances of his infallibility. If he enjoins upon the hierarchy of Ireland to withstand mixed education, this is no exercise of his infallibility'.[37]

The inclusion of the *Biglietto* speech in the Supplement was aimed at undermining a different set of accusations against Newman: that his writings were informed by an incomplete grasp of Catholic teaching and practice, and consequently were a danger to the life of the Church. Further background explanation is needed to contextualise this assertion.

When Newman was preparing for the priesthood in Rome in 1846–47, he was shocked by the poor state of both philosophy and theology, there being no proper study of Aristotle or St Thomas Aquinas. But within a decade or two there were clear signs of a scholastic revival in the Catholic

---

36 'Memorandum about my Connection with the Catholic University', *AW*, p. 320.
37 *Certain Difficulties felt by Anglicans* ii, p. 332.

Church. Consequently, Newman went out of favour as his writings were considered to be incompatible with scholasticism. Newman's thought remained an interesting alternative to the resurgent neo-scholasticism, as it engaged with the post-Enlightenment world in areas where Thomism had little to say; his mode of thinking was more in tune with modernity, but his thoughts were couched in a language many could not understand. Quite understandably, in times of intellectual confusion most Catholics opted for the safety of neo-scholasticism.

Up until the First Vatican Council, Newman's main propagator among German Catholics was the church historian Ignaz von Döllinger, but when he refused to accept the declaration on papal infallibility and was excommunicated, Newman's reputation suffered. When Newman's *Lectures on the Prophetical Office of the Church* (1837) were republished in 1878, the leading Ultramontane journal in Germany *Der Katholik* urged that Newman's writings should not be published without a good scholastic commentary, as they were theologically suspect and tainted with Protestant prejudices. [38] The revival of neo-scholasticism and its establishment as the dominant way of doing theology was boosted when Leo XIII brought out his encyclical *Aeterni Patris* (1879) on the restoration of Christian philosophy in the spirit of the Angelic Doctor, and created the Pontifical Academy of St Thomas Aquinas; he also gave instructions for the compilation of a critical edition, the so-called Leonine Edition, of the complete works of St Thomas.

Nevertheless, Newman's theology had not been officially censured, and so it presented an interesting alternative to the triumphant neo-scholasticism which appeared to some as static, unhistorical and overly-

[38] Claus Arnold, 'Newman's Reception in Germany: from Döllinger to Ratzinger', Newman lecture at Oriel College, Oxford, 2011.

intellectual theology. In France, from the 1880s onwards, there was widespread use, in theological and philosophical circles of the term *newmanisme*. Modernists, in particular, expressed enthusiasm for his ideas, to the point where Newman was labelled the 'father of modernism', a phrase which really applied to the biblical scholar and historian Alfred Loisy. There were certainly many superficial likenesses to modernism in Newman, but his writings simply did not support their arguments other than when they were quoted out of context or selectively. In 1896, the year when *My Campaign in Ireland, Part I* appeared, there were already signs of the modernist crisis.

The Protestant theologian Auguste Sabatier was the first to view Newman's *Essay on Development* (1845) from a modernist perspective: *The Apostle Paul: A Sketch of the Development of his Doctrine* appeared in translation in 1891 and *The Vitality of Christian Dogma* in 1898. A few years later, Loisy wrote for the *Revue du Clergé Français* on 'Christian Development According to Cardinal Newman' (1898–1901). When Pius X used *Lamentabili Sane Exitu* (1907) to condemn modernist errors in the exegesis of Holy Scripture and in the history and interpretation of dogma, his main target was the statements of Loisy. In response to two letters to *The Times* from the Irish priest George Tyrrell claiming that some of Newman's most cherished teachings were thereby condemned, referring to the 'toast' in Newman's *Letter to the Duke of Norfolk*, Pope Pius X wrote to refute the claim in a letter to the Bishop of Limerick, Edward O'Dwyer.[39] Another modernist who used Newman for his own agenda was Henri Bremond in the *Mystery of Newman* (1907).

The only modernist, if he was one – this is disputed –

---

[39] This letter can be found in full on the Newman Reader website at: http://www.newmanreader.org/controversies/index.html <accessed 22 July 2020>.

who understood Newman properly was the Baron Friedrich von Hügel, the learned son of an Austrian diplomat who had settled in England. He visited Newman at the Birmingham Oratory, and corresponded with him during the period 1874–84, thereafter continuing to meet and to correspond with Newman's successor at the Birmingham Oratory, Ignatius Ryder. Von Hügel encouraged and advised Bremond, Loisy and Tyrrell about which books of Newman to read; unlike Loisy and Tyrrell, he was not excommunicated.[40]

Given these and other developments affecting Newman's legacy, it was prescient of Neville to insert the *Biglietto* speech into the Supplement of *My Campaign, Part I*, as it makes a clear statement about Newman's lifelong struggle against liberalism in religion. Nine years later the *Biglietto* speech appeared in *Addresses to Cardinal Newman* (1905), the collection of addresses and replies given during the years 1879–81, after Newman was made a cardinal.

One further complication that Neville faced as editor of *My Campaign, Part I* was the private instruction (dated 3 December 1882) that Newman had left him about his papers; it concerned Ignatius Ryder, Newman's successor as provost of the Birmingham Oratory, and read:

> If it were necessary in my defence to publish any paper etc of mine, whether for my doctrine, for my conduct, or any other reason, I forbid Fr Ignatius Ryder being allowed to see it or to judge of it with a view to its publication. Of course I do *not* wish *him* to know of this prohibition — but I insist upon it, because his mind is so differently constructed from mine. I don't recollect him ever showing sympathy with any thing I

[40] These three paragraphs draw on H. F. Davis, 'The Catholicism of Cardinal Newman', *John Henry Newman: Centenary Essays* (London: Burns, Oates & Washbourne, 1945), pp. 36–52; K. Beaumont, 'The reception of Newman at the Time of the Modernist Crisis', *Receptions of Newman* (Oxford: OUP, 2015), pp. 156–76.

> have said or done <(My conscience bears me witness I have ever been doing kind things to *him*)> — he is sure to take a contradictory view — he has never taken my side — it is his rule to trip me up. I am not complaining but explaining. I suppose I have borne this, and without showing my pain, for 25 years.[41]

This put Neville in an almost impossible situation, since Ryder, as provost of the Oratory, would necessarily have had a say over the contents of *My Campaign, Part I* and its publication. Just a few weeks after Newman's death and after Ryder had become provost, Ryder read a memorandum to the Congregatio Deputata (which comprised Lewis Bellasis, Paul Eaglesim, William Neville and Thomas Pope) about 'the relationship between the Congregation & Fr Wm Neville (sole literary executor of the late Cardinal) as regards the editing & publication of the Cardinal's life and letters':

> The Congregation thinks it would be well that Fr Wm Neville should keep it informed, so far as this is possible, of the progress of the plan he is carrying out for editing the Cardinal's Catholic letters. This is the more appropriate seeing that the Congregation will consider itself bound to exercise an ultimate censorship both of the selected letters and of the biographical record to which they may be attached, and this whether the whole is Fr William Neville's sole work, or embraces in a more or less degree the work of other collaborators, but from the whole of which Fr Neville

[41] *LD* xxviii, p. 93n. The sentence in angle brackets <> is an interlinear explanation written by Newman. Meriol Trevor comments that 'Newman was anxious Ryder should not know of the prohibition, and probably never did know it, for he died before Neville. It was a fact that he often felt differently from Neville on the subject of Newman's papers and his biography, and that he altered many things in the House after Newman's death.' (*Light in Winter*, p. 544). Trevor makes a mistake here: Ryder died in 1907, two years after Neville.

> undertakes the recognised responsibility. Besides the rule enacting that any literary work of a member of the Congregation should be submitted before publication to the judgment of the Congregation, it must be obvious that in this instance the credit of the congregation is especially involved, and that in the eyes of the public, its responsibility will be inalienable.[42]

When *Meditations and Devotions* was published in 1893 Neville wrote in the Prefatory Notice (p. xiii) that he was indebted to Ryder and Eaglesim 'for some important suggestions and curtailments, for the sake of greater clearness'. This was a result of a resolution by the Congregatio Deputata on 27 March 1893 'that leave be given to Father Wm Neville to publish a volume of our Cardinal's Devotional papers, the Father [i.e. Ryder] & Fr Paul Eaglesim being appointed [as censors].'

When it came to *My Campaign, Part I*, it seems that Neville was able to avoid the 'ultimate censorship' of the Congregation by having the volume printed rather than published, and then distributed by 'private circulation'. This would have enabled him to comply with the strict letter of the ruling of the Congregatio Deputata and to prevent any interference with his selection of content or with his lengthy introduction. Not that there was anything controversial in the papers comprising *Part I*, for he writes in the Advertisement (p. [xxxv]) that Newman 'thought that they might be published at any time, for there was nothing compromising in them to any one.' (Not so, *Part II*.) The private circulation strategy gives us a picture of a deliberate, very cautious and defensive strategy on the part of Neville: to defend Newman's reputation in setting up and running the Catholic University, but to do so in a private way,

---

42 This entry in the Minute Book of the Birmingham Oratory is dated 10 November 1890.

avoiding public controversy.[43] Printing the volume in Aberdeen would have been a way of keeping it from attracting public notice.

More needs to be said about Ryder. When he became provost after Newman's death the atmosphere in the Birmingham Oratory changed noticeably. Ryder had studied at the English College in Rome and so had been formed in a very different way from Newman; he was also related to Manning, being his nephew by marriage. Despite having published pamphlets against the leading Ultramontane W. G. Ward, defending the moderate interpretation of the 1870 definition of papal infallibility, he was of the Manning stamp intellectually and was actually rather wary about some aspects of Newman's thought, or at least how it might be interpreted.[44]

Various strong reasons have been given for not printing *Part II*. An additional one is that the 'Memorandum about my Connection with the Catholic University' contains the following comment about Ryder: 'I am not, and have never been particularly intimate or open-hearted with Ignatius. He is not quite of my sort, and one does not make new friends, when one is old.'[45]

Since the printing of *Part II*, with Newman's comments about Pius IX's ignorance of Ireland and the various shortcomings of Archbishop Paul Cullen, would have been explosive, it is no surprise that it remained hidden away in the archives until it was published in *Autobiographical Writings* (1956).

---

[43] Referring to the 'great demand' to see Newman's correspondence, the Oratorian Henry Bellasis comments: "I suppose it is "Private Circulation Only". I always laugh when I read the word "only"; it is so emphatic and is so clearly to me the outcome of worry about "publication" or "no publication" (H. L. Bellasis to W. P. Neville, 2 May 1898, B034-F002-D001, BOA).

[44] I am grateful to Andrew Nash for pointing out these facts about Ryder.

[45] *AW*, p. 266.

As regards this edition of *My Campaign, Part I*, minor errors that appeared in the original text, such as inaccurate quotations – but not Newman's 'loose' quotations – have been corrected silently. Some of the more disconcerting nineteenth-century punctuation has been modernised: thus, for instance, 'Pius IX.' is given as 'Pius IX'. In addition, English translations have been supplied for letters that were originally in Latin. I have tried to refer to the original documents wherever possible, but as many of these are no longer available (lost or not extant) the text necessarily uses Neville's original volume of 1896 as *editio princeps*.

I am grateful to Tom Longford for asking me to undertake this critical edition for the Newman Millennium Edition. As Gracewing published *The 'making of men': the* Idea *and reality of Newman's university in Oxford and Dublin* (2014), Tom already knew of my research into Newman's practical contribution to university education. I am, nevertheless, honoured to be asked to take on this task. I am grateful to Dr Paul Haffner for his editorial encouragement, and to Dr Peter Damian Grint for his editorial advice, as well as his help, along with Jim Mirabal, with the translations from Latin into English. To Dr Andrew Nash I am greatly indebted for his patience and skill in handling the text and turning it into the handsome product that it is; he took great care in typesetting this volume to ensure that it approximated as closely as possible with the original. I also thank Dr James Tolhurst, the general editor of the Millennium Edition, who, along with Andrew Nash, encouraged me to enlarge this Introduction by urging me to explain the editorial decisions of Neville.

I am grateful to the Fathers of the Birmingham Oratory for allowing me access to the Newman archive and for looking up entries in their Minute Books and allowing me to quote from them. I would also like to thank Lawrence Gregory, the archivist at the Birmingham Oratory, for assisting me on my visits there to look at the Newman papers, and Daniel Joyce who deputised for Lawrence in his absence; also Prof. Teresa Iglesias, for her first-class work in cataloguing over 2,400 documents within the Dublin Papers sub-collection of the main Newman archive. Lastly I would like to thank a former pupil of mine, Bertie McIntosh, for his generous gift to me of an original copy of *My Campaign in Ireland, Part I*: his way of saying thanks for three year's teaching prior to heading off to Oriel College, Oxford. Little did he know how useful his gift would prove to be!

Paul Shrimpton

A NOTE ON THE TEXT

The typography and layout of the original printing of 1896 have been followed in this Gracewing edition as closely as is practicable, apart from the addition of editorial footnotes. To enable scholars to continue to refer to the page numbers of the original, they are shown in square brackets in the margins. All the cross-references in the footnotes use these page numbers in square brackets.

The final piece, a 'Note on Cardinal Newman's Preaching and Influence at Oxford', was separately paginated in the original. In order to avoid confusion, those marginal original page numbers are asterisked to indicate that they did not run on from the main text.

The original footnotes by Newman or Neville are those containing [JHN] or [WPN] respectively; any additional editorial content follows these initials. Footnotes without those initials are by this volume's editor.

[Original title page]

MY CAMPAIGN IN IRELAND

PART I.

CATHOLIC UNIVERSITY REPORTS

AND OTHER PAPERS

BY

CARDINAL NEWMAN

OF THE ORATORY

PRINTED FOR PRIVATE CIRCULATION ONLY

BY A. KING & CO.

PRINTERS TO THE UNIVERSITY, ABERDEEN

1896

ADVERTISEMENT

This volume contains various papers by the late Cardinal Newman relating to the Catholic University in Dublin, the Reports of which to the Archbishops and Bishops, being official papers, give the collection its title. Some extracts from the Letters of Pius IX,[1] and of Propaganda,[2] which are appended to this Advertisement, will help to show how the movement for a Catholic University in Ireland originated; Pius IX's earnestness for its commencement; and what led to Dr Newman's employment therein. The papers which are placed under the head of Supplement have previously been isolated and forgotten, but gathered together they have an interest of their own, and with the Reports and the Letters may serve to form a Memorial of events hitherto but little known, and now fast passing into oblivion. The whole will be preceded by an extract from Principal Shairp's *Studies in Poetry and Philosophy*, as giving an account of Dr Newman's preaching and influence in the University of Oxford, by one who, though an eye witness of what went on, was without personal acquaintance with him, and was unbiased by sympathies of country or religion.[3]

---

[1] Giovanni Maria Mastai Ferretti (1792–1878) was elected Pope in 1846 and served for over thirty-one years.

[2] The *Sacra Congregatio de Propaganda Fide* (Sacred Congregation for the Propagation of the Faith) was established for missionary work in 1622. Its title is often abbreviated to Propaganda Fide or just Propaganda. The United Kingdom (including Ireland from 1833) was regarded as missionary territory and under the jurisdiction of Propaganda until the early twentieth century. Propaganda was renamed in 1967 as the Congregation for Evangelisation of Peoples.

[3] Principal Shairp was a Scotchman, born in 1819. He held a Snell Exhibition at Balliol College, Oxford, residing there from 1840–1845. He was a layman, and throughout life a Presbyterian. He had not even thought of going to hear Newman preach until a college friend almost made him accompany him, and thus it was that, having followed up that

[x] There are three of these Reports, and they are here reprinted with their Appendices.

They were made by Dr Newman as Rector, in accordance with a Decree of the Archbishops and Bishops assembled in Dublin by order of Pius IX, May, 1854, requiring the Rector to send annually to the Archbishops, or to the *Cœtus Episcoporum*, if sitting, a Report on the University. But, it may be asked, why, since he was Rector during seven years, from November, 1851, to November, 1858, are there but three Reports?

Some explanation of this will be found in Report I, but the reasons shall be stated here more fully, together with other circumstances, some of which, though prior to his appointment, are connected therewith; and it will be done without pretence of exhausting what could be said on the subjects which occur.

Great anxiety had arisen in Ireland in consequence of the dangerous influence which was found to be affecting Catholics frequenting the Queen's Colleges recently established by Sir
[xi] Robert Peel[4] at Belfast, Cork, and Galway.[5] These colleges had

---

occasion, he was able to give the impression Newman made on him, and his estimate of him. They met for the first time at Trinity College, on Trinity Monday, 1880. The extract is taken from Principal Shairp's *Studies in Poetry and Philosophy*, published by David Douglas, Castle Street, Edinburgh. For other mention of Newman by Shairp, *vide Principal Shairp and his Friends*, by Professor Knight, St Andrews, published by John Murray; also Shairp's *Aspects of Poetry*, published by Douglas.

N.B.—The extract has been withdrawn. It will be found between pages 240 and 256 of Principal Shairp's book of *Studies*. [WPN]

In the event, the extract *was* printed as part of *My Campaign in Ireland, Part I* and so is included in this volume too; it appears after the Supplement, not before.

[4] Robert Peel (1788–1850) was Prime Minister 1834–5 and 1841–6.

[5] The prospect of founding a Catholic university in Ireland in the mid-nineteenth century would have been unthinkable to the vast majority of Catholics in the United Kingdom. Ironically it was the British government which provided a major incentive for Catholics to undertake the project when, in 1845, it decided to establish the secular and non-denominational Queen's Colleges. If this was the proximate cause for the establishment of a Catholic university, the more remote and deeper one was the need to address a grievance shared by the vast majority of Irishmen: the provision of suitable

almost every advantage that the State could give; well-endowed scholarships and prizes were attached to them. Moreover, at this time, while the other places of education recognized by the State were practically, if not professedly, closed against Catholics, these colleges offered themselves as accessible to them by ignoring religion altogether. To very many, therefore, the Queen's Colleges seemed to meet all that could be required, for as the people of Ireland had preserved their faith under persecution, it was not to be expected that that faith would suffer when religious subjects were excluded.[6] This, however, was not the opinion of all; there were those who feared the gift of colleges, such as these, planted amidst people distinctly Catholic, as was the case at Cork and Galway; they dreaded the infidelity that lay implicitly beneath what looked so fair. But it was not easy to foresee what would be a practicable remedy. This subject had occupied the mind of Pope Gregory XVI, but the death of that Pontiff, and the troubles in Rome which followed, had hindered any important action being taken to counteract the evil.[7] However, after the return of Pius IX from exile, and on the arrival of Dr Cullen[8] in Ireland as Primate

---

higher education that Catholics could attend. Together with the resolution of the 'land question' and the disestablishment of the Irish Church, the 'university question' constituted one of the three main demands of Irish Catholics after the Catholic Emancipation Act of 1829.

[6] The question of 'mixed' (i.e. Catholic–Protestant) education had already led to deep divisions within the Irish episcopate in the debate over the national schools, which pitted 'Castle' or pro-Westminster bishops against 'patriot' ones; now, with the prospect of the Queen's Colleges, they were split again, even though rescripts from Rome in 1847, 1848 and 1850 upheld official opposition to mixed education and forbade the bishops to cooperate with the new colleges. See pp. [lxxiii–lxxvi] for these rescripts.

[7] Pope Gregory XVI died in 1846. In 1848 there were uprisings in the Italian states aimed at driving out the Austrians from the north and uniting the states in the Italian peninsula. Pope Pius IX was forced to flee Rome, where a republic was proclaimed under Garibaldi, but it only lasted until July 1849 when the republican forces were defeated by French and Austrian forces.

[8] Paul Cullen (1803–78) had received a fine Classical education at Carlow College before leaving, at the age of seventeen, for the College of Propaganda Fide in Rome, where after eight years of theological studies he was ordained to the priesthood. After lecturing in Rome for three

and Apostolic Delegate,[9] vigorous measures were taken which resulted in the Bishops, assembled, 1850, in the National Council or Synod of Thurles, resolving to erect a Catholic University.[10] A Committee was at the same time solemnly announced to have been appointed by the Synod to act in its name and by its authority in examining into the details of the project, and carrying it into execution. It bore the name of *The Catholic University Committee.*[11]

---

further years, he became Vice-Rector of the Irish College, one of the many national colleges for students studying for the priesthood at the Roman universities. There he was responsible for the priestly formation and general welfare of the students; at the same time he acted as an agent for the Roman authorities in their dealings with the Irish hierarchy.

[9] In 1850 the vacant primatial See of Armagh was filled by Paul Cullen, Rector of the Irish College in Rome and the leading supporter of Rome's university plan for Ireland. Granted the title of 'apostolic delegate' and commissioned by the Holy See to convene the first synod in Ireland for over two centuries, Cullen was Rome's choice to sort out the tempestuous Irish Church.

[10] At the synod of Thurles, the bishops voted by narrow margins—two and four votes respectively—to prohibit their clergy from holding office at the Queen's Colleges and to warn the laity strongly against attending them. Despite the divisions over whether to cooperate or not with the Queen's Colleges, Cullen managed to secure unanimous approval for a Catholic university. (See E. Larkin, *The Making of the Roman Catholic Church in Ireland, 1850–1860* (Chapel Hill: University of North Carolina Press, 1980), p. 30).

[11] The Catholic University Committee comprised the four archbishops and one other bishop from each of the four provinces, each of whom had the right to co-opt one priest and one layman. For the list of its members, see p. [436]. For a detailed register of the Committee's activities, see the Minute Book of the Catholic University Committee, CU1, UCDA.

At the first meeting of the Catholic University Committee in October 1851 Archbishop John MacHale objected to the eight bishops on it being in a minority, and argued that responsibility for the University should be vested in the bishops as a body. After opposing Cullen's policy at the committee's third meeting, in January 1852, MacHale wrote to explain his opposition, arguing that the committee was 'only provisionally established and for preparatory arrangements'. When he refused to sign the petition to the Pope asking for a Brief to authorise the erection of the Catholic University, Cullen sent the petition to Rome without his signature

In coming to this resolve the Bishops acted (as it would seem [xii] from the Letters) in obedience, rather than in concurrence of mind with Rome. They were necessarily Irishmen, brought up in Ireland, used to their countrymen as having ministered to them as priests, and having as Bishops a still wider knowledge of the country generally; it was clear to their minds that they could gauge the temper and the resources of the country with respect to the subject before them, and, taken individually, the judgment of an influential number of them was against the practicability, at least at that time, of carrying out the principle laid down by Rome against Mixed Education in connection with University Education. Of this, at least later on, they made no secret; nevertheless they so did their best to provide the funds necessary for attempting it by means of a University, that between the autumn of 1850–51, £26,000 in Donations and £500 in Annual Subscriptions was collected in Ireland alone for the purpose,[12] notwithstanding a bad season.[13]

Dr Cullen, on the other hand, having from boyhood lived in Rome, was at this time almost equally a stranger to his country and to the Bishops. From early in life he had ruled undisputed over his college in Rome, and he was unused to defer to difficulties presented by others. He was in the confidence of

---

(Larkin, *Making of the Roman Catholic Church in Ireland*, pp. 124, 130–4).

[12] *Vide* also Statement of Accounts in the Appendix to the volume. [WPN] See p. [435].

[13] Remarkably, the lion's share came not from the middle or upper classes, but from the Irish poor. This uneven yield from the Irish national collection reflected a lack of enthusiasm for the project among the bishops in the wealthier areas such as Dublin, but it was also an indication of the lukewarm support for episcopal projects among the better-off laity. John Coolahan has pointed out that 'unlike England there was no tradition among the Irish landowning classes of public service towards education' (*Irish Education: its History and Structure* (Dublin: Institute of Public Administration, 1981), pp. 19–20).

During the Great Famine, 1845–49, more than a million people died in Ireland and in the immediate aftermath around one and a half million emigrated. The cause of the famine was the potato blight, which affected Ireland's one main crop. Potato production began to improve after 1849, but only gradually.

Rome, he was zealous against Mixed Education, and he had come from Rome with extraordinary powers for the furtherance of the Holy Father's wishes. A Catholic University, therefore, having been resolved upon, he proceeded to carry out the project.[14]

[xiii] With this object before him, Dr Cullen consulted Dr Newman as to the best way of setting about it;[15] and, in July, 1851, made the proposal to him that he should allow himself to be nominated Rector.[16] Left to himself, Dr Newman would have preferred a

---

[14] The description of Archbishop Cullen as an autocratic Ultramontane has a good deal of truth in it.

[15] Cullen already knew Newman from Rome, where he had assisted him on a number of occasions, so it was only natural that Cullen should now turn to him for advice (Cullen to Newman, 15 April 1851, *LD* xiv, p. 257n). Initially Cullen thought that, as a priest should be Rector, 'we hope that the Vice-Rector will be one of the University of Oxford converts and a layman' (Cullen to Kirby, 18 March 1851, quoted in Larkin, *Making of the Roman Catholic Church in Ireland*, p. 121). Evidently Cullen hoped that if he secured one of the leading Oxford converts he would enhance the university's reputation and attract English support; it would also enable him to avoid having to appoint a native Irishman, who could hardly avoid falling foul of the feuds within the Irish Hierarchy. Newman duly provided Cullen with eleven names—all Converts, nine from Oxford and two from Cambridge—while at the same time commenting that none of them really struck him as suitable to act as Vice-Rector (Newman to Cullen, 28 April 1851, *LD* xiv, pp. 267–70). Meanwhile Cullen reasoned that 'If Dr Newman could be persuaded to come, he would at once give a name and fame to the good work' (Cullen to Kirby, 16 April 1851, quoted in C. Barr, *Paul Cullen, John Henry Newman, and the Catholic University of Ireland, 1845–1865* (Leominster: Gracewing, 2003), p. 64).

[16] Cullen stayed overnight with Newman on 8 July 1851 en route to London, where he had a meeting with three recent converts: Henry Edward Manning, the future cardinal of Westminster; William Monsell, MP for Limerick and the future Baron Emly; and James Hope (later Hope-Scott), a Parliamentary barrister who was an expert on ecclesiastical and educational matters. After the converts had talked over the plan for the projected university—location, residential arrangements, structure and professors—they agreed that the best method of proceeding would be to refer all these matters to Newman, and that 'he should be requested to consider the best means of establishing the University' and 'frame a report for publication as the basis for all further discussions'

subordinate position, and suggested that of Prefect of Studies, as one which would afford him great opportunities for service, unshackled by the responsibilities and anxieties of the Rectorship.[17] But his friends thought such a position unadvisable, and they pressed upon him to be Rector. Mr Hope (afterwards Mr Hope-Scott)[18] writes to him thus:—

July 24*th,* 1851

> I am very clearly of opinion that you should be Rector, not on account of the dignity, though that deserves consideration; but because it is most important in my view that you should be, both in name and fact, at the head of the institution. In the

---

('Memorandum on the subjects discussed at a meeting of several gentlemen with the Primate relating to the establishment of a Catholic University in Ireland', 13 July 1851 [misdated 1852], Cullen Papers, 45/3/6, DDA). Cullen readily accepted their recommendation to devolve the whole matter to Newman and, confirmed in his conviction that Newman was the man with the energy, administrative skills and vision to see through this highly ambitious scheme, broke his return journey to Dublin to offer Newman the Rectorship on 18 July.

[17] For Newman's recollection of the meeting with Cullen on 18 July see his 'Memorandum about my Connection with the Catholic University', *AW*, p. 280. For his letter to Cullen (23 July 1851, *LD* xiv, p. 316), see the footnote on p. [xiii].

[18] James Robert Hope (1812–73), was the son of the governor of the Royal Military Academy, Sandhurst and MP for Linlithgowshire. He was educated at Eton and Christ Church, Oxford, and became a Fellow of Merton College, where he was a keen Tractarian and a close friend of Newman's. In the 1840s he helped to rescue St Columba's College, the 'infant Eton or Winchester' in County Meath which William Monsell and Lord Adare had helped to found, for the Irish Protestants; and along with Gladstone he helped to found Trinity College, Glenalmond, in Scotland. In 1847 Hope married a grand-daughter of Sir Walter Scott, and on the death of his brother-in-law inherited Abbotsford and assumed the name Hope-Scott. In 1851 he was received into the Catholic Church, and was followed by his wife and other relations. Approached by Cullen about setting up the Catholic University, Hope told him: 'First get Newman.' Hope was Newman's constant adviser on a whole range of matters, not just the Catholic University. In recognition of his 'early researches and the munificence of his later deeds' – his £5000 was the largest single gift to the University – Newman dedicated *The Office and Works of Universities* (1856), the collected volume of his university sketches, to Hope. (*ODNB*)

> discussions which we had with Dr Cullen, it seemed agreed that the University should be started without statutes or any formal constitution, and that the Rector and his assistants should govern according to their discretion, until experience had given the data for establishing it in a regular manner. Our whole idea depends upon the men who start the University, and a great part of it on your being the foremost. So pray do be Rector.[19]

Still Dr Newman did not pledge himself to either office, but became one of a Committee of *three*, charged with the duty of reporting to the Committee of the Synod on the best mode of commencing the University, on the course of studies, etc. For this purpose he went to Ireland, and, in conjunction with his
[xiv] colleagues, Dr Leahy,[20] afterwards Archbishop of Cashel, and Mr Myles W. O'Reilly,[21] drew up a paper which will be found in the

---

[19] This letter is a reply to Newman's, dated 23 July, in which he seeks the advice of Hope (*LD* xiv, p. 317).

[20] Patrick Leahy (1806–75) was educated at the Classical day school in Thurles, then at Maynooth, and was ordained in 1833. Leahy served on the original University Committee at a time when he was vicar-general of Cashel and President of St Patrick's, Thurles. He became Professor of Exegetics at the Catholic University and the first Vice-Rector, while also acting as parish priest of Cashel. On becoming Bishop of Cashel in 1857, he resigned the vice-rectorship. In 1866 and 1867 he acted on behalf of the Irish Catholic bishops in negotiating with Lord Mayo, the chief secretary for Ireland, over the proposed endowment of the Catholic University. A man of great courtesy and dignity, he acted as a buffer between the dictatorial Cullen and the wary episcopate. (*DIB*, *ODNB*)

[21] Myles O'Reilly (1825–80) was born in Ireland and educated at Ushaw. He graduated from the University of London and gained an LLD from Rome, then returned to Ireland where he assumed the part of a country gentleman who bred horses and prize cattle. He was a member of the original Catholic University Committee, as well as the subcommittee of three. He once acted as examiner in Classics at the Catholic University, agreed to lecture on the philosophy of law, and was one of the authors of the *Report on the Condition and Circumstances of the Catholic University of Ireland, Presented by a Committee of Senate* (1859). O'Reilly joined the Louth Rifles militia, holding a captain's commission, then entered the papal army with the rank of major and was appointed to

Appendix No. I to Report II.[22] It was read to the Committee November 12th, 1851, and on the same day Dr Newman was named Rector by unanimous acclamation; his appointment to the office to be thereby fixed, subject only to his acceptance of it. He wrote from Birmingham on November 14th, accepting the office,[23] and the Cardinal Prefect of Propaganda, Cardinal Fransoni,[24] wrote formally to Dr Cullen, congratulating him on this appointment. Later on, the Holy Father, while approving of this act of the Archbishops and Bishops, made Dr Newman's appointment, over and above their act, an act of his own.

How momentous he felt the duties involved in this nomination to be, may be gathered from a few lines written by him in the *Catholic University Gazette* of November 9th, 1854.

> Considering the disorders to which Universities have incidentally given rise in former times, and the jealousy expressed in this *extract*[25] of their action upon the clergy, it is

---

command the Irish brigade; in September 1860 the Battalion of St Patrick gallantly defended Spoleto against Piedmontese troops, but was forced to surrender. On his return to Ireland, O'Reilly was elected MP for County Longford, 1862–79, and was a prominent speaker in parliament on Irish, military and educational matters. He wrote pamphlets and articles on the question of university education, and on renouncing his seat in Westminster was appointed Assistant Commissioner of intermediate education. (*DIB*, *ODNB*)

[22] This paper, as given, is not quite as Dr Newman had left it on his return to England, it having been somewhat altered by Dr Leahy (so Dr Leahy wrote word), previous to its being presented to the Committee. [WPN]

[23] In fact, Newman replied on 16 November, saying that the appointment gave him a great deal of pleasure as well as anxiety, and asking if there was 'any way of putting the University under the patronage of our Blessed Lady' (Newman to Cullen, *LD* xiv, pp. 425–6). For Cullen's letter, see *AW*, p. 283.

[24] Giacomo Filippo Fransoni (1775–56) was Prefect of the Sacred Congregation of Propaganda Fide from 1834 until 1856. Newman was ordained a priest by Cardinal Fransoni on 30 May 1847.

[25] Dr Newman is alluding to an *extract* from a dissertation on "Education in the Middle Ages," abridged and translated from No. 2 of the *Analecta Juris Pontificii* for January, 1854—*vide Catholic University Gazette*, Nos. 20, 22, 24, 1854. [WPN]

a remarkable evidence of the confidence placed by the Holy See in the people of Ireland that it should recommend to them
[xv] at this day an institution, which it has for centuries rather tolerated as established than taken the initiative in establishing. The instances of Louvain and Quebec, striking as they are, are less significant, inasmuch as the University of Louvain was only a revival,[26] and the University of Quebec had already existed, or was founded, under the form of a college.[27] In the case of Ireland the nation itself is taken as a sufficient safeguard that its University will be loyal to Catholicism.

And next we may remark, that these cases of Louvain, Quebec and Dublin, to say nothing of the Seminario Pio,[28] seem to suggest to us that a change of policy is in progress in Rome on the subject of methods of education. We are not then concerned in an isolated, experimental or accidental attempt, but sharing in a great movement, which has the tokens of success in its deliberateness and its extent.[29]

---

[26] A university had been founded at Louvain in 1425 and it flourished until the French Revolutionary Wars, which resulted in the Netherlands coming under French rule and the university being suppressed. It was reopened as a state university in 1816, but in 1830 Belgium seceded from the Netherlands and in 1834 the Belgian bishops founded a Catholic university in Mechlin; the following year it moved to Louvain, where the state university had been closed, and it was renamed the Catholic University of Louvain. The new university took over the buildings of the ancient one. There had been a strong Irish connection with the old Louvain and during the sixteenth, seventeenth and eighteenth centuries Ireland supplied the university with around 1200 students, most of whom belonged to one of the four Irish colleges at Louvain, three religious and one secular.

[27] The Université Laval was founded in Quebec in 1852 out of the Seminary of Quebec (Séminaire de Québec), which itself was founded in 1663 by Bishop François de Laval, the first bishop of New France.

[28] This refers to the Roman seminary established by Pope Pius IV in 1565.

[29] 'State of Seminaries and other schools in the sixteenth century and since', *CUG* 24 (9 November 1854), p. 191.

Some extracts taken as spoken from his first address to the Irish people, will show the spirit in which he entered upon his duties. They indicate also some of the difficulties which made it necessary to prepare people, as he was asked to do, for a Catholic University.

> I know quite well that there are multitudes of Protestants who are advocates for Mixed Education to the fullest extent, even so far as to desire the introduction of Catholics themselves into their colleges and schools; but then, first, they are those for the most part who have no creed or dogma whatever to defend, to sacrifice, to surrender, to compromise, to hold back, or to 'mix,' when they call out for Mixed Education. There are many Protestants of benevolent tempers and business-like minds, who think that all who are called Christians do in fact agree together in essentials, though they will not allow it; and who, in consequence, call on all parties in educating their youth for the world to eliminate differences, which are certainly prejudicial, as soon as they are proved to be immaterial. …
>
> I can conceive the most consistent men, and the most [xvi] zealously attached to their own system of doctrine, nevertheless consenting to schemes of Education from which Religion is altogether or almost excluded, from the stress of necessity, or the recommendations of expedience. Necessity has no law, and expedience is often one form of necessity. It is no principle with sensible men, of whatever cast of opinion, to do always what is abstractedly best. Where no direct duty forbids, we may be obliged to do, as being best under circumstances, what we murmur and rise against, while we do it. We see that to attempt more is to effect less; that we must accept so much, or gain nothing; and so perforce we reconcile ourselves to what we would have far otherwise, if we could. Thus a system of Mixed Education may, in a particular place or time, be the least of evils; it may be of long standing; it may be dangerous to meddle with; it may be professedly a temporary arrangement; it may be in an improving state; its

disadvantages may be neutralized by the persons by whom, or the provisions under which, it is administered.[30] …

Viewed as a matter of argument, judgment, propriety, and expedience, I am not called upon to deny that in particular cases a course has been before now advisable for Catholics, in regard to the education of their youth, and has been, in fact, adopted, which was not abstractedly the best, and is no pattern and precedent for others. Thus, in the early ages, the Church sanctioned her children in frequenting the heathen schools for the acquisition of secular accomplishments, where, as no one can doubt, evils existed, at least as great as can attend on Mixed Education now. The gravest Fathers recommended for Christian youth the use of pagan masters; the most saintly Bishops and most authoritative Doctors had been sent in their adolescence by Christian parents to pagan lecture halls. And, not to take other instances, at this very time, and in this very
[xvii] country, as regards, at least, the poorer classes of the community, whose secular acquirements ever must be limited, it has approved itself not only to Protestant state Ecclesiastics, who cannot be supposed to be very sensitive about doctrinal truth, but, as a wise condescension, even to many of our most venerated Bishops, to suffer, under the circumstances, a system of Mixed Education in the schools called National.

On this part of the question, however, I have not to enter; for I confine myself to the subject of University Education. But, even here, it would ill have become me to pretend, simply on my own judgment, to decide on a point so emphatically practical, as regards a state of society about which I have much to learn, on any abstract principles, however true and important. It would have been presumptuous in me so to have acted, nor am I so acting. It is my happiness, in a matter of Christian duty about which the most saintly and the most able may differ, to be guided simply by the decision and recommendation of the Holy See, the judge and finisher of all controversies. That decision, indeed, I repeat, shall not enter into my argument; but it is my own reason for arguing. I am

---

[30] For comments on these two paragraphs from Discourse I, see the footnotes on pp. [224–5].

trusting my own judgment on the subject, because I find it is the judgment of him who has upon his shoulders the government and the solicitude of all the Churches. I appear before you, gentlemen, not prior to the decision of Rome on the question of which I am to treat, but after it. My sole aspiration—and I cannot have a higher under the heavens—is to be the servant of the Vicar of Christ. He has sanctioned, at this time, a particular measure for his children who speak the English tongue, and the distinguished persons by whom it is to be carried out have honoured me with a share in their work. I take things as I find them; I know nothing of the past; I find myself here; I set myself to the duties I find here; I set myself to further, by every means in my power, doctrines and views, true in themselves, recognized by all Catholics as such, familiar to my own mind; and to do this quite apart from the [xviii]
consideration of questions which have been determined without me and before me. I am here the advocate and the minister of a certain great principle; yet not merely advocate and minister, else had I not been here at all. It has been my previous keen sense and hearty reception of that principle, that has been at once the cause, as I must suppose, of my selection, and the ground of my acquiescence. I am told on authority that a principle is necessary, which I have ever felt to be true. As the royal matron in sacred history consigned the child she had made her own to the charge of its natural mother, so truths and duties, which come of unaided reason, not of grace, which were already intimately mine by the workings of my own mind, and the philosophy of human schools, are now committed to my care, to nurse and to cherish, by her and for her who, acting on the prerogative of her divinely inspired discernment, has in this instance honoured with a royal adoption the suggestions of reason. …

If I have been expressing a satisfaction that opinions, early imbibed and long cherished in my own mind, now come to me with the Church's seal upon them, do not imagine that I am indulging a subtle kind of private judgment, especially unbecoming a Catholic. It would, I think, be unjust to me were any one to gather from what I have been saying that I had so established myself in my own ideas and in my old notions, as

> a centre of thought, that, instead of coming to the Church to be taught, I was but availing myself of such opportunities as she gave me, to force principles on your attention which I had adopted without her.[31]

But with Dr Newman's acceptance of the Rectorship there came a great hindrance to his work. It was necessary that the Rector, before entering upon the administration of the University,
[xix] should profess the Creed of Pius IV, and take the oaths of fidelity and obedience. But any such formal act of recognition or installation as Rector, so absolutely necessary to enable him to start on his work and to act with authority, was delayed nearly three years.[32] In May, 1854, it was enjoined by the Archbishops

---

[31] For comments on these three paragraphs from Discourse I, see the footnotes on pp. [128–31].

[32] During this time, Cullen had his share of difficulties with the University project, as he was trying to walk a tightrope in his dealings with the Irish episcopate over the matter. Most troublesome of them was the Archbishop of Tuam, John MacHale (1791–1881), who argued vehemently that the body of bishops, and it alone, had the right to set up and govern the Catholic University; from February 1852 MacHale objected to everything the University Committee proposed and did his level best to block its decisions. The first modern bishop to be educated entirely in Ireland, MacHale was by the mid-1840s the most popular man in Ireland after Daniel O'Connell. A political radical and an uncompromising champion of the poor and underprivileged, MacHale combined his stand on social justice with a commitment to cultural and political nationalism. On account of his pugnacious and confrontational tactics in his dealings with the representatives of British rule, he was widely known as the 'Lion of the West'.

In 1852, when Cullen could count on the support of only seven of the twenty-eight bishops, MacHale spread the view that Cullen was Attempting to control the University Committee—as indeed he undoubtedly was. Moreover, at a time of strong anti-English feeling, MacHale's objection to the appointment of Englishmen caused further problems for Cullen.

Another reason for the delay was Cullen's preoccupation with dissension among the hierarchy over Irish nationalism and the thorny issue of the limits of clerical involvement in the political question. The newly-formed Tenant League, set up to champion security of tenure and a fair rent for the workers on the land, received widespread support from

and Bishops that this should be done in the hands of the Archbishop of Dublin; and it took place on Whit-Sunday, June 4th, 1854, at High Mass in the Cathedral of Dublin, the Archbishop making him, as Dr Newman expresses it, "a most touching address".[33] He never learnt the cause of this delay.

In this long interval, although he could act only in a private capacity, he nevertheless spared no pains to hasten the progress of his work.[34] He resided from time to time in Dublin and there made intimate acquaintance with many of its leading residents. Also, on his acceptance of the Rectorship, he at once devoted himself to the preparation of the Discourses on University Education, which he undertook at the suggestion of Dr Cullen[35] and others, in order, as has been said, to prepare the Catholic public for the project of a University; the first five of these he delivered in Dublin in the months of May and June, 1852; the remainder were published in the autumn.[36] Moreover, in spite of the difficulties of travelling in those days, he began a great round in Ireland in the early winter of

---

both clergy and laity, but the country became sharply divided by the two factions within it: those who advocated an independent political movement and those who argued for an alliance with one of the major political parties – which, in practice, meant the Whigs. Besides splitting the country, the division caused dissension within the ranks of the Catholic clergy, pitting Cullen against MacHale.

33 *CUG* 3 (15 June 1854), p. 18. This is from Newman's account of his inauguration as Rector, which can also be found in *LD* xxxi, pp. 87–9.

34 For a full analysis of the way Newman sought to adapt his vision of the university to the Irish situation, see chapter 3, 'Searching for an educational *via media*' in Shrimpton, *MM*, pp. 107–72.

35 Newman's educational classic had its origins in Cullen's request: 'if you could spare time to give us a few lectures on education, you would be rendering good service to religion in Ireland' (Cullen to Newman, 15 April 1851, *LD* xiv, p. 257n). Yet it was Newman's friend, the priest Robert Whitty, who had suggested to Cullen on 12 April 1851 that Newman could be asked to give some lectures on university education (*NU*, pp. 104–5).

36 Newman delivered the first five lectures to the general public on five successive Mondays, starting on 10 May 1852; the rest were ready by the autumn, but never given. All ten were published the same year, first separately as pamphlets and then together in a single volume under the title *Discourses on the Scope and Nature of University Education*.

1854 to call on the Archbishops and Bishops in their respective Sees, so that their want of personal acquaintance with him might not be a drawback to success.[37] Later on he projected a visit to America; this intention, however, was not carried out.[38] The Table

[37] The tour began on 18 February but, after less than a month and with only six bishops seen, the worst winter in decades caused it to be cut short. Newman encountered largely negative reactions to the prospect of a Catholic university from the clergy he met on the tour; though he was greeted everywhere with welcoming hospitality, he could not but notice a general expectation that the enterprise would fail. In Dublin, John Curtis, the Provincial of the Irish Jesuits, told him that the class of students required for a university did not exist in Ireland; his advice was to go to Cullen and 'say, "Don't attempt the University—give up the idea"'. (University journal, 8 February 1854, A34.2, BOA; reproduced in *AW*, p. 323). As for the laity, the few willing to consider the university project at all were decidedly gloomy about it. Peers such as the Earl of Fingall, the Earl of Kenmare and Viscount Castlerosse refused even to give their names as honorary members (i.e. patrons) of the Catholic University, while the Dublin lawyers were lukewarm at best and justified their position by claiming consistency with the bishops' previous policy of toleration of mixed education in the national schools negotiations of the 1840s. The two members of the University Committee who (unofficially) represented the wealthier landed gentry, Michael Errington and James More O'Ferrall, were despondent about the University's prospects. The latter showed Newman a letter from his brother Richard, a politician and colonial administrator, which prophesied that the 'Protestant party will endeavour to raise a cry in which many Catholics are disposed to join, that the new University is got up for the purpose of placing Catholic education entirely in the hands of the Clergy and for the exclusion of the Laity from all interference' (R. M. O'Ferrall to J. M. O'Ferrall, 5 May 1854, *LD* xvi, p. 128n).

[38] John Hughes (1797–1864), the first Archbishop of New York and the leading Catholic Irishman in the United States, had called on Newman at Birmingham in 1846, and in 1853 had arranged for a collection to be made to meet the costs of Newman's Achilli trial. Hughes was very optimistic as to the money and students that would flow to the Catholic University from the United States, and he invited Newman to cross the Atlantic for a lecture tour before the term opened in November 1854; he told Newman that he hoped to send between 60 and 120 students within a year or two. It is likely that Newman decided against the tour because he could not afford the two months such a trip would require; he had earlier considered touring major cities of North America, from New York to

of Receipts at the end of the volume shows the large sum that was [xx]
contributed by the United States of America for the University.[39]

But though Dr Newman was not as yet in a position to act for the University, there were others who through their connexion with the *Catholic University Committee* were able to do so. This Committee, originally consisting of eight, the four Archbishops and four Bishops, and afterwards, by its own powers, increased to twenty-four,[40] had not yet been dissolved, and, through those members who acted in its name, still exercised the powers conferred upon it. Thus it was that the locality in Dublin for the University was fixed by the purchase of premises in Stephen's Green for academical purposes;[41] whereas Dr Newman considered the higher ground of the opposite side of the Liffey altogether preferable for the site of a University, for among other advantages it was the more ecclesiastical quarter; the Archbishop resided there, and the establishments of the Jesuits and the Dominicans were at hand; moreover, it was out of the glare of the town.[42]

This purchase in Stephen's Green, which was good in itself and suitable for its purpose, would not be mentioned here but that it affords an instance of the important transactions that could be decided on and carried out independently of the Rector, while his summons to the administration remained in abeyance.[43]

New Orleans, even though he dreaded the inconvenience such a trip would cause him (Newman to Flanagan, 9 February 1854; Newman to Stanton, 28 February 1854; Newman to H. Wilberforce, 12 July 1854: *LD* xvi, pp. 40, 65, 196; Cullen to Newman, 14 November 1854, *Paul Cullen and his Contemporaries: with their Letters from 1820–1902*, ed. P. MacSuibhne (Naas: Leinster Leader, 1965) iii, p. 198).

[39] See p. [435].

[40] For the names *vid.* Appendix to the volume. [WPN] See p. [436].

[41] In February 1853 Cullen saw to it that the University Committee chose 86 St Stephen's Green as the site for the University and purchased it for the grand sum of £3500. Astonishingly, Newman was not consulted about the matter.

[42] Like everyone else involved in the university project, Newman was wary about a city location because of the dangers it presented to student life. For more on the discussion about a suitable site, see *MM*, p. 98, n8, as well as the relevant footnote on p. [85].

[43] The Rector-in-waiting watched anxiously from across St George's Channel, awaiting a summons, exasperated with the slowness and

Other projects were also put into motion, and since some of
[xxi] these if accomplished were likely seriously to affect the future well-working of the University, and even the continuance of his connexion with it, they became the occasion of grave anxieties to him. A letter which he entitled *The Statement of August* 14*th*, 1852,[44] gives some insight into what he had, in his anomalous position, to encounter from causes such as these. This *Statement*, being a letter to Dr Cullen, properly belongs to Dr Newman's correspondence, but, as he himself separated it from the rest, it is inserted here to show, *inter alia*, his clear perception of the difficulties of a University situated in a capital, and the methods by which he proposed to meet them. His solicitude in this respect, though the letter does not touch upon it, extended even to providing for the legitimate enjoyment by the students of the recreations of the town. The theatre, for instance, would be a pleasure, he said, so attractive to the students, that considering its proximity to them, he desired to meet any difficulty rather than that they should be harassed by an absolute prohibition from it. For this purpose he contemplated licensing a theatre, and thus bringing it under the control of the University, a plan which he had reason to believe would be, not only practicable, but likely to receive a hearty support in the town.[45] This plan, so far as is known, was not pursued, being only contemplated with others in anticipation of the future development of the University. Mention

---

ineffectualness of the University Committee, and unaware how divided the episcopal body had become. On the question of how to begin the university, a majority of the Committee favoured a well-staffed professoriate and imposing buildings as a means of exciting interest and showing the intent to match the foundations of Trinity and the Queen's University (the degree-awarding body erected in 1850 for the three Queen's Colleges). Those favouring a modest start were in a minority, but they included Cullen and Newman, as well as James Hope.

[44] *Vide* Supplement. [WPN] See pp. [271–8].

[45] There was a widespread view at the time that the theatre was liable to corrupt youth. Undergraduate theatricals, which had been banned at Oxford in the seventeenth century, revived in the 1860s, but they took place outside the city until the ban was lifted in the 1880s. On account of its location in Dublin and its largely non-residential student population, Trinity had long been unable to restrict student access to the theatre.

of it is therefore made only as illustrating the earnestness with which Dr Newman threw himself into the preparation for the great work which he had before him, and which Pius IX was so anxious [xxii] to see begun.

With this desire of the Holy Father no one was more in sympathy than the Rector, but its fulfilment was scarcely promoted by the action of the Committee. He had at once made all the preparations he could foresee for an early commencement, and he had in hand what would follow; but his position confined him to merely conditional steps, and called for all possible vigilance to keep any ground he had gained. Most especially was this the case with regard to the selection of his fellow-workers. This was a duty which belonged to his office, and, at this critical time for the University, one which ought not to be anticipated by others. But here again he found the Committee taking advantage of his position.[46]

Of all the offices that of Vice-Rector was considered by Dr Newman the most important. He had written to Dr Cullen about this office and kindred subjects some weeks previous to *The Statement of August* 14*th*, but nothing is known of this letter except what is contained in a fragment of the rough copy. He there speaks of the Vice-Rector as one who would be "most intimately near me and involved in my doings and responsibilities. ... He takes my place when I am absent, and I depend upon him simply. It is not enough that I should have full confidence in his zeal, and his desire to act with me. He must see things from the same point of view as I do. If there is any one office of which I ought to have the absolute appointment it is this."[47] And in a Note upon these remarks written in 1872, he [xxiii]

---

[46] In July 1852 Newman had explained to Cullen that, since the Vice-Rector needed to be someone who saw things from the same point of view as the Rector, and since Newman could think of no-one suitable at the time, it was better not to appoint. But two months later—without any warning—Cullen appointed James Taylor as vice-Vice-Rector. In the event, James Taylor (1805–75), a former President of Carlow College, acted as the General Secretary of the University Committee and left before the University got going.

[47] Two decades later, Newman wrote: 'Since the need, and the choice of a Vice-Rector runs through nearly all my correspondence with Dr Cullen,

and gave colour and shape to the termination of my Rectorship, it is worth while to note that is was my first as well as my last difficulty' ('Memorandum about my Connection with the Catholic University', *AW*, p. 290). For this reason, Newman's letter to Cullen needs to be quoted in full:

> I wish to put you in possession of my feelings about the appointment of a Vice-Principal […]
>
> As to the Professors, since our state is to be at first provisional and *they* will not have anything to do with the government, I have no personal interest in their appointment, and do not care who they are, so that they are good ones and creditable to the University.
>
> But it is different with those immediately about me, who are to help me and share my responsibilities. I must have perfect confidence in them, and power over them. I mean the Vice President, the Deans, the Tutors, and perhaps the Lecturers. These are the *working body* who will be, at least at first, and for a time, the real life of the Institution.
>
> Of these, the Vice President is the most intimately near me, and most involved in all my doings and responsibilities. He takes my place when absent—I depend on him simply. It is not enough even that I have full confidence in his zeal and desire to act with me—he must see things from the same point of view as I do.
>
> If there is one office, of which I ought to have the absolute appointment, it is this.
>
> But I do *not* wish to have it, for this simple reason, that, knowing so few persons, I have not the *power* of choosing, though I had leave to do so. I am obliged to depend on the choice of others.
>
> Yet the difficulty is *how can* others choose for me? how can they prophesy who will get on with me, and who will not?
>
> The difficulty, of getting a person who would pull well with me, is all in *addition* to the difficulty of finding a person possessing the requisite qualities for the *office* – which is very great. We want a person of method, of resource, of business like habit, of firmness yet gentleness, and of largeness of mind.
>
> The conclusion I come to from all this, is, that it is *inexpedient* to appoint a Vice President at once. It may be ruining every thing.
>
> Would it be possible to appoint a 'Prefect of Studies?', *an office which might die a natural death at any moment*, its holder being translated to a professorship, lectureship or the like? (4 July 1852, *LD* xv, pp. 117–18).

Years later Newman commented: 'Dr Cullen never wrote a word to me in answer to this letter' ('Memorandum about my Connection with the Catholic University', *AW*, p. 291).

says: "There was a reason *a fortiori* for urging this point, that I was not to reside uninterruptedly in Ireland. The Holy Father had expressly laid on me the duty of being half the year in England. It was indispensable then that I should have a resident *locum tenens*[48] with whom I was most familiar and confidential."[49]

For this office of Vice-Rector, Dr Manning,[50] by his reception into the Church in the earlier part of 1851, had been, as it might have seemed, providentially provided. To him Dr Newman wrote, as soon as his own nomination to the Rectorship was free from doubt, asking him to join in the work of the University as its Vice-Rector. Dr Manning, however, found himself obliged to decline, since he had resolved not to bias his future by inclining to any one work till he had been to Rome, whither he was soon starting. He did so in effect in the accompanying letter, and more definitely in another that followed.

---

[48] The expression *locum tenens* means someone temporarily taking the place of another.

[49] When Cullen offered Newman the Rectorship, Newman replied, 'What I should desire, is to do as much work for the University as possible with *as little absence as possible* from this place' (Newman to Cullen, 23 July 1851, *LD* xiv, p. 316). By 'this place' Newman meant the fledgling Oratory at Birmingham, of which he was Provost. This concern turned out to be Newman's single most serious constraint on his involvement in the university project; it was one Cullen never learnt to come to terms with.

The Pope granted Newman only three years' absence from Birmingham, in response to Newman's request for seven months per year for three years (Newman to Wiseman, 5 June 1854; Newman to Walker, 8 January 1855, *LD* xvi, pp. 146, 345). In 1857 the Birmingham Oratorians claimed that during the previous six years the Catholic University had had two thirds of his time.

Newman's Note of 1872 has not been found. The passage quoted appears in *LD* xv, pp. 117–18n, but the reference is to *MC*.

[50] Henry Edward Manning (1808–92) was educated at Harrow School and Balliol College, Oxford, then became a Fellow of Merton College. He took Anglican orders and became Archdeacon of Chichester, but in 1851 he became a Catholic and was ordained a priest ten weeks later. After serving as Provost of Westminster Cathedral, he became Archbishop of Westminster in 1865 and a cardinal ten years later.

Thus began a series of disappointments in connexion with this office of Vice-Rector which accompanied Dr Newman throughout his Rectorship.[51]

From Dr Manning to Dr Newman

14 QUEEN STREET, MAYFAIR,
October 21*st,* 1851

MY DEAR NEWMAN,

Your note has set me wishing to do anything you bid me; but I do not know what to say. Many doubts about myself and such a work occur at once.

Above all, the desire and I may say resolution I have had
[xxiv] not to incline to any one work more than another till I have been to Rome.

This has made me avoid even speaking of the future. But your words are too weighty with me to be passed by; and I will both think of them, and ask others who can guide me better than I can myself.

I need not say that old affections and many debts draw me strongly towards you.

On 3rd November, I trust to start for Rome. Do not forget me.

I shall not fail to go and look down from the Pincian and think of you.

Ever yours affectionately,
H. E. MANNING[52]

As to the other offices, leaving the choice of the Theological Professors to the Archbishops, as more suitably belonging to

[51] Years later Newman commented: 'It is plain from what took place in 1852 etc that Dr Cullen's idea of a Vice-Rector from the first was, not as an official who would represent me but one who would represent the Archbishop against me, as a regulator of my movements' (*LD* xviii, p. 221n). See also the comment in his 'Memorandum about my Connection with the Catholic University', *AW*, p. 294.

[52] Letters: Ireland 1851, 48(1).16, C.6.37.1, BOA. This letter is quoted in full in W. Ward, *Life of John Henry Cardinal Newman* (London: Longman's, Green & Co., 1912) i, p. 319.

them, he entered into correspondence for Professors, Lecturers, and Tutors, and as far as the uncertainty of the time of opening the University would allow, their services were secured.

This uncertainty, however, caused most serious difficulty. Dr Newman had contemplated making a start, though on a small scale, in the autumn of 1852, but neither then nor at other times between it and the summer of 1854, when he was installed, was he able to bring about any such progress. Consequently a diffidence of the ultimate success of the University grew up in some who had looked forward to devoting themselves to its service, and they found themselves obliged to turn to other pursuits. The lapse of time naturally brought other disappointments which he had to face. Death and ill-health, for instance, deprived him of some whose assistance he had hoped [xxv]
for, vocation to the ecclesiastical state lost him others.

Dr W. G. Ward[53] he tried to gain for any Chair he would take; but a recent increase of duties at St Edmund's College, where he held the office of Professor of Theology, had made his residence there too constant to allow him to accept the offer.

Dr Ward writes thus:—

> So you see I shall be really *more* occupied than ever; as I must always, even when away, be ready to return at a day's notice. I fear, therefore, it is impossible to avail myself of your offer; which would have been particularly to my taste otherwise, and which I feel as *a very great* kindness. I should have greatly enjoyed otherwise working with you. I am not sure, however, but that I might have got you into hot water in Dublin in the *political* line. Here my violent politics don't

[53] William George Ward (1812–82), the son of William Ward, MP, Director of the Bank of England, and proprietor of Lord's cricket ground, was educated at Winchester College and Christ Church, Oxford. He was President of the Oxford Union and later became a Fellow of Balliol, lecturing in logic and mathematics. One of the most extreme of the Tractarians, he was condemned by the Oxford Convocation and stripped of his degrees for his *Ideal of a Christian Church* (1844). Ward was received into the Catholic Church with his wife in 1845 and then taught philosophy and theology at St Edmund's, Ware. (*ODNB*)

matter. So perhaps you are well rid of me.

May 23rd, 1853[54]

Mr Henry Wilberforce,[55] Dr Northcote,[56] Mr Healy Thompson[57] and others, were obliged to add to these disappointments;[58] Dr Jerrard,[59] and later on Mr Robert

---

[54] WPN gives the year of this letter as 1853, but McGrath corrects this to 1855 (*NU*, p. 356n), presumably because of its location: Letters: Ireland 1853, 48(3).13, C.6.37.3, BOA. However, based on *LD* xvi, p. 480n; xxxii, p. 86, the year was probably 1854.

[55] Henry Wilberforce (1807–73) was the fourth and youngest son of the 'emancipator', and the brother of Robert, who had been a tutor with Newman at Oriel. Henry was a pupil of Newman's at Oriel and read with him in vacations, taking a First in Classics. He married, took Anglican orders then became a Catholic in 1850. After two years in Dublin as secretary of the Catholic Defence Association, he turned to journalism and became proprietor, then editor, of the *Catholic Standard*, which amalgamated with the *Weekly Register* the following year. (*ODNB*)

[56] James Spencer Northcote (1821–1907) studied at Corpus Christi College, Oxford and gained a First in Classics. A friend of Newman, he took Anglican orders, then in January 1846 followed his wife into the Catholic Church. He travelled in Italy, becoming an authority on Christian antiquities, and was editor of *The Rambler*, 1852–54. After his wife's death in 1853 he studied for the priesthood and became President of Oscott, 1860–76.

[57] Edward Healy Thompson (1813–91) studied at Emmanuel College, Cambridge before taking Anglican orders. Under Newman's influence he became a Catholic in 1846, and together with his wife devoted himself to literary, religious and translation work.

[58] A problem the three of them shared was that they had literary or scholarly ambitions and children to feed—though Newman held out the prospect of lectureships on top of the tutorships. Wilberforce accepted the tutorship, but resigned in April 1854; Northcote declined the offer; and Thompson, after initially accepting it, pulled out for reasons of health.

[59] Joseph Henry Jerrard (1801–53) was a scholar, then Fellow, of Caius College, Cambridge (1824–44). He became the first Principal of Bristol College, 1831–38, then Examiner in Classics at London University, from 1838 until his death. He became a Catholic in April 1851 and was consulted by Newman and the Subcommittee about the organisation of

Wilberforce,[60] were carried off by death. Nevertheless, when the time of opening did come, Dr Newman found he had gathered round him a body of teachers who entered upon their work *con amore*, and of whom, as he said, he had reason to be proud.[61] The following letter, received since this was put into type, gives an instance of the disinterested zeal for the University that was to be found amongst them. It is an instance, too, of the Rector's thoughtfulness for them.

15*th June,* 1858 [xxvi]

MY DEAR DR LYONS,[62]

I have read with great pleasure and interest the Report of your Faculty, and will gladly accompany it with a letter of my own. ...

Have you shown the Report to Mr Flanagan?[63] That he is not now drawing an income from the Funds of the University,

---

the Catholic University. Newman had hoped to appoint him to a professorship.

[60] Robert Isaac Wilberforce (1802–57), the second son of the 'emancipator', gained a double First at Oriel College, Oxford and became a Fellow. From 1828 he was a tutor at Oriel with Newman and R. H. Froude and helped to establish the modern tutorial system. He became a Catholic in October 1854 and soon afterwards enquired about teaching at the Catholic University. (*ODNB*)

[61] Newman stressed to Thompson that it was 'important that every one should begin our work con amore' (7 September 1853, *LD* xv, p. 419).

[62] Robert Spencer Dyer Lyons (1826–86) was the son of Sir William Lyons, the mayor of Cork. He studied medicine at Trinity College Dublin and became a member of the Royal College of Surgeons in Ireland. He went out to the Crimea as pathologist-in-chief in 1855, and reported on diseases in the trenches; later that year he was appointed Professor of Physiology and Pathology at the Catholic University. He wrote widely on subjects in medicine, education, and forestry: of note are *A handbook of hospital practice* (1859); *Intellectual resources of Ireland: supply and demand for an enlarged system of Irish university education* (1873); *Forest areas in Europe and America* (1884). A Young Irelander in his youth, Lyons served on Gladstone's Commission (1870) to inquire into the treatment of Irish political prisoners in English gaols, and became a Liberal MP for Dublin, 1880–85. He married the daughter of D. R. Pigot, Chief Baron of the Exchequer in Ireland. (*DIB*, *ODNB*)

[63] Professor of Civil Engineering. [WPN]

and is offering his talents and experience to such few students as choose to avail themselves of him, is simply owing to his great forbearance, for which I am very grateful. I suspect he has lost by the University, for I brought him from Lisbon, and wished him to open an office—but he preferred the good of the University to an arrangement which would be an immediate gain to himself. For this reason, I should be sorry, if he had not an opportunity of concurring in the acts of his Faculty. I am assuming you do not know his direction, and therefore have not had an opportunity of consulting him. His address is Terence Woulfe Flanagan, Esq. ...

I am, my dear Dr Lyons,

Very sincerely yours,

JOHN H. NEWMAN[64]

The names and some little notice of all who formed this first teaching staff must not be passed by. Such a notice was provided by Dr Newman in anticipation of the St Malachy's Day, 1854, and it will be found in the Appendix to this book.[65] There is one name in it which has already been mentioned, Mr Healy Thompson. His health had recently begun to fail, and in fact he never came into actual work. Besides what that notice contains about another, Mr
[xxvii] Robert Ornsby,[66] a few lines must be added here, for, to Mr Ornsby's correspondence with Dr Newman, we are indebted for

[64] The full letter can be found in *LD* xviii, pp. 379–80.

[65] See pp. [425–8].

[66] Robert Ornsby (1820–89) studied at Lincoln College, Oxford and became a Fellow of Trinity College, Oxford. Newman considered him 'an excellent man' and thought highly of him academically, having examined him at Oxford. Ornsby took Anglican orders, and in 1847 became a Catholic; his wife followed him a year later. Ornsby moved to Dublin, where he assisted Frederick Lucas in editing *The Tablet*. In 1854 he was appointed Professor of Classical Literature and a tutor in Classics at the Catholic University, where he stayed until 1866. After a spell as tutor to the fifteenth Duke of Norfolk, Ornsby returned to his old post in Dublin in 1874, and in 1882 became a Fellow of the Royal University of Ireland. He published *The Greek Testament, from Cardinal Mai's edition of the Vatican Bible, with Notes, Chiefly Philological and Exegetical* (1860) and *Memoirs of James Robert Hope-Scott* (2 vols, 1884). (*ODNB*)

much knowledge of interesting incidents in the early life of the University; as for instance in connexion with what has been recently described, and is shown in the extracts from Dr Newman's letters which will presently follow.

Mr Ornsby, formerly Fellow of Trinity College, Oxford, was one whose services would have been greatly valued by any University, yet there was danger of Mr Ornsby being another of those lost to that which was rising in Dublin. Gentle, and somewhat retiring, Mr Ornsby was for his ability, his culture and refinement, for his opinion on University matters generally, and for his zeal, simply invaluable to the new University and to Dr Newman. He looked forward most truly to serving the University *con amore*, and to being entirely at Dr Newman's disposal. His circumstances, however, made the uncertainty as to the time of his being employed a serious anxiety to him, indeed, one impossible to be borne indefinitely. Still Dr Newman had no better consolation to give than by telling him of his own position. Thus:—

EDGBASTON, *Feb.* 23, 1853

MY DEAR ORNSBY,

I wish I could tell you more about the University—but you know I have at present no more to do with it than you—I am not even a member of the Committee. I hope this state of things will soon end—indeed it must, for I must either be able to act, or be able to retire. I think my friends will not allow this state of suspense to continue longer. You shall know as soon as I have anything to tell. ...

Ever yours affectionately in Christ,

JOHN H. NEWMAN,

Of the Oratory[67]

EDGBASTON, *March* 7, 1853 [xxviii]

MY DEAR ORNSBY,

I confidently rely on getting to work soon after Easter, and am doing all I can to prepare beforehand. I wish I saw my way

---

[67] *LD* xv, p. 309. Newman added at the end, 'I *expect* to have every thing my own way—but of course I cannot tell—and therefore I am cautious of speaking'.

to give you any certainty how far I could avail myself, or in what way, of persons like yourself. Such I *must* have, but till I am on the spot, as you would understand, if I could talk with you, I do not see my way to any definite plan. ...

Ever yours affectionately in Christ,

JOHN H. NEWMAN[68]

EDGBASTON, *June* 1, 1853

MY DEAR ORNSBY,

... I had supposed I should have been called to Dublin long ago. You of course have no light to throw on the delay. I don't understand it. ...

Ever yours affectionately in Christ,

JOHN H. NEWMAN,
Of the Oratory[69]

In his choice for the appointments to the University offices and in other matters in which, as a stranger to Ireland, he required advice, Dr Newman had an invaluable friend in the late Dr Moriarty,[70] President of All-hallows College near Dublin, and afterwards Bishop of Kerry, whose memory should be kept up, even at the cost of some digression. Dr Newman makes acknowledgment of Dr Moriarty's kindness in his letter, October

---

[68] *LD* xv, p. 324. Newman went on to tell Ornsby about his plan for lodging houses and suggested that Ornsby set himself up as a tutor in Dublin; by doing so, Newman would be more able to involve him in the University plans. Newman also asked him to make various enquires relating to his plan to build a University Church (*LD* xv, pp. 324–5).

Since Ornsby was living in Dublin, Newman had frequent recourse to him for advice about Ireland and the situation there.

[69] *LD* xv, p. 375. The letter continues: 'I do not understand it for this reason, that the facts will remain, as far as the Archbishop of Tuam goes, as difficult to deal with 6 months hence as now. Is the new Primate and the Maynooth Commission the difficulty?'. This refers to the Royal Commission of enquiry into the management and government of the College of Maynooth, which published its findings in 1855.

[70] David Moriarty (1814–77) was president of the missionary college of All Hallows (1846–54) and became a bishop in 1856. (*ODNB*)

23rd, 1872, dedicating *Historical Sketches*, volume i, to him as follows:—

THE ORATORY, BIRMINGHAM, [xxix]
October 23, 1872

MY DEAR LORD,

If I have not asked your Lordship for your formal leave to dedicate this volume to you, this has been because one part of it, written by me as an Anglican controversialist, could not be consistently offered for the direct sanction of a Catholic bishop. If, in spite of this, I presume to inscribe your name in its first page, I do so because I have a freedom in this matter which you have not, because I covet much to be associated publicly with you, and because I trust to obtain your forgiveness for a somewhat violent proceeding, on the plea that I may perhaps thereby be availing myself of the only opportunity given to me, if not the most suitable occasion, of securing what I so earnestly desire.

I desire it, because I desire to acknowledge the debt I owe you for kindnesses and services rendered to me through a course of years. All along, from the time that the Oratory first came to this place, you have taken a warm interest in me and in my doings. You found me out twenty-four years ago on our first start in the narrow streets of Birmingham, before we could well be said to have a home or a church. And you have never been wanting to me since, or spared time or trouble, when I had occasion in any difficulty to seek your guidance or encouragement.

Especially have I cause to remember the help you gave me, by your prudent counsels and your anxious sympathy, when I was called over to Ireland to initiate a great Catholic institution. From others also, ecclesiastics and laymen, I received a hearty welcome and a large assistance, which I ever bear in mind; but you, when I would fill the Professors' chairs, were in a position to direct me to the men whose genius, learning, and zeal became so great a part of the life and strength of the University; and, even as regards those whose high endowments I otherwise learned, or already knew myself, you had your part in my appointments, for I ever tried to guide myself by what I had gained from the conversations and [xxx] correspondence which you had from time to time allowed me. To you, then, my dear Lord, more than any other, I owe my introduction to a large circle of friends, who faithfully worked with me in the course of my seven years of connection with the University, and who now, for twice seven years since, have generously kept me in mind, though I have been out of sight.

There is no one, then, whom I more intimately associate with my life in Dublin than your Lordship; and thus when I revive the recollections of what my friends there did for me, my mind naturally reverts to you; and again in making my acknowledgments to you, I am virtually thanking them.

That you may live for many years, in health, strength, and usefulness, the centre of many minds, a blessing to the Irish people, and a light in the Universal Church, is,

My dear Lord,
The fervent prayer of
Your affectionate friend and servant,
JOHN H. NEWMAN[71]

This was not all. While still in Ireland and Rector, when the desirableness of his retiring from the Rectorship had become clear to him, the one above all others whom he would have chosen for his successor was Dr Moriarty. Dr Newman's letters written at that time show how readily, for the well-being of the University, he would have given place to (could he have brought it about), and himself have worked under, Dr Moriarty (Bishop of Kerry, as he had become), whom he looked upon as having all the qualities for a good Rector—a Bishop, moreover, and an Irishman. Writing confidentially to Mgr Manning, January 11th, 1857, in answer to a New Year's letter, he says:—

---

[71] *Historical Sketches* i (1872; London: Longmans, Green & Co, 1907), pp. v–vii; *LD* xxvi, pp. 186–7. Moriarty did not see this dedicatory letter until he received his copy of the book. On 18 December 1872 he replied, 'The kindness of your letter is overwhelming. It was all dictated by the heart. I am grateful indeed' (*ibid*, p. 187n). This volume of *Historical Sketches* comprises: 'Lectures on the History of the Turks, in their relation to Europe'; 'The personal and literary character of Cicero'; 'Apollonius of Tyana'; and 'Primitive Christianity'.

> Your letter is just brought me as I am waiting to preach a University sermon, and though I shall not get through many lines first, I take up my pen to begin an answer. A happy New Year to you, in all best senses of the wish. How many New Years am I to have? This makes me rush in *medias res*. ... [xxxi]

Then after speaking of the circumstances of the time in the University, "the chronic state of things," as he calls it, he continues:—

> Dr Moriarty, Bishop of Kerry, ought to be Rector ... to deal with the Hierarchy a Bishop is wanted. Dr Moriarty is the man; a calm, prudent, firm man—has had much to do with governing—and is a friend of all parties.

And further on:—

> Were Dr Moriarty Rector, of course I would aid him—if he wished it, as much as ever I could.

But it was not within Dr Newman's sphere to move in the choice of his successor, especially since his choice would have involved the withdrawal of a Bishop from his Diocese. The letter continues thus:—

> Though always thinking Dr Moriarty the best man, it never would have occurred to me to entertain the thought of our having him here. I should have thought it a liberty to contemplate him—and indeed I still think it *would* be a liberty in me to do so. What has made me hope for him, has been the fact that has come to my knowledge, that he *has* been mentioned at Rome. And then again it strikes me, that no one *would* have taken such a liberty with him without having got his negative permission. But on this point I am quite in the dark. ...[72]

[72] The full letter can be found in *LD* xvii, pp. 491–3.

Dr Moriarty never was Rector; he died October 1st, 1877, aged 67.

[xxxii] Two passages from a letter to a friend, will serve to illustrate difficulties attending his choice of assistants. The first refers to the Editorship of the *Catholic University Gazette*, the burden of which ultimately fell upon Dr Newman. Writing with the freedom of intimacy to Mr Henry Wilberforce, whom he wished to attach to the University in close connexion with himself, as Editor of the *Gazette*, and Lecturer, he says:—

> (a) If you *take* to the *Gazette*, you will do well. All depends on that. I suppose you will from what you say, but I *protest* against your undertaking things '*to help me*'. It will not be enough, however affectionate the motive—you must do things *con amore*, or not at all. I shall be ruined if people come forward to help me—they must come forward to help the object as a *τέλος τελειότατον*.[73] You will love and serve me best, by not thinking of me, and measuring your actions by your zeal for the cause.
>
> But I take it for granted you will be taking up the *Gazette* with zeal; and on this assumption I advise you to go at once to Duffy,[74] as from me, and have a talk with him.

Then after speaking of subjects for articles, etc., and referring to his plans for Professorships, etc., he goes on to the second passage:—

> (b) Now here you can do me a service. Go to Dr Moriarty, and ask him *in confidence* what his cool judgment is about my asking Brownson[75] to give a *course of Lectures*,—tell him in the first place I am not sanguine at all that he would come,—but if he came, he would come as 'Lecturer Extraordinary,' which is simply that he would give a course of Lectures—that

---

[73] That is, an end in itself.

[74] James Duffy (1808/9–71) was a publisher of religious books in Dublin.

[75] Orestes Brownson (1798–1880) was a well-known North American convert, the pugnacious owner-editor of the controversial *Brownson's Review*, which criticised the North American bishops (and Newman, too).

> my object would be in engaging him: (1) to give *éclat* in Dublin and Ireland to the University; (2) to interest Americans in it—tell him the only objection *I* see is, what some people have urged on me, that he would be sure to lecture against me—but I think this *impossible*—he could but advance truths [xxxiii] which he fancied I did not hold, or would, as he fancied, tell against me—moreover, that he *would* be limited by the subject of his Lectureship—lastly, which is the most important question for Dr Moriarty to have before him, *viz.*, the subject of his lectures—ask him if he can suggest to me a province. What he would think of Logic? Or Ethnology? Or Antiquities? Or Geography[76] (which might be a great subject)?[77]

Such an offer, after the subject had been brought before Dr Cullen, was eventually made by Dr Newman; and it was accepted. But Dr Brownson, having meantime become at variance in politics with his patrons and others at home, first deferred his coming indefinitely, and ultimately declined. This was done in a frankly written letter of painful and touching interest, but it would require to be accompanied by too much correspondence to allow of its insertion here. The conclusion, however, of this letter (dated Sept. 13th, 1854) hardly can be omitted. Dr Brownson says:—

> Allow me, in changing the subject, to say that I have just read for the first time *Loss and Gain*.[78] If I had seen that work

---

[76] Newman wrote in his diary (15 December 1853, *LD* xxxii, p. 75), 'My letter to Brownson offered him the subject of Geography, political, moral, and physical, and enlarged on the breadth and fertility of the subject'.

[77] The full text of this lengthy letter to Henry Wilberforce, dated 23 November 1853, can be found in *LD* xv, pp. 483–7.

[78] Published March, 1848. [WPN] Newman's first novel, *Loss and Gain: the Story of a Convert*, was among the first of the genre of university novels – and the first to directly link the protagonist's personal growth to a university experience. The picture Newman paints of Oxford is a self-contained learning environment inhabited by earnest young men who are forming their life views, casting them into words, putting them on an intellectual basis, and testing them out on others. In describing how students mature both morally and intellectually, Newman draws the distinction between those who come to form a coherent 'view' and those

> at an earlier date, many things which I have written concerning you and your friends, the Oxford Converts, would never have been written. I have taken occasion in my *Review* for October to say as much, and to do what I could to repair the injustice I had unwittingly done to men whom I love and reverence, and with whom I wish in my heart sincerely to co-operate in the defence of our holy religion. Forgive me. Reverend Father, whatever injustice I have done you, and ask them in my name to forgive me also. Believe me, I was moved by no personal consideration, and thought I was only doing my duty.[79]

[xxxiv] In after years, even in the year of Dr Newman's death,—before and after that event—this offer was widely and strongly

---

who come to acquire an insubstantial 'viewiness', which perhaps remains with them all their lives. Some students develop a comprehensive perspective of the landscape of life by painstakingly piecing together fragments of vision, experience and action, and thereby construct a coherent picture of the world which gives them the possibility of living a coherent life. Others 'have no consistency in their arguments'; they argue one way today, and another the next. 'Their lines of argument diverge; nothing comes to a point; there is no one centre in which their minds sits, on which their judgment of men and things proceeds.' (*Loss and Gain*, p. 18).

Though Newman's hero is less well-read and knowledgeable than a college friend, the friend turns out to be too quick to form a view, impatient to reduce things to a system and over-fond of argument, and ends up as glib and superficial; it is, instead, the protagonist who acquires a consistent and true view of things by means of patient questioning, the careful sifting of facts and discernment of principles, a refusal to take intellectual shortcuts or to make do with simplistic explanations. Implicit in the story is that what makes this process possible is the residential nature of a university which provides for such formative opportunities outside the lecture hall; by means of the collegiate structure and the human scale of domestic arrangements, the right conditions are provided for the flourishing of the individual student through the companionship and friendship nurtured there.

For more see the critical edition published by Gracewing in 2014, edited by Sheridan Gilley.

[79] *LD* xvi, p. 257n; *NU*, p. 218. Both sources give the date as 12 (not 13) September 1854, and both quote from other parts of this letter.

commented upon, as showing a "craven spirit" very prejudicial to his estimation as Rector of the University. It will suffice here to mention his own remarks on these comments a few months before his death. They were to this effect. That an author, by the very fact of publishing a work, challenges criticism on it; he must therefore take what comes, and he has no right to complain if it goes against him; that Dr Brownson, therefore, was within his right in animadverting in his *Review* (*Brownson's Review*) on his (Dr Newman's) volume, *The Development of Christian Doctrine*. As to Dr Brownson's behaviour towards him, the irrelevant personalities interspersed in his series of articles, etc., of these Cardinal Newman went on to say, that, to himself, it was incomprehensible that people could have supposed him capable of sacrificing the great interests of the University by letting his feelings as to what was so personal to himself weigh against the distinction that Dr Brownson's name would have brought to the University. Had Dr Brownson, he continued, made a wrong use (which he did not think he would) of his Chair, he would have been told that he must *not*, and had he then repeated the offence, he would have had to be dealt with.[80] So thoroughly in earnest was Dr Newman in his purpose to draw Dr Brownson to Dublin, and for all to go well, that, in the summer of 1854, when planning for the leasehold of a house for himself, he included in it rooms for Dr Brownson, and for a table in common with himself for Dr [xxxv]
Brownson and two or three others. But it must not be supposed that Dr Newman was indifferent to, or that he did not properly estimate the effect of Dr Brownson's conduct towards him. This incident led the Cardinal to refer to his Dublin University papers generally, and to say that the whole collection might be called *My Campaign in Ireland*.[81] It consists of a variety of papers—also, a

---

[80] On 14 November 1854, Cullen wrote to Newman from Rome: 'Dr Hughes [Archbishop] of New York says it is most fortunate that Brownson did not go to Ireland, as he is hot-headed and obstinate, and it would not be easy to handle him' (*NU*, p. 218n). See also *LD* xvi, p. 234, n3.

[81] There is no reference to this in *LD*. The closest Newman came to using this phrase was when thanking Ornsby for sending him his letters about the University: 'what a capital history I found your letters to me to be of the University campaign' (9 September 1872, *LD* xxvi, p. 164).

brief *Narrative of Events*, and correspondence. He thought that they might be published at any time, for there was nothing compromising in them to any one.

His attention was by no means confined to filling the various offices. He anticipated the time for practical work by all kinds of preliminary inquiries and organization. For instance, in speaking of the Faculty of Law, he says: "I was able to do nothing for the Faculty of Law, but it was not for not trying. The practical difficulty was the premium there was on attending Trinity College Lectures, in the shortening it gave of the course of years requisite for being called to the Bar.[82] As early as February 16th, 1854, I offered to Mr T. O'Hagan, now Lord O'Hagan, 'any Lectureship he would take, and asked him to recommend men from the Bar'.[83] By 22nd March, I had gained Bowyer's[84] consent to helping me
[xxxvi] by delivering a course of Lectures. About April or May in the

[82] The premium on attending Trinity or the Queen's Colleges meant it shortened the time needed for the Bar by two years. In the absence of any alternative, Catholics studying for the Bar continued to go to Trinity.

[83] Thomas O'Hagan (1812–85) was the first Catholic to become Lord Chancellor of Ireland since the reign of James II.

[84] Sir George Bowyer, Bt, of Radley Park, Berks, was born in 1811. Originally educated for a military career, he became a cadet of the Royal Military College, Woolwich; but afterwards determining to adopt the legal profession, he was admitted in 1836 a member of the Middle Temple, and was called in 1839. In the same year he received from the University of Oxford the honorary degree of MA, and in 1843 that of DCL In 1850 he was appointed Reader to the Middle Temple. In that year, too, his conversion to the Catholic Faith was announced, and from that time he took an active and prominent part in whatever the ecclesiastical authorities brought forward to promote its interests. He was the author of several legal works of reputation, among others, *Dissertations on the Statutes of the Italian Cities* and *Commentaries on the Constitutional Law of England*. He sat as a Liberal for Dundalk from 1852 to 1868, and was returned for County Wexford in 1874, but he did not seek re-election in 1880. Sir George Bowyer was a Knight of Malta and also Grand Cross of the Pontifical Order of St Gregory. He was also a Magistrate and Deputy-Lieutenant for Berks. The large and beautiful Chapel of the Hospital of St John of Jerusalem and St Elizabeth in Great Ormond Street, London, was paid for by Sir George Bowyer. He died 7th June, 1883. [WPN]

same year, I had gained Myles O'Reilly's consent to undertake other Lectures. By November he had named his subject, 'Natural Law, or the Philosophy of Law,' and Mr Pigot[85] had undertaken conditionally, 'The Law of Real Property'."[86]

It was by forethought such as this, that at length when the oaths were administered, he was able to open the University without delay. This he did the following 3rd November, St Malachy's Day, as soon as people had reassembled in Dublin after their vacation, he himself matriculating and locating the students, and starting their lectures. It is much to be regretted that the address which he made to the students on the occasion of their assembling for the first time, was not preserved by him except in some notes of his own. These, imperfect though they are, are included in the Supplement. Twelve months later, however, the then Editor of the *Catholic University Gazette* inserted in it a Note on this gathering. It will be found at page 319.

The Rector's Fourth Report (for 1857–58) is wanting. This, [xxxii] there is reason for saying, was occasioned by a Report he had received from the Faculty of Science, superseding, as may be believed, what he himself was preparing. This Report was so ably

---

85 John Edward Pigot (1822–71), son of the Chief Baron of the Exchequer, was called to the Bar in 1845. He was a Young Irelander and became one of the poets of the movement; he was also a member of the Repeal Association, but left and joined the newly-founded Irish Confederation, serving on its council. After the failed Young Irelander rebellion of 1848, Pigot focused his energy on cultural rather than political matters. Newman's offer of a position was on condition that Pigot did not bring politics into his lectures, an arrangement which Pigot willingly signed up to. (*DIB*)

86 Unable to set up a Faculty of Law for November 1854, despite his best efforts, Newman hoped that John O'Hagan (1822–90), a barrister who had been educated at Trinity College Dublin, would combine his lectureship in political economy with one in law. O'Hagan acted as Dean of the Faculty of Law when the University Council first met in November 1855. Three years later, on his 'University annual expenses' (11 November 1858) Newman allocated £100 for jurisprudence, to be taught by John O'Hagan, with the comment that the arrangement 'has not yet come into effect, though it ought to settled at once. I heartily and earnestly wish it carried out' (enclosed with Newman to Anderdon, 16 November 1858, *LD* xviii, p. 584).

drawn up by Dr Lyons, the Dean of the Faculty, and the subjects on which it treated were so important, and so peculiar to that Faculty, that Dr Newman considered it advisable to let it stand by itself, rather than risk the diminution of its force by introducing it among other matters in a Report of his own. Moreover, it was urgent that the Report should be brought before the *Cœtus Episcoporum*, then close at hand; consequently, he forwarded it to the Archbishop, with the letter in explanation which follows:—

The Very Rev. the Rector, to His Grace the Archbishop of Dublin, President of the Cœtus Episcoporum, etc., etc.

THE ORATORY, BIRMINGHAM,
June 17*th,* 1858

MY DEAR LORD ARCHBISHOP,

The Dean and Faculty of Science have sent me their Report on the wants and requirements of the Faculty, with a request that I would submit it to the Archbishops and Bishops of Ireland, with such recommendation as I might think fitting.

As they suggest that it should be laid before the next Episcopal meeting, I feel I am best giving expression to their wish by addressing myself, as I now do, to your Grace as the formal President of the *Cœtus Episcoporum*.

No remarks which I could offer on their Report would be in themselves of any value, considering the matters of which it
[xxxiii] treats; but, since I am *still* Rector, there is both a fitness in the Professors addressing the Archbishops and Bishops through me, and a call on me to declare my full concurrence in the step they have taken, founded on my intimate sense of the claim which the Faculty has on the zealous and munificent patronage of those who, like the Archbishops and Bishops of Ireland, have come forward in the sight of Europe as the founders of a great University. I am encouraged in this strong expression of opinion by the recollection that when I was in Rome two years since, persons there of the highest consideration urged upon me the duty, under which I lay as Rector, of furthering to the best of my power the interests of Physical Science.

I am, my dear Lord Archbishop,

With profound respect,
Your Grace's most faithful servant in Christ,
JOHN H. NEWMAN,
Of the Oratory

His Grace the most Rev. the Archbishop of Dublin, etc.[87]

Dr Newman certainly at one time had it in mind to let one Report supersede the other, but it is not unlikely that he afterwards resumed writing his own, for in a letter to Professor Ornsby dated 19th September, 1858, when the usual time (October) for presenting his own drew near, he says; "I am glad you have moved *in re bursaria*. I have put it into my Report."[88] This then is a reason, along with others, for hoping that a Fourth Report may yet be found, though at present there is no trace of it, nor any record of its presentation.[89]

---

[87] Cullen replied on 27 September to express his concern that Newman's letter and the printed Report from the Dean of the Faculty of Science, though marked 'proof', were now in circulation. The Report contained an appeal to increase the number of professors, but, commented Cullen, this was not possible because the University was running at a loss. Besides there were complaints that there were too many professors. 'Under these circumstances, I doubt whether it would be prudent to publish the report, as it would only attract attention to wants which cannot at present be supplied.' (*LD* xviii, p. 467n)

[88] This fragment comes from a letter from Newman to Ornsby dated 19 September 1858 (*LD* xviii, p. 460 n1). Ornsby wanted the annual grant for burses for medicine and science to be increased from £80 to £100.

[89] A breach of etiquette had unfortunately been committed by Dr Lyons by his sending his Report to the Archbishop in print instead of in manuscript. As this was brought before the notice of the Rector, it is likely that his own Fourth Report never was printed but was sent in manuscript. [WPN]

Lyons, the Dean for 1857/58, explained to Newman on 1 October that copies of his report were printed for the meeting of the bishops expected in the summer (which in the end did not take place), and that copies were sent to some of the bishops, as well as friends and supporters of the University, but that the report was not in 'any sense published' (*LD* xviii, p. 468n).

[xxxix] At this time, and for long past, grave matters relating to the University had been weighing upon Dr Newman; two of these shall be mentioned, as probably they would have been dealt with in his missing report.

(1) His estimation of the importance of the office of Vice-Rector has already been seen, yet it hardly can be said that he had ever had a Vice-Rector's assistance.[90] This want had become

---

By 1858, the struggle with MacHale had unnerved Cullen to the point that he suffered a second physical and mental breakdown—the first was In 1855—which required a protracted convalescence of some seven months in Rome. As he was out of Ireland from 28 September 1858 to 1 June 1859 and as Newman left the University in November 1858, it is probable that Newman did not write more than an introduction to Lyon's report.

[90] Patrick Leahy was the first Vice-Rector, while also acting as parish priest of Cashel—with an indult from Rome allowing him to reside for much of the year in Dublin. When in Dublin, he did not stay near the University but in outlying Dalkey. During Newman's visit to Rome on Oratorian business, 26 December 1855 to 11 February 1856, Leahy was Left in charge of the University—the only occasion 'in which a Vice Rector was a reality', Newman commented at the time (*LD* xvii, p. 99, n1). Laurence Forde substituted as Vice-Rector in January 1857, when Dr Leahy was ill, but Newman found him impossible to deal with. Moreover, he was unpopular and had little understanding of Newman's idea of a university, and when Cullen tried to make Forde the Vice-Rector, Newman effectively blocked the appointment; Newman later confided to a friend that to appoint Forde Vice-Rector would be 'simply inadmissible. I should be a traitor to the University if I concurred in such a choice' (Newman to Monsell, 9 October 1857, *LD* xviii, p. 140).

On Leahy's appointment as Archbishop of Cashel, the University lost its (mainly non-resident) Vice-Rector that summer, and finding a replacement was to prove highly problematic. Having offered his resignation as Rector in April 1857, Newman only agreed to stay on for a fourth year with partial residence 'of say nine weeks' provided a Vice-Rector was appointed. O'Reilly was offered the job, but turned it down, after which the archbishops decided to postpone the appointment. With no Vice-Rector and a largely absent Rector, it was hardly surprising that disciplinary problems should have arisen during Newman's fourth and final year in office (1857/58). See *LD* xvi, p. 551 n2; *AW*, pp. 294–5 for more about Newman's difficulties over a vice-Vice-Rector. For details about the disciplinary problems in 1857/58, see *MM*, pp. 324–35, 343–5.

especially trying to him. The discipline of the University was one of the duties belonging to that office, but in default of the proper official it in great measure devolved upon himself; he assumed it perforce, until the appointment of a Vice-Rector, to which he was continually looking forward. It was, however, a duty which neither belonged to, nor became his office, nor was compatible with it; conscience, therefore, would not allow him to acquiesce in the continuance of this deficiency, and he made most earnest applications that the Vice-Rectorship might be filled up.[91] He failed, however, of success.

(2) An authoritative audit and acceptance of the University accounts was also a subject which pressed upon him as an urgent need. About £5000 annually passed through his hands in a complicated arrangement of cheques, and the liability to be called upon by the Archbishops and Bishops to account at a moment for an expenditure, however far back it may have been, oppressed him more and more with the increase of time. He knew, he said, the treachery of memory when suddenly called upon, and he felt it [xl] was not right to let himself be exposed to such risks.[92] But as was the case with respect to the Vice-Rectorship, so, here too, his applications failed of success.[93]

---

[91] As Dean of his college at Oxford and Pro-Proctor, Dr Newman had had considerable experience in the maintenance of University discipline, which at Dublin inclined him to leniency unless authority or substantial decorum was threatened. [WPN] Newman was Pro-proctor of Oxford University from 21 April 1830 until 13 April 1831. There are many diary entries during this term of office which mention 'walking [i.e. patrolling] the streets'. Newman was elected Dean, and therefore Vice-provost, of Oriel on 17 October 1833, a position he occupied for two years.

[92] As Treas. at Oriel he had been used to punctuality and exactness. [WPN] Newman was appointed Junior Treasurer of Oriel on 16 October 1824, and four years later took over the Senior Treasurer's work. He ceased to be Treasurer of Oriel on 15 October 1831, but he took up the position of Junior Treasurer again on 16 October 1838 for one more year.

[93] Despite his best efforts, Newman failed to relieve himself of some of the financial administration of the Catholic University by establishing a lay finance committee. In the summer of 1854 he told Cullen, who had just returned from Rome, where he had been for nine months, that 'some soreness exists on the part of the educated and upper class through Ireland on the ground that they are allowed so little share in the

A letter to Fr O'Reilly, S.J., will show how seriously he viewed the want of a Vice-Rector.

April 22nd, 1858

MY DEAR FATHER O'REILLY,

Though you had so little success in persuading the members of the Council[94] to meet some two months ago, I fear I must once more trouble you to make the attempt. The want of a Vice-Rector is ruining the University. The best rules of discipline will do nothing, unless there is some one to enforce them. I do not consider this to be the Rector's duty; and I feel that it is as little *my calling*, as you (most intelligibly) felt it to be yours.

---

management of the money matters of the University. I think they would have joined us before now, if they had been more definitely recognised' (Newman to Cullen, 26 July 1855, *LD* xvi, pp. 514–15). In a draft of this letter (p. 514n) he expressed himself more strongly, writing that he had reason to believe that 'a strong opinion and much soreness exist on the subject [of a lay committee to manage the University accounts] among the laity of the educated class, and we shall not gain the names of the Catholic gentry, till the money matters of the University are in their hands'. It was not until 8 September that Cullen replied.

Among the letters Newman received on the subject was one from a lay member of the University Committee, who complained that 'the tendency is to make the University a close borough of clergymen and a clerical College', and pointed out that this had not been the intention of those who had assisted Newman at the start (J. M. O'Ferrall to Newman, 17 December 1854, *LD* xvi, p. 515 n3. A 'close borough' means one having the right of sending a member to Parliament, whose nomination is in the hands of a single person). Newman's request for greater lay involvement was turned down on this and later occasions. A sub-committee had been set up by the University Committee in October 1853 to represent it, especially in financial matters, and it comprised Cullen, Patrick Leahy, Michael Errington, James More O'Ferrall and Myles O'Reilly. It met only once.

A separate matter from a finance committee was the compilation of the annual report of the accounts of the Catholic University, which was carried out by two auditors, Charles Bianconi and Michael Errington.

[94] The role of the Rectorial Council was to advise the Rector on academic matters; it was composed of the Deans of faculties and the Vice-Rector. Newman defines its role in Report II and its appendices: see pp. [59–63, 79–80, 101–9].

Now, in the absence of this most necessary office, what is to be done? I can think of nothing better than that the Council should give their authority to a set of rules which they should *impose* on the Deans.[95] You cannot expect the Deans to act without some one to fall back upon. They must be able to say to the members of their Houses: 'We are obliged to do so and so'.

Now, what I think best is this—for a small Committee to be appointed, consisting of the Deans (who practically acknowledge the authority of the University in their Houses), *viz*., Mr Flannery[96] and Mr Penny[97] (Father Bennett,[98] I am

---

[95] Not to be confused with the Deans of faculties, the 'Deans of Houses' were the heads of the collegiate houses. In the fourth year of the University there were four collegiate houses: St Patrick's, St Mary's, St Laurence's and Our Lady of Mount Carmel.

[96] Michael Flannery (1818–91) was Professor of Moral Theology at All Hallows, 1845–51, and Vicar-General of Killaloe, 1853–59. At Cullen's indication, he was appointed Dean of St Patrick's House in 1854 and remained there until he became coadjutor Bishop of Killaloe in 1858, succeeding a year later. He was unsuited to running a collegiate house as he had little idea of how to manage students (*MM*, pp. 155, 297–303, 327–9, 335–42). As a bishop he threw himself into his work, which was considerable in the post-Famine years, and within four years was burnt out; he moved to Paris in 1863 for health reasons, while his diocese was managed consecutively by three coadjutor bishops until his death.

[97] William Goodenough Penny (1815–*c*.85) was educated at Westminster School and Christ Church, Oxford, where he gained the top mark in his year in mathematics and became a Student (i.e. a Fellow). He took Anglican orders, became a Catholic in 1848, then joined Newman at Littlemore, Maryvale, and then Rome, where he was ordained. He left the Oratory in 1851 (but not the priesthood), and remained a good friend of Newman. Newman invited him to a tutorship in mathematics at the Catholic University, and a year later he became the University Catechist; in 1856 he succeeded Newman as Dean of St Mary's House, but resigned after two years. Penny succeeded Butler as Professor of Mathematics, 1860–73. He was a popular tutor and lecturer, and took a great interest in student sport, acting as a rowing coach and umpire.

[98] Thomas Bennett was educated at the University of Louvain and became the Provincial of the Calced Carmelites in Ireland, acting for a time as Vice-President of All Hallows. He became Dean of the Carmelite House of Our Lady of Mount Carmel when, in 1855, the older students of

told, has hardly any of our students just now), with one or two of the Professors of the Faculty of Ph. and L.,[99] with, say, Dr MacDermott,[100] etc. (but I am not suggesting of course, only illustrating what I mean)—and that they should draw up some rules to submit to the Council, and that they should come out with the Council's authority.[101]

I have great dread of this great long Summer term. I hear
[xli] that some of the Students skip dinner, and dine in coffee-houses. There are the long evenings too.[102] On these and other accounts, considering there is no chance of a Vice-Rector before the long vacation, I feel I should be wanting in a duty unless I wrote you this letter.

I remain, my dear Father O'Reilly,

Most sincerely yours in Christ,

---

the Carmelite secondary school became members of the Catholic University. However, fewer than a dozen students joined the University.

[99] That is, Philosophy and Literature.

[100] Robert MacDermott (1829–59) was educated at Clongowes Wood and studied Classics at Trinity College Dublin, before studying medicine. He was appointed Professor of Materia Medica (i.e. Pharmacology) at the Catholic University in 1855 and had the reputation of being the best lecturer of his day.

[101] The committee of three Deans of Houses and four academics drew up some rules of discipline which were effectively a graded system of penalties and fines. Only Flannery warmed to the new rules. Penny had grave misgivings about them, and James Quinn (the Dean of St Laurence's) was sufficiently astute to notice 'that such a system of management is not in harmony with the views which presided over the Formation of the little collegiate bodies—like families'; he thought the rules imprudent and ill-adapted to their actual circumstances (Dunne to Newman, 31 May 1858, *LD* xviii, p. 369 n1). In the end the Council rejected the system, and instead proposed that Newman write to the Deans to insist on the observance of the Rules and Regulations.

Quinn's name was deliberately omitted from the committee by Newman, but as O'Reilly thought it advisable to include him, his name was added. See *LD* xviii, p. 329n.

[102] For a full account of the disciplinary problems at the Catholic University see chapter 6, 'The problems of keeping house', in *MM*, especially the section entitled 'Discipline wears thin' (pp. 324–35).

JOHN H. NEWMAN,
Of the Oratory[103]

It must be here observed in connexion with these anxieties that Dr Newman had to act under great disadvantage from the very first; and this in two ways especially. One has already been noticed, his having in the earlier years of his Rectorship to act in a private capacity; but this was brought to an end by his installation in May, 1854. He was subject to the other, from his nomination to his retirement. As Rector of the University he had to deal with the highest authorities of the Church; but being himself merely a priest, he could not press his opinion, nor contend beyond a certain point for what he thought necessary; both in liberty of speech, and opportunity of access to such dignitaries, he was within very restricted limits.

But a remedy at one time seemed to be forthcoming. In the winter of 1853–54 Cardinal Wiseman,[104] himself a most rigid enforcer of the rules of ecclesiastical etiquette, perceived, perhaps by intuition, the difficulties which had already arisen, or would be likely to follow from Dr Newman's anomalous position; and in consequence, after consulting Dr Cullen and obtaining his hearty concurrence, he personally suggested (January, 1854) to Pius IX [xlii] that His Holiness would be pleased to create Dr Newman a Bishop *in partibus*—"which," he said to Dr Newman, "would at once give you a right to sit with the Bishops in all consultations, would raise you above all other officers, professors, etc., of the University, and would give dignity to the University, and to its Head".[105] The Holy Father assented, and recurring to the subject at a subsequent audience, named the See to which he would elevate

---

[103] *LD* xviii, pp. 329–30.

[104] Nicholas Wiseman (1802–65) was Rector of the English College in Rome (1828–40) when Newman called on him twice during his visit there in 1833. Wiseman visited Newman at Oriel in 1841. He followed the Tractarian Movement closely, and welcomed the converts into the Catholic Church. In 1849 he became the last Vicar Apostolic of the London District, and following year was made the first Archbishop of Westminster and a cardinal.

[105] The full letter from Wiseman can be found in *LD* xvi, pp. 31–2.

him. Permission was at the same time given Dr Newman to make use of the information. This was on January 20th, 1854.

Writing with appreciation of this act of Cardinal Wiseman, he says:—

> I really did think that the Cardinal had hit the right nail on the head, and had effected what would be a real remedy against the difficulties which lay in my way.[106]

To Dr Grant, Bishop of Southwark, who had congratulated him, he speaks of it thus:—

> I never could have fancied the circumstances would exist such as to lead me to be glad to be made a Bishop, but so it was, I did feel glad, for I did not see how without some accession of weight to my official position I could overcome the inertia or opposition which existed in Ireland on the project of a University.[107]

His Bishop, Dr Ullathorne,[108] also congratulated him most warmly.

Nothing further followed; no further communication was made to him. Having had occasion in later years to write on this subject, he says of it, "it faded out of my mind".[109]

[xliii] Indeed, except that in kind remembrance of the donors, he may once and again have shown the presents of pectoral crosses and chains, such as are not unfrequently made by friends to a Bishop-Elect, those about him hardly could have realized that his name had ever been connected with such a dignity.[110]

---

[106] 'Memorandum about my Connection with the Catholic University', *AW*, p. 316.

[107] This is taken from a memorandum of the letter. [WPN] 'Memorandum about my Connection with the Catholic University', *AW*, p. 316.

[108] William Ullathorne (1806–89) was the first Bishop of Birmingham.

[109] 'Memorandum about my Connection with the Catholic University', *AW*, p. 320.

[110] For Newman's account of the affair, see section 6 of his 'Memorandum about my Connection with the Catholic University', *AW*, pp. 312–20. At the time everyone thought the idea to be a good one, as it

There were other and very different subjects, directly and indirectly relating to the University, which caused him much serious thought about himself and his work; the more so as he had it continually before him that, though still in his best years, he could not count upon strength in the future to make up for the loss of any one of them. Two letters will show something of what was working unseen throughout his Rectorship. Both letters are addressed to personal friends; the first is to a member of Parliament closely connected with the Ministry of the day.

EDGBASTON, BIRMINGHAM, *February 3rd*, 1853

MY DEAR _____[111]

---

would facilitate Newman's dealings with the Irish bishops; but on Cullen's recommendation the prospect was at first postponed, until the University was started, then effectively dropped by the summer of 1855 (though most people did not realise this until later). Cullen's argument for the postponement was that the time was not right and that it might cause opposition. Cullen's actions only became known with the publication of: V. F. Blehl, 'Newman and the missing mitre', *Thought: Fordham University Quarterly* 35:136 (Spring 1960), pp. 111–23; and J. H. Whyte, 'Newman in Dublin: fresh light from the archives of Propaganda', *Dublin Review* 483 (Spring 1960), pp. 31–9. For a summary and discussion of the episode, see Barr, *Paul Cullen*, pp. 111–16; I. Ker, *John Henry Newman: a Biography* (Oxford: Clarendon Press, 1988), pp. 402, 405, 408, 417.

[111] William Monsell (1812–94), first Baron Emly, is the person referred to here. Educated at Winchester and Oriel College, Oxford, he was MP for Limerick 1847–74 and from 1855 held various offices in the Liberal government, though he never reached the Cabinet. Along with William Sewell and Lord Adare (whose sister he married), he helped to found St Columba's College in County Meath for the Irish Protestants. He became a Catholic, and together with Hope-Scott and Manning advised Cullen in 1851 about the Catholic University. Although he had no official attachment to the Catholic University, he and Newman exchanged many letters about it; and after Newman's departure, he acted energetically for the University to gain a charter and endowment, most notably in the scheme Gladstone brought forward in 1873. Newman dedicated to him *Lectures and Essays on University Subjects* (1859), the second half of the *Idea*, as 'a memorial of work done in a country which you so dearly love, and in behalf of an undertaking in which you feel so deep an interest'. A regular contributor to *The Rambler*, he was a close friend of the French

I have thought over the question you put me, and I think I have my answer, tho' it is no very helping one in the difficulty in which we find ourselves.[112]

The Pope has resolved on a Catholic University in Ireland—money is collected for it—and a President appointed. He has done this in opposition to certain Government Colleges. And he has put a mark on those Colleges, forbidding priests to teach there. Now, for him to withdraw his censure, is simply asking him to extinguish the projected University, for both cannot flourish. Why not then ask him *directly* to do so? That is intelligible, and may be right, or may not—but still is respectful. But it seems to me greatly wanting in consideration
[xliv] to him, so to ignore his acts and intentions as coolly to ask him to do a thing which will neutralize them. I cannot conceive it will be taken well—tho' of course I only give you my own impression on the suggestion you made.

Then again, I do not see how Ireland (or England either) can possibly supply professors for *three* Colleges. Either you will have incompetent men to fill the Chairs, or you will of necessity bring in a set of quasi-unbelievers. On the other hand, if you cut down the staff, you have three incomplete schools of learning.

Moreover, while you have professors of different religions, you never can have a *genius loci*—and the place is no longer a genuine University.

And again, I feel sure the Holy See will never agree to any plan which mixes up Catholic *youth* with Protestants, let alone the Professors.

I lament as much as any over the present fix—but I do not see how it is possible for the Church in any way to recognize the Colleges—and for myself, unless I am better advised, I do not see how I could ever come into any plan of the sort.

---

liberal Catholic leader Montalembert. He became Vice-Chancellor of the Royal University of Ireland. (*DIB*, *ODNB*)

[112] Newman feared that the government of Lord Aberdeen—to which Monsell acted as Clerk of the Ordnance—was seeking a compromise over the Queen's Colleges.

Also, unless it is putting what I have said merely in another form, it seems to me to be disrespectful to the Holy See, for the State to ask it to *recognize* the State Colleges, while the State steadily persists in *ignoring* the Holy See's University.

The establishment of the Queen's University is an additional difficulty.[113]

Ever yours affectionately in Christ,

JOHN H. NEWMAN[114]

The second is to Dr Grant, Bishop of Southwark, who had often shown great interest in the University. A few lines in explanation of this letter must precede it.

Until eighteen months before the date of the letter to Dr Grant, Oxford had been absolutely closed to Catholics, but on 7th [xlv] August, 1854, an Act was passed which provided that it should not be necessary for any person upon matriculating in the University or upon taking the degree of Bachelor in Arts, Law, Medicine, or Music, to make or subscribe any declaration or take any oath. Henceforth a Catholic could obtain admission to the University if he could obtain admission into a College, for it was through a College that admission was obtained to the University, and the Colleges had full liberty as to their admission of applicants. Now as very few Colleges would receive Catholics, the University still remained practically closed to Catholics. At the Colleges, the one or two, where admittance to Catholics was allowed, it was only to two or three at a time as a special personal favour, with the understanding that their religion was to be kept out of sight.[115] So special a favour was this, that it may be said to

[113] The Queen's University had been established by Letters Patent in 1850. Presumably Newman thought that the formal incorporation of the three Colleges as parts of a non-denominational university made it more difficult to modify their constitutions.

[114] *LD* xv, pp. 283–4. At the top of this letter is the phrase '(sent pretty much the same)'.

[115] About twenty Catholics entered Oxford University in the first decade after the removal of the religious test.

have been granted only to youths of some distinction, and sometimes there would be not one even, in residence.[116]

Now one of Dr Newman's objects was to attract youths of the higher classes to the Catholic University in Dublin, for hitherto they had had no such place for completing their education, and he therefore adapted his own house in Harcourt Street, Dublin, to that purpose.[117] This House was known as St Mary's, and it was carried on upon the lines indicated in the Reports and papers. A number of such youths had collected there.[118] But the opening at

---

[116] It was not till 1865 that Oxford was prohibited to Catholics by Rome. [WPN] This is not quite true; in February 1865 Propaganda Fide instructed the English bishops to *dissuade* Catholics from attending non-Catholic universities. (Note that the instruction did not apply to Irish or Scottish Catholics.) Two years later Propaganda issued a stronger warning, declaring that English Catholics sending their sons to the national universities would be guilty of exposing them to a proximate occasion of grave sin; the bishops were charged to communicate the decision to the faithful through pastoral letters. Four years after the closure of the Catholic University College, Kensington (1875–82), the warning was reiterated. The policy was reversed in 1895, after the death of Cardinal Manning. For a fuller account of the 'university question', see P. A. Shrimpton, *A Catholic Eton*? *Newman's Oratory School* (Leominster: Gracewing, 2004), pp. 220–33.

[117] Towards the end of October 1854 Newman decided to rent 6 Harcourt Street, and to furnish it at his own expense. By opening up the Rector's house to students he thought he could help solve one of the 'actual difficulties – viz the necessity of beginning with *several* houses for different classes of students' (Newman to H. Wilberforce, 5 July 1854, *LD* xvi, p. 188). By way of explaining the large difference in fees between his house St Mary's (£60, £80 or £100) and St Patrick's (£42), Newman placed a notice in the *CUG* (12 October 1854) which stated that the availability of more expensive residential arrangements would not divide the student body as regards 'academic advantages, social equality, and unity of discipline'.

[118] Newman used every connection he had to drum up support for the University from the English constituency and beyond, urging friends to assist the enterprise by recommending students for it. Although he had anticipated receiving mainly sons of Englishmen of the professional classes, he found himself overseeing a cosmopolitan household with considerable social éclat. By the end of the first term the student residents at St Mary's comprised two Englishmen, two Scottish cousins of noble

Oxford, such as it was, brought him great anxiety, not only as to his raising up a Catholic University for English-speaking Catholics, but in connexion with these youths in particular, for it would be to such as these that the permission to enter a College at Oxford would be likely to be granted, and thus, perhaps, render Pius the Ninth's strongly expressed wishes and commands of but little weight, at least as regards the class for whom the University in Dublin was especially intended. [xlvi]

Among the earliest to look towards taking advantage at Oxford of the Act of 1854, was a youth to whom Dr Grant[119] had either a quasi-guardianship, or at least a consultative voice with respect to his education. He had, moreover, been commended by a dying parent to the remembrance of Dr Newman.

The letter to Dr Grant which this occasioned will show that Dr Newman had full ground for anxiety, and will supply whatever more need be said on the subject.

From Dr Newman to Dr Grant, Bishop of Southwark

6 HARCOURT STREET, DUBLIN,
March 7th, 1856

MY DEAR LORD,

If the report is true which I hear, that ____[120] is intended by his Guardian for Oxford, I am sure your Lordship is in

---

blood, two Irishmen (one of them a baronet), and two titled Frenchmen. No wonder Newman could say, 'we have quite a galaxy of high people in this house' (Newman to de Lisle, 7 May 1855, *LD* xvi, p. 462). At Christmas 1854, it looked as though more rooms would be needed for French, Belgian and Polish youths. For more about St Mary's see *MM*, pp. 183–97, 211–17.

[119] Thomas Grant (1816–70) studied at the English College, Rome and acted as its Rector, 1844–51. In 1851 he became the first Bishop of Southwark.

[120] Francis Scawen Blunt (1839–72) is the person referred to here. He was received into the Catholic Church, along with his brother Wilfred (later famous as a poet and politician) in 1852, two years after his mother, who was by then a widow. The boys attended Stonyhurst then Oscott. Before she died, their mother entrusted them to Bishop Grant, but the Court of Chancery appointed two Protestant relatives as wards. The boys

considerable anxiety—and with the hope that you will not be displeased by my setting before you some suggestions, supposing your mind not to be made up on the subject, I have, after several days of uncertainty and fidget to myself, taken up my pen to write to you.

Speaking according to my knowledge of Oxford, I should say that it was a place very dangerous to a young man's faith—and though he might be preserved from defection, he might be indelibly stamped with indifferentism, which would be his character through life.

[xlvii] He would be saved from this, if there were a Catholic *Hall* or *College* there, but this leads me to another aspect of the subject, which is my real reason for writing to you,

Every one looks at things from his own point of view, so your Lordship must make allowances for me, if I am personally alarmed at the notion of the Bishops of England allowing (should they allow) young Catholics to go to the English Protestant Universities. What is Ireland to me, except the University here is a University for England, as well as for Ireland? I wish to do good, of course, to all Catholics if I can, but to *English* Catholics as my duty. I have left England for a while, for what I conceive to be a great *English* interest. But, if I went by my own wishes and tendencies, of course I would far rather do good to English Catholics in Oxford than in Dublin.

However, the Holy See decided that Dublin was to be the place for Catholic education of the upper classes in these islands, and, under this decision, I acquiesced in the wish of the Irish Bishops to have me here. But, if there is a College for Catholics in Oxford, or anything approaching to it, I am at once loosened from this place. And I should give as my reason, that I have a call nearer home. Oxford is close to Birmingham.

Not only as regards myself would the allowance of Catholic youths to go to Oxford unsettle this nascent

---

were allowed to stay on at Oscott, but Grant feared to suggest they join the Catholic University in case they were moved to a Protestant school. Neither of them went to Oxford.

University. You may easily fancy that Catholic youths here look up with admiration and curiosity to Oxford. The Irish as well as English youths, would wish to go there, and this University [at Dublin] would have to seek not only Rectors and Professors but students altogether. As it is, I am very much alarmed, and have been for this year past, lest our youths, having spent a year or two here, should transfer themselves to Oxford, and make us merely tutors or providers of a Protestant Institution—but, if it is known here that a Catholic youth actually is in Oxford with the leave of a Catholic Bishop, the consequences may be serious.

For myself, I have only to look, and I hope I do look, at [xlviii]
what the Holy See wishes. It has fixed on Dublin as the seat of Catholic Education—and, till it undoes its work, it is of course my duty to do all I can to advance it.

Whatever judgment you form of this letter, I am sure you will kindly give it the attention suitable to the sincerity with which I trust it is written.

I am, my dear Lord,

Begging your Lordship's blessing,

Ever yours affectionately,

JOHN H. NEWMAN,

Of the Oratory[121]

These two letters, besides serving as instances of the difficulties which beset him, show also how far even his friends were from grasping the main object of the University, and the danger of that object being missed in a variety of aims and interests. Dr Newman had long seen how infidelity, taking advantage of the philanthropic spirit of the day, was advancing in every direction, and nowhere did exertion in anticipation of its approach seem to him more needful than in Ireland. The intellectual gifts of the people, their desire to avail themselves of advantages for their improvement, their history in the past,—all this, with his own increasing personal knowledge of them, helped to warn him of their danger, and to animate him the more to serve

[121] *LD* xvii, pp. 178–9.

them in that particular.[122] His deep religious interest in them, together with his good hopes for them, are well brought out in his Address (2 November 1858) on *Discipline of the Mind*,[123] to the young men of the evening classes;[124] he thus speaks to them and of their country:—

[xlix] If I do homage to the many virtues and gifts of the Irish people, and am zealous for their full development, it is not simply for the sake of themselves, but because the name of Ireland ever has been, and, I believe, ever will be, associated with the Catholic Faith, and because, in doing any service, however poor it may be, to Ireland, a man is ministering, in his own place and measure, to the cause of the Holy Roman Apostolic Church. …

Ireland is the proper seat of a Catholic University, on account of its ancient hereditary Catholicity, and again of the future which is in store for it.[125] It is impossible, Gentlemen, to

---

[122] It could be said that Newman did not give the Irish bishops the university they *wanted*, but the university he thought they *needed*. I owe this insight to Alasdair MacIntyre from a lecture he gave at Notre Dame University on 1 November 2006 in the series 'God, philosophy, universities' (from the lecture notes of Brian Boyd).

[123] This is one of the ten occasional lectures and essays that comprise the second half of the *Idea*.

[124] Evening classes were arranged at the Catholic University in 1854/55, but not the following year, as Newman judged it was premature to offer them. When they were restarted in April 1858, 105 students enrolled; the following term 179 registered. Thanks to a statute Newman had passed through the Council in January 1857, those attending were able to proceed to degrees. After this promising start, numbers at the evening classes fell, and in 1865 the classes were discontinued. See also *AW*, p. 323.

[125] Newman had written in similar fashion in one of his university sketches: 'I desiderate […] a more central position than Oxford […] I look for a city less inland […] and a country closer upon the highways of the seas. I look towards a land both old and young; old in its Christianity, young in the promise of its future […] I dimly see the island I am gazing on, become the road of passage and union between two hemispheres […] The capital of the prosperous and hopeful land is situate in a beautiful bay and near a romantic region […] Thither […] students are flocking

doubt that a future is in store for Ireland, for more reasons than can here be enumerated. …

That this momentous future, thus foreshadowed, will be as glorious for Catholicity as for Ireland we cannot doubt from the experience of the past; but, as Providence works by means of human agencies, that natural anticipation has no tendency to diminish the anxiety and earnestness of all zealous Catholics to do their part in securing its fulfilment. And the wise and diligent cultivation of the intellect is one principal means, under the Divine blessing, of the desired result.

Gentlemen, the seat of this intellectual progress must necessarily be the great towns of Ireland; and those great towns have a remarkable and happy characteristic, as contrasted with the cities of Catholic Europe. Abroad, even in Catholic countries, if there be in any part of their territory scepticism and insubordination in religion, cities are the seat of the mischief. Even Rome itself has its insubordinate population, and its concealed free-thinkers; even Belgium, that nobly Catholic country, cannot boast of the religious loyalty of its great towns. Such a calamity is unknown to the Catholicism of Dublin, Cork, Belfast, and the other cities of Ireland; for, to
say nothing of higher and more religious causes of the [1]
difference, the very presence of a rival religion is a perpetual incentive to faith and devotion in men who, from the circumstances of the case, would be in danger of becoming worse than lax Catholics, unless they resolved on being zealous ones.

Here, then, is one remarkable ground of promise in the future of Ireland, that that large and important class,[126] members of which I am now addressing,—that the middle classes in its cities, which will be the depositaries of its increasing political power, and which elsewhere are opposed

---

from East, West and South […] with the ease and rapidity of a locomotion not yet discovered […] all speaking one tongue' (*HS* iii, pp. 31–2).

126 The 'young men of the Middle Class' who Newman refers to were typically shop employees (Newman to Ornsby, 20 February 1858, *LD* xviii, pp. 263–4).

in their hearts to the Catholicism which they profess,—are here so sound in faith, and so exemplary in devotional exercises, and in works of piety.

And next I would observe, that, while thus distinguished for religious earnestness, the Catholic population is in no respect degenerate from the ancient fame of Ireland as regards its intellectual endowments. It too often happens that the religiously disposed are in the same degree intellectually deficient; but the Irish ever have been, as their worst enemies must grant, not only a Catholic people, but a people of great natural abilities, keen-witted, original and subtle. This has been the characteristic of the nation from the very early times, and was especially prominent in the middle ages. As Rome was the centre of authority, so, I may say, Ireland was the native home of speculation.[127] In this respect they were as remarkably contrasted to the English as they are now, though, in those ages, England was as devoted to the Holy See as it is now hostile. The Englishman was hard-working, plodding, bold, determined, persevering, practical, obedient to law and precedent, and, if he cultivated his mind, he was literary and classical rather than scientific, for Literature involves in it the idea of authority and prescription. On the other hand, in Ireland the intellect seems rather to have taken the line of Science, and we have various instances to show how fully this was recognized in those times, and with what success it was
[li] carried out. 'Philosopher,' is in those times almost the name for an Irish monk. Both in Paris and Oxford, the two great schools of medieval thought, we find the boldest and most subtle of their disputants an Irishman,—the monk John Scotus Erigena,[128] at Paris, and Duns Scotus,[129] the Franciscan friar, at Oxford.

---

[127] Newman develops this idea in his essay 'The Benedictine Schools' which he wrote for *Atlantis* (January 1859). For the relevant section, see *Historical Sketches* ii (1872; London: Longmans, Green & Co, 1906), pp. 481–5.

[128] Newman contends that John Scotus Erigena 'is the palmary specimen of the philosophical party among the Irish monks', and in his *De divisione naturæ* 'accounted reason, not only as the ultimate basis of

Now, it is my belief, Gentlemen, that this character of mind remains in you still. I think I rightly recognize in the Irishman now, as formerly, the curious, inquisitive observer, the acute reasoner, the subtle speculator. I recognize in you talents which are fearfully mischievous, when used on the side of error, but which, when wielded by Catholic devotion, such as I am sure will ever be the characteristic of the Irish disputant, are of the highest importance to Catholic interests, and especially at this day, when a subtle logic is used against the Church, and demands a logic still more subtle on the part of her defenders to expose it.

Gentlemen, I do not expect those who, like you, are employed in your secular callings, who are not monks or friars, not priests, not theologians, not philosophers, to come forward as champions of the faith; but I think that incalculable benefit may ensue to the Catholic cause, greater almost than that which even singularly gifted theologians or controversialists could effect, if a body of men in your station of life shall be found in the great towns of Ireland, not disputatious, contentious, loquacious, presumptuous (of course I am not advocating inquiry for mere argument's sake), but gravely and solidly educated in Catholic knowledge, intelligent, acute, versed in their religion, sensitive of its beauty and majesty, alive to the arguments in its behalf, and aware both of its difficulties and of the mode of treating them. And the first step in attaining this desirable end is that you should submit yourselves to a curriculum of studies, such as that which brings you with such praiseworthy diligence within these walls evening after evening; and, though you may not be giving attention to them with this view, but from the laudable love of knowledge, or for the advantages which will accrue to you personally from its pursuit, yet my own reason for [lii]
rejoicing in the establishment of your classes is the same as that which led me to take part in the establishment of the University itself, *viz.* the wish, by increasing the intellectual

religious truth, but the direct and proper warrant for it' (*Historical Sketches* ii, p. 483).

[129] The tradition that Duns Scotus was born in Ireland is now discredited.

force of Ireland, to strengthen the defences, in a day of great danger, of the Christian religion.[130]

But any allusion to the possibility of such a danger as trials to faith, was thought strange,—nay, more. Even in conversation such an allusion was too unwelcome to be repeated; sympathy of thought on the subject, whether in Ireland or in England, he found little or none. A full though condensed expression of his mind on this danger,—on the subject of Liberalism generally,—will be found in a letter to Canon Longman[131] written in 1878; more especially will it be found in his speech in Rome (known as the *Biglietto* speech) on his elevation to the Cardinalate in May, 1879. This introduction of matter of such recent date, and so long after Dr Newman's retirement from Dublin, may have the appearance of being the introduction of a new subject, but it is not really so. They are the embodiment of his thoughts and of his often repeated words in years far back, and they give so well the key to his mind and to his acts in connexion with his work in Dublin, that there can be no more appropriate place for them than in this volume. The letter to Canon Longman will follow; the speech in Rome will be found in the Supplement.

THE ORATORY, *May* 28*th*, 1878

MY DEAR CANON LONGMAN,

Fr Ryder[132] tells me you have asked him to a meeting of
[liii] the Mission Clergy with a view of considering the expedience of their taking part in the Temperance movement here, and he has urged me to state to you my own opinion upon it.

I have certainly a strong opinion on the subject, though, from my want of mission experience, one-sided.

The question is, I believe, whether in October next the clergy should take any part, formal or informal,

[130] From the first half of 'Discipline of Mind', *Idea*, pp. 482–7.

[131] Thomas Tucker Longman (1818-92) was educated at Oscott College before being ordained a priest. He worked in the Midlands, and from 1867 was at St Chad's Cathedral; in 1873 he was made a Canon and Vicar-General.

[132] Henry Ignatius Ryder (1837–1907), a priest at the Birmingham Oratory.

contemporaneous, collateral, or sympathetic, whether in recognition of, or in understanding with, the Alliance;[133] and I wish I could in a few words which alone are possible in a letter, do justice to what seems to me the gravity of the question.

For the last fifty years, since 1827, there has been a formidable movement among us towards assigning in the national life political or civil motives for social and personal duties, and thereby withdrawing matters of conduct from the jurisdiction of religion. Men are to be made virtuous, and to do good works, to become good members of society, good husbands and fathers, on purely secular motives. We are having a wedge thrust into us which tends to the destruction of religion altogether; and this is our misery, that there is no definite point at which we can logically take our stand, and resist encroachment on principle. Such is the workhouse system, such was the Civil Marriage Act.[134] On this account I looked with jealousy even on Dr Miller's October Hospital Collections;[135] yet it was impossible to refuse to take part in them. The proceedings of the School Board are only a more pronounced form of what really is the Pelagian heresy.[136] Such of course are the Irish Queen's Colleges. Such teetotalism.[137]

---

[133] This refers to the United Kingdom Alliance, a temperance movement founded in 1853 which worked for the prohibition of the trade in alcohol.

[134] Lord John Russell secured the passage of this Act in 1836.

[135] John C. Miller (1814–80), Rector of St Martin's, Birmingham, and a liberal evangelical, was chiefly responsible for the Hospital Sunday Fund in October, which began in 1859.

[136] Newman explains in a sermon that, 'speaking popularly, I may call [the Pelagian heresy] the belief, that "holy desires, good counsels, and just works", can come of *us*, can be *from* us, as well as *in* us: whereas they are from God only; from whom, and not from ourselves, is that righteousness, sanctification, and redemption, which is in us,—from whom is the washing away of our inward guilt, and the implanting in us of a new nature. But when men take it for granted that they are natural objects of God's favour,—when they view their privileges and powers as natural things,—when they look upon their Baptism as an ordinary work, bringing about its results as a matter of course,—when they come to Church without feeling that they are highly favoured in being allowed to come,—when they do not understand the necessity of prayer for God's

As I have said, the misery is that the wedge works its way. Plausible innovations introduce serious ones. I never should be surprised if we are forced to give in on this Alliance question, as we may, perhaps, be forced to make terms with the School Board; but I do not see that we are obliged yet, and we may gain experience of the necessary safeguards by waiting.

I am, my dear Canon,

Most truly yours,

JOHN H. NEWMAN[138]

[liv] Dr Newman's paper, *University and King's Colleges in London*, taken from the *Catholic University Gazette* of May, 1855, will be read with interest in connexion with the above subject. It has been placed for chronological order at page 325.

---

grace,—when they refer everything to system, and subject the provisions of God's free bounty to the laws of cause and effect,—when they think that education will do everything, and that education is in their own power,—when, in short, they think little of the Church of God, which is the great channel of God's mercies, and look upon the Gospel as a sort of literature or philosophy, contained in certain documents, which they may use as they use the instruction of other books; then, not to mention other instances of the same error, are they practically Pelagians, for they make themselves their own centre, instead of depending on Almighty God and His ordinances. ('Righteousness not of us, but in us', *Plain and Parochial Sermons* v, pp. 135–6)

[137] A year after writing this letter, on 9 August 1879, Newman received an Address from the Members of the Catholic Total Abstinence League of the Cross. In his reply he said: 'I look upon you as a remarkable body—in its spirit almost a religious body—for you have upon you a certain Religious character from the special obligation under which the members of your association lie.' He added that the League 'is so singularly contrasted with the secular schemes and institutions with the same object which are external to the Church'. (*Addresses to Cardinal Newman with his Replies*, ed. W. P. Neville (London: Longmans, Green & Co., 1905), pp. 162–3). But Newman had doubts about any teetotalism. When his brother Francis invited him to share a platform with Manning and himself at a meeting in Manchester against the drink trade, Newman declined: 'I have heard that some also of our Irish bishops think that too many drink-shops are licensed. As for me, I do not know whether there are too many or too few' (October 1867, *LD* xxiii, 363).

[138] *LD* xxviii, pp. 363–4.

Another difficulty may be named over and above the two grave matters mentioned at p. xxxix,—a difficulty, or better say, a drawback, arising from difference of race, may be more than surmised to have existed, which would not have made Dr Newman's work the easier.

That this would naturally have been the case, may easily be inferred, with knowledge of the many instances of occasions of it, which forty and fifty years ago were common topics in conversation. Forty-five years ago the severities of the penal laws would be remembered with a sensitiveness producing (often, perhaps, unconsciously), an antagonistic disposition towards even those whose sympathy, while most heartfelt and active, was not that of race. How natural this disposition was may be gathered from the letter a little further on (p. lv) of May 7th, 1855, which though written under satisfaction at the religious results of the circumstances to which it refers, is sufficiently suggestive. It is the more appropriate to this place, inasmuch as it relates to the University House in Stephen's Green.[139] As regards himself it would show itself at times amid much that was joyful and most hearty towards him, but it not the less seemed to bring home to him that there must therein, in the nature of things, exist an impediment to the advancement of the work.

For instance:—Dr Ryan,[140] Bishop of Limerick, though he [lv]
considered the success of a University independent of the State to be impossible, welcomed Dr Newman to Limerick with a banquet, and there, in the midst of his clergy, did him the extraordinary honour of proclaiming him a Vicar-General of the Diocese. Clamorous applause accompanied this act of the Bishop, and presently it burst out into the songs of '98.[141] Never before had Dr

---

[139] The imposing mansion at 86 St Stephen's Green was built at a time when Ireland had a substantial aristocracy. The ground floor, the *piano nobile* and the grand staircase are all decorated with rococo plasterwork by Robert West, Dublin's premier stucco artist. St Patrick's House occupied the upper two floors, reached by the back staircase, while the lower, grander rooms acted as the official rooms of the University for lectures and meetings.

[140] John Ryan (1781–1864).

[141] Newman describes this visit in a letter to J. S. Flanagan, 28 February 1854, *LD* xvi, p. 63.

Newman been present at such a scene. Greatly overcome by its novelty and kindliness, he, nevertheless, read in it a still more serious estimate of the gravity of his task than he had hitherto formed, and, moreover, of its greater difficulty from the goodwill towards himself personally. Nor was he, in the event, mistaken, for, among some memoranda in 1872 he has written as a reason for resigning "because the hope of the University being English as well as Irish was quite at an end".[142]

7th May, 1856

VERY REVEREND SIR,

Seeing by the advertisement that you are to preach on Sunday next in the Church of the University, I take the liberty of intruding on your notice what I think you will consider as another manifestation of the Providence of the Almighty towards His Holy Church.

Something better than a hundred years ago my great-grandfather was domestic physician to the Prince of Hesse Darmstadt; while in that service he saved some money and returned to his native land, Ireland; he embarked his money in partnership with a man named Whaley in the purchase of a copper mine by which they expected to be able to transmute iron into copper by aid of the spring or water found in the mines, the impregnating power of which had been observed by my ancestor or some one else. However, when the matter was
[lvi] in full working order Whaley said to my progenitor: 'You are a Papist, and according to the laws of these kingdoms you cannot possess land': and taking advantage of those penal laws Whaley robbed my great-grandfather and prospered on his ill-gotten plunder. He next took an active part in persecuting Papists in general, and earned a title not yet forgotten by the

---

The Irish Rebellion of '98, i.e. 1798, was an uprising against British Rule lasting from May to September 1798. It was suppressed by the British forces with a death toll of around 20,000. In response to the rebellion, the Act of Union was passed in August 1800 and came into effect on 1 January 1801.

[142] This memorandum has not been located. See *MM*, pp. 322–3, 421, 423–4 for examples of similar comments by Newman and a contextual explanation; and *AW*, p. 330.

old, that of *Burn Chapel Whaley*.[143] Wealth still flowed to him, and some of your near neighbours could tell you of his splendour and prince-like magnificence. Yet see the end of all; a Catholic Chapel in the very palace of him who burned chapels, his family scattered in obscurity, no one knows where; the Almighty thus proving as He proclaimed, 'Vengeance is Mine, and I will repay'.

If, Very Reverend Sir, you think this matter worthy of comment you might just add that the man who was robbed had two sons, one of whom became a priest of the Most High, and for forty years was pastor of Rathangan in the county of Kildare, where some of the very old people might perhaps recollect Father Stephen Bolger.

I am, Very Rev. Sir,

Your most obedient servant,

JOHN BOLGER

The Very Rev. Dr Newman,
Catholic University[144]

But difficulties and drawbacks were regarded by Dr Newman as inevitable with so great a work. With the hand of the Pope upon him, he allowed nothing of the kind to abate his energy. *The Idea of a University, The Rise and Progress of Universities*[145] and

---

143 Mr Richard Chappell Whaley died between June, 1768 and April, 1769. [WPN] The building that became University House had been his home, then that of his son, the no less notorious Tom 'Buck' Whaley, who had used it for meetings of the dissolute Hell-Fire Club.

144 Catholic University journal and other papers, M 7.16, A 34.2, BOA.

145 Newman wrote twenty articles for the *CUG* in 1854 which were like historical snapshots telling the tale of the organic growth and development of the university. The essays were published together as *Office and Work of Universities* (with an alternative subtitle, *University Teaching, Considered in a Series of Historical Sketches*) in 1856, then—More appropriately—as the *Rise and Progress of Universities* in 1872, the first and major part of *HS* iii (1872, pp. 1–251). Though the 'university sketches' are far less well known than the Dublin lectures, Newman scholars have argued that they are vital for a full understanding of Newman's educational views. In his preface to *University Sketches. Text of 1856* (Dublin, [1952], p. vii) Michael Tierney argues that the sketches form 'a very important part of a coherent body of thought'. In

other writings[146] are evidence, among other things, how well his energy was sustained. Once or twice he had half prepared courses
[lvii] of Lectures to supply the place of likely absentees. Moreover, he was ready to have undertaken the Professorship of Ecclesiastical History.

In 1857, perceiving the apathy prevalent in England respecting the University, he made an attempt to raise an interest in it by introducing it into public discussion; this, however, failing to have the desired effect, he wrote in the following year some newspaper articles with the same object. These articles are here reprinted under the title of *The Catholic University, its Defence and its Recommendation*, with the omission of only two or three short passages of ephemeral importance.[147] They serve to show much of what took place in the last year of his Rectorship, and to some extent supply the want of his Official Report. This mode of bringing the University before the public was adopted by him in compliance with the wish of Dr Cullen, who was disappointed that certain of the Professors had not already made more use of the newspaper press for that purpose. These Professors not seeing their way to follow the Archbishop's wish, Dr Newman thus relieved them of the task.

NU (p. 319) Fergal McGrath goes so far as to assert that they are as valuable as the *Idea*, if not more so. For a fuller analysis of the sketches, see Katherine Tillman's preface to *The Rise and Progress of the Universities and Benedictine Essays* (1856); ed. M. K. Tillman (Leominster: Gracewing, 2001).

[146] It was never Newman's intention for the Dublin lectures to be taken in isolation from what he saw as three companion volumes on university education: the Dublin lectures (1852); the occasional lectures and essays (1859); and the university sketches (1856). In the advertisement to the second edition of the *Discourses* (1859), Newman refers to 'his two other volumes on University Teaching': two of them coalesced to form the *Idea of a University*, but the third, *Office and Work of Universities* (1856), was published separately. While only the first two constitute the *Idea*, all three examine the idea of a university: the first as the idea *defined*, the second as the idea *illustrated*, and third as the idea *lived out* in history.

[147] For the six articles and the background to them, see pp. [345–81].

The starting of the *Atlantis* magazine[148] was another occupation of 1857–58. The value to the University of this publication will be seen in Supplement, pp. 367–374, and Appendix, pp. 429–434.

In the letter to Dr Cullen, of June 17th, 1858, given p. xxxvii, Dr Newman alludes to his intended retirement from the Rectorship, of which he had long previously given notice to the [lviii] Archbishops and Bishops; and he was then, as he had been for many months past, holding the office only provisionally, until they could determine upon his successor. This notice had been first given in August, 1857, and he renewed it more formally in February, 1858, ceasing, at the same time, to draw further salary, and naming November 14th as the latest day to which he could defer giving effect to his resignation. Because the Holy Father wished it, and for the sake of the University, he had broken himself off from his employments, and from his plans, from his literary labours and recreations, from those who knew him best, and from his home. He had, in his own mind (and had said so in conversation), lent himself to the University for seven years, and his three years of weary waiting in suspense, his toils and anxieties, had told upon him sufficiently to remind him that if the threads of the past were to be gathered up again, the task must not be indefinitely postponed. To use his own words—"the claim of my duties to my own home" so pressed upon him, that, the seven years having expired, and the University having now taken root and its prospects become good, to his home he returned. Dr Newman did, in fact, retire on the day he had named, November 14th, 1858.[149]

[148] *Atlantis, a Register of Literature and Science Conducted by Members of the Catholic University,* was launched in January 1858 as a biannual journal for the scholarly output of the teaching staff. As a heavyweight academic journal under the editorship of W. K. Sullivan, Dean of the Faculty of Science, *Atlantis* provided an outlet for those academics who had few students to challenge and excite them, and it served to raise the academic tone of the University and set its sights high.

[149] Technically speaking, Newman was Rector until the beginning of August 1859, when the bishops formally accepted his resignation.

This distinct mention of his actual resignation has necessarily been made because Dr Gartlan,[150] who, under the title of Vice-Rector, had succeeded Dr Newman, opens his first Report to the Archbishops, June 14th, 1859, by speaking of himself as acting only "*in the absence of the Very Rev. Dr Newman, Rector of the University of Ireland*," etc., and further on he expresses his hope "*that the Rector of the University may be released from engagements elsewhere and resume the full exercise of his office* [lix] *in Ireland*". There was no overlapping of authority such as this mistake may seem to indicate; moreover, Dr Newman, when resigning, was well on his guard lest his former accessibility to the Professors and others, and his intimacy with many of them, should lead to complications which would be injurious to the welfare of the University, and make his retirement unreal. His determination in this respect cannot be better shown than by a few lines from one of his letters to Professor Ornsby, thus:—

> THE ORATORY, BIRMINGHAM,
> 16*th November*, 1858
>
> I cannot answer resolution 3, for I am *not* Rector—and the Archbishops must clearly understand I am not playing at make-believe, which ____[151] and others will be sure to suspect.[152]

Dr Gartlan's mistake must have arisen from his being a stranger to the University and to Dr Newman until after his arrival

---

[150] After Newman's departure, nearly three academic years were to pass before a new Rector could be found. The Vice-Rector during this *interregnum* was the elderly James Gartlan, a former Rector of the moribund Irish College in Salamanca, who had arrived at the end of November 1858 and taken over from William Anderdon, the temporary Vice-Rector. Gartlan was an able man, though not in good health, and on the whole acquitted himself well in what was a difficult situation, but being a stop-gap he was reluctant to take the initiative or assume responsibility for a situation that was not of his making. When a new Rector was appointed in April 1861 Gartlan immediately retired; he was not replaced.

[151] Newman refers to James Quinn.

[152] *LD* xviii, p. 515. Resolution 3 is about applying for a charter.

as Vice-Rector; or, it may be, that his undoubted wish to be working under Dr Newman deceived him as to the reality of the situation, although Dr Newman, in reply to a letter from Dr Gartlan, had said:—

> ... At the same time I am unable to respond to its courteous and friendly advances, as I am no longer Rector of the University, having resigned my office into the hands of the Archbishops several weeks ago.[153]

Of the papers included in the Supplement besides those already mentioned, there are also the following:—

The *Cathedra Sempiterna* is placed the first of these papers, [lx] because it was partly with these words that he first introduced the object of his work to the Catholics of Dublin.

This paper was not written as it stands until the year 1867, when Dr Newman put it together from passages in No. i of the Discourses which he had delivered in Dublin in 1852 on University education. It was his contribution to Fr Cardella's (S.J.) book called *Omaggio Cattolico ai Principi degli Apostoli Pietro e Paolo*, to be presented to Pius IX in honour of his Jubilee.[154] Some disappointment, arising from most kind thoughts about him, was expressed among his friends that he had not written anything new for the purpose. His reply, however, was, that when originally composing the Discourse from which this paper was extracted, he had done so with great devotion to St Peter and with exceeding pains to do his uttermost in the Saint's honour. And further, that he had there said all that he felt and had to say; try how he would he could not do better, and he did not think his contribution the less suitable because it was a repetition of his words and thoughts of very many years before. The whole of the Discourse No. i will follow the *Cathedra Sempiterna*.

---

[153] This letter (*LD* xviii, pp. 520–1) is dated 30 November 1858. From Gartlan's letter to Newman the previous day (*LD* xviii, p. 521n), it seems that Gartlan thought that Newman was still Rector.

[154] Newman's contribution can be found in *Omaggio Cattolico in Varie Lingue ai Principi degli Apostoli Pietro e Paolo nel XVIII Centenario dal loro Martirio* (Rome, 1867), pp. 82–4. For the reasons Newman subsequently regretted its publication, see the first footnote on p. [211].

There is another Discourse which may very suitably be reprinted in this volume. This was Lecture No. v of the above-mentioned University Discourses, as published in their first edition. It is entitled "General Knowledge Viewed as One Philosophy".

He had had great difficulty in preparing his Discourses in
[lxi] consequence of his being a stranger to the people and to their modes of thought. He had begun, so it seemed, very happily, but it was afterwards brought home to him that he was on the wrong tack if he hoped to carry the Clergy along with him. This was a great disappointment; for, had he been left alone, he said, and heard to the end, they would have found themselves in accord with him. An influence so great as this could not be let go. This obliged him to alter what he had prepared, and, indeed, the scheme of the whole course; in doing this, by adjusting, for instance, part to part, No. v became, in his opinion, both spoilt and out of keeping with the rest, and he therefore withdrew it. This was not done as condemning the Discourse, for he purposed including it, after corrections, in an intended volume of Pamphlets and Papers.[155] He did not include No. i in this intention, for having taken *Cathedra Sempiterna* from it for Fr Cardella's book, he thought it would be unfair to the sale of that book to reprint this Discourse by itself.

Both these Discourses, *viz.*, No. i and No. v, are here reprinted from the first edition, with only some verbal alterations which he

---

[155] Dwight Culler suggests that Neville was mistaken here: 'Writing after the lapse of nearly fifty years, Neville has evidently confused two events, first, Newman's trouble with Discourse VI, which *did* arise from the fact that, in his serial mode of publication, he felt the clergy would not hear him "to the end" before they began to criticize, and secondly, the alteration of the times of the delivered lectures. It will be recalled that Newman wrote the first three discourses to be delivered as a unit, close together, and that he then intended to go on with what is now Discourse VI. When the lectures were scheduled at weekly intervals, however, he found that it was neither wise to drop the old subject so quickly nor was there time to begin a new one before the [Achilli] trial. Therefore he simply gave further illustrations in IV and recapitulated in V' (A. D. Culler, *The Imperial Intellect: a Study of Newman's Educational Ideal* (New Haven: Yale University Press, 1955), pp. 315–16).

had written in pencil and are now enclosed in brackets.[156] The alterations are too roughly written to have been intended as final.

In the Advertisement of the edition which he published under the title of *The Scope and Nature of University Education, or University Teaching*, he says of the volume of Discourses that "it gave me less satisfaction, when written, than any of my volumes".[157] This opinion he never changed.[158]

The following letter, written while he was composing the [lxii] Discourses, will partly explain the cause of the difficulties above mentioned.

THE ORATORY, BIRMINGHAM,
April 14*th*, 1852

MY DEAR ORNSBY,

... My immediate cause of writing to you is this—my Lectures have taken me more trouble than any one could by a stretch of fancy conceive. I have written almost reams of paper; finished, set aside, then taken up again, and plucked them, and so on. The truth is, I have the utmost difficulty of writing to people I do not know, and I commonly have failed when I have addressed strangers. …

Now my first Lecture starts with *Oxford*—I have done so very deliberately and with good reasons. One I proceed to give, *viz*., that I am going to treat the whole subject, not on the assumption of Catholicism, but in the way of reasoning, and as men of all religions may do. Then, after this, I go on to protest against the notion that, *because* I do so, I am but using the sanction of the Holy See as a sort of lever or permit for private

---

[156] As Ian Ker has noted in his critical edition of the *Idea* (p. xxxvii), not all Newman's pencil corrections have been accurately transcribed from the copy in the Birmingham Oratory (A 16.5, BOA).

[157] In a letter of December 1852 Newman describes the *Discourses* as one of 'my two most perfect works, artistically', the other being his *Lectures on the Present Position of Catholics in England* (1851) (*LD* xv, p. 226). In 1969 he refers to the *Discourses* as among his '5 constructive books' (*LD* xxiv, pp. 398–9). See Culler, *Imperial Intellect*, pp. 154–5 for more on this.

[158] Commenting on this assertion, Ker points out that 'writing long after the event, Neville is by no means infallible' (*Idea*, ed. Ker, p. xviii, n1).

judgment, instead of that sanction being a positive authority or ground in reason.[159]

It struck me, and my judgment was confirmed on consulting another, that, as I was addressing the English party, I mean the Dublin Barristers, etc. etc., I was rhetorically safe in appealing to my antecedents. And then again I found the view variously brought out by old Catholics, that 'the new University must be *as good as* Oxford'. And then again, why was I chosen except as having been connected with the English Universities? But now what you say frightens me again—and if you can give me more light on the subject, I should be glad.[160]

I assure you I have no security to myself that the Lectures will not be from beginning to end a failure, from my not knowing my audience.

Yours affectionately in Christ,

JOHN H. NEWMAN[161]

[lxiii] The letter to Fr St John which follows seems to have been inspired by the apparent gratification with which his first Discourse was received.

22 LOWER DORSET STREET, DUBLIN,
May 11*th*, 1852

CHARISSIME,

You are all expecting news and I have to be my own trumpeter.

The Lecture, I suppose,[162] has been a hit—and now I am beginning to be anxious lest the others should not follow up the blow. The word 'hit' was Dr Cooper's word.

---

[159] This passage was in the original version of Discourse I—see p. [231]—but was omitted from the *Idea*.

[160] Ornsby obliged with a long letter (16 April) in which he describes the four classes of Dublin society. This letter is given almost entirely in *NU*, pp. 143–8. See also *LD* xv, p. 71.

[161] *LD* xv, pp. 66–7.

[162] A slightly different version of this letter is given in *LD* xv, pp. 83–4; after 'The Lecture, I suppose' comes the phrase 'thanks to our dear Lady'.

The room was very good for my purpose, being very small.[163] It was just the room I like, barring want of light. I cannot make myself heard when I speak to many, nor do the many care to hear me; *paucorum hominum sum.* The room holds (say) 400, and was nearly full. Mr Duffy,[164] whom I met in the train to Kingstown after it, said he had never seen so literary an assemblage; all the intellect, almost, of Dublin was there. There were thirteen Trinity fellows, etc., eight Jesuits, a great many clergy, and most intense attention.

When I say that Dean Meyler[165] was much pleased, I mean to express that I did not offend Dr Murray's[166] friends. Surgeon O'Reilly,[167] who is the representative perhaps of a class of laity, though too good a Catholic perhaps for my purpose, and who, on Saturday, had been half arguing with me against the University, said, when the Lecture was ended, that the days of Mixed Education were numbered.

Don't suppose that I am fool enough to think I have done any great things yet; it is only good as far as it goes. I trust it

---

[163] This was the Exhibition Room in the Rotunda. The Rotunda, built in 1764, was where fashionable gatherings, musical events and public meetings of Dublin took place; the New Assembly rooms, where Newman spoke, were added in 1784.

[164] Charles Gavan Duffy (1816–93) was the leader of the Young Irelanders. For his comments on the lectures, see *My Life in Two Hemispheres* ii (London: Fisher Unwin, 1898), pp. 26–7.

[165] Walter Meyler (1784–1864) was Vicar-General of the archdiocese of Dublin.

[166] Daniel Murray (1768–1852) was Archbishop of Dublin from 1823 until his death. Along with William Crolly, the Archbishop of Armagh, he considered that there was more to be gained from cooperation with the British government than from confrontation, and was generally supportive of the National Schools and the Queen's Colleges – and therefore uninterested in, even opposed to, the prospect of a Catholic University. He was strongly opposed by those like Archbishop MacHale who would not accept a compromise with the government and regarded Murray as 'pro-Castle'. Progress with the establishment of a Catholic University could only be made after his death, in February 1852.

[167] John O'Reilly later became one of the Demonstrators in Anatomy at the Catholic University.

could not be better *so far as* it goes, but it goes a very little way.

The Lectures are to be *in extenso* in the *Tablet*,[168] and I am going to publish them at 6d apiece; and then, I think, I shall have a Library edition.

[lxiv] Dr Moriarty, whom I made censor of the Lecture before delivery,[169] was the first who gave me encouragement, for he seemed much pleased with it, and spoke of its prudence, and said it went with the Queen's College party just as far as was possible.

I was heard most distinctly, or rather my voice so filled the room, and I had so perfect confidence that it did, that people *would not believe* I could not be heard in a great church—but I know myself better. It was just the room I have ever coveted and never have had.

My own object is that of *hastening* on these University matters. Three new and stronger Rescripts on the subject[170] have just come from Rome.

Ever yours affectionately,

JOHN H. NEWMAN

The whole of this course of Discourses was at one time in danger of being relinquished before it had actually come into form. It happened thus, and perhaps in connexion with whatever it was that had delayed his installation. After his acceptance of the Rectorship in 1851, he had found himself so strangely left alone with regard to his going to Ireland that in the following spring he fixed a day to himself when he would resign, unless, meanwhile, a letter of some sort (this is the way he happened to put it to himself) came to him from Ireland. The day had come without his having received any such letter; his letter of resignation was written, but in the course of the day a letter *did* come from Dr

[168] Only the first lecture appeared in full in *The Tablet* 13 (5 May 1852), pp. 307–9, as Newman was told that it would be anti-Irish to have them published in an English newspaper (*LD* xv, p. 86).

[169] David Moriarty was President of All Hallows, where Newman stayed before his lecture.

[170] Two of these Rescripts are reproduced in his volume, on pp. [lxxvii–lxxix, lxxxiv–lxxxv].

Cullen, which, though not *apropos* to anything calling him to Ireland, nevertheless broke the stipulation he had made with himself. He regarded this circumstance as an indication of the will of Providence that he should go on with the work, and, thereon, [lxv] with a most remarkable cheerfulness and contentment, though mixed with a no less striking sadness, he put aside thoughts for himself, which, as things were, he could have wished for himself, to be harnessed to the work in Dublin (these were his words) as a horse to a cart. This was at the close of April or in the early days of May, 1852.[171]

The Inauguration of the University, or Dr Newman's admission to its administration.—The relation of what took place in connexion with that event is taken from the *Catholic University Gazette* of 1st June, and 15th June, 1854, Nos 1 and 3. These two papers are given as having been written by Dr Newman, inasmuch as the earlier numbers of the *Gazette* were entirely his own work.[172] No. 1 records the Synodal meeting in Dublin which preceded his admission, and No. 3 gives an account of what took place at the ceremony itself. The intervening number relates to the same subject.

What I aimed at belongs to the papers connected with Dr Newman's Dublin correspondence, to which it is an introductory paper. It has been taken with some reluctance from its proper place and included in the Supplement for the interest of readers, as preferable to withholding it from them until the uncertain time

---

[171] It would seem that this episode occurred around Christmas 1853, not in April/May 1852. For Newman's thoughts about resigning, see his memorandum dated 29 December 1853 (*AW*, pp. 305–7); his correspondence at the time (*AW*, pp. 307–12); and his diary entries (*LD* xxxii, pp. 75–6).

[172] The weekly periodical the *Catholic University Gazette* was edited by Newman from 1 June 1854, the eve of his installation as Rector, until the end of the calendar year. Besides notices about university regulations and proceedings, the eight-page *Gazette* featured leading articles by Newman that were intended to familiarize people with the idea of a university by presenting snapshots of it in different historical eras.

of the publication of that correspondence.[173] As will be seen, it is from a rough and unfinished copy.

The University Church occupies so prominent a place in this paper, *What I aimed at*, and it was considered by Dr Newman of such very great importance, that a record of various other
[lxvi] circumstances connected with it may fitly be introduced into this volume. The writer of the Advertisement has therefore given as a Note a narrative of what, as far as he can trust his memory, he knew at the time and learnt from the Cardinal. This Note was roughly made a few years back without any thought to its present use and without reference to the Cardinal's papers. Some little discrepancy may be found between it and those papers, but it can be explained thus:—that with change of circumstances and prospects, and in long length of time, Dr Newman's thoughts and plans changed also, and sometimes to and fro. In this way some matters become difficult to follow in their exact sequence—and this is the case in one instance with regard to the University Church where the Note differs from the paper *What I aimed at*, for a question might be raised as to the order of the first two plans for providing such a Church. They in fact sometimes ran concurrently. But this is a trivial matter. The Note will be found at p. 305.

There is another subject in this paper *What I aimed at* on which additional information will be interesting. It relates to the foundation of the Chair of Irish History and Archaeology to which Mr O'Curry was appointed. Besides what is found in Dr Newman's paper, *The Catholic University: its Defence and Recommendation*, more is supplied by an extract from Mr O'Curry's Preface to the first volume he published, *Lectures on the MS Materials of Ancient Irish History.* The extract follows next after the Note on the University Church.

[lxvii] The *Senate* is given here because it was the last Senate at which Dr Newman presided, and the only Senate of which he is known to have left a written record. This Senate was held January 15th, 1857.

---

[173] The correspondence Newman refers to is the collection of papers which was intended to become *My Campaign in Ireland, Part II.*

The papers, *Contemporary Events*, are taken from the columns under this head in the *Rambler* of May and July, 1859, written by Dr Newman during the period of his Editorship. They are interesting as relating to the movement at that time for obtaining a Charter for the University.[174]

The *Replies* which the Cardinal made to the Addresses received from Ireland on the occasion of his elevation to the Sacred College, have been inserted to close the volume as being a not unfitting place for their preservation, indicating, as they do, the widespread appreciation in Ireland of his endeavours to serve that country; and also his own gratitude for the almost affectionate remembrance of himself after more than twenty years' retirement from the University.[175] The Addresses to the Cardinal precede [lviii]
each Reply, and, with one exception, they are given in full,

---

[174] Dr Newman's contribution to the series of "Current Events" in the *Rambler* (a bimonthly magazine) is confined to the May and July numbers of 1859. In behalf of four Bishops (the Committee on the Education Question) Cardinal Wiseman, Dr Errington, Dr Grant, and Dr Ullathorne, he had for some months been engaged in correspondence with the proprietors of the Rambler, and finally, as the only way of bringing their difficulties to an end, he, after pledges from both parties, undertook its editorship himself.

After the issue of his first number, Dr Ullathorne called upon him (22nd May), and expressed his wish that he would give up the editorship after the next number, viz., that of July. Accordingly Dr Newman gave it up, returning it to those from whom he had received it, and whose property the magazine was.

The series of "Foreign Affairs" in the same numbers is also by Dr Newman. [WPN]

For a fuller account of the *Rambler* episode see Ker, *Newman: a Biography*, pp. 472–89, 514–5, 517–19, 579.

[175] In his reply to the Rector and Senate of the University Cardinal Newman alludes to a service done him by Cardinal Cullen. The knowledge of this reached him in May, 1867, through a verbal message from Pius IX, who called it out to Fr Ambrose St John as he was leaving the Holy Father's room. What precisely the circumstance was, or when it occurred, was not named. It may be supposed that Dr Cullen had on other occasions, also unknown to Dr Newman, befriended him. [WPN]

Ambrose St John, Newman's right-hand man at the Birmingham Oratory, was at the time Headmaster of the Oratory School and had been sent to Rome by Newman to prevent the school being closed down.

although he had some difficulty in appropriating to himself all the kind things they say of him.

WM. P. NEVILLE
Visitation of the Blessed Virgin Mary,
July 2, 1896.

POSTSCRIPT

It may be asked where is now the University which cost so much toil to build up, and which Dr Newman left already rooted, and with every hope and prospect of growth.[1] Its history is not closed. It has held its way under various vicissitudes. The classes which were carried on under the Faculty of Philosophy and Letters have been kept up with unbroken activity, and the evening classes have grown more and more flourishing. The Medical School still maintains the credit which accompanied its earlier years,[2] and it has from time to time sent forth men who have become eminent in

[1] Neville does not present a realistic description of the state of the Catholic University after Newman's departure in November 1858. Newman's departure was a severe blow for a young institution that had depended so heavily on the inspiration and energy of its founding Rector, and, as a result, over the next two decades its survival became precarious. In the short term, as the supply of overseas students dried up and the English element of the professoriate drained away, the University became solidly Irish in composition and middle- to lower-middle-class in intake. Nearly three academic years were to pass before a new Rector could be found, and during this time the University dwindled. In 1858/59 there were thirty-six matriculated students in the arts faculty, but by the second year the number had dropped to below thirty, with barely twenty in residence at any one time. The appointment of the forty-two-year-old priest Bartholomew Woodlock as Rector in April 1861 breathed new life into the University, and when the new academic year began, numbers in the arts faculty had risen to eighty. See *MM*, pp. 369–420 for a full analysis of the University after Newman's departure.

[2] The School of Medicine, which had continued to expand after Newman's departure, was absorbed into the newly-established University College Dublin in 1909. In terms of student numbers the Catholic University Medical School was by then the largest of the six medical schools in Ireland.

their profession.[3] Great changes have, however, taken place. The whole nation, it may be said, when once the University had been put before it, had come forward to do for it that which—with respect to Universities—may be considered a prerogative of kings and princely persons to do—itself providing the funds for its first starting and for its maintenance, by contributions in the Churches—a circumstance perhaps unique in history, and in which the peasantry had been particularly prominent. From the first, however, even friends of Dr Newman had predicted that the work would be too difficult without the aid and countenance of the State, and this has shown itself to be the case. The want of a Charter enabling the University to grant Degrees recognized by the State, became a great discouragement, and necessitated
[lxx] recourse to shifts to meet that difficulty. The state of the country, too, changed from the times when Dr Newman could say, "As to Ireland herself, the overflowing, almost miraculous liberality of the poorer classes makes no anticipation of her prospective contributions extravagant".[4] The decrease of population, the destitution which from time to time prevailed, the many troubles of the country, all these helped gradually to deprive the University of its main source of support, and, on this account, other shifts had to be resorted to. In this way, and from the lapse of time, the work, as begun by Dr Newman, has become very much lost to sight; it lives on, however, awaiting favourable opportunities for its fuller development. To advance this, the Archbishop of Dublin is now devoting himself, with brightening hopes of the eventual fulfilment of Dr Newman's anticipations of it.[5]

---

[3] Thomas Maunsell (1839–1937) was one of the first students of the Catholic University Medical School. He joined the British Army in 1860, serving in the Burma and Chitral campaigns, and became surgeon-general in 1895; he was made a Companion of the Order of Bath. He retired in 1899, and in 1911 founded what became the Guild of Catholic Doctors, on account of which he was decorated with the papal Cross of Honour.

[4] *Vide Rise and Progress of Universities*, chapter on Macedonian and Roman Schools in "Historical Sketches," vol. iii. [WPN]

[5] Neville refers to William Joseph Walsh (1841–1921), the son of a Dublin watchmaker and jeweller, who entered the Catholic University in 1856, where he studied for two years on a mathematical exhibition, leaving after taking the scholar's exam. He proceeded to Maynooth and,

How necessary a Charter has been for the University may be seen from the Petition of 1872 to Mr Gladstone.[6] This Petition is given,[7] as being of more recent date than that mentioned in [lxxi]

after he was ordained, taught dogmatic and moral theology there until he became the President. He became Archbishop of Dublin in 1888 and for the next quarter of a century was the dominating personality of the Church in Ireland; a champion of Catholic educational interests, he was made the first chancellor of the National University of Ireland in 1909. (*DIB, ODNB*)

[6] William Gladstone (1809–98) served as Prime Minister 1868–74, 1880–85, 1886 and 1892–94.

[7] 1872. To the Right Hon. W. E. GLADSTONE, M.P., First Lord of Her Majesty's Treasury, etc., etc.

The Memorial of the Rector, Professors, Officers and Students, present and past, of the Catholic University of Ireland,

Showeth: That the Catholic University was opened in the year 1854, and that the Memorialists have been connected with it for various periods since that date.

That in the persons of the Memorialists 'civil disabilities' are still imposed on Irish Catholics on account of religious opinions.

That such of your Memorialists as 'profess to teach the liberal arts,' are not only liable to be restrained in their office by the Court of Chancery at the instance of the University of Dublin, but are, moreover, legally subject to severe penalties, in virtue of the penal clauses of certain Acts of Parliament.

That others of your Memorialists, as Students of an unrecognized University, are denied those substantial aids to education which the State affords so abundantly to their Protestant fellow-countrymen, and also are refused Academical privileges and Degrees which bring with them social distinction, as well as professional and other valuable advantages.

That all your Memorialists feel it to be a grievance and an injustice, that through their connection with this University they should be unfairly weighted in the race of life, as against the members of other institutions, upon which the State has lavished, and continues to lavish, its bounty, its honours and its favours.

That although this University was founded, and its Statutes framed for the Catholics of Ireland, it imposes no religious test on Students who do not profess the Roman Catholic faith, and does not require them to attend any instruction or comply with any observance of the Roman Catholic religion, and as a matter of fact, non-Catholic Students have not only received its instruction, but have also enjoyed its prizes and emoluments.

Current Events to Mr Disraeli, which was in 1859.

W. P. N.

That for many years your Memorialists, in common with the whole Catholic people of Ireland, have, in accordance with the repeated declaration of Her Majesty's Ministers, expected the settlement of the Irish University question, and they venture to express their earnest desire that this settlement be no longer deferred.

In conclusion, your Memorialists pray Her Majesty's Government to introduce early in the present Session of Parliament such a scheme of University Education as will secure to the Catholics of Ireland Denominational Education, and equality with their fellow-countrymen in Collegiate endowments, University honours and emoluments, examinations, government and representation.

Dublin, 7th February, 1872. [WPN]

Gladstone's Liberal government came near to clinching a solution to the Irish University question in 1873, but the Bill for affiliation to a Dublin University, along with Trinity College and two of the Queen's Colleges, was defeated by a majority of three in Parliament – and precipitated the fall of the government.

INSTRUCTIONS FROM THE HOLY SEE RELATING TO THE ERECTION OF THE UNIVERSITY[1]

RESCRIPT FROM THE SACRED CONGREGATION OF PROPAGANDA FIDE
ABOUT THE QUEEN'S COLLEGES[2]

I[3]

Most Illustrious and Most Reverend Lord,[4]

It will, perhaps, appear strange that the reply of the Sacred Congregation on the subject of the academical colleges should have been so long delayed; but the deep importance of the question at issue, and the great variety of matters to be considered, rendered it necessary that much time should be spent in duly

---

[1] The nine documents in this final section of the Advertisement were all in Latin in the original printing of *My Campaign in Ireland, Part I*. For ease of reading, they have been replaced by translations into English.

[2] The Irish bishops were divided over how to react to the secular and non-denominational Queen's Colleges which the British government decided to erect in 1845, so they decided to submit the matter to Rome in November that year. Pope Gregory XVI died in June 1846 and was succeeded by Pius IX. Archbishops MacHale and Slattery wrote to the new Pope urging him to take action against the Colleges (*NU*, pp. 60–3). See also T. Twiss, *The Letters Apostolic of Pope Pius IX Considered with Reference to the Law of England and of Europe* (London: Longman, Brown, Green & Longmans, 1851), p. 107.

[3] This translation has been taken from the *Royal Commission Endowed Schools* (1858) ii, Documents, p. 388. The Latin text can be found in *Decreta Synodi Plenarie Episcoporum Hiberniæ apud Thurles habitæ Anno MDCCCL* (Dublin: Duffy, 1851), pp. 73–5. Parts of this letter are quoted (in English, though using a different translation) in *NU*, pp. 63–4. Both the Latin and an English translation were published in *Battersby's Catholic Directory* (1848), pp. 247–50.

[4] Though this letter is addressed to the Archbishop of Cashel, identical letters were sent to the other three archbishops.

examining the documentary proofs and reasons on both sides, before judgement could safely be delivered. First of all we deem it our duty to declare that the Sacred Congregation never imagined that the Bishops who appeared to be in favour of establishing the colleges proposed to do what they believed to be incorrect, for long experience has proved their probity; and the Congregation considers that they were only impelled to take that view through the hope of effecting a greater good, and promoting the prosperity of religion in Ireland. However, the Sacred Congregation having considered the matter maturely and in all its bearings, dares not presume to promise itself fruits of that kind from the erection of such colleges; it even dreads that grievous peril to the Catholic Faith would thence arise; in one word, it considers that institutions of the sort would be detrimental to religion.

Therefore it admonishes the archbishops and bishops of Ireland to have no part whatever in carrying them out. But as it could have wished that some bishops, before treating with the Government to obtain an amendment of the law regarding the colleges in question, and other matters, in their favour, had first solicited the decision of the Holy See; so also, it does not doubt,
[lxxiv] so great has been the obedience which the Bishops of Ireland have ever professed to the Head of the Church, but that those same bishops will retract what they may have done to the contrary. But all this notwithstanding, any of your body who may have anything of greater moment, and requiring further notice to communicate, will be at liberty to disclose it to the Sacred Congregation, that in all things a right judgement may be given.

The Sacred Congregation is well aware how important it is that provision should be made for the scientific instruction[5] of the young, especially of the higher classes; it therefore exhorts Your Grace, together with your Suffragan Bishops, to use every legitimate means within your power to promote that object. It will be yours to take care that the Catholic colleges which are already in existence may flourish more and more, by adding those more useful chairs, particularly in the philosophical department, which may, possibly, be yet wanting, and to enlarge the accommodation,

---

[5] By 'scientific instruction' is meant a teaching which is systematic and organised.

so that a greater number may enter according to the wants of the surrounding districts. Of all things, the Sacred Congregation would deem it most advantageous that the bishops, uniting their exertions, should erect in Ireland a Catholic Academy on the model of that which the prelates of Belgium founded in the city of Louvain.[6]

. . . .
. . . .[7]

This we believe you will do with the greatest earnestness, because the same are in every respect the views of our Most Holy Lord Pius IX. When he had accurately informed himself respecting the whole circumstances of the case, he ratified the council of the Sacred Congregation, and added to it the supreme weight of his own authority.

In the meantime we pray God
that he may grant Your Grace a long and
happy life.
Your Grace's most obedient servant,

College of the Sacred Congregation of Propaganda Fide, Rome, 9th October, 1847.

J. PHIL CARDINAL FRANSONI, P.D.P.F.
ALEXANDER BARNABÒ, Pro-Secretary

Most Illustrious and Most Reverend Lord,
MICHAEL SLATTERY[8]
Archbishop of Cashel

---

[6] Emmet Larkin makes a telling observation on the choice of Louvain: the Secretary of Propaganda, Barnabò, preferred the Roman model for the Catholic University with a cardinal as its head, whereas the Pope had suggested the Louvain model (*Making of the Roman Catholic Church in Ireland*, p. 126).

[7] The missing paragraph reads: 'And that all these things may be successfully carried out, the Sacred Congregation exhorts the Bishops to cultivate, as far as possible, mutual union, and the greatest concord; not to permit themselves to be carried away by partisan zeal on matters which have nothing to do with the worship of God, the good of religion, and the salvation of souls.'

[8] Michael Slattery (1785–1857).

[lxxv]

II[9]

Most Illustrious and Most Reverend Lord,

Some extracts from the statutes compiled for the new colleges in Ireland, and the opinions given by the Bishops regarding them, have afforded the Sacred Congregation an occasion of again treating of the aforesaid colleges, chiefly under that aspect, and of weighing diligently and maturely what it should deem its duty to answer regarding the spiritual interests of the Catholic people of Ireland. For though the aforesaid statutes are in such a form that it is difficult to ascertain their authority, considering the constitution of the English realm, still, all things maturely weighed, the Sacred Congregation could not be induced on account of the grievous and intrinsic dangers of the same colleges to mitigate the decision passed on them, and, with the sanction of the Most Holy Lord, communicated to the four Metropolitans in the month of October, last year.

But since it is manifest with what zeal the Clergy and the entire people labour for those things which have for their object to promote the good of the Church, their Eminences judged that the erection of a Catholic University should not be despaired of; nay, they have again and again recommended a project of this sort, in order that all may lend their best endeavours towards its execution,[10] and that thus sufficient provision be made for giving the Catholics more ample instruction, without their religion suffering danger from that source.

---

[9] This translation has been taken from the *Royal Commission Endowed Schools* (1858) ii, Documents, pp. 388–9. The Latin text can be found in *Decreta Synodi Plenarie Episcoporum Hiberniæ*, pp. 75–8. Both the Latin and an English translation were published in *Battersby's Catholic Directory* (1849), pp. 313–16.

[10] For an alternative English translation of the first part of this paragraph, see *NU*, pp. 89–90.

This decision of the Sacred Congregation, with all prudence and maturity weighed, our Most Holy Lord has resolved to sanction and confirm with the weight of his own authority, and has willed that it should be sent to the four archbishops, to be by them communicated to their respective Suffragans.

. . . .

Given at Propaganda Fide, Rome, 11th October, 1848.

J. PH. CARD. FRANSONI, PREFECT
AL. BARNABÒ, Secretary

Most Illustrious and Most Reverend Lord,
MICHAEL SLATTERY
Archbishop of Cashel

[lxxvi]

III[11]

Most Illustrious and Most Reverend Lord,

. . . .

. . . . Meanwhile, I have thought it should be signified, through your Grace, to the bishops, that it appears astonishing after the answers already given on the colleges that some should not have hesitated to assert that it is lawful for priests to undertake certain offices in the said colleges; for if it has been declared that the aforesaid colleges will prove detrimental to religion, by reason of their grave and intrinsic dangers, if the bishops have been warned to have no share in carrying out their establishment, it is certainly evident that neither is it lawful for other ecclesiastical persons to discharge any function having reference to the said colleges.

As to other controversies raised on the subject of the said colleges, it will be the business of the bishops, after having diligently weighed the above-mentioned rescripts, to frame such rules to be observed everywhere for withholding the faithful from frequenting those colleges, as will correspond with the said rescripts, and be conformable to the equity and benignity which the Apostolic See itself ever enforces by its example.

. . . .

Given at Rome, from the College of the Sacred Congregation of Propaganda Fide, 18th April 1850.

Your Grace's most obedient servant,

J. PH. CARD. FRANSONI, PREFECT
ALEXANDER BARNABÒ, Secretary

R. P. D., PAUL CULLEN,
Archbishop of Armagh

---

[11] This translation has been taken from the *Royal Commission Endowed Schools* (1858) ii, Documents, p. 389.

LETTERS FROM POPE PIUS IX TO THE IRISH BISHOPS

I[12]

TO THE VENERABLE BROTHERS, ARCHBISHOPS, AND BISHOPS OF IRELAND

PIUS PP. IX

Venerable Brothers, Greetings and Apostolic Benediction. . . . We are anxiously concerned to learn by what strategies the ancient enemy strives to damage and weaken your union of minds, since at present he is inciting dissensions. We have such an opinion of your devotion that We do not doubt at all that you will bravely resist the snares of the enemy and fight constantly and prudently, with ever greater zeal, for God and Church. Yet because of Our office of Apostolic ministry and because of the great love We entertain for you and for your faithful people, We cannot but impress upon you again and again the need of mutual concord. . . . You are daily bound together by a most stringent covenant of love, and you are obligated to spread the glory of God, to safeguard the doctrine of the Catholic Church, to fight for its rights, to protect the safety of the flocks entrusted to you, to overthrow the plots and errors of the enemies, and to satisfy the other serious episcopal duties. Therefore, from the depths of our hearts, We exhort, even beg you to be more of one mind each day, unified in the same perceptions and in the same judgments, and concerned with preserving the unity of spirit in the bond of peace.[13]

---

[12] This translation is taken from https://www.papalencyclicals.net/pius09/p9nemoce.htm accessed 3 July 2020.

[13] Newman comments (*AW*, p. 321) that this letter was issued just a month after the death of the Archbishop of Dublin; 'and it quotes the

In your wisdom you know well how much this sacerdotal and [lxxviii] trusting agreement of minds, wills, and judgment is necessary and advantageous to the good of the Church and the profit of the faithful. Therefore We are convinced by your exceptional piety and virtue that you will consider nothing more important than to continually cultivate such concord, not only among yourselves, but also with other Venerable Brothers, especially with the Bishops of England and Scotland. . . . . . .

.

. . . We trust, Venerable Brothers, that you will always be eager for such concord, since We joyfully recall with what unanimity you signed the Acts of the Synod of Thurles in 1850, called to protect the affairs of the Catholic Church in Ireland. And here is something related to that synod. You will recall the letter that twelve of your number sent to Us following the Synod on 11 September 1850. It was also signed by the Venerable Brother Daniel, Archbishop of Dublin, over whose death We grieve. There was the particular question in the letter about the Queen's Colleges, as they called them. Nor are you unaware of the decree, prepared by Our Congregation for the Propagation of the Faith, which We published after due consideration of the matter. Since We wanted you to know how, in this important matter, We had written to the same Archbishop of Dublin in a personal letter dated 17 November of the preceding year, We decided to use the same words in this letter. They are as follows: "Concerning the Queens Colleges you spoke of in your letter, We are pleased to learn, Venerable Brother, that after the decree of the Apostolic See concerning this important matter was published, you promptly agreed to obey it. We are convinced that you will carefully execute the decree and do so with every zealous effort. We know that you will see to it that the bishops who signed the 11 September letter along with you, will respect and obey this decree, complying with it promptly and zealously. This decree

---

severe words which had been addressed to him from Rome for his direct disapproval of the attempt to establish a University, a disapproval so undisguised, that it could hardly have been commenced in Dublin during his lifetime'. After quoting words of Pope St Gregory the Great—omitted in this paragraph—the letter 'then applies the lesson to them', i.e. to the Irish bishops.

was always dear to Us. We greatly desire that it be earnestly and religiously observed by all, since in it there is the question of safeguarding Catholic doctrine, and nothing can be or should be more important for us." From this you can easily understand how [lxxix] that venerable brother, admonished and encouraged by Us, applied all his energies to seeing that the decree would be diligently observed both by himself and by others. Because he died, he perhaps was unable to complete the task that We had intended; therefore We again commend and urge all of you that for the sake of your religion, the decree under consideration be observed with diligence and accuracy by all.[14] . . . . . .

. . . .

We praise you because in the assembly at Thurles mentioned above, solicitous for the salutary, Catholic education of youth, you wisely agreed to erect a Catholic university in Ireland as quickly as possible. There, young men, without danger to their Catholic faith, will be taught literature and the more austere disciplines. We encourage you to spare no zealous attention so that this most salutary work may rapidly achieve its desired success. We gladly approve the foundation of this same Catholic university with the promised Apostolic letters. We rejoiced greatly when We learned that the faithful of Ireland seconded your splendid plans with ready good will and liberality, so that substantial subsidies have already been received to bring your plans to fruition. Therefore while We greatly congratulate you and the faithful, We certainly entertain the hope that this Catholic university with God's help will rise in prosperity and happiness as soon as possible, according to Our and your desires.

. . . .

Given at Rome, at St Peter's, 25th March 1852, in the sixth year of Our Pontificate.

---

[14] Newman comments on this paragraph: 'Then the Brief proceeds, as an admonition to those who were backward among the Bishops in their zeal against the Queen's Colleges, to quote the Pope's words to the late Archbishop Murray in the preceding November, three months before his death, on the occasion of a memorial on the subject addressed by the Archbishop and some other Bishops in the September before it' (*AW*, p. 321).

II

TO THE VENERABLE BROTHERS, THE ARCHBISHOPS AND BISHOPS OF IRELAND[15]

---

[15] Cardinal Wiseman had spoken of the prospect of a Brief from Rome when writing to Cullen on 27 December 1853 (*AW*, p. 313); a fortnight later Cullen asked Taylor to pass on this letter to Newman. On 20 January 1854 Wiseman wrote directly to Newman mentioning that the Pope had told him in an audience that he had commissioned a Brief to be drawn up establishing the Catholic University, naming Cullen as Chancellor, and making Newman a bishop *in partibus* (*AW*, p. 315).

This Brief contained two guiding principles which concerned Newman. One was the stress that the Catholic religion should be 'the soul of the entire institution of learning', which he interpreted to mean that the Catholic faith should be '*the form*'; that all disciplines 'are to go forward in the most *strict league* with religion, that is, with the assumption of Catholic doctrine in their *intrinsic* treatment'. The other concern was with the Brief not only urging that the professors should give the students good example by their lives, but that a priority 'should be shaping the minds of the youth to piety, decency, and every virtue'; this meant, in Newman's words, that the professors should mould 'the youth to piety and virtue, and to ground them in literature and science in conformity with the Church's teaching'. This forced him to think carefully about whether the line he had adopted in his Dublin lectures, particularly the fifth, might be inconsistent with the papal Brief, and therefore whether his ideas were at odds with those of the Holy See. He had, after all, argued that in *essence* a university was concerned with imparting a liberal education and that its aim was not, strictly speaking, a directly moral one (*AW*, pp. 322–3).

After a good deal of reflection Newman came to the conclusion that the apparent disparities between the papal Brief and his lectures came about partly because of the different approaches taken (on account of their different concerns) and partly because of language used (due to their different cultural backgrounds), and hence that they were not in fact inconsistent. For further explanations see: Culler, *Imperial Intellect*, pp. 264–6; *NU*, pp. 274–91.

Venerable brothers, greetings and Apostolic benediction.

You know very well how great Our joy and consolation was [lxxx]
when We first learned that in your devotion, you willingly followed Our advice and that of the Holy See. In the Synod of Thurles, held in 1850, you decided, among other things, to establish a Catholic *Lyceum*[16] as soon as possible. There the youth of your illustrious nation could be shaped in piety and every virtue and educated in letters and in the more difficult disciplines free from any danger to their faith. You also remember clearly how We approved both the acts of that synod and the establishment of this *Lyceum* in Our Apostolic letter published on 23 March 1852. Then in Our encyclical letter of 25 March 1852, which We sent to you, We gave thanks regarding this plan for the advancement of religion and knowledge. We also gave well-deserved praise to those faithful people who had already contributed substantial aid in support of that Catholic *Lyceum* in Ireland.

As We greatly desired to see this Catholic *Lyceum* or University [*Lyceum seu Universitas*] founded quickly in Ireland, We recommended in Our Apostolic letter to Paul, who was then Archbishop of Armagh, that the office of Apostolic Delegate be prolonged. By this office he could see to it that the decrees of the Synod of Thurles were diligently observed and especially that the establishment of the Catholic *Gymnasium* which that synod approved and which We confirmed was brought quickly to the desired result. Therefore, when that venerable brother was transferred to govern the archiepiscopal church of Dublin, it seemed appropriate to Us that he should continue in the office of

---

[16] Newman was unsettled by the variations in nomenclature for the new institution: in this Brief the term *universitas* is used eight times, but is substituted by the terms *lyceum* three times and *gymnasium* twice—though Newman seems to have overlooked the implied equivalence in the phrase '*Lyceum seu Universitas*'. Newman was anxious that the phrasing might have the effect of limiting or modifying his idea of a university, a fear derived in part from considering the effect the text might have on Irish ecclesiastics in encouraging them to think in terms of a college, not a university (*AW*, p. 322). 'It is not clear to me', he wrote to Henry Wilberforce, 'that the Committee will not shirk off into a College instead of a University, from ignorance and from fear' (30 September 1853, *LD* xv, p. 444).

Apostolic Delegate in the same manner as We set forth in Our Apostolic letter of 3 May 1852. We thought for certain, that you would put your hand to the task without delay and that you would apply all of your understanding and enthusiasm toward the speedy founding of this *Gymnasium*. We trust that great benefits will flow from it to the faithful.

Thus, it was with great annoyance that We learned that this Catholic University, which We and all good people desire, has not yet been founded, although you already have all the necessary
[lxxxi] materials to build it. Therefore, we write this letter to you and implore you to put aside all hesitation and to direct all your thoughts and attention with redoubled efforts toward the construction of this Catholic University. With the goal of accomplishing this pious and salutary work more quickly, We command all of you to hold a meeting within a period of three months after you receive this letter with Paul, the Archbishop of Dublin. We name him as Apostolic Delegate; he will preside over this meeting. You will meet there and convene according to the rule of the sacred canons. After your plans have been discussed again without public celebration and you are all of one mind, may you arrange everything which pertains to the quick building and opening of the University.

It will be your episcopal concern in this meeting to adopt appropriate plans so that this University may live up to the sanctity and dignity of the Catholic name with which it is adorned. Therefore, see to it that divine religion is regarded as the soul of the entire institution of learning [*divina nostra religio tamquam anima totius litterariæ institutionis*].[17] For that purpose

---

[17] Although Newman worried about whether this sentence was at odds with the line he adopted in his discourses, it does echo part of his final lecture, where he states: 'it is no sufficient security for the Catholicity of a University, even that the whole of Catholic theology should be professed in it, unless the Church breathes her pure and unearthly spirit into it, and fashions and moulds its organization, and watches over its teaching, and knits together its pupils, and superintends its action' (*Idea*, p. 216).

The consistency of Newman's approach with the Church's traditional teaching on the essential unity of religious and secular knowledge is brought out in 'The Tamworth Reading Room' (1841): 'Christianity, and

encourage the fear of God and His worship so that the sacred trust of faith may be preserved and all studies [*omnes disciplinas*] may proceed, joined in a close bond with religion. Thus may the shimmering rays of Catholic doctrine illuminate all kinds of intellectual pursuits. Decorous language should be firmly maintained so that whatever is Catholic, whatever proceeds from this See of Saint Peter, the safe harbour of the whole Catholic communion[18] and the mother and teacher of all churches,[19] may be welcomed and believed. May whatever is against it be rejected, so that every error and profane novelty may be repelled and eliminated. The professors of this University should show themselves to be models of good works in doctrine, in purity, and in seriousness. Their primary concern should be shaping the minds of the youth [*totis viribus adolescentium*][20] to piety, decency, and every virtue; instructing them in the finest matters; and educating them carefully in letters and studies according to the teachings of the Catholic Church, which is the pillar and chief support of truth.[21]

---

nothing short of it, must be made the element and principle of all education. Where it has been laid as the first stone, and acknowledged as the governing spirit, it will take up into itself, assimilate, and give a character to literature and science. Where Revealed Truth has given the aim and direction to Knowledge, Knowledge of all kinds will minister to Revealed Truth' (*Discussions and Arguments* (London: Longmans, Green & Co., 1872; 1907), p. 274).

[18] St Jerome, Epistle 16.

[19] Council of Trent, session 7 on Baptism, canon 3.

[20] In *AW* (pp. 322–3) Newman writes, 'again the Pope exhorts the Bishops to make "divina nostra religio *tamquam anima* totius litterariæ institutionis" in the University; that is, *the form*. "Omnes disciplinæ" are to go forward in the most *strict league* with religion, that is, with the assumption of Catholic doctrine in their *intrinsic* treatment: and the Professors are directly to mould "totis viribus", "the youth to piety and virtue, and to ground them in literature and science in conformity with the Church's teaching". I wrote on a different idea my "Discourses on University Education" in 1852, vid especially the original 5th Discourse.' The italics have been added by Newman. For the fifth Discourse, see pp. [243–70], and for the use of the word 'form', see pp. [251–5].

[21] The apparent conflict between the Pope (in this passage) and Newman (in his Dublin lectures) over moral formation and training at a Catholic

As We know that you have already chosen Our beloved son,
Father John Henry Newman, to govern that University, We want
[lxxxii] to approve your choice that this priest [*volumus, ut idem*
Presbyter], blessed with such wonderful gifts of mind and soul
and endowed with piety, sound doctrine, and zeal for the Catholic
religion, assume the care and governance of this University and
preside over it as Rector [*ejusdem Universitatis curam et regimen*
suscipiat, eique veluti Rector præsit].[22]

. . . .

---

university can be resolved by observing that in the discourses Newman was treating of a faith-based university in the abstract, while the Pope was dealing with a Catholic university in practice. Though Newman's metaphysical distinction separated liberal knowledge from moral formation, this did not imply that the university's essential task of securing mental culture precluded the overall end of education including moral formation and training.

Arguing from history, Newman contended that it was subsidiary bodies within the university, such as colleges and halls, that were the chief promoters of morality. Arguing first in a strictly philosophical sense, then on the basis of historical fact, Newman wrote: '*I do not think that a University has to do with morals*. [...] Nor do I think that the Church on the whole employs a University for morals, (except as *teaching* them, but *that* comes under faith) but I think she uses small bodies in the Universities, Colleges and Halls, etc etc. as the preservative of *morals*, more naturally. In short, as a Bishop's jurisdiction *foro exteriore* is to a priest's over his penitent in *foro interiore*, in an analogous way is the University to the College. [...] The University takes care of faith in fullest sense – the College of morals' (Newman to Moriarty, 23 July 1852, *LD* xv, pp. 136–7).

[22] In *AW* (p. 322) Newman writes that, 'though the Bishops had already elected me, the Pope says "*Volumus* ut idem Presbyter [...] ejusdem Universitatis curam et regimen suscipiat, eique *velut*[*i*] *Rector* præsit." This certainly is as if the Pope appointed me—but if really he had put down on me his hand, how was it that I was able to leave without his distinct permission?' The italics have been added by Newman.

Given in Rome at St Peter's on 20th March 1854, the eighth year of Our Pontificate.[23]

PIUS PP. IX

[23] The last third of this letter was omitted by WPN. Newman received a copy of this Brief on 15 April and not long afterwards set off for Dublin, where he remained until the bishops had finished their synod (18–20 May). Prior to the meeting, he submitted to the bishops his blueprint for the university in a second major memorandum (pp. [93–100]).

III

LETTER FROM POPE PIUS IX TO THE ARCHBISHOP OF DUBLIN

PIUS PP. IX

Venerable brother, greeting and the Apostolic blessing.

With this Our letter you will receive Our encyclical letter written this day to those Venerable Brothers the Bishops of Ireland, by which we order them to assemble with you, so that without any delay whatever a Catholic *Gymnasium* or University may be swiftly set up in that place, and at the same time there be carried out a consultation concerning things that may pertain to the spiritual benefit and the procuring of the ever greater prosperity of this people, just as you can clearly and openly understand from the same encyclical letter.

And because we considered it entirely appropriate that you, venerable brother, should preside at this episcopal gathering, on that account we send you this letter, by which through Our Apostolic Authority We choose, establish, and depute you as Our and this Holy See's Delegate, and We grant you all the necessary and convenient faculties, so that you may assemble and hold in your presence this gathering of all the Bishops of Ireland according to the norms of the sacred canons, although without employing any public solemnity. In the same gathering you can and may freely and licitly exercise the functions of Apostolic Delegate, notwithstanding whatever may be to the contrary in the canonical sanctions and Apostolic constitutions, even those worthy of particular and special mention and derogation.

But as we well know what is your religion, devotion, prudence, and wisdom, so we hold as certain that you, with God's
[lxxxiii] aid, will place all care and attention also in this same task, and will achieve it in the most praiseworthy manner. And We place our trust that the Catholic University so much desired in this place

will be set up and opened as soon as possible, and that the decrees of the Synod of Thurles, approved and ratified by Us, will be most carefully observed by all.

For as we have these things very much in Our heart, so by this letter We extend the term of your office as Apostolic Delegate, with which We previously decided to grant you Our and this Apostolic See's authority by Our two Apostolic letters, signed by the Fisherman's Signet and published on the 23rd March and 3rd May, by which you may continue to carry out your useful and diligent work, especially in those things that concern the observance of the decrees of the above-mentioned synod celebrated in Thurles and also the setting up of the Catholic University.

Finally, nothing is more pleasing to Us than to take advantage of this occasion to again bear witness to and confirm the special benevolence with which We embrace you in the Lord. And We wish to be a most certain sign of this benevolence the Apostolic blessing which we impart with heartfelt affection to yourself, venerable brother, and to the flock entrusted to your most loving vigilance.

Given in Rome at St Peter's on 20th March 1854, the eighth year of Our Pontificate.

PIUS PP. IX

[lxxxiv]

ABOUT THE CATHOLIC UNIVERSITY
TO BE ESTABLISHED IN IRELAND
PIUS PP. IX
FOR A PERMANENT RECORD OF THE MATTER

As something that was highly opportune and advantageous for the reinvigoration and strengthening of the Catholic Faith in Ireland, we ardently desired that there should take place and be completed, by the blessing of Our Lord, a Synod of the Archbishops and Bishops of Ireland in Thurles in 1850, whose acts and statutes having been sent to this Apostolic See, and having sent some amendments, already on 23rd May 1851 by decree of the Congregation our Venerable Brother the Cardinal of Propaganda Fide, We ratify and confirm the propositions. Further concerning those acts and statutes together with the amended prescriptions that were issued, and additionally our Apostolic letters in the form of Briefs, as well as decrees and letters of the above-mentioned Congregation to the same celebration of the Synod, or pertaining to the matters studied in it, We, by the counsel of our Venerable Brothers, have ordered that Apostolic letters be published on this matter, so that there may be a memorial of solemn approval by Our Pontificate. Furthermore, through this letter we again approve and confirm by Our Apostolic Authority all the acts and statutes of the above-mentioned synod held at Thurles published after correction, and others by the decree of the said Congregation approved and validated by Us on Our own initiative, with certain knowledge and mature deliberation, and We instruct and command by Our said Authority that the same statutes mentioned above, once published, are to be inviolably observed by each and every one to whom it regards or will regard. So, then, among those things that have been decreed in the above-mentioned by the Bishops of Ireland for the benefit of the good and increase of the Catholic religion, it is especially commendable that, after consultation, a

Catholic University in Ireland should be quickly established, in [lxxxv] which young men may certainly be formed in the fine arts and sciences without the danger of losing the faith. The piety and generosity of the Irish nation has responded admirably to this zeal of the Catholic Bishops by the collection of no small sum for its support. And as requests have been made to Us in the name of many of the Bishops that We might deign to approve the establishment of this Catholic University by Our special Apostolic Authority, on the advice of the same venerable brothers of Ours, We willingly resolve to consent to such prayers offered. Therefore, We approve and confirm the establishment of the aforesaid University, which the Irish Bishops promote, by Our Apostolic Authority by means of the present Letters. Indeed, We beg the Father of mercies, from whom all good things proceed, that the Decrees of the above-mentioned Synod, through the inspiration of His heavenly grace, the commands being carried out by all those concerned, may attain the desired result, and that the work of the Catholic University may be happily completed; by which the Catholic offspring of this nation, nourished by true doctrine, may grow up in increase of true religion and in the glory of God.

Given at Rome under the Fisherman's Ring, 23rd March 1852, in the sixth year of Our Pontificate.

On behalf of H.E. CARDINAL LAMBRUSCHINI[24]

A. PICCHIONI, Sostituto

[24] Luigi Lambruschini (1776–1854) had been Secretary of State (1836–46) under Pope Gregory XVI and at time of this letter was Prefect of the Congregation for Studies and Vice-Dean of the College of Cardinals.

[lxxxvi]

DECREE OF THE SACRED CONGREGATION OF PROPAGANDA FIDE

The statutes composed by the archbishops and bishops of Ireland for a Catholic University, and submitted to the judgement of the Holy See in a general meeting of the Sacred Congregation on 31st July 1854 by his Eminence the Most Reverend Cardinal Constantine Patrizi, Bishop of Albano, were evaluated, some changes having been made following the instruction to be given,[25] it was agreed that the same be handed over to the rectorate of the above-mentioned University to be carried out; asking, too, from our most Holy Father for the hoped-for faculty for this University of confering academic degrees by the Rector, observing what must be kept.

This judgement of the Sacred Congregation was reported by the undersigned Secretary to our most Holy Father Pius IX, by Divine Providence Pope, in an audience on 6th August 1854, and His Holiness ratified it and kindly granted the required indult; anything to the contrary notwithstanding.

---

[25] The original synodal decrees vested control of the University in the Irish episcopate as a whole, but in arranging for them to be ratified by Rome, Cullen secretly negotiated for a change—to the fury of Archbishop MacHale—which saw control given to the four archbishops instead. Since Cullen was assured of the support of Archbishop Dixon, and had the casting vote, he now effectively controlled the University. The downside of this manoeuvre was the loss of the remaining support from the bishops (Larkin, *The Making of the Roman Catholic Church*, pp. 246, 248–9, 252, 261–2). When Cullen wrote to Newman to inform him that the Pope had approved the regulations that the bishops had submitted, he omitted to say that changes had been made, on account of his unilateral recommendations. He did, however, tell Newman that MacHale had done everything he could in Rome to prevent the regulations being confirmed (20 December 1854, *LD* xvi, pp. 339–40n).

Given at Rome from the Sacred Congregation of Propaganda Fide, 3rd October 1854

J. PH. CARD. FRANSONI, PREFECT
ALEXANDER BARNABÒ, Secretary

[Original title page]

CATHOLIC UNIVERSITY

REPORTS

TO THEIR LORDSHIPS

THE ARCHBISHOPS AND BISHOPS OF IRELAND

FOR THE YEARS 1854–55, 1855–56, 1856–57

BY

THE VERY REV. J. H. NEWMAN, D.D.
Rector

REPORT I [3]

FOR THE YEAR 1854–55[1]

MY LORDS,

I offer to your Lordships my hearty congratulations that time has so far advanced since the foundation of your University, that it becomes incumbent on its Rector, in obedience to the provisions contained in your Decrees for its regulation,[2] to lay before the *Cœtus Episcoporum* his first annual statement of its proceedings and its existing condition. I indeed, if any one, should seem to be the fit person to tender to you such congratulations, for you have condescended to make me in this matter a partaker of your anxieties; and it is with no ordinary satisfaction that I make over to your Lordships a record of acts, or at least of results, which have been the chief occupation of my mind for the [4]

---

[1] This report is one of the six foundational documents for the Catholic University. A measure of its importance is that Newman arranged for it to be translated into Italian and printed. Copies were taken to Rome by George Talbot (1816–86) with instructions to pass them on to the Pope, Cardinals Barnabò, Brunelli and Reisach, 'and any other official persons known to me'. (Newman to St John, 27 June 1856, *LD* xvii, p. 299)

[2] "Singulis annis Rector amplam et fidelem relationem de Academiæ Statu Episcoporum Cœtui, cum congregabitur, vel si conventus Episcoporum non habeatur, quatuor Archiepiscopis subjiciat." V *Acta et Decreta*, Rep. ii, App. ii.

"Archiepiscopi de statu et gestione Universitatis descriptionem elucubrandam curent, quo singulis Episcopis pro opportunis animadversionibus tradatur"—*Letter of the S. Congr. de P. F.* (*ibid.*). [WPN]

'Every year, the Rector shall submit a full and faithful account of the state of the academy to the assembly of bishops, when it shall be in session, or if no gathering of bishops takes place, to the four archbishops'; 'The archbishops shall see to the drawing up of an account of the state and management of the University, which shall be sent to every bishop for appropriate comments' (trans., *LD* xxxii, p. 116n).

last four years. This, without further introduction, I now proceed to do.

1. Scarcely had I consented, in the year 1851, to accept the important and honourable post which your Lordships' Committee offered to me, when, at the advice of several persons whom it was incumbent on me to consult, I engaged myself in an inquiry into the nature of University Education, with a view of directing the attention of Catholics to the subject. This was done in a series of Discourses, which (after some of them had been delivered before audiences of distinction in this city) were successively published, and ultimately collected into one volume.[3] They treated of the connection of Education with Religion, of the claims of Theology to take its place among the sciences, of the idea and scope of Liberal Education, and of similar topics. This was the work of the year 1851–52.

2. In the year that followed I was not in a position to do more than institute private inquiries, as I did at Louvain[4]

---

[3] The first five lectures were delivered to the general public in May and June 1852; the rest were written by the autumn, but never given. All ten were published in 1852, first separately and then together in a single volume under the title *Discourses on the Scope and Nature of University Education, Addressed to the Catholics of Dublin*. Most people are familiar with the *Discourses* as the first part of *The Idea of a University: Defined and Illustrated* (1873).

[4] The University of Louvain is mentioned because the Holy See had recommended it as a model for the Catholic University in Ireland. See the rescript from Propaganda Fide to the Irish bishops, 9 October 1847, p. [lxxiv].

Newman obtained pamphlets and reports from Louvain, and had questions answered about the arrangements there: the power of rector, whether their academic/pastoral system was provisional, the proportion of lay students, and whether the professors were laymen. The notes he took between August and October 1851 are preserved in the file 'University of Louvain, its working and routine with questions and answers in detail' (C.6.3, BOA). For Newman's list of thirty-two questions about Louvain, see his 'Memorandum on the University of Louvain', [1851] (*LD* xxxii, pp. 49–50).

and elsewhere,[5] and to make general preparations in various ways, with reference to the work which I was to commence.

3. In the beginning of June, 1854, I was admitted to the office of Rector by his Grace the Archbishop of Dublin. The [5]
University may be said then to have commenced, and from that date this Report, which I have to present to your Lordships, properly begins.

I at once started a small weekly publication, which I called the *University Gazette*.[6] It consisted of only a few pages, and was divided into two portions,—official and non-official. This division corresponded to the twofold object to which the work was directed. In the first place, it seemed to me desirable thereby to provide for the University an organ, distinct from the public journals, in which announcements of regulations successively made by its authorities, and a statement of its proceedings, might be contained; and considering that, in the first beginnings of any institution, the need of such advertisements is recurring and frequent, it was expedient that it should appear at not longer than weekly intervals. The other object which such a publication answered, was one cognate to that which was contemplated in the Discourses, of which I have already made mention. For, as those Discourses attempted to determine the abstract nature of University Education, so the Essays which were introduced into the *Gazette*, treated of actual Academical Institutions, past or present, in their historical characteristics and several fortunes.

In April 1853 Newman sent his fellow Oratorian Ambrose St John to Louvain to meet the rector, Mgr de Ram, and his assistants so as to learn about the university there. For the 'Additional questions' that St John was to ask about the functioning of the university church, see *LD* xv, p. 357n.

[5] Newman also consulted the German theologian Ignaz von Döllinger and Joseph Jerrard, as well as his close friends, T. W. Allies and James Hope, both experts on education, especially the latter.

[6] This pre-dated the *Oxford University Gazette*, which began in 1870.

I think I adhered all through these Essays to the intention
[6] expressed in the Introductory Number, *viz.* to present to the reader "a description and statement of the nature, character, work, and peculiarities of a University; the aims with which it is established, the wants it supplies, the methods it adopts; what it involves and requires, what are its relations to other institutions, and what has been its history".[7] I have reason to believe that this publication has had its fair measure of success for the purpose with which it was projected. I kept the management of it in my own hands till the beginning of this year, when the direct business of the University obliged me for a time to give it up altogether, and afterwards only partially to write in it; and I fear that the expense necessarily involved in putting it into other hands will oblige me to bring it to an end.[8]

4. While thus endeavouring to illustrate on paper the true character and principles of a University, I was also anxiously engaged in reducing those general views to practice in the Institution itself which I had to form. Here the initial question was, in what way were we to commence it? were we in the first instance to give to it the form of a University, or that of a mere College, which, as time went on, might be gradually expanded into a University? It was not to be denied that the latter was the course which
[7] Universities had for the most part historically pursued.

---

[7] 'On the objects of the Essays which are to follow', *CUG* 1 (1 June 1854), p. 4; *HS* iii, p. 4.

[8] When Ornsby took over the editorship in January 1855, it was announced that the *Gazette* would be expanded and feature articles dealing with universities both at home and abroad; with school education insofar as it prepared for university; and with practical suggestions for those at, or preparing for, university. The change of editorship was not announced, but attentive readers observed the change in style and the circulation dipped during 1855. The difficulty of meeting the ambitious target he had set himself forced Ornsby to turn the *Gazette* from a weekly into a monthly publication after his first ten numbers. It cost the University £10 to produce each weekly number (*LD* xvi, p. 371).

"Such an institution," it was observed, in the publication from which I have already quoted, "has, generally speaking, grown up out of schools, colleges, seminaries, or monastic bodies, which had already lasted for centuries; and, different though it be from them all, has been little else than its natural result and completion. While then it has been expanding into its peculiar and perfect form, it has at the same time been educating subjects for its service by anticipation, and has been creating and carrying along with it the national sympathy."[9] This is what history tells us; and it is reasonable to suppose that especial advantages attach to what has been the matter of fact.

However, to comply with such historical precedents was simply out of the question, from the very circumstances of the case. I suppose a College is a domestic establishment or community, in which teachers and taught live together as one family; sufficient for itself, and with little or no direct bearing upon society at large. I suppose a University is a collection of Professors and Schools, independent of each other, though united under one Head and by one code of laws, addressing all comers, acting on the world, and assuming a national aspect. Now, if a College be so different from a University, how would it have been fulfilling the intentions of the Holy See or the Irish [8]
Episcopate, which contemplated a University, to set about founding a College? What would have been the need of Apostolic Letters and Synodal Meetings to commence a merely local institution, which, long after the present generation was passed, might, if so be, be turned at length by the accidental influences of centuries to come into something besides, which those then obsolete Letters and

[9] 'On the objects of the Essays which are to follow', *CUG* 1 (1 June 1854), p. 3; *HS* iii, p. 2.

Meetings could hardly be said to have had any part in creating?[10]

This was my first consideration. And next I reflected that the Irish Bishops had condescended to call me from England, in order to do something, for which they were so indulgent as to think I had definite qualifications. I had for nearly thirty years of my life resided in a University founded in the medieval period, and retaining a certain measure of medieval traditions.[11] In this I differed from others; but it would have been presumption in me to fancy that I had recommendations for the presidency of a College above those of a hundred well-known and honourable names that might be mentioned.

Moreover, I had submitted to the previous Synod Meeting a sketch of the plan which I proposed to pursue,[12]
[9] and this plan was framed on the idea of a University, not a
College. In that sketch I contemplated making provision at

---

[10] Here Newman is attempting to convince the Irish ecclesiastics reading the *Report* why a university had been founded and not a college.

[11] Newman was an undergraduate at Trinity College, Oxford, 1817–20, a private tutor in Oxford, 1821–22, and a Fellow of Oriel College, 1821–45. Oriel was the pre-eminent college at Oxford, leading the reform of the University, and Newman played a crucial part in this; he introduced written exams at Oriel in 1828 and, along with Hurrell Froude and Robert Wilberforce, provided 'the germ of the modern tutorial system' at Oxford (M. G. Brock, 'The Oxford of Peel and Gladstone, 1800–1833', *History of the University of Oxford* vi, ed. M. G. Brock & M. C. Curthoys (Oxford: OUP, 1997), p. 61). As well as being a tutor, dean of discipline and senior and junior treasurer at Oriel, Newman acted as a University Examiner in the academic year 1827/28.

[12] "Lecta est relatio Rev. D. Newman, Universitatis Rectoris designati, de modo quo Universitas constitui debet."—*Acta et Decreta*, 1854. (*Ibid.*) [WPN]

'There was read the report of the Revd Dr Newman, Rector-designate of the University, on the manner in which the University ought to be drawn up' (trans., *LD* xxxii, p. 119n). For the 'Substance of the Memorandum of the Rector, read in the Synodal Meeting, May 20, 1854', see pp. [93–100].

once for both the liberal and the professional education of the various classes of the community. Here at once was an object far beyond the reach of any College, and only to be reached by a University; but I added other objects still larger as well as various in their nature, those for instance of providing philosophical defences of Catholicity and Revelation, of creating a Catholic Literature, of influencing the general education of the country, of giving a Catholic tone to society, and of meeting the growing geographical importance of Ireland.[13]

Whether, then, I considered your Lordships' expressed intentions, or your act in calling me here, or the representations I had laid before you already, it seemed to me clear that, desirable as it was to feel our way as we went, and let the Institution grow into shape, as time went on, by a natural process, still we were bound to begin with a University, not with a College. And there was this incidental advantage in such a decision, that, though, on any course of proceeding whatever, a considerable outlay would be required, nevertheless the first expenses of a University are less than those of a College. A few thousand pounds will put into working order the establishments necessary for the former, whereas the material fabrics and architectural [10]
display necessary for a large College render it a very costly undertaking.

5. Having discarded the proposition of beginning merely with a Collegiate Institution, I had obviously to consider next, what was the sort of commencement proper to a University. This was an historical question, and it was as easy to answer as it was imperative to contemplate it. To open the Schools in Arts, was indeed essential; first, simply as being a mode of beginning the University; next, because students proceed through Arts, as a preliminary, before they

[13] See pp. [93–4] for a fuller consideration of the objects of the University.

attach themselves to a particular profession;—at the same time it had to be borne in mind that Lectures in Greek, Latin, French, and the Elements of Mathematics, which are commonly understood by the Studies in Arts, were the work of a College, and more was to be done at once, if we were to lay the foundation of a University. The first step in such a work was to provide a large body of Professors, who, as being eminent each in his own department, should, by means of that very eminence, be advertising the Institution, and drawing to it public attention.

This method of proceeding is stated at greater length in a passage of the Paper, which I submitted to your Lordships
[11] at the Synodal Meeting. "Since students are to be gained," it said, "by means of the celebrity of the Professors, Professors must be appointed in great measure prior to the students who are to employ them. This has been the case in the history of Universities generally. Learned men came and opened schools, and their existing reputation drew followers. Schools rose into importance, not simply by royal favour, by civil privileges, by degrees, or by emoluments; but by the enthusiasm kindled by distinguished teachers, and the popularity and recognized utility of the subjects of which they treated."

I went on to draw the practical conclusion as follows: "We must commence by bringing into position and shape various extensive subjects of study; by founding institutions, which will have a value intrinsically, whether students are present or not. This, if we can manage to effect it, will have a double advantage,—such institutions, first, will attract students; next, will have a sufficient object, and a worth in themselves, even before students come."

This is the principle, then, which I have attempted to keep steadily in view, in all my proceedings. I have aimed at laying the foundation of academical institutions, useful in themselves and attractive to the public.

6. Before entering into the details of these proceedings, I think it right, after thus bringing before your Lordships the principle on which I have acted, to mention also the [12]
assistance which was supplied to me, in the midst of great practical difficulties, for carrying it out.

Your Lordships gave me a singular and most acceptable token of your confidence, in putting the measures necessary for commencing entirely into my sole hands, both as regards their planning and their execution;[14] with equal kindness and consideration your Committee, appointed at the Synod of Thurles,[15] at the very meeting in which it invited me over to commence the work, selected some friends, ecclesiastical and lay, to aid me in it. The Resolution of the Committee runs as follows:—

"That, as financial and other questions will require constant communication with the Rector, the following constitute an acting Sub-committee for these purposes: *viz.*—

[14] Realising that the committee that would oversee his work and exercise overall control was scattered around Ireland, Newman sought an assurance that he would be given the freedom of action he needed. In a letter to Cullen, which he sent via James Hope so that his friend could add his comments, Newman agreed that the rector should be subordinate to the board of archbishops, but he went on to argue that he should be 'autocrat: Two authorities will ruin the attempt'. The rector should have the power of choosing his associates, 'especially *lecturers* and *tutors*'. Once the University was set up and a system established, then after two or three years of 'an autocracy', different influences would be beneficial (Newman to Cullen, 11 October 1851, *LD* xiv, pp. 382–3).

Newman had long been opposed to the dead hand of committees: 'Living movements do not come of committees, nor are great ideas worked out through the post, even though it had been the penny post', he writes in his *Apologia pro Vita Sua* (1865; London: Longmans, Green & Co., 1908, p. 39).

[15] The synod, the first for over two centuries, was commissioned by the Holy See and convened by Cullen at St Patrick's College, Thurles in August 1850.

THE ARCHBISHOP OF DUBLIN,
THE VERY REV. DR LEAHY,
JAMES O'FERRALL, ESQ.,
MICHAEL ERRINGTON, ESQ."[16]

As time went on, a doubt arose, whether the subsequent Synodal Meeting had not superseded the functions of the Committee itself, from which this smaller body derived its powers; however, I was able to use the advice of its members individually even though they did not meet together; and, whenever this was impossible, I had recourse to members of the larger Committee.

[13] On his Grace the Archbishop's going abroad,[17] he mentioned to me three friends whom I might consult, as circumstances might require, instead of himself; an instruction of which I gladly availed myself.[18]

I have also taken advantage of the judgment of Right Rev. Prelates, Priests, and other members of the Irish Church, according as the occasion made it necessary.

It has been my practice never to take any measure of consequence without securing the advice, which I consider most apposite, or which I was best able to command. In saying this, I am not putting away from me the responsibility, in whole or part, of anything I have done. I am much indebted to the superiors and friends to whom I have referred, and I wish here to acknowledge my

[16] This sub-committee was set up in October 1853 and met only once, on 4 October 1855; when invited to attend, O'Ferrall did not know that the committee existed (*LD* xvi, p. 539n).

[17] Cullen went to Rome in October 1854, along with other Irish bishops, for the Declaration of the Immaculate Conception, and stayed there for nine months.

[18] Cullen recommended Thomas MacNamara, superior at Phibsborough, and Philip Dowley, superior at Castleknock College, both founding members of the Vincentian Congregation in Ireland (*LD* xvi, p. 272n).

obligation; but the acts which followed my correspondence or communication with them were my own.

And here I hope your Lordships will allow me to dwell for a short time on the real concern I feel at the news of Dr Leahy, the Vice-Rector's, projected retirement, and on the pleasant and grateful recollections with which I shall ever invest my thoughts of him.[19] It is now four years since I first acted with him on the business of the University, and I have always found him ready to give me faithful counsel in matters where I was ignorant, and prudent direction when I [14]
had occasion to avail myself of it. His suggestions have been always valuable, and I trust I have ever turned them to account. Our loss of him would be one of the few things which would sincerely grieve me in the history of the year; and, though I know well the greater claims his own part of Ireland has on him, yet this rather justifies than reconciles us to his departure.[20]

7. I avail myself of this place also to speak of our academical government and administration, so far as either have existed. I thus limit the mention of them, because the University is too little advanced even into its childhood, to have either of them properly speaking. There have been very few students to be the subjects of government, nor are the Faculties yet formed with Deans at their heads, nor is a Council appointed. Under existing circumstances, I have observed the following rule. During term time, the Vice-Rector, or myself, or both of us, have been in residence; in the Vacations, though we were away, still the Secretary's office was kept open daily from 10 till 2 o'clock. For

---

[19] In the appendix to his 'Memorandum about my Connection with the Catholic University', Newman made a note which he marked '*Very Private*': 'I always got on very well with him—from first to last—we never had even a momentary misunderstanding—no sharp or cold word ever passed between us' (*LD* xvi, p. 551).

[20] Leahy had been appointed parish priest of Cashel and dean of the diocese, but in the event Leahy continued on as Vice-Rector.

myself, I was in Ireland from September to July, forty-six continuous weeks, six Sundays alone being deducted at various times.[21]

[15] 8. On the 3rd of November, the feast of St Malachy, the books of the University were opened for the reception of the names of students, and, at the very time and in the act of entering them, the rudiments of as many as three Colleges were laid down.[22]

On the following Monday, the Professors in the Faculty of Philosophy and Letters, or what is commonly called the School of Arts, commenced their Lectures.[23]

Professors and Lecturers in various departments of science and research had already been recommended either to the *Cœtus Episcoporum*, or to the Four Archbishops, and some of these gentlemen proceeded to give Inaugural Lectures, open to the public, in the weeks which

---

[21] Newman stresses the amount of time he had spent in Dublin because Cullen had recently written to him, 'there are great complaints here that no-one is doing any thing for the University, and no one is charged to give information about what is to be done next year'. Newman replied that the University Secretary was present in his office at University House 'from 10 to 2—and either by application then or by letter will answer all questions'. This had been advertised in the *CUG* and in the newspapers (Cullen to Newman, 27 September; Newman to Cullen, 28 September 1855, *LD* xvi, pp. 550–1). That September Newman was in Birmingham dealing with important Oratory business.

[22] The Catholic University Student Register has columns for name, age, place of birth, father's name, where educated, date of admission, collegiate house, date of taking name off the University books. The first name entered in the University Register is that of Daniel O'Connell, grandson of the 'liberator', who on account of his ancestry was awarded a scholarship which enabled him to reside at University House and attend lectures free of charge for four years (Student Register 1854–79, CU6, UCDA).

[23] On the first day of term the students attended lectures in Classics and mathematics at University House, and, two days later, began lectures in modern languages. For details about the earliest surviving lecture list, see the relevant footnote on p. [322].

immediately ensued.[24] A second series of public lectures took place in the month of June of the present year. The former course was given by the Professor of Holy Scripture, the Professor (designated and provisional) of Classics, the Lecturers on Poetry and on the Philosophy of History, and the Lecturers (designated and provisional) on French, and on Italian Literature:[25] the latter course by the same two Professors, the Professor of Archaeology and Irish History, the Professor (designated and provisional) of Natural Philosophy,[26] and the Lecturers (designated and provisional) on Geography, on Political Economy, on Political and [16]
Social Science, and on the Fine Arts.[27] It is not surprising, but it is gratifying, to be able to state, that the abilities displayed by these gentlemen have created a marked impression in the public mind in favour of the nascent University.[28]

9. I shall have occasion, before I conclude, to ask the indulgence of your Lordships to confirm by your definite

---

[24] During the first year most of the evening display lectures (which were open to the general public, including women) took the form of inaugural lectures, the first of which was given by Newman on Thursday, 9th November, 'On the place held by the Faculty of Arts in the University Course'. This was published as 'Christianity and Letters' in the *Idea* (pp. 249–67).

[25] The other inaugural lectures were given by the Vice-Rector Patrick Leahy (Professor of Holy Scripture) on 'The Church and the Bible'; Robert Ornsby (Professor of Classical Literature) on 'The Utility of Classical Studies'; Denis MacCarthy (Professor of Poetry and English Literature) on 'The Nature and Meaning of Poetry'; T. W. Allies (Professor of Modern History) on 'The Object and the Idea of the Philosophy of History'; Peter le Page Renouf (Professor of Ancient History) on 'The Literary History of France'; and Augustus Marani (Professor of Italian and Spanish) on 'The Origin and Rise of the Italian Language and Literature'.

[26] By 'natural philosophy' is meant natural or empirical science.

[27] The others referred to are: Eugene O'Curry, Henry Hennessy, James Robertson, John O'Hagan, Aubrey de Vere and John Hungerford Pollen.

[28] Articles about these inaugural lectures appeared in the Irish press.

nomination the selections and provisional appointments of Professors and Lecturers, which I have made. Here, however, I am called upon to offer some explanation of the rules which I have laid down to myself both in the establishment of particular chairs and the designation of individuals to fill them. First of all, it is obviously the paramount necessity of this University, from its peculiar position, to secure Professors, who, while sincerely devoted to Catholicism, have reputation sufficient to command the deference and confidence of the world in their respective departments of teaching. Long established institutions, foundations maintained and protected by the State, recognized and chartered bodies, can afford to dispense more or less with professorial merit or fame; but such attributes are the very life of a University which has to make its way without secular patronage to station and authority. Yet, on the other hand, this tentative and
[17] experimental character (if I may so speak) which attaches to it, makes it just as difficult as it is imperative, to interest distinguished men in an undertaking, which, for what they know, is ephemeral. Belief in a Catholic University requires an enthusiasm, which we have had neither right to demand nor time to justify. It seemed unreasonable to ask men of name to commit themselves at once to our intellectual, social, and moral responsibilities, and to undertake new and untried engagements, which might dispossess them of old and sure ones. It would have been no cause of surprise, had they been suspicious of plans which might ultimately be superseded or changed, and mistrustful of pledges which it might have been impossible for the parties making them to redeem. That, under these circumstances, I have found in matter of fact so many generous, high-minded, and zealous men to share my labours, was not to be anticipated; and, while it has a claim on my special acknowledgments, it is an omen of our ultimate success. But, the less careful they

were of themselves, the more I was bound to consult for them, and to see that they did not disregard the obvious dictates of prudence, and sacrifice existing duties to an enterprise. I was bound to view the difficulties I have named as really existing, and as likely to operate as time goes on, though they may be but partially felt at the moment; and I notice them here to account for various [18] provisions or modes of acting on my part, which otherwise may be considered awkward or superfluous.

To meet, then, the difficulties which stood in the way of a satisfactory arrangement of the Professorial Chairs, I have acted as follows:—I have taken as few irrevocable steps as possible; and, in such steps as I have taken, I have attempted very little of rule or uniformity. Sometimes, while distinctly declaring my subordination to the *Cœtus Episcoporum* and my limited powers in the selection and retention of Chairs and Professors, I have not hesitated to declare, what I believe to be the fact, that your Lordships would not reverse any designation of mine, except on the ground of some real and substantial objection to it, approving itself to the *Cœtus Episcoporum*; and I have given my assurance that, though a Professor occupies his Chair only *durante bene-placito*,[29] yet in matter of fact he never will be displaced by any act of your Lordships, while he does not offend against faith, in moral conduct, or in obedience to the authorities of the University. As to the salary, sometimes I have assigned none at all; and generally I have named a sum far short of that which the Committee of Thurles has set down, either because the Professor was not yet in full work, or because certain of his hearers paid fees for attending his Lectures. Sometimes I have not [19] appointed Professors at all, but only Lecturers, in order that the office might be provisional; and that, for the convenience of gentlemen undertaking the office, as well as

[29] That is, during our good pleasure.

of our own. It sometimes has happened that men of reputation could assist us for a time, or to a certain point, but not permanently or with a complete devotion to our interests; and there seemed no reason why such persons should not be induced to join us, though they should not be able to reside among us, or to do much more than give us their name, and deliver a few brilliant lectures in the course of the year.

One remark I have great satisfaction in making. It is natural that, out of reverence to a nation so tried in its devotion to Catholicity, I should wish to take the first Professors and Lecturers of the University principally from among the natives of Ireland;—though your Lordships, in founding a University for all who speak the English tongue, were far indeed from having any such intention, as is plain, if in no other way, from the simple fact of your having selected an Englishman for the first Rector. However, it so happens, that I have been able to secure what you have been too generous to exact; for, putting aside Lecturers in particular languages (which would most suitably be assigned to persons who spoke them as their mother
[20] tongues), out of twenty-one Professors and Lecturers hitherto appointed, all the resident and salaried teachers but two are of the Irish nation; the Professor of Classics being English, and the Lecturer in Ancient History Scotch.[30] Again, even including the Lecturers in particular languages, and those who are non-resident and non-salaried, of twenty-three in all, only seven, that is, less than one-third, whether salaried or resident, or not, are of any nation whatever but the Irish.

10. I now come to mention to your Lordships those University Establishments, as I have called them, to which I

---

[30] Newman refers to Robert Ornsby and James Stewart, respectively. Cullen had not wanted Newman to appoint either of them (*LD* xv, p. 262n).

have directed my care, as having the promise of use in themselves, and of doing us credit with the public for their own sake, even though for the moment there were few University students to avail themselves of them.

The Medical Faculty was naturally one of the first which gained my attention. At the recommendation of some of the principal Catholic practitioners of Dublin, aided by the concurrence of the members of the Sub-committee and other friends, I effected a purchase of the well-known Medical School in Cecilia Street.[31] I have every reason to be satisfied with the transaction; the situation is central; the house was in fair repair; and its internal arrangements have a convenience and completeness not to be surpassed elsewhere in Dublin or any other part of Ireland. The [21]
University Schools have already opened there with great promise of success,[32] though only those Professors are as yet appointed who were absolutely necessary for the commencement.

11. After making this purchase, I next turned my thoughts to the possibility of providing a lodging house, in which Catholic students of Medicine might be offered

[31] Over the summer of 1854 Newman pulled off the greatest coup of his rectorate by purchasing the Cecilia Street Medical School, which had been running since 1837 and was recognised by the Royal College of Surgeons in Ireland. In 1854, after two of its most able staff departed, the proprietor decided to sell up, and when the fully-equipped premises came onto the market, Newman empowered Andrew Ellis, who had been Professor of Surgery at Cecilia Street since 1837, to purchase the school on behalf of the Catholic University, which he did for £1,500. The transaction was carried out without the proprietor realising he was effectively selling to Catholics; if he had known, he would not have sold to Ellis. But Newman was unable to staff the medical school at short notice, which meant that the opening was delayed until the start of the second academic year.

[32] The Medical School was opened to students on 1 October 1855; practical anatomy classes began on 7 October and lectures on 1 November (Record of transactions, pp. 23–4, CU10, UCDA).

rooms at a moderate rate, and exempted from the various inconveniences, material and moral, which befall them in a great city. I have been told that a house of this kind would certainly fill, if once it was opened; but, having already incurred a large expense in the purchase of the Medical School itself, I did not think it prudent to venture on the new expenditure which would have been hazarded on its rent and furniture. I advertised for the names of prospective candidates of admission into it, in the event of its being established; but these advertisements have not hitherto been successful.[33]

12. Expecting in no long time to be able to present to your Lordships a Professor of Chemistry, I have thought it right to take measures for providing a chemical apparatus suitable to the requirements of his chair. I have put this matter into the hands of a scientific gentleman of great distinction,[34] who has kindly undertaken it, and I have the
[22] best reasons for anticipating that the purchases will be both judiciously and economically made.

13. Mathematical and Natural Science is another of the Faculties, which your Lordships have designed for your University. For the moment, the Professor of Natural Philosophy[35] will take possession of one of the rooms of the University House, though he certainly ought to be more advantageously situated, in order to carry out the duties of

---

[33] The lodging house was advertised in the *CUG* 18 (28 September 1854) as receiving the sanction of the University, but without a formal connection, which meant that its residents were not subject to its rules or barred from attending lectures at other medical schools in Dublin. Even though the charge was a modest £7 per quarter (reduced to £6 in the *CUG* of 12 October 1854), there was insufficient demand and the scheme was temporarily shelved.

[34] Newman offered the position to William Sullivan on 26 April 1855, but Sullivan declined the position as he was already Professor of Chemistry in the School of Science at the Museum of Irish Industry in Dublin; he accepted the offer the following year.

[35] Henry Hennessy.

so extensive a department of Science. I have committed to him the task of providing the apparatus necessary for his chair, and I believe he has procured it in Paris at a price scarcely more than half of that which it would have cost in England.

When this gentleman, if definitely nominated by your Lordships, shall be suitably placed with his due apparatus and instruments about him, I have good reason for anticipating that an Institution in Physical Science will have been created, which has no parallel at present in the United Kingdom.

14. The Engineering School is another Institution which, when it is once in operation, cannot fail to be popular. Some delicacy and care will be required for its establishment, considering the difficulty of combining academical residence with the practical studies and the experience in Field Works which the science requires. The School opens [23]
in the ensuing Session, and the Professor[36] has drawn up a Prospectus,[37] with the object of meeting the difficulty to which I have alluded.

15. I ought here to make mention of the Theological School, of which so great a promise exists in the person of the Professors whom your Lordships have already nominated.[38] When it is once fairly in operation, it is my

---

[36] Terence Flanagan (1817?–59), a cousin of the Oratorian John Flanagan, studied for eighteen months at Trinity College Dublin, then worked for three years at an engineering office. He acted as the chief engineer of several railway lines, and was elected a member of the Institute of Civil Engineers. (For more details, see p. [426].) In 1850 Newman chose him as the architect for the Oratory house in Birmingham, and in 1855 he appointed him as Professor of Civil Engineering at the Catholic University.

[37] Prospectus for the Catholic University School of Engineering, 1855–56 (Catholic University, 1850–60, VI(27), Cullen Papers, 45/3, DDA).

[38] Newman had initially been keen to start the University with a Faculty of Theology, but he changed his mind once he realised there would be no demand at the outset. Newman regarded the theology faculty as being in

intention, with your Lordships' sanction, to endow it with several burses or exhibitions,[39] in favour of various schools in Ireland and England, by means of sums which I have the good fortune to have in my possession; but, till its prospects are more distinct, it would be rash to take any definitive steps in this direction.

16. An institution of a directly religious character, which I have been very anxious to establish, though there have been delays in bringing it into operation, is that of stated University Preaching. I have obtained the assistance of some of the most eminent divines both in Ireland and in England, including the important aid of some of your Lordships' body.[40] The difficulty lay in providing a Church for their reception.[41] It is inexpedient that the University

---

The bishops' hands—if not entirely in Cullen's—and he was reluctant to get involved. Newman thought the faculty should be established close to the seminary college of All Hallows, and that the lectures should form an advanced course, 'beyond the routine of a Seminary course'; O'Reilly disagreed, proposing instead a regular course for those preparing for the priesthood (Newman to O'Reilly, 27 April 1855; O'Reilly to Newman, 30 April 1855, *LD* xvi, p. 453).

[39] An exhibition is a type of award or bursary, normally given on the grounds of merit, and typically worth less than a scholarship.

[40] Newman's only stipulations to those invited to preach was that they were to avoid political topics and to abide by the forty-minute time-limit. Preachers could also make use of Newman's thoughts on the subject: his open letter to Bishop Moriarty 'On the Subject of University Preaching' (*CUG* 41 (8 March 1855, pp. 394–400)), which formed the basis of his essay 'University Preaching' in the *Idea* (pp. 405–27). In response to this letter, Ornsby wrote an article entitled 'Preaching With or Without a Book' (*CUG* 42 (5 April 1855), pp. 416–19).

[41] See 'The University Church' on pp. [305–9] for a summary of Newman's efforts to find a suitable location. Before the University opened, Newman had hoped ultimately to make the University Church and the collegiate houses into a personal diocese, either with the Rector as its bishop, or else with the Archbishop of Dublin as its bishop and the Rector as its vicar apostolic (Newman to Stanton, 12 March 1854, *LD* xxxii, p. 84). Newman relied on the Oratorian Richard Stanton to help him decide on arrangements for the University Church. 'Part of my plan,

should commit itself to a definite site and fabric at so early a stage of its proceedings, and to the great outlay which would be required for a Temple suitable to so great an [24] Institution. In consequence, I have taken upon myself the entire cost of erecting and furnishing a temporary Church,[42] of which I propose to give the University the use, on payment to me of a rent, till such time as it seems advisable to your Lordships to provide a structure of dimensions and costliness adequate to the dignity of a Catholic University. The site, which I have chosen, with the consent of the Ordinary and the Parish Priest, is the spot of ground next the University House, the lease of which I have purchased.[43]

I cannot well exaggerate the influence, which a series of able preachers, distinguished by their station and their zeal, will exert upon the young men entering into life, externs and interns, and the students of various professions, who will constitute the mass of University residents. Moreover, such an institution will give a unity to the various academical foundations, some of which I am enumerating, and that unity, too, a unity of a religious character. It will force the University upon public notice, and raise it in public estimation by the presence of the most sacred of all schools, the school of faith and devotion; and it will

---

if I have my way, is to have rather a magnificent ceremonial; good preachers, confraternities etc.', he told him, 'and I wish to get them hot from Rome' (24 February 1853, *LD* xv, p. 311). In the process of consulting Stanton about academic dress and the University Church, and whether they should follow Rome or Louvain, he wrote: 'I want the whole *imposing*' (12 March 1854, *LD* xvi, p. 83).

[42] Having failed to borrow from the University funds the £3,000 he estimated it would cost, Newman decided to pay from his own pocket, using money left over from the Achilli trial fund, in the expectation that he would recoup the outlay through collections over twenty years.

[43] This small piece of land lay behind 87 St Stephen's Green, adjacent to University House. Newman was not deterred by the limited space available as he considered that university sermons were best suited to a church where the preacher was not distanced from the congregation.

maintain and symbolize that great principle in which we glory as our characteristic, the union of Science with Religion.[44]

[25] 17. Another of the Academical Establishments of which the rudiments are already laid, is a University Library;[45] and this seems likely to grow into shape of itself, with little more expense on our part than that of providing rooms and cases for holding it. The munificence or the providence of friends has already shown us how easily it will be formed. We are in possession of the Library of the late Most Rev. Prelate, Dr Murray, Archbishop of Dublin. An Irish Priest, lately deceased, the Rev. M. Dillon, has left us as many as five hundred volumes. A select and valuable collection of books, principally on Canon and Civil Law,[46] has been presented by Mr James R. Hope Scott, Q.C., late Fellow of Merton College, Oxford, and more are to come. Several voluminous and valuable works[47] in excellent condition have been presented by Mr Robert J. Wilberforce, late Fellow of Oriel College, and others by his brother, Mr Henry Wilberforce, late Secretary to the Defence Association. The Rector and Professors of the University of

---

[44] The union of science and religion was one of the themes of Newman's first sermon in the University Church: see the relevant footnote on p. [120]. The essential harmony between science and religion is an argument that features in 'Christianity and Scientific Investigation, a Lecture Written for the School of Science', *Idea*, pp. 473–7.

In 1865, six years after founding the Oratory School in Birmingham, Newman felt able to 'boast' to one of his co-founders that the school really had solved 'the problem of combining a good intellectual education with Catholic morality', which had been the aim from the outset (Newman to Hope-Scott, 28 April 1865, *LD* xxi, p. 454).

[45] The University Secretary took on the task of cataloguing books and acting as librarian. The Special Collection of the UCD library contains a three-volume subject catalogue for the Catholic University that Scratton began in 1858.

[46] There were 192 volumes in this collection.

[47] Robert Wilberforce gave eight volumes of Luther's works and twenty-nine on French ecclesiastical assemblies.

Louvain have testified the interest they take in our undertaking by presenting the works which have proceeded, on various scientific subjects, from members of their body.[48]

18. Lastly, I have been anxious to establish a Printing Press for University purposes; and, though from various circumstances, I have not succeeded as I had hoped, yet I [26]
trust to have a Press at command in some way or other. The publication of scientific registers or literary works will bring us into correspondence with the centres of intellect throughout Europe, and, by exchanging our publications with theirs, we shall receive an important accession of stores to the University Library. I think I may state to your Lordships three works which already are preparing or ready for publication; one on Irish Antiquities,[49] one on a subject connected with the Literature of Poetry,[50] and one on investigation in the department of Mathematical Physics.[51]

19. There is one other Institution of a public character, though not to be classed among those of which I have been speaking, which is almost involved in the very idea of a University, and the mention of which in this place will carry us forward to the remaining subjects to which I have to ask your Lordships' attention. This is the system and the collation of Academical Degrees.

---

[48] This collection of publications was 'on various scientific subjects'.

[49] Eugene O'Curry's lectures were published as *Lectures on the Manuscript Materials of Ancient Irish History* (1861).

[50] It is unclear what this was, as most of Professor MacCarthy's original work and his translations from Spanish, German, French, Italian, Greek and Latin poetry were published in periodicals.

[51] This probably refers to a publication of Henry Hennessy. While teaching at the Catholic University, he published three books: *On the Study of Science in its Relation to Individuals and Society* (1858); *On the Freedom of Education* (1859); and *The Relation of Science to Modern Civilisation* (1862). He also published many original and valuable papers in British and foreign scientific journals, in terrestrial physics, meteorology and climatology, and devised several mechanical inventions.

Your Lordships have given to the Rector power, under sanction of the Holy See, to confer any Academical Degrees whatever. So far the Institution in question exists and needs nothing for its completion; but, on the other hand, it is difficult to find an instance in the history of Universities,
[27] though such may occur, in which Academical Degrees were not accompanied by state recognition and civil privileges, or at least in which they were not conferred under the expectation of their ultimately attaining these advantages. So far this function of a University is not simply in our own hands; it may be necessary then to say a few words on the subject, as it practically affects us at the moment.

There are points of view in which the circumstance which I have mentioned affects us unfavourably, and I wish to state to your Lordships, as accurately as I can, how far the inconvenience extends.

First, it is plain that public opinion, and individual impression, must be regarded and treated as facts; and that if the absence of legal sanction to our degrees is judged an evil, it is so far forth an evil, whatever be the value of the judgment. It is also plain that, in proportion as public opinion changes, the evil so far vanishes; and therefore, while we do not at all deny that it is a real difficulty in our way to be thought to be in a difficulty, still we must leave that impression alone,— not denying, I say, but not caring for it,—with the expectation that, if the opinion has no solid basis, it will in course of time disappear of its own accord, dying as it has arisen, without our having anything to do with it.

[28] Next, as to the deficiency itself,—how far does it really stand in our way? Not much, I think, when steadily looked at. The worth of a Degree is twofold,—first, as far as it is a testimony of merit; next, as being a qualification. A University prize, for instance, is a testimony of merit, but no qualification; University residence is a qualification, but no

testimonial; a Degree is both a testimonial of having passed an examination, and a qualification for certain situations.

Now, considering the degree as a testimonial of merit, its worth depends simply and entirely on ourselves. It is an honour *laudari a laudato*.[52] If, my Lords, your Examiners and Examinations claim the respect of the public, your degrees will be necessarily a testimony of merit; if they do not, they will not be so. If you choose able, zealous men for your Professors and other officials, the world cannot help respecting those who go forth into it decorated with the marks of your approbation; and if you did not choose men of the first talents, name, attainments, energy, for your servants, the world would think little of your diplomas, even though they had a legal sanction.

And to tell the truth, there never was a time when the legal sanction was of less avail than at the present,—never a time when we could more easily dispense with it. This war[53] [29]
itself has given a rude shake to all patents and monopolies of civil advancement, and has shown candidates for distinction or emolument that their hopes must rest on a base more logically cogent than their belonging to established Universities. If there was a moment when we need not sacrifice anything for the sake of state recognition it is when appointments in the Artillery and Engineers and in the Civil Service of our Indian Empire are offered to a free *concursus*,[54] and may be gained by our students, as well as the students of the most venerable and time-honoured Academies, provided our youths do but beat theirs in fair fight within the lists of an examination hall.[55]

---

[52] This expression, 'to be praised by a man who has been praised', was quoted several times by Cicero from the early Roman poet Naevius.

[53] The Crimean War. [WPN] England and France declared war against Russia in March 1854; hostilities ceased in February 1856.

[54] That is, open competition.

[55] The rise of a meritocracy and the gradual acceptance in society of those who were not members of the Established Church were reflected in new

What is so emphatically true of that new order of things which is opening upon us, is becoming more and more the case continually, even as regards those portions of the ancient regime, in which degrees are still necessary qualifications for employment or recognition. A degree may be considered at present to do little for the Student in Law, and next to nothing at all for the Student of Medicine. A Student of Medicine who graduated at the Catholic University, would find himself precisely in a similar
[30] position, with respect to practising, as if he had taken his degree at Oxford or Cambridge. No one practises in Medicine on an Oxford Degree. That Degree is a testimonial that the possessor has had a liberal education and has lived among gentlemen; but it has no direct bearing on his being recognized as a physician, on his receiving patients, and taking fees. He goes up to London, passes an examination before the College of Physicians, and on the diploma there obtained, not on his Oxford Degree, he practises. The simple question then is, whether students from our Medical School will be allowed to present themselves for examination before bodies who have the

---

legislation which opened up positions to all educated subjects of the Crown, as exemplified by the India Act (1853) which opened up to competition appointments to the India civil service. Newman did not hesitate to use the pages of the *Gazette* to provide up-to-date information on the new employment opportunities that were opening up to Catholics. The *Gazette* provided details of the new exam regulations, and when it was announced that the East India Company's administrative training college at Haileybury was to have its monopoly on employment in India broken up, the implications for the Catholic University were spelt out. See 'The Throwing Open of Haileybury', *CUG* 35 (18 January 1855) and 'The Examination for the East India Civil [Service] Appointments', *CUG* 47 (6 December 1855). Just as Macaulay's *Report* (1854) laid down rules for the India civil service exams, which were adopted in full, the recommendations of the *Northcote–Trevelyan Report* (1854) were taken up by the Civil Service Commission which was set up in 1855 to oversee open recruitment and end patronage for the home civil service.

power of granting diplomas; and, though it would be going into unsuitable details to prove this here, I believe there is no doubt that such recognition will be granted to them.[56] As to the Faculty of Law, certainly here we shall be at some disadvantage, for a Degree at a recognized University is, I believe, a saving of Terms at the Inns of Law; but it will be some time before we are in a situation to feel this disadvantage.

20. It must not be forgotten, moreover, that the only Degrees we shall need for a while are the Degrees in Philosophy and Letters, the Faculty in which every one must graduate before he goes into one of the higher Faculties. In this Faculty I should recommend the establishment of three Degrees, those of Scholar, Bachelor, [31]
and Master.[57] Few youths, after leaving school, have much time, to speak generally, for University Education; and the problem we have to determine is this,—how to consult for the interests of the majority, who are soon to be engaged in the business of life, without sacrificing the definitiveness and completeness of the Academical system, and the just demands of those to whom knowledge itself is a

[56] The opening of the medical school was something of a gamble, because it began without any official recognition, but at the end of the first term the recognition was forthcoming and with that the success of the school was guaranteed. The story of the medical school is told in F. O. C. Meenan, *Cecilia Street: the Catholic University Medical School, 1855–1931* (Dublin: Gill & Macmillan, 1987). See also W. Doolin, 'Newman and his medical School', *Studies: an Irish quarterly review* 42 (1953), pp. 151–68.

[57] After taking advice from counsel, Newman decided not to use the titles 'BA' and 'MA' for degrees as that was deemed to be illegal. Among the supporters and staff of the University opinion was evenly divided about whether or not to defy the British government: the Young Irelanders wished to push ahead; others preferred to wait for a charter. On account of the lack of unanimity Newman adopted the more cautious approach, even though Rome had given the University permission to award degrees.

profession.[58] I have attempted to meet the difficulty in the following way.

Sixteen is considered to be the age of entrance.[59] After passing an examination, the candidate for admission is entered on the University books, and is called a Student, and is submitted to a course of liberal, not professional, study. At the end of two years he will be eighteen, and of the age when it is to be expected he will wish to pursue his particular profession, whether he be intended for the ecclesiastical state, for law, for medicine, for engineering, or for trade. If this be his wish, he gives up of course the prospect of the *curriculum* of the University, whether he transfers himself to some professional department of the University, or retires from residence altogether. In either case he will have gained two years' education, though he go no further; but to give completeness to his course of study, I
[32] have arranged that he should pass an examination and take a degree, and thus have something to show for the time he has spent in the Faculty he is quitting. This degree it is proposed to call the Scholar's Degree, after the manner of some

---

[58] By advocating an acquaintance with all disciplines and a deep study of a few or one, Newman has been accused of wanting the best of both worlds but of proposing a scheme that would foster neither. By offering a liberal education instead of a professional training, Newman has also been accused of serving Ireland badly (see T. Corcoran, *Newman's Theory of Liberal Education* (1929) and *Newman: Selected Discourses on Liberal Knowledge* (1929); also V. A. McClelland, *English Roman Catholics and Higher Education 1830–1903* (1973)). Most commentators agree with Fergal McGrath, who argued that Newman managed to solve the problem of how to combine the interests of all parties: a balance between protecting the initial years for a liberal education and some degree of specialisation in line with future professional studies (*NU*, pp. 21, 299–307).

[59] The ages of the students in Newman's collegiate house were: fifteen, sixteen, seventeen (four of them), eighteen and twenty-one. At the time, students in Scotland began their university studies at fifteen or sixteen; the University of London similarly fixed its minimum age for entry at fifteen when it opened in 1828.

Foreign Universities, the examination necessary for it being made upon such subjects of study as had employed him during his residence.

If, however, he does not yet turn aside to any particular profession, a second course of liberal studies is allotted to him, and lasts for two years, at the end of which he undergoes a corresponding examination for the Degree of Bachelor. This is at the end of his fourth year of residence, and when he has completed his twentieth year.

At the end of another three years, or at the end of seven years from entrance, when he is twenty-three years old, he is in a condition to receive the Degree of Master in Philosophy and Letters, of Doctor in Theology, in Law, and in Medicine, his diploma in Engineering, and whatever honourable distinction is determined on for proficiency in the Faculty of Mathematical and Physical Science.

Besides these Degrees, which imply a certain residence within the limits of the University, I have proposed, at the suggestion of persons who felt the desirableness of
extending our influence as far as possible, to give a [33]
certificate or diploma of merit, though short of a degree, to any persons who, coming with due testimonials of respectability, are desirous, without residence, to submit themselves to an examination in Philosophy and Letters.[60]

---

[60] When, in 1840, the University of London gained its charter enabling it to act as an examining body for teaching institutions that wished to affiliate, Seven Catholic colleges—six English and one Irish—did so immediately, and others followed soon after. St Patrick's, Carlow affiliated in 1840, St Kieran's, Kilkenny, followed suit in 1844, and St Patrick's, Thurles, in 1849 (F. M. G. Willson, *Our Minerva: the Men and Politics of the University of London, 1836–1858* (London: Athlone, 1995), appendix II). The University of London effectively became an 'open' or distance-learning university in 1858, when the stipulation of attendance at affiliated institutions was dropped. The result was that only 15% of those who graduated were educated there. A campaign to turn it back into a teaching university eventually made it not just a metropolitan university, but a national and imperial one.

21. But to return to the student or freshman of the University. On admission to the university, he is at once put under discipline, and he is required to join himself to some particular House or Community, of which he becomes a member. These Houses are each under the rule of a Dean or President, and are furnished with Tutors in proportion to the number of students. Each House has its chapel and common table. The following is the course of a student's day: attendance at Mass at 8 A.M.; breakfast; attendance at Lectures from 9 to 1 or 2; dinner at 5; presence indoors by a fixed hour in the evening, according to the season. Moreover, there will be examinations once or twice a term, and the examination for the degree at the end of the course of study.

Besides these intern members of a House, it should be in the power of the Dean or President, under sanction of the Rector, to permit young men to live at the houses of their parents or friends, if they wish it; but in the case of such
[34] externs, their home, or abode, whatever it is, must be considered as a licensed lodging house, or rather as an integral part of the academical domicile; so that the young men so situated are as simply under the jurisdiction of the Dean as if they resided under his roof.[61]

And lastly, each House should be self-supporting; independent of the University in all money matters, and taking nothing from the University; though at the commencement of so large and complicated a system, there always must be exceptions to the strict rule.[62] Moreover, all

---

[61] In the Oxbridge system, the usual way of becoming a member of the university was by first being accepted by a college or hall. Newman adapted this to the Irish situation by allowing Irish students who expected to live at home or with friends of the family to be attached to a collegiate house.

[62] The plan for each collegiate house to be financially independent of the University proved to be unworkable in the early years. With all his experience, even Newman struggled in the first year to balance the books

the Houses, both as regards superiors and subjects, would be under the supreme jurisdiction of the University, the Dean and Tutors being in every case appointed by the Rector, and subject to his visitation and interposition.

22. Of such Houses there are already three in existence;[63] the House attached to the University, which happens to be the largest of them, and of which the Very Rev. Mr Flannery is Dean; the Rector's House, in Harcourt Street; and Dr Quinn's[64] House, also in Harcourt Street, of whose school the senior members have been entered at the University.[65]

---

of the house he oversaw and had to contribute £300 to its running costs to make it break even (see *MM*, pp. 188–9).

[63] All three occupied Georgian mansions. That such fine properties should be associated with an impoverished institution might seem surprising, but it should be remembered that until the Act of Union (1800) Dublin was a European city which boasted fine buildings and a thriving social life; after 1800, decline set in and fifty years later there were plenty of large properties on the market at reasonable prices.

[64] James Quinn (1819–81) studied under Cullen at the Irish College in Rome, where he first met Newman. When his school – see the following footnote – was affiliated to the Catholic University in 1854, Quinn became the Dean of St Laurence's House. In 1859 he was consecrated the first bishop of Brisbane, Australia.

[65] This collegiate house, also known as St Laurence's, was formed within an existing seminary school located at 16–17 Harcourt Street, a Georgian mansion once owned by the Earl of Clonmel. St Laurence O'Toole's Seminary and Catholic Day School—as it was styled in *Battersby's Catholic Directory* – catered for local boys living at home and boarders intended for the priesthood, and was run by the recently ordained James Quinn. In 1854 the older boys were enrolled as members of the University and, under the deanship of Quinn, formed a collegiate house which shared the same premises as the school. The school, named after St Laurence O'Toole, the twelfth-century Archbishop of Dublin, had been opened in 1850 and within three years had twenty-seven boarders and forty-three day boys. (D. Kerr, 'Dr Quinn's School and the Catholic University, 1850–67', *Irish Ecclesiastical History* 108 (1967), pp. 89–101)

Besides the intern and extern members of the University, and here too with a view of opening the advantages of the University to the furthest possible extent, I have allowed
[35] studious persons to attend the Lectures without entrance, on the payment of a fee.[66]

The whole number of students in Lecture attached to these Houses, including a few who attended the Lectures without entrance, in the course of last Session was forty-three;[67] and of these, ten passed their Examination for the Scholar's Degree at its termination in July.[68] They were enabled to do so, at the end of their first instead of their second year, in consequence of a provision I made in favour of existing classical schools through Ireland and England; *viz.*, that residence in any of them for any time under two years, with certificate of good conduct, should count as residence for an equal length of time in the University.

Houses, such as I have been describing to your Lordships, on principle small and numerous, are thus instituted in order to the enforcement of discipline upon young men, who are at a very anxious time of life, and

---

[66] In later documents Newman refers to these students as 'auditors'.

[67] During the first term the numbers on the lecture list rose from seventeen to twenty-seven; further additions over the Christmas vacation meant that the Lent term began with thirty-seven, and, despite several departures over the Easter vacation, the summer term began with forty. In total, around sixty were on the University books during that first year, though there was a fair amount of coming and going. In addition to those who matriculated there were others who only attended the 'evening display lectures', which were advertised in the press and aimed at attracting new students.

[68] The examining for the scholar's degree took place on 16–17 July 1855 in University House. Besides the two examiners, one internal (Professor Edmund O'Reilly, an Irish priest who had lectured at Maynooth for over a decade) and one external (Edward Walford, a former scholar of Balliol College, Oxford), there were also present the Rector, the Archbishop of Dublin and various other clerics. At the end of the second day a handwritten notice in Latin confirmed that ten of the students were successful (University transactions 1854–80, p. 20, CU10, UCDA).

come to us under very anxious circumstances; and, as this subject is one of the most important ones we have to consider, I hope I shall not be trespassing upon your Lordships' patience, if I enter into it at some length.[69]

23. It is assuredly a most delicate and difficult matter to manage youths, and those lay youths, in that most dangerous and least docile time of life, when they are no [36]
longer boys, but not yet men, and claim to be entrusted with the freedom which is the right of men, yet punished with the lenience which is the privilege of boys. In proposing rules on this subject, I shall begin with laying down, first, as a guiding principle, what I believe to be the truth, that the young for the most part cannot be driven, but, on the other hand, are open to persuasion, and to the influence of kindness and personal attachment; and that, in consequence, they are to be kept straight by indirect contrivances rather than by authoritative enactments and naked prohibitions. And a second consideration of great importance is, that these youths will certainly be their own masters before

---

[69] At both Oxford and Cambridge the undergraduate population had always been broken down into smaller units because of the system of colleges and halls. When Newman was an undergraduate there were around sixty undergraduates at Trinity College, and when at Oriel as Fellow about the same number. In 1825–26 Newman acted as Vice-Principal of Alban Hall, an independent academic hall with a dozen students.

The idea of breaking down the school population into smaller units by means of the house system had been a major part of the reforms introduced by Dr Arnold at Rugby School in the 1820s and was soon copied by other public schools. This strategic change reflected a general feature of the Victorian era, the slow but progressive divorce of the public school from its surroundings: instead of boys eating and sleeping in town, in boarding or dames' houses, they came to be lodged in central buildings or boarding houses contiguous to them. The change had two crucial advantages: it brought boys under the power of the masters, and it ensured that boarding profits remained within the school. Although Newman did not attend a public school he was well aware of this development and its advantages.

many years have passed, as they were certainly schoolboys not many months ago. A University residence, then, is in fact a period of training interposed between boyhood and manhood, and one of its special offices is to introduce and to launch the young man into the world, who has hitherto been confined within the school and the play-ground. If this be so, then is it entrusted with an office as momentous as it is special; for nothing is more perilous to the soul than the sudden transition from restraint to liberty. Under any circumstances it is a serious problem how to prepare the young mind against the temptations of life; but, if
[37] experience is to be our guide, boys who are kept jealously at home or under severe schoolmasters till the very moment when they are called to take part in the business of the world, are the very persons about whom we have most cause to entertain misgivings. They are sent out into the midst of giant temptations and perils, with the arms, or rather the unarmed helplessness, of children, with knowledge neither of self nor of the strength of evil, with no trial of the combat or practice in sustaining it; and, in spite of their good feelings, they too commonly fail in proportion to their inexperience. Even if they have innocence, which is perhaps the case, still they have not principle, without which innocence is hardly virtue. We could not do worse than to continue the discipline of school and college into the University, and to let the great world, which is to follow upon it, be the first stage on which the young are set at liberty to follow their own bent.[70] So proceeding, we should

[70] By arguing for a different kind of discipline over the student than that exercised by the home tutor or schoolmaster, Newman was addressing a concern he only fully appreciated towards the end of his rectorate, when he had come to realise the extent to which Irish Catholics failed to see the need for a gradation of liberties as the young man approached adulthood – what might be termed a progressive 'education in freedom'. The right mixture of liberty and restraint was scarcely possible either at the colleges run by religious orders or at the seminary colleges which

be abdicating a function, and letting slip the opportunities of our peculiar position. It is our duty and our privilege to be allowed to hold back the weak and ignorant a while from an inevitable trial;—to conduct them to the arms of a kind Mother, an Alma Mater, who inspires affection while she whispers truth; who enlists imagination, taste, and ambition on the side of duty; who seeks to impress hearts with noble and heavenly maxims at the age when they are most [38]
susceptible, and to win and subdue them when they are most impetuous and self-willed; who warns them while she indulges them, and sympathizes with them while she remonstrates with them; who superintends the use of the liberty which she gives them, and teaches them to turn to account the failures which she has not at all risks prevented; and who, in a word, would cease to be a mother, if her eye were stern and her voice peremptory. If all this be so, it is plain that a certain tenderness, or even laxity of rule on the one hand, and an anxious, vigilant, importunate attention on the other, are the characteristics of that discipline which is peculiar of a University. And it is the necessity of the exercise of this "Lesbian Canon," as the great philosopher calls it,[71] which is the great difficulty of the governors of

---

compensated for the absence of tertiary education by offering extra courses for those of university age. Undoubtedly these makeshift arrangements were better than nothing, but for Newman they were no substitute for an 'education in freedom' in a university setting.

[71] In *An Essay in Aid of a Grammar of Assent* (London: Longmans, Green & Co., 1870; 1898, p. 355) Newman writes: 'State or public law is inflexible, but this mental rule is not only minute and particular, but has an elasticity, which, in its application to individual cases, is, as I have said, not studious to maintain the appearance of consistency. In old times the mason's rule which was in use at Lesbos was, according to Aristotle, not of wood or iron, but of lead, so as to allow of its adjustment to the uneven surface of the stones brought together for the work. By such the philosopher illustrates the nature of equity in contrast with law, and such is that *phronesis*, from which the science of morals forms its rules, and

such an institution. It is easy enough to lay down the law and to justify it, to make your rule and keep it; but it is quite a science, I may say, to maintain a persevering, gentle oversight, to use a minute discretion, to adapt your treatment to the particular case, to go just as far as you safely may with each mind, and no further, and to do all this with no selfish ends, with no sacrifice of sincerity and frankness, and with no suspicion of partiality.

The formal discipline of a University, then, being, from
[39] the nature of the case, defective, and needing personal influence for (what I may call) its *integrity*,[72] I have thought

---

receives its complement.' See also *LD* xxxii, p. 133 for a summary of Aristotle's use of *phronesis* in the *Nicomachean Ethics*.

[72] One of Newman's original contributions to educational thinking is the way he applies the idea of flourishing not to an individual but to an institution, the university, employing the Aristotelian distinction between the *essence* of something and its *integrity*. The essence of an object refers to what is necessary for its nature, whereas integrity (*eudemonia*) refers to what is required for its harmonious functioning or well-being; it is a gift added to its nature. Without it that nature is indeed complete, and can act and fulfill its end, though not with ease. For Newman, the essence of a university consists in the communication of knowledge, in lecturers and students, in the professorial system; but the influence of professors alone is insufficient for its well-being, for a rich and full life and all that the term *eudemonia* connotes. 'For its sure and comfortable existence we must look to [...] the collegiate system' (*HS* iii, p. 74).

The separation of functions between a university and college, a professor and a tutor, is only referred to once in the *Idea* (in the Preface), and there Newman makes a different distinction, arguing that a University was in *essence* a place of teaching and that it carried out its function independently of its relation to the Church. In practice, however, it was unable to fulfill its purpose properly without the aid of the Church, since the Church was necessary for its *integrity*. In his university sketches Newman argues that 'Colleges are the direct and special instruments, which the Church *uses* in a University, for the attainment of her sacred objects'. By combining the two antitheses, university–college and professor–tutor, Newman arrives at his conclusion: 'The Professorial system fulfils the strict idea of a University, and is sufficient for its *being*, but it is not sufficient for its *well-being*. Colleges constitute the *integrity* of a University' (*HS* iii, pp. 182–3).

to meet the difficulty in our own case in the following ways:—

(i) I propose, as I have already implied, to lodge the students in communities of limited accommodation, so that no great number will live together. A large College of lay students will be found impenetrable and unmanageable by even the most vigilant authorities. Personal influence requires personal acquaintance, and the minute labour of a discretionary rule is too fatiguing to be exercised on a large number. And this especially holds good, when an Institution is in its first beginnings.

(ii) Next, it is of great importance to create among the young men a good academical spirit, which may be carried on by tradition. It is scarcely too much to say that one-half of the education which young people receive is derived from the tradition of the place of education. The *genius loci*, if I may so speak, is the instructor most readily admitted and most affectionately remembered.[73] The authorities cannot directly create it; still they can encourage, and foster, and influence it. One special means of operating upon it is the establishment of lucrative places or exhibitions, to be given

[73] Newman felt that everything in a long-established institution was influenced by this intangible but all-important power, which he called the *genius loci* (the 'spirit of the place'). It has been described as combining 'in itself the power of discipline with the power of influence, for though its ways were secret and indirect and personal, it had all the authority of law and all the consistency of a living idea' (Culler, *Imperial Intellect*, p. 166). Newman's audience would have been familiar with the concept from the Dublin lecture in which he describes how a youthful community naturally gives birth to a living teaching, which in course of time takes the shape of a self-perpetuating tradition 'which haunts the home where it has been born, and which imbues and forms, more or less, and one by one, every individual who is successively brought under its shadow'. It constituted 'a sort of self-education', and was clearly visible in the academic institutions of Protestant England (*Idea*, p. 147).

away on *concursus*.[74] It will generally happen that the most
[40] studious are the best principled and most religiously minded of the young men; at least a certain share of self-command, good sense, and correctness in deportment they must have; and, by bringing them forward in the way I am proposing, the respect due to successful talent comes in aid of order and virtue, and they become the centre of influence, who are likely to use influence well. Moreover, it ought to be a condition that youths enjoying such honourable emoluments should be interns; they should exercise certain collegiate functions, for instance, such as holding the place of sacristan, serving at Mass, assisting the Professors and Tutors in the promulgation of the Lecture List; they should have certain slight privileges, as having a separate table in the refectory, admittance to the library, an *entrée* into the Dean's and Tutors' rooms, and their special confidence; and thus, without having a shadow of jurisdiction over the rest, they would constitute a middle party between the superiors and the students, break the force of their collisions, and act as an indirect and spontaneous channel of communicating to the students many an important lesson and truth, which they would not receive, if administered to them from the mouth of a superior.[75]

---

[74] That is, on open competition. To modern ears there is nothing particularly novel about the idea of open competition, but at the time it was an innovatory practice. It saw the old order of privilege and sponsorship giving way to meritocracy. At Oxford, reformers in the 1850s battled to open up scholarships, exhibitions and bursaries to ordinary students without ties of kin, school, geographical location or parental status.

[75] There is more than an echo here of the prefect system introduced by Thomas Arnold at Rugby which played a key part in reforming the public-school system. During the middle decades of the nineteenth century it gradually became accepted that character training was enhanced by a delegation of authority to the boys themselves and that, besides instilling virtues, self-government had two practical advantages: it made the headmaster's job easier, and it prevented rebellion by uniting some of the most influential boys with the masters. Though theologically at odds with

Here too a beginning has been made. An anonymous Benefactor, through the Most Reverend Prelate the Archbishop of Dublin, gave two exhibitions last November [41]
for proficiency in Classics and Mathematics;[76] to which I ventured to add two on my own responsibility on the part of the University.[77] Of the four successful candidates, three were interns and one extern. Two are in the number of those who creditably passed their examination for the Scholar's Degree. Ill health, I am sorry to say, deprived us for some months of another, who, I trust, will soon return to residence for the ensuing Session.

(iii) I expect much from the influence of the Tutors; though, from the nature of the case, some years must pass before the objects I wish them to answer can be really carried into effect. They should be young men, not above two or three years older than their pupils, and such as have lately passed their own course of study in the University, and gained honours on examination, or are holders, or lately were holders, of the lucrative places or exhibitions of which I have been speaking.[78] They would be half companions,

---

Arnold's latitudinarianism, Newman clearly admired his use of surrogate authority and employed it himself.

[76] By the end of the second academic session the University had awarded just one academic scholarship for a free place; in this instance the recipient was supposed to be a mathematical genius, but later it was found that his 'habits of intemperance' were such that they could not keep him (Newman to Moriarty, 30 August 1856, *LD* xvii, p. 369).

[77] Restricted to native Irishmen, these were advertised in the *Gazette* and elsewhere, together with sample questions. As funds for scholarships were limited, Newman hoped to make them self-financing, by awarding them to students on condition that the recipients worked as assistant librarians.

[78] At the end of his final year as Rector Newman was able to appoint someone who fitted this description. The academic star of St Patrick's, Augustus Keane, had gained honours in the licentiate exam and in 1858 became a tutor at St Patrick's. Keane had won a Classical scholarship to the Catholic University in 1856, as well as three university prizes, and had therefore risen through the system.

half advisers of their pupils, that is, of the students; and while their formal office would be that of preparing them for the Professors' Lectures, and the Examinations, or what in this place is technically called "grinding," they would be thrown together with them in their amusements and recreations; and, gaining their confidence from their almost
[42] parity of age, and their having so lately been what the others are still, they may be expected to exercise a salutary influence over them, and will often know more about them than any one else.[79]

(iv) And I should hope a good deal from the influence of the Professors; though of course they must be left to their own discretion and inclination in this matter. Still, I should hope that the Professors will without effort, and almost spontaneously, draw around them such young men as, from a turn for a particular study, or in other ways, are open to their influence.

(v) Above all, incalculable benefit will, I trust, accrue from the institution of University Sermons. I doubt whether it would not defeat their influence if the students were under an obligation to assist at them; but, seats and the attraction of good preachers being supplied to them, it will become a fashion, or rather a rule of the place, to attend the University Church, and, through the divine blessing, their hearts will receive indelible impressions.[80]

---

[79] This description of the role of the tutor has similarities with the Arnoldian role of the school prefect: in both cases a beneficial influence was to be exerted by those who were a little older and, hopefully, wiser. Since such a system of young tutors was impractical at the start, Newman decided that *pro tem* the tutorial work should be committed to three or four older academics, who would also carry out tasks necessary for the commencement of the University, such as organising the plan of studies and compiling a list of set texts and the course of reading to be recommended to the students.

[80] A year after Newman's departure from the Catholic University, Cullen commissioned a *Report on the Condition and Circumstances of the Catholic University of Ireland, Presented by a Committee of Senate* (1859). Those on

(vi) It is desirable too that confessionals for the students should be provided in the Church; and that a religious Confraternity should be erected there; and that opportunity should be given for the cultivation of particular devotions.[81]

(vii) I should add that an academical gown, to be worn at Lecture, at Church, in Refectory, and on other formal [43] attendances, would much subserve the cause of discipline; and academical solemnities at stated times, whether religious or of a secular character.[82]

24. And now I have but two subjects more on which I have to ask your Lordships' attention, though they are subjects of no slight moment. The first is that of the expenditure of the year.

---

the committee (six laymen and a priest) identified so strongly with Newman's emphasis on freedom in matters of religious observance, that they argued (p. 86) that practices of piety were better 'enforced by a sense of belonging to an institution where religion was recognised and honoured as its basis, than by a compulsory compliance' by means of detailed rules. Nevertheless, the new Dean of St Patrick's House had instituted compulsory attendance at morning prayer at 7.30 am and observance of the 'short silence' after night prayer at 10 pm (Record of Proceedings at St Patrick's House 1858–61, Woodlock Papers, 106/5, DDA).

[81] To complement the provision at the collegiate houses for the students' spiritual needs, Newman wanted the University Church to supply confessionals, at least one religious confraternity, and the opportunity for the cultivation of particular devotions. In a private letter he wrote, 'we hope to act upon the young men, instead of using strict *rules of* discipline – which in a University is impossible. To bring out my idea of a University fully, I must establish some confraternity or the like to *win* young minds instead of driving them.' He explained that this would require priests not connected to the University 'to act on the University men' (Newman to Wenham, 24 November 1856, *LD* xxxii, p. 161).

[82] Despite his intention for students to wear an academic gown—as at Oxford—during lectures, at dinner and on other formal occasions, whether of a religious or secular nature, Newman did not act on this particular idea. The introduction of academic dress was the result of a petition addressed to the rector in 1855 and signed by forty-one students, at that time virtually the entire student body of the University (A 34.2, BOA).

The expenditure naturally divides itself under two heads;—that which is current and ordinary, and that which is extraordinary and belongs to the first establishing of the University.

(i) Of the extraordinary expenses, the bulk of which takes place once for all,

α. First, I have to mention the fitting up the Lecture Rooms in the University House, as Schools especially of the Faculty of Philosophy and Letters,—the Professors of which are accustomed to lecture with books and maps or boards, but without instruments or apparatus. These are the rooms on the ground and first floors of the House No. 86 Stephen's Green.

β. Cases for the University Library have been fitted round one of these rooms; they were required at once, in order to receive the books of the late Archbishop of Dublin.

γ. A far more considerable expense has been that of putting into habitable condition the upper storeys and
[44] basement of No. 86, in order to adapt them to the purposes of an Academical House or Hall. It has been in some instances necessary to divide the rooms, which were too large and too few for the use to which we had to put them. A refectory had to be gained, drains to be repaired or made; the whole house had to be painted, and the rooms papered. A kitchen range and other fixtures had to be supplied or put to rights. The roof of the stables had to be renewed. The whole had to be furnished. There still remains a great deal to do; a chapel is needed; and the courts at the back of the house are still in disorder.

δ. With a view of withdrawing the students from the society found at the public rooms, I have borrowed a sum from the University for forming a billiard room out of one of the stables. The Loan altogether will be about £160, and it will be gradually repaid by the incomings from the use of the table.[83]

ε. This Academical House being already full, I have, with the advice of others, obtained a lease of nineteen years, without fine, of the premises No. 87 at a rent of £57 15s a year. This new house will afford accommodation for about a dozen students more, and the expense of fitting it up will not be considerable.[84]

ζ. Next, as to the Rector's House in Harcourt Street. To this House I have added a chapel[85] and a new building [45]

---

[83] This was not a sop to student whims but a carefully considered response to a problem that had developed during the first academic year, when the students took to the tables in nearby Dawson's Lane, at what was regarded as the great billiards place in Dublin. Though it was kept by a good Catholic who professed to keep a strict eye on the students, and though priests played there in private, the danger for the students was that they were likely to form undesirable acquaintances there and become involved in betting. Rather than simply issue a ban on frequenting the place, Newman sought to acquire a table for the University with the intention of formally licensing a 'keeper' and then forbidding the young men to go elsewhere, but the expense and want of a room delayed the plan. Although Newman knew it 'won't quite answer the purpose, for *the youths wish to see play*', he decided to push ahead over the first summer vacation using a loan of £160 from the University (Newman to Flanagan, [June 1855], *LD* xvi, p. 496). Upon completion the *Gazette* (1 November 1855) announced that a spacious room had been set up 'to serve as a billiard room, for the recreation of the students', and that it was open from noon until 5 pm under the care of 'a respectable and efficient marker, who has orders to prevent all gaming and betting'.

Cullen complained to Rome that Newman had spent 'a very large sum on billiards', and that while such things might be done at Oxford, 'here it is really too bad for us to throw away the money of the poor on such trifles' (Cullen to Kirby, 15 January 1856, quoted in Barr, *Paul Cullen*, p. 145). In fact, a second-hand billiard table was acquired, and the billiard room made a handsome profit of £20 in 1857/58.

[84] The works enabled provision at the University House to expand from fifteen to twenty-seven places; as part of the works, a passage linking Nos 86 and 87 was constructed.

[85] It was over the Christmas vacation of 1854/55 that Newman completed the process of converting the stables of the Rector's House into a chapel.

consisting of four rooms. I have made various necessary additions to the house, and have in a good measure furnished it. The furniture, etc., has cost me £274; the new buildings and additions £265; and the chapel £110: altogether, in round numbers, £650. Of this sum, which I have actually paid or owe, I propose to take a moiety upon myself, that is, £325. The other half I propose to ask of the University; but of this sum, £325, thus paid me back, I intend to put £275 to the credit of the New Church Fund. Thus, on the whole, I shall be expending on University objects out of my own means, £600. I am or shall be enabled to do this by means of the liberal salary which is assigned to me as Rector.

η. The third house, Dr Quinn's, has been no expense to us whatever. Certain of the senior students have been entered members of the University and have attended the Lectures. Their free admission has been their gain; ours has been the advantage of an increase of numbers, the addition of some clever youths, one of whom gained an Exhibition, and another an extraordinary prize, an opening in our favour to a class in Dublin society who otherwise might not send their sons to us at all, and the satisfaction of connecting
[46] ourselves with an existing institution of the place,[86] which is presided over by clergymen of great consideration.

θ. Another source of initial or extraordinary expense has been the Medical School in Cecilia Street. We bought it for

---

Asked if he had news about the University for the Pope, Newman instructed Lord Henry Kerr to inform the pontiff that the Blessed Sacrament was now reserved at his house (Newman to Kerr, 30 January 1855, *LD* xvi, p. 370). In fact, from January 1855 onwards Mass was said there daily and attended by several of the residents.

[86] Both the University House and Dr Quinn's were ideally placed to draw students from the locality, and by the end of the second academic year Newman was quite optimistic as he felt the two schools were 'working' Dublin well.

£1450; we have spent in the course of the last year £152 10s. for fixtures, repairs, and furnishing.

(ii) Passing on to the ordinary and recurring charges, I have to mention:—

α. The Professors and Lecturers; the charge for whom will of course increase year by and year according as the Faculties are supplied with their complement of Chairs. I think it very desirable that most of them should ultimately be paid in part by means of fees. The Medical Professors will gain a portion of their salaries in this way from the first. There are Chairs, however, which, as demanding the whole devotion of the persons who fill them to the subjects themselves which they profess, and depriving them of the emoluments of a secular calling, must ever look to the University for their support. There are other Chairs which it is politic to pay well in the beginning of the institution.

β. The rent, taxes, rates, gas, firing, waiting, etc., incurred by that part of the House No. 86 Stephen's Green, which is devoted to University Lecture Rooms and Library, form another head of ordinary expense, and have amounted [47]
in the last year to about £163 3s. 9d.

γ. Next may be mentioned the payment of the Exhibitions, which during the first year has cost no more than £50, with the expense in addition of a set of books given as a prize to a candidate who came close upon the successful ones.

δ. There ought to be little more of ordinary expenditure; but here I am brought to a subject of some anxiety, to which I am obliged to ask your Lordships' particular attention. A strong opinion has been expressed, ever since a University was seriously contemplated, that a student's expenses must be very low, if the laity of Ireland were to take advantage of the education it offered. In the advertisement put out shortly before our opening in November last, fifty guineas was proposed as the pension of an intern for the Session; but a

decided judgment was at once pronounced by friends of the Institution against even so moderate a sum. I defended it on the ground that, while an Academical House was small, or rather when its members were most numerous, it could not pay its expenses at a lower rate per head; and that, to lower it, was merely to call on the University to pay part of them. I was answered that, the University being intended for the special benefit of Ireland, and the contributions coming
[48] principally from Ireland, it was fit that the youth of Ireland should receive some portion of their maintenance from the University Funds. I felt the force of this argument, and lowered the terms to forty guineas for the Session;[87] that is, as regards Mr Flannery's House, the only House of which the University was itself the founder. The event has been, as it was not difficult to foresee; the most anxious and praiseworthy economy has been exercised by Mr Flannery, but the expenses have come to nearly twice the receipts. In other words, it has been impossible to meet the rent, taxes, and rates of a house so situated, the remuneration of Dean and Tutors, the board, coals, lights, washing, servants, and other charges of from five to thirteen students (the house having but gradually filled), at a pension per head under £80 a year.

The experiment of the Rector's House tends to the same conclusion. I have had about eight young men in it, and have been paid more than £80 a piece; yet, while I have not been able to provide a Dean, Tutor, or Chaplain, but have taken these offices on myself,[88] I have hitherto had a serious

[87] The fees for University House were announced in the *Gazette* (28 September 1854) as fifty guineas, 'including board, lodging, firing, servants, public lectures, and private tuition'; a fortnight after the first announcement the fees were lowered to forty guineas. See Newman to M. O'Reilly, 23 September 1854, *LD* xvi, pp. 256–7.

[88] Although St Mary's did have Renouf as a resident Tutor, Newman undertook some of the work himself. After Newman's death, Charles de la Pasture recalled, 'I learnt more as to the writing of Latin from a few

overplus in the current expenditure, though, as I am now increasing my numbers at the same pension, I am sanguine, not only of meeting the expense in future, but of getting back what I have lost.[89]

However, such is the fact, that Mr Flannery's House is involved in a debt of £460 12s, which the University has accordingly to pay. The question follows, what is to be done henceforth?—is the pension to be raised? On this subject I shall offer a suggestion before I conclude. [49]

25. Here then I am brought to the last point to which I have to ask your Lordships' attention; and that is, our prospects, and the measures for which I respectfully hope to obtain your Lordships' sanction.

(i) I beg hereby to present to your Lordships the names of the gentlemen whom I have designated to Chairs in the various Faculties, trusting to obtain for them your Lordships' definitive nomination *durante bene-placito*.

1. Dogmatic Theology, the Rev. Father Edmund O'Reilly, D.D., S.J.[90]

---

classes given privately to the men of his own house by Newman as its tutor than I did from a longer course' of lectures under the two professors of Latin, Ornsby and Stewart. He added, 'to read the Greek tragedians in the same manner with Newman was, indeed, a classical treat I love to recall' (letter to the editor, *The Tablet* 114:3618 (11 September 1909), p. 416). At St Mary's, the students seem to have gone to Newman for confession and spiritual direction, though they were free to choose another confessor.

[89] Unlike the other houses, Newman gave wine at dinner, and in some instances paid for extra tuition; he also factored into his calculations a cost for wear and tear on furniture and fittings.

[90] Edmund Joseph O'Reilly (1811–78) was educated at Clongowes Wood before he studied for the priesthood, first at Maynooth then at the Irish College, Rome, where he made friends with Cullen. After gaining a doctorate in theology, he held the chair of theology at Maynooth until 1851, when he decided to become a Jesuit. His revised *Catechism of Scripture History* (1852) and theological lectures at the Jesuit college of St Beuno's in Wales led Newman to appoint him Professor of Dogmatic

2. Holy Scripture, the Very Rev. Patrick Leahy, D.D.

3. Archaeology and Irish History, Eugene Curry, Esq., M.R.LA., etc., etc.[91]

4. Political Economy, John O'Hagan, Esq., M.A.[92]

5. Geography, J. B. Robertson, Esq.[93]

Theology, though he did not draw a salary for the first three years, as there were no students. Newman regarded him as 'one of the first theologians of the day' and wanted him to be made the Pro-Vice-Rector in 1857. In 1859 O'Reilly was withdrawn from the University and appointed superior of a new Jesuit retreat at Milltown, near Dublin, where he remained for the rest of his life. (*DIB*, *ODNB*)

[91] Eugene O'Curry (1796–1862) has a prominent place in the development of Irish studies. From 1830 he worked for the historical and topographical section of the Irish Ordnance Survey. In the process of cataloguing and transcribing Irish manuscripts for Trinity College Dublin, the Bodleian Library Oxford, and the British Museum, he established his reputation as an authority on Irish language and history. He was elected to the Royal Irish Academy in 1851, and in 1854 Newman appointed him Professor of Irish History and Archaeology. (*DIB*, *ODNB*)

[92] John O'Hagan (1822–90) was a graduate of Trinity College Dublin and qualified as a barrister, becoming a Justice of the High Court. A poet and noted Young Irelander, he wrote patriotic songs and contributed to *The Nation*. Newman appointed him a Lecturer in Political Economy in 1854, though he declined a salary, and the two became close friends. He was a good scholar and published in *Atlantis*. O'Hagan became commissioner to the Board of National Education in 1861, and in 1881 Gladstone appointed him Chief Judicial Commissioner for the Irish Land Commission. He married a daughter of Thomas, later Lord, O'Hagan. (*DIB*, *ODNB*)

[93] James Burton Robertson (1800–77) was born to a Catholic mother and a Scottish Presbyterian father who was a landed proprietor in Granada. He was educated at St Edmund's, Ware, trained for the law, and was called to the Bar but moved to France to study literature, philosophy and theology under the direction of Lamennais. He published a translation of Schlegel's *Philosophy of History* (2 vols, 1835), which sold tens of thousands of copies, and between 1836 and 1854, and was an assiduous contributor to the *Dublin Review* and other periodicals. He spent seventeen years in Belgium and Germany and published a translation of Möhler's *Symbolism* (2 vols, 1843); this and his work on Schlegel gained him a European reputation. In 1855 Newman appointed him Professor of

6. Classical Literature, Robert Ornsby, Esq., M.A.

7. Ancient History, James Stewart, Esq., M.A.[94]

8. Philosophy of History, Thomas W. Allies, Esq., M.A.[95]

9. Political and Social Science, Aubrey de Vere, Esq.[96] [50]

Geography and Modern History, to which was added English Literature in 1862. He was the butt of student jokes on account of his eccentricities, but respected for his immense learning; he was a regular visitor to 6 Harcourt Street, where Newman lived. He published two sets of *Public Lectures Delivered before the Catholic University of Ireland*, the first on ancient and modern history (1859), the second on modern history and biography (1864). There followed *Writings of Chateaubriand, and on the Illuminati, Jacobins, and Socialists* (1864); *Lectures on the Life, Writings, and Times of Edmund Burke* (1869); and a translation of Hergenröther's *Anti-Janus* (1870), with an introduction on the history of Gallicanism. He received a civil pension of £90 p.a. in recognition of his services to English literature and in 1873 was made a Doctor in Philosophy by Pope Pius IX. (*DIB*, *ODNB*)

[94] James Stewart (c.1816–91) was educated at Merischal College, Aberdeen, then Trinity College, Cambridge. He took Anglican orders, acted as a schoolmaster for six years at Houghton-le-Spring, then as a tutor and curate in Suffolk. On becoming a Catholic in 1849 he went to teach in Mauritius, returned to England in 1852 and became a tutor again. Newman appointed him Lecturer in Ancient History, then Professor of Greek and Latin Languages, 1857–91. In 1882 he became a Fellow of the Royal University of Ireland.

[95] Thomas William Allies (1813–1903) was educated at Eton and Wadham College, Oxford, where he became a Fellow. While an Anglican curate, he made a deep study of the Catholic Church and its educational systems in France, Germany and Italy on several tours abroad, and in 1850 he became a Catholic. He acted as secretary to the sub-committee on the organization of the Catholic University in 1851, and was appointed Professor of Modern History in 1855; though he resigned shortly afterwards, because of a dearth of students, the lecture course he prepared under Newman's encouragement formed the basis of his voluminous *The Formation of Christendom* (8 vols, 1865–95). He was secretary of the Catholic Poor School Committee for the period 1853–90 and actively promoted Catholic elementary education in England, in the process setting up three teacher training colleges. A small dapper man with a pugnacious disposition, he was known among friends as 'bantam cock'. (*ODNB*)

10. Poetry, D. Florence MacCarthy, Esq.[97]
11. The Fine Arts, J. H. Pollen, Esq., M.A.[98]

---

[96] Aubrey Thomas de Vere (1814–1902) was born on the family estate of Curragh Chase, Adare, the third son of Sir Aubrey de Vere and Mary Rice, sister of the first Lord Monteagle. He was privately tutored then studied metaphysics and theology at Trinity College Dublin, though he did not proceed to holy orders. He visited Oxford in 1838 and met Newman, whom he described as a 'youthful ascetic of the middle ages'; and in 1839 he visited Cambridge, where he discovered an entirely different intellectual climate at the Apostles Club. In 1841 he met Wordsworth, by then Poet Laureate, and was invited to his extended household in the Lake District, where he fitted in easily. De Vere published *The Waldenses and Other Poems* (1842) and *The Search after Proserpine and Other Poems* (1843). He also became a friend of Browning, Carlyle and Tennyson. From his involvement in famine relief and emigration schemes after the potato blight of 1846 came his study of the Anglo-Irish political economy, *English Misrule and Irish Misdeeds* (1848), where he called for systematic emigration from a rural society that was uneconomic, as well as the redevelopment of agriculture along efficient lines. In 1851 he and Manning made a study of St Thomas Aquinas and Dante, and on their way to Rome de Vere became a Catholic, despite the warnings of Carlyle. Newman appointed him Professor of Political and Social Science in 1855, but having no students de Vere resigned in 1858. The lectures he prepared at the Catholic University were published in substance in *Essays, Chiefly Literary and Ethical* (1889). De Vere never married and spent the rest of his life at the family home, writing poetry and about Irish political questions. (*DIB*, *ODNB*)

[97] Denis Florence MacCarthy (1817–82) studied for the priesthood at Maynooth, before switching to law at Trinity College Dublin. He was called to the Irish Bar but devoted himself to literature. He was a prominent Young Irelander, contributing regularly to *The Nation* and writing on the history and religion of the Irish, and on ballad poetry. Most of MacCarthy's original work and his translations from Spanish, German, French, Italian, Greek and Latin poetry were published in periodicals. He was appointed Professor of Poetry and English Literature by Newman in 1854, resigning (possibly for reasons of health) in 1856. He wrote an *Early Life of Shelley* (1872), and was elected a member of the Real Academia of Spain in recognition of his work in translating the plays of Calderón. (*DIB*, *ODNB*)

[98] John Hungerford Pollen (1820–1902) was the great-great-nephew of Pepys and the nephew of the architect C. R. Cockerell. After an education

12. Logic, David Dunne, Esq., D.D.[99]
13. Mathematics, Edward Butler, Esq., M.A.[100]
14. Natural Philosophy, Henry Hennessy, Esq., M.A.[101]

---

at Eton and Christ Church, Oxford, he became a Fellow of Merton and came under the influence of the Tractarians. In the summer of 1847 Pollen travelled to France with T. W. Allies in order to discover how the Catholic Church dealt with the poorest parts of the community, before they moved on to Italy and Germany. Pollen was an Anglican curate at St Saviour's, Leeds, but turned down a wealthy living to become a Catholic in 1852; thereafter he devoted himself to art and architecture. In 1855 he was appointed Professor of Fine Arts by Newman, married that year and settled in Dublin. He worked closely with Newman on the building of the University Church, and became one of Newman's most devoted friends. Pollen's lectures on art in 1856 were later published in *Atlantis*. In 1857 he moved to London, where he had a large family, and worked with the Pre-Raphaelites Edward Burne-Jones, J. E. Millais and D. G. Rossetti. Pollen became assistant keeper at the South Kensington (now the Victoria and Albert) Museum, 1863–76, and then acted as private secretary to the Marquis of Ripon (who had become a Catholic and, in 1880, was appointed Viceroy of India). In 1889 Pollen helped to found the United Arts and Crafts Guild. (*DIB*, *ODNB*)

[99] David Basil Dunne (1828?–92) gained doctorates in philosophy and theology at the Irish College in Rome, but did not become a priest. He was appointed a Lecturer in Logic at the Catholic University in 1854 and acted as Tutor at St Patrick's. He began lecturing in the Catholic University Medical School in June 1858 and, after training as a barrister, became Professor of Law and Logic. Dunne married in 1855 and had five children. In 1879, when the Catholic University became part of the Royal University, he displaced Scratton as Secretary.

[100] Edward Butler (d. 1902) was educated at Trinity College Dublin and became Chief Inspector of the National Board of Education but gave up the position (and accepted a drop in salary) to become Professor of Mathematics at the Catholic University in 1854. He was the first Dean of the Arts faculty. In 1859, on being appointed Principal of the Training Department for teachers at Marlborough Street, Dublin, by the Commissioners of National Education, he left the Catholic University.

[101] Henry Hennessy (1826–1901), the librarian at Queen's College, Cork, was invited by Newman in May 1855 to become Professor of Natural Philosophy, charged with the task of setting up a physics laboratory in the newly acquired medical school. Henry, the brother of the politician and colonial administrator Sir John Pope Hennessy, had been deprived of a

15. Civil Engineering, Terence Flanagan, Esq., M.I.C.E.
16. French Literature, M. Pierre le Page Renouf.[102]
17. Italian Literature, Signor Marani.[103]

---

university education on account of being a Catholic. He was elected a Fellow of the Royal Society in 1858, and was the vice-president of the Royal Irish Academy, 1870–73. Although he was active in trying to promote the study of science among Catholics, he transferred his services to the Royal College of Science, Dublin in 1874 and acted as its Dean in 1880 and 1888. (*DIB*, *ODNB*)

[102] Sir Peter le Page Renouf (1822–97), of an old Guernsey family, was educated at Pembroke College, Oxford, and came under the influence of the Tractarians. He became a Catholic in 1842 and, after teaching at Oscott, acted as private tutor to the son of the Comte de Vaulchier, traveling with the family and continuing his studies. In 1854 he was appointed Lecturer in French at the Catholic University and his tutee entered as a student; a year later he became Professor of Ancient History, then Professor of Oriental Languages and began his studies in Egyptology. Renouf published several articles in *Atlantis* and helped Newman and Sullivan to edit the journal in 1859; he replaced Newman as its literary editor in 1862 and 1863. After Newman's departure, he hoped to take Catholic pupils at Oxford, but instead became an inspector of Catholic schools, 1864–85. He contributed to the liberal Catholic *Home and Foreign Review*, edited by Acton, and briefly served as a sub-editor; later he contributed to its successor, the *North British Review*. He opposed the defining of papal infallibility, and his pamphlet about it was put on the Index, but he remained in the Church after the First Vatican Council, though he stayed in touch with those who left, such as Döllinger and his brother-in-law Franz Brentano. He became a member of the Society of Biblical Archaeology in 1872 and became its president from 1887 to his death. He contributed to the Society's publications, as well as publishing *An Elementary Grammar of the Egyptian Language* (1875). In 1886 he was appointed Keeper of the Egyptian and Assyrian Antiquities at the British Museum, where he carried on the work of arranging, modernizing, and enlarging the Egyptian and Assyrian collections. His most important work was *The Book of the Dead* (1890); his shorter works were republished under the supervision of his widow as *The Life-work of Sir Peter Le Page Renouf* (4 vols, 1902–7). He was knighted in 1896. (*ODNB*)

[103] Augustus Caesar Marani (b. *c.*1815), a supporter of Young Italy, was educated at the Jesuit College and University in Modena, Italy, before coming to Ireland. He became Professor of Italian at Trinity College Dublin and acted as a private tutor. In 1854 he accepted Newman's

18. Practice of Surgery, Andrew Ellis, Esq., F.R.C.S.[104]

19. Anatomy (1), Thos. Hayden, Esq., F.R.C.S.I.[105]

20. Anatomy (2), Robert Cryan, Esq., L.R.C.S.I., and K. and Q.C.P.I.[106]

21. Physiology and Pathology, Robert D. Lyons, Esq., M.B.T.C.D. and L.R.C.S.

---

invitation to the chair of Italian and Spanish at the Catholic University, and stayed on after Newman's departure.

[104] Andrew Ellis (1792–1867) was the son of a gentleman farmer in Wicklow. He became surgeon to St Mary's Hospital, Dublin in 1821 and that year began lecturing on anatomy. From 1837 he was Professor of Surgery at the medical school in Cecilia Street; when it closed in 1854, he helped Newman acquire it for the Catholic University. The leading Catholic surgeon of his day, he was made Professor of the Theory and Practice of Surgery at the Catholic University Medical School when it opened in 1855. He published several books, including *Lectures and Observations on Clinical Surgery* (1846), and was a member of the Royal College of Physicians.

[105] Thomas Hayden (1823–81) had a Protestant father and a Catholic mother who was related to the Duke of Wellington. He was Professor of Anatomy and Physiology at the Catholic University from 1855 until his death; he was also the physician at the Mater Misericordiae Hospital from its foundation, and had a private practice too. Known as 'gentle Thomas' on account of his courtesy and charm, he contributed articles to medical journals and to *Atlantis*, and was Vice-President of the College of Physicians in Ireland, 1875–77; his major book on *Diseases of the Heart and Aorta* (1875) broke new ground. He lived in fashionable Merrion Square, where he entertained regularly. His daughter Mary Theresa was the academic historian and campaigner for women's causes, who was the only female founder-member of the senate of the new National University of Ireland in 1909. (*DIB*)

[106] Robert Cryan (1826–81) was appointed Professor of Anatomy and Physiology at the Catholic University in 1855, having been Lecturer in Anatomy and Physiology at the Carmichael School of Medicine, Dublin. He was a member of the Royal College of Physicians and of the Royal College of Surgeons. When the president of Queen's College, Cork, claimed in the press that there was little difference between Cork and the Catholic University, because the latter admitted Protestants too, Cryan wrote to clarify the matter (*Freeman's Journal*, 21 November 1856).

22. Demonstrator in Anatomy, Henry Tyrrell, Esq., L.R.C.S.I.[107]

23. Demonstrator in Anatomy, John O'Reilly, Esq., L.R.C.S.I.

(ii) Next I wish to bring before your Lordships the desirableness of our becoming connected with the existing schools in Ireland, such, that is, as undertake what is called secondary instruction. Such a measure would strengthen the
[51] University through the country; it would encourage and elevate the schools which joined us; it would consolidate and advance the whole system of Irish education, and bring it into its due relation to the Church; and, if there be any movement elsewhere to extend an opposite system, based on principles short of religious, and breathing an uncatholic spirit, it would be the surest bulwark against its encroachments. We should be able to give certain privileges to the schools which we affiliated, and in turn we should ask to exercise a power of visitation over them.[108]

(iii) It would be a great satisfaction to me, and facilitate the discharge of my duties, if your Lordships would appoint some persons as a committee of finance, who would meet statedly in Dublin, and with whom I might treat, when I am in want of means for the objects which I may have in contemplation. During the past year I have been in considerable difficulty from the circumstance that there was no authorized board or body to whom I could go for money. Nothing could exceed the kindness of the Most Rev. and Right Rev. the Trustees, whenever I brought the subject

---

[107] Henry Tyrrell (1833–79) was educated at Clongowes Wood and the Original School of Medicine, Dublin. He was a surgeon first at the Jervis Street Hospital, then at the Mater Misericordiae Hospital; in 1855 Newman appointed him one of the Demonstrators in Anatomy at the Catholic University Medical School. He was proactive in setting up St Luke's House, the residence for medical students, and acted as its Dean.

[108] Newman fleshed out this proposal in later documents.

before any of their members, and of many other persons, especially the Vice-Rector, Mgr Yore, V.G., and Mgr Meagher, V.G.,[109] who were informed of my need; and I am glad of this opportunity of making my acknowledgment to those many zealous friends; still, the whole responsibility of [52]
the expenditure was thrown upon me, and I was, as it were, dipping my hand into a bag, and taking out what I wanted at random. The four Trustees and the four Archbishops were, either not in the country, or in their own respective parts of it; and I had not the means of consulting them, or explaining what I was contemplating. It would be otherwise, if during term time three or four men of business met together, say once a month, or more frequently when there was occasion, before whom I could present myself, state my needs, and consult with them to what extent they should be met. Should this *desideratum* be supplied, it will be superfluous for me to make now any calculation of the expenses of the ensuing year,—a difficult undertaking, which at best I should but unsatisfactorily discharge. A board of finance in Dublin would receive my application for pecuniary means from time to time, as the necessity arose.[110]

(iv) Next, as to Mr Flannery's house. As its members increase, its annual debt will diminish; but I very much fear that in one shape or other it must look to the University Fund for assistance, while the pension is so low as forty guineas. I suggest then to your Lordships' better judgment the following scheme; *viz*., that you should consider it an endowed house for the natives of Ireland, and should yourselves exercise the right of presentation to it, subject, of [53]
course, in the case of every youth presented, to the

[109] William Yore (1781–1864) was parish priest of St Paul's, Arran Quay, Dublin, and William Meagher (d. 1881) parish priest of Rathmines; both were vicars-general.

[110] For more on the state of financial affairs and the need for a finance committee, see the relevant footnote on p. [xl].

condition of his passing the Examinations, and otherwise satisfying the authorities of the University. It might be called St Patrick's House or Hall, and would thus come into connection with the whole of Ireland.

(v) Considerable misgiving exists of the stability of the Medical School, under the notion that after a few years it may come to an end, from deficiency in the annual contributions to the University. This uncertainty, which is doing us no little harm, would be removed at once, if your Lordships thought right to endow the Medical Faculty to the extent of £300 or £400 a year; I mean, to create a trust, or virtual trust, and assign certain sums to be applied to the benefit of the University Medical School for ever, or for a certain fixed term of years.

(vi) I cannot help wishing to have your Lordships' sanction to the establishment of a lodging house in connection with the same Faculty, which might ultimately become a University Hall for Medical Students. My plan would be, to begin with a simple lodging, if not a boarding house, where young men would find comfort and economy united. Such qualifications, I have understood, are much needed in the lodgings of Dublin, and the want of them is
[54] not the worst of the evils to which medical students are exposed. Our own anxiety to provide them with what is better in a social point of view, would of course be subordinate to the higher object of removing them from the temptations which surround young men who are thrown without protection on a large town. The details of my plan would be submitted to the projected finance board, of which I have already spoken.[111]

(vii) Lastly, I should suggest to such a board the advisableness of granting £50 for the next year towards the expenses of the *University Gazette*. I had proposed to bring it to an end before this date, as it is uncertain whether it will

[111] See p. [21] and the relevant footnotes on pp. [297, 343].

pay its expenses; but have hitherto been delayed, from representations made to me, that it had done and was doing good, and that, moreover, if it stopped, that very circumstance would look like a failure, and prejudice the interests of the University.

And now nothing remains for me but to return to your Lordships my best thanks for having allowed me to occupy so much of your time; but, in an undertaking so anxious and important as that in which we are engaged, and on the first occasion of my presenting myself before you, I have judged it better that my Report should be too circumstantial, than incur the imputation of meagreness or vagueness. To approve myself to your Lordships in what I have undertaken [55]
is to me a sacred duty; and the great consideration with which you have all along honoured me, the zeal you have shown in my behalf, and the feelings of personal affection which so many of your Lordships have allowed me to entertain for them, have also made it an intimate and earnest wish of my heart. My only regret is, that the time is so limited, which, at my age, and with my engagements elsewhere, I can hope to be allowed to employ in securing it; and this feeling has been the reason of my looking with anxiety at those delays, which after all are inseparable from the commencement of any great undertaking. I have the most simple confidence of our ultimate success, and have ever felt it: such an Institution is wanted in that wide world in which the English tongue is spoken; and Ireland is evidently the soil to produce it, and Dublin is its natural seat. The determination of the Holy See, the energy of an ancient and famous hierarchy, are but supplying a great demand. An Institution which has already attracted teachers from other countries, has given the earnest that it will attract students from them also. Its aims are as large as they are high; and the wonderful Providence which has watched over this country is our ground for a humble but sure confidence,

[56] that it will be blessed with successes as lasting as they are widespreading.

Begging your Lordships' blessing,
I have the honour to be,
My Lords,
Your Lordships' faithful servant in Christ,
JOHN H. NEWMAN,
Of the Oratory

October 13, 1855

[57]

REPORT II

FOR THE YEAR 1855–56

MY LORDS,

I have now to report to your Lordships, according to the Rule prescribed in the Synodal Meeting of 1854, the proceedings of the second year of your University. These proceedings have been mainly directed towards the settlement of its constituent parts, which are the essential conditions and the sole tokens of its existence in fact, however high are the sanctions and privileges which it has received by anticipation from ecclesiastical authority. Last year I scarcely can be said to have addressed your Lordships, as its Rector, but as one out of various labourers, though a principal one, all of whom were engaged together in laying down its rudiments; and in my Report I was obliged simply to pass over the subject of academical government and administration, for those elementary functions of a constituted body were not at that time in operation. The Professors were neither members of any consultative board, nor distributed into Faculties; those of them, moreover, whose services were principally put into [58]
requisition, were only provisionally appointed. Statutes or regulations there were none, for there were neither offices to call for them, nor authorities to enact them. Nor was any provision made for those external forms, which invest an institution with the attribute of unity in the public estimation, and with dignity in the eyes of its members. The past year has been devoted to the supply, as far as is yet possible, of these deficiencies.

And in this work I placed before myself, as closely as our circumstances allowed, the pattern of the University of Louvain. This pattern had been suggested to your

Lordships, nine years ago, by the first Rescript which came to Ireland on the subject from Propaganda. "Of all things", it said, "the Sacred Congregation would deem it the most advantageous, if the Bishops, uniting their exertions, should erect in Ireland a Catholic Academy, on the model of that which the Prelates of Belgium have founded in the city of Louvain".[1] The organization of that University seems to have been designed as a type, to which Universities might be generally conformed in the present age of the Church.[2] The experience of twenty years has proved the accuracy of
[59] the judgment, by which its outlines were described; a great success has followed the experiment:[3] I had evidently nothing more to do than, in accepting what was already provided for me, to adapt it, in certain of its details, to our own peculiar circumstances, with some portion of the judgment with which it had been originally founded. Of such an adaptation your Lordships had already set me the example; for your Decrees of 1854, while they follow the decisions, sometimes even the language, of the Louvain

---

[1] Thus quoted in the Address of the Thurles University Committee. Sept. 9, 1850. [WPN]

The original letter, from Propaganda Fide, dated 9 October 1847, can be found on pp. [lxxiii–lxxiv].

[2] The University of Louvain was set up with the sanction of Pope Gregory XVI as a 'free university' – that is, its administration, teaching, and budget were independent of the State. The Belgian episcopate had overall control of the institution and appointed the rector, who governed with the assistance of a council, the most important members of which were the deans of the faculties (theology, law, medicine, philosophy and letters); the professors were appointed by the bishops on the presentation of the rector and grouped into faculties, each of which elected its own dean; the rector was assisted by a vice-rector, whose special charge was the care of the students.

[3] Having begun in 1834 with 86 students, Louvain had grown to 754 within twenty-five years. This rapid success owed a great deal to the favourable arrangement for granting decrees: the Belgian state recognised and convalidated the degrees awarded in all subjects except theology, which was recognised instead by Rome.

Statutes, do not scruple from time to time to depart from them.[4]

I have proceeded as follows: I have formed two bodies for transacting the business of the University, a Senate, and a Rectorial Council. The Council, which is intended for the support of the Rector, is composed of Vice-Rector and Deans of Faculties, after the pattern of Louvain; however, with this difference, that, besides the Dean of Philosophy and Letters, three Professors of that Faculty have seats in it, with a vote between them.[5] This addition was suggested, partly by the prominent position which has always been allowed in Universities to the Faculty in question;[6] secondly and principally, by the number of its Professors and the range of its subjects, viewed in comparison with other Faculties. It might indeed even claim to be subdivided into two: one department for those sciences which are included under the head of Philosophy; the other for the studies [60]
(these again differing in kind from each other) which go under the general name of Letters. This Faculty, moreover,

---

[4] Newman gladly accepted the model of Louvain as providing an ideal blueprint for the organisation of the Catholic University in Dublin. At the same time, he also borrowed from the Oxbridge collegiate system and its emerging tutorial practice. Some commentators have ignored the Louvain pattern at the Catholic University and only seen a replica of Oxford. Newman's remark to Catherine Froude about how extraordinary it would be 'if Oxford is imported into Ireland, not in its members only, but in its principles, methods, ways and arguments' (14 October 1851, *LD* xiv, p. 389), has been taken too literally by some; what Newman meant was that he hoped to renew the battle against liberalism that he once conducted in Oxford.

[5] By contrast, the Hebdomadal Board at Oxford had been composed of heads of houses, to the exclusion of the professoriate. This changed with the Oxford University Act (1854): the Hebdomadal Board was replaced by an elected Hebdomadal Council (six heads of house, six professors and six others), which took over the executive role.

[6] Newman argued in the *Idea* (p. 249) that 'a University, after all, should be formally based (as it really is), and should emphatically live in, the Faculty of Arts'.

as if not satisfied with its own ample province of knowledge, appropriates to itself portions of the subject-matter of other Faculties also; as, for instance, Christian Knowledge and Mathematics, and makes them subservient to its own end. These are imperative reasons why it should be fully represented at the Rector's council table.

The Council, thus constituted, has been of the greatest assistance to me, ever since its appointment. It has given me the benefit of its advice in every measure which came into consideration in the course of the year past; and its members have never spared themselves, when work was to be done. I take this opportunity of expressing to your Lordships my gratitude for the patient and ungrudging zeal, with which they have placed their time and labour, their talents and their experience, at my disposal.

What has principally occupied them, has been the examination of the body of Rules and Regulations, which naturally became the next subject of arrangement, after the appointment of the Council itself. As these Rules are necessarily of a provisional character, I should have proposed their actual trial for a while,[7] before submitting
[61] them to your Lordships, had it not been for the coincidence of the sitting of the long and anxiously expected Synodal

[7] Over the first long vacation Cullen asked Newman to provide him with rules of discipline but almost immediately changed his mind and asked Newman to draw up statutes instead. This was not to Newman's liking, as he thought that statutes 'must be the slow work of time': if Cullen insisted on having statutes immediately, Newman's recommendation was that they should simply adopt the Louvain statutes in their entirety *pro tem* (Newman to Cullen, 25 October 1855, *LD* xvii, p. 20). But Cullen rejected this suggestion, insisting that they must have new statutes of their own, and so when the new academic session began in November 1855, Newman established that the main business of the University Council's weekly meetings should be the drafting of a 'Scheme of Rules and Regulations'. It turned out to be a slow business, for it was not until 9 May that a printed draft was ready for Newman to circulate to the professors, lecturers, deans and tutors.

Meeting just upon the time that they were in the hands of the Rectorial Council.[8] It seemed hardly respectful to your Lordships, under such circumstances, or responsive to your just expectations, not to lay before you, for your immediate inspection and approval, at least some specimens of our proceedings, and of the results at which we had arrived. Accordingly, a portion of the body of Rules was submitted to the Synodal Meeting: it is gratifying to me to have good grounds for hoping that, out of that portion, only two Regulations failed to recommend themselves to it. Of these two, one was on the subject of the affiliation of country schools,[9] the other on that of model and training schools. These two Regulations fall back, accordingly, into the number of those, as for instance the Regulations about the Examinations, which have never been presented to your Lordships at all. They will be subjected, as well as those others, to the test of experience; and, should they come before your Lordships again, they will have had the trial of several years in their favour. Meanwhile, I have great satisfaction in being able to state, that some of your Lordships have already given us an opportunity of making that trial, by affiliating their own schools to the University.[10]

After the Synodal Meeting, the whole body of the Rules [62]
and Regulations were provisionally accepted by the Academical Senate, which had been brought into existence

[8] The bishops met for their synod, 20–26 June 1856, and approved Newman's statutes for three years; in July the provisional statutes were duly sanctioned by the Senate at its first meeting. They were formally ratified by the bishops at their annual meeting in the autumn.

[9] For more on the affiliation of schools, see pp. [122–3, 147] and the relevant footnote on p. [349].

[10] The schools that affiliated during Newman's rectorate were: St Munchin's, Limerick; St Kieran's, Kilkenny; the Diocesan School, Tralee; St John's, Waterford; and St Peter's, Wexford (Newman to Dixon, 15 December 1856, *LD* xvii, p. 477; *NU*, p. 373).

for the purpose of taking them into consideration.[11] As the Senate, however, may naturally be expected in course of time to alter and add to them, before presenting them as a whole for your Lordships' sanction, on this account, though they have been printed as they stand at present, for the convenience of members of the University, I have thought it best, since no edition of them could be considered as permanent, to append them to this Report in the shape they originally wore before the Rectorial Council took them in hand; because the rough draft, inferior as it is in all other respects, embodies various enunciations of principle, which were necessarily out of place when that draft became a formal collection of Statutes.[12]

In the composition of the Senate, as well as of the Council, there is some innovation on the pattern of Louvain. In addition to the official persons who have seats in it in that University, we have opened it to those whom we have denominated Fellows of the University, *viz.* such as have what elsewhere would be called the Degree of Doctor in any of the five Faculties. This addition has been made in anticipation of any risk occurring in time to come, of the
[63] Supreme Power of the University (for such the Senate may be considered) falling into the hands of the Resident Body, that is, of such Professors and other authorities, as are necessarily on the spot. The evil indeed of such an oligarchy might find a corrective in the fact that the Senate, as well as every other function and department of the University, is ultimately responsible to your Lordships; but it was our business to make the constitution of the University as

[11] The Senate sanctioned the provisional statutes at its inaugural meeting on Monday 14 July, which took place in the University Church, following the medieval custom (as revived by Louvain). For Newman, this was 'almost the coming into constitutional existence of the University' (Newman to Holmes, 14 July 1856, *LD* xvii, p. 323).

[12] The 'Scheme of Rules and Regulations submitted to the Council in April 1856' can be found on pp. [101–45].

perfect as possible in itself, and as little dependent as might be on the interposition of external authority. In so great and anxious an undertaking, it would be wrong not to contemplate even improbable contingencies; and, by giving votes in the Senate to a number of learned persons scattered through the country (for such would be the effect of this provision) we obtain a check upon the power of the Senate, such as the Senate is itself upon any tendency to arbitrary spirit on the part of the Rulers and Officials of the University. And thus, while the ordinary power rests, as it ought to rest, with those who have the ordinary work, your Lordships will be put in possession of a principle of adjustment and correction in your respective dioceses, which may be brought into operation without your direct interference, whenever the prospect arises of the University degenerating into a party, and committing itself to measures which do not carry with them the judgment of the educated [64]
classes.[13]

There has been one other occasion, besides that of sanctioning the provisional Statutes, of convoking the Academical Senate. It was one of the last acts of the Session, and its interesting object was to confer the prizes on those gentlemen who had passed the best examination in the Medical School. His Grace the Archbishop of Dublin did us the most acceptable favour of presiding at the meeting, which was held in the University Church,[14] as he

---

[13] Newman was fully aware of the situation in Oxford and knew that with the Oxford University Act (1854) the effective power passed from Convocation, made up by all MAs but dominated by the country clergy, to Congregation, which consisted only in resident MAs.

[14] The Senate met for its first public assembly on Wednesday 16 July. In the presence of the Archbishop of Dublin (who presided), other bishops, the University authorities, students and the general public, Newman distributed prizes to the medics who had passed their first-year exams. Afterwards there were speeches from Newman and the archbishop (University transactions 1854–80, pp. 45–6, CU10, UCDA).

had already honoured us with his presence at the commencement of the Session, when the same School was formally opened by an Inaugural Address by the Dean of Faculty, Andrew Ellis, Esq., Professor of the Practice of Surgery.[15]

As the purchase of the Buildings in Cecilia Street was one of the earliest of our successes, so the establishment of the Faculty of Medicine is one of the most important and encouraging. Did our efforts towards the foundation of a Catholic University issue in nothing beyond the establishment of a first-rate Catholic School of Medicine in the metropolis, as it has already done, they would have met with a sufficient reward. Such a school has not only not existed in Dublin or elsewhere, but it could not exist, from
[65] the natural but inordinate influence which the State religion exercises over the existing schools of the country. The medical establishments have been simply in the hands of Protestants; and, without going out of my way to complain of the fact, I may fairly record it as a reason for feeling satisfaction at the prospects which are now opening upon us of its alleviation. I understand that, at this time, out of all the Dublin Hospitals, only three have any Catholic practitioner in them at all, and that even in these three the Catholic officials do not exceed the number of Protestant. On the other hand, out of sixty-two medical officers altogether in the various Hospitals, the Catholic do not exceed the number of ten. Again, out of five Medical Schools in Dublin (exclusive of our University) three have no Catholic Lecturers at all; and the other two have only one each; so that, on the whole, out of forty-nine Lecturers, only two are Catholic. Putting the two lists together, we find that, out of one hundred and eleven Medical Practitioners in

---

[15] The dean of the new faculty officially opened the medical school on 2 November; dissection work had begun on 1 October 1855.

situations of trust and authority, twelve are Catholic, and ninety-nine Protestant.

And, while the national religion is so inadequately represented in the existing Schools of Medicine, so on the other hand, in a Catholic population there is an imperative call for Catholic practitioners. To enter into this subject would be beside my purpose; suffice it to say, that, while [66]
Medicine and Surgery, considered as Arts, are confronted, at the great eras of human life, at birth and at death, with a higher teaching, and are forced, whether they will or no, into cooperation or collision with Theology; so again the Practitioner himself is the constant companion, for good or for evil, of the daily ministrations of religion, the most valuable support, or the most painful embarrassment, of the parish-priest, according as he professes or abjures the Catholic Religion. Nor is the importance of establishing a Catholic Medical School less grave, when Medicine is viewed as a Science, though it be less immediate and less widely felt. Any study, exclusively pursued, tends, from the very constitution of our minds, to close them against such truths as lie beyond its range; and, unless the claims of Revealed Religion be recognized in the Schools of Philosophy, they will be regarded as simply disproved, merely because they are beyond the reach of its investigations. And thus the presence, though not the interference, of Theology is necessary in the lecture-halls and theatres of Medical, as of other Science, by way of rescuing scientific teaching, whatever be its subject-matter, from a narrowness of mind, of which indifference to religion is only one specimen. The Catholic University, then, will have done a great service to Medical Students, if it secures them against the risk of forgetting the existence of

[67] theological truth, and its independence of the teaching of Philosophy and Science.[16]

The number of students in our Medical School was forty-three last year; in the Session which is now beginning they already amount to fifty-three. At present, as is unavoidable, they almost entirely belong to the class of Auditors, who are neither subjects of the University, nor have passed the Examinations in the Faculty of Philosophy and Letters. There will indeed be always a number of students so circumstanced, nor is it at all desirable to shut our lecture-rooms against those, who, even without a University education, will, under our Medical Professors, have the benefit of a much healthier atmosphere of thought than is to be found in other places. But, this being fully granted, still our object obviously is something more than this. Our object is, to form a school of medical practitioners, who not merely avail themselves of our classes, but are identified with Alma Mater as her children and her servants, and who will go into the wide world, as specimens and patterns of a discipline which is at once Catholic and professional. With a view, then, to the furtherance of this important object, I proposed to your Lordships in June last, to establish a number of burses, to be held for two years, in the Faculty of Philosophy and Letters, for young men who
[68] propose ultimately to betake themselves to the Medical and other Faculties.[17] This measure, I trust, will secure to us, in the course of a few years, a body of Medical Students, whom we may truly call our own; and it involves no additional outlay, for it tends to fill the rooms of St Patrick's

[16] The last of the ten lectures and essays in the second half of the *Idea*, 'Christianity and medical science', was originally published as *Relations between Medical Science and Theology. Address Delivered to the Students in the Faculty of Medicine of the Catholic University* (1858).

[17] To entice the medical students to go through the two-year arts course Newman arranged that those with two years' standing were remitted the fees, which were £2 2s per medical course.

House, which, from the want of inmates, is an existing burden upon us.[18]

As to my own House, I have great reason to be satisfied with the resolution I took of increasing its availableness for students, by building additional rooms. They are filled, and more are even wanted. There is reason to hope that a feeling is making progress on the Continent in favour of what is called an English Education, as presenting advantages to the youthful mind, which are not to be found elsewhere. Our University is likely to reap the benefit of this movement. We have the prospect of youths of high family and station, French, Belgian, and Polish,[19] renewing the custom of past

---

[18] Anxious to provide suitable accommodation for the medical students, but without funds at his disposal for doing so, Newman decided in the meantime to make use of St Patrick's, which was unable to fill itself. He argued that since the University had laid out large sums on No. 86, it was better to get something out of it than nothing; and that if there were additional students, who received bursaries and paid a nominal sum, the house only stood to gain. His plan involved allocating ten rooms at St Patrick's for those studying the two-year arts course prior to their medical studies, and using a sum of £400 p.a. to fund ten medical bursaries whose recipients would be nominated by the ten most important ecclesiastical sees in Ireland, the remaining unfilled places being allotted by open competition. In doing this, Newman argued that he was increasing the overall number of students and laying the foundations for both the medical school and its future halls of residence. In December 1855 the Council approved this proposal, to take effect from November 1856, as well as agreeing to an increase in the fees at St Patrick's to £60 (including the £10 academic fee). By these measures, Newman effectively ensured that those who could pay their way did so, while those in need of bursaries obtained them. Nevertheless, there were those on medical bursaries who struggled to pay even £20 p.a. (i.e. the £60 fees less the £40 bursary).

[19] Louis, Vicomte de Vaulchier, (1837–1910), the only child of the comte and grandson of the Marquis de Vaulchier, was already at St Mary's. In 1856 three other titled students entered Newman's house: two princes, Charles (1837–1914) and his younger brother Edouard (1839–1911), sons of Eugène, ninth Prince de Ligne, by his third wife Hedwig, Princess Lubomirska, Eugène being President of the Belgian Senate, 1852–78,

ages, and having recourse for their final studies to the Irish schools. What makes such a result the more important, is, that to students of this description it will be obviously of no consequence, whether the State recognizes our acts or no, while their position in society will do more to raise us in public opinion, than any legal power of granting degrees.[20]

[69] In addition to the St Laurence's House, among the students of which, meritorious from the first, are now to be found some of the most promising youths of the University, we are now able to congratulate ourselves on the commencement of a fourth House, under the governance of Father Bennett, O.C.C.[21] We have good reason to believe, that, by establishments such as these, a great portion of the rising generation of Dublin will ultimately be brought into our classes.

---

and one of the most powerful financiers in Europe; and Count Etienne Zamoyski (1837–99), whose family came from Austrian Poland but were living in exile in France.

[20] A resident at St Patrick's at the time comments that St Mary's was the 'swell' house, since it was 'a sort of fellow-commoner's preserve' and contained all the 'personages'. The residents of St Patrick's looked up to those from St Mary's, but looked down on St Laurence's, which they 'patronisingly regarded as a mere upper school, and not an orthodox college' (J. A. O'Shea, *Roundabout Recollections* ii (London: Ward & Downey, 1892), p. 95).

[21] Two of the day-pupils (both 'intended' for the priesthood) from the Academy of St Mary of Mount Carmel, the Carmelite secondary school in Lower Dominick Street, entered the University in November 1855 and they were joined by a further seven the following January; they formed the House of Our Lady of Mount Carmel under the deanship of Fr Thomas Bennett, Provincial of the Order of Calced Carmelites and Vice-President of the missionary seminary of All Hallows. Bennett attempted to open a separate collegiate house in 1861, but it closed a year later. It was not until 1863 that the Carmelite house was able to contribute more students to the Catholic University. Bennett was one of the first graduates of the University of Louvain, where he would have seen a rudimentary collegiate structure in operation.

Of the Exhibitions and Prizes opened to competition during the Session, Four have been gained by members of St Patrick's House, and Five by members of the Rector's.[22]

Of our prospect of affiliating schools through the country to the University, I have already spoken. These will tend, as they increase in number, both to raise the standard of the instruction already given, and to create a bond of interest and sympathy between the country and the University.

On Ascension Day, May 1, the Church was opened, (with the sanction and presence of the Archbishop of Dublin), which I had built for the use of the University.[23] I have in my former Report given some of my reasons for thinking a University Church to be of great and various importance, nor need I enlarge on them now. I had originally intended to propose to the Trustees to build it [70]
with University money; but, as the expenditure was sure to be considerable, and the negotiation, by which it was to be authorized, would be necessarily slow, and the issue of it was uncertain, and as months, or rather years passed, and I felt the time to be slipping away during which I was to be connected with the University, I determined, with advice of persons, on whose judgment I could fully rely, to make the risk my own, and build at once, with the hope that the University would in the event relieve me of it. Till then I had no idea at all of anything else but a University Church: when, however, the responsibility of finding means for it

---

[22] When the exhibitions and prizes were advertised, the students were warned that not all would be awarded if applicants or entries failed to reach the required standard. On 3 December 1855 three visiting examiners interviewed candidates for the four exhibitions, two each in Classics and mathematics, worth either £35 or £18. The examiners found only one worthy candidate, James Molloy of St Patrick's, who received an £18 exhibition in Classics (Record of transactions, p. 35, CU10, UCDA).

[23] For more see the 'University Church' on pp. [305–9].

became my own, I began to contemplate also the possibility of the Archbishop considering it useful to the city, whether as the Church of a Dublin Oratory, or of some religious Order. It is scarcely possible either to calculate or to control adequately the expenses of a building in progress; and by the time it grew near its completion, it had cost almost half as much again as the utmost sum to which I had originally hoped to confine them. The final settlement of account will show the expenditure to be not much under £6000. In the extreme difficulty, existing just now, of raising money, and in the case of a building which could not furnish a strictly marketable security for repayment, I then hoped to effect a
[71] loan at a low interest from the University funds, to be repaid by fixed periodical instalments, for such a portion of my liabilities, as were to me a cause of anxiety, not to say distress. Being disappointed in that natural expectation, I am obliged to turn to the Sunday collections as a means of meeting the interest of the serious debt in which the building has involved me; nor shall I have recourse to the University itself for aid, till these are found to come short. Meanwhile, as long as I am Rector and the Church is in my own hands, I will freely lend it to the University, whether for sacred or for academical functions, nor will I charge the Trustees anything for the use of a beautiful and imposing structure, which was built simply out of zeal for the University, and which has given it a sort of bodily presence in Dublin. One prospect I am obliged to forego,— the promise I made to myself in my Report of last year, of making a gift towards the building from my personal means.

Much has been done in the course of the year towards putting the Chairs of Chemistry and Natural Philosophy in a state befitting their importance, by the purchase of apparatus and by other necessary outlay. More, however, has still to be done. The most serious difficulty under which we lie, is the want of large rooms for Professorial Lectures, for specimens and apparatus, and for books.[24]

I have now enumerated the principal matters which call [72] for observation in the proceedings of our Second Session. I have never flagged in my confident anticipation of the success of the undertaking which your Lordships have committed to us. If it has become even stronger than it was, this has been owing to the satisfaction with which I have witnessed the zeal in its behalf of the Professors and others associated in it, and the good understanding and fellow-feeling and mutual sympathy which prevails among them. There is no surer indication and instrument of success in an institution, than an *esprit de corps*: and without it there can be no real life at all. This potent principle, open to abuse and excess, but admirable when acting within its due limits, exists strongly and in its purest form among us. We have faith in our cause and in each other; we know what we have to aim at, and what we have to do. While we are thus true to ourselves, nothing can happen externally to harm us; and while we take a religious view of our mission, and are true to its demands on us, even trial will but turn to our advance and aggrandisement.[25]

---

[24] When in Rome on Oratorian business (12 January–4 February 1856), Newman was urged to further to the best of his power the interests of physical science at the University (Newman to Cullen, 17 June 1858, *LD* xviii, p. 385).

[25] Newman was well-placed to harness and drive his academic and administrative team, both because the men were largely his appointments, and because his own talents were such that he had their utmost respect. Newman told the Bishop of Kerry, who had helped him select the Irish lecturers, 'I have the utmost confidence in them. […] the difficulty of ruling them only arises from the existence of zeal and talent, pulling, as is natural, in the course of time, in various directions' (Newman to Moriarty, 25 November 1856, *LD* xvii, p. 461).

The lecturers and professors were all too aware of the onerous task Newman had taken on in attempting to set up the institution almost single-handedly. They knew from personal experience that virtually

It is the sight of this internal consolidation, which is in progress not only among Professors and other officers, but among the students also, that reconciles me to the inevitable prospect of my own eventual separation from so noble an
[73] undertaking; but One only both began and consummated the work with which He was charged. We, His followers, are abundantly blessed, if we are allowed to lay any portion whether of the foundation or the superstructure. For me, it will be more than enough of honour and privilege, to have had my small share, or my brief toil, in a great design, which is destined, as we may trust, to exert an influence on the distant future and to the ends of the earth.

Begging your Lordships' blessing upon our exertions in this great cause,

I have the honour to be,

My Lords,

---

every aspect of life at the University came into being through his hands. Besides overseeing academic affairs, the financial administration, the launching of new faculties and schools, editing the *Gazette*, delivering lectures each term and preaching sermons, Newman also acted as the academic and moral conscience of the University. Despite all the administrative pressures bearing down on him, he managed to give priority to his dealings with the academic staff. This emphasis resonated with his abiding concern for the pastoral well-being of the University, because if its main task was to 'make men', then the makers of men themselves needed to be encouraged, reassured and given direction. Despite the many difficulties pressing round him, Newman injected a spirit of optimism into the whole enterprise and gave orientation to them all.

Towards the end of the second academic session Newman introduced weekly soirées for the academic staff, when tea was served in the library of University House. Newman's private correspondence with friends outside the University confirms what he thought about his team of fellow workers and the way they pulled together. 'We have hitherto been in most perfect harmony', he told Hope-Scott, the loyal and trusted friend he usually turned to for advice (24 December 1857, *LD* xviii, p. 214). In 1858 Newman wrote: 'There can't be a set of men with a better spirit or more zeal' (Newman to Monsell, 9 May 1858, *LD* xviii, p. 343).

Your Lordships' faithful servant in Christ,

JOHN H. NEWMAN,

Of the Oratory

October 31, 1856

[75]

APPENDIX

SESSION—NOVEMBER 3, 1855, TO JULY 22, 1856

IN this Appendix are contained various Documents belonging to the last five years, which may be considered as successive steps towards the formation of the constitution of the University. It is almost superfluous to say, that No. 2, and it alone, is authoritative. Such portions of No. 4 as are marked with an asterisk, will become authoritative, so far as they shall be eventually sanctioned by the Synodal Meeting of last June, which has not yet published any statement of its proceedings.

1. *Extracts from the Minutes of the Thurles Committee in* 1851.
2. *Ex Decretis Conventûs Epp. Hiberniæ,* 1854.
3. *Substance of the Rector's Memorandum, submitted to the Synodal Meeting,* 1854.
4. *Scheme of Rules and Regulations,* 1856.
5. *Rector's Memorandum submitted to the Synodal Meeting,* 1856.
6. *Rector's Letter to the Dean of the Faculty of Philosophy and Letters,* 1856.

APPENDIX

No. I

Extracts from the Minutes of the Committee of Archbishops and Bishops, Clergy and Laity, appointed by and under the authority of the National Synod held at Thurles in A.D. 1850.

August 12, 1851

Resolved that the Rev. Dr Newman, the Rev. Dr Leahy, and Myles W. O'Reilly, Esq., be requested to draw up a report on the organization of the University, consulting any or all the following persons: his Grace the Primate, the Archbishop of Cashel, the Archbishop of Tuam, the Rev. Dr O'Hanlon, Rev. Dr Manning, Rev. Dr Cooper,[1] Mr Hope, Dr Jerrard, Dr Döllinger,[2] Dr F. X. de Ram;[3] and that Mr Allies be requested to act as Secretary.

---

[1] Peter Cooper (1798?–52), a native of Dublin, spent most of his priestly life working as curate of the pro-cathedral. One of the secretaries of the Synod of Thurles, he became a member of the Catholic University Committee and was very helpful to Newman until his untimely death in December 1852.

[2] J. J. Ignaz von Döllinger (1799–1890) was a Church historian at Munich who took a great interest in English affairs.

[3] Pierre François Xavier de Ram (1804–65) was the Rector of Louvain from its re-foundation in 1834 until his death; he was a successful administrator who managed to combine his office with his own academic research as an historian.

November 12, 1851

The Report of the Sub-committee on the Organization of the University was read by the Very Rev. Dr Leahy, and was considered and approved of, subject to the alterations in the copy submitted to the Committee.

[77] *Report on the Organization of the Catholic University of Ireland*[4]

MY LORDS AND GENTLEMEN,

Having been appointed to consider and report on the future organization of the Catholic University, we have the honour to lay before you the following suggestions:—

I. FACULTIES—The University should consist of Four Faculties. 1. Arts, divided into (1) Letters; (2) Science. 2. Medicine. 3. Law. 4. Theology.[5] As, however, the Faculty of Arts only can be founded at once, we shall detail only its branches and extent.

---

[4] This document was drawn up by Myles O'Reilly, Patrick Leahy and Newman, who formed a sub-committee of three appointed by the Synod of Thurles, T.W. Allies acting as secretary. The committee first met at the Oratory House, Alcester Street, Birmingham on 27 August 1851, O'Reilly and Leahy 'bringing with them a list of questions which they had drawn up in Ireland, and intending, after their consultations with me to proceed to our friends in London for the same purpose, and then to return to me for a second conversation'. The committee also asked de Ram, Jerrard, Döllinger and others for advice based on the same list of questions. At the end of September, Newman and Allies set off for Thurles where they met Leahy and O'Reilly for a final consultation. Newman then took the report to Cullen at Drogheda in time for the meeting of the Catholic University Committee on 15 October (*AW*, pp. 281–2).

[5] Like the recently founded University of Louvain, the Catholic University was to be framed on the medieval model, with the lower faculty of arts leading on to the higher faculties of theology, law and medicine.

II. FACULTY OF ARTS—The time embraced by the course up to the B.A. degree should be four years, as this period appears best suited to the various subjects to be learned, to the development of character, the probable age of the student entering, and the prosecution of future professional studies. More years of study should be required for the attainment of the M.A. degree.

The branches of study embraced by the Faculty of Arts, are:—

In the division of Letters:—Latin; Greek; the Semitic and Modern Languages; History, Ancient and Modern, both National and Ecclesiastical; Archæology, Christian and Profane; English Literature, and Criticism.

In the division of Science:—Logic, Metaphysics, Ethics, including Economy and Politics; Philosophy of Religion; Mathematics; Natural Philosophy; Chemistry; Natural History; Mineralogy and Geology, etc., etc.[6]

Subsidiary to the Faculty of Arts should be organized a [78]
School of Engineering.

III. GOVERNMENT—1. Following the Encyclical Letter of the Belgian Bishops for erecting the University of Louvain, which says:—In order that things really work well, so that one and the same person rules firmly and steadily in academic matters, we delegate and depute the whole direction of our University to the Rector as our Vicar General,[7]—we recommend that the government of the University be committed to a Rector nominated during the first ten years by the Episcopal Body, and revocable by them.

---

[6] This broad curriculum showed that Newman's mental horizons were not confined to Oxford, which had a narrowly Classics-based curriculum, and that his affection for Oxford did not blind him to its educational shortcomings.

[7] This sentence has been translated from the Latin original in *MC*.

2. The Vice-Rector shall be nominated in a similar manner.

3. There shall be Deans of Discipline, a Secretary, a Bursar, and other officers, appointed by the Rector, and revocable by him, subject to the approval of the Archbishops.

4. The instruction of the students shall be provided for by a certain number of Professorial Chairs[8] and Lectureships, to be created as hereafter determined.

5. The Archbishops, acting in the name of the Episcopal Body, shall, during the first ten years, nominate the Professors and Lecturers on the recommendation of the Rector.

6. The Professors of each Faculty shall elect annually out of their own body, by a plurality of votes, their Dean and Secretary. Each division of the Faculty of Arts shall have a Dean and Secretary.

7. The Deans shall convoke and preside over the
[79] Sessional Meetings of their respective Faculties. In these meetings, the Professors will discuss the interests of their Faculty, and draw up the Sessional Programme of Studies. This Programme must be submitted to the approbation of the Rector.

8. The Deans of Faculties, with the Vice-Rector, will form the Rectorial Council, to be assembled by the Rector when he deems it necessary.

9. The Academic Senate shall consist of the Rector, the Vice- Rector, the Secretary of the University, the Professors of the respective Faculties, and at the end of ten[9] years from

---

[8] At Oxford, and indeed Trinity College Dublin, the professors were on the periphery of the teaching system and possessed no administrative functions, though both universities would subsequently alter this state of affairs following investigations by Royal Commissions. In advance of these changes, Newman granted his professors a central role and status.

[9] An earlier draft had specified a period of two years, not ten (*LD* xxxii, p. 52n).

the establishment of the University, such a number of Graduates annually appointed by the Graduates of their respective Faculties, as shall not exceed one-fourth of the whole body.

10. The Salaries of the Professors and the several officers shall be determined by the Archbishops in the name of the Bishops, with the advice of the Rector.

11. Should it be deemed advisable in the course of time to add to the number of Chairs or Lectureships, the erection of new ones is to rest with the Archbishops in the name of the Bishops, with the advice of the Rector.

IV. POWERS AND DUTIES OF THE GOVERNING BODY—1. The Rector is authorized to take all measures which the interest of the University may require. He regulates the course of studies and duties of Professors; and with the advice of the Vice-Rector and the Deans of Discipline, forms Rules of Internal Discipline. He summons and presides over the Rectorial Council and Senate. He is to [80]
make annually a detailed Report to the Episcopal Body upon the state of the University.

2. The Vice-Rector will assist the Rector in the discharge of ordinary business, and will replace him provisionally in case of absence, sickness, or death. He will conform in all things to the instructions of the Rector.

3. The Deans of Discipline will be in all things subject to the Rector.

4. As all academic instruction must be in harmony with the Principles of the Catholic Religion, the Professors will be bound, not only not to teach anything contrary to Religion, but to take advantage of the occasion the subjects they treat of may offer, to point out that Religion is the basis of Science, and to inculcate the love of Religion and its duties. The full salaries of the Professors shall be

guaranteed to them from year to year for some time,[10] after which they shall depend in part on fees.

5. The Rectorial Council will assist the Rector with their advice in all matters of studies.

6. To the Senate shall be entrusted the determination of graver matters, such as the framing of Statutes, and such other extraordinary subjects as the Rector may refer to their consideration.

7. All the Officers and Professors of the University shall be required upon entering into possession of their office to make a Profession of the Catholic Faith according to the form of Pope Pius IV.[11]

V. THE STUDENTS—They shall be interns, so far as circumstances may permit.[12]

[81] During the provisional constitution of the first ten years, a power will reside in the Episcopal Body to alter whatever may work wrongly. After that period it is hoped that the constitution of the University will have been so developed and matured as to admit of a greater degree of self-action.

Signed, etc.

October, 1851[13]

---

[10] Instead of 'from year to year for some time', an earlier draft read 'for a certain number of years' (*LD* xxxii, p. 53n).

[11] Instead of 'according to the form of Pope Pius IV', an earlier draft read 'into the hands of the Primate or some person delegated by him' (*LD* xxxii, p. 53n).

[12] Instead of 'so far as circumstances may permit', an earlier draft read 'except in cases of special dispensation to be granted by the Rector' (*LD* xxxii, p. 53n).

[13] An earlier draft had an extra line at the end which read: 'Dublin chosen as the site of the University, with the understanding that the principal Colleges in the Provinces shall be incorporated with it at an early day' (*LD* xxxii, p. 53n).

[82]

POSTSCRIPT

Having presented to the Committee[14] a sketch of the Organization of the University, we think it desirable to add, in the form of an appendix, a few considerations which ought to be borne in mind.

We hold it to be specially important that there be in the teaching and governing body of the New University, while it is yet untried and unformed, a perfect unity of purpose and operation, that no strength may be wasted by intestine division, and that the force and capacity of each agent be at the free disposition of the Superior, to direct as need requires. A working, rather than a theoretical constitution is needed at first. It is easy to appoint a number of Professors with different titles and subjects of study; but the harmonious action of these, their growth into one body, and their production of a real education for those under their care, is quite another thing. This can only be brought out in

---

[14] The original Catholic University Committee of 1850 comprised the four archbishops together with one bishop from each of the four provinces: John Cantwell of Meath (Ulster), Francis Haly of Kildare and Leighlin (Leinster), Nicholas Foran of Waterford (Munster) and John Derry of Clonfert (Connaught). In 1851 they were joined by eight priests and eight laymen. The priests were Dean Meyler, vicar-general of Dublin; Dominic O'Brien, vicar-general of Waterford; Patrick Leahy, vicar-general of Cashel and president of Thurles College; Peter Reynolds, president of St Jarlath's College, Tuam; Peter Cooper, of the pro-cathedral, Dublin; John O'Hanlon from Maynooth; James Maher, parish priest of Carlow (and Cullen's uncle); and Patrick Brennan, parish priest of Kildare. The laymen were Myles O'Reilly; Charles Bianconi of Longfield House, Clonmel; Sir Michael Dillon Bellew of Mount Bellew, Galway; Thomas Boylan of Hilltown House, Dundalk; James More O'Ferrall of Kingstown; Thomas Meagher, MP for Waterford; Michael Errington of Kingstown; and William Skelly of Dublin.

action after much toil, and, it may be, partial failures, alterations, and substitution of plans; in short, by experience, and not on paper. Again, there is the necessity of meeting the actual state of the pupils, as to knowledge, and moral and intellectual training, which it is impossible to know beforehand. Time must elapse before the University can create around it a certain atmosphere, a standard either
[83] of acquisition in knowledge or of moral character. In the meantime it must take the youth as it finds them, and make the best of them, which entails a certain period of experimental action. Then there is the necessity of immediate commencement. Catholics in Ireland should be at once assured that the requisite steps have been taken, and that their children can be received in January next.

With a view to this, we recommend the immediate appointment of a Rector with a certain number of working Professors, who are to be Tutors also, and to help each other. These, when the *personnel* is completed and at full work, will stand thus: Rector, Vice-Rector, two Deans of Discipline, Secretary, Bursar. Professors of, 1. Logic and Metaphysics, 2. Ethics and Politics, 3. Philosophy of Religion, 4. English Literature, 5. Latin, 6. Greek, 7. Ancient History, 8. Modern History, 9. Pure Mathematics, 10. Criticism. Also Lecturers should be appointed for the following subjects: Chemistry, Botany and Zoology, Experimental Philosophy, French, Irish, Italian, German. In the beginning, two or more of the preceding subjects could be taught by one and the same person, if need were. It is also to be observed that the entire number of Professorships and Lectureships might not be required at once.[15]

---

[15] On 19 October 1851 Leahy wrote to Newman, 'I made a few alterations with Mr O'Reilly's concurrence, (having had yours already) to adapt our Report in a few particulars to the Primate's views. One or two little observations (I?) added—that two or more of the subjects to be taught by our Professors and Lecturers might for a time be taught by one person; also, that the *personnel* for the Faculty of Arts needs not to be

This way of starting has suggested the recommendations.[16] First, it will show a determination to go to work at once. Secondly, it will give time to ascertain by experience what are the real wants and the real way of [84]
supplying them, before the Church becomes committed to a formal institution. The whole thing will be provisional, and we shall have at once the best means of deciding how to make the future University successful, and the best excuses for failures and defects, should any such occur at the first starting.

It will be observed that we propose to blend at this commencement the Professorial and Tutorial systems.[17] The same person will in fact act as one and the other, to the same students. The two systems have each advantages, which perhaps may thus be united. For their application depends much on the subject matter; for instance, the Physical Sciences require a Professor, the Languages a Tutor. Again, a Professor is required to set forth the objects and limits of a science, and to give a preliminary view upon it, to those who have not thought on it. Professorial Lectures also are valuable as bringing the Professor before external judges, and keeping him up to the mark. On the other hand, the work of a Professor is not sufficient by itself to form the pupil. The catechetical form of instruction and the closeness of work in a small class, are needed besides. Without these, even supposing the Professor to be a man of genius and to interest his hearers, the acquirements carried away from him

---

completed at the outset, because the course of studies being spread over four years, some of the subjects would not come to be treated for some time' ('Memorandum about my Connection with the Catholic University', *AW*, p. 287).

[16] Thus transcribed into the Minute Book; qu.: "This way of starting, as suggested, has these recommendations". [WPN]

[17] The ideas in this paragraph were developed in the article 'Professorial and Tutorial systems' (*CUG* 10 (3 August 1854), pp. 75–80, which became 'Professors and Tutors' in *HS* iii.

will often be very superficial. No doubt, wherever the mind is really interested, it is also led in some degree to exert itself, and there is fruit; but if this is trusted to, the result will be undisciplined and unexercised minds, with a few
[85] notions, on which they are able to show off, but without any judgment or any solid powers. So that the principal making of men must be by the Tutorial system. But, in the scheme recommended we propose to combine the two, and that every Professor shall be bound to deliver a certain number of public lectures in the year. While this regulation will secure the advantages of a Professor on the one hand, on the other the same persons, acting on a smaller number at a time, and by the catechetical method, will be able to exert those personal influences, which are of the highest importance in the formation and tone of character among the set of students, as well as to provide that the student shall actually prepare the subject for himself, and not be a mere listener at a lecture. And the Professors, whatever their particular title, will hold themselves generally disposable for the good of the undertaking, according to the guidance of the Rector.[18] . . . [19]

---

[18] The ideas contained in this paragraph and the style of writing are undoubtedly Newman's.

[19] This missing section, about the pros and cons of a country or Dublin location, is reproduced in *LD* xxxii, pp. 56–7:

'With regard to the site we recommend that the University be ultimately fixed at Dublin. The Capital unites upon the whole recommendations with which it is impossible for any other place to compete. But as to the *Provisional Site*, and considering the great desirableness of commencing not later than January next, We wish to state for the Judgement of the Committee what may be said in favor of Dublin and in favor of a Provincial site it is urged

1st—That some existing colleges might be used at once;

2nd—That it would present every facility for carrying out a perfect system of Catholic Discipline offering such accommodation that all the probable number of students who will come at first can be interns;

3rd—That it would be remote from the temptations of a city;

As to salaries, we recommend that there be given to the Rector not more than £400 a year with Rooms and Commons;[20] to the Professors not more than £300 a year with Rooms and Commons;[21] to the Lecturers £100 a year; to the Deans of Discipline £150 a year; to the Bursar £150 a

---

4—That some colleges are connected with the London University affording the opportunity of using the degrees of that University;
5—That the Railways in many instances afford easy means of communication;
6th—That some provincial Colleges might be had at a moderate rent without binding the University to any long tenure.
On behalf of Dublin it is urged, if the University is commenced elsewhere—
1st. The loss of Libraries Museum etc;
2nd. The very large number of students in or near Dublin who are ready to enter an Institution situated there;
3rd. The reluctance of the students to go elsewhere than to the centre of learning civilisation etc;
4. The necessity of moving when the Faculty of Arts has been commenced elsewhere;
5—That the Lecturers part of whose services at a much smaller expense might be secured in Dublin, must elsewhere be wholly devoted to the University and paid accordingly;
6—That the poorer students would be deprived elsewhere than at Dublin of any means of earning somewhat towards their expenses;
7—The great difficulty of supplying means of amusement elsewhere to a large number of young men;
8—That the commencement at any other place but Dublin will act unfavourably on the minds of Catholics, in England, America, and the Colonies as well as in Ireland;
9—The good effect upon the higher and intellectual classes which may be expected to attend the Establishment of a University at Dublin.'

As president of St Patrick's College, Thurles, it is likely that Leahy was in favour of beginning there. In general, it has to be borne in mind that none of the Irish bishops had had a university education; they were all used to the seminary colleges in Ireland, Rome or elsewhere, which were run strictly.

[20] An earlier draft stated '£500 a year' without the additional phrase 'with Rooms and Commons' (*LD* xxxii, p. 57n).

[21] An earlier draft stated '£400 a year and Lodging' without the additional phrase 'with Rooms and Commons' (*LD* xxxii, p. 57n).

year. The Vice-Rector to be a Professor[22] with an addition of £50 a year. To the Librarian, Secretary, etc., as they will probably be Professors, a small additional salary will be sufficient. …[23]

We would suggest the great advantage of founding, as soon as possible, Exhibitions and Scholarships for the
[86] respective Dioceses, Counties, and Towns, which may serve as an encouragement of the poorer and meritorious class of students.

For the purpose of carrying out the above recommendation as to the immediate commencement of the University, we think a very small committee should be appointed, consisting of the Primate, the Rector, and a layman, to whom a grant may be made of such sums as may be required for provisional payments, and who should make a Report of their proceedings at the end of a year; whilst the ordinary funds received for the foundation of the University should continue to be managed as before.

Should the University be commenced in Dublin, we wish to point to the advantages that some of the existing Colleges present for any object that may arise in connection with the University. For instance, were it thought advisable to establish preparatory schools or colleges in connection with the University, some of the existing colleges could be employed to great advantage for such a purpose.[24] Many

---

[22] An earlier draft stated 'Professor or a Dean of Discipline' instead of 'Professor' (*LD* xxxii, p. 57n).

[23] The two short missing paragraphs can be found in *LD* xxxii, pp. 57–8.

[24] This sentence originally read, 'For any object that may arise in connection with the University, as, for instance, a preparatory School or College, such Institutions would be most useful' (*LD* xxxii, p. 58n).

In the event, some colleges proved reluctant to cooperate in this fashion. Before the foundation of the Catholic University – and in the absence of any university education suitable for Catholics – the Catholic colleges in the United Kingdom had sought to retain lay boys for higher studies by allowing them to follow the first two years of seminary training, the philosophy course. Tertiary education was most developed at Stonyhurst, which had up

Catholic young gentlemen would require a course specially adapted to prepare them for the University; others, again, coming from a distance, from America, England, and other places, might not be found fit to enter upon the University course, and yet could not well be sent away. A preparatory college would supply a course of education suited to all such persons, which, being, it is presumed, of the very best sort, would also lead to the improvement of the Preparatory Education imparted in the Catholic Schools and Colleges of Ireland; a thing, it will be admitted, very much to be [87]
desired. We may further add, that, when the Faculty of Theology shall have been established, some one of the Provincial Colleges would be a suitable place for ecclesiastical students preparing for graduation.

We may add, that we feel strongly the importance of naming at least some of the Professors and Officers of the University with all despatch. This would at once alleviate the anxiety of those who are hoping to avail themselves of so great a good, and dissipate the adverse rumours which are circulated by its enemies.

Signed, etc.

October, 1851

---

to fifty young men (including some from Ireland) aged between seventeen and twenty-one in its 'philosophy department': some studying philosophy proper, some following London University courses, and others completing their education under private tuition. These 'gentlemen philosophers', as they were called, provided colleges like Stonyhurst with a useful stream of income; understandably, the colleges were reluctant to see them leave for the Catholic University. The story of the Stonyhurst philosophers is told in H. J. A. Sire's *Gentlemen Philosophers: Catholic Higher Studies at Liège and Stonyhurst College, 1774–1916* (1988).

[88]

No. II[1]

From the Decrees of the meeting of the Bishops of Ireland, which took place in Dublin at the request of Pope Pius IX on 18th May 1854

Meeting together by Apostolic authority, we decide that the aforementioned University should open at once, and, that it be administered properly, should incorporate the following things that we have decreed:

1. By virtue of the Apostolic Letters already sent and the Decrees of the Synod of Thurles approved by the Apostolic See, a University (*Studiorum Universitatis*) shall be erected and founded under our supreme jurisdiction and perpetual care to govern and promote (subject in all things to the authority of the Holy See) the five Faculties to be formed: of which the first in dignity is Theology, the second Law, the third Medicine, the fourth Philosophy and Letters, the fifth Mathematics and Natural Sciences.

2. It will greatly facilitate the proper administration of everything, in order that academic matters are governed by one and the same person firmly and constantly, in accordance with the statutes and ordinances that shall be determined on by the Body of Bishops (*Cœtus Episcoporum*) at some future date, if the whole direction of our University is given to the cleric we choose, marked with the dignity of the priesthood, and dignified with the title of Rector, whose nomination and dismissal will always be reserved to ourselves.

[1] The whole of this section (i.e. No II) was originally in Latin.

3. We enjoin on this Rector that before undertaking the [89] administration of the University he shall make a profession of faith according to the form of Pius IV, and a promise of fidelity and obedience to the Body of Irish Bishops, and that he shall solemnly promise to care for the good standing and health of the Academy according to the same proscribed form.

4. We determine the power of the Rector to be such that, subject to the authority of the Holy See, he be empowered to confer academic degrees, and that freely and lawfully, according to the statutes sanctioned by the Body of Irish Bishops, he be able to adopt in matters relating to the teaching of the sciences or what pertains to discipline, such measures as shall seem necessary for the well-being and progress of the University, always subject to the superior right (*supremum ius*) of the Bishops to change anything done by him.

5. The Rector shall annually present to the Body of Bishops, when they meet, or if no episcopal meeting be held, to the four Archbishops, a full and faithful report on the condition of the Academy, according to the indication given by the Sacred Congregation on this matter.[2]

6. There shall be a Vice-Rector to assist and advise the Rector and to take his place provisionally in case of absence, illness or death, so that there is no harm done to the Academy. The appointment to this office and dismissal from it shall be vested with the bishops.

7. We defer consideration of the number and duties of the Professors until a more suitable time. In general, however, for the present and until the Body of Bishops sees otherwise, the Rector shall be empowered to designate and present the Professors, whether ordinary or extraordinary, [90] whilst the definitive appointment (*definitiva nominatio*) will

[2] See the footnote on p. [lxxxvi] for an explanation of the modifications made to this decree.

remain with us. We decree that each of the Professors shall make the profession of faith according to the form of Pius IV, as well as promising, in the form prescribed by ourselves, to give due honour and assistance to the Rector and to care for the well-being of the academy.

8. If anyone among the teachers should fail in some way in his duties and promises – may God prevent it – we reserve to ourselves the right to dismiss him; until that time the Rector has the power to suspend him from his post.

9. For the moment, and until otherwise seen by the Body of Bishops, we decree that the nomination of the Secretary and all other officials of the Academy shall belong to the Rector. He has the right to incur academic expenses, with the consent of the Bishops, in setting up Houses of Residence [*Collegia seu Paedagogia*] whose Heads [*Praesides*] he shall appoint and whose regulations he shall establish.

10. As soon as possible we shall take care to determine the rules and ordinances to be laid down for the administration and progress of our University and for the constitution of each of its Faculties.

11. The Rector shall have the power, for the cause of honour [*honoris caussâ*], to inscribe on the books of the University the names of persons distinguished for their piety, learning, or some other merits, providing they agree, and to present them to the four Archbishops for honorary degrees.[3]

[91] 12. Since it will be necessary to gather funds for the University, we decree that each year in every parish there should be a collection on the first Sunday of October. If any Bishop finds that that day is inconvenient, he can establish another Sunday in his Diocese.

13. Finally, that all may know that this University which is to be set up shall be for the building up of the Body of

---

[3] For the implementation of this decree, see the footnote on p. [283].

Christ and by that means the glory of His spouse, the column and foundation of truth, we consider that the professors and students are, as taught by the Lord, to hold with heart and deed and adhere firmly to the Catholic faith and the chair of Peter, upon which the Church is founded, and, being strangers to profane novelties which stain the integrity of faith, to follow that knowledge which builds up with charity and be guided by that wisdom whose beginning is the fear of God.[4]

From the Acts of the meeting of the Bishops of Ireland, which took place in Dublin on 18th May 1854

The submission by the Rev. Dr Newman, the designated Rector of the University, about the manner in which the University ought to constituted, was read out (vid. infra, *p.* 93).

---

[4] Newman had feared that the bishops might be contemplating something less than a university, but the use of *universitas* eight times and *academia* twice (for the sake of variety), and the absence of the terms *lyceum* and *Gymnasium*, shows that Newman's fears were unfounded—as were his concerns over the vexed question of the 'soul' of education. Considerable powers were 'reserved to the hierarchy, but none that exceed the *summum ius* exercised by the Belgian bishops over Louvain' (*NU*, p. 296). The one disappointment was that the decrees had not given him the appointment of the Vice-Rector.

After some significant modifications, the decrees were approved by Propaganda on 31 July, and on 6 August confirmed by the Pope, who at the same time granted the rector power to confer academic decrees (*NU*, p. 296).

The modifications were made after Cullen appealed to Rome and petitioned for changes to the decrees. As a result the bishops' meetings were to be held every five years or, for exceptional reasons, every three; in other years the Rector's report would be made to the four archbishops, not the whole episcopate, and the archbishops would make any necessary decisions about the University; the rules of the University, borrowed from Louvain, would be confirmed for six years. See Larkin, *Making of the Roman Catholic Church in Ireland*, pp. 247–52.

From the Acts of the same meeting, 20th May

It was established that, as well as a profession of faith, the Rector should make the following promise:—

"I, N., the appointed Rector of the Catholic University, will be faithful and obedient to the Body of Irish Bishops, and will endeavour with all my strength to secure the reputation and success of the University, in accordance with their intentions."

[92] The formula for the promise of the Vice-Rector, Professors and other officials is as follows:—

"I, N., the appointed Vice-Rector (or Professor, etc.) of the Catholic University, will observe faithfully its statutes and ordinances. I promise to give all due respect and support to the Rector: and will also endeavour with all my strength to secure the reputation and success of the Academy."

It is decreed that the Rector, Vice-Rector, and Professors should make a profession of faith according to the form of Pius IV, the Rector before the Most Reverend Archbishop of Dublin, and the others before the Rector.

If the Rector needs the work of others to promote the University matter [besides the list read by the Most Illustrious President] let it be established that provisionally he use other learned men, without giving them any right to acquire professorships.

Appendix – II

ADDENDUM

From a letter of his Eminence and Most Reverend Prefect of the Sacred Congregation of Propaganda Fide to the Archbishop of Dublin

Care should be taken that the meeting of Archbishops should take place at a time by which the conferring of academic degrees has taken place: that the same Archbishops take care to obtain a description of the state and performance of the University, which will be passed on to the individual Bishops for their opportune comments.

It is truly pleasing to add that the Catholic University should be placed under the protection of the Blessed Virgin Mary, who is honoured as Seat of Wisdom (*Sedes Sapientiae*).

[93]

No. III

Substance of the Memorandum of the Rector, read in the Synodal Meeting, May 20, 1854,[1] *as referred to above, p.* 91

The Rector wrote to the following effect:—

I beg leave to submit to the Most Reverend and Right Reverend Prelates, the Archbishops and Bishops of Ireland, the following remarks in furtherance of the great design, which is at present on their hands, of founding a University for the Catholics of Ireland, and of other countries which speak the English tongue.

§ 1.

Their object, I conceive, in setting up this their University, is to provide for Catholic Education (in a large

[1] This was Newman's second major memorandum and it contains his blueprint for the university, which he submitted to the bishops prior to their meeting. On 15 April Newman had received a copy of the Brief of 20 March 1854 formally appointing him as rector and ordering the Irish bishops to meet in synod within three months to decide on the measures necessary for the immediate opening of the University.

The original MS, dated 29 April, is reproduced in *LD* xvi, pp. 557–61, but it was the above corrected version which was read at the synod. The first version was approved by Cullen, though he suggested, through Dr Taylor, 'that it would be well to lay it down in express terms that the University is the property of the Archbishops and Bishops of Ireland'; Newman altered the final paragraph accordingly. But he felt he had already provided for Cullen's other suggestion, 'that the faculty of Theology should be particularly mentioned as an integral part of the University' (*LD* xvi, p. 557n).

sense of the word "education")[2] in various respects, in which at present we have to depend upon Protestant institutions and Protestant writings.

For instance, it is proposed:—

1. To provide means of finishing the education of young men of rank, fortune, or expectations, with a view of putting them on a level with Protestants of the same description.

2. To provide a professional education for students of law and medicine, and a liberal education for youths destined to mercantile and similar pursuits, as far as their [94] time will admit it.

3. To develop the talents of promising youths in the lower classes of the community.

4. To form a school of theology and canon law suited to the needs of a class of students who may be required to carry on those sciences beyond the point of attainment ordinarily sufficient for parochial duty.

5. To provide a series of sound and philosophical defences of Catholicity and Revelation, in answer to the infidel tracts and arguments which threaten to be our most serious opponents in the era now commencing.

6. To create a national Catholic literature.

7. To provide school books, and generally books of instruction for the Catholics of the United Kingdom,[3] and of the British Empire, and of the United States.

---

[2] The expression 'in the large sense of the word "education"' is very telling, because it emphasises that Newman was interested in giving a deep human and Christian formation at one and the same time. Then, as now, there was a common mistake of viewing education as the imparting of knowledge rather than the training of the mind, character formation, and the acquisition of habits. The danger of this tendency is that it diminishes what education is about and neglects important dimensions of it. Newman uses this or similar expressions on a number of other occasions, e.g. 'from first to last, education, in this large sense of the word, has been my line' (Journal entry, 21 January 1863, *AW*, p. 259).

8. To raise the standard, and systematize the teaching, and encourage the efforts, of the schools already so ably and zealously conducted throughout the country.

9. To give a Catholic tone to society in the great towns.

10. To respond to the growing importance of Ireland, arising from its geographical position, as the medium of intercourse between East and West, and the centre of the Catholicism of the English tongue,[4] with Great Britain, Malta (perhaps Turkey or Egypt), and India, on one side of it, and North America, and Australia, on the other.[5]

§ 2.

The means by which these great objects must be attempted by those to whom the Most Reverend and Right
[95] Reverend Prelates entrust their accomplishment, is the appointment of *Professorial Chairs* for the most important and attractive subjects of instruction, and of *men of high name* to fill them.

Considering we have the whole weight of Government, not only against us, but in favour of a rival system, it is imperative that the Professors appointed should be men of

---

[3] The term United Kingdom was shorthand for the United Kingdom of Great Britain and Ireland.

[4] On one occasion, when consulting Manning about his rights as Rector and how to exercise them, Manning replied, 'If you should find the national element in Ireland insuperable, would it not be well to re-consider the site of the University? All your arguments of centrality would apply to the West Coast of England as much as to the East Coast of Ireland. […] England is even more central to the Anglo-Saxon Race than Ireland' (12 April 1855, *LD* xvi, p. 440n).

[5] By the end of the nineteenth century, most lists of the overall objectives of a university would have included, in one form or another, the following four ends: the preservation and diffusion of culture, and the raising of the cultural level of society; preparation for the professions and the higher branches of commerce and industry; the advance of knowledge and research of every kind; and the development or maturation of the individual student, including what is required for social living. With the exception of research, these ends are found in this memorandum.

celebrity. Such celebrity is the only (human) inducement to bring students to us in preference to the Government colleges. Even able men, if they have not yet made a name, will be unequal to the special necessity of the moment. It would be better to leave some of the chairs empty for a time, than to fill them with men whose names will not be in themselves an attraction. Nay, it is desirable to substitute at first *pro tempore* Lecturers, instead of Professors, in order thereby to be able to secure the services of men of name, whose existing engagements are inconsistent with that simple devotion to the duties which is involved in the office of a Professor.

§ 3.

An important conclusion follows from the same consideration. Since students, as has been said, are to be gained specially and pre-eminently by means of the celebrity of the Professors, it is plain that the Professors must be appointed independent of, and prior to, the presence of students. This has been the case in the history of all Universities. Learned men came and opened schools, and their existing reputation drew followers. Even when schools were set up by sovereigns, the process was the same. They
rose into importance, not simply by royal favour, by civil [96]
privileges, by degrees or emoluments, but by the enthusiasm kindled by distinguished teachers, and the popularity and recognized importance of the subjects on which they lectured.[6]

---

[6] This is one of the key themes running through Newman's historical university sketches, where he uses the device of attributing change in the historical development of the university project to the shifting fortunes of two rival powers, which he calls 'influence' and 'system'. The first teachers were like preachers or missionaries, who attracted disciples by means of personal influence – which Newman describes as the absence of rule, 'the action of personality, the intercourse of soul with soul, the play of mind upon mind' (*HS* iii, p. 88). But individual action is fickle and

§4.

This brings us to another practical conclusion. We must commence by bringing into position and shape various large departments of knowledge; by founding institutions, which will have their value intrinsically, whether students are present or not. This, if we can manage to do it, will have a double advantage; such institutions, first, will attract students; next, they will have a sufficient object before students come.

As instances of such institutions (whether possible or not one by one in *fact*, for I am only illustrating what I mean and aim at), I would mention—

1. A school of useful arts, developing and applying the material resources of Ireland; that is, comprising the professorships of engineering, mining, agriculture, etc., etc., being a scientific treatment of such subject matters as are, for instance, provided in the Government Museum in Stephen's Green.[7]

2. Another such institution, if possible, would be an Observatory, with the Professorships it would involve.[8]

3. Another would be an archæological department, employing itself principally on the language, remains, MSS, etc., of ancient Ireland, with a special reference to Catholicity.

---

unreliable, and it needs the steadying hand of system to preserve the gains made. For more, see *MM*, pp. 124–8.

[7] This is the Museum of Irish Industry, founded in 1854 and dedicated to the exhibition of materials from the mining and manufacturing industries of Ireland. In addition, the museum organised lectures for the general public on related subject matters, thereby challenging the previous monopolisers of scientific study and instruction in Ireland: Trinity College Dublin and the Royal Dublin Society.

[8] Newman wrote on 5 May 1854 to his friend Manuel Johnson, the Radcliffe Observer at Oxford, to ask for advice about setting up an Observatory and about the state of the Dublin Observatory under the mathematician William Rowan Hamilton (*LD* xvi, pp. 123–4).

4. Another would be the medical staff of an Hospital, which would be the basis of a professoriate for students in [97] medicine.

I do not say that such institutions are all of them possible all at once, but some of them are; and these, and such as these, I repeat, might set to work, and would be producing results, before, and during, and until, the actual formation of classes of students in each department, for whose sake they are really set up. Astronomical observers, professors of medical science, the decipherers and editors of ancient writings, chemists and geologists, would in various ways subserve the social interests of Ireland, even though their lecture-rooms at first were but partially filled.

§5.

Such institutions could not of course be contained under one roof; and this leads me to observe that, a definite local position in a city or town is rather the attribute of a College than of a University. A University may be said to fill the city where it is placed, as we see from the ancient Universities of Paris, Louvain, and Oxford.

§ 6.

The *Unity* of the University, thus locally divided in its departments, will consist in the unity of the Catholic dogma and spirit. I conceive their Most Rev. and Right Rev. Lordships will see the desirableness of providing a University Church, which will be the place for all those high occasional ceremonies in which the University is visibly represented. But, besides this, it will be the place for [98] ordinary preaching on Sundays and holydays, on which occasions the pulpit will be filled by some distinguished theologian or sacred orator, called for that purpose from the scene of his labours in Ireland or England. No one can over-estimate the influence of an instrument of this kind in inculcating a loyal and generous devotion to the Church in the breasts of the young.

But of course the more obvious means of securing Catholic unity in this great Institution, is that of throwing the students into small communities, in the neighbourhood of the lecture-rooms which they would have principally to attend. These communities could be formed as students come, and should consist of about twenty students a-piece. They should be presided over by a Dean, who would be a Priest, who would enforce the necessary discipline and would serve the community chapel.

The Dean of these small communities should have with him two or three young men taken out of those, who have passed the public examinations, and are therefore of several years standing. These should be the private Tutors (or "Grinders" as they are sometimes called in Dublin) of the twenty students who constitute the community, in their preparation for those Lectures of Professors which they are attending.

Such Tutors, from the nature of the case, cannot be provided at once. I should propose meanwhile to be allowed to commit the whole Tutorial work to three or four good
[99] scholars, who will also perform a work necessary for our commencement, *viz.*, systematize a plan of studies and form a list of the editions, critical works, and the course of reading to be recommended to the students.

§ 7.

As to the charges to which a pupil will be subject, it is impossible as yet to estimate them fairly. I should recommend to their Lordships the institution of a certain number of burses or money prizes, to be obtained by *concursus*, which may at once stimulate exertion and diminish to those who obtain them the expenses of education.

§ 8.

I conceive the normal age of coming to the University will be 16. For the first two years the student will be engaged in classics, the elements of mathematics and logic, ancient history, etc. At the age of 18, he will pass an examination which will gain him an initial degree. We must, at this age, contemplate losing the majority of our students. Those who are destined for business will nevertheless have gained a certain amount of liberal education, without any unreasonable postponement of the time when they are to enter on the duties of their particular calling.[9]

Those who remain on, will give themselves for the space of a second two years to a course of modern history, political economy, law, metaphysics, etc., which will terminate when they are of the age of 20, after an examination, in the degree of B.A.

After this none would remain on, except such as desired, at the end of three additional years, a degree of M.A., or the [100]
Doctorate in one of the three faculties; the degree of M.A. being the ordinary qualification for a Professorial Chair.

Modifications and exceptions in these rules will occur in particular cases, but they are too minute to enter upon here.

§ 9.

I must not conclude without mentioning to the Most Reverend and Right Reverend the Archbishops and Bishops, what I conceive will be the cost of their starting so great an institution. Whatever, then, may be the degree of

---

[9] Newman's use of 'particular calling', a term normally associated with a calling to the priesthood or religious life, reflects his understanding of the 'professional vocation' of the ordinary Christian within their general calling (or vocation) to holiness. For two stories which show how Newman regarded preparation for the world on the same footing as for the priesthood and one calling for a serious and appropriate training, see Shrimpton, *A Catholic Eton?*, pp. 213–14.

success on starting, which attends upon the undertaking, greater or less, I beg to suggest that the Prelates themselves and the parties immediately engaged in it, should make up their minds to the necessity of a resolute trial of it for a sufficient length of time, say seven years. And during that time of experiment they must not be unwilling to reckon on its involving, for its ordinary charges, an annual outlay of £5000.

April 29, 1854

No. IV

Scheme of Rules and Regulations, submitted by the Rector to the Council in April, 1856, *afterwards to be adapted to University use*[1]

N.B.—Those sections, paragraphs, or sentences, to which an asterisk is prefixed, came before the Synodal Meeting of Prelates held in Dublin, June 20, 1856.

---

[1] The 'Scheme of Rules and Regulations' was Newman's longest and most complete document – written with the assistance of the Council – about the working of the University. Its four main sections deal with the constitution of the Catholic University, its discipline, the academic course, and the examinations; a separate, fifth section deals with the short-term aims of the University and its finances. The version presented to the bishops in June 1856 was a lengthy document which contained 'general enunciations of principle', some of which were excerpts from the articles Newman had written for the *Gazette* in 1854. When this provisional version became a formal collection of statutes, the 'general enunciations of principle' were omitted, as they were when the sections on the constitution and discipline appeared in *The Tablet* (16 & 23 August 1856).

When the definitive *Constitution and Statutes of the Catholic University of Ireland* was approved by the bishops and published in 1869, they embodied Newman's Rules and Regulations almost verbatim. This latter document included two additional statutes: one constituting the four archbishops as Visitors, who were to elect a Chancellor from among themselves; the other prescribing that for professorships the Rector would propose three candidates for the bishops to choose from (*NU*, p. 383n).

The origins of this foundational document have been described on pp. [60–2].

I. CONSTITUTION OF THE UNIVERSITY

* § 1. *The Authorities and Officials of the University*

These are (1) the Rector, and Vice-Rector; (2) the Professors and Deans of Faculties; (3) the Heads and Tutors of Collegiate Houses; (4) the Senate; (5) the Rectorial Council; and (6) the Secretary, Bursar, Librarian, and Curators of Museums.

The Senate is composed of the Vice-Rector and Secretary, the Professors, the Heads and Tutors of Collegiate Houses, and the Fellows of the University, convoked and presided over by the Rector.

The Rectorial Council consists of the Vice-Rector, the Deans of Faculties, and three additional members of the Faculty of Philosophy and Letters, with one vote between the three, which goes with the majority.

[102] Each Faculty has its own deliberative body, consisting of its Dean and Professors, under the presidency of its Dean; which acts as a standing subcommittee of the Council, for the purpose of its particular Faculty, in concurrence with the Rector. Each Collegiate House is presided over by a head, at present called a Dean, supported, at his option, by one or more assistants, called Tutors, or combining the office of Tutor with his own, when there is no Tutor.

* § 2. *The mode of appointing the Authorities and Officials*

The Rector and Vice-Rector are appointed by the *Cœtus Episcoporum*, or by the Archbishops acting for it, with power of revocation.

The Professors are designated and presented to the *Cœtus Episcoporum* by the Rector, or to the Archbishops acting for it, and by it or them definitely appointed, and by it or them alone revocable.

The Secretary, Heads of Collegiate Houses, Tutors, and all other officials, are appointed by the Rector.

The Deans of Faculties are elected annually by the Professors of the respective Faculties, and are presented for definite appointment to the Rector.

All these authorities and officials, though subject to removal by the same power that appointed them, are secure of the permanence of their appointments, till they forfeit them by some offence against religion or morals, by
insubordinate conduct, contentiousness, incapacity, or other [103]
obvious disqualification, according to the judgement of the *Cœtus Episcoporum*, or the Archbishops acting for it.

§ 3. *The several provinces of the Authorities and Officials*

* The Rector has the government of all classes, and the direction of all matters, in the University, according to the Statutes and Regulations of the same.

* The Vice-Rector assists the Rector, both by counsel and in act, and is his provisional *locum-tenens* in the event of his absence, sickness, or death.

* The Senate is the body representative of the University.

* The Council acts as the ordinary adviser of the Rector, in preparing measures, deciding questions, and other current business.

* The Secretary has the execution of the current business of the University, external and internal, under the direction of the Rector, Senate, and Council, as hereafter provided.

* The Professors are put in trust of the particular science or department of learning which they undertake.

They are bound to give themselves to the study of it, to extend its cultivation to the best of their power, to be alive to its interests, and to deliver in their lectures and by means of the Press,[2] clear and adequate expositions of its principles and subject matter.

* They will ever recollect in all they say and write, to keep in view the glory of Almighty God and the honour and edification of His Church.

[104] * The Head or Dean of a Collegiate House is bound to rule and guide the students committed to his charge with firmness and tenderness, and to minister to the best of his power to their religious and intellectual advancement.

§ 4. *The Faculties*

* There are five Faculties in the University, *viz*., Theology, Law, Medicine, Philosophy and Letters, Science.

* The Faculty of Theology will be represented by Professors of Holy Scripture, Dogmatics, Morals, Biblical Languages, Canon Law, and Ecclesiastical History. The Faculty of Medicine, by Professors in Medicine, Surgery, Anatomy, Pathology, Medical Chemistry, Physiology, Materia Medica,[3] etc. The Faculty of Philosophy and Letters, by Professors in Classical Literature and Languages, Ancient and Modern History and Geography, English Literature, Modern Languages, Logic, Metaphysics, Ethics, Political Economy, Irish Archæology, etc. The Faculty of Science, by Professors in Mathematics, Natural Philosophy, Natural History, Physical Chemistry, Engineering, Agriculture, etc. The Faculty of Law is not constituted yet.

* Each Faculty will be represented by its Professors, who meet together, and pass regulations for the purposes of

---

[2] Newman was asked to explain what 'by means of the Press' meant at a meeting of the Senate on 15 January 1857. See pp. [336–8]. See also the footnote on p. [345] for the similar views of Cullen.

[3] That is, pharmacology.

the Faculty, such as Sessional Tables of Lectures, subject to the confirmation of the Rector in Council.

Every member of the University begins with the Faculty of Letters, and is debarred from the Schools, Examinations, and Ranks of any of the other Faculties, till he has become a Scholar in this Faculty.

§ 5. *Ranks or Qualifications in the several Faculties* [105]

By Rank is meant a qualification for certain privileges. Of these Ranks there are altogether five—Student, Scholar, Inceptor, Licentiate, and Fellow; but, as a Student is an incipient Scholar, and an Inceptor is an incipient Licentiate, they may be reduced to three—Scholar, Licentiate, and Fellow; of which the two latter are analogous to Bachelor and Master or Doctor, as Degrees are arranged in other Universities.

A Student is made such by the act of entrance, which is the qualification for entering the School of Philosophy and Letters, and follows upon the entrance examination.

A Scholar becomes such, when he receives the certificate of his having passed the Scholarship examination, *viz.*, at the end of the second session, as explained below, which certificate is his title for entering the schools of any of the other Faculties.

He becomes an Inceptor, when he has passed the first examination for his Licence, which takes place at the end of his third session.

He becomes a Licentiate, when he has passed his second examination, which takes place at the end of his fourth session.

He becomes a Fellow of the University, when, being not less than seven sessions standing, he has passed the requisite examination or other test of proficiency; and he has a seat in the Senate, and participates in the government of the University.

[106] ## § 6. *The Rector*

The Rector's jurisdiction is supreme throughout the University.[4] Nothing can be done without his concurrence, whether in the Faculties or Collegiate Houses; nor is any University act formal, except by virtue of his direct participation.

It is his part to encourage and support every Official, both of the University and of the Colleges, in the performance of his duty, and to enforce such duty, wherever it is neglected, in such ways as are in accordance with the sentiments, and carry with them the sympathy, of the Academic Body.

To him falls the duty of supplying what is accidentally not provided for in the Statutes and Rules. He has to act in great emergencies, which require sudden measures. He has to do what falls upon no one else; and to him revert the powers which the proper Professor is not in circumstances to exercise.

He has the power of giving leave of absence to an Official, and of dispensing him from any part of his duty *pro hac vice*,[5] and of suspending *pro hac vice* any of the provisional Rules and Regulations of the University; provided always that he refers the case to the Council at their next meeting, and, on their declining to entertain the consideration of it, to the Senate, convoked within a week for that purpose.

---

[4] This followed the pattern at Louvain, where the effective government of the University was in the hands of the rector, assisted by the professors. The situation was very different at Oxford, where the heads of house were the supreme rulers within their colleges and the University was barely more than an examining body and powerless to act.

[5] That is, for or on this occasion.

He can suspend an Official from the exercise of his office, first, however, formally stating his reasons to his Council, till the next meeting of the *Cœtus Episcoporum* or of the Archbishops.

He confers academical degrees. He has the power of [107]
setting up or dissolving Collegiate Houses. He signs and authorizes all diplomas and certificates. He signs all money orders. He presides at all University meetings, and is curator of all the University buildings.

He may not act contrary to the Statutes and Rules of the University, nor in matters of importance without the advice of his Council, nor against two-thirds of its votes.

Should he himself on any occasion seem deserving of censure, or require to be stopped in any course of action, any one of the Faculties, assembled under its Dean, may, without consulting him, privately refer the matter to the four Archbishops, or to the presiding Archbishop, informing the Rector at the same time of the fact.

§ 7. *The Vice-Rector*

The Vice-Rector has, when the Rector is present, the routine administration of the University; and in his absence fulfils those higher duties also which ordinarily are peculiar to the Rector, under the authority, if possible, of letters from him, occupying the Rectorial seat, and receiving Rectorial honours in Church, in the Senate, and in the Schools. In subordination to the Rector, he superintends the discipline both of the University and of the Collegiate Houses. He has jurisdiction over their Heads, and, with the Rector's consent, can even interfere in a particular case with their internal administration. He has the ordinary care of the [108]
extern Students of the University; and, at the instance of their Head, removes interns from their House, gives them leave of absence, and awards honours or punishments for

their conduct, on the more extraordinary occasions. He appoints and dismisses the University servants, has the superintendence of them, and fixes their salaries.

§ 8. *The Senate*

The Senate is the representative of the collective University, and is charged with those acts which especially belong to it. Its presence is the presence of the University, and its acts are University acts. It is the formal organ of the University in its external relations and external proceedings. It speaks and acts for the University, when word or deed is demanded. It represents the University in all matters of religion and morals. It prescribes the course of studies, and the subjects and form of examination. It presents to the Rector candidates for degrees, according to the qualifications specified below. It passes Rules and Regulations; it prepares and presents addresses and petitions; it concurs with the Rector in expelling from the University. It has jurisdiction over the University Press; it appoints committees; it appoints auditors of accounts.

In the meetings of the Senate, the initiative of measures and the moving of amendments lie with the Rector, and any Dean of Faculty who is seconded by a Professor of another Faculty.

[109] ### § 9. *Rectorial Council*

The Rectorial Council, as its name implies, has for its object to give counsel and support to the Rector. It originates nothing, and executes nothing; but the Rector avails himself of its assistance, and listens to its advice, in all the ordinary business of the University, holds it at least once a month in term time, and cannot do any public act, except the suspension of Professors, or carry out any public measure, against two-thirds of its votes.

§ 10. *The Secretary*

The Secretary attends at his office in term time daily, excepting Sundays and other feasts of obligation, and in the week previous to the commencement of the Session; during the two recesses of Christmas and Easter, and when the schools are closed, at the seasons of Carnival and Corpus Christi, on Wednesdays and Saturdays; and on Saturdays in the Long Vacation, except during the months of August and September.

He issues the summonses for meetings of the Senate and the Council, and takes minutes of their proceedings. He prepares all documents, sends out all notices, keeps the University books, carries on the University correspondence, and makes a record of University transactions. He receives University dues, and prepares and registers money orders for the Rector, till a Bursar is appointed, and draws up a
yearly balance-sheet of receipts and expenditure. He brings [110]
before the Rector from time to time the state of the University buildings, and has charge of them during the vacations.

§ 11. *The Professors*

A Professor is not to be overburdened with lectures, that he may have time for the steady pursuit and thorough mastery of the department of science or learning, which he has undertaken. His main office is to expound and illustrate it; to deepen its principles and to enlarge its stores;[6] and to

[6] In his Preface to the *Discourses on the Scope and Nature of University Education* (1852) Newman asserts that the university is 'a place of *teaching* universal *knowledge*', which implies that its object entails 'the diffusion of knowledge rather than its advancement. If its object were scientific and philosophical discovery, I do not see why a University should have students' (*Idea*, p. ix). In distinguishing between the tasks of teaching and researching, Newman goes on to argue that the capacities for undertaking both are not commonly found in one and the same

erect what may be called a real objective image of it, such as may have value in itself, as distinct from the accidents of the day. He is not bound by duty, though he may be advantageously induced by circumstances, to adapt himself to his particular hearers, and to bring down his teaching to their capacity: on the other hand, they are required to prepare themselves for what may be at first above them, and to raise themselves towards the level of his view and the standard of his intellect. His Lectures are emphatically public, and his hearers take part in his publicity. They are called on to construe, translate, and answer questions before their companions, and with a sort of emulation one against another.[7] They are, from exercises of this nature, to gain

---

person, since research demands isolation and concentration, and teaching an external involvement; the proper home of research lies outside the university, albeit in institutions closely connected with it (*Idea*, pp. xii–xiv).

Not a few have concluded from these passages that Newman was against research being conducted at university. With hindsight, it seems that in emphasising that the primary purpose of a university is to teach, Newman made a sharper distinction between teaching and research than he intended; after all, his medical school incorporated both functions.

Newman's practice in Dublin shows he did not set himself against the idea of research, as he tried to ensure that academics at the Catholic University focus on their special fields of research and cultivate them; that they publish their findings; that the University set up practical or technical schools such as engineering, mining and agriculture, a school of Irish language and history, an astronomical observatory, and science laboratories – 'institutions which will have their value intrinsically, whether students are present or not' (p. [96]). He also started the journal *Atlantis* to showcase the research being carried out at the University.

For more on Newman's ideas on research, see Ker, 'Newman's *Idea of a University*. A Guide for the Contemporary University?', *The Idea of a University*, ed. D. Smith & A. K. Langslow (1999), pp. 12–16; *MM*, pp. xxxviii, 113–15, 241, 475–8.

[7] When Newman was an undergraduate at Oxford and later when a Fellow, students were supposed to attend two or three hours of college lectures a day. During these, a college tutor would typically oversee a group

habits of self-possession, presence of mind, quickness, clearness, and accuracy of thought, power of grasping ideas, and steadiness of contemplation; and they are to be formed one and all upon one model by the intellectual excitement and mutual sympathy which his teaching elicits.

Nor are his duties confined to the lecture hall: in this [111] day, especially, he may be quite as usefully employed with the pen as with the tongue;[8] and if there is one *desideratum* greater than another just now, which may employ him, it is that of text-books in literature and science for the use of students, written on a Catholic basis and with a scrupulous avoidance of all matter of a vicious and immoral tendency.

§ 12. *Moderator of Studies*

It is the office of the Moderator of Studies to assist the Rector in vindicating, applying, adjusting, advancing, and perfecting the subjects and the method of academical teaching and examination already adopted by the Senate in the five Faculties. He is to take on himself, in a nascent and unformed Institution, those conservative duties, which, when it is established, are supplied by tradition, prescription, and the prevailing and authoritative sentiment of the Professorial and Tutorial body. He is selected by the Senate, and is presented to the Rector for nomination, who has, of course, the right to decline their choice, should he think fit.

---

of up to fifteen students translating Latin and Greek texts, to which he might add a commentary of a grammatical, historical or philosophical nature.

[8] The copy of the 'Scheme of Rules and Regulations' at the Birmingham Oratory contains in the margins the phrase 'Professors to write books' (Culler, *Imperial Intellect*, p. 311).

§ 13. *Examiners*[9]

Three Examiners are appointed by the Rector for the examinations in each Faculty. The same person may be Examiner in various Faculties at once. One goes out every year. They must not be taken from the Professors or
[112] Collegiate Heads or Tutors. One of them is sufficient for conducting the Entrance Examination; all three must be present at the rest. The Entrance Examination may take place at any time; in the Faculty of Letters, the other Examinations take place twice a year, in Term time, before the Feast of the Conversion of St Paul (January 25), and after the Feast of Mount Carmel (July 16).

For the Licentiate Examination in Letters, which takes place in Full Term, about the Feast of St Columba (June 9),

---

[9] Among his many contributions to education, one that is rarely recognised is that Newman was an examiner all his adult life, whether at Oxford, Dublin or, later, at the Oratory School in Birmingham. It should be noted that the role of the examiner in the days of oral exams was, if carried out diligently, an exacting one, and required the person to become thoroughly acquainted with the material being examined. A conscientious examiner could have a great influence on the way in which the set books were studied. One of the reforms Newman had undertaken at Oxford was to introduce written work into the termly college exams at Oriel; and as an Oxford University examiner he had sought to ensure that examining was made more rigorous.

In the months prior to the opening of the Catholic University Newman immersed himself in all the details of the entrance exams, which were devised by three of the lecturers. While he strongly disliked cramming and superficial learning, he maintained that regular tests had a specific use in training the intellect: 'they impart self-confidence, they serve to bring home to a youth what he knows and what he does not, they teach him to bring out his knowledge and to express his meaning clearly' (Newman to Northcote, 23 February 1872, *LD* xxvi, p. 26). For this reason he felt that at Dublin, 'The Examination system is the key to the whole University Course, and the Examiners should be as formal Officers of the University as Professors' (Newman to MacDermott, 21 August 1858, *LD* xviii, p. 445).

an extra Examiner shall be added, who, if possible, shall be unacquainted with the University lectures and examinations.

The Examiners for the Exhibitions, Burses, and Prizes shall be three, of whom one shall be a Professor and another a Tutor.

The appointment of Examiners must in every case be confirmed by the Senate.

[113]

II. DISCIPLINE

§ 14. *Heads of Houses*

* Any Priest coming with letters from his Ecclesiastical Superior and with the approbation of the Archbishop of Dublin, or Graduate of the University, with the same approbation, has the power, with permission of the Rector, to set up and govern a Collegiate House, which forthwith becomes an integral part of the University. He undertakes it on the condition of making it self-supporting, though the Rector is at liberty to entertain an application for pecuniary assistance, and to hear pleas in its behalf. He may keep the whole charge of his House in his own hands or not. In the former case, he has on his hands the accounts, the tuition, and the daily Mass, as well as the discipline. In the latter, he appoints a Sub-Dean, Bursar, or Chaplain, as the case may be, and avails himself of the services of one or more Tutors, or of extern Teachers; always with the consent of the Rector. In every case the Chaplain must reside in the House, and be a priest approved by the Archbishop. In matters of discipline he is under the jurisdiction of the Vice-Rector, whose rules he carries out with a power of appealing to the Rector, and to whom he reports his students in cases of bad conduct.

[114] At present the University allows at the rate of £50 per annum to every Collegiate House, as an aid towards its expenses; to be made up to £100 when it has on quarter-day above five intern students; to £150 when it has above twelve; and to £200 when it has above twenty. The object of

this grant is to relieve the difficulties which at present press upon the finances of the Collegiate Houses. It also has respect to the expenses which a Head will at present incur in providing Tutors, for the accurate grounding of his students, and to prepare them for the Lectures of the Professors, as is to be mentioned presently.

* The Heads of Houses are charged with the moral and intellectual advancement of the Students of Houses, who are strictly committed to them as *pupilli*, and are under their tutelage. They are responsible for their religious and correct deportment, for their observance of the Rules both of the House and of the University, and for their acquitting themselves adequately both before the Professors and the Examiners.

* In case of the absence or illness of any Head or Dean, the Rector provides a substitute for him.

Perhaps it may be allowable to quote here a passage on the subject of the management of Students, which the Rector had occasion to put into print last autumn.[10] It runs as follows:—

"It is assuredly a most delicate and difficult matter to manage youths, and those lay youths, in that most dangerous and least docile time of life, when they are no longer boys, but not yet men, and claim to be entrusted with [115]
the freedom which is the right of men, yet punished with the lenience which is the privilege of boys. In proposing rules on this subject, I shall begin with laying down, first, as a guiding principle, what I believe to be the truth, that the young for the most part cannot be driven, but, on the other hand, are open to persuasion and to the influence of kindness and personal attachment; and that, in consequence, they are to be kept straight by indirect contrivances rather than by authoritative enactments and naked prohibitions.

---

[10] This passage is copied from section 23 of Newman's first Report (pp. [35–8]), though a few minor variations are introduced.

And a second consideration of great importance is, that these youths will certainly be their own masters before many years have passed, as they were certainly schoolboys not many months ago. A University residence, then, is in fact a period of training interposed between boyhood and manhood, and one of its special offices is to introduce and to launch the young man into the world, who has hitherto been confined within the school and the playground. If this be so, then is it entrusted with an office as momentous as it is special; for nothing is more perilous to the soul than the sudden transition from restraint to liberty. Under any circumstances it is a serious problem how to prepare the young mind against the temptations of life; but, if experience is to be our guide, boys who are kept jealously at home or under severe schoolmasters, till the very moment when they are called to take part in the business of the world, are the very persons about whom we have most cause to entertain misgivings. They are sent out into the
[116] midst of giant temptations and perils, with the arms, or rather with the unarmed helplessness, of children, with knowledge neither of self nor of the strength of evil, with no trial of the combat or practice in sustaining it; and, in spite of their good feelings, they too commonly fail in proportion to their inexperience. Even if they have innocence, which is perhaps the case, still they have not principle, without which innocence is hardly virtue. We could not do worse than to continue the discipline of school and college into the University, and to let the great world, which is to follow upon it, be the first stage on which the young are set at liberty to follow their own bent. So proceeding, we should be abdicating a function, and letting slip the opportunities of our peculiar position. It is our duty and our privilege to be allowed to hold back the weak and ignorant a while from an inevitable trial;—to conduct them to the arms of a kind mother, an Alma Mater, who inspires affection while she

whispers truth; who enlists imagination, taste, and ambition on the side of duty; who seeks to impress hearts with noble and heavenly maxims at the age when they are most susceptible, and to win and subdue them when they are most impetuous and self-willed; who warns them while she indulges them, and sympathizes with them while she remonstrates with them; who superintends the use of the liberty which she gives them, and teaches them to turn to account the failures which she has not at all risks prevented; and who, in a word, would cease to be a mother, if her eye were stern and her voice peremptory. If all this be so, it is plain that a certain tenderness, or even indulgence[11] on the
one hand, and an anxious, vigilant, importunate attention on [117]
the other, are the characteristics of that discipline which is peculiar to a University. And it is the necessity of the exercise of this elastic Rule, as in a good sense of the term it may be called, which is the great difficulty of its governors.[12] It is easy enough to lay down the law and to justify it, to make your rule and keep it; but it is quite a science, I may say, to maintain a persevering, gentle oversight, to use a minute discretion, to adapt your treatment to the particular case, to go just as far as you safely may with each mind, and no further, and to do all this with no selfish ends, with no sacrifice of sincerity and frankness, and with no suspicion of partiality."[13]

---

[11] The earlier version has 'laxity of rule' for 'indulgence'.

[12] In the earlier version this sentence reads: 'And it is the necessity of the exercise of this "Lesbian Canon", as the great philosopher calls it, which is the great difficulty of the governors of such an institution.'

[13] This passage was eventually incorporated into the *Constitution and Statutes of the Catholic University of Ireland* (1869) (45/5/V(4), DDA).

§ 15. *The Tutors*[14]

* The Tutor is an assistant of the Ruler of a House, chosen by him (with approbation of the Rector), and living with him. His duty is, certainly the moral, but more directly the intellectual care of his pupils, of which he relieves the Head or President.[15] His chief work is to prepare them for the Professorial Lectures and the Examinations.

It will be prudent in him to anticipate, in the case of many of his charge, little love of study and no habit of application, and, even in the case of the diligent, backwardness and defective or ill-grounded knowledge. Towards them, as well as towards the studious and

---

[14] Newman's idea of the Tutor's role touches on much that makes him special as an educational thinker – and much that is characteristic of him as a person: his recognition of the importance of education for the development of young people; his love of his fellow human beings; his *caritas*; his stress on the formative value of personal influence; his appreciation for the personal element in the process of understanding and embracing knowledge and faith; his patience with human weakness in the fitful process of maturation; his grasp of the obligations and rewards of the universal; his insistence on the practical. In particular, Newman held that moral and religious truths were best communicated and most likely to stir the heart by the power of personal influence, and that tutorials should be conducted on this basis. These views were not the outcome of research or reading, but rather the result of many years in education, during which he had tried to live out his high ideals and to observe and ponder on what he saw around him.

[15] During Newman's years as an Oxford college Tutor (1826–31) the Laudian statutes of 1636 were technically still in force; and although the Tutor's main task had become that of a college lecturer, enough of the old associations lingered on to convince most people that the task should continue to be undertaken by unmarried clergymen. The Laudian Code decreed that the Tutor should imbue the students committed to his charge with good morals and instruct them in approved authors, above all in the rudiments of religion and the Thirty-Nine Articles; he was also to be responsible for his students' behaviour. Newman interpreted this to mean that 'a Tutor was not a mere academical Policeman, or Constable, but a moral and religious guardian of the youths committed to him' (*AW*, p. 91).

advanced, he will have to address himself according to the needs of each.[16] He will select for them their course of reading, recommend them the lectures which they are to [118] attend, and the books and subjects which they are to present for examination.

As to the more promising, he will superintend their reading. He will set them off, for instance, in private informal lectures and conversations, at the commencement of new and difficult authors. He will then let them go a while, and bid them bring him their difficulties. He will keep his eye upon them, and from time to time examine them, take them in hand again when they come to more difficult portions, and bring to their notice points which would otherwise escape them. He will direct them to works in illustration of their subject, help them with analyses and abstracts, or teach them how to make them; and, as their examination draws near, he will go over the ground again with them, and try them to and fro in their books.

On the other hand, in the case of the backward, he will ascertain their weak points, and set them on remedying them. He will force upon them the fact of their want of grounding and other defects, and, without annoying them, will be jealous and importunate on the subject in proportion to their indisposition to amend. He will try to keep them up to the mark of the Professors' Lectures which they attend, and prevent them from showing ill there. As to the idle, he will be in the practice of sending for them, will ask them if they have prepared to-morrow's lectures, oblige them to

---

[16] Newman speaks from experience. In 1825 he was appointed Vice-Principal of Alban Hall, an independent academic hall in Oxford, and acted as Tutor and Dean of the dozen undergraduates, giving most of the lectures, setting weekly compositions, and dining with them three times a week. This brought him into contact with some of the University's most idle men, for Alban Hall was regarded as Oxford's Botany Bay. In his first year as a Tutor at Oriel he came up against a set of gentlemen-commoners who were notoriously rowdy. For more, see *MM*, pp. 14–32.

come at a certain hour for examination in them, treating them throughout with good-humour, but with the steadiness
[119] of a superior. In like manner, he will bring before them their approaching examination, confront them with the disgrace of failure, and impress upon them their ever-accumulating loss of time, and the extreme difficulty of making up for it.[17]

All this involves a real occupation on the part of the Tutor, but it is close rather than great, and continual rather than continuous; it does involve, however, a sustained solicitude, and a mind devoted to his charge. And because of the serious importance, and the really interesting nature of the office, when understood and entered into, and again, of the difficulty some persons have in understanding it, its duties have here been drawn out somewhat in detail. The way to a young man's heart lies through his studies, certainly in the case of the more clever and diligent.[18] He

---

[17] Newman could be sternly demanding of his pupils, especially if he saw they were wasting their talents and could take a strong reprimand. On one occasion he reproached Henry Wilberforce for wasting two terms. Henry was told that 'if you feel ashamed of yourself for having wasted time, some permanent good may ensue and you may be induced to correct a bad habit'; Newman hoped that his feelings of self-reproach would be lasting, as 'you have not done your duty like an honest man and a Christian'. After his scolding, Henry was given detailed advice about what he should be reading in preparation for his exams, and warned: 'Beware of repenting indeed of idleness in the evening, but waking next morning thoughtless and careless about it' (9 July 1827, *LD* ii, p. 23).

[18] Newman speaks from his own experience. At Ealing School he was befriended by Dr George Nicholas, the scholarly headmaster, and deeply influenced by the sermons, conversations and suggested reading of the Rev. Walter Mayers, the senior Classics master and a devout evangelical. In the aftermath of the collapse of his father's bank in March 1816, Newman spent the summer vacation at school, where he was thrown into the company of Mayers, and during this time he fell seriously ill. That autumn Newman experienced the religious conversion that he regarded as the most momentous event of his life and from which he emerged as a believing Christian.

At Trinity College, Oxford the Junior Tutor, the Rev. Thomas Short, lent Newman a book and invited him to breakfast, as soon as he realised he had a

feels grateful towards the superior, who takes an interest in the things which are at the moment nearest to his heart, and he opens it to him accordingly. From the books which lie before them the two friends are led into conversation, speculation, discussion: there is the intercourse of mind with mind, with an intimacy and sincerity which can only be when none others are present. Obscurities of thought, difficulties in philosophy, perplexities of faith, are confidentially brought out, sifted, and solved; and a pagan poet or theorist may thus become the occasion of Christian advancement. Thus the Tutor forms the pupil's opinions, and is the friend, perhaps the guide, of his after life. He becomes associated with the pupil's brightest and pleasantest years, and is invested in the hues of a past youth.

In this idea of a College Tutor, we see that union of [120]
intellectual and moral influence, the separation of which is the evil of the age. Men are accustomed to go to the Church for religious training, but to the world for the cultivation both of their hard reason and their susceptible imagination. A Catholic University will but half remedy this evil, if it aims only at professorial, not at private teaching. Where is the private teaching, there will be the real influence.[19]

---

genuine scholar on his hands. As a timid young Fellow at Oriel, Newman was taken walking and riding over the summer of 1822 by Richard Whately, who conversed with him at length. As Newman recounts, Whately 'was the first person who opened my mind, that is, who gave it ideas and principles to cogitate on' and taught him to think for himself (Newman to Monsell, 10 October 1852, *LD* xv, p. 176).

[19] In his first sermon at the Catholic University Church, Newman spoke at length about the disjunction of the academic and moral as the evil of the age: 'I wish the intellect to range with the utmost freedom, and religion to enjoy an equal freedom; but what I am stipulating for is, that they should be found in one and the same place, and exemplified in the same persons. I wish the same spots and the same individuals to be at once oracles of philosophy and shrines of devotion. It will not satisfy me, what satisfies so many, to have two independent systems, intellectual and religious, going at once side by side, by a sort of division of labour, and

* To fulfil this idea, however, the Tutor must have no part in College discipline, nor any academical authority over his pupils. Should he be invested with these additional duties, he will often find it expedient to commit the Tutorial care of certain of his pupils to externs; on the principle on which the offices of Ruler and Confessor are separated in Religious communities.[20]

---

only accidentally brought together. It will not satisfy me, if religion is here, and science there, and young men converse with science all day, and lodge with religion in the evening. It is not touching the evil [...] if young men eat and drink and sleep in one place, and think in another: I want the same roof to contain both the intellectual and moral discipline. [...] I want the intellectual layman to be religious, and the devout ecclesiastic to be intellectual.'

'This is no matter of terms, nor of subtle distinctions. Sanctity has its influence; intellect has its influence; the influence of sanctity is the greater on the long run; the influence of intellect is greater at the moment. Therefore, in the case of the young, whose education lasts a few years, where the intellect is, *there* is the influence. Their literary, their scientific teachers, really have the forming of them' ('Intellect, the Instrument of Religious Training', sermon preached on 4 May 1856, *Sermons Preached on Various Occasions* (London: Longmans, Green & Co, 1874;1908), pp. 13–14).

[20] In May 1855 Newman and Ornsby hit upon a way of explaining the role of the Oxbridge private tutor, through reproducing in the *CUG* extracts from Charles Bristed's *Five Years in an English University* (1852). Bristed's account of life at Trinity College, Cambridge had been intended to provide his fellow North Americans with an accurate depiction of university life there and to counter the image evoked by fictional works such as the widely-read *Adventures of Mr Verdant Green, an Oxford Freshman* (which first appeared in serialized form in the *Illustrated London News* in 1851). Bristed's was one of the earliest accounts to provide detailed descriptions of the academic lifestyle of the serious student and, more importantly, to explain the role of the tutor. Intended to inform a North American public uninitiated in the mysteries of the tutorial system, Bristed's account was well suited for Irish consumption.

The two articles entitled 'The University of Cambridge' (*CUG* 43 (3 May 1855) & 44 (7 June 1855)) describe how the teaching was left to private tutors at the two ancient universities. Thrown upon his own resources, the student naturally turned for guidance and sympathy to

* § 16. *Discipline in the Collegiate Houses*

The following is to be the course of a Student's day, except on Holydays, in a Collegiate House:—

Attendance at Mass, 7 or 8 A.M.; breakfast; attendance at Lectures from 9 to 1 or 2; dinner; presence indoors by a fixed hour in the evening, varying with the season; sometimes lectures in the evening.

The Student furnishes the Head of his Society with the name of his Confessor at the beginning of the Session, and is expected to frequent the Sacraments. He attends the University High Mass, and such devotions as his Head appoints for him.

* § 17. *Externs* [121]

Extern members must reside in a house approved of by the Rector, and must be indoors by ten o'clock at night.

---

those who had recently distinguished themselves in their BA exams and remained in college in the hope of obtaining a fellowship. Two or three years older than their pupils, they were ideally placed to impart 'the best rules and cautions' for exam success; they were the undergraduates' 'saints', though as yet not 'canonized' with a fellowship. The influence these officially unrecognised teachers exercised was great, since they became the students' 'advisers, confidants, and real instructors'. Moreover, they were 'the very seat of that academical tradition and sentiment' which made the university what it was; they were 'the oracles of the rising generation', who would in time carry the country forward.

The passages selected for the *CUG* provide readers with a picture of university life that was busy and purposeful, all the more so as they focus on the society of the private tutors. This select breed of scholars had common traits: they took regular, daily exercise; they lived frugal lives; and they were serious in the views they espoused. These characteristics, as well as the warm comradeship of graduate society, are conveyed by Bristed's description of an animated dinner party—a description that offsets the more forbidding elements of their academic asceticism, and was chosen as it would appeal to the young Irishman thinking of applying to the Catholic University.

They attend the University High Mass, and are expected to observe their religious duties as exactly as the interns. They are under the superintendence of the Vice-Rector, to whom they are amenable in cases of violation of rule or misconduct.

* § 18. *Lectures*

The Professors send weekly notices to the Vice-Rector and the Heads of the Houses, of the attendance and conduct at Lecture of the Students who form their classes; that is, to the Vice-Rector in the case of externs, to the Heads or Deans in the case of their own interns respectively.

* § 19. *Punishments*

As discipline is in the hands of the Rector, Vice-Rector, and Heads or Deans of Houses, only they can inflict punishment.

The lighter punishments—(1) admonition, (2) prohibition to pass into the town, (3) confinement to the House, (4) imposition, (5) fine,—are in the hands of the Vice-Rector and of the Heads or Deans. The graver punishments—(1) loss of term, (2) *consilium abeundi*,[21] (3) expulsion,—are in the hands of the Rector, who inflicts the

---

[21] The *consilium abeundi* (literally 'advice to leave') was a term in common usage, particularly at German universities, for a punishment whereby the convicted student was not formally expelled, but unofficially required to leave the university. At some institutions, re-matriculation was possible after a year; besides, a student in this position was allowed to register at any other university, as *consilium abeundi* did not carry any imputation on the morals of the student: it was generally inflicted for youthful imprudence. Expulsion, the ultimate sanction, was for more serious offences, and meant that the student could not matriculate elsewhere.

second in Council, the third with the concurrence of the Senate.

§ 20. *Fees* [122]

The Fee of £1 is paid to the Secretary of the University by every intern member, and £5 by every extern, on his entrance; also on his taking his Scholarship, his Licentiate, and his Fellowship, severally.

The Annual Fee of £10 is paid to the Secretary, as lecture money, in half-yearly portions, and in advance, by every Student and Scholar in the Faculty of Letters and Philosophy; *viz*., £5 on St Malachy's Day, and £5 on St Patrick's.

§ 21. *Auditors*

Any person not a member of the University, may attend, as an Auditor, the Lectures of the Faculty of Philosophy and Letters, on a letter of the Vice-Rector to the Secretary and the previous payment of £10 a year; and any one of the Courses, on a like letter and a fee varying with its subject matter.[22]

The Rector in Council may, under special circumstances, allow Auditors, who wish to become members of the University, to count the terms in which they have already attended Lectures, towards their Scholarship.

[22] In the long vacation of 1856, just after the Rules and Regulations received provisional approval, Newman had to deal with a parent who wanted his two sons to attend the University while living at home, in Booterstown outside Dublin. According to the regulations they had to attend as Auditors, rather than Externs, because living outside Dublin Meant they were not under the Vice-Rector's jurisdiction—unless the Senate exempted them. But this was far from ideal and approximated to the situation at London University which Newman so strongly deplored. (See his article 'University and King's Colleges in London', pp. [325–34]). Unavoidable, however, was the status of the non-Catholic medical students, who could only join the Catholic University as Auditors.

Such persons may be received as interns of a Collegiate House on leave being obtained from the Rector, by its head.[23]

§ 22. *Affiliation of Schools*

Grammar Schools, which come up to a standard
[123] hereafter to be determined, may be affiliated to the University, at the recommendation of their respective Diocesans. Affiliation involves the following conditions and privileges:—

1. An Affiliated School is subject to the formal inspection of the University.

2. The pupils of an Affiliated School are examined once a year in the studies prosecuted in the year past, by persons deputed by the University for that purpose.

3. A prize is given by the University to the pupil who acquits himself best in the examination.

4. A certain number of full burses, lasting during the four first years of residence in the University, are offered every year to the competition of the pupils of Affiliated Schools, who are over sixteen years of age.

§ 23. *University Halls*

A certain number of Grammar Schools and Colleges, or the lay portions of them, to be determined by circumstances, may, with the consent of their respective Diocesans, be constituted University Halls.

The government, course of study, management, and whole expenses of these Halls, the appointment of teachers, and the school fees, shall be entirely in the hands of the University; the Diocesan or other negotiating party finding,

---

[23] In this case, Auditors had to submit to the *house* regulations, as distinct from the University regulations.

where it is practicable, a master's house, lodgings for the intern pupils, and school accommodation.

Each Hall shall be divided into two schools, one for [124] pupils under, the other for pupils over, thirteen years of age. The lower school shall be devoted chiefly to a commercial, and the upper to a higher education.

Free places, to be held for two years, will be offered to the competition of pupils over the age of sixteen; the successful candidates being obliged to reside in the Master's House, and being employed for a portion of each day in teaching the lower school. Holders of free places, who reside the full two years, and wish to proceed to the University, will be allowed to count them for the Scholarship.

[125]

III. ACADEMICAL COURSE

§ 24. *The Session and its Terms*

The Session lasts from St Malachy, November 3, to St Mary Magdalen, July 22, following. Two recesses occur in the course of it, which divide it into three Terms.

The First Term of the Session extends from St Malachy, November 3, to St Thomas, December 21; and is followed by the Christmas Recess, which lasts to the Saturday after the Feast of the Epiphany.

The Second Term extends from the Saturday after the Epiphany to the Saturday before Palm Sunday; and is followed by the Easter Recess, which lasts to the Saturday after Low Sunday.

The Third Term extends from the Saturday after Low Sunday to the end of the Session, the Feast of St Mary Magdalen, July 22.

When Quinquagesima is after February 17, the Schools are closed from the Thursday before it to Shrove Tuesday inclusive.

When the Feast of Corpus Christi is before June 6, the Schools are closed from that day to the Octave, inclusive.

In each Term or Term-time, there is a portion called Full Term, which is considered as its most solemn and formal
[126] portion, *viz*., from St Malachy, November 3, to St Andrew, November 30, from the Purification, February 2, to St Patrick, March 17, and from the Auxilium Christianorum, May 24, to the Visitation, July 2.

§ 25. *Members of the University*

First shall be stated in a few words the general character of the Academical Course. The normal age of entrance is sixteen years. The Student commences in the School of Letters and Philosophy. At the end of two years, being then eighteen, he becomes Scholar. He then either retires from the University, if it be necessary, or he continues the course of letters; or he passes into the Schools of Medicine, of Science, etc.; receiving at the end of two years, being then of the normal age of twenty, the Academical Licence. Three years more carry him, at the age of twenty-three, to his Fellowship. The same number of years lead in the other faculties to the Licence and the Fellowship. Such is the general delineation of the University Course, which must now be described more in detail.

§ 26. *Candidates for Examinations*

The Candidate for Entrance must bring with him letters from the persons who have had last the care of his education, and must present them to the Vice-Rector, if he wishes to be an extern, or to the Governor of the Society which he desires to join. From him he proceeds, with a paper of recommendation, to one of the Examiners, to undergo the Entrance Examination. This paper, [127]
countersigned by the Examiner, is the Secretary's voucher, on his presenting it, for the insertion of his name in the University Catalogue, which always is the act of the Rector. Before doing this, the Rector exacts of him a declaration of obedience to the authorities of College and University.[24]

[24] The Form of Promise devised by Newman read: 'I A.B. promise to the Rector and Senate of this University that I will dutifully obey those who are in authority over me, and, as far as in me lies, will observe the Rules

When entered, he resides at once; or he remains in any licensed College or Colleges for any part of the first two Sessions, with the leave of his University Head.

At the end of two Sessions, he presents himself for the Scholar's Examination; at the end of three Sessions, for the Inceptor's; and at the end of four Sessions, for the Licentiate's.

The Candidate for these several examinations calls on the Secretary, who, on receiving from him the necessary papers, places his name on the Examination List.

These papers are—1, a permission from the Governor of his House; 2, a certificate from him that he is already a Student, a Scholar, or an Inceptor, as the case may be; and 3, that he is of two Sessions' standing, or, as the case may be, has resided one full Session since his Scholarship, or one full Session since his Inceptorship, in the University.

After satisfying the Examiners, each Candidate receives a testimonial to that effect. A Scholar or Inceptor may present himself for his examination for Inceptor or for Licentiate in that term which completes the Session necessary for his standing; and an Inceptor, examined for his Licence, keeps the whole term by the act of obtaining his Examination certificate.

---

and Regulations of the place' (Newman to Scratton, 4 October 1856, *LD* xvii, p. 397).

§ 27. *Exhibitions and Prizes in Letters*[25] [128]

An Exhibition of £____[26] will be given, for classical proficiency, by *concursus* every November.

The Exhibition lasts for two years. It cannot be enjoyed except during residence; nor be attempted except by Students, not yet Scholars, who intend to reside the full period for the Academical Licence.

The list of books, in which the Examination is to take place, will be published early in the foregoing July; *viz.*, three Greek and three Latin books. The candidates will construe and translate on paper out of them. They will also translate from English prose into Latin prose; will write an English theme; and be examined orally and in writing on (1) Greek and Latin Grammar; (2) Ancient History from the battle of Marathon to death of Alexander, and from the creation of Tribunes to death of Sylla; (3) Ancient Chronology and Geography.

Another Exhibition will be proposed under the same circumstances (except the requirements for success, which

---

[25] As early as October 1851 Newman had insisted on having a good fund for scholarships and prizes to help 'the deserving students and create a sort of model set of men, who would form the nucleus of a good tradition'. This emphasis on merit and the worthy student can be traced back to Newman's days at Oriel when he fiercely opposed the unearned privileges and immunities that the gentlemen-commoners enjoyed; but an additional reason for founding bursaries to help 'the poorer and meritorious class of students' was to counter the effect of the generous scholarships made available by the British government in order to entice students into the Queen's Colleges (Newman to Cullen, 14 October 1851, *LD* xiv, p. 389).

From the outset, the three Queen's Colleges each offered forty-five junior scholarships worth £30 p.a., and there was the promise of senior ones worth £50 p.a. to follow. During the period 1851–58 the average annual number of matriculations between them was 134.

[26] The missing amount is £35.

of course will be higher), to the competition of Scholars who are not yet Inceptors.

No one can compete for an Exhibition without the permission of his Head, forwarded to the Rector.

Five prizes of £5 each will be proposed for competition every July, to be decided in November, the exercises required being in writing.[27]

* § 28. *Medical and Scientific Burses*

Any gentleman, till the number of ten is filled up,
[129] presenting himself to the Rector with a letter of nomination from his Bishop and a written declaration to the effect that he is preparing to study Medicine or other science in the University Schools, and wishes to pass two years previously in the School of Philosophy and Letters, will, on satisfying the entrance examination, be furnished with a room in St Patrick's House, and £40 a session towards his board and other expenses for the space of two years.[28] The first £20 will be put to his credit on his passing his entrance examination and completing one Term in the House; the second on his completing his first Session; the third on his

---

[27] As a spur to academic endeavour over the summer of 1855, Newman had announced that seven prizes of five guineas each were open for competition. The requirement for applicants were: an essay in English comparing the views of named Classical authors; a translation into English of a passage from Virgil; a Greek exercise; a composition in Latin describing the death of Alexander the Great; an account in English of the conversion of Ireland; knowledge of MacLaurin's account of Newton's discoveries; and knowledge of conic sections geometrically illustrated. The first five were to be submitted to the Rector on return after the summer, candidates being 'bound in honour to offer only what is bona fide the result of their own labour'; the latter two were to be decided by examination at the beginning of November (University transactions 1854–80, p. 21, CU10, UCDA). The students were warned that prizes would not be awarded if entries failed to reach a minimum standard.

[28] See the footnote on p. [68].

completing the first Term of his second Session, and the fourth and last on his completing his second Session and passing his Scholar's examination.

[130]

IV. EXAMINATIONS

§ 29. *First or Entrance Examination*

The subjects of this Examination are, Latin and Greek construing and parsing, one classical work in each language being presented by the candidate for the purpose; translation into Latin; general knowledge of Greek and Roman history; the elements of geography; the first book of Euclid's elements; the rules of arithmetic, proportion, fractions, decimals, and square root; and the matter of the Gospel according to St Matthew, and of any approved Catechism. Deficiency in Greek may be compensated by proficiency in mathematics.

The main object of an Entrance Examination is simply this, *viz*., to ascertain whether a candidate for admission is in a condition to profit by the course of study, to which on admission he will be introduced. Such examination need not go *beyond*, but it must go *as far* as this. A University does not take the charge of boys, or the first steps in education; it professes to continue, and, in a certain sense, to complete, the education of those who have already done with school, but are not yet fully prepared for the business of life and intercourse with the world. Education is a process steadily carried on through years, on fixed principles, towards a
[131] definite end; as is its termination, so must have been its beginning, and its continuation is according to its course hitherto. A desultory method of study (if method it can be called), in which one part has no connection with another, is not education: if it were, an Examination at Entrance either

would be superseded altogether, or certainly would have some object of its own, which those who advocated such a mode of education would have to define and recommend. Those, however, who adopt the ordinary, and (as it may be presumed) the obvious view, that it is the same in kind from first to last, and that its later stages are but the scope of its earlier, and that its earlier were traversed in order to its later, will easily understand, that, if a University professes to teach the classics, mathematics, and other branches of study, it must have the assurance, provided it is conscientiously to fulfil its promise, that the students, whom it takes in charge, are already well grounded in the *elements* of those studies. The Entrance Examination, then, to which Candidates for admission into a University are subjected, is, from the reason of the case, an examination in *those subject matters*, on which the University course of teaching is to be employed, and is an *elementary* examination in them.

When, for instance, it is said that one of the subjects of the Entrance Examination is to be "the elements of geography," it means that the Candidate will be expected to know the general facts necessary for the prosecution of that study, such as a Lecturer will be disposed naturally and fairly to take for granted. It would be preposterous indeed, if [132]
a University expected the Candidate for Entrance to have studied such subjects as the physical formation of the Earth, its rocks and minerals, its peculiarities of heat and cold, of dryness and moisture, its productions, and its races, whether of brute animals or men; such study is his very business at the University. On the other hand, it is not unreasonable, rather it is very necessary, that a Professor of this great department of knowledge should be allowed to take for granted, that the students he is addressing have some general knowledge, such as that the Earth is round, and not square, that it is of a certain size, that the relative positions of places on it, and distances from point to point, are

expressed by means of certain received, though artificial, standards and measures, *e.g.* latitude and longitude; that its sea and land are scientifically divided into oceans, seas, channels, continents, islands, peninsulas, and so on, with certain recognized names; and that it has certain chains of mountains, isolated peaks, volcanoes, capes, lakes, and rivers; and that all these have their names, and that such and such are the names appropriated to the principal of them. To lecture to young men not knowing as much as this, is like talking English to a Frenchman who has never studied our language.

Another subject of examination set down above is "general knowledge of Greek and Roman history,"—*e.g.*, to take the simplest case, what the state of the world was when our Lord came on the earth, who were the ruling people,
[133] under what Emperor He was born, under whom He suffered: again, what were the principal revolutions of Pagan Rome; what the principal wars during the growth of its power. And so as regards Greece: the principal states into which it was divided; the several characters of the greatest of them; and the great events of its and their history;—and further, the principal heroes and worthies of both Greece and Rome;—who was Leonidas, who Socrates, who Epaminondas, who Scipio, who Julius Caesar.

As to "the elements of Latin and Greek Grammar," here some explanation is perhaps necessary, from the ambiguity of the word "grammar". In the ancient sense of the word, grammar is almost synonymous with "literature". A professor of grammar in Roman and Medieval times was one who lectured on the writers of Greece and Rome; and in this sense "grammar" was accounted one of the seven great departments of knowledge. But there is another sense, more familiar in this day; as when we speak of a Greek or Latin Grammar. In a word, Grammar, in this sense, is the scientific analysis of language, and to be conversant with it, as regards a particular language, is to be able to understand the meaning and force of that language when thrown into sentences and paragraphs.

This is the sense in which the word is used, when it is proposed to examine Candidates at entrance, in the "elements of Latin and Greek Grammar"; not, that is, in the elements of Latin and Greek literature, as if they were to have a smattering of the classical writers in general, and were to be able to give an opinion about the eloquence of [134]
Demosthenes and Cicero, the value of Livy, or the existence of Homer; or need have read half a dozen Greek and Latin authors, and portions of a dozen others:— though of course it would be much to their credit if they had done so; only, such proficiency is not to be expected, and cannot be required, of a Candidate for entrance:—but it means examination in their knowledge of the *structure and characteristics* of the Latin and Greek languages, that is, in their *scholarship*.[29]

It is for the same reason that one book of Euclid's elements of geometry is set down among the subjects of examination. If a Candidate has mastered the process of reasoning as contained in one book, he will be able to proceed with profit; he has crossed and surmounted the main difficulty in the science, by the mere circumstance of having begun. He who has possessed himself of the fifth

---

[29] Academics at the Catholic University would have learnt what Newman meant by superficial knowledge when reading 'The Entrance Examination a trial of accuracy', which describes an oral exam in Latin and Greek and illustrates the importance of the principle of 'really know what you say you know' (*CUG* 4 (22 June 1854), p. 26; *Idea*, p. 335). The article conveys Newman's view that precise and accurate reading, rather than merely wide reading, is the key to educational progress; it encapsulates the approach that Newman championed against those who urged a superficial omniscience (*Idea*, pp. 142, 146, 149). For another article, 'On Latin Composition', which concludes with a classic statement of Newman's education theory, see *CUG* 34 (18 January 1855), p. 296; *Idea*, p. 371.

proposition, may be wanting indeed in diligence and resolution, but not in ability, to overcome the sixth and seventh.

And in like manner, even if "arithmetic" does not contain the elements of algebra, at least it is a necessary preliminary to the study, smoothing its first difficulties. It is discouraging to a Tutor to discover, after proceeding some way in algebra with a pupil, that he has no knowledge of vulgar and decimal fractions, and does not understand what is meant by extracting the square root. University teaching has a claim to be secured against this inconvenience.

Lastly, an examination into the Candidate's knowledge of the elements of Revealed Religion is proposed on
[135] account of the evident congruity of requiring it. By "elements" is meant the main facts and doctrines on which Christianity is established. It would be a reproach to a Christian University if its students were well furnished and ready in the details of secular knowledge, without a corresponding acquaintance with those divine truths which alone give to secular knowledge its value and its use. Nor need we go far for the information we are seeking. In the Gospel we have an inspired record of the Lord's life and mission; and in the authorized catechisms of the Church we are furnished with infallible information as to the great mysteries to which His life and mission were directed. It is not much to ask of the Candidate for admission into a Catholic school of learning, that he should be familiar with our Lord's discourses, miracles, and parables, and with those doctrines the knowledge of which is necessary directly or indirectly to his own salvation.

§ 30. *Second Examination, viz., for the Scholarship*

The following is the scheme of the Examination at present proposed for Candidates for the Scholarship, being considered eighteen years old, and having passed two Sessions already under the superintendence of responsible masters and tutors.

The Candidate will present *three* out of the following *four* subjects of examination; he may take his choice of the first and fourth, the second and third are fixed.

1. The text and matter of one Greek book; *e.g.*

(1) Xenophon, Anabasis, seven books.
(2) Herodotus, two books. [136]
(3) Thucydides, one book.
(4) Homer, four books.
(5) Euripides, four plays.
(6) Sophocles, two plays.
(7) Æschylus, Agamemnon.
(8) Xenophon, Memorabilia; etc., etc.

2. The text and matter of one Latin book; *e.g.*

(1) Livy, five books.
(2) Tacitus, Germania, Agricola, and De Claris Oratoribus.
(3) Cæsar, de Bello Gallico.
(4) Cicero, Select Orations (half).
(5) Cicero, Orationes Verrinæ.
(6) Cicero, Tuscul. Quæst.
(7) Cicero, de Officiis.
(8) Cicero, de Natura Deor.
(9) Virgil, Æneid, six books.
(10) Virgil, Bucolics and Georgics.
(11) Horace, Odes.
(12) Horace, Epistles; etc., etc.

3. (1) Philosophy:—

e.g., Cardinal Wiseman's Scientific Lectures; Fénelon on the existence of God; Schlegel's Philosophy of History.[30]

(2) Criticism:—

e.g., Burke on the Sublime and Beautiful; André, Sur le Beau; Lowth, de Poesi Hebræorum; Portions
[137] of the Theatre of the Greeks: Müller's History of Greek Literature; Copleston's or Keble's Prelections.[31]

(3) Geography:—

e.g., Arrowsmith's Grammar of Ancient Geography; Adams' Summary of Geography and History; Paul and Arnold's Handbook of Ancient Geography.[32]

(4) Chronology:—

e.g., Portion of Clinton's Fasti Hellenici.[33]

(5) Mathematics:—

---

[30] The books in question are: N. Wiseman, *Twelve Lectures on the Connexion between Science and Revealed Religion* (1836), F. Fénelon, *Evidence of the Existence of God* (trans. 1779) and F. Schlegel, *Philosophy of History* (trans. 1835).

[31] E. Burke, *On the Sublime and Beautiful* (1801), Y.-M. André, *Sur le Beau* (1767), R. Lowth, *De Sacra Poesi Hebræorum* (1753), M. Müller, *History of the Literature of Ancient Greece* (1836, trans. 1840), E. Copleston, *Praelectiones* (1813) and J. Keble, *Praelectiones* (1842).

[32] A. Arrowsmith, *Grammar of Ancient Geography: Compiled for the Use of King's College School (*1832), A. Adams, *Summary of Geography and History both Ancient and Modern* (1794) and W. Pütz, *Handbook of Ancient Geography and History* (trans. 1849, R. B. Paul and T. K. Arnold).

[33] H. Clinton, *Fasti Hellenici* (1824).

e.g., Six books of Euclid; Algebra to Quadratics, inclusive; Trigonometry, etc.

(6) Logic:—
e.g., Murray's Compendium of Logic, by Wheeler.[34]

(7) Physical Science:—
e.g., Arnott's Physics; Whewell's History of the Inductive Sciences; Herschell's Outlines of Astronomy, etc.[35]

4. One modern language and literature.

Besides these three subjects of examination, every Candidate must be prepared with an exact knowledge of the matters contained in some longer Catechism and in the four Gospels, and with a general knowledge of ancient history, geography, chronology, and the principles of composition, as already specified at the Entrance Examination. A more exact and a wider knowledge of religious matters will be required of those who are proposing, after the Scholarship, to pass on to any of the other four Faculties.

SPECIMENS OF EXAMINATION LIST TO BE GIVEN IN BY CANDIDATES FOR THE SCHOLARSHIP, IN ACCORDANCE WITH THE ABOVE SCHEME [138]

1. Xenophon's Anabasis—Cicero's Offices—Logic, etc.
2. Xenophon's Memorabilia—Horace's Odes—Logic.
3. Herodotus—Georgics and Bucolics—Euclid.
4. Herodotus—Æneid—Algebra.

---

[34] *Murray's Compendium of Logic* (1847) with commentary by J. Walker and explanatory notes by G. B. Wheeler.

[35] N. Arnott, *Elements of Physics* (1827), W. Whewell, *History of the Inductive Sciences* (1837), and J. F. W. Herschel, *Outlines of Astronomy* (1849).

5. Homer—Horace's Epistles—Geography.

6. Euripides—Tacitus, as above—French Language and Literature.

7. Horace's Epistles—Conic Sections—French Language and Literature.

8. Cicero's Offices—Differential Calculus—German Language and Literature.

9. Bucolics and Georgics—Lowth, de Poesi Hebræorum—Italian language and Literature.

10. Cicero, de Finibus—Melchior Canus, de locis Theol.—French Language and Literature.

11. Cicero, de Natura Deorum—Vincent of Lerins, Commonitorium —Italian Language and Literature.

12. Æschylus, Agamemnon—Cicero's Verrine Orations—Dixon on Scripture.

13. Thucydides—Cicero, Select Orations, as above—Brown's Greek Literature.

14. Æschylus, Choephorœ—Æneid—Becker's Gallus.

It will be observed from these examples, that the list can be adapted to the classical student, the ecclesiastic, or those who are intended for engineering, for business, etc.

[139] § 31. *The Third and Fourth Examinations for Licentiate in Letters*

All members of the University, till they become Scholars, pursue the same studies and the same intellectual discipline. If there are to be exceptions to this rule, as in the case of Agriculture,[36] they do not come into consideration here. The School of Letters, and the Scholarship with its

---

[36] A School of Agriculture was never opened. There was one at Queen's College, Galway, but the commissioners recommended closing it because it was not a success (*Royal Commission Queen's Colleges* (1858), p. 22).The Benedictines founded an agricultural college in Leopardstown near Dublin in 1867, and it was affiliated to the Catholic University for the period 1874–77, but it closed down in 1888.

two previous Examinations, are the ordinary approach to the other Schools. And then those who are destined for Civil Engineering, Manufacture, and similar pursuits, betake themselves to the Faculty of Science; while the Students in Theology, Law, and Medicine, go off to the Faculties which bear those names respectively. The Studies and Examinations proper to other Faculties will be described elsewhere: here we proceed with the School of Letters, about which one or two remarks are first to be made.

1. It must be observed that portions of certain subjects belonging to other Faculties, being parts of a Liberal Education, still come into its teaching, as in the former Sessions; such as, for instance, theological and mathematical works.

2. Next, it is important that the School of Letters has now lost those who never really belonged to it, and who used it by constraint, as the way to other Schools. It now addresses none but those who voluntarily attend its classes as an end; and its peculiar studies gain accordingly, and the character of its Examination is materially affected.

3. Moreover, this Examination, which is the qualification [140]
for the Academical Licence, and takes place at the end of the fourth Session from entrance, has a double scope, *viz*., to ascertain whether the examinee's knowledge is sufficient, on the one hand, for the Licence, or has a claim for honours on the other. Perhaps he presents extra books, and extra subjects; and if his trial ends favourably to him, he is not only *satisfactory*, but *meritorious*. This being the case, it has been thought best to divide the Licentiate Examination into two, and to place the first portion of it earlier, *viz.,* at the end of the Third Session, with the name of the Examination for Inceptor. Its object is to find whether the Candidate is in the way to *satisfy* the Examiners; though as the Examination is not complete and finished till the end of the Fourth Session, he is after all only an Inceptor. The Examination

for *merit* is left wholly to the second Examination at the end of the Fourth Session. According to this arrangement, Inceptor and Licentiate, with their Examinations, will somewhat correspond to Student and Scholar.

The subject matter on which both Examinations are engaged, is fourfold: 1. Christian Knowledge; 2. Philosophy; 3. Literature; 4. History. How these departments of study are to be employed for the ascertainment of (1) sufficiency and (2) merit, shall next be explained.

I. STANDARD OF NECESSARY PROFICIENCY FOR THE LICENCE IN LETTERS

The four Heads of examination mentioned at the end of the foregoing paragraph, when applied to Candidates who
[141] aim only at *satisfying* the Examiners, stand as follows:—

1. Knowledge of the Four Gospels and the Acts of the Apostles; of the history of the Old Testament; and of an extended Catechism.
2. Logic; six books of Euclid; Algebra to Quadratics.
3. One Greek and one Latin Historian or Orator; *i.e.*, a sufficient portion of their works.
4. One out of the six tercenaries of Profane History since the Christian era; (1) from A.D. 1 to 300; (2) 300–600; (3) 600–900; (4) 900–1200; (5) 1200–1500; (6) 1500–1800.

Of these four subjects the Candidates, whether for the necessary or meritorious standard, present, at the end of the Third Session, for their Inceptorship, (1) knowledge of the Four Gospels, Acts, etc.; (2) Logic, six books of Euclid, Quadratics; and (3) Latin Historian. They reserve (3) Greek Historian, and (4) Profane History, to the end of the Fourth Session, when they receive their Licence.

Appendix – IV

SPECIMENS OF EXAMINATION LIST FOR NECESSARY PROFICIENCY

1st Head—Four Gospels, etc., as prescribed,
2nd—Logic, etc., as prescribed,
3rd—(1) Latin Historian or Orator—
e.g., Sallust,
or Livy, half decade,
or Cicero, Select Orations,
or Cicero, Verrine,
or Cicero, Philippics,
or Tacitus, Annals,

(at Inceptor examination)

(2) Greek Historian or Orator— [142]
e.g., Xenophon's Hellenics,
or Herodotus—i–iv, or v–ix,
or Thucyd.—i–iv or v–viii,
or Speeches from Thucydides,
or Lysias,
or Demosthenes and Æschines, etc.,
or Polybius, etc.,

(at Licentiate examination)

4th—300 years of Profane History, as prescribed.

II. STANDARD OF MERITORIOUS PROFICIENCY FOR THE LICENCE IN LETTERS

The four Heads of Examination, when viewed as the trial for honours, stand as follows:—

1. Christian Knowledge.
   (1) The Church. (2) Holy Scripture. (3) Literature of Religion. (4) Philosophy of Religion.

2. Philosophy
(5) Logic. (6) Metaphysics. (7) Ethics. (8) Schools of philosophy, ancient and modern. (9) Politics and Law of nations. (10) Political economy. (11) Political geography. (12) Ethnology. (13) Polite criticism and Science of taste. (14) Philology. (15) Geometry.

[143] 3. Literature
(16) Latin classics. (17) Greek classics. (18) Celtic language and literature. (19) English language and literature. (20) Two foreign literatures. (21) Hebrew.

4. History.
(22) Ancient history—Greek. (23) Do. Roman. (24) Medieval—Eastern. (25) Do. Western. (26) Modern. (27) Ecclesiastical.

Of these 27 subjects, one under each Head is absolutely necessary for being a Candidate for honours.

The Examination for honours is at the end of the Fourth Session, previous to the Academical Licence.

Each subject, both in the necessary and meritorious Examinations, that is, the Examinations both for Inceptor and Licentiate, has a certain number of marks attached to it, greater or less, varying with the particular subject. The details of the performances of each Candidate are also determined by marks.

SPECIMENS OF EXAMINATION LISTS FOR MERITORIOUS PROFICIENCY

The following are specimens of the smallest admissible lists, with the smallest admissible new matter, in addition to that required for the necessary examination; for this is all that need be determined. Of course the *more* that is presented, the *more* meritorious, provided it be done well.

I. Christian Knowledge.
Dixon on Holy Scripture.[37]

2. Philosophy. [144]
Copleston, de Quatuor Fontibus Poeseos (say, already presented for Scholarship).

3. Literature.
(1) 7 plays of Euripides (say, 4 of them already at Scholarship).
(2) 5 books Herodotus (required for *necessary* Examination, even without attempting meritorious).
(3) Virgil's Æneid (say, six books of it already at Scholarship).
(4) Cicero's Philippics (say, already at Inceptor Examination).

4. Medieval history, *i.e.* A.D. 800 (Charlemagne)—1454 (Mahomet II)—(of which 300 years, *e.g.* A.D. 900–1200, is already required for *necessary* examination).
1. Christian Knowledge. Clarke on the Attributes.[38]
2. Philosophy. Enfield's History of Philosophy.[39]

---

[37] This is probably M. C. Dixon, *Tables and Suggestions, Intended to Promote a Thorough and Profitable Reading of the Holy Scriptures* (1853).

[38] S. Clarke, *A Demonstration of the Being and Attributes of God and Other Writings* (1705).

[39] W. Enfield, *The History of Philosophy, from the Earliest Times to the Beginning of the Present Century: drawn up from Brucker's Historia Critica Philosophiæ* (1819).

3. Literature.

Greek only. Homer's Iliad, xii books (four of these already for Scholarship).

Sophocles, vii plays (required for necessary examination).

Xenophon's Hellenics.

Xenophon's Memorabilia.

4. History.

Ecclesiastical (No. 27 above), by which is meant, Say
(1) outline and chronology of principal events,
(2) general knowledge of the principal Popes,
[145] (3) of the General Councils,
(4) of persecutions,
(5) of national conversions and spread of the Gospel,
(6) of heresies,
(7) of chief episcopal sees,
(8) of principal Fathers.

Together with Profane History of A.D. 1–300, as required for necessary examination.

[146]

No. V

Memorandum of the Rector, addressed to the Synodal Meeting of June 20, 1856

MY LORDS,

Though I hope to be able, by word of mouth, to satisfy any questions on the subject of the arrangements of the University, which your Lordships may condescend to put to me, yet I trust I shall have your Lordships' sanction if I prefer to put down upon paper some suggestions I wish to make on one or two very important and practical points to which your thoughts will naturally be turned, as soon as the subject of the University engages them, and which are better dealt with when taken together and reduced to writing, than when they are brought forward in desultory conversation.

I consider then, that, omitting abstract views and objects, of whatever kind, you will now be asking from me, *what*, at this moment, the University definitely aims at effecting for the Catholic Church and for Ireland, *what sums* are requisite for such purposes, and *how* these sums are to be brought together. These are the questions on which I propose to submit to you a few observations.

I. *Immediate objects to be compassed by the University* [147]

1. I contemplate, then, first of all, cooperating with and aiding the present system of education and the schools throughout the country; and that with an especial view of preserving the Catholic population of the middle and higher ranks from the formidable anti-Catholic influences (which need not be more particularly described) which are likely soon to be brought against them. This is to be done by the

affiliation of schools to the University, and other similar measures.

Secondly, I would provide a library of educational works for the schools of the middle and upper classes. This will be done by means of the Professors.

A third object is that of preparing, by suitable instruction, the Catholic youth of this country successfully to compete for the places lately thrown open by the Government and Legislature in the engineering and artillery departments,[1] in the civil service, and in the India appointments. This also will be done by means of the Professors.

And a fourth is that of securing the moral and liberal education of the Medical Profession, a profession which can, of all others, be an aid and support to the parish priests in the country at large. This is to be done by establishing a Medical School in Dublin, and by providing burses for students in connection with it.

[148] In addition to these objects are others, which, if they have not the same direct and tangible utility, yet obviously approve themselves to the mind; such as the encouragement of Irish Archaeology, and again of the Physical Sciences, an object which was especially urged upon me when I lately was at Rome.[2]

---

[1] The prospectus of the Engineering School for 1855/56 describes the first-year course at the Catholic University and the provision made for the Woolwich entrance exams (Cullen papers, 45/3/VI(27), DDA). In 1856 P. F. Gallwey, a student at the Catholic University, passed the entrance exams for the College of Military Engineering at Woolwich. Advertisements were placed in the Catholic press in October 1856 to the effect that pupils were prepared at the Catholic University for the entrance exams of the Royal Artillery and Royal Military Academy at Woolwich.

[2] Despite Rome's encouragement for Newman to promote the physical sciences at the Catholic University, the Irish bishops showed little or no interest. Professor W. K. Sullivan, by reputation a leading scientist, came close to resigning in 1858 out of frustration with the bishops, because he

An additional and most momentous object which might be mentioned, is that of theological teaching; but I prefer to leave that sacred science to the charge of your Lordships, who are its legitimate guardians; and in the remarks I proceed to make, I shall contemplate only those secular Faculties, which, though they never should be severed from religion, have Professors and Schools of their own, and from the very circumstance that their subject matter may so easily, and is so commonly, directed against the Church, have a greater claim on the attention and solicitude of the Rector of a University.

II. *Expenses of the University*

1. *Ordinary Expenses*

Of the Secular Faculties, Law cannot at present be provided for; we must like the Queen's Colleges, contemplate only three, Medicine, Philosophy and Letters, and Science. These three Faculties will cost £4000 a year; *viz*., Medicine, £1000; Philosophy and Letters, £2000; and Science, £1000. Adding to this sum, the cost of administration and accommodation, which includes Rector, [149]
Vice-Rector, Secretary, and other officers, Church room, affiliation of schools, and similar expenses, we have a total

---

felt they had no idea what teaching science meant and of the level of investment it required. When he left in 1873 to become president of Queen's College, Cork, he wrote to the politician William Monsell, 'The bishops' ideal of a University is certainly not mine. [...] The bishops want a Seminary or rather a number of Diocesan Seminaries under their absolute control. With them Science and secular learning are naturally secondary objects', and while they spotted dangers to faith in these disciplines, they did not see their 'importance as an element of secular education' (16 June 1873, quoted in Larkin, *Consolidation of the Roman Catholic Church, 1860–1870* (Chapel Hill: University of North Carolina Press, 1987), pp. 381–2).

of ordinary expenses of £5000. And this is the sum which I mentioned to your Lordships, as likely to be necessary for our ordinary expenses, in the paper which I presented to you at the Synodal Meeting two years ago.

It is certainly a large sum for secular instruction; but, when it is analysed, I trust it will be acquiesced in by your Lordships, as I have reason to hope was the case at the date to which I have referred.

I would beg to submit, first of all, that there are other methods you might have pursued, which to no one would have seemed extraordinary, and which would have involved you in far great expenses. It would have been natural, had I recommended your Lordships to build a college, as the Government has done at Cork and elsewhere. But such a building must have been spacious and handsome, with a Church as part of the plan, as becomes the dignity of the Hierarchy and Church of Ireland. Here would have been an outlay in site, building, and furnishing, of perhaps £50,000. Say part of it was first built, at the cost of £30,000; here would have been a loss of interest to the amount of £1050 a year. Moreover, in a building, consisting of a multitude of rooms, and inhabited by young men, who have no care even of their own property, the yearly deterioration of fabric and furniture is not to be rated under £1 per cent, or £300 a year. Here at once is an annual expense of £1350, with nothing to
[150] put against it but the room-rent to be derived from the students, if in the first years of the erection of the fabric there were students to fill it.

And, after this had been done, still the payment of Professors would have had to engage our consideration, as a second and fresh head of expenditure, towards which the outlay on building contributed little or nothing, beyond lodgings for some of them, and lecture-rooms for their classes.

In considering, then, the sum above set down for the due establishment of the Secular Faculties, it will be equitable to bear in mind, that, even granting I am proposing an unusual outlay in Professorial Chairs, I have avoided an outlay in another direction. But I do but propose what is moderate and reasonable, as a little explanation will show.

A University, such as ours, is of a character far more comprehensive than that of the Government Colleges; moreover, those Colleges are able to offer to men of intellect and attainments various inducements peculiar to themselves. It is not indeed to be supposed that any persons, who vacillated between Institutions so different, and were swayed this way or that by temporal motives, would be fit candidates for the chairs of a Catholic University. Still, all remuneration goes upon the principle of recognized standards; and the advantages on the whole which we offer to distinguished talent should not be inferior, as far as we can hinder it, to those which are held out elsewhere. This implies in some cases a money payment even higher than [151]
that which is fixed at the Government Colleges: and it would not be surprising if our annual expenditure for the Academical Staff, were even greater than theirs. This, however, is not the case. The annual cost of Queen's College, Cork, is £5350; £350 above the sum which I have fixed for the University.

The details of comparison between the two institutions run as follows:—The administration at Cork (by which I mean the President, Registrar, Bursar, and other officers), comes to £1900 a-year; ours is at present somewhat above £700. On the Faculty of Science £1400 is expended at Cork; I allot to the same Faculty in the University, £1000. Medicine at Cork costs £600; I have assigned £1000 as the annual expense of our Medical School; but this sum will gradually decrease with increase of pupils; and it will be observed, moreover, that the increase of outlay here (£400) is not more than the sum which we save, in comparison with Cork, in the Faculty of Science; so that, taking the two Faculties of Medicine and Science together, I propose the very same sum in our own case, which is devoted to them at the Queen's College, *viz*., £2000.

In Philosophy and Letters, I own I exceed the expenditure of the Government institution; there the Professors come to £1450; with us they cost £400 more, nay, from first to last, perhaps they will run up to £2000 altogether. But here several material considerations have to
[152] be carefully weighed: first, the important subject of History is almost omitted from the Government system of teaching, and that of necessity, it being impossible to treat this great province of learning in a College of mixed education.[3] Remarkable it is, that the vast range of Ancient and Modern History is there a mere appendage to the Chair of English Literature; but this, disadvantageous as it is to a School of Letters, is certainly a considerable saving of expense. Again, Irish Archaeology, a subject especially interesting to the Church of this country, has a chair in our University, but not at Cork. It must be added that, in order to ensure in the case of our students a knowledge of their religion befitting a Catholic University, I have appointed a Lecturer in Holy Scripture and Catechism.[4] This measure has already been attended with the most salutary effects; but, though the

---

[3] It is worth noting that when Gladstone introduced his scheme to reform Irish university education in 1873, he included 'gagging clauses' by which he sought to exclude not just theology and philosophy but even modern history (R. Shannon, *Gladstone: Heroic Minister, 1865–1898* (London: Penguin, 1999), p. 123).

[4] When William Penny started acting as University Catechist in Creed and Scripture in Michaelmas Term 1855, all interns were required to attend the catechetical instructions he gave four evenings a week, as well as the course of lectures he gave on the Roman Catechism at 10 am on Sundays, before High Mass.

salary is low, it is of course an addition to the expense of the Faculty to which it is attached.

It is simply impracticable, taking things as they are, to secure first-rate men for the purposes of the University, without giving them an income sufficient for their decent maintenance. The standard of a Professor's remuneration, as sanctioned by the Committee appointed at the National Synod, is £300, with certain additions; as yet I have only in a few cases, and in these for special reasons, risen to this sum. In the whole number of chairs, only four have £300 a year assigned to them: two Professors, besides, fill chairs in distinct schools, which, united, give them the same income. Only four Professors more have as much as £200. Of the fourteen Professors in the Faculty of Philosophy and Letters, ten only receive salary of any kind: taking the whole expense of the Faculty, as I have stated it, at £1850, [153]
the average of salaries is not more than £185.

The University of Louvain pays its Professors better than any of the Government Universities of Belgium; and I am told that, probably, there is no lay Professorship under £500 a year. There is a case—an extraordinary one certainly, but I relate it on the authority of a friend,—of one Professor of Law who received an annual income of £800 sterling from the University, with a pension of £500 to his widow on his death. Mœhler was offered at Bonn a Chair of Theology at 5000 dollars a year—more than £700. At Bonn, the father of Professor Windischmann, who filled the chair of Moral Philosophy, had a salary of £300 a year, which, I am told, is equal to £450 in this country. At Edinburgh, I am told, the Professor of Physiology has £1200. Under these circumstances, our rate of remuneration, though heavy for our funds, is not excessive.

The only plausible objection which might be urged against the above representations, is that however reasonable such a University scheme may be in itself, it

cannot be expected here for some time to produce fruit proportional to the labour, ability, and expense which it supposes. And certainly I must grant that the students who come to the University will not at once be adequate to the staff of Professors. But this difficulty is in the nature of the case; whenever a great object is to be attained, there must be a considerable previous outlay. In the world, such an outlay
[154] for a prospective advantage is called a speculation; and a risk which is grounded on reasonable expectations, is not considered reprehensible or absurd. In our case certainly the difficulty is greater than that of a common enterprise, inasmuch as we have in great measure to make the public sensible of the existence of the want, which we profess to supply; yet those who are acting under the Holy See and a Catholic Hierarchy need have no fear, lest ventures made in faith, however anxious, should be ultimately unsuccessful.[5]

[5] Reflecting in 1870 on the predicament of the Catholic University and its many problems, Newman concluded that if the Holy See had been better informed it would never have promoted the project in the first place. It had always seemed to Newman that 'a gift of sagacity had in every age characterized' the Holy See, 'so that we might be sure, as experience taught us, without its being a dogma of faith that what the Pope determined was the very measure, or the very policy, expedient for the Church at the time it was determined'; but events in Ireland led him to think that if the Pope had known more about the state of things there, 'he would not have taken up the quarrel about the higher education which his predecessor had left him, and, if he could not religiously have found a way of recognising the Queen's Colleges, then at least he would have abstained from decreeing a Catholic University' ('Memorandum about my Connection with the Catholic University', *AW*, p. 320).

2. *Extraordinary Expenses*

There are certain outlays of money which will happen once and not again, or which cannot be exactly calculated; such was the fitting up of the University House; such was the purchase of the Medical School Buildings in Cecilia Street (the cost of which was defrayed by a private benefactor). Such would be the apparatus necessary for the Lectures of certain Professors; such again is preaching money, such printing; such again, prizes and burses, the number and value of which will vary according to circumstances, and some of which may be sustained (as I have noticed in one instance), by the munificence of friends. It is impossible to calculate the sum to which these items of expenditure will amount.

Against these expenses must be put, as a means of satisfying them, not only the special benefactions alluded to, but the fees paid by the students. According to the Regulations which the Rector and Professors have made, each student will in future pay an annual £10 to the
University as lecture money. If we have 50 students, we [155]
should have £500; if 100, £1000 for the purposes of Burses, Prizes, and similar other extraordinary calls upon our funds. And it is to be borne in mind that, whilst the extraordinary expenses will decrease as time goes on, the lecture fees, it is to be hoped, will be greater and greater every year.

III. *Mode of meeting the Annual Expenditure*

Against the *extraordinary* expenses, and the cost of the *Theological Faculty*, I would put, first, the annual fees students (as I have already said), say at present £600, and, secondly, the interest of the capital of the University, say £1200. £1700 will be more than enough to meet these two heads of expenditure.

What I have called the *ordinary* cost of the University remains, *viz.*, £5000, and it is that which has to be raised from the country.

At present we are under a great disadvantage, in consequence of having no organisation for interesting the people in our wants.

I propose, then, to your Lordships a Committee of three persons, and a clerical Secretary, all of whom shall be presented by the Rector for the approval and nomination of the Archbishops. This Committee shall have the duties of corresponding with the clergy, of advocating the cause of the University through the country, of stimulating and facilitating the payment of contributions into the Trustee Fund, and of receiving from the Trustees the sum assigned by them yearly for University purposes.[6]

[156] They should have an account at the Bank, and should receive from the Trustees yearly: 1. The interest of the Trustee Fund, say, £1200; 2. £5000 for ordinary expenses; and 3. From the Students, the annual fees which are due from them to the University. This should be called the Committee Fund, and the Committee shall pay out of it: 1. The salaries of the Professors, and other ordinary expenses; 2. Such sums to the Theological Faculty as the Archbishops might determine; and 3. They shall be empowered, on application from the Rector, to grant him, according to their own discretion, such sums for extraordinary purposes, as they can give him, without bringing the Fund into debt.

The Committee should be subject to an annual audit of account, and the Clerical Secretary, who will be the chief instrument of collecting contributions for the University

---

[6] This proposal would have fallen on deaf ears as it entailed surrendering control to laity. Cullen was of the view that the University should be firmly in the control of the hierarchy.

from the country, should be remunerated, year by year, by a percentage on the yearly collections.[7]

I would conclude by asking your Lordships, if you approve of these arrangements, as regards the Faculties, the Professors and their salaries, the Committee of Expenses and their powers, to allow them to be tried till your next meeting, with an understanding that the Archbishops will interfere, in case of any unexpected difficulties arising in the way of carrying them out.

Begging your Lordships' blessing on our labours,

I am, etc., etc.

DUBLIN, June 19, 1856[8]

---

[7] For the outcome of Newman's plea for a finance committee, see the relevant footnote on p. [xl].

[8] Newman appeared before the bishops on 26 June, and the following day the synod was concluded. Newman told Allies that they 'have approved of all I have done, have passed all my appointments, and agreed to all my prospective expenditure for three years. They were unanimous' (6 July 1856, *LD* xvii, p. 310).

[157]

No. VI

Letter of the Rector to the Dean of Faculty of Philosophy and Letters on the Introduction of Religious Teaching into the Schools of that Faculty[1]

MY DEAR PROFESSOR,

You have recalled my attention to a subject which has come before us several times,—the place which religious instruction may be considered to hold in the School of Philosophy and Letters. We have certainly felt it ought to have a place in the School, yet the subject is not without its difficulty.[2] The place, if it is to have one, should of course be determined on some intelligible principle, which, while it justifies its introduction into a secular faculty, will preserve it from becoming an intrusion by fixing the limits to which it is to be subjected. There are many who would make over

[1] As Dean of the Arts Faculty, Edward Butler was the recipient of this open letter. After some alterations, it became part four of 'Elementary Studies', under the subtitle 'General Religious Knowledge', in *Lectures and Essays* (pp. 178–86), then in the *Idea* (pp. 372–80). Editorial comments on it can be found in *Idea*, ed. Ker, pp. 646–9.

[2] Ornsby understood from this letter that Newman was thinking of including the teaching of religion in the current business of such professors as Stewart and himself; he reported that Edmund O'Reilly, Professor of Dogmatic Theology, was 'jealous' about some parts of the letter and that he objected to them teaching controversial matters (Ornsby to Newman, 7 August 1857, Dublin Papers 32/7, BOA).

For religious instruction, Newman was able to rely on several Oxbridge graduates who had been Anglican clergymen. Newman's reliance on the laity for religious instruction can be traced back to 1827, when in referring to elementary schools he maintained that 'It seems indeed to be a fundamental mistake in a system of education, when the instructors of youth in general knowledge are not also their religious instructors.' ('On General Education as Connected with the Church and Religion', sermon preached on 19 August 1827, BOA)

the subject of religion to the theologian exclusively;[3] there are others who allow it unlimited extension in the province of Letters. The latter of these two classes is not large, though it is serious and earnest; it considers that Classics should be superseded by the Scriptures and the Fathers, and that Scholastic Theology should be taught to the youthful aspirant for University honours.[4] I am not here concerned [158]
with opinions of this character, which I respect, but cannot follow. Nor am I concerned with that large class on the other hand, who, in their exclusion of religion from the lecture-rooms of Philosophy and Letters, are actuated by scepticism or indifference, but there are other persons, much to be consulted, who arrive at the same practical conclusion as the sceptic and unbeliever, from real reverence and pure zeal for the interests of Theology, which they consider sure to suffer from the superficial treatment of lay-professors, and the superficial reception of young minds, as soon as,

---

[3] In his article in *The Rambler* (July 1859) 'On Consulting the Faithful in Matters of Doctrine', Newman expressed his misgivings about a Church which 'cuts off the faithful from the study of her divine doctrines [...] and requires from them *fides implicita* in her word, which in the educated classes will terminate in indifference, and in the poorer in superstition' (p. 230).

[4] Jean Joseph Gaume (1802–79), a French priest, ignited a lively controversy in France with *Le Ver Rongeur des Société Modernes, ou Paganisme dans l'Éducation* (1851), which appeared in English as *Paganism in Education* (1852). Gaume argued that the revival of interest in pagan antiquity during the Renaissance had paved the way for the Revolution and other social ills; he wanted pagan authors (who had been taught in the Catholic colleges for three centuries) to be largely excluded from the curriculum and replaced by Christian ones. The Gaume controversy had just begun when Newman started his Dublin lectures, and Newman spoke out clearly against the new theory: while acknowledging the opinable nature of the question, he felt that 'the Church's true policy is not to aim at the exclusion of Literature from Secular Schools, but at her own admission into them. [...] She fears no knowledge, but she purifies all; she represses no element of our nature, but cultivates the whole.' (*Idea*, pp. 233–4)

and in whatever degree, it is associated with classical, philosophical, and historical studies. From respect for their opinion, it is necessary for me to state why I have thought it right, in the scheme of Rules which I am submitting to the Senate, to make religious knowledge a subject of examination for the Scholarship and the License.

Here I waive the authority for my proceeding, which I seem to derive from the words of Bishops in May 1854, who expressly enjoin all the teachers and students of the University, 'being strangers to profane novelties which stain the integrity of faith, to follow that knowledge which builds up with charity and be guided by that wisdom whose beginning is the fear of God',[5] a direction, which scarcely will be fulfilled, if a youth can go through our academic course without any direct teaching of a religious character. I waive this authoritative injunction, because mere authority, however sufficient for my own guidance, is not sufficient
[159] for the definite direction of those who have to carry out the matter of it in practice.

In the first place, then, it is *congruous* certainly that youths, who are prepared in a Catholic University for the general duties of a secular life, or for the secular professions,[6] should not leave it without some knowledge of their religion; and, on the other hand, it does, in matter of fact, act, in the world and in the judgment of men of the world, to the disadvantage of a Christian place of education,

---

[5] For the full passage, see section 13 on p. [91].

[6] Implicit in such a statement is an understanding of the laity which affirms their role. Attempts to define the laity within the Church have usually lapsed into negative definitions; but here Newman defines the lay role in positive terms. Newman is one of several theologians credited with the formulation of a 'theology of the laity' *avant la lettre*, though not in any systematic fashion. One of his most telling contributions was his insistence that the laity should assert their freedom and realise their responsibility; another was his insistence that they should be offered an education adapted to lay needs.

and is a reproach to its conductors, and even a scandal, if it sends out its pupils accomplished in all knowledge except Christian knowledge; and hence, even though it were impossible to put the introduction of religious teaching into the secular lecture-rooms upon any scientific principle, the imperative necessity of its introduction would remain, and the only question would be, what matter was to be introduced and how much.

And next, considering that, as the mind is enlarged and cultivated generally, it is capable, or rather is desirous and has need, of fuller religious information, it is difficult to maintain that the knowledge of Christianity which is sufficient for entrance at the University, is all that is incumbent on students who have been submitted to the academical course. So that we are unavoidably led on to the further question, *viz*., shall we sharpen and refine the youthful intellect, and then leave it to exercise its new powers upon the most sacred of subjects, as it will, and with the chance of its exercising them wrongly; or shall we proceed to feed it with divine truth, as it gains an appetite for knowledge?

Religious teaching, then, is urged upon us in the case of [160]
University students, first, by its evident propriety; secondly, by the force of public opinion; thirdly, from the great inconveniences of neglecting it. And, if the subject of religion is to have a real place in their course of study, it must enter into the *examinations* in which that course results; for nothing will be found to impress and occupy their minds, but such matters as they have to present to their Examiners.

Such, then, are the reasons which oblige us to introduce the subject of religion into our secular schools; and in fact I think we can do so without any sacrifice of principle or of consistency, as, I trust, will appear, if I proceed to explain the mode which I propose to adopt for the purpose.

I would treat the subject of religion in the school of Philosophy and Letters, simply as a branch of knowledge. If the University student is bound to have a knowledge of history generally, he is bound to have inclusively a knowledge of sacred history as well as profane; if he ought to be well instructed in ancient literature, Biblical literature comes under that general description as well as classical; if he knows the philosophy of men, he will not be extravagating from his general subject, if he cultivate also the philosophy of God. And as a student is not necessarily superficial, though he has not studied all the classical poets or all Aristotle's philosophy, so he need not be dangerously superficial, if he has but a parallel knowledge of religion.

[161] However, it may be said that the risk of theological error is so serious, and the effect of theological conceit is so mischievous, that it is better for a youth to know nothing of the sacred subject, than to have a slender knowledge, which he can use freely for the very reason that it is slender.

This objection is of too anxious a character to be disregarded. But in the first place it is obvious to answer, that one great portion of the knowledge here advocated is, as I have just said, historical knowledge, which has little or nothing to do with doctrine. If a Catholic youth mixes with educated Protestants of his own age, he will find them conversant with the outlines and the characteristics of sacred and ecclesiastical history as well as profane: it is desirable that he should be on a par with them, and able to keep up a conversation with them. It is desirable, if he has left our University with honours or prizes, that he should know as well as they, the great primitive divisions of Christianity, its polity, its luminaries, its acts, and its fortunes; its great eras, and its course to this day. He should have some idea of its propagation, and the order in which the nations, which have submitted to it, entered its pale; and the list of its Fathers, and of its writers generally, and the

subjects of their works. He should know who St Justin Martyr was, and when he lived; what language St Ephraim wrote in; on what St Chrysostom's literary fame is founded; who was Celsus, Ammonius, Porphyry, Ulphilas, Symmachus, or Theodoric. Who were the Nestorians; what was the religion of the barbarian nations who took [162]
possession of the Roman Empire: who was Eutyches, or Berengarius, who the Albigenses. He should know something about the Benedictines, Dominicans, or Franciscans; about the Crusades, and the chief movers in them. He should be able to say what the Holy See has done for learning and science; the place which these islands hold in the literary history of the dark age; what part the Church had, and how its highest interests fared, in the revival of letters; who Bessarion was, or Ximenes, or William of Wykeham, or Cardinal Allen. I do not say that we can insure all this knowledge in every accomplished student who goes from us, but at least we can admit such knowledge, we can encourage it, in our lecture and examination halls.

And so in like manner, as regards Biblical knowledge, it is desirable that, while our students are encouraged to pursue the history of classical literature, they should also be invited to acquaint themselves with some general facts about the canon of Holy Scripture, its history, the Jewish canon, St Jerome, the Protestant Bible; again, about the languages of Scripture, the contents of its separate books, their authors, and their versions. In all such knowledge I conceive no great harm can lie in being superficial.

But now as to Theology itself. To meet the apprehended danger, I would exclude the teaching *in extenso* of pure dogma from the secular schools, and content myself with enforcing such a broad knowledge of doctrinal subjects as is contained in the catechisms of the Church, or the actual [163] writings of her laity.[7] I would have them apply their minds to such religious topics as laymen actually do treat, and are thought praiseworthy in treating.[8] Certainly I admit that, when a lawyer, or physician, or statesman, or merchant, or soldier sets about discussing theological points, he is likely to succeed as ill as an ecclesiastic who meddles with law, or medicine, or the exchange. But I am professing to contemplate Christian knowledge in what may be called its secular aspect, as it is practically useful in the intercourse of life and in general conversation; and I would encourage it as it bears upon the history, literature, and philosophy of Christianity.

It is to be considered, that our students are to go out into the world, and a world not of professed Catholics, but of inveterate, often bitter, commonly contemptuous Protestants; nay of Protestants who, so far as they come from Protestant Universities and public schools, do know their own system, do know, in proportion to their general attainments, the doctrines and arguments of Protestantism. I should desire, then, to encourage in our students an intelligent apprehension of the relations, as I may call them, between the Church and society at large; for instance, the difference between the Church and a religious sect; between the Church and the civil power; what the Church claims of necessity, what it cannot dispense with, what it can; what it

---

[7] In a letter to *The Rambler* entitles 'Lay Students in Theology' Newman comments that this passage 'agrees pretty nearly with a judgement which I heard, and to which I defer, viz. that laymen may study the Treatises *de Religione* and *de Ecclesia*; but had better keep clear of the high mysteries of faith and of the subject of grace' ('H' [Newman] to *The Rambler* (July 1859), *LD* xix, p. 544).

[8] 'I am opposed to laymen writing Theology, on the same principle that I am against amateur doctors and still more lawyers—not because they are laymen, but because they are *άυτόδιδακτι* [self-taught]. [...] I don't exclude myself. I have not written on dogmatics or asceticism since I have been a Catholic' (Newman to J. M. Capes, 19 January 1857, *LD* xvii, p. 504).

can grant, what it cannot. A Catholic hears the celibacy of the clergy discussed; is that usage of faith, or is it not of faith?[9] He hears the Pope accused of interfering with the [164]
prerogatives of her Majesty, because he appoints an hierarchy.[10] What is he to answer? What principle is to guide him in the remarks which he cannot escape from the necessity of making? He fills a station of importance, and he is addressed by some friend who has political reasons for wishing to know what is the difference between Canon and Civil Law, whether the Council of Trent has been received in France, whether a Priest cannot in certain cases absolve prospectively, what is meant by his *intention*, what by the *opus operatum*;[11] whether, and in what sense we consider Protestants to be heretics; whether any one can be saved without sacramental confession; whether we deny the reality of natural virtue, and what worth we assign to it.[12]

---

[9] Newman writes, 'Heroic, by which I mean self-sacrificing, virtues are, as a general rule, less applicable to fathers of families, simply because all duties are relative, the duty of a man to his wife and children comes before a larger number of more distant duties. This it is which has led, in the Catholic Church, to the celibacy of the clergy; which is no dogma, but a mere consequence of what I may call *the division of labour* consequent on a more developed state of Christian civilisation.' (Newman to *The Rambler* (July 1859), *LD* xix, p. 540).

[10] The restoration of the Catholic hierarchy in England and Wales in 1850 and the manner in which it took place produced a strong 'No Popery' reaction. Protestant outrage was vented from the pulpit and the press, anti-Catholic demonstrations were mounted across the country, and the allegiance of Catholics to the Crown was questioned publicly. The storm of indignation aroused by this 'papal aggression' prompted Newman to deliver his *Lectures on the Present Position of Catholics in England*, ed. A. Nash (1851; Leominster: Gracewing, 2000), p.390.

[11] This refers to the Tridentine formula *ex opere operato* (from the deed done) for the working of the sacraments, which confer grace whatever the merits of the person administering them. For the validity of the sacrament, the person administering it must have the right intention, that is, must have the purpose of doing what the Church intends.

[12] Newman's quotes at length from this open letter to Butler when he writes to *The Rambler* (July 1859, pp. 238–42) a letter entitled 'Lay

Questions may be multiplied without limit, which occur in conversation between friends, in social intercourse, or in the business of life, where no argument is needed, no subtle and delicate disquisition, but a few direct words stating the fact. Half the controversies which go on in the world arise from ignorance of the facts of the case; half the prejudices against Catholicity lie in the misinformation of the prejudiced parties. Candid persons are set right, and enemies silenced, by the mere statement of what it is that we believe. It will not answer the purpose for a Catholic to say, "I leave it to theologians", "I will ask my priest"; but it will commonly give him a triumph, as easy as it is complete, if he can then and there lay down the law. I say
[165] "lay down the law"; for remarkable it is, that, even those who speak against Catholicism, like to hear about it, and will excuse its advocate from alleging arguments, if he can gratify their curiosity by giving them information. Generally speaking, however, as I have said, such mere information will really be an argument also. I recollect some twenty-five years ago three friends of my own, as they then were, clergymen of the Establishment, making a tour through Ireland. In the West or South they had occasion to become pedestrians for the day; and they took a boy of thirteen to be their guide. They amused themselves with putting questions to him on the subject of his religion; and one of them

---

Students in Theology', signed 'H' (*LD* xix, pp. 546–7). He concludes the letter by quoting (anonymously) from a letter from the theologian Victor du Buck, which was passed on to him by a third party: 'My opinion is, which many others share, that at present laymen of a certain rank have more need of knowing *dogmatic* theology, ecclesiastical history, and canon law, than priests. The reason is, that in lay company the deepest and most difficult problems in those subjects are discussed. This is seldom done when any priest is present. Moreover, in your country, laymen have better opportunities than priests to correct a thousand false notions of Protestants.' For the origin of this quotation, see Simpson to Newman, 19 May 1859, *LD* xix, p. 139n.

confessed to me on his return that that poor child put them all to silence.[13] How? Not of course by any course of argument, or refined theological disquisition; but merely by knowing and understanding the answers in his catechism.

Nor will argument itself be out of place in the hands of laymen mixing with the world. As secular power, influence, or resources are never more suitably placed than when they are in the hands of Catholics; so secular knowledge and secular gifts are then best employed when they minister to divine revelation. Theologians inculcate the matter and determine the details of that revelation; they view it from within; philosophers view it from without, and this external view may be called the Philosophy of Religion, and the office of delineating it externally is most gracefully performed by laymen. In the first age laymen were most commonly the Apologists. Such were Justin, Tatian, [166]
Athenagoras, Aristides, Hermias, Minucius Felix, Arnobius, and Lactantius. In like manner in this age some of the most valuable defences of the Church are from laymen: as de Maistre, Chateaubriand, Nicolas, Montalembert, and others.[14] If laymen may write, lay students may read. They

---

[13] Newman refers to this incident in a letter to Froude: 'Dornford was […] pleased with what he saw in Ireland […] He met some very clever Irish lads (Roman Catholics) who knew a great deal about their own tenets, and argued well.' (15 August 1829, *LD* ii, p. 158)

[14] Newman had spoken at length about the need for an educated laity in his last lecture in Birmingham on 1 September 1851. He told his listeners that what was needed were 'men who know their religion, who enter into it, who know just where they stand, who know what they hold, and what they do not, who know their creed so well, that they can give an account of it, who know so much of history that they can defend it. I want an intelligent, well-instructed laity; [...] I wish you to enlarge your knowledge, to cultivate your reason, to get an insight into the relation of truth to truth, to learn to view things as they are, to understand how faith and reason stand to each other' (*Lectures on the Present Position of Catholics in England* (London: Longmans, Green & Co., 1851;1896), p. 390).

may surely study other works too, ancient and modern, whether by ecclesiastics or laymen, which, although they do contain theology, nevertheless, in their structure and drift, are polemical. Such is Origen's great work against Celsus; and Tertullian's Apology; such some of the controversial treatises of Eusebius and Theodoret; or St Augustine's City of God; or the tract of Vincentius Lirinensis. And I confess that I should not even object to portions of Bellarmine's Controversies, or to the work of Suarez on Laws, or to Melchior Canus's treatise on the Loci Theologici. On these questions in details indeed, which are, I readily acknowledge, very delicate, opinion may differ, even when the general principle is admitted; but, even if we confine ourselves strictly to the Philosophy, or the external contemplation of Religion, we shall have a range of reading sufficiently wide, and as valuable in its practical application as it is liberal in its character. In it will be included what are commonly called the Evidences; and, what is an especially interesting subject at this day, the Notes of the Church.[15]

But I have said enough in illustration of the point which has given occasion to my writing to you. One more remark I make, though it is implied in what I have been saying:—
[167] whatever the students read in the province of religion, they read, from the very nature of the problem, under the superintendence, and with the explanations, of those who are older and more experienced than themselves.

I am, etc., etc.

June, 1856

---

[15] Newman wrote to Lucy Agnes Phillips, 'The more *obvious* reasons for believing the Church to come from God are its great notes, as they are called—such as its antiquity, universality, its unchangeableness through so many revolutions and controversies, its adaptation to our wants' (5 June 1851, *LD* xiv, p. 292). The four 'notes' of the Church are usually expressed by saying that she is One, Holy, Catholic and Apostolic.

[169]

REPORT III

FOR THE YEAR 1856–57

MY LORDS,

In bringing before your Lordships the proceedings of your University during the third year of its establishment, I have again to notice, as I noticed when I last addressed you, a material advance in its condition, compared with that which it presented at the end of the foregoing year,—an advance, of which a significant evidence will be afforded by the very character which the Report assumes, on which I am now engaged.

This time last year, I had occasion to remark, that the Session then concluded had been successfully occupied in settling the constituent parts of the University, and in providing a system of academical government and administration. This had constituted the advance of the second year upon the first, during which, as I observed at the same time, we had proceeded, as best we could, without Academical Senate, or Rectoral Council, without any sufficient distribution of the Professors into Faculties, without the support of Statutes, and without any religious [170]
rites, or a place where they might be celebrated.

The advance of the third year upon the second consists in this, that the various departments brought into operation in the University, which were then provided, have by this time so fully come into operation, that the Reports, which have been sent in to me by their respective Deans and Professors, of the proceedings which have severally taken place in them, have not merely furnished me with matter for my own Report to your Lordships, but have even superseded the necessity of my giving expression to it, by supplying the very words in which my Report is to be made.

I beg leave to refer your Lordships especially to the Reports of the Deans of two Faculties, of Dr Hayden, Professor of Anatomy and Physiology, the Dean of the Faculty of Medicine, and Mr Butler, Professor of Mathematics, the Dean of the Faculty of Philosophy and Letters.

1. Dr Hayden, Professor of Anatomy and Physiology, Dean of the Faculty of Medicine, in the year now closing, writes to me as follows:—

"The number of students entered for lectures in the Medical School in its first Session", which was the second Session of the University, "was comparatively small,
[171] amounting to 43. To this result many causes contributed, perhaps the most potent was the fear, entertained by students and fostered by those interested in the success of rival institutions, that our lectures would not be recognized by the licensing bodies."

"Nothing less than the actual demonstration of its groundlessness would have sufficed to remove this impression: accordingly, the Faculty, towards the approach of last Winter Session (1856–7), formally sought recognition of its lectures from the several chartered Medical bodies in Ireland, and had the satisfaction of being able to set forth in its Sessional Prospectus, a complete recognition of all these bodies, without a single exception. The privileges of the school are now, therefore, co-extensive with those of any similar institution in the United Kingdom, because of the conventional rule which makes recognition of any school by the Colleges of the country in which it is situated *primâ facie* evidence of its title before all the others. As a confirmation of the above statement, the

Faculty is now in a position to point to several of its pupils who have passed the examination and obtained the Licence of the College of Surgeons in London, as well as in Dublin, and also to a few who have already entered the public service."

The Dean of Medicine continues: "The Winter Session [172]
commenced in November and ended in April. The total number of students entered for lectures at the closing of the Register on the 25th of November was 59.[1] The course of instruction consisted of Lectures in Anatomy and Physiology, and Demonstrations, and Dissections: of Lectures on Surgery, Chemistry, Practice of Medicine, and Medical Jurisprudence. The Summer Session commenced about the middle of April, and terminated on the 15th of July; the classes amounted in the gross to 21. Lectures were given on Practical Chemistry, Materia Medica, and Medical Jurisprudence.

"Three Gold Medals were awarded by the University in the last year; two in the Winter and one in the Summer Session. Of the former, one was given to the best answering in Anatomy, Physiology, and Chemistry combined, the other in Surgery and Practice of Medicine, whilst the third was awarded in the three subjects of the Summer course. This combination of subjects the Faculty thinks entitled to special notice, as being a novel feature in prize-examinations. It has the advantage of grouping together, in the order in which they engage the attention of the student, the subject of the first and second two years of his studies respectively." The Dean adds that the experiment has been attended with complete success, and he goes on to speak
with high praise of "the industry and good conduct of the [173]
classes," to which he has to notice hardly any exception.

---

[1] The numbers of medical students enrolled in the following three sessions were, respectively, 73, 95 and 110.

After mentioning the lectures of the Professors of Anatomy and Physiology in the latter of these sciences, the Dean proceeds to speak of the Professor of Chemistry, who, he says, "reports most satisfactorily of his class. In this difficult department of science," he continues, "the proficiency attained by the candidates for honours was very remarkable and promises well for the future; a student in the Faculty of Philosophy and Letters, and a native of France, obtained the second prize."

He then notices in succession the reports of the Professors of Surgery, Practice of Medicine, Materia Medica, and Medical Jurisprudence,[2] "which are all of a satisfactory and encouraging character".

I think it well to notice here one remark of the Professor of the Practice of Medicine. "I wish," he says, "to take this opportunity of observing that it is absolutely out of my power to do justice to the important branch of medical education committed to my care, without having that store of *materiel* for illustration to draw upon, that can only be supplied by an Hospital. I have no hesitation in forcibly stating that, until the above deficiency be supplied,
[174] shortcomings are unavoidable in attempting to teach a practical subject like mine." This statement, I doubt not, will recommend itself to the minds of your Lordships, as it does to my own; but it depends, of course, upon the state of the funds of the University whether a remedy can be applied to the deficiency to which it draws your attention. But on this subject the Dean himself will speak presently.

After some observations in detail on the state of the classes, the Dean of Medicine proceeds to speak of the

---

[2] The Professor of Medical Jurisprudence was Stephen Myles MacSwiney (1821–90). He had pursued his medical studies at the Apothecaries' Hall, Cecilia Street, then at St Vincent's Hospital, Dublin. When Newman appointed him he was a member of the Royal College of Surgeons, England, a Doctor of Medicine at St Andrews University, and a Licentiate at the Royal College of Physicians.

Chemical Laboratory. "This important adjunct of the school," he says, "is now in a state of completeness that may safely challenge comparison with anything of a similar kind in these Islands, and the good effects it is likely to produce on the interests of the school can scarcely be overrated;" and he adds a suggestion as to the advisableness of completing the professorial corps by filling up the vacant Chairs of Midwifery and Botany.

With the following extended remarks on the state of the Medical Museum, the need of an Hospital, and the receipts from Students, the Dean brings his observations to an end:—

"The state of the Museum has been the subject of grave and anxious thought to the Faculty. In the present uncertainty as to the exact state of the Finances of the University, the Faculty would be slow to press this subject [175]
on the attention of the authorities, did it not feel the want to be of so urgent a nature as not to admit of longer postponement."

The *materiel* for illustrating the Lectures on Physiology, Pathology, Zoology, and Comparative Anatomy, is sadly defective; and, although in the infant period of the existence of the University, such deficiencies were to be expected, yet now that the School is about entering on its third Winter Session, the classes will naturally require greater effectiveness in the experimental and demonstrative power of these courses, than the meagre collection now at their command enables the Professors to give them. It may be more convenient for the University to grant small sums of money towards the Museum from year to year, as wants are felt in each department, than to advance the whole sum necessary at once. This plan would be found equally convenient, and in the end probably more advantageous to the school; for the collection thus made, having grown with the school, and consisting of objects each of which had been actually found essential or useful, would possess the greatest value at the least expense to the University. It is hoped that, as a beginning, something will be done before the next Session. An advance of even a few hundred pounds would supply the present wants, and enable the Professors to keep faith with the classes."

[176] "The want of an Hospital connection, to which attention has been already directed in the report of the Professor of the Practice of Medicine, is one that is sensibly felt by the Faculty.[3] Its pupils are scattered abroad amongst the Hospitals of the city, where they are often exposed to influences hostile to the interests of the school. Independently of this, unity of instruction, which can only be obtained from the same teachers in the Hospital and School, would seem to require a union of the kind indicated. The value of such a connection has been already so fully appreciated by those most competent to judge, that the late Commission of Inquiry into the Hospitals of this city has strongly recommended it in every instance, and actually made it an essential condition of Government support in the

[3] In June 1856 Newman tried to forge a link between the Catholic University and St Vincent's Hospital, Stephen's Green, which was run by the Sisters of Charity, but failed. (See the correspondence in *LD* xvii, pp. 287, 289n, 334–6, 374; xviii, pp. 107, 110, 144, 523.) Newman was fully involved in the early growth of all the faculties and schools, and had to deal with many petty problems which cumulatively absorbed much of his time and made endless demands on his reserves of diplomacy. The medical school in particular was a drain on his time because he had to encourage doctors to join the concern, negotiate rates of pay, resolve rival claims for titles, and forge links with hospitals. Regarding the latter, Newman also explored links with two hospitals associated with the Sisters of Mercy: the Jervis Street Hospital, where the Sisters took over the nursing and internal management in 1854; and the Mater Misericordiae Hospital, which they had founded in 1852. The latter did not open its doors until 1861, after Newman's departure from Dublin. Thomas Hayden became physician to the Mater Misericordiae Hospital while continuing as Professor of Anatomy and Physiology at the Catholic University.

case of a school recently founded in Dublin. Without the advantage and support to be derived from such an alliance, the Faculty feels it cannot long successfully contend against the powerful and hostile combinations by which it is surrounded. An Hospital and a School are parts of the same system; they are mutually sustaining; what is theoretically taught in the one is demonstrated in the other; pathological specimens are supplied by the Hospital to furnish the Museums, and illustrate the Lectures in the School, which, in return, sends students to the Hospital, whence it derives these advantages."

After observing that, from various accidental causes, the [177]
income derived from the students of the school during the last two sessions is not in the usual proportion to the number entered for Lectures, the Dean proceeds to say that the total sum "during the last year is £290 0s 2d. On this sum a discount of 10 per cent, paid to the University by the Professors would amount to £29. Some members of the Faculty are not bound by agreement to pay this rate of discount; but they have consented to do so for the sake of uniformity, and in order to diminish as much as possible the expense of the School to the University. The debts due to the School are already very considerable, amounting in the aggregate to £253 9s. Of these a large portion is expected to come in before the next Report."

The Laboratory, which has been alluded to in one part of the Dean's Report, requires to be brought more distinctly under the notice of your Lordships.

It has been fitted up, as the Professor of Chemistry informs me, upon the plan of those established in connection with several of the German Universities, and is designed to meet the wants of three classes of students: 1. those who propose to study chemistry for purely scientific purposes, among which may be named chemico-physiological investigations; 2. those who require a [178] knowledge of chemistry for practical purposes, as agriculture, mining, metallurgy, the various chemical manufactures, bleaching, dyeing, tanning, brewing, distilling, sugar-boiling, paper-making, etc., and civil engineering; 3. students of medicine, who are required to attend one or more courses of lectures on practical chemistry during the summer months. The course of instruction is adapted to the objects which each class of students may have in view.

Besides the regular University lectures on Chemistry, special lectures are given from time to time, on such branches of chemical science as may appear to be necessary to meet the requirements of particular laboratory students, and which are not comprised in the regular University courses.

With the view of affording students of Medicine, etc., an opportunity of acquiring a knowledge of practical pharmacy, a very complete steam apparatus has been fitted up, and the Laboratory is open for their use throughout the session.

I have also thought it advisable to purchase for the Medical Faculty, a library, which was on private sale at Munich, and is one of the most celebrated on the continent.[4] This library is the result of the united collections made since
[179] an early period of the last century by some eminent medical philosophers of Germany. It has been most recently enriched by the additions of Dr von Ringseis, Rector of the University of Munich, from whose hands it has passed directly into the possession of the Catholic University of Ireland. It comprises over 5000 volumes, including some of

[4] The negotiations were undertaken by the Professor of Ancient History, Peter le Page Renouf, who visited Munich in the summer of 1856. The collection was being sold for £300. See *The Letters of Peter le Page Renouf (1822–1897)* iii, ed. K. J. Cathcart (Dublin: UCD Press, 2003), pp. xviii, 27, 41.

the richest and most *recherché* works in medical literature, from the earliest periods of printing. It may be said to represent the select medical literature of the chief schools which have flourished in Europe. The languages which it comprises are Greek, Latin, French, German, Dutch, Italian, and English.

2. The review of the year, taken by the Dean of Philosophy and Letters[5] and the Professors of that Faculty, equals in importance and in interest, if not altogether in result, the Report from which I have given the foregoing extracts.

Your Lordships will be glad to receive his testimony to the improvement of various kinds which has taken place in the body of the students. "It is but right to say," he observes, "that a general improvement in the bearing and demeanour of the students during the Lectures has been remarked by the Professors; and, though complaints of carelessness and inattention have been made from time to time, yet it is gratifying to be able to state that on the whole the students have bestowed greater pains on preparation for the Lectures, [180]
and given a greater amount of attention to their delivery."

His Report is as encouraging of the mode in which they have acquitted themselves in Examinations. "Every succeeding term, the Entrance and other Examinations have exhibited some improvement in the character and amount of acquirements on the part of the candidates, and the matter of the Lectures has been better got up."

The other Professors speak on the same subject, in corroboration of the Dean's remarks. The Professor of Logic[6] observes: "So far from expressing dissatisfaction with the progress of the class who attended my Lectures on Metaphysics, I am led to congratulate the University and the Students on having accomplished so much. From the

---

[5] Edward Butler.

[6] David Dunne.

success which has attended our exertions during the past year, I am inclined to draw the best auguries for the future; provided the obstacles which have hitherto impeded us be removed, or at least diminished." In like manner, the Professor of Classical Literature[7] speaks of his class in Thucydides as having "pleased him very much," of "the history having been carefully studied," and "the state of the grammatical knowledge of the students having much improved". The Professor of Italian and Spanish[8] too reports
[181] that the students in his Italian class "have improved so much as to understand his explanations in Italian, and to answer his questions in that language"; while in Spanish the improvement of his class "has been very surprising," as the students can translate any passage without the least hesitation, and understand the spoken language, and speak it themselves". He adds that "the general attendance of the pupils has been very regular".

I must not, however, conceal from your Lordships, that this is only one side of the presentations which the Professors have felt it their duty to make to me. They consider, that though there is an advance in the diligence and attainments of the students, yet most of them scarcely possess the qualifications necessary for any real and substantial improvement. They complain generally of the serious want of grounding in the learned languages, in history, and in sciences, with which the students come to the University, and they imply, though they do not explicitly say it, that real professorial instruction would in most cases be simply thrown away upon them, from the want of that familiarity with the first elements of knowledge, without which it is impossible duly to understand or to appreciate or to appropriate the Lectures of highly educated men. It is

[7] Robert Ornsby.
[8] Augustus Marani.

obvious how discouraging such a state of things must be to zealous and able Professors.

Their remarks on this important subject are reserved for [182]
the Appendix.

I will but add that, though some of the holders of the Scientific Burses have shown themselves quite worthy of the patronage of your Lordships, this (as one of the Professors remarks) has not been the case with all of them. The suggestion has been made that it would be a great improvement if they were given away on *concursus* in each diocese as its turn came.

3. The Report which I have received from the Dean of the Faculty of Science[9] shows that the Professors have not been in a position to advance much beyond printing a scheme of studies and examination for the use of such students as profess to enter the course. This scheme also is subjoined in the Appendix.

4. It is impossible not to feel some anxiety at the state of things suggested by my last two paragraphs. As to the Professors of Medicine, they, indeed, are not only in active work, but in work which is of a character adequate to their zeal and their talents; but the Faculty of Science has scarcely begun to form classes; and, though the Faculty of Philosophy and Letters numbers above sixty students in its lecture rooms,[10] very few are of that calibre which is adapted to excite the interest and task the ability of a
University Lecturer. In this difficulty, it seemed incumbent [183]
on the Rector to find some means by which the Professors in these two Faculties should be able to direct their powers and extensive attainments to those public benefits for which

[9] W. K. Sullivan.

[10] By the end of the third academic session (1856/57) there were ninety matriculated students at the Catholic University, including twenty-eight who had passed the Scholar's exam, six who had passed the Inceptor's exam, and two their Licentiate, and around 130 attending lectures.

the University has been established. This has led me to contemplate a periodical work as the record of their investigations in literature and science. I am happy to say it starts with the full promise of success. It is to be called the *Atlantis*, and to be published for the present half-yearly, beginning with the first of January, 1858. (*Vid.* Supp., *What I Aimed At.*)[11]

5. Though no building is as yet provided for the various collections illustrative of antiquities, fine arts, and physical sciences, which constitute a Museum, the nucleus of such collections has already been formed. The University has received from the late Mgr Bettachini, of the Oratory of St Philip Neri, Bishop of Jaffna, a great number of specimens of the birds, amphibia, and recent shells of Ceylon; and a very interesting collection of Greek *terra cotta* vases, etc., from Major Patterson, the result of his own excavations in the neighbourhood of Athens.[12]

[184] And now, my Lords, having thus briefly but distinctly set before your Lordships the main points in the proceedings of our third Session which seemed to call for notice, I feel there is no reason why I should detain you longer from that more minute and practical information on subjects which are so interesting to you, which is contained in the Appendix.

---

[11] See pp. [290–304].

[12] Major (afterwards Lieut.-General) W. T. L. Patterson was for some time with his regiment the 91st Argyle Highlanders (now Princess Louise's own) in Greece. During the Crimean War that country was occupied jointly by English and French troops; and Major Patterson, who was a well read and accomplished soldier, occupied his leisure in antiquarian researches. He had a special and appreciative knowledge of all Dr Newman's works, and a profound respect for his character, and was greatly regarded by him. He and his brother the Rev. J. L. Patterson, M.A., of Trinity College, Oxford, now Bishop of Emmaus, always a staunch friend to Dr Newman, were among the converts of the year 1850, and owed their conversion to the Oxford movement. [WPN]

I am, my Lords,
Begging your Lordships' blessing,
Your Lordships' faithful servant in Christ,

JOHN H. NEWMAN,
Of the Oratory.

October 31, 1857

[185]

APPENDIX

SESSION—NOVEMBER 3, 1856, TO JULY 22, 1857

PROFESSORS' REPORTS TO THE RECTOR[1]

1. *From the Professor of Classical Literature.*
2. *From the Professor of Classical Languages.*
3. *From the Professor of Logic.*
4. *From the Professor of Ancient History.*
5. *From the Theological Catechist.*
6. *Table of Lectures.*
7. *From the Dean of the Facility of Science.*

[1] These official reports are revealing, since they illustrate the extent to which the lecturers and tutors shared Newman's educational thinking, even in the manner in which they tackled their students' deficiencies. It is evident that they were one with him in placing great store on rigorous learning and in training their students to think. In fact, their annual reports reveal a sense of frustration and disappointment at the general backwardness and lack of application of the students.

It must be appreciated that if Newman was to put theory into practice he had to rely on those he had appointed, whether they were lecturers, tutors or examiners, to enter into his way of thinking, to give it some practical expression, and even to embody it. Using his position as rector – talking with the professors informally, delivering the occasional lecture, and presiding at the internal examinations and collections (academic interviews at the end of term or year)—Newman was able to explain his meaning and teach by example.

[186]

APPENDIX

No. I

From the Professor of Classical Literature[2]

My classes have not been numerous, but, as the nature of the subjects caused them to be attended by some of the most promising of the Students, and as I hope they have generally shown an interest in what I have been enabled to place before them, I feel, on the whole, encouraged by a review of the Session. I proceed to offer some remarks which suggest themselves to me in making such a review.

In several of the subjects I have proposed for my lectures, I have had in view the circumstance, that some at least of the Students likely to join the classes cannot but hereafter mix more or less in public life. Now the studies which especially belong to the formation of the intellectual habits which such young men require, are books like Aristotle's Ethics, Rhetoric and Politics, Thucydides, Tacitus, and other great writers of this stamp—serious studies, without which it will be difficult for a young man to play a considerable part in life, or to rival those who have had a complete training founded upon them. A difficulty, as you are aware, awaited us here, for at the commencement of our labours it was unadvisable to introduce some of these books into our curriculum, the preliminary training of our

[2] Robert Ornsby had been a Lecturer in Rhetoric at Trinity College, Oxford, as well as a private tutor for four or five years, and had held the University office of Master of the Schools.

youths in Greek and Latin scholarship not having been such as to allow of their being introduced, at least immediately, into the highest classics. Hence, several most important [187]
works have been hitherto reserved; for example, Aristotle's Rhetoric, although in this I think a class may well be formed next term. By way of a substitute for this, I, last Session and the commencing term of the present Session, went through the principal parts of Cicero de Oratore. It is a diffuse treatise, and what it contains of a scientific nature has to be picked out and presented to the Student in a different form from that in which it appears in the work; nevertheless it abounds in valuable matter and suggestive views. I believe I may say that several of the class got up this work very creditably and usefully to themselves.

On the Demosthenes class I bestowed a good deal of pains, though I cannot say with visible results that gave me equal satisfaction. Whilst I believe that the classics hardly afford a more profound study than the writing of that orator, it is very difficult to make young men, at least at the stage in which ours are, seize the idea of getting them up in a scientific manner. The history they contain is so scattered, especially in the absence of any great contemporaneous continuous account of the same transactions, that their attention is divided, and I am afraid they forget almost as rapidly as they learn. At least, I conceived myself to have fallen short of my wishes in making them feel a real interest in the subject, although some of them took it up for their degree. The introduction, however, to so great and prominent a department of Greek literature cannot fail to have been a useful part of their education.

Cicero's Letters to Atticus may be compared to the Orations of Demosthenes, as containing a great deal of [188]
history in a scattered form; but as the details they give are immensely more numerous, and the facts more brought together, they present greater facilities for acquisition. I

believe this work is not much used in University education, but I can safely say that I have found it a most useful instrument, so far, in developing the minds of those Students whom I have been allowed to instruct in it. The *style* is not hard, whilst the allusions are singularly difficult, and hence, it is especially a book to be lectured upon. A youthful Student would find it almost impossible to get it up unassisted; but, with the help of a lecturer, the difficulties themselves add to its interest. It is copious in political wisdom, and idiomatic, beyond almost any other, in its Latin. Hence, the expectations I formed of its utility have not been disappointed, and I think the terminal examinations will show that several of our best men have derived much profit from the study.

I wish I could speak with equal confidence as to the lectures upon Tacitus, a book quite as useful and important, but our progress in which has been impeded by circumstances over which I had not control. The class contained two distinct elements which I found it very difficult to amalgamate—some advanced and some backward Students. Either, separately, I could have dealt with more or less satisfactorily, or with both together in a larger class; not so in a small one, such as mine has been. However, something has been done; the class is improved, and a beginning made of a difficult book. I should be sorry if we failed to make up a class in Tacitus next term, for I
[189] look upon the historical works of that author as among the most advantageous books a classical Student can take up.

The Thucydides class has pleased me very much, and was the largest as well as one of the most satisfactory of my classes. The history has, I think, been carefully studied by several of the Students, and the general state of their grammatical knowledge is much improved. I find it rather difficult to convey my exact impression as to their attainments. On the one hand, the general style of translating and getting up the book is perhaps superior to what would be shown by the same number of average men in other places of education. On the other hand, I am afraid they are frequently ignorant of points which ought to lie at the very foundation of all classical learning, and without perfect accuracy in which—without a sense, if I may use the expression, of the *enormity* of not knowing them—scholarship, properly so called, cannot exist. Further, I think even our best men are deficient in their *idea* of what classical proficiency, at their age and in their position, really means—of the extent to which they might and really ought, without aiming at a very high standard, carry it. A part of this deficiency, for example, is caused by their not, so far as I can make out, generally possessing or attempting to study the *adminicula* of real classical learning, such as the larger Greek grammars and other philological books, or similar aids in the antiquarian and historical departments of the classics.

I have attempted to remedy a part of this deficiency by two courses of lectures on the History of Greek Literature. In the first I went over the history from the Homeric period to that of Pericles inclusively; and am at present going over [190]
the same ground with another class, using for my basis in both courses Müller's History of Greek Literature,[3] the most accurate and copious with which I am acquainted. These lectures have been attended by very limited numbers; but I can certainly say that in none of my lectures have notes been more carefully taken, and I, therefore, am in hopes that I have succeeded more or less in giving them an idea of how great and interesting a pursuit may be made of classical literature, and how much the development of their taste and general mental cultivation depends upon it.

[3] C. O. Müller, *History of the Literature of Ancient Greece*, 2 vols (1840–2), trans. G. C. Lewis & J. W. Donaldson.

In conclusion, I may remark that my lectures on the Characteristics of Demosthenes more or less fall in with other public lectures I have delivered, in particular with those on the Greek Sophists, and on the Life and Characteristics of Cicero. The public, to whom they are addressed, cannot be expected to be familiar with the reading to which such subjects refer; and the only way, therefore, to interest them in these is to bring as much as possible into relief the *modern* aspect of the classical literatures and ages, and to show that they were as essentially human as our own—in form far more complete, in material fully as abundant, and hence fraught with utility as well as interest, not only to the scholar, but also to the man of the world—to those at least who have been taught by a University education, the only means of attaining such an end, how to apply the intervals of leisure which life may afford to studies so great and ennobling.

No. II

From the Professor of Classical Languages[4]

The Latin Composition has all along been rather up-hill work, from the want of previous training in schools; and this, in my opinion, is the grand defect in our schools. If some of Arnold's books were introduced into them, beginning with Henry's First Latin Book for prose, and Arnold's First Verse Book for verse,[5] we should soon see a great improvement in this respect.

---

[4] James Stewart had been a schoolmaster for six years, then a private tutor. After he became a Catholic, he taught in Mauritius, returned to England and became a tutor again. Besides acting as Professor of Classical Languages, Stewart was also a tutor at St Patrick's House.

[5] These were published by T. K. Arnold in 1839 and 1841 respectively.

[192]

No. III

From the Professor of Logic[6]

With a view to the improvement of the Students, by exercising them on the subject of the lectures, we have held disputations in Psychology and Natural Theology, generally once in each week. These disputations were conducted in Latin. One Student *defended* a leading position, such as the *immortality of the soul*, its *simplicity*, the *existence of free will*, the *unity of God*, etc. He opened the disputation by a short Latin preface, which stated briefly the principal arguments in support of the position. Two other Students then *objected*, proposing, in syllogistic form, difficulties in opposition: these difficulties the defendant answered also in logical form. I think that most of those engaged in these exercises have profited by them; they have been improved in precision and in readiness of expression.

I am sorry that I cannot report of the general progress of the Students as favourably as I should have wished. The impediments with which we have had to contend have been chiefly two. I shall state them very briefly.

First, *shortness of time*. It was proposed to us to go over in 120 lectures—and those interrupted, as has been already mentioned —the same quantity of matter, to which, for

---

[6] David Dunne had studied at the Irish College in Rome, where he gained doctorates in philosophy and theology. Besides acting as Professor of Logic, Dunne tutored at St Patrick's and St Mary's. He was a much-liked lecturer and tutor, though demanding, and had great admiration for Newman, with whom he kept in touch after his departure from Dublin.

example, 270 lectures are devoted in the Roman College. It [193]
was impossible in such circumstances to treat the different subjects entrusted to my charge with the fulness of detail, which is both necessary to enable the student to understand them accurately, and by which other institutions are in a position to prosecute their study with success and honour.

A second difficulty in our way was the extremely imperfect preparatory training of almost all the Students. This one difficulty includes in itself many: I shall endeavour to distinguish them.

I. The great youth of several amongst the Students.

II. Their very imperfect acquaintance with Logic or Geometry—the only sciences which could have prepared their minds for that close reasoning, without which Metaphysical information will always be inaccurate, and generally most dangerous.

III. Their neglect (in several cases) of attending to Mathematical studies concurrently with their Metaphysical. For, as previous intellectual discipline is a condition *sine quâ non* for entering on the study of Metaphysics; so, there is an indispensable necessity of keeping up this training to a proper standard, which can only be done by that constant practice which Logic or Mathematics will ensure.

IV. The very defective *Latin* education (if I may be allowed such a phrase) of most of the Students—nay, I might say, in some respects, of all. And, when I characterize it as "*very defective*," I am rather understating the fact. It had been arranged that Latin should be the school language.
But there were Students who could neither express a [194]
thought of their own in Latin, nor understand the Latin speech of others: some even could but slowly and painfully decipher the meaning of an author whose treatise was written in Latin. Under such a pressure it became unavoidable to have recourse largely to English, and to devote much time to mere grammatical explanations, which,

under more favourable circumstances, would have been altogether dispensed with.

The first difficulty enumerated above cannot be removed; but it may be obviated. It is quite impossible to compass the whole course of Metaphysics within one University Session; and the claims of other sciences forbid devoting a longer period to it. It only remains, then, to select judiciously those questions which may be treated in lecture with most profit and advantage to the Students. They can easily, with the aid which they may expect to receive from their respective houses, complete the subject by their private study.

As to the second class of difficulties, time will no doubt remove them; but meanwhile their remedy lies unquestionably, in a great measure, with the Heads of Houses. So long as youths, who are too immature to appreciate even the difficulty of mastering an abstruse science, will be sent to the school of Metaphysics, it is vain to expect that the subject can be treated with the gravity and research which adorn its teaching elsewhere, or that it can be presented to the Student otherwise than in the rudimentary form of a mere outline.

[195] The same observation will apply to the absence of previous intellectual discipline and logical training. Where this is wanting, the student cannot fix his attention on the precise point on which the question hinges, for he is incapable of perceiving it; his mind wanders about through a series of crude, confused notions; and he knows not how to set himself on the right path, how to correct his own mistakes, or detect the fallacies of others. The loose, undecided information (it cannot be dignified with the title of *knowledge*), which such a Student may collect, can only be to him the fruitful source of most dangerous errors. The obvious remedy in this case is, not to permit any Student to enter on a course of Metaphysics, unless he has previously

satisfied his Head or Tutor of his sufficient knowledge of logic.

A similar remedy will at once suggest itself for what I have enumerated as the third of this class of difficulties. If the Student of Metaphysics attend contemporaneously some mathematical lecture, he will be obliged to keep up to its proper standard the accuracy already acquired, and will be prevented from gradually falling into that vague discursiveness which is the besetting fault of young Metaphysicians. I know no book whose study I would more earnestly recommend to the philosophical Student than Euclid; it ought to divide with his text-book the highest place in his consideration.

As to what we may call the "*Latin*" difficulty, its consequences are so obvious, that they need no comment. This is not the occasion when one might usefully inquire if the advantages arising from the use of Latin as the school [196]
language in Philosophy be really superior to those secured to us by the use of English— even could such an inquiry be entered on with propriety. But it is plain, that, as long as Latin is the favoured tongue, it is simply a matter of necessity that the Students be in a position (as far as regards their practical acquaintance with it) little, if at all, inferior to that in which they would find themselves were English the language of the schools.

The remarks which I have hitherto made apply chiefly to the Metaphysical classes. I may now make one or two observations with regard to those Students who have attended my lectures on Dialectics. These lectures were delivered regularly three times a week during the entire Session. Their subject was the *Art* of Logic, or, as it is sometimes called, *Instrumental* Logic. They were delivered in English. You will perceive that what I have denominated the Latin difficulty has no place here; nor indeed have the other difficulties enumerated above much influence, unless *mutatis mutandis*, and in a very modified form. On the contrary, as we proceeded slowly, illustrating and developing our subject as copiously as we could, there was ample opportunity afforded of mastering it, even to those whose abilities were very moderate.

Under these circumstances, it pains me to be obliged to speak of the progress of these Students in terms less favourable than I should use with regard to the Metaphysicians; and I am the more pained because the shortcomings of the latter are much extenuated by difficulties which did not exist in the case of the former.

[197] I fear, I must say, that the character of the class of Dialectics (with one or two honourable exceptions) was a general indisposition to study, frequently degenerating into idleness. And amongst those who have least profited by my lectures, I am very sorry to be compelled to enumerate young men from whom the University has a right to expect steadiness and good example—some of them even occupants of *Burses*. The want of application apparent in these youths—their general carelessness, inattention, and negligence—has considerably interfered with the progress of others.

Considering our condition generally, there is another deficiency which has impeded our progress; but which I mention rather for the sake of completeness than for the special influence which it has exercised over us. I allude to the *absence of a tradition*. This is a deficiency shared by other departments, but which affects philosophical schools particularly. By tradition I do not mean a *traditio docens*—one which would direct the Professor in his teaching. For, although such a tradition would doubtless have been very valuable, nevertheless, our sphere of subjects was so limited, that we missed it not—especially as we had for our guide the more general tradition of Catholic Philosophy all over Europe. But I mean a *traditio docta*, if I may be

allowed the use of such an expression; one which would address itself to the Students, animating them, guiding them, assisting them. Such a tradition, the result of the labours, the experience, the lights of years—in some instances of centuries—has been elsewhere the most valuable agent of instruction possessed by the Schools of [198]
Philosophy. Placing before the Student the example of the long list who have preceded him, pursuing the same course, treading in the same path, in which he now finds himself, telling him what and how they studied, what helps they used, what methods they followed, their defects, the origin of their failures, the cause and measure of their success, appealing to his judgment through his feeling and imagination and sense of honour:—such a tradition, embodying in its practice the history of the body to which he belongs, does for the Student what no Professor can ever do; just as traditionary discipline meets requirements which no Superior can ever satisfy. More than this, strong in its independence of all personal contingencies, it will be to the school a source of strength in the midst of individual weakness, securing the stability and furthering the progress of science, even when its interests are imperilled by the errors, or neglect, or shortcomings of its Professed Interpreters.[7]

Such a tradition, the unwritten history of the school, the record of its labours, transmitted in some undefinable way through successive classes of Students, is obviously of great consequence to every discipline; for it gives unity to its efforts, harmonizes its movement, and directs the action of those who devote themselves to its pursuit. But on it the actual teaching and progress of Metaphysics and Ethics (as these sciences are understood and taught on the Continent)

---

[7] It is evident that Dunne had identified closely with Newman's description of and stress on the *genius loci* of a place of education. For Newman's thoughts on this, see p. [39].

much more intimately depend, than can be said of any other subject taught by the University. Its absence, then, was to us
[199] a more serious drawback than a similar absence could have been to any other of our schools. Moreover, our commencement has been made under less propitious circumstances, and with elements less capable of adaptation, than has occurred in other departments. Hence, not merely we have had no past tradition to look back to for guidance, but we can scarcely be said to have laid the foundations of one which may assist in our future direction. However, as this valuable gift can come to us in time only, we must await patiently the course of events which years may develop.

There is another matter, not unconnected with this traditionary direction, which has influenced our movement, and which must continue to affect seriously the fortunes of the Schools of Metaphysics and Ethics. I shall allude to the matter *historically* only; otherwise its discussion does not properly come within the Professor's province.

I mean the small encouragement which the University extends to these sciences; or, to speak more correctly, the absence of all encouragement. According to the present system of studies and examinations, a Student of the University may pass through his whole course and attain the highest honours without having attended a single lecture on Metaphysics, or having read a single line on the subject. Now, I think, I may venture to say, that this is not the case in a single Continental University. There, attendance on a regular course of Metaphysics and Ethics (or Natural Right as it is sometimes termed) is exacted as a *sine quâ non* not to honours only, but even to the ordinary degree. In fact, no
[200] one there would be considered to have received a University education, who had not attended such a course.

Side by side with this absence of encouragement in our University there exists a relative discouragement. Amongst all the subjects which are at present taught in the Faculty of Philosophy and Letters, there is not one which does not, in one way or another, enter at some period into every Student's course, with the single exception of Metaphysics. It would betray ignorance of human nature to expect under these circumstances that Students would follow a subject which was not obligatory, and which would demand an amount of time and attention, that could ill be spared from lectures of a more immediately useful character.

These circumstances will explain a fact, which in its turn is a witness of the practical tradition of the University. I mean the fewness of Metaphysical Students, and the exclusively personal motive and reasons of those who attended. Now, as each Student attends those lectures which are assigned him by his Tutor, we may fairly conclude that the Tutors do not regard Metaphysics as occupying a very prominent or important position in the University system.

These remarks, as I have already stated, I make historically only; for, doubtless, there are weighty reasons why each department of knowledge should hold the place actually assigned to it.

And now, looking back on all these difficulties and disadvantages, against which we have had to struggle, I am inclined to modify considerably the opinion stated at first; [201]
and so far from expressing dissatisfaction with the progress of the class who attended my lectures on Metaphysics, I am led to congratulate the University and the Students for having accomplished so much. From the success which has attended our exertions during the past year, I am inclined to draw the best auguries for the future; provided the obstacles which have hitherto impeded us be removed, or, at least, diminished. But it is clear, that as long as this state of things continues, our School of Metaphysics will never be able to compete with those of the Continent, will never get beyond a rudimentary condition. It will be poor in numbers and low

in knowledge; dependent even for existence on a few stragglers who may find it advantageous for their own individual objects to attend a course of lectures on the subject.

No. IV

From the Professor of Ancient History[8]

Those lectures which I have delivered this term have not, in general, either as to their matter or their method, come up to what I consider the true type of the University lectures. But this is the fault of no one. Had I simply followed this ideal type, without reference to my audience, I might with equal profit have lectured in an unknown tongue.

A University Professor has the right, under ordinary circumstances, to take it for granted that his hearers have *some* knowledge, however imperfect, of the matter upon which he lectures. This has *not* been my good fortune, at least as far as regards an important portion of my hearers, and it would have been idle to have plunged into the abyss of historical erudition, or to have indulged in the flights of speculation, in presence of gentlemen who have yet to learn such elementary truths as that Jerusalem is not in Africa, that the Helots did not dwell on the shores of the Red Sea, and that the Patriarch Jacob lived and died before the Babylonish Captivity.

---

[8] Peter le Page Renouf was also a tutor at St Mary's House. He had previously taught at Oscott College and been a private tutor.

[203]

No. V

From the Theological Catechist[9]

As to religious instruction, I have in general found the young men who come here pretty well informed as to matters of doctrine; but in anything that relates to the *history* of Christianity, whether its original institution, or its subsequent course, they are for the most part surprisingly deficient; and accordingly during the past year the lectures on these subjects have been chiefly of a historical kind. New Testament History and the History of the early Church have principally formed the subject of them; the progress of some of the gentlemen has been very satisfactory; yet, I regret to say, that with others it has not been so, especially during the Summer Term.

---

[9] Besides acting as University Catechist, William Penny was a Tutor in mathematics and Dean of St Mary's.

No. VI

Table of Lectures

	FIRST TERM	SECOND TERM	THIRD TERM
Mr Ornsby	Thucyd. II Cic. de Orat. III	Thucyd. III Hist. of Greek Lit. Tac. Germ. Agri. Dem. Olynth. Phil. Cic. Ep. ad Att. I, II	Thucyd. IV, V Hist. of Greek Lit. Tacitus, Hist. I, II Cic. Ep. ad Att. III IV, V
Mr Stewart	Xen. Mem. Arist. Clouds Greek Accent Ov. Fasti I, II Latin Comp.	Arist. Frogs and Knights Hellenics I, II Greek Accent Ov. Fasti III, IV Latin Comp. Prose Latin Comp. Verse	Hellenics III Æsch. Chœph. Eumen. Greek Prose Comp. Hor. Ep. I, II and Ars. Poet. Latin Prose Comp. Latin Verse Comp.
Mr Arnold	English Lit.	English Lit.	English Lit.
Signor Marani	Italian Spanish	Italian Spanish	Italian Spanish

		FIRST TERM	SECOND TERM	THIRD TERM
	Abbé Schürr	French German	French German	French German
	Mr Renouf	Ancient Hist. and Geog.	Ancient Hist. and Geog.	Ancient Hist. and Geog.
[205]	Mr Robertson	Modern Hist. and Geog.	Modern Hist. and Geog. Italy, Germany, France, England, from 1550 to 1650	Modern Hist. and Geog. European States from 1650 to 1750
	Mr Butler	Algebra Trigonometry	Spherical Trig. Calculus Euclid, I II III IV V Mechanics	Calculus Co-ordinate Geom. Euclid, V VI XI Conic Sections Mechanics
	Dr Dunne	Logic	Logic. Dialectics Logic. Alt. Psychology	Dialectics Ontology Nat. Theology

[206]

No. VII

From the Dean of the Faculty of Science

VERY REV. FATHER RECTOR,

Up to the year 1856–57 the Faculty of Science was represented by only three professors, of which only two actually officiated in the University. The existence of a Faculty of Science, in a proper sense, may therefore be said to have commenced with the establishment of the Chairs of Chemistry and Physiology; because, although there were still no professors of Zoology, Botany, Geology, etc., yet the great divisions of the mathematical, physical, and observation sciences might be looked upon as more or less represented.

The course of study not having been arranged, and the Faculty of Philosophy and Letters, through which matriculated students must pass before entering that of Science, having been too short a time in operation to enable any students to join us, the Faculty was not formally opened with an inaugural address like the other Faculties in operation.

At the commencement of the Session the Faculty discussed the subject of a scheme of studies and examinations; but before entering upon its preparation, it was considered desirable that we should get together as much information as possible about the systems of
instruction adopted in other Universities, especially those of [207]
Catholic countries. The Dean was accordingly instructed by the Faculty to apply to the proper authorities for copies of

the various programmes and reports which may have been recently issued regarding superior instruction in France, Belgium, and Austria. This was accordingly done, and after some time we received from the Belgian Government a very complete series of documents. These, with such others relative to France and Germany as the members of the Faculty happened to have possessed, enabled us to enter at once upon the preparation of our scheme. When fully discussed, it was submitted for your approval, and with your and the Rectorial Council's sanction was printed at the end of the session.[10]

Several subjects are included in this scheme, which do not properly come under any of the chairs now established. But as the scheme would be obviously incomplete without them, the members of the Faculty undertook to give lectures upon those subjects, until such time as their teaching could be more effectually provided for, by the establishment of special professorships.

The Professor of Natural Philosophy, having got together the nucleus of a first-class Physical Cabinet, was enabled to give a complete course of lectures on Physical Science, during the session, to such students of the University generally as desired to attend.

The other professors of the Faculty, actually officiating, did not give any lectures in connection with the Faculty; but being members of other Faculties, they were fully occupied with their duties in those Faculties.

[208] The General Chemical Laboratory, for the use, conjointly, of the Faculties of Science and Medicine, was fitted up during the session.

Although the duty more properly devolves upon my successor in office, I cannot help alluding to the great wants

[10] This report urged the immediate establishment of Chairs of Botany and Zoology, and of Geology and Mineralogy, and the expenditure of £20,000 on scientific laboratories (*NU*, p. 372).

which paralyze the action and progress of the Faculty of Science. Those wants are:—1. The establishment of a Science House, provided with physical, chemical, mineralogical, geological, and natural history cabinets, laboratories for physical, chemical, and physiological research, and an observatory; 2. The establishment of chairs of Natural History and Geology; and 3. The allocation of some fund for scientific researches, and the establishment of burses which shall be offered to public competition in some of the chief towns of Ireland.

I remain, Very Rev. Father Rector,
Yours faithfully,
WILLIAM K. SULLIVAN,[11]

---

[11] William Kirby Sullivan (*c.*1821–90) a native of Cork, had studied chemistry under von Liebig at Giessen, Germany, where he completed his doctorate. While chemist to the Museum of Irish Industry in Dublin, he investigated ways of using the industrial resources of Ireland and published *The Manufacture of Beetroot Sugar in Ireland* (1851). He was appointed Professor of Theoretical and Practical Chemistry at the newly-founded School of Science Museum in 1854 and retained some of his duties when he was appointed Professor of Chemistry and Dean of the Faculty of Science at the Catholic University in November 1855.

He championed Newman's idea of a university and cherished the hope that the University would become a preeminent centre for science, but his hopes were thwarted, first by Newman's resignation, then by the attitude of the Irish bishops. He strongly opposed the gradual clericalisation of the University, and threatened his resignation several times. When the opportunity arose, Sullivan took a leading part in the negotiations with the government for a charter and endowment.

Besides his scientific papers, he became a competent Gaelic scholar and an accomplished philologist, and edited E. O'Curry's *Lectures on the Manners and Customs of the Ancient Irish* (3 vols, 1873) for publication; he also edited the University journal *Atlantis* (1858–59, 1862–63, 1870). He became secretary of the Royal Irish Academy, then Professor of Theoretical Chemistry at the Royal College of Science, founded in 1867. When the Jesuits were given the running of St Patrick's House in 1873, he resigned in protest and took up the presidency of Queen's College,

Dean of Faculty of Science (for the Session of 1856–1857), and on behalf of the Faculty

The Very Rev. the Rector of the
Catholic University of Ireland

Cork. There he actively promoted its science departments. He married the sister of Henry Hennessy and they had five children. (*DIB*)

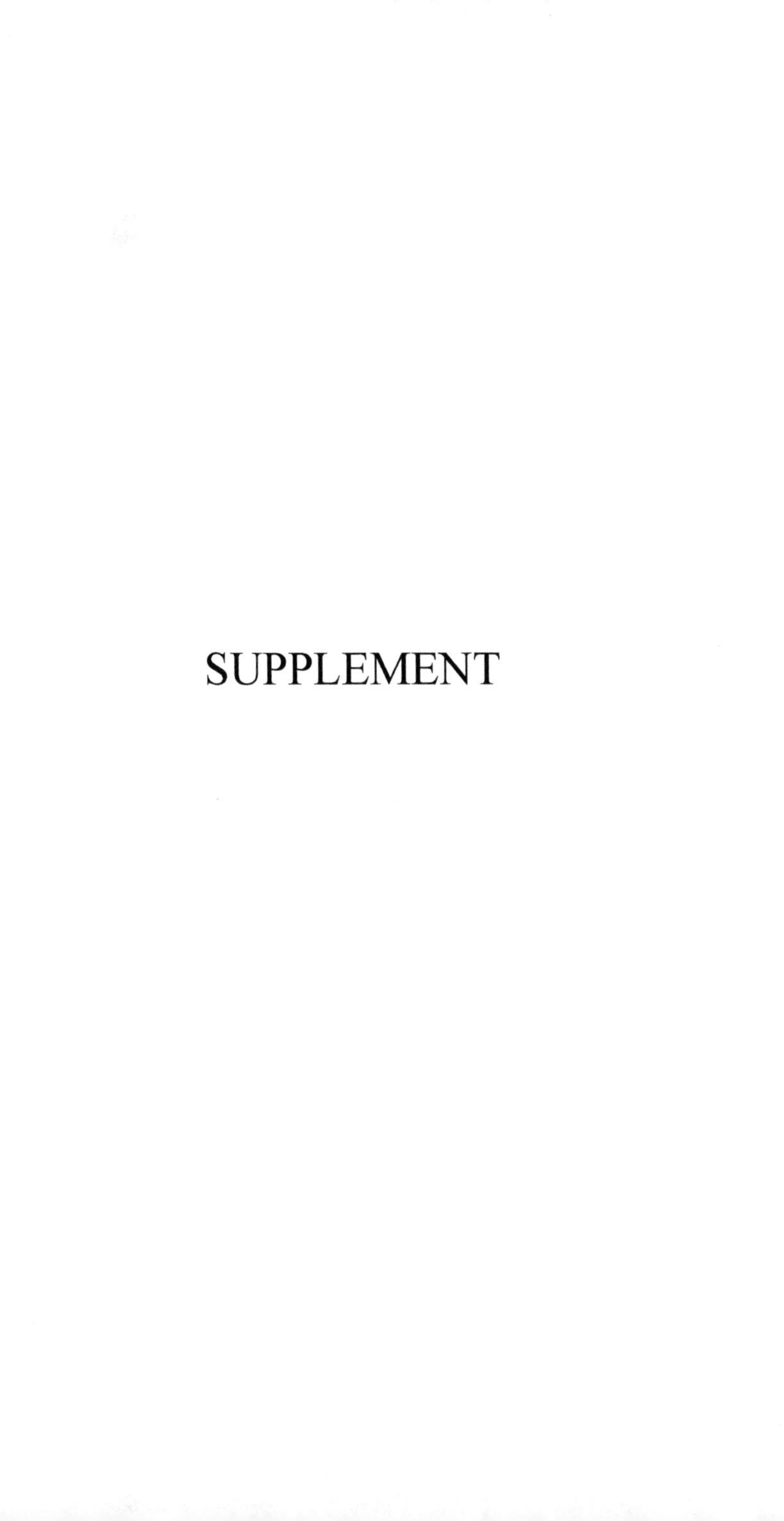

SUPPLEMENT

SUPPLEMENT

CATHEDRA SEMPITERNA[1]

DEEPLY do I feel, ever will I protest, for I can appeal to the ample testimony of history to bear me out, that, in questions of right and wrong, there is nothing really strong in the whole world, nothing decisive and operative, but the voice of him, to whom have been committed the keys of the kingdom and the oversight of Christ's flock. The voice of Peter is now, as it ever has been, a real authority, infallible when it teaches, prosperous when it commands, ever taking the lead wisely and distinctly in its own province, adding certainty to what is probable, and persuasion to what is certain. Before it speaks, the most saintly may mistake; and after it has spoken, the most gifted must obey.

Peter is no recluse, no abstracted student, no dreamer about the past, no doter upon the dead and gone, no

[1] This was put together in 1867 from passages taken from Discourse I (*Discourses on the Scope and Nature of University Education* (1852), pp. 22, 25–28), as described on pp. [lix–lx].

Subsequently Newman regretted its publication. He explained to John Wallis, the former editor of *The Tablet* (1856–68), that 'a Jesuit Father got up a volume of testimonies from living writers to the Pope's Infallibility. I like a fool gave him a passage of my own, since I had ever held the doctrine – but I saw afterwards the meaning to the project when the question of the Definition was suddenly mooted in the Council, a measure which I had never wished.' (24 August 1873, *LD* xxvi, p. 356)

Newman in fact modified his ideas on the perennial sagacity of the papacy, as expressed here (see Editor's Introduction, p. xxviii). Also see the Advertisement, pp. [xxi, xxxii–xxxiii] for why Neville nevertheless included 'Cathedra Sempiterna' in this volume.

projector of the visionary. Peter for eighteen hundred years has lived in the world; he has seen all fortunes, he has encountered all adversaries, he has shaped himself for all emergencies. If there ever was a power on earth who had an eye for the times, who has confined himself to the
[212] practicable, and has been happy in his anticipations, whose words have been deeds, and whose commands prophecies, such is he in the history of ages, who sits from generation to generation in the Chair of the Apostles, as the Vicar of Christ and Doctor of His Church.

It was said by an old philosopher, who declined to reply to an emperor's arguments, "It is not safe controverting with the master of twenty legions." What Augustus had in the temporal order, that, and much more, has Peter in the spiritual. When was he ever unequal to the occasion? When has he not risen with the crisis? What dangers have ever daunted him? What sophistry foiled him? What uncertainties misled him? When did ever any power go to war with Peter, material or moral, civilized or savage, and got the better? When did the whole world ever band together against him solitary, and not find him too many for it?

All who take part with Peter are on the winning side. The Apostle of Christ says not in order to unsay; for he has inherited that word which is with power. From the first he has looked through the wide world, of which he has the burden; and according to the need of the day and the inspirations of his Lord, he has set himself, now to one thing, now to another, but to all in season and to nothing in vain. He came first upon an age of refinement and luxury like our own; and in spite of the persecutor, fertile in the resources of his cruelty, he soon gathered, out of all classes of society, the slave, the soldier, the high-born lady, and the sophist, to form a people for his Master's honour. The
[213] savage hordes came down in torrents from the north,

hideous even to look upon; and Peter went out with holy water and with benison, and by his very eye he sobered them and backed them in full career. They turned aside and flooded the whole earth, but only to be more surely civilized by him, and to be made ten times more his children even than the older populations they had overwhelmed. Lawless kings arose, sagacious as the Roman, passionate as the Hun, yet in him they found their match, and were shattered, and he lived on. The gates of the earth were opened to the east and west, and men poured out to take possession; and he and his went with them, swept along by zeal and charity, as far as they by enterprise, covetousness, or ambition. Has he failed in his enterprises up to this hour? Did he, in our fathers' day, fail in his struggle with Joseph of Germany and his confederates—with Napoleon, a greater name, and his dependent kings—that, though in another kind of fight, he should fail in ours? What grey hairs are on the head of Judah, whose youth is renewed as the eagle's, whose feet are like the feet of harts, and underneath the Everlasting Arms?

"Thus saith the Lord that created thee, O Jacob, and formed thee, O Israel. Fear not, for I have redeemed thee, and called thee by thy name! Thou art Mine.

"When thou shalt pass through the waters, I will be with thee, and the rivers shall not cover thee.

"When thou shalt walk in the fire, thou shalt not be burned, and the flame shall not kindle against thee.

"For I am the Lord thy God, the Holy One of Israel, thy [214]
Saviour.

"Fear not, for I am with thee, I am the first, and I am the last, and besides Me there is no God."

JOHN HENRY NEWMAN

It is not altogether irrelevant to mention here that in January, 1856, Dr Newman, having occasion to go to Rome on business of very great anxiety, he at once, on alighting from the diligence, went with Father St John to make a visit of devotion to the shrine of St Peter, going there the whole way barefoot. The time was the middle of the day, when, as was the case in those years, the streets were very empty, and thus, and screened by his large Roman cloak, he was able to do so unrecognized and unnoticed—nor was it ever known except to Father St John and another.[2]

His friend Dr Clifford (the Hon. William J. H. Clifford, late Bishop of Clifton), who with his father Lord Clifford, had travelled with him from Siena, and with whom he dined that day in Rome, knew nothing of this until it was mentioned to him on occasion of his preaching the Cardinal's funeral sermon in 1890.

---

[2] This 'other' was William Neville, who recorded the incident, noting that it was the time of the siesta and that their long cloaks hid their feet (Meriol Trevor, *Newman: Light in Winter* (London: Macmillan, 1962), p. 103). Newman's diary entry for Saturday 12 January 1856 simply says: 'arriving at Rome in evening 47 Piazza di Spagna'.

DISCOURSE I[1]

[1] Discourse I was abridged and incorporated into Discourse II for the 1859 edition of the *Discourses*: the passages on mixed education were omitted, as well as one long and two shorter passages on the perennial wisdom of the Papacy. In the first edition of the *Idea* (1873) the first half of Discourse I was restored; the lengthy eulogy of the papacy remained considerably shortened, but 'the central argument for the practicality of the University from the Pope's authority was restored, together with the peroration on the joint mission of England and Ireland under Papal auspices' (*Idea*, ed. Ker, pp. xxxvii–xxxix).

These alterations should be seen in the context of the various editions of the *Discourses*. Originally, Newman planned to give three Discourses at the outset, but for various reasons they became five. These he delivered in May and June 1852, before heading back to England for the Achilli trial. The other five Discourses were composed later that year but not delivered. All ten were published separately that year, and then together as *Discourses on the Scope and Nature of University Education* (1852).

Around 800 textual changes were made for the 'abridged' edition, *The Scope and Nature of University Education; or University Teaching Considered in its Abstract Scope and Nature* (1859), as a companion volume to *Lectures and Essays on University Subjects* (1859). Another 240 changes were made for the publication of the Discourses as the first part of *The Idea of a University: Defined and Illustrated* (1873). The last edition of the *Idea*, the ninth, appeared in 1889. Ian Ker's critical edition charts and cites all the changes in the eleven editions of the Discourses. See the section 'History of the Text', *Idea*, ed. Ker, pp.xxix–xli; and the 'Textual Apendix', pp. 493–573.

Newman explains the reason for the cuts: 'I […] omitted […] large portions of the volume, as of only temporary interest, and irrelevant to the subject of University education' (Newman to the editor of *The Guardian*, 20 September 1872, *LD* xxvi, p. 167). In other words, the alterations can be attributed to the change from a local, Dublin audience and the specific purpose of preparing the way for the foundation of a university to forming part of a treatise on university education for a universal audience.

Discourse I

From *The Scope and Nature of University Education* (ed. 1852)[2]

INTRODUCTION[3]

IN addressing myself to the consideration of a question which has excited so much interest, and excited so much discussion at the present day, as that of University Education, I feel some explanation is due from me for supposing, after such high ability and wide experience have been brought to bear upon it in both countries, that any field remains for the additional labours either of a disputant or of an inquirer. If, nevertheless, I still venture to ask permission to continue the discussion, already so protracted, it is because the subject of Liberal Education, and of the principles on which it must be conducted, has ever had a hold upon my mind;[4] and because I have lived the greater part of my life in a place which has all that time been occupied in a series of controversies among its own people and with strangers, and of measures, experimental or definitive, bearing upon it. About fifty years since, the Protestant University, of which I was so long a member, after a century of inactivity, at length was roused, at a time when (as I may say) it was giving no education at all to the
[216] youth committed to its keeping, to a sense of the

---

[2] Changes from the 1852 text of *Discourses on the Scope and Nature of University Education* are shown in square brackets. The original text is given in the footnote, unless the change is a mere addition, in which case no footnote is needed.

[3] For Ian Ker's explanatory notes on the text of this discourse (as it appeared in the ninth edition of the *Idea*), see *Idea*, ed. Ker, pp. 575–91.

[4] In the 1852 appendix Newman cites several passages from the sermon 'The Religion of the Day' that he preached on 26 August 1832 to illustrate what he had said 'concerning the long hold which the class of opinions' being advocated 'have had upon my mind' (*Idea*, ed. Ker, p. 487). This sermon can be found in *Parochial and Plain Sermons* i (1834).

responsibilities which its profession and its station involved;[5] and it presents to us the singular example of an heterogeneous and an independent body of men, setting about a work of self-reformation, not from any pressure of public opinion, but because it was fitting and right to undertake it. Its initial efforts, begun and carried on amid many obstacles, were met from without, as often happens in such cases, by ungenerous and jealous criticisms, which were at that very moment beginning to be unjust. Controversy did but bring out more clearly to its own apprehension, the views on which its reformation was proceeding, and throw them into a philosophical form.[6] The course of beneficial change made progress, and what was at first but the result of individual energy and an act of the academical corporation, gradually became popular, and was taken up and carried out by the separate collegiate bodies, of which the University is composed. This was the first stage of the controversy. Years passed away, and then political adversaries arose, and a political contest was waged; but still, as that contest was conducted in great measure through the medium, not of political acts, but of treatises and pamphlets, it happened as before that the threatened dangers, in the course of their repulse, did but

---

[5] Newman describes the state of things in *HS* iii, pp. 235–8, 316–17.

[6] The University of Oxford was heavily criticised in three articles in the *Edinburgh Review* in 1808–9. The provost of Oriel, Edward Copleston, widely regarded as 'the representative man of university culture', (Pattison, *Memoirs* (1885; London: Centaur, 1969), p. 8) defended Oxford to brilliant effect in his lengthy *Reply to the Calumnies of the Edinburgh Review* (1810), and over the following two decades inspired an intellectual renaissance in Oriel College and Oxford in general. See M. G. Brock, 'The Oxford of Peel and Gladstone, 1800–1833', *History of the University of Oxford* vi, pp. 10–11; A. Briggs, 'Oxford and its critics, 1800–1835', *ibid.*, pp. 134–6. Newman deals at length with the controversy in the *Idea*, pp. 153–77.

afford fuller development and more exact delineation to the principles of which the University was the representative.[7]

Living then so long as a *witness*, though hardly as an actor, in these scenes of intellectual conflict, I am able, Gentlemen, to bear *witness* to views of University
[217] Education, without authority indeed in themselves, but not without value to a Catholic, and less familiar to him, as I conceive, than they deserve to be. And, while an argument originating in them may be serviceable at this season to that great cause in which we are just now so especially interested, to me personally it will afford satisfaction of a peculiar kind; for, though it has been my lot for many years to take a prominent, sometimes a presumptuous, part in theological discussions, yet the natural turn of my mind carries me off to trains of thought like those which I am now about to open, which, important though they be for Catholic objects, and admitting of a Catholic treatment, are sheltered from the extreme delicacy and peril which attach to disputations directly bearing on the subject matter of Divine Revelation.

What must be the general character of those views of University Education to which I have alluded, and of which I shall avail myself, can hardly be doubtful, Gentlemen, considering the circumstances under which I am addressing you. I should not propose to avail myself of a philosophy which I myself had gained from an heretical seat of learning, unless I felt that that philosophy was Catholic in its ultimate source, and befitting the mouth of one who is taking part in a great Catholic work; nor, indeed, should I refer at all to the views of men who, however distinguished in this world, were not and are not blessed with the light of true doctrine, except for one or two special reasons, which will form, I trust, my sufficient justification in so doing.

---

[7] For more about the controversy in the 1830s, see Culler, *Imperial Intellect*, pp. 102–15; *Idea*, ed. Ker, p. 580.

One reason is this: It would concern me, Gentlemen, were I [218]
supposed to have got up my opinions for the occasion. This, indeed, would have been no reflection on me personally, supposing I were persuaded of their truth, when at length addressing myself to the inquiry; but it would have destroyed, of course, the force of my testimony, and deprived such arguments, as I might adduce, of that moral persuasiveness which attends on tried and sustained conviction. It would have made me seem the advocate, rather than the cordial and deliberate maintainer and witness of the doctrines which I was to support; and while it undoubtedly exemplified the faith I reposed in the practical judgment of the Church, and the intimate concurrence of my own reason with the course she had authoritatively sanctioned, and the devotion with which I could promptly put myself at her disposal, it would have cast suspicion on the validity of reasonings and conclusions which rested on no independent inquiry, and appealed to no past experience. In that case it might have been plausibly objected by opponents that I was the serviceable expedient of an emergency, and never could be more than ingenious and adroit in the management of an argument which was not my own, and which I was sure to forget again as readily as I had mastered it. But this is not so. The views to which I have referred have grown into my whole system of thought, and are, as it were, part of myself. Many changes has my mind gone through; here it has known no variation or vacillation of opinion, and though this by itself is no proof of truth, it
puts a seal upon conviction, and is a justification of [219]
earnestness and zeal. The principles, which I can now set forth under the sanction of the Catholic Church, were my profession at that early period of my life, when religion was to me more a matter of feeling and experience than of faith.[8]

[8] In a sermon preached to the parishioners of St Clement's Church, Oxford, shortly before his twenty-fifth birthday, Newman shows that he

They did but take greater hold upon me as I was introduced to the records of Christian Antiquity,[9] and approached in sentiment and desire to Catholicism; and my sense of their truth has been increased with the experience of every year since I have been brought within its pale.

And here I am brought to a second and more important reason for introducing what I have to say on the subject of Liberal Education with this reference to my personal testimony concerning it; and it is as follows: In proposing to treat of so grave a matter, I have felt vividly that some apology was due from me for introducing the lucubrations of Protestants into what many men might consider almost a question of dogma, and I have said to myself about myself: "You think it, then, worth while to come all this way, in order, from your past experience, to recommend principles which had better be left to the decision of the theological schools!" The force of this objection you will see more clearly by considering the answer I proceed to give to it.

Let it be observed, then, that the principles I would maintain on the subject of Liberal Education, although those as I believe of the Catholic Church, are such as may be

---

had thought deeply about the nature and purpose of education, and that he had already discerned in outline many of his key educational principles. See 'On Some Popular Mistakes as to the Object of Education', sermon preached on 8 January 1826, reproduced in J. Arthur & G. Nicholls, *John Henry Newman. Continuum Library of Education Thought* xviii (London: Continuum, 2007), pp. 205–13; for the variants introduced when the sermon was preached a second time on 27 August 1826, see the original sermon (no. 128, A 17.2, BOA).

[9] Newman elaborates on the influence on him of the Christian humanism of the Alexandrian school in the *Apologia* (p. 36): 'The broad philosophy of Clement and Origen carried me away. […] Some portions of their teaching […] came like music to my inward ear, as if the response to ideas, which, with little external to encourage them, I had cherished so long. […] pagan literature, philosophy, and mythology, properly understood, were but a preparation for the Gospel. The Greek poets and sages were in a certain sense prophets'.

gained by the mere experience of life. They do not simply come of theology—they imply no supernatural discernment—they have no special connection with [220]
Revelation; they will be found to be almost self-evident when stated, and to arise out of the nature of the case; they are dictated by that human prudence and wisdom which is attainable where grace is quite away, and recognized by simple common sense, even where self-interest is not present to sharpen it; and, therefore, though true, and just, and good in themselves, though sanctioned and used by Catholicism, they argue nothing whatever for the sanctity or faith of those who maintain them. They may be held by Protestants as well as by Catholics; they may, accidentally, in certain times and places, be taught by Protestants to Catholics, without any derogation from the claim which Catholics make to special spiritual illumination. This being the case, I may without offence, on the present occasion, when speaking to Catholics, appeal to the experience of Protestants; I may trace up my own distinct convictions on the subject to a time when apparently I was not even approximating to Catholicism; I may deal with the question, as I really believe it to be, as one of philosophy, practical wisdom, good sense, not of theology; and, such as I am, I may, notwithstanding, presume to treat of it in the presence of those who, in every religious sense, are my fathers and my teachers.

Nay, not only may the true philosophy of Education be held by Protestants, and at a given time, or in a given place, be taught by them to Catholics, but further than this, there is nothing strange in the idea, that here or there, at this time or that, it should be understood better, and held more firmly by Protestants than by ourselves. The very circumstance that it [221]
is founded on truths in the natural order, accounts for the possibility of its being sometimes or somewhere understood outside the Church, more accurately than within her fold.

Where the sun shines bright, in the warm climate of the south, the natives of the place know little of safeguards against cold and wet. They have, indeed, bleak and piercing blasts; they have chill and pouring rain; but only now and then, for a day or a week; they bear the inconvenience as they best may, but they have not made it an art to repel it; it is not worth their while; the science of calefaction and ventilation is reserved for the north. It is in this way that Catholics stand relatively to Protestants in the science of Education; Protestants are obliged to depend on human means solely, and they are, therefore, led to make the most of them; it is their sole resource to use what they have; "Knowledge is" their "power" and nothing else;[10] they are the anxious cultivators of a rugged soil. It is otherwise with us; *funes ceciderunt mihi in prœclaris*.[11] We have a goodly inheritance. The Almighty Father takes care of us; He has promised to do so; His word cannot fail, and we have continual experience of its fulfilment. This is apt to make us, I will not say, rely too much on prayer, on the Divine Word and Blessing, for we cannot pray too much, or expect too much from our great Lord; but we sometimes forget that we shall please Him best, and get most from Him, when we use what we have in nature to the utmost, at the same time that we look out for what is beyond nature in the confidence
[222] of faith and hope. However, we are sometimes tempted to let things take their course, as if they would in one way or another turn up right at last for certain; and so we go on, getting into difficulties and getting out of them, succeeding certainly on the whole, but with failure in detail which might be avoided, and with much of imperfection or

---

[10] The expression *ipsa scientia potestas est* (knowledge itself is power) appears in F. Bacon's *Meditationes Sacrae* (1597). The phrase *scientia potentia est* was first used by his secretary, Thomas Hobbes, in the Latin edition of *Leviathan* (1668), chapter 10.

[11] 'The measuring lines have fallen for me in pleasant places' (Ps 16:6); the second half of the verse reads: 'yes, I have a goodly heritage'.

inferiority in our appointments and plans, and much disappointment, discouragement, and collision of opinion in consequence. We leave God to fight our battles, and so He does; but He corrects us while He prospers us. We cultivate the innocence of the dove more than the wisdom of the serpent; and we exemplify our Lord's word and incur His rebuke, when He declared that "the children of this world were in their generation wiser than the children of light".

It is far from impossible, then, at first sight, that [even on that question which comes first in the controversy],[12] Protestants may have discerned the true line of action, and estimated its importance aright. It is possible that they have investigated and ascertained the main principles, the necessary conditions of education, better than some among ourselves. It is possible at first sight, and it is probable in the particular case, when we consider, on the one hand, the various and opposite positions, which they enjoy relatively to each other; yet, on the other, the uniformity of the conclusions to which they arrive. The Protestant communions, I need hardly say, are respectively at a greater and a less distance from the Catholic Church, with more or with less of Catholic doctrine and of Catholic principle in them. Supposing, then, it should turn out, on a survey of [223]
their opinions and their policy [as regards one of the two main subjects of which I have been speaking], that in proportion as they approach, in the genius of their religion, to Catholicism, so do they become clear in their enunciation of a certain principle in education, that very circumstance would be an argument, as far as it went, for concluding that in Catholicism itself the recognition of that principle would, in its seats of education, be distinct and absolute. Now, I conceive that this remark applies [to one of the two portions of the controversy,—the former of the two,][13] to which I am

[12] The original has 'on the subject before us'.

[13] The original has 'in the controversy'.

addressing myself. I must anticipate the course of future remarks so far as to say what you have doubtless, Gentlemen, yourselves anticipated before I say it, that the main principle on which I shall have to proceed is this—that Education must not be disjoined from Religion, or that Mixed Schools, as they are called, in which teachers and scholars are of different religious creeds, none of which, of course, enter into the matter of instruction, are constructed on a false idea. Here, then, I conceive I am right in saying that every sect of Protestants, which has retained the idea of religious truth and the necessity of faith, which has any dogma to profess and any dogma to lose, makes that dogma the basis of its Education, secular as well as religious, and is jealous of those attempts to establish schools of a purely secular character, which the inconvenience of religious differences urges upon politicians of the day. This circumstance is of so striking a nature as in itself to justify me, as I consider, in my proposed appeal in this controversy to arguments and testimony short of Catholic.

[224] Now, Gentlemen, let me be clearly understood here. I know quite well that there are multitudes of Protestants who are advocates for Mixed Education to the fullest extent, even so far as to desire the introduction of Catholics themselves into their colleges and schools; but then, first, they are those for the most part who have no creed or dogma whatever to defend, to sacrifice, to surrender, to compromise, to hold back, or to "mix," when they call out for Mixed Education. There are many Protestants of benevolent tempers and business-like minds, who think that all who are called Christians do in fact agree together in essentials, though they will not allow it; and who, in consequence, call on all parties in educating their youth for the world to eliminate differences, which are certainly prejudicial, as soon as they are proved to be immaterial. It is not surprising that clear-sighted persons should fight against

the maintenance and imposition of private judgment in matters of public concern. It is not surprising that statesmen, with a thousand conflicting claims and interests to satisfy, should fondly aim at a forfeited privilege of Catholic times, when they would have had at least one distraction the less in the simplicity of National Education. And next, I can conceive the most consistent men, and the most zealously attached to their own system of doctrine, nevertheless consenting to schemes of Education from which Religion is altogether or almost excluded, from the stress of necessity, or the recommendations of expedience. Necessity has no law, and expedience is often one form of necessity. It is no principle with sensible men, of whatever cast of opinion, to [225]
do always what is abstractedly best. Where no direct duty forbids, we may be obliged to do, as being best under circumstances, what we murmur and rise against, while we do it. We see that to attempt more is to effect less; that we must accept so much, or gain nothing; and so perforce we reconcile ourselves to what we would have far otherwise, if we could.[14] Thus a system of Mixed Education may, in a particular place or time, be the least of evils; it may be of long standing; it may be dangerous to meddle with; it may be professedly a temporary arrangement; it may be in an improving state; its disadvantages may be neutralized by the persons by whom, or the provisions under which, it is administered.[15]

---

[14] This is an important guiding principle of Newman's, one which explains why he sometimes appears inconsistent in his actions. While he saw the need of delineating the great principles of education, he was also quite prepared to admit that education involves 'questions not merely of immutable truth, but of practice and expedience' (*Idea*, p. 8). Rather than feel constrained by the principles he so eloquently describes in the Dublin discourses, Newman was down to earth in the way he went about applying them when setting up the Catholic University.

[15] It has been argued that Newman dropped his opposition to mixed education after he left the Catholic University (J. Coulson, *Newman and*

Protestants then, in matter of fact, are found to be both advocates and promoters of Mixed Education; but this, as I think will appear on inquiry, only under the conditions I have set down, first, where they have no special attachment to the dogmas which are compromised in the comprehension; and next, when they find it impossible, much as they may desire it, to carry out their attachment to them in practice, without prejudicial consequences greater than those which that comprehension involves. Men who profess a religion, if left to themselves, make religious and secular Education one [and the same]. Where, for instance, shall we find greater diversity of opinion, greater acrimony of mutual opposition, than between the two parties, High Church and Low, which mainly constitute the Established Religion of England and Ireland? Yet those parties,
[226] differing, as they do, from each other in other points, are equally opposed to the efforts of politicians to fuse their respective systems of Education with those either of Catholics or of sectaries; and it is only the strong

---

the Common Tradition: A Study in the Language of Church and Society (Oxford: Clarendon Press, 1970), p. 97). Yet two days before leaving Ireland for good, Newman was still speaking of his 'great dislike of mixed education' (Newman to Denison, 2 November 1858, *LD* xviii, pp. 500–1). Later, in 1868, he told William Monsell, 'No one doubts, at least I don't, that the true normal condition of things would be a Catholic University for Catholic students' (12 January 1865, *LD* xxi, p. 384). Likewise he told Woodlock, his successor as Rector, that 'A Catholic University, recognised as such by the State, is [...] the normal instrument of high education and of literary and scientific proficiency within the pale of the Church' (23 February 1868, *LD* xxiv, pp. 40–1). See also: *LD* xxi, pp. 234, 339, 384, 407; xxiii, pp. 75, 101; xxiv, pp. 39–40; xxvi, pp. 58, 61, 75; xxvii, p. 155. Also, Ker, 'Did Newman Believe in the Idea of a Catholic University?', *Downside Review* 93 (January 1975), pp. 39–42.

Elsewhere in the *Idea (*pp. 382–3), Newman argued that, far from conceding that a Catholic university might be unworkable in an intellectual climate which was inhospitable to Christian truth, he considered that in some respects it might be easier to found one in such a climate than in times when society was fully permeated by Catholicism.

expedience of concord and the will of the state which reconcile them to the necessity of a fusion with each other. Again, we all know into what various persuasions the English constituency is divided—more, indeed, than it is easy to enumerate; yet, since the great majority of that constituency, amid its differences, and in its several professions, distinctly dogmatizes, whether it be Anglican, Wesleyan, Calvinistic, or so-called Evangelical (as is distinctly shown, if in no other way, by its violence against Catholics), the consequence is, that, in spite of serious political obstacles and of the reluctance of statesmen, it has up to this time been resolute and successful in preventing the national separation of secular and religious Education. This concurrence, then, in various instances, supposing it to exist, as I believe it does, of a dogmatic faith on the one hand, and an abhorrence of Mixed Education on the other, is a phenomenon which, though happening among Protestants, demands the attention of Catholics, over and above the argumentative basis, on which, in the instance of each particular sect, this abhorrence would be found to rest.

While, then, I conceive that certain Protestant bodies may, under circumstances, decide, more successfully than Catholics of a certain locality or period, a point of religious philosophy or policy, and may so far give us a lesson in perspicacity or prudence, without any prejudice to our [227]
claims to the exclusive possession of Revealed Truth, I say, they are in matter of fact likely to have done so in a case like the present, in which, amid all the variety of persuasions into which Protestantism[16] necessarily splits, they agree together in a certain practical conclusion, which

[16] For the first edition of the *Idea* (1873), Newman amended or deleted many of the references to Protestantism (mostly in Discourse I). His use of the word in the original needs to be seen against the contemporary background of the mixed education controversy, the repression of Irish Catholics, and the 'No Popery' agitation.

each of them in turn sees to be necessary for its own particular maintenance. Nor is there surely anything startling or novel in such an admission. The Church has ever appealed and deferred to testimonies and authorities external to herself, in those matters in which she thought they had means of forming a judgment: and that on the principle *Cuique in sua arte credendum.*[17] She has ever used unbelievers and pagans in evidence of her truth, as far as their testimony went. She avails herself of heretical scholars, critics, and antiquarians. She has worded her theological teaching in the phraseology of Aristotle; Aquila, Symmachus, Theodotion, Origen, Eusebius, and Apollinaris, all more or less heterodox, have supplied materials for primitive exegetics. St Cyprian called Tertullian his master; Bossuet, in modern times, complimented the labours of the Anglican Bull; the Benedictine editors of the Fathers are familiar with the labours of Fell, Ussher, Pearson, and Beveridge. Pope Benedict XIV cites according to the occasion the works of Protestants without reserve, and the late French collection of Christian Apologists contains the writings of Locke, Burnet, Tillotson, and Paley. If, then, I come forward in any degree as borrowing the views of certain Protestant schools
[228] on the point which is to be discussed, I do so, not, Gentlemen, as supposing that even in philosophy the Catholic Church herself, as represented by her theologians or her schools, has anything to learn from men or bodies of men external to her pale; but as feeling, first, that she has ever, in the plenitude of her divine illumination, made use of whatever truth or wisdom she has found in their teaching or their measures; and next, that in particular times or places some of her children are likely to profit from external suggestions or lessons which are in no sense necessary for herself.

[17] Every man should be trusted in his own art or trade.

And in thus speaking of human philosophy, I have intimated the mode in which I propose to handle my subject altogether. Observe, then, Gentlemen, I have no intention of bringing into the argument the authority of the Church at all; but I shall consider the question simply on the grounds of human reason and human wisdom.[18] And from this it follows that, viewing it as a matter of argument, judgment, propriety, and expedience, I am not called upon to deny that in particular cases a course has been before now advisable for Catholics in regard to the education of their youth, and has been, in fact, adopted, which was not abstractedly the best, and is no pattern and precedent for others. Thus in the early ages the Church sanctioned her children in frequenting the heathen schools for the acquisition of secular accomplishments, where, as no one can doubt, evils existed, at least as great as can attend on Mixed Education now. The gravest Fathers recommended for Christian youth the use of Pagan masters;[19] the most saintly Bishops and most

---

[18] Culler writes in *The Imperial Intellect* (p. 145) that Newman's 'rationalistic approach was chiefly designed for the lawyers and doctors of Dublin. Many of them were already skeptical of the university as a project desired by the clergy for their own purposes, and therefore to be told that its principles were attainable simply by practical wisdom and good sense and that these principles had long been entertained by a university that was not even Catholic, though it was the greatest in the English-speaking world—this was as forceful an argument as any that could be devised, and certainly by the mid-point of his lecture Newman must have had the liberal party convinced of his absolute good faith'.

[19] In *HS* iii, pp. 151–2, Newman says that during the Roman Empire the Church, 'for the most part confined herself to the education of the clergy, and their ecclesiastical education; the laity and secular learning seem to have been still, more or less, in the charge of the State;—not, however, as if this was the best way of doing things [...] but because she found things in a certain state and used them as best she could. Her aim was to make the Empire Christian, not to revolutionize it [...] But when society was broken up, and had to be constructed over again, the case was different. [...] Henceforth, as all government, so all education, was to be founded

[229] authoritative Doctors had been sent in their adolescence by Christian parents to Pagan lecture halls.[20] And, not to take other instances, at this very time, and in this very country, as regards at least the poorer class of the community, whose secular acquirements ever must be limited, it has approved itself not only to Protestant state Ecclesiastics, who cannot be supposed to be very sensitive about doctrinal truth, but, as a wise condescension, even to many of our most venerated Bishops, to suffer, under the circumstances, a system of Mixed Education in the schools called National.[21]

On this part of the question, however, I have not to enter; for I confine myself to the subject of University Education. But even here it would ill have become me to pretend, simply on my own judgment, to decide on a point so emphatically practical, as regards a state of society, about which I have much to learn, on any abstract principles, however true and important. It would have been presumptuous in me so to have acted, nor am I so acting. It is my happiness in a matter of Christian duty, about which

---

on Revealed Truth. Secular teaching was to be united to sacred; and the Church had the supervision both of lay students and of profane learning.'

[20] *Vide* M. l'Abbé Lalanne's recent work. [JHN] Newman refers to *Influence des Pères de l'Église sur l'Éducation Publique pendant les Cinques Premiers Siècles de l'Ére Chrétienne* (Paris: Sagnier & Bray, 1850), pp. 52–6.

Elsewhere in his Dublin lectures, Newman contends with the Intellectual descendants of John Locke—such as his pupil Lord Shaftesbury, the *Edinburgh Review* circle, the utilitarian Jeremy Bentham, and politicians like Lord Brougham and Sir Robert Peel—who championed 'useful knowledge' and held that education alone was needed to make the public moral, thereby making religious teaching redundant. But Newman also contends with ecclesiastics who tended to be interested in education only insofar as it ministered to religion and the Church. This tendency manifested itself in an extreme form in the writings of the French priest Jean Gaume. For more, see the relevant footnote on p. [157].

[21] For an explanation of the National System and the opposition to it, see *NU*, pp. 28–39; Barr, *Paul Cullen*, pp. 10–22.

the most saintly and the most able may differ, to be guided simply by the decision and recommendation of the Holy See, the judge and finisher of all controversies. That decision indeed, I repeat, shall not enter into my argument; but it is my own reason for arguing. I am trusting my own judgment on the subject, because I find it is the judgment of him who has upon his shoulder the government and the solicitude of all the Churches. I appear before you, Gentlemen, not prior to the decision of Rome on the [230]
question of which I am to treat, but after it. My sole aspiration—and I cannot have a higher under the heavens—is to be the servant of the Vicar of Christ. He has sanctioned at this time a particular measure for his children who speak the English tongue, and the distinguished persons by whom it is to be carried out have honoured me with a share in their work. I take things as I find them; I know nothing of the past; I find myself here; I set myself to the duties I find here; I set myself to further, by every means in my power, doctrines and views, true in themselves, recognized by all Catholics as such, familiar to my own mind; and to do this quite apart from the consideration of questions which have been determined without me and before me. I am here the advocate and the minister of a certain great principle; yet not merely advocate and minister, else had I not been here at all. It has been my previous keen sense and hearty reception of that principle, that has been at once the cause, as I must suppose, of my selection, and the ground of my acquiescence.[22] I am told on authority that a principle is

[22] Newman had acted as the champion of the credal university in his leading role in defending the University of Oxford as an Anglican institution. A major national grievance at the time came from the growing number of non-Anglicans who found themselves excluded from the two ancient universities by the religious test barriers there, which were originally devised to exclude Catholics. At Oxford, students were required to subscribe to the Thirty-Nine Articles both on matriculation and on taking a degree; at Cambridge, the tests were only required for the latter. The

necessary, which I have ever felt to be true. As the royal matron in sacred history consigned the child she had made her own to the charge of its natural mother; so truths and duties, which come of unaided reason, not of grace, which were already intimately mine by the workings of my own mind, and the philosophy of human schools, are now committed to my care, to nurse and to cherish, by her and
[231] for her who, acting on the prerogative of her divinely inspired discernment, has in this instance honoured with a royal adoption the suggestions of reason.

Happy mother, who received her offspring back by giving him up, and gained, at another's word, what her own

---

needs of these Dissenters were partially met in 1828 by the foundation of London University, established as a secular institution.

After a long period of Tory rule, the incoming Whig administration of the early 1830s presented the reforming Liberals with the opportunity to challenge vested interests. In 1834 a Bill was introduced in Parliament to remove the religious tests at Oxford and Cambridge, triggering a pamphlet war that lasted for two years. The first pamphlet was written by Newman, and it argued that religion was so much part of the very fabric of an Oxford education, with its daily routine of morning and evening chapel, that to admit Dissenters would destroy the whole. After this Newman left to others the task of penning the pamphlets, and joined Edward Pusey and William Sewell on the committee that ran the campaign, using the structures that had recently been put in place for distributing the *Tracts for the Times*.

Largely thanks to the united front it put up, Oxford was able to see off calls for reform inspired by Whig influence outside the University, but shortly after the Bill's defeat in Parliament, bitter controversy erupted within the University over proposals to replace subscription to the Thirty-Nine Articles with a Declaration of Conformity. The battle over the reform of the religious tests raged for a decade, pitting liberal reformers against the rising Tractarian party, each side arguing for a set of beliefs which concerned the whole spirit and method of education. The religious tests were eventually removed, partially in 1854, then fully in 1871 (See P. Nockles, 'An Academic Counter-revolution: Newman and Tractarian Oxford's Idea of a University', *History of Universities* 10 (1991), pp. 137–97; 'Lost Causes and … impossible loyalties: the Oxford Movement and the University', *History of the University of Oxford* vi, pp. 195–267).

most jealous artifices had failed to secure at home! Gentlemen, I have not yet ended the explanations with which I must introduce myself to your notice. If I have been expressing a satisfaction that opinions, early imbibed and long cherished in my own mind, now come to me with the Church's seal upon them, do not imagine that I am indulging a subtle kind of private judgment, especially unbecoming in a Catholic.[23] It would, I think, be unjust to me, were any one to gather, from what I have been saying, that I had so established myself in my own ideas and in my old notions, as a centre of thought, that, instead of coming to the Church to be taught, I was but availing myself of such opportunities as she gave me, to force principles on your attention which I had adopted without her [aid]. It would, indeed, be a most unworthy frame of mind, to view her sanction, however it could be got, as a sort of leave or permit, whereby the intellect obtains an outlet, which it is ever coveting, to range freely once in a way, and to enjoy itself in a welcome, because a rare, holiday. Not so; human wisdom, at the very best, even in matters of religious policy, is principally but a homage, certainly no essential service to Divine Truth. Nor is the Church some stern mistress, practised only in refusal and prohibition, to be obeyed grudgingly and dexterously overreached; but a kind and [232]
watchful teacher and guide, encouraging us forward in the path of truth amid the perils which beset it. Deeply do I feel, ever will I protest, for I can appeal to the ample testimony of history to bear me out, that, in questions of right and wrong there is nothing really strong in the whole world,

---

[23] Having recourse to private judgement was, according to Newman, almost what typified the Protestant mind, to the extent that it is a recurring theme in his sermons and correspondence. Newman takes the opportunity of his first Dublin discourse to counter the lurking suspicion among cradle Catholics that the Oxford converts had not shed their Protestant modes of thinking and that they were potentially a dangerous influence.

nothing decisive and operative, but the voice of him, to whom have been committed the keys of the kingdom and the oversight of Christ's flock. That voice is now, as ever it has been, a real authority, infallible when it teaches, prosperous when it commands, ever taking the lead wisely and distinctly in its own province, adding certainty to what is probable, and persuasion to what is certain. Before it speaks, the most saintly may mistake; and after it has spoken, the most gifted must obey.

I have said this in explanation; but it has an application if you will let me so say, far beyond myself. Perhaps we have all need to be reminded, in one way or another, as regards our habitual view of things, if not our formal convictions, of the greatness of authority and the intensity of power which accompany the decisions of the Holy See. I can fancy. Gentlemen, among those who hear me there may be those who would be willing to acquit the principles of Education which I am to advocate of all fault whatever, except that of being impracticable. I can fancy them to grant to me, that those principles are most correct and most obvious, simply irresistible on paper, yet, after all, nothing more than the dreams of men who live out of the world, and who do not see the difficulty of keeping Catholicism anyhow afloat on
[233] the bosom of this wonderful nineteenth century. Proved, indeed, those principles are to demonstration, but they will not work. Nay, it was my own admission just now, that, in a particular instance, it might easily happen that what is only second best is best practically, because what is actually best is out of the question. This, I hear you say to yourselves, is the state of things at present. You recount in detail the numberless impediments, great and small, threatening and vexatious, which at every step embarrass the attempt to carry out ever so poorly a principle in itself so true and ecclesiastical. You appeal in your defence to wise and sagacious intellects, who are far from enemies, if not to

Catholicism, at least to the Irish Hierarchy, and you simply despair, or rather you absolutely disbelieve, that Education can possibly be conducted, here and now, on a theological principle, or that youths of different religions can, in matter of fact, be educated apart from each other. The more you think over the state of politics, the position of parties, the feelings of classes, and the experience of the past, the more chimerical does it seem to you to aim at anything beyond a University of Mixed Instruction. Nay, even if the attempt could accidentally succeed, would not the mischief exceed the benefits of it? How great the sacrifice, in how many days, by which it would be preceded and followed!—how many wounds, open and secret, would it inflict upon the body politic! And, if it fails, which is to be expected, then a double mischief will ensue from its recognition of evils which it has been unable to remedy. These are your deep misgivings; and, in proportion to the force with which they [234]
come to you, is the concern and anxiety which they occasion you, that there should be those whom you love, whom you revere, who from one cause or other refuse to enter into them.

This, I repeat, is what some good Catholics will say to me, and more than this. They will express themselves better than I can speak for them—with more nature and point, with more force of argument and fulness of detail; and I will frankly and at once acknowledge, Gentlemen, that I do not mean here to give a direct answer to their objections. I do not say an answer cannot be given; on the contrary, I may have a confident expectation that, in proportion as those objections are looked in the face, they will fade away. But, however this may be, it would not become me to argue the matter with those who understand the circumstances of the problem so much better than myself. What do I know of the state of things in Ireland that I should presume to put ideas of mine, which could not be right except by accident, by the

side of theirs, who speak in the country of their birth and their home? No, Gentlemen, you are natural judges of the difficulties which beset us, and they are doubtless greater than I can even fancy or forebode. Let me, for the sake of argument, admit all you say against our enterprise, and a great deal more. Your proof of its intrinsic impossibility [at this time] shall be to me as demonstrative as my own of its theological correctness. Why then should I be so rash and perverse as to involve myself in trouble not properly mine? Why go out of my own place? How is it that I do not know
[235] when I am well off? Why so headstrong and reckless as to lay up for myself miscarriage and disappointment, as though I had not enough of my own?

Considerations such as these might have been simply decisive in time past for the boldest and most able among us; now, however, I have one resting point, just one, one plea which serves me in the stead of all direct argument whatever, which hardens me against censure, which encourages me against fear, and to which I shall ever come round, when I hear the question of the practicable and the expedient brought into discussion. After all, it is St Peter who has spoken. Peter is no recluse, no abstracted student, no dreamer about the past, no doter upon the dead and gone, no projector of the visionary. Peter for eighteen hundred years has lived in the world; he has seen all fortunes, he has encountered all adversaries, he has shaped himself for all emergencies. If there ever was a power on earth who had an eye for the times, who has confined himself to the practicable, and has been happy in his anticipations, whose words have been deeds, and whose commands prophecies, such is he in the history of ages who sits on from generation to generation in the Chair of the Apostles as the Vicar of Christ and Doctor of His Church.

Notions, then, taught me long ago by others, long cherished in my own mind, these are not my confidence.

Their truth does not make them feasible, nor their
reasonableness persuasive. Rather, I would meet the
objector by an argument of his own sort. If you tell me this
work will fail, I will make answer, [that] the worker is apt to [236]
succeed, and I trust in my knowledge of the past more than
in your prediction of the future. It was said by an old
philosopher, who declined to reply to an emperor's
arguments, "It is not safe controverting with the master of
twenty legions". What Augustus had in the material order,
that, and much more, has Peter in the spiritual. Peter has
spoken by Pius, and when was Peter ever unequal to the
occasion? When has he not risen with the crisis? What
dangers have ever daunted him? What sophistry foiled him?
What uncertainties misled him? When did ever any power
go to war with Peter, material or moral, civilized or savage,
and get the better? When did the whole world ever band
together against him solitary, and not find him too many for
them?

These are not the words of rhetoric, Gentlemen, but of
history. All who take part with Peter are on the winning
side. The Apostle says not in order to unsay, for he has
inherited that word which is with power. From the first he
has looked through the wide world, of which he has the
burden, and according to the need of the day, and the
inspirations of his Lord, he has set himself, now to one
thing, now to another, but to all in season, and to nothing in
vain. He came first upon an age of refinement and luxury
like our own, and in spite of the persecutor fertile in the
resources of his cruelty, he soon gathered, out of all classes
of society, the slave, the soldier, the high-born lady, and the
sophist, to form a people for his Master's honour. The
savage hordes came down in torrents from the north,
hideous even to look upon; and [St] Peter went out with
holy water and with [blessing][24] and by his very eye he [237]

[24] The original has 'benison'.

sobered them and backed them in full career. They turned aside, and flooded the whole earth, but only to be more surely civilized by him, and to be made ten times more his children even than the older populations they had overwhelmed. Lawless kings arose, sagacious as the Roman, passionate as the Hun, yet in him they found their match, and were shattered, and he lived on. The gates of the earth were opened to the east and west, and men poured out to take possession; and he and his went with them, swept along by zeal and charity, as far as they by enterprise, covetousness, or ambition. Has he failed in his successes up to this hour? Did he, in our fathers' day, fail in his struggle with Joseph of Germany and his confederates, with Napoleon, a greater name, and his dependent kings, that, though in another kind of fight, he should fail in ours? What grey hairs are on the head of Judah, whose youth is renewed like the eagle's, whose feet are like the feet of harts, and underneath the everlasting Arms?

In the first centuries of the Church all this was a mere point of faith, but every age as it has come has stayed up faith by sight; and shame on us if, with the accumulated witness of eighteen centuries, our eyes are too gross to see what the Saints have ever anticipated. Education, Gentlemen, involved as it is in the very idea of a religion such as ours, cannot be a strange work at any time in the hands of the Vicar of Christ. The heathen forms of religion thought it enough to amuse and quiet the populace with spectacles, and, on the other hand, to bestow a dignity and
[238] divine sanction upon the civil ruler; but Catholicism addresses itself directly to the heart and conscience of the individual. The Religion which numbers Baptism and Penance among its sacraments, cannot be neglectful of the soul's training; the Creed which opens and resolves into so majestic and so living a theology, cannot but subserve the cultivation of the intellect; the Revelation which tells us of

truths otherwise utterly hid from us, cannot be justly called the enemy of knowledge; the Worship which is so awful and so thrilling, cannot but feed the aspirations of genius, and move the affections from their depths. The Institution which has flourished in centuries the most famed for mental activity and cultivation, which has come into collision, to say no more, with the schools of Antioch and Alexandria, Athens and Edessa, Saracenic Seville, and Protestant Berlin, cannot be wanting in experience what to do now, and when to do it. He whom the Almighty left behind to be His representative on earth, has ever been jealous, as beseemed him, as of God's graces, so also of His gifts. He has been as tender of the welfare and interests of human science as he is loyal to the divine truth which is his peculiar charge. He has ever been the foster-father of secular knowledge, and has rejoiced in its growth, while he has pruned away its self-destructive luxuriance.

Least of all can the Catholics of two islands,[25] which have been heretofore so singularly united in the cultivation and diffusion of Knowledge, under the auspices of the Apostolic See, we surely, Gentlemen, are not the persons to distrust its wisdom and its fortune when it sends us on a
similar mission now. I cannot forget, Gentlemen, that at a [239]
time when Celt and Saxon were alike savage, it was the See of Peter that gave both of them first faith, and then civilization; and then, again, bound them together in one by the seal of that joint commission which it gave them to convert and illuminate in turn the pagan Continent. I cannot forget how it was from Rome that the glorious St Patrick was sent to Ireland, and did a work so great, that he may be said to have had no successor in it; the sanctity, and learning, and zeal, and charity which followed being but the result of the one impulse which he gave. I cannot forget

---

[25] This and the following paragraphs were aimed at mollifying the anti-English sentiment among his listeners and readers.

how, in no long time, under the fostering breath of the Vicar of Christ, a country of heathen superstitions became the very wonder and asylum of all people;—the wonder by reason of its knowledge, sacred and profane; the asylum for religion, literature, and science, chased away from the Continent by barbaric invaders. I recollect its hospitality freely accorded to the pilgrim; its volumes munificently presented to the foreign student; and the prayers, and blessings, and holy rites, and solemn chants, which sanctified the while both giver and receiver. Nor can I forget how my own England had meanwhile become the solicitude of the same unwearied Eye; how Augustine was sent to us by Gregory; how he fainted in the way in terror at our barbarian name, and, but for the Pope, had returned as from an impossible expedition; how he was forced on "in weakness, and in fear, and in much trembling," until he had achieved the conquest of all England to Christ. Nor, how it came to pass that, when Augustine died and his work
[240] slackened, another Pope, unwearied still, sent three great Saints from Rome to educate and refine the people he had converted. Three holy men set out for England together, of different nations; Theodore, an Asiatic Greek, from Tarsus; Adrian, an African; Bennett alone a Saxon, for Peter knows no distinction of races in his ecumenical work; they came with theology and science in their train; with relics, and with pictures, and with manuscripts of the Holy Fathers and the Greek classics; and Theodore and Adrian founded schools, secular and religious, all over England, while Bennett brought to the north the large library he had collected in foreign parts, and, with plans and ornamental work from France, erected a church of stone, under the invocation of St Peter, after the Roman fashion, "which," says the historian,[26] "he most affected". I call to mind how St Wilfrid, St John of Beverley, St Bede, and other saintly

[26] Cressy. [JHN]

men, carried on the good work in the following generations, and how from that time forth the two islands, England and Ireland, in a dark and dreary age, were the two lights of Christendom; and nothing passed between them, and no personal aims were theirs, save the interchange of kind offices and the rivalry of love.

O! memorable time when St Aidan and the Irish Monks went up to Lindisfarne and Melrose, and taught the Saxon youth, and a St Cuthbert and a St Eata repaid their gracious toil! O! blessed days of peace and confidence, when [Celtic] Mailduf penetrated to Malmesbury in the south, which has inherited his name, and founded there the famous school which gave birth to the great St Aldhelm! O! precious seal [241]
and testimony of Gospel charity, when, as Aldhelm in turn tells us, the English went to Ireland "numerous as bees"; when the Saxon St Egbert and St Willibrod, preachers to the heathen Frisons, made the voyage to Ireland to prepare themselves for their work; and when from Ireland went forth to Germany the two noble Ewalds, Saxons also, to earn the crown of martyrdom. Such a period, indeed, so rich in grace, in peace, in love, and in good works, could only last for a season; but, even when the light was to pass away, the two sister islands were destined not to forfeit, but to transfer it. The time came when [the][27] neighbouring country was in turn to hold the mission they had so long and so well fulfilled; and, when to it they made over their honourable office, faithful to the alliance of two hundred years, they [both participated in the solemn act].[28] High up in the north, upon the Tyne, the pupil of St Theodore, St Adrian, and St Bennett, for forty years [had][29] Bede [been] the light of the whole western world; as happy, too, in his scholars round about him, as in his celebrity and influence

[27] The original has 'a'.
[28] The original has 'did the solemn act together'.
[29] The original has 'was'.

in the length and breadth of Christendom. St John of Beverley, [too], a generation before him, taught by the same masters, had for thirty years been shedding the lustre of his sanctity and learning upon the Archiepiscopal school of York. Among the pupils of these celebrated men the learned Alcuin stood first; and Alcuin, not content even with the training which Saints could give him, betook himself to the sister island, and remained a whole twelve years in the Irish
[242] schools. And thus, when Charlemagne would revive science and letters in his own France, to England he sent for masters, and to the cloisters of St John of Beverley and St Bede; and Alcuin, the scholar both of the Saxon and the Celt, was the chief of those who went forth to supply the need of the Great Emperor. Such was the foundation of the school of Paris, from which, in the course of centuries, sprang the famous University,[30] the glory of the middle ages.

The past never returns; the course of things, old in its texture, is ever new in its colouring and fashion. Ireland and England are not what they once were, but Rome is where it was; St Peter is the same; his zeal, his charity, his mission, his gifts, are the same. He, of old time, made us one by giving us one work, making us joint teachers of the nations; and now, surely, he is giving us a like mission, and we shall become one again, while we zealously and lovingly fulfil it.

---

[30] In *HS* iii, p. 152 Newman comments, 'whether his school at Paris be called a University or not, he [Charlemagne] laid down principles of which a University is the result, in that he aimed at educating all classes, and undertook all subjects of teaching.'

DISCOURSE V[1]

[1] Discourse V (not to confused with Discourse V, 'Knowledge its Own End', in the *Idea*) was published separately then as part of *Discourses on the Scope and Nature of University Education* in 1852, but was omitted from the 1859 edition and from the *Idea* (1873). Why? One reason, it seems, was that Newman was uneasy about the wording of the Papal Brief of 20 March 1854 to the Irish bishops, which appeared to be at variance with passages in this Discourse. (For explanations, see *AW*, pp. 322–3; *NU*, pp. 275–8, 286; *Imperial Intellect*, pp. 264–6, 315–6; *Idea*, ed. Ker, pp. xxxiv-xxxviii. See also WPN's comments about Discourse V on p. [lxi] and Culler's questioning of them in the relevant footnote.) Culler gives another, more succinct reason to explain the omission of Discourse V; he says that, 'if V was later dropped, it was because it was never needed in the first place' (*Imperial Intellect*, p. 316).

However, Ker agrees with Culler that Newman did not suppress Discourse V as being 'dangerous'. After all, as Neville notes, 'he purposed including it, after corrections, in an intended volume of Pamphlets and Papers' (p. [lxi]). Moreover, one of Newman's plans (dated 25 Feb 1857) was to compress the first five Discourses into two for an edition to be called *The Genius, Scope, and Method of Universities*, which was to be a companion volume to *The Office and Works of Universities* (1856). It entailed keeping one third of Discourse I, nearly one third of Discourse III, two-thirds of Discourse IV and the first half of Discourse V (pages 135–6, 140–53 of *Discourses*), including the two potentially controversial passages (*Imperial Intellect*, p. 316. N.B. McGrath read the same MS document as Culler and concluded that only five pages of Discourse V were to be retained in this compressed edition, *NU*, p. 288.) Ker points out that Discourse V provides 'a devastating contrast between modern fragmented secularist education and an integrated liberal education in the Christian tradition', and is therefore 'one of the most eloquent parts of the Discourses' (*Idea*, ed. Ker, p. xxxviii). However, it did not fuse easily with the other parts of the 1859 and 1873 editions (*Idea*, ed. Ker, p. xxxvi).

A separate plan of Newman's was to 'Leave out the whole of this *Discourse*, except *perhaps* some little bits' (*NU*, p. 288). In the Advertisement to *The Scope and Nature of University Teaching; or*

Discourse V

From *The Scope and Nature of University Education* (ed. 1852)[2]

[UNIVERSAL][3] KNOWLEDGE VIEWED AS ONE PHILOSOPHY[4]

IT is a prevalent notion just now, that religious opinion does not enter, as a matter of necessity, in any considerable measure, into the treatment of scientific or literary subjects. It is supposed, that, whatever a teacher's persuasion may be,

---

University Teaching Considered in its Abstract Scope and Nature (1859), Newman explains that, 'He has removed from the text much temporary, collateral, or superfluous matter, and has thus reduced it to the size of his two other volumes on University Teaching'. Moreover, as Ker points out, a large part of Discourse V is taken up with arguments and illustrations drawn from religion. Among the Discourses, 'the fifth contains the most allusions to theological doctrine and controversy, of the kind that the author was to be at pains to omit or alter in his revisions of 1859 and 1873' (*Idea*, ed. Ker, p. xxxvii). Although Discourse I *was* partly restored in the 1873 edition, Discourse V was not: there were simply too many corrections required in order to amend controversial and peripheral religious material.

For a full discussion of Discourse V, see *Idea*, ed. Ker, pp. xxxiv-xxxviii; *NU*, pp. 274–92.

[2] Changes from the 1852 text of *Discourses on the Scope and Nature of University Education* are shown in square brackets. The original text is given in the footnote, unless the change is a mere addition, in which case no footnote is needed.

[3] The original has 'General'.

[4] The 1852 edition of the *Discourses* included an appendix which provides references to the authorities and sources that Newman had consulted. The fourth section, entitled 'The Branches of Knowledge Form One Whole', is relevant to Discourse V. It begins as follows: 'It is curious how negligent English writers seem to be just now of the necessity of comprehensiveness and harmony of view, in their pursuit of truth in detail. The very Encyclopædia ought to suggest it to them; but the alphabetical order has assimilated the great undertaking so designated to a sort of Dictionary of portions and departments of knowledge. Coleridge indeed, a man of philosophical mind, has felt the evil, and planned the Encyclopædia with which he was connected, on a truer idea' (*Idea*, ed. Ker, pp. 446–7). The reference is to Samuel Taylor Coleridge.

whether Christian or not, or whatever kind or degree of Christianity, it need not betray itself in such lectures or publications as the duties of his office require. Whatever he holds about the Supreme Being, His attributes and His works, be it truth or error, does not make him better or worse in experiment or speculation. He can discourse upon plants, or insects, or birds, or the powers of the mind, or languages, or historical documents, or literature, or any other such matter of fact, with equal accurateness and profit, whatever he may determine about matters which are entirely distinct from them.

In answer to this representation I contended last week, that a positive disunion takes place between Theology and Secular Science, whenever they are not actually united. Here, not to be at peace is to be at war; and for this reason: The assemblage of Sciences, which together make up Universal Knowledge, is not an accidental or a varying heap of acquisitions, but a system, and may be said to be *in* [244]
equilibrio as long as all its portions are secured to it. Take away one of them, and that one so important in the catalogue as Theology, and disorder and ruin at once ensue. There is no middle state between an *equilibrium* and chaotic confusion; one science is ever pressing upon another, unless kept in check; and the only guarantee of Truth is the cultivation of them all. And such is the office of a University.

Far different, of course, are the sentiments of the patrons of a divorce between Religious and Secular Knowledge. Let us see how they spoke twenty-five years ago in the defence formally put out for that formidable Institution, formidable, as far as an array of high intellects can make any paradox or paralogism formidable, which was then set up in London on the basis of such a separation. The natural, as well as the special, champion of the then University of London, and of the principle which it represented, was a celebrated Review, which stood at the time, and, I suppose, stands still, at the head of our periodical literature. In this publication, at the date of which I speak, an article was devoted to the exculpation of the Institution in question, from the charges or suspicions which it incurred in consequence of the principle on which it was founded. The Reviewer steadily contemplates the idea of a University without Religion; "From pulpits, and visitation dinners, and combination rooms innumerable, the cry," he says, "is echoed and re-echoed, An University without religion"; and then he proceeds to dispose of the protest by one or two simple illustrations.

[245] Writing, as he does, with liveliness and wit, as well as a profession of serious argument, this Reviewer can scarcely be quoted with due regard to the gravity which befits a discussion such as the present. You must pardon me, Gentlemen, if, in my desire to do justice to him and his cause in his own words, I suffer him to interrupt the equable flow of our discussion with unseasonable mirth; and in order to avoid, as much as possible, a want of keeping between his style and my own, I will begin with the less sprightly illustration of the two. "Take the case," he says, "of a young man, a student, we will suppose, of surgery, resident in London. He wishes to become master of his profession, without neglecting other useful branches of knowledge. In the morning he attends Mr McCulloch's Lecture on Political Economy. He then repairs to the Hospital, and hears Sir Astley Cooper explain the mode of reducing fractures. In the afternoon he joins one of the classes which Mr Hamilton instructs in French or German. With regard to religious observances, he acts as he himself, or those under whose care he is, may think most advisable. Is there anything objectionable in this? is it not the most common case in the world? And in what does it differ from that of a young man at the London University? Our surgeon,

it is true, will have to run over half London in search of his instructors. ... Is it in the local situation that the mischief lies?"[5] Such is the argument; need I point out the fallacy? Whatever may be said of Political Economy, at any rate a surgical operation is not a branch of knowledge, or a process of argument, or an inference, or an investigation, or [246] an analysis, or an induction, or an abstraction, or other intellectual exercise: it is a grave practical matter. Again, the primer, the spelling book, the grammar, construing and parsing, are scarcely trials of reason, imagination, taste, or judgment; they can scarcely be said to have truth for their object at all; anyhow, they belong to the first stage of mental development, to the school, rather than to the University. Neither the reduction of fractures, nor the Hamiltonian method can be considered a branch of Philosophy; it is not more wonderful that such trials of skill or of memory can safely dispense with Theology for their perfection, than that it is unnecessary for the practice of gunnery or the art of calligraphy.

So much for one of this Reviewer's illustrations: the other is more infelicitous still, in proportion as it is more insulting to our view of the subject. "Have none of those," he asks, "who censure the London University on this account, daughters who are educated at home, and who are attended by different teachers? The music master, a good Protestant, comes at twelve; the dancing master, a French philosopher, at two; the Italian master, a believer in the blood of St Januarius, at three. The parents take upon themselves the office of instructing their child in religion. She hears the preachers whom they prefer, and reads the theological works which they put into her hands. Who can

---

[5] *Edinburgh Review*, Feb., 1826. [JHN] The relevant article, 'Thoughts on the Advancement of Academical Education in England', *Edinburgh Review* 86, pp. 318–19, was written by either T. B. Macaulay or H. Brougham.

deny that this is the case in innumerable families? Who can point out any material difference between the situation in which this girl is placed, and that of a pupil at the new
[247] University?" I pass over the scoff at a miracle to which the writer neither gave credence himself, nor imagined it in others; looking simply at his argument, I ask, is it not puerile to imply that music, or dancing, or lessons in Italian, have anything to do with Philosophy? It is plain that such writers do not rise to the very idea of a University. They consider it a sort of bazaar, or pantechnicon, in which wares of all kinds are heaped together for sale in stalls independent of each other; and that to save the purchasers the trouble of running about from shop to shop; or an hotel or lodging house where all professions and classes are at liberty to congregate, varying, however, according to the season, each of them strange to each, and about its own work or pleasure; whereas, if we would rightly deem of it, a University is the home, it is the mansion-house, of the goodly family of the Sciences, sisters all, and sisterly in their mutual dispositions.

Such, I say, is the theory which recommends itself to the public mind of this age, and is the moving principle of its undertakings. And yet that very instinct of the intellect of which I spoke last week, which impels each science to extend itself as far as it can, and which leads, when indulged, to the confusion of Philosophy generally, might teach the upholders of such a theory a truer view of the subject. It seems, as I then observed, that the human mind is ever seeking to systematize its knowledge, to base it upon principle, and to find a science comprehensive of all sciences. And sooner than forego the gratification of this
[248] moral appetency, it starts with whatever knowledge or science it happens to have, and makes that knowledge serve as a rule or measure of the universe, for want of a better, preferring the completeness and precision of bigotry to a

fluctuating and homeless scepticism. What a singular contrast is here between nature and theory! We see the intellect in this instance, as soon as it moves at all, moving straight against its own conceits and falsities, and upsetting them spontaneously, without effort, and at once. It witnesses to a great truth in spite of its own professions and engagements. It had promised, in the name of the patrons of our modern Colleges and Universities, that there need not be, and that there should not be, any system or philosophy in knowledge and its transmission, but that Liberal Education henceforth should be a mere fortuitous heap of acquisitions and accomplishments; however, here, as it so often happens elsewhere, nature is too strong for art. She bursts violently and dangerously through the artificial trammels laid upon her, and exercises her just rights wrongly, since she cannot rightly. Usurpers and tyrants are the successors to legitimate rulers sent into exile. Forthwith Private Judgment moves forward with the implements of this or that science, to do a work imperative indeed, but beyond its powers. It owns the need of general principles and constituent ideas, by taking false ones, and thus is ever impeding and preventing unity, while it is ever attempting and thereby witnessing [to] it. From the many voices crying "Order" and "Silence," noise and tumult follow. From the very multiplicity and diversity of the efforts after unity on every side, this practical age has thrown up the notion of it [249]
altogether.

What is the consequence? that the works of the age are not the development of definite principles, but accidental results of discordant and simultaneous action, of committees and boards, composed of men, each of whom has his own interests and views, and, to gain something his own way, is obliged to sacrifice a good deal to every one else. From causes so adventitious and contradictory, who can predict the ultimate production? Hence it is that those works have

so little permanent life in them, because they are not founded on principles and ideas. Ideas are the life of institutions, social, political, and literary; but the excesses of Private Judgment, in the prosecution of its multiform theories, have at length made men sick of a truth, which they recognized long after they were able to realize it. At the present day, they knock the life out of the institutions they have inherited, by their alterations and adaptations. As to their own creations, these are a sort of monster, with hands, feet, and trunk moulded respectively on distinct types. Their whole, if the word is to be used, is an accumulation from without, not the growth of a principle from within. Thus, as I said just now, their notion of a University is a sort of bazaar or hotel, where everything is showy, and self-sufficient, and changeable. "Motley's the only wear." The majestic vision of the Middle Age,[6] which grew steadily to perfection in the course of centuries, the University of Paris, or Bologna, or Oxford, has almost gone
[250] out in night. A philosophical comprehensiveness, an orderly expansiveness, an elastic constructiveness, men have lost them, and cannot make out why. This is why: because they have lost the idea of unity: because they cut off the head of a living thing, and think it is perfect, all but the head. They think the head an extra, an accomplishment, the *corona operis*, not essential to the idea of the being under their

[6] In the *Imperial Intellect* (pp. 251–2) Culler writes, 'It is in the *Rise and Progress of Universities* [*HS* iii, pp. 1–251] that Newman shows himself most conscious of his medieval heritage [...] he regarded his own work as repeating in some sense the work of the Middle Ages. He saw a deep and pervasive analogy between the intellectual problem of the twelfth century and that of his own day, for both periods were confronted with the task of bringing a vast body of new knowledge, suddenly acquired, into harmony with the more traditional wisdom of a rather different character; and he hoped that in the great synthesis of the thirteenth century [...] he might find a means of adjusting the claims of science and religion in the modern world.'

hands. An idea, a view, an indivisible object, which does not admit of more or less, a form, which cannot coalesce with anything else, an intellectual principle, expanding into a consistent harmonious whole,—in short, Mind, in the true sense of the word,—they are, forsooth, too practical to lose time in such reveries![7]

Our way, Gentlemen, is very different. We [do but] adopt a method, founded in man's nature and the necessity of things, exemplified in all great moral works whatever, instinctively used by all men in the course of daily life, though they may not recognize it, discarded by our opponents only because they have lost the true key to exercise it withal. We start with an idea, we educate upon a type; we make use, as nature prompts us, of *the faculty* which I have called an intellectual grasp of things, or an inward sense, and which I shall hereafter show is really meant by the word "Philosophy". Science itself is a specimen of its exercise; for its very essence is this mental formation. A science is not mere knowledge, it is knowledge which has undergone a process of intellectual digestion. It is the grasp of many things brought together in one, and hence is its power; for, properly speaking, it is Science that is power, not Knowledge. Well then, this is [251]
how [I would][8] act towards the Sciences taken all together; we view them as one and give them an idea; what is this but an extension and perfection, in an age which prides itself upon its scientific genius, of that very process by which science exists at all? Imagine a science of sciences, and you have attained the true notion of the scope of a University. We consider that all things mount up to a whole, that there

[7] For Alasdair MacIntyre's championing of Newman's idea of the unity of knowledge, or 'more accurately of the unity of understanding', see 'The very idea of a university: Aristotle, Newman and us', *British Journal of Educational Studies* 57:4 (December 2009), pp. 347–62.

[8] The original has 'Catholics'.

is an order and precedence and harmony in the branches of knowledge one with another as well as one by one, and that to destroy that structure is as unphilosophical in a course of education, as it is unscientific in the separate portions of it. We form and fix the Sciences in a circle and system, and give them a centre and an aim, instead of letting them wander up and down in a sort of hopeless confusion. In other words, to use scholastic language, we give the various pursuits and objects, on which the intellect is employed, a *form*;[9] for it is the peculiarity of a form, that it gathers up in one, and draws off from everything else, the materials on which it is impressed.

Now here, Gentlemen, I seem in danger of a double inconvenience, *viz.* of enlarging on what, as a point of scholasticism, is too abstruse, and, as put into familiar language, is too obvious, for an auditory, [like the present,] which claims of me what is neither rudimental on the one hand nor technical on the other. And yet I will rather ask your indulgence to allow me in a very familiar illustration of a very scholastic term, than incur the chance, which might otherwise fall out, of being deficient in my exposition of the subject for which I adduce it.

[252] For instance, we all understand how Worship is one idea, and how it is made up of many things, some being essential to it, and all subservient. Its essence is the lifting up of the heart to God; if it be no more than this, still this is enough, and nothing more is necessary. But view it as brought out in some solemn rite or public ceremonial; the essence is the same, and it is there on the occasion I am supposing;—we will say it is Benediction of the Most Holy Sacrament, or a devotion in honour of some Saint;—it is there still, but, first, it is the lifting up, not of one heart, but of many all at once; next, it is the devotion, not of hearts only, but of

[9] See the text of the 1854 Papal Brief on p. [lxxxi] (and the corresponding footnote) for the differing approaches of Newman and Pope Pius IX.

bodies too; not of eyes only, or hands only, or voices only, or knees only, but of the whole man. And next, the devotion passes on to more than soul and body; there are vestments there, rich and radiant, symbolical of the rite, and odorous flowers, and a flood of light, and a cloud of incense, and music joyous and solemn, of instruments, as well as voices, till all the senses overflow with the idea of devotion. Is the music devotion? as the Protestant inquires; is the incense devotion? are candles devotion? are flowers? are vestments? or words spoken? or genuflections? Not any one of them. And what have candles to do with flowers? or flowers with vestments? or vestments with music? Nothing whatever; each is distinct in itself, and independent of the rest. The flowers are the work of nature, and are elaborated in the garden; the candles come of the soft wax, which the "Apis Mater" (as the Church beautifully sings), which the teeming bee fashions; the vestments have been wrought in the looms of Lyons or Vienna or Naples, and have been brought over [253]
sea at great cost; the music is the present and momentary vibration of the air, acted upon by tube or string; and still for all this, are they not one whole? are they not blended together indivisibly, and sealed with the image of unity, by reason of the one idea of worship, in which they live and to which they minister? Take away that idea, and what are they worth? the whole pageant becomes a mummery. The worship made them one; but supposing no one in that assemblage, however large, to believe, or to love, or to pray, or to give thanks, supposing the musicians did but play and sing, and the sacristan thought of nothing but his flowers, lights, and incense, and the priest in cope and stole, and his attendant ministers, had no heart, nor lot in what they were outwardly acting, let the flowers be sweetest, and the lights brightest, and the vestments costliest, still who would call it an act of worship at all? Would it not be a show, a make-belief, an hypocrisy? Why? Because the one idea was away,

which gave life, and force, and an harmonious understanding, and an individuality, to many things at once, distinct each of them in itself, and in its own nature independent of that idea.

Such is the virtue of a "form": the lifting up of the heart to God is the living principle of this solemnity; yet it does not sacrifice any of its constituent parts, rather it imparts to each a dignity by giving it a meaning; it moulds, inspires, individualizes a whole. It stands towards the separate elements which it uses as the soul is to the body. It is the presence of the soul which gives unity to the various
[254] materials which make up the human frame. Why do we not consider hand and foot, head and heart, separate things? Because a living principle within them makes them one whole, because the living soul gives them personality. It brings under the idea of personality all that they are, whatever they are; it appropriates them all to itself; it makes them absolutely distinct from everything else, though they are the same naturally, so that in it they are not what they are out of it; it dwells in them, though with a greater manifestation and intensity in some of them than in others, yet in all in sufficient measure; in our look, our voice, our gait, our very handwriting. But as soon as it goes, the unity goes too, and not by portions or degrees. Every part of the animal frame is absolutely changed at once; it is at once but a corpse that remains, and an aggregate of matter, accidentally holding together, soon to be dissolved. What were its parts, have lost their constituting principle, and rebel against it. It was life, it is death.

Thus a form or idea, as it may be called, collects together into one, separates utterly from everything else, the elements on which it is impressed. They are grafted into it. Henceforth they have an intercommunion and influence over one another, which is special; they are present in each other; they belong to each other even in their minutest

portions, and cannot belong to any other whole, even though some of those portions might at first sight seem to admit of it. You may smash and demolish the whole, but you cannot otherwise find a way to appropriate the parts. A human skeleton may resemble that of some species of brutes, but the presence of the soul in man makes him differ [255]
from those animals, not in degree, but in kind. A monkey or an ape is not merely a little less than human nature, and in the way to become a man. It could not be developed into a man, or is at present a man, as far as it goes; such a mode of speech would be simply unmeaning. It is one whole, and man is another; and the likeness between them, though real, is superficial, and the result of a mental abstraction.

[Hence it is that great theologians say][10] that no action is indifferent; what [do they][11] mean? surely there are many actions which are quite indifferent; to speak, to stop speaking, to eat and drink, to go hither and thither. Yes, they are indifferent indeed in themselves; but they are not at all indifferent, as referable to this or that whole in which they occur, as done by this or that person. They are not indifferent in the individual: they are indifferent in the abstract, not in the concrete. Eating, sleeping, talking, walking, may be neither good nor bad, viewed in their bare idea; but it is a very different thing to say that this man, at this time, at this place, being what he is, is neither right nor wrong in eating or walking. And further, the very same action, done by two persons, is utterly different in character and effect, good in one, bad in another. This, Gentlemen, is what is meant by saying that the actions of saints are not always patterns for us. They are right in them, they would

[10] In the original the paragraph begins, 'Here I am reminded of a doctrine laid down by the Angelical Doctor, which illustrates what has been said. He says that no action …'. The reference is to St Thomas Aquinas, *Summa Theologica*, Ia–IIae, xviii, 8–9.
[11] The original has 'does he'.

be wrong in others, because an ordinary Christian fulfils one idea, and a saint fulfils another. Hence it is that we bear things from some people, which we should resent, if done by others; as for other reasons, so especially for this, that
[256] they do not mean the same thing in these and in those. Sometimes the very sight of a person disarms us, who has offended us before we knew him; as, for instance, when we had fancied him a gentleman in rank and education, and find him to be not so. Each man has his own way of expressing satisfaction or annoyance, favour or dislike; each individual is a whole, and his actions are incommunicable. Hence it is so difficult, just at this time, when so many men are apparently drawing near the Church, rightly to conjecture who will eventually join it and who will not; it being impossible for any but the nearest friends, and often even for them, to determine how much words are worth in each severally, which are used by all in common. And hence again it happens that particulars which seem to be but accidents of certain subjects, are really necessary to them; for though they may look like accidents, viewed in themselves, they are not accidents, but essentials, in the connection in which they occur. Thus, when man is defined to be a laughing animal, every one feels the definition to be unworthy of its subject, but it is, I suppose, adequate to its purpose. I might go on to speak of the singular connection, which sometimes exists, between certain characteristics in individuals or bodies; a connection which at first sight would be called accidental, were it not invariable in its occurrence, and reducible to the operation of some principle. Thus it has been said, rightly or wrongly, that Whig writers are always Latitudinarians, and Tory writers often infidels.

But I must put an end to these illustrations:—coming at
[257] last to the point, for the sake of which I have been pursuing them, I observe that the very same subjects of teaching, the

Evidences of Christianity, the Classics, and much more Experimental Science, Modern History, and Biography, may be right in their proper place, as portions of one system of knowledge, suspicious, when detached or in bad company; desirable in one place of education, dangerous or inexpedient in another; because they come [in a different prominence,][12] in a different connection, at a different time, with a different drift, from a different spirit, in the one and the other. And hence two Universities, so called, may almost concur in the lecture-papers they put out and their prospectus for the year, that is, in their skeleton, as man and certain brute creatures resemble one another, and yet, viewed as living and working institutions, not as preparations in an anatomical school, may be simply antagonistic.

[This then is the obvious answer to][13] the objection with which I opened this Discourse. I supposed it to be asked me, how it could matter to the pupil, who it was [that] taught him such indifferent subjects as logic, antiquities, or poetry, so that they [*be*][14] taught him. I answer that no subject of teaching is really indifferent in fact, though it may be in itself; because it takes a colour from the whole system to which it belongs, and has one character when viewed in that system, and another viewed out of it. According then as a teacher is under the influence, or in the service, of this system or that, so does the drift, or at least the practical effect of his teaching vary; Arcesilas would not teach logic as Aristotle, or Aristotle poetry as Plato, though logic has its fixed principles, and poetry its acknowledged classics; and [258]
in saying this, it will be observed I am claiming for Theology nothing singular or special, or which is not

[12] The original has 'differently'.

[13] In the original the paragraph begins 'Thus, then Gentlemen, I answer the objection ...'.

[14] No emphasis in the original.

partaken by other sciences in their measure. As far as I have spoken of them, they all go to make up one whole, differing only according to their relative importance. Far indeed am I from having intended to convey the notion, in the illustrations I have been using, that Theology stands to other knowledge as the soul to the body; or that other sciences are but its instruments and appendages, just as the whole ceremonial of worship is but the expression of inward devotion. This would be, I conceive, to commit the very error, in the instance of Theology, which I am charging other sciences, at the present day, of committing against it. On the contrary, Theology is one branch of knowledge, and Secular Sciences are other branches. Theology is the highest indeed, and widest, but it does not interfere with the real freedom of any secular science in its own particular department[15] [except in such sense as they also interfere with it]. This will be clearer as I proceed; at present I have been only pointing out the internal sympathy which exists between all branches of knowledge whatever, and the danger resulting to knowledge itself by a disunion between them, and the object in consequence to which a University is dedicated. Not Science only, not Literature only, not
[259] Theology only, neither abstract knowledge simply nor experimental, neither moral nor material, neither metaphysical nor historical, but all knowledge whatever, is taken into account in a University, as being the special seat of that large Philosophy, which embraces and locates truth of every kind, and every method of attaining it.

However, much as lies before me to clear up, ere I can be said to have done justice to the great subject on which I

---

[15] It would be plausible to call Theology the *external* form of the philosophical system, as charity has been said to be of living faith, *vid.* Bellarm. *de Justif.*, but then, though it would not *interfere* with the other sciences, it could not have been *one* of them. [JHN] For Fergal McGrath's comments on this footnote, see *NU*, pp. 167–8.

am engaged, there is one prevalent misconception, which what I have been to-day saying will set right at once; and though it is scarcely more than another form of the fallacy which I have been exposing, it may be useful, even for the further elucidation of the principles on which I have exposed it, to devote what remains of this Discourse to its consideration. It is this: As there are many persons to be found who maintain that Religion should not be introduced at all into a course of Education, so there are many too, who think a compromise may be effected between such as would and such as would not introduce it, *viz*., by introducing a certain portion, and nothing beyond it; and by a certain portion they mean just as much as they suppose Catholics and Protestants to hold in common.[16] In this way they hope, on the one hand to avoid the odium of not teaching religion at all, while on the other they equally avoid any show of contrariety between contrary systems of religion, and any unseemly controversy between parties who, however they may differ, will gain nothing by disputing.

Now I respect the motives of such persons too much not to give my best attention to the expedient which they propose: whether men advocate the introduction of no [260]
religion at all in education, or this "general religion," as they call it, in either case peace and charity, which are the objects they profess, are of too heavenly a nature not to give a sort of dignity even to those who pursue them by impossible roads; still I think it very plain that the same considerations which are decisive against the exclusion of Religion from Education, are decisive also against its

[16] Attempts were made to satisfy the various parties after the introduction of mixed education in Ireland in the 1830s by such measures as the introduction of instruction which was to be 'moral and religious [...] without being sectarian', and the reading of Scripture without comment. This form of 'common, so-called fundamental religious instruction' was condemned by Rome in 1841 (*NU*, pp. 30, 35).

generalization or mutilation, for the words have practically the same meaning. General Religion is in fact no Religion at all. Let not the conclusion be thought harsh, to which I am carried on by the principles I have been laying down in the former part of this Discourse; but thus it stands, I think, beyond dispute, that, those principles being presupposed, Catholics and Protestants, viewed as bodies, hold nothing in common in religion, however they may seem to do so.

This is the answer I shall give to the proposition of teaching "general religion". I might indeed challenge any one to set down for me in detail the precise articles of the Catholic Faith held by Protestants "in general"; or I might call attention to the number of Catholic truths which anyhow must be sacrificed, however wide the range of doctrines which Protestantism shall be made to embrace; but I will not go to questions of mere fact and detail: I prefer to rest the question upon the basis of a principle, and I assert that, as all branches of knowledge are one whole, so, much more, is each particular branch a whole in itself; that each is one science, as all are one philosophy, and that to
[261] teach half of any whole is really to teach no part of it. Men understand this in matters of the world, it is only when Religion is in question that they forget it. Why do not Whigs and Tories form some common politics, and a ministry of coalition upon its basis? does not common sense, as well as party interest, keep them asunder? It is quite true that "general" tenets could be produced in which both bodies would agree; both Whigs and Tories are loyal and patriotic, both defend the reasonable prerogatives of the Throne, and the just rights of the people; on paper they agree admirably, but who does not know that loyalty and patriotism have one meaning in the mouth of a Tory, and another in that of a Whig? Loyalty and patriotism, neither quality is what it is abstractedly, when it is grafted either on Whig or Tory. The case is the same with Religion; the

Establishment, for instance, accepts from the Catholic Church the doctrine of the Incarnation; but at the same time denies that Christ is in the Blessed Sacrament and that Mary is the Mother of God; who in consequence will venture to affirm that such of its members as hold the Incarnation, hold it by virtue of their membership? the Establishment cannot really hold a Catholic doctrine, a portion and a concomitant of which it puts on one side. The Incarnation has not the same meaning to one who holds and to one who denies these two attendant verities. Hence, whatever he may profess about the Incarnation, the mere Protestant, [he who is a Protestant and nothing more, who limits his Christianity to his Protestantism], has no real hold, no grasp of the doctrine; you cannot be sure of him; any moment he may be [262]
found startled and wondering, as at a novelty, at statements implied in it, or uttering sentiments simply inconsistent with its idea. Catholicism is one whole, and Protestantism has no part in it. In like manner Catholicism and Mahometanism are each individual and distinct from each other; yet they have many points in common on paper, as the unity of God, Providence, the power of prayer, and future judgment, to say nothing of the mission of Moses and Christ. These common doctrines we may, if we please, call "Natural Religion," or "General Religion"; and so they are in the abstract; and no one can doubt that, were Mahometans or Jews numerous in these countries, so as to make it expedient, the Government of the day would so absolutely take this view, as to aim at establishing National Colleges on the basis of such common doctrines; yet, in fact, though they are common doctrines, as far as the words go, they are not the same, as living and breathing facts, for the very same words have a different drift and spirit when proceeding respectively from a Jewish, or a Mahometan, or a Catholic mouth. They are grafted on different ideas.

Now this, I fear, will seem a hard doctrine to some of us. There are those, whom it is impossible not to respect and love, of amiable minds and charitable feelings, who do not like to think unfavourably of any one. And when they find [a man of another denomination][17] differ from them in religious matters, they cannot bear the thought that he differs from them in principle, or that he moves on a line, on which did he progress for centuries he would but be carried
[263] further from them, instead of catching them up. Their delight is to think that he holds what they hold, only not enough; and that he is right as far as he goes. Such persons are very slow to believe that a scheme of general education, which puts Religion more or less aside, does *ipso facto* part company with Religion; but they try to think, as far as they can, that its only fault is the accident that it is not so religious as it might be. In short they are of that school of thought, which will not admit that half a truth is an error, and nine-tenths of a truth no better; that the most frightful discord is close upon harmony; and that intellectual principles combine, not by a process of physical accumulation, but in unity of idea.

However, there is no misconception perhaps, but has something or other true about it, and has something to say for itself. Perhaps it will reconcile the persons in question to the doctrine I am propounding, if I state how far I can go along with them; for in a certain sense what they say is true and is supported by facts. It is true that youths can be educated at Mixed Colleges, of the kind I am supposing, nay at Protestant Colleges, and yet may come out of them as good Catholics as they went in. Also it is true, that Protestants are to be found, who, as far as they profess Catholic doctrine, do truly hold it, in the same sense as that in which a Catholic holds it. I grant all this, but I maintain at the same time, that such cases are exceptional; the case of

[17] The original has 'another'.

individuals is one thing, of bodies or institutions another; it is not safe to argue from individuals to institutions. A few words will explain my meaning.

There are then doubtless such phenomena as what may [264]
be called inchoate truths, beliefs, and philosophies. It would be both unreasonable and shallow to deny it. Men doubtless may grow into an idea by degrees, and then at the end they are moving on the same line, as they were at the beginning, not a different one, though they may during the progress have changed their external profession. Thus one school or party comes out of another; truth out of error, error out of truth; water, according to the proverb, chokes, and good comes from Nazareth. Thus, eternally distinct as orthodoxy is from heresy, the most Catholic Fathers and the worst of heresiarchs [have sometimes belonged][18] to the same teaching, or the same ecclesiastical party. St Chrysostom comes of that Syrian theology, which is more properly represented by the heterodox Diodorus and Theodore. Eutyches, Dioscorus, and their faction, are closely connected in history with St Cyril of Alexandria. The whole history of thought and of genius, is that of one idea being born and growing out of another, though ideas are individual. Some of the greatest names in many various departments of excellence, metaphysical, political, or imaginative, have come out of schools of a very different character from their own. Thus, Aristotle is a pupil of the Academy, and the Master of the *Sentences* is a hearer of Peter Abelard. In like manner, to take a very different science: I have read that the earlier musical compositions of that great master, Beethoven, are written on the type of Haydn, and that not until a certain date did he compose in the style emphatically his own. The case is the same with public men; they are called inconsistent, when they are but [265]
unlearning their first education. In such circumstances, as in

[18] The original has 'belongs'.

the instance of the lamented Sir Robert Peel,[19] a time must elapse before the mind is able to discriminate for itself between what is really its own and what it has merely inherited.

Now what is its state, whatever be the subject-matter on which it is employed, in the course of this process of change? For a time perhaps the mind remains contented in the home of its youth, where originally it found itself, till in due season the special idea, however it came by it, which is ultimately to form and rule it, begins to stir; and gradually energizing more and more, and growing and expanding, it suddenly bursts the bonds of that external profession, which, though its first, was never really its proper habitation. During this interval it uses the language which it has inherited, and thinks it certainly true; yet all the while its own genuine thoughts and modes of thinking are germinating and ramifying and penetrating into the old teaching which only in name belongs to it; till its external manifestations are plainly inconsistent with each other, though sooner in the apprehension of others than in its own, nay perhaps for a season it maintains what it has received by education the more vehemently, by way of keeping in check or guarding the new views, which are opening upon it, and which startle it by their strangeness. What happens in Science, Philosophy, Politics, or the Arts, may happen, I [grant],[20] in Religion too; there is such a thing as an inchoate faith or incomplete creed, which is not yet fully Catholic,
[266] yet is Catholic as far as it goes, tends to Catholicism, and is in the way to reach it, whether in the event it actually is happy enough to reach it or not. And from the beginning

---

[19] Peel accepted Catholic Emancipation in 1829, went along with the Reform Bill in 1832, and repealed the Corn Laws in 1846, all of which were against traditional Tory policy. It was said of him that he had 'lost a party, but won a nation'.

[20] The original has 'say'.

such a creed, such a theology was, I grant, the work of a supernatural principle, which, exercising itself first in the rudiments of truth, finished in its perfection. Man cannot determine in what instances that principle is present and in what not, except by the event; but wherever it is, whether it can be ascertained by man or not, whether it reaches its destination, which is Catholicity, or whether it is ultimately frustrated and fails, still in every case the Church claims that work as her own; because it tends to her, because it is recognized by all men, even enemies, to belong to her, because it comes of that divine power, which is given to her in fulness, and because it anticipates portions of that divine creed which is committed to her infallibility as an everlasting deposit. And in this sense it is perfectly true that a Protestant may hold and teach one doctrine of Catholicism without holding or teaching another; but then, as I have said, he is in the way to hold others, in the way to profess all, and he is inconsistent if he does not, and till he does. Nay, he is already reaching forward to the whole truth, from the very circumstance of his really grasping any part of it. So strongly do I feel this, that I account it no paradox to say, that, let a man but master the one doctrine with which I began these Discourses, the Being of a God, let him really and truly, and not in words only, or by inherited profession, or in the conclusions of reason, but by a direct apprehension, be a Monotheist, and he is already three- [267]
fourths of the way towards Catholicism.

I allow all this as regards individuals; but I have not to do with individual teachers in this Discourse, but with systems, institutions, bodies of men. There are doubtless individual Protestants, who, so far from making their Catholic pupils Protestant, lead on their Protestant pupils to Catholicism; but we cannot legislate for exceptions, nor can we tell for certain before the event where those exceptional cases are to be found. As to bodies of men, political or

religious, we may safely say that they are what they profess to be, perhaps worse, certainly not better; and, if we would be safe, we must look to their principles, not to this or that individual, whom they can put forward for an occasion. Half the evil that happens in public affairs arises from the mistake of measuring parties, not by their history and by their position, but by their accidental manifestations of the moment, the place, or the person. Who would say, for instance, that the Evangelical Church of Prussia had any real affinities to Catholicism; and yet how many fine words do certain of its supporters use, and how favourably disposed to the Church do they seem, till they are cross-examined and their radical heterodoxy brought to view! It is not so many years since, that by means of their "common doctrines," as they would call them, they persuaded an ecclesiastical body, as different from them, as any Protestant body which could be named, I mean the ruling party in the Establishment, to join with them in the
[268] foundation of an episcopal see at Jerusalem, a project, as absurd, as it was odious, when viewed in a religious aspect.[21] Such too are the persevering attempts, which excellent men in the Anglican Church have made, to bring about a better understanding between the Greeks or Russians and their own communion, as if the Oriental Church were not formed on one type, and the Protestant Establishment on another, or the process of joining them were anything short of the impossible exploit of fusing two individuals into one. And the case is the same as regards the so-called approaches of heterodox bodies or institutions towards Catholicism. Men may have glowing imaginations, warm feelings, or benevolent tempers; they may be very little aware themselves how far they are removed from

[21] Newman refers to the Anglican–Lutheran agreement for a joint bishopric in Jerusalem. For more see Ker, *Newman: A Biography*, pp. 234–6; Newman, *Apologia*, pp. 141–3.

Catholicism; they may even style themselves its friends, and be disappointed it does not recognize them; they may admire its doctrines, they may think it uncharitable in us not to meet them half way. All the while, they may have nothing whatever of that form, idea, type of Catholicism, even in its inchoate condition, which I have allowed to some individuals among them. Such are the liberal politicians, and liberal philosophers and writers, who are considered by the multitude to be one with us, when, alas! they have neither part nor lot with the Catholic Church. Many a poet, many a brilliant writer, of this or the past generation, has taken upon himself to admire, or has been thought to understand, the Mother of Saints, on no better ground than this superficial survey of some portion of her lineaments. This is why some persons have been so taken by surprise at the late outburst against us in England, because they fancied men would be better than their [269] systems. This is why we have to lament, in times past and present, the resolute holding off from us of learned men in the Establishment, who seemed or seem to come nearest to us. Pearson, or Bull, almost touches the gates of the Divine City, yet he gropes for them in vain; for such men are formed on a different type from the Catholic, and the most Catholic of their doctrines are not Catholic in them. In vain are the most ecclesiastical thoughts, the most ample concessions, the most promising aspirations, nay, the most fraternal sentiments, if they are not an integral part of that intellectual and moral form, which is ultimately from divine grace, and of which faith, not carnal wisdom, is the characteristic. The event shows this, as in the case of those many, who, as time goes on, after appearing to approach the Church, recede from her. In other cases the event is not necessary for their detection, to Catholics who happen to be near them. These are conscious in them of something or other, different from Catholicism, a bearing, or an aspect, or

a tone, which they cannot indeed analyze or account for, but which they cannot mistake. They may not be able to put their finger on a single definite error; but, in proportion to the clearness of their spiritual discernment or the exactness of their theology, do they recognize, either the incipient heresiarch within the Church's pale, or the unhopeful inquirer outside of it. Whichever he be, he has made a wrong start; and however long the road has been, he has to go back and begin again. So it is with the bodies,
[270] institutions, and systems of which he is the specimen; they may die, they cannot be reformed.

And now, Gentlemen, I have arrived at the end of my subject. It has come before us so prominently during the course of the discussion, that to sum up is scarcely more than to repeat what has been said many times already. The Catholic Creed is one whole, and Philosophy again is one whole; each may be compared to an individual, to which nothing can be added, from which nothing can be taken away. They may be professed, they may not be professed, but there is no middle ground between professing and not professing. A University, so called, which refuses to profess the Catholic Creed, is, from the nature of the case, hostile both to the Church and to Philosophy.[22]

---

[22] This line of thinking is the complete opposite of the contention that a 'Catholic university' represents a contradiction in terms. In his *Suggestions on Academical Organisation, with Special Reference to Oxford* (Edinburgh: Edmonston & Douglass, 1868, p. 301), Newman's former friend Mark Pattison asserted that 'Catholic schools there may be, but a Catholic university there cannot be'.

THE STATEMENT OF AUGUST 14TH, 1852

DR NEWMAN TO ABP. CULLEN[1]

THE ORATORY, BIRMINGHAM,
August 14*th*, 1852

MY DEAR LORD,

This is for your Grace to read at your leisure. Having heard from Dr Cooper that you and he are making inquiries about buildings and Professors for the University,[2] I am unwilling you should not have before you my own views

[1] Although Newman decided against sending this letter to Cullen, and instead sent a brief note, the document provides a crucial insight into the development of Newman's plans. Among other points it contains a fully worked-out scheme for accommodating the students in small lodging houses and shows Newman's fertility of mind in devising a solution for the particular need in question. But as he foresaw that the scheme was running ahead of itself and stood to complicate the lives of both Cullen and the Committee, he divulged its contents only to his English friends, whose advice he sought and whose interest he hoped to awaken.

Written as a letter, but *not* sent, this document was effectively a memorandum which summarised Newman's ideas at the time. It was not unusual for Newman to act in this way. As on other occasions, the document served as a means for helping him sort out his ideas, as Newman found that he thought best with a pen in his hand, and it also enabled him to discuss them confidentially with his friends.

[2] Peter Cooper had informed Newman that the University Committee had decided on two things: on 'the feasibility of getting houses in a desirable position of the city'; and on Cooper's being authorized to approach the likes of Ignaz von Döllinger about whether they might be willing to 'come over and take chairs in the University' (1 August 1852, *LD* xv, p. 144n). Newman probably only received this letter on 10 August, on his return to Dublin.

about them, and I set them down with the greater alacrity, because I believe your Grace is likely to concur in them.

As to buildings, what is wanted first is a house for Lecture-rooms, and other *public* rooms for examinations, etc., and for an office and clerks. I do not conceive that it would be possible to engage rooms for *Professors*, for they may be married men. Next, I should be very sorry if an attempt were made to collect the students into *one* house; we should not get a house large enough, and, even if we could, we cannot prophesy how many students will come. Then, again, every student must have, at least, one room *to himself.*[3] Even the largest houses will cut up badly under this condition—for it is not a common thing to find a large
[272] number of fair rooms in one house. If we attempt to *alter* and *adapt* a great deal of money goes. But I have a far stronger and a moral reason for disliking large houses.[4] *The only way* to hinder the disorder incident upon a University in a town is to do what they were forced to do at Oxford and other Universities in the middle ages—to open *Inns* or *Halls*, as they were called (which, when endowed, became Colleges). We shall be as bad as Trinity,[5] unless we do the same—and here we can let our apparent difficulty be an excuse for what is a direct and substantive benefit. We shall seem to be forced by necessity into a number of what will seem like lodging-houses, but which will really be separately organized establishments in and under the University.

I would have these lodging-houses or halls large enough to hold twenty students each. A Dean should preside over

---

[3] In the mid-1860s, after Newman's departure, the capacity of St Patrick's House was increased when students began to double and triple up in rooms (Account book of St Patrick's House, 1859–68, Woodlock Papers, 106/6, DDA).

[4] By 'large houses', Newman probably means large institutional buildings that could accommodate eighty or a hundred students.

[5] That is, Trinity College Dublin.

them, or some other officer (I do not care about the names) if the Dean was Confessor, one or two Lecturers, and the Tutors of the Community (*i.e.* 20) should lodge there too. Thus there would be some sort of governing body in each house, or what would ultimately become such. There should also be two or three scholars, *i.e.*, youths holding burses, in each of the Communities, if possible, who would act as a sort of medium between the governing body and the independent students. This, however, would be the gradual work of time; and need not be talked of at first ("lodging-houses" alone would be talked of at first). Then, in a little while, some of these lodging-houses then become Inns, or Halls, Hostels, or Entries (all names were used in the middle [273]
ages); one of them should be called St Patrick's, as if by way of giving it a *name*; another St Lawrence's, another St Columba's, etc. Each of these should have its private Chapel (and the Chaplain might be the Confessor).[6]

A plan like this I conceive to be *indispensable* for discipline—the experience of ages has shown it; but there will be another great advantage. Not only is it the way to make the large body of students *manageable*, but it will introduce a spirit of emulation, an *esprit de corps*.

Further, it will interest different parts of the country in the undertaking—for, as in the middle ages, each diocese may have its hall (for Priests, or Lay, or both); and this will be a way of getting bursaries founded.

In like manner the Dominicans, or the Oratorians, might have an establishment; or your Grace might have a selection of your own Clerks or Priests, whom you wished to have a

[6] This is the first time that Newman explains in detail the plans for residential arrangements that he had been nurturing since he had been invited to join the university project. Culler (*Imperial Intellect*, p. 165) claims that Newman's collegiate plans for the Catholic University were largely the outcome of discussions he had had with Froude and Pusey in the 1830s, but he provides no evidence to back up his assertion.

literary education, as I believe the Archbishop of Paris has done at the Carmes.[7]

So, again, separate faculties might have separate Inns, as the S. Esprit is for theology at Louvain.

I am mentioning, I repeat, not what can be done at once, but what is to be aimed at; and I mention it now, because it must be aimed at from the first, and a false step now may render the whole project simply impracticable.

And it is for the same reason, that, hearing that Dr Cooper is to inquire about Professors, I put down on paper my thoughts here, some of which your Grace has allowed me to put before you before. It never will do, if things are
[274] done, or begin to be done, from distinct sources of action. There must be Unity—nothing can be done without it. I cannot help being jealous of these initial inquiries, even on the part of your Grace, and for the simple reason, that, unless your Grace undertakes *every* thing, you will do nothing, and will only lose time which can ill be spared. Your Grace's inquiry here, Dr Cooper's there, will issue in nothing, or in something not at unity with itself. And what is so true of these initial movements, is still more certain as regards the government of the nascent Institution, when it first comes into operation. Dr Cooper is searching for Professors, but *what* are Professors to do?

Now, I have heard your Grace's opinion on this subject already, and I say it therefore more confidently than I should speak otherwise, that the Rector must be supreme and sovereign (under the Bishops) for some time, or nothing will do well. On the other hand, unless we start with Professors of name,[8] nothing will go well. It is, I know, a

---

[7] This is the seminary known as the Écoles des Carmes, now the seat of the Institute Catholique in Paris.

[8] In a copy of this letter Newman wrote above this '(if we have Professors at all?)' (*LD* xv, p. 147n).

very perplexing problem how to combine these *two* conditions, but it must be done.

Professors *of name*, not merely able men, are absolutely necessary. *What* is our bait for students to come to us? We have no direct temporal motives; we have the weight of Government against us; we must have *names*; Trinity College, the Queen's Colleges, have, I doubt not, able Professors, but they have not *names*; I doubt if they have any, or more than one or two, whose names are known out of Ireland. It will be a great thing, for the success of the Institution, to get Professors whose names are known to the Continent, to the world.

At the moment, I know scarcely more than one Irishman [275]
who answers to this condition, and that is Mr Aubrey de Vere. His name is high in England as a poet. At present he is abroad; whether he would be willing to take part in our plan, I know not. If he did, he ought to be Professor of the *Belles Lettres*, or Poetry, or Rhetoric, or English Literature, or whatever other title be given to the subject matter which these titles denote.

In saying this, I am not therefore forbidding other Chairs to be given to Irishmen, but they should be those which are not for display, and which require Priests, for which able, though not distinguished, persons can be found in Ireland; *e.g.* logic, metaphysics, theology, chemistry, experimental philosophy, and the physical sciences (I would have all the *Deans* Irishmen).

I can only name at the moment two Englishmen, Mr H. Wilberforce and Mr Allies. Mr H. Wilberforce ought to have the Chair of Political Economy, or of Modern History, and Mr Allies that of Greek or Latin Literature, or of Modern History or Ancient; but I am not certain whether Mr Allies has not embarked in some other plan.

If Professors of Greek or Latin, besides, are wanted from England they can be found; but I have mentioned two gentlemen whose names are known in England, Ireland, and abroad.

Mr Ornsby, from his residence in Ireland, is half an Irishman. *He is a very able man* and if you take a *supplemental* Englishman, I would have him. I could mention others, as Mr Northcote, who would be most
[276] excellent Professors, for *themselves*, though they are not *well known*.

If we can get several distinguished foreigners it will be a great gain. But, after all, what is the chance of it? Not much, I fear; yet it is well to make the trial.

There is one way in which I think it might be done, *viz*. by getting foreigners, who would consent to give *courses of lectures* remaining perhaps fourteen weeks in the year in Dublin, at two distinct times. I do not feel sanguine about this, but neither do I feel sanguine of getting them at all.

There are two difficulties: 1. The distance. I allow it. 2. It may be said that it will hardly look like holding a Professorship merely to give two courses of Lectures. Perhaps so in Ireland, I do not know; in England, that is, at Oxford, at this moment it would be quite sufficient, and it is what is usual. The late Dr Arnold, whose lectures on Modern History made so much noise, was Master of Rugby School at the time;[9] he merely came to Oxford for several weeks and delivered his lectures, and went away. Mr Keble[10] delivered his Poetry lectures in like manner as a non-resident; so, again, Mr Senior, his lectures on Political Economy,[11] etc., etc. The real working men are, not the Professors, but the Tutors—and so it must be now with us, with some exceptions—and this brings me to what I have to

---

[9] Thomas Arnold (1796–1842) was (visiting) Professor at Oxford in 1841/42.

[10] John Keble (1792–1866) was a Fellow of Oriel College, Oxford, and one of the leaders of the Oxford Movement.

[11] Nassau Senior (1790–1865) was Professor of Political Economy, 1825–30 and 1847–52.

say of the working and influential portion of the University, and those who should assist me, and be the practical managers of the whole, and, that is, the Lecturers and Tutors.

I have *no need* to have the appointment of *Professors* if [277]
they are to be what I have described them. I *must* have the appointment of Lecturers (in the vacancy of a Professor) and Tutors.

By Professors I mean persons of name, who will give a *tone* to the studies in their department, who perhaps will *publish books*, who will take part in the *examinations*. Some of them may be non-residents, coming to Dublin for courses of lectures; others resident. If they are resident, they will have immediate superintendence of the Lecturers in their department. I think nearly all the Professors had better be Laymen.

By Lecturers, I mean either pro-Professors, *i.e.*, acting Professors, before the Chair is filled up, or assistant Professors, acting under the Professors. By Tutors, I mean young men who go through the drudgery of preparing the students for examination, and see that they profit by the Professors' Lectures. They should live in the Hall to which their pupils belong.

The state of things, then, I contemplate is such as this:—

We start, say, on such a day in Lent, 1853. At that time we have secured: 1. A Greek Professor; 2. Modern History; 3. Logic, and (non-resident) *i.e.*, only giving courses of Lectures; 4. Philosophy of Religion, or Christian Evidences; 5. Political Economy; 6. Chemistry, etc.

The Rector of the University undertakes to supply the deficit. He provides Lectures for the vacant Chairs of Latin, Ancient History, English Literature, etc. He gets a number
of Tutors for the different lodging-houses, or Halls. He [278]
appoints Deans and Chaplains for each Hall. And so he sets off.

You will observe my principle would be, not to fill up a Professorship, till I found a really good Professor, but to go on for a time with a Lecturer.

I am ashamed to take up your Grace's time with so long a letter, nor should I dream of troubling you with so much detail, except I find that *something is doing*. I really do think the simplest thing would be *to do nothing* till a sub-committee is appointed.

Begging your Grace's blessing,

I am, my dear Lord,

Your affectionate friend and servant in Christ,

JOHN H. NEWMAN[12]

---

[12] In a separate letter to Cullen written the same day, Newman writes: 'I have written you so long a letter, and so full of detail, that I am ashamed to send it. It seems to me, it will only plague your Grace, considering how much your thoughts are employed. And yet I must do so, if any thing is doing in the way of fixing on sites or inquiring about Professors. That is, I fear least something should be done which *commits* us.'

'When Dr Cooper spoke to me about it, I thought the difficulty might be got over, by my writing to you. Now when the letter is written, I very much doubt whether you would have time to study it. And therefore I come to the conclusion, that is would be well to do nothing till a sub committee is appointed. It is only the delay of a few weeks.' (*LD* xv, p. 150)

This letter is also marked 'not sent', though Newman states in *AW* (pp. 291–2) that he *did* send it and that no answer came from Cullen.

THE INAUGURATION OF THE UNIVERSITY

OR DR. NEWMAN'S ADMISSION TO ITS ADMINISTRATION

From *The Catholic University Gazette*[1]

No. I

1*st June*, 1854

NOTICES[2]

AS the late Synodal Meeting of the Archbishops and Bishops of Ireland has given occasion to this publication, it has an obvious claim to be the first subject recorded in our columns. It was held on Thursday, the 18th of May last, and following days, under the presidency of Dr. Cullen, Primate of Ireland and Apostolic Delegate, at the Presbytery in Marlborough Street. All the Bishops of the country (except the Rt. Rev. Dr. Keane, of Ross, for some time in Rome), were present, either in person, or by their respective representatives; and, considering the momentous measures in which their deliberations issued, it may be expedient, for the information of future times, to enumerate their names and sees.

[1] Newman was the editor of the *Gazette* until January 1855 and the author of most of the articles in it during this time. These three Notices were the first article in each of the first three issues.
[2] *CUG* 1 (1 June 1854), pp. 1–2.

THE ARCHBISHOPS AND BISHOPS OF IRELAND,

As present at the Synodal Meeting, held in Dublin,
May 18–20, 1854

The Most Rev. Dr. Cullen, of Dublin, Apostolic Delegate and Primate of Ireland.

[280] The Most Rev. Dr. Dixon, of Armagh, Primate of all Ireland.

The Most Rev. Dr. Slattery, of Cashel.

The Most Rev. Dr. MacHale, of Tuam.

The Rt. Rev. Dr. Browne, of Kilmore.

The Rt. Rev. Dr. M'Gettigan, of Raphoe.

The Rt. Rev. Dr. Ryan, of Limerick.

The Rt. Rev. Dr. Browne, of Elphin.

The Rt. Rev. Dr. Cantwell, of Meath.

The Rt. Rev. Dr. Denvir, of Down and Connor.

The Rt. Rev. Dr. Haly, of Kildare and Leighlin.

The Rt. Rev. Dr. Foran, of Waterford and Lismore.

The Rt. Rev. Dr. Feeny, of Killala.

The Rt. Rev. Dr. M'Nally, of Clogher.

The Rt. Rev. Dr. Walshe, of Ossory.

The Rt. Rev. Dr. Delany, of Cork.

The Rt. Rev. Dr. Derry, of Clonfert

The Rt. Rev. Dr. Murphy of Ferns.

The Rt. Rev. Dr. Kelly, Administrator Apostolic of the Diocese of Derry.

The Rt. Rev. Dr. Vaughan, of Killaloe.

The Rt. Rev. Dr. Durcan, of Achonry.

The Rt. Rev. Dr. Fallon, of Kilfenora and Kilmacduagh.

The Rt. Rev. Dr. Kilduff, of Ardagh.

The Rt. Rev. Dr. Moriarty, Coadjutor of the Rt. Rev. Dr. Egan, of Kerry.

The Rt. Rev. Dr. Blake, of Dromore, represented by the Very Rev. Dr. O'Brien.

The Rt. Rev. Dr. Murphy, of Cloyne, represented by the

Very Rev. Dr. Yore.
The Rt. Rev. Dr. O'Donnel, of Galway, represented by the [281]
Very Rev. Dr. Roche.

SECRETARIES OF THE SYNOD

The Very Rev. Dr. O'Brien, of Waterford, and
The Very Rev. Dr. Leahy, of Thurles.

The principal object of the Meeting was that of taking the steps immediately necessary for the establishment and commencement of the new Catholic University. For that purpose, following the pattern of the Belgian Bishops twenty years ago, in the erection of the University of Louvain, their Lordships, after recording their past nomination, made by means of the University Committee, and already confirmed by his Holiness, of the Very Rev. Dr. Newman, Priest of the Oratory of St Philip Neri, to the office of Rector, proceeded to commit to him the execution of the great work which it will be, in years to come, the glory of their Lordships' time to have designed; that is, under their control and with their sanction, and with an annual meeting to receive and to consider the Rector's report.

They then proceeded to the selection of the Vice-Rector, which they made in favour of the Very Rev. Dr. Leahy, President of the College of Thurles; an appointment, which, it is scarcely necessary to say, will give general satisfaction to the Catholic body.

It is understood that the Rector is already taking measures for securing the services of various distinguished or rising men, to fill the offices of Professors or Lecturers; but the negotiations are not in that state, which enables him to communicate their results to the public.

[282]

No. II

8th June, 1854

NOTICES[3]

THE University House in St Stephen's Green is undergoing such adaptations as are necessary for its fulfilling the purposes to which it is to be devoted. It will form two separate establishments; the one of which consists of a suite of Lecture Rooms, for the use of Professors and Lecturers, situated on the ground and first floors, and connected with the grand staircase. The upper stories, reached by a separate staircase, will be converted into a Lodging-house or Hall for students, of whom there is room for as many as from fifteen to twenty. Other houses will be got ready, according as the number of names of candidates sent in make further steps necessary.

The great inconvenience, which will be occasioned by uncertainty how many are likely to present themselves, an uncertainty which will lead either to engaging houses now at a venture, or to being overtaken in November by deficiency of accommodation, is a reason for earnestly pressing on parents and friends of young men, whom it is proposed to send to the University, to acquaint the authorities with their intention as soon as possible. Such a procedure would by no means commit them actually to fulfil their intention when the time came; it would only imply that they had a *bona fide* intention when they expressed it.

---

[3] *CUG* 2 (8 June 1854), pp. 9–10.

As the University will be for some years in a merely provisional state, and statutes for its governance will be the work of time, the teachers appointed will hardly have a claim to the name of Professors, and will rather be in the situation of Lecturers, both from the want of an academical constitution to define their rights, and of a sufficient academical body to demand their superintendence. Moreover, it is not to be expected that the able and distinguished persons, whose cooperation it is hoped to secure, will feel themselves justified, before the University has grown a little more into shape, in devoting themselves to it unreservedly and for good. An engagement for a definite period is the utmost which either they or the governing authorities can deem advisable at present. [283]

Various influential persons have expressed a wish to be allowed to place their names on the University Books; and there are reasons for anticipating that this kind and respectful feeling towards the Institution will spread beyond the United Kingdom. The subject of conferring honorary or *ad eundem* degrees will be considered, as soon as the necessary powers for that purpose are conferred on the Rector. Since, from the nature of the case, some time must elapse before the list is completed, the names actually forwarded to the University authorities, will be published, as they are received.[4]

---

[4] The names of eminent men who lent their names as supporters of the enterprise appeared in the weekly instalments of the *Gazette*. The first names appeared in *CUG* 19 (5 October 1854): besides those of Cullen and four bishops, two Irish and two English, the names were of: de Ram and two deans from the University of Louvain; J. O'Connell MP, C. de Zulueta, J. R. Hope Scott, Serg. Bellasis, G. Bowyer MP, J. R. Wegg Prosser, Earl of Shrewsbury, Hon. P. Stourton, H. E. Manning, M. O'Reilly, C. W. Russell, D. O'Brien, Hon. W. Clifford, and W. Dodsworth. Besides bishops, the most well-known names were those of Döllinger, Sir John (later Lord) Acton, and Montalembert. All these names appeared in the *Catholic University of Ireland, Calendar for 1855–56* (Dublin: J. F. Fowler, 1855). Newman discussed with a lawyer

It is also proposed to open a University Church, for the solemn exercises of the Academical Body, as time goes on, and for sermons on Sundays and other great Festivals at
[284] once. A list of University preachers is in preparation, and will appear with as little delay as possible.[5]

Two exhibitions for students have already been given by an anonymous benefactor. From three to six others are in contemplation, to be called "the Exhibitions of St Philip Neri".

A collection of books towards the formation of a library has been liberally offered by the executors of the late Most Reverend Prelate who filled the See of Dublin; another, rich in Fathers of the Church, has been given in reversion, by a venerable Priest of the Archdiocese; and a third, chiefly consisting of valuable books on ecclesiastical law, has been presented by James R. Hope-Scott, Esq., of Abbotsford, N.B. The University of Louvain also has manifested the interest it takes in the establishment of a sister Institution in

---

friend the possibility of giving some of them an honorary degree (Newman to Badeley, 17 May 1854, *LD* xvi, pp. 134–5). In this connection, see section 11 on p. [91].

In the 1870s, referring to 'the list of honorary members of the University, principally laymen from Ireland or elsewhere' that he was trying to form, Newman comments that 'the plan was not viewed without jealousy by Dr Cullen, and at Rome they gave it no countenance ('Memorandum about my Connection with the Catholic University', *AW*, p. 326). A decade earlier Newman noted that 'nearly the only alteration the Propaganda made in the details which I put before them, was to hinder me from associating laymen even as *honorary* members'. In the same letter he wrote, 'It is so discouraging to see the educated laity, (lawyers etc) getting more and more separated from the clergy and tending to a worse state than that of Italy' (Newman to Ornsby, 8 November 1861, *LD* xx, p. 63).

[5] The list that appeared in *CUG* 24 (9 November 1854) comprised two bishops and twenty-seven priests; they hailed from England as well as Ireland, and included religious as well as secular priests.

Dublin, by taking the earliest opportunity of sending its publications.[6]

[6] See p. [25] for more details about these early library acquisitions.

[285]

No. III

15th June, 1854

NOTICES[7]

WE have not till now had the opportunity of recording the late inauguration, as it may be called, of the Catholic University; for such ought reasonably to be accounted the public appearance of the Rector in the Metropolitan Church at High Mass on 4th June, to take the necessary oaths, previously to his entering upon the duties of his office. No festival in the whole year could be so suitable for the purpose, as the day selected, the Feast of Pentecost, commemorative, as it is, of the descent from heaven of the Holy Ghost in His sevenfold Presence to enlighten and fortify the hearts of the faithful; nor, amid the many honoured names which adorn the Episcopate and Priesthood of Ireland, could one more suitable have been found, to offer the Holy Sacrifice on the occasion, than the revered Prelate who was the celebrant, Dr. Moriarty, of All Hallows College, the new Coadjutor Bishop of the Diocese of Kerry, and that, not only as having been for some years past a personal friend of Dr. Newman's,[8] but especially because the institution, which he is now leaving, so flourishing yet so young, affords both a memorable instance of what Irish faith can effect, and a pattern and a promise of good hope to

---

[7] *CUG* 3 (15 June 1854), pp. 17–18.

[8] Moriarty first met Newman on 24 May 1849 when he visited the Oratory in Alcester Street, Birmingham.

those who are charged with the great undertaking which was put under the sanction of the Festival of the day.

The Mass was sung *coram Archiepiscopo*; and, on its [286] termination, it was before him, as Apostolic Delegate and natural representative on the occasion, from his local position, of the whole Hierarchy, that the Rector presented himself to make his profession of faith. To this profession, commonly called the Creed of Pope Pius,[9] the Fathers of the Synodal Meeting had added, after the example of Louvain, an engagement, which runs pretty much as follows:—"Ego, N., nominatus Rector Universitatis Catholicæ, fidelis et obediens ero cœtui Episcoporum Hiberniæ, et pro viribus juxta illorum mentem curabo honorem et prosperitatem dictæ Universitatis".[10]

His Grace's sermon followed;[11] in which the Most Reverend Prelate, in commemoration of the subject of the Festival, enlarged on the wonderful transformation of mind and spirit exhibited in the Apostles on the first Pentecost; how twelve men, selected from the poorest and most illiterate class, without any of the human qualifications specially necessary for their prodigious undertaking, were gifted with a divine power, which exalted them in their views, their aspirations, their resolves, and their deeds, above those earthly politics and governments, which were to be the scene of their labours. He then proceeded to speak of the office of teaching which was at the same time committed to them and of the blessing which went forth with them and their successors wherever they preached; and

---

[9] This is the *Professio fidei Tridentinae*, imposed by Pius IV on holders of ecclesiastical offices.

[10] 'I, N., nominated Rector of the Catholic University, will be faithful and obedient to the conference of the bishops of Ireland, and, according to my ability and powers, I will guard the honour and prosperity of the said University according to their intentions' (trans. from *LD* xxxii, p. 88).

[11] For the full version see *Paul Cullen and his Contemporaries* ii, pp. 163–5.

of their success in bringing to their feet the haughty world, in the persons of its wisest and its most learned, forced into the attitude of hearers and disciples, and in exacting of
[287] intellects great as Origen, Athanasius, or Augustine, recognition of their divine mission, and obedience to their word. Thence he took occasion to remind his audience that the Church, far from being hostile to the progress of knowledge (as was so absurdly and unfairly reported among her enemies), had ever been, on the contrary, its most remarkable patron, and the promoter and foster-mother of every good and useful and beautiful art, and of every honourable science; and that to her these later ages, the very ages which speak against her, were indebted both for the preservation of ancient literature, and for their present civilization. All that she exacted and provided was, what common sense as well as the interests of knowledge themselves suggested, that the investigations of the intellect should not be allowed to extravagate and waste themselves in false conclusions, by ignoring and running against truths, already known and infallibly certain,—those, namely, which the Christian Dispensation has either confirmed or revealed.

Such is a meagre sketch in our own words of the Archbishop's discourse, which naturally terminated in a reference to the event of the day, and in a most touching address to the ecclesiastic in whom it was represented,—an address conceived in that noblest style of eloquence, which is the unstudied effusion of a mind, animated by divine faith and charity, urged forward by a sense of duty, and aiming at nothing else but simply the greater glory of God. We quote it from the report contained in the *Freeman's Journal*:—

"And you, Very Reverend Father, to whom the
[288] execution of so great a work is committed by the Church of Ireland, allow me to exhort you to meet the difficulties and trials which you shall have to encounter, with courage and

determination. You will have with you the blessing of the successor of St Peter, the sanction and cooperation of the Church of Ireland, and the fervent prayers of the faithful. All difficulties will gradually vanish, and a fair and open field will be presented to you for your labours. Teach the young committed to your care to cultivate every branch of learning, to scan the depths of every science, and to explore the mysteries of every art; encourage the development of talent and the flight of genius; but check the growth of error, and be a firm bulwark against everything that would be prejudicial to the interests of religion and the doctrines of the Holy Catholic Church. In all circumstances, and at all times, let it be your care to infuse a strong Catholic spirit, a true spirit of religion, into the tender minds of youths; to make them understand the value of that element, of that *aroma scientiarum*, without which the sciences only corrupt the heart, and spread baneful influences around them. In this way your labours will tend to restore the ancient glories of this Island of Saints; you will enrich the State with obedient, faithful, and useful subjects, and give to the Church devoted and enlightened children. Your praises will be in all the churches, and an imperishable crown prepared for you in heaven. May the Holy Spirit, who on this day descended on the Apostles, descend on all here present, purify our hearts, and give us that true wisdom, whose beginning is the favour of the Lord, and which is necessary to guide us in working [289]
our eternal salvation."

The services of the morning were concluded with Benediction of the Blessed Sacrament. The large church was crowded from end to end, and those who had means of giving an opinion were unanimous in reporting, that on no other occasion had they ever seen it so full. The poor seemed equally interested in the ceremony as the more educated class; and their prayers, it may be confidently expected, will have as great a share in the success of an undertaking, which only indirectly concerns them, as the donations and active exertions of those on whom it will visibly depend.

[290]

"WHAT I AIMED AT"[1]

I WANT if I can here to set down various measures I had in purpose, as means of setting off the University, a most difficult problem from the circumstance that there was so little precedent to go by; for Universities commonly have been spontaneously born, grown, matured, and at length, and then only, been recognized, and not been made to order, as the one committed to my handicraft.

The first expedient which suggested itself to me was the erection, or the provision, of a University Church. I suppose I had it in mind as early as, or earlier than, any other work.

I thought—(1) Nothing was a more simple and complete advertisement of the University than a large Church open for worship; the cheapest advertisement, since, if self-supporting, it cost the University nothing, yet was perpetual and in the face of day. (2) It symbolized the great principle of the University, the indissoluble union of philosophy with religion. (3) It provided for University formal acts, for Degree-giving, for solemn lectures and addresses, such as those usual at the opening and closing of the Academical year, for the weekly display of the University authorities, etc., a large hall at once, and one which was ennobled by
the religious symbols which were its furniture.[2] (4) It [291]

[1] The background to this 'rough and unfinished' paper is given in the Advertisement on p. [lxv]. An MS autograph with corrections can be found in the BOA.

[2] In this, not only was Newman following the *contemporary* example of the University Church in Oxford, but also the *medieval* custom. Note that there was a separate Blessed Sacrament chapel in the University Church in Dublin.

interested the clergy in the University, the preachers being taken from all parts of the country.

Further than this, I connected it in my anticipations, with the idea I had, and which Hope-Scott suggested in his letter at the end of December, 1853, of founding an Oratory at Dublin.[3] My notion was that an Oratory would be the religious complement of an Intellectual School; that it would not take part in the work proper to a University, but that it would furnish preachers and confessors for the University body, establish confraternities, and in all the many ways which the Church employs, counteract the dangers incident to a high school of learning and science, and a large collection of young men entering into life. When I went to Rome on Oratory business at Christmas, 1855–56, I brought the matter before Cardinal Barnabò, with the sanction and promise of aid of Dr Cullen. He was to obtain for me a Brief. Whether he gave me a letter or promised to write to Rome about it, I do not know. Nothing came of my application.

---

[3] Newman had written to Hope-Scott on 28 December 1853 to ask his advice about whether the time had come for him to say he would be forced to resign unless he was installed as Rector. Replying on 30 December, Hope-Scott urged him not to resign. Mentioning that he had heard from Bishop Grant that Newman was thinking of establishing an Oratory in Dublin, Hope-Scott said that he agreed with the bishop's suggestion that Newman could set up an Oratory independently of the University: this would give him a standing in Dublin; he could begin lectures at the Oratory; and in this way he would prepare the way for the University (*LD* xv, pp. 514–5; xvi, p. 3n).

Newman did not agree. He felt that the Oratory should follow the University as 'its natural attendant, as being what may be called the School of Devotion for its members'. Moreover, to begin with an Oratory 'would have been to impress upon the Dublin public that I had a private and personal end in coming there, not the good of Ireland'. Nor did he think that Cullen would, in practice, have borne with an Oratory, a group of secular priests 'independent of the Bishops'. Besides, he thought the idea of the Oratorians being 'in any shape academic Lecturers' incongruous (*AW*, pp. 308–9; *LD* xvi, p. 3).

As early as 10th February, 1854, I find I got Dr Moriarty to give me a list of preachers.[4] In the second number of the *University Gazette*, 8th June, I say: "It is also proposed to open a University Church, for the solemn exercises of the Academical body, as time goes on, and for sermons on Sundays and other great Festivals at once. A list of University preachers is in preparation, and will appear with as little delay as possible."

I wished a Church at once; how was this to be effected? [292]
At first I thought of the ground at the back of my house in Harcourt Street. I thought that without any great expense it might serve a temporary purpose, paying itself, I suppose, by weekly receipts. This does not seem at first sight to have been a very happy scheme, though I have not yet come across any memoranda explanatory of it. I thus notice it in my Journal, under date of 27th November, 1854: "Mr Bianconi does not like the idea of the University spending money on a temporary Church next to No. 6 Harcourt Street, where I am. I suspect the reason is that he bought the University House, and had a notion of the University being all in one place; for he wanted me to build a temporary Church in the stable there; or to build a permanent Church on Judge Ball's ground" (which was next to the University House, on the farther side from Harcourt Street). "So I am offering [asking] on good [Achilli money] security to borrow of the University £3000 for building, to be repaid in twenty years, at 3 per cent, interest."[5] Then I arrange the account thus:—

[4] Newman dined with Moriarty at All Hallows that day and had a 'long talk' with him about possible preachers and lecturers (*LD* xvi, p. 40).

[5] Newman refers to the money left over from the fund raised to offset the expenses incurred in the Achilli trial. Subscriptions to the 'Newman Defence Fund' came to £12,932, while costs amounted to £9,289, leaving a surplus of £3,643 (*LD* xv, p. 389n). Of this £2600 was spent on the University Church, though Newman's hopes were dashed when costs for

Profits of Church—200 sittings at 1s for 38 weeks	£380
Rent of ground, £30 to	£40
Gas, coal, and cleaning,	60
Interest of £3000,	90
Instalment of repayment in 20 years,	150
	£340

[293] This leaves £40 margin [I have omitted the expense of preachers, etc.].[6]

I then went off to the notion of an existing Church, to be used for University purposes, as St Mary's at Oxford. There were several large Churches in Dublin, and, with the Archbishop's sanction, I had some correspondence with Mr Mooney of St Audeon's, High Street, who (19th December, 1854) answered me that "any accommodation his Church could afford me was at my immediate disposal, the Archbishop to fix the compensation". But nothing came of this,[7] nor could a Parish Church in a low part of Dublin answer those various purposes of a University Church which I have enumerated above.

---

the Church rose to £5600 – and he faced soaring interest rates after the Crimea War.

For an account of the Achilli trial, see Ker, *Newman: A Biography*, pp. 372–5, 397–9.

[6] Newman had had experience of financing new churches before. When curate of St Clement's, Oxford, he oversaw the collecting of around £5,500 for building a new church; and as vicar of St Mary's he oversaw the collecting of around £650 for a church at the hamlet of Littlemore.

[7] See Newman to Flanagan, 6 December 1854; Newman to Cullen, 24 January & 23 February 1855; Newman to Mooney, 9 & 22 April 1855, *LD* xvi, pp. 318, 358, 389, 438–9, 444–5.

Next I conceived the notion of purchasing the lease of the house and grounds next to the University House in Stephen's Green, and building there. I think the lease had only forty years to run; but there was, I understand, very little freehold property in Dublin; and, on the other hand, it was unheard of, and would be impossible for a landlord to refuse renewal of lease in the case of a place of worship. On the other hand, it had to be recollected that the landlords in this case were the Trustees of the Blue Coat School, who were Protestants, and greatly adverse to Catholic interests. The Archbishop, who seemed to me throughout to show great coldness to the project of a University Church, owned that a Church was wanted there, but that a longer lease was necessary, and I suspect was afraid that a Church there would not be acceptable to the Parish Priest of Francis
Street, in whose district the site in question lay. I was left to [294]
my own decision and resources, and I determined to purchase the lease and to erect a Church. I had devoted the Achilli money to Scholarships; I now determined to spend it in the first instance on a Church. In November, 1854, I got acquainted with Mr Pollen, Professor (honorary) of the Fine Arts, and I employed him as my architect, or rather decorator, for my idea was to build a large barn, and decorate it in the style of a Basilica, with Irish marbles and copies of standard pictures. I set about the building at once, and it was solemnly opened on May 1st, 1856. For the details of the building I must wait till I examine more my correspondence—its further history enters into the account of the matters which passed between Dr Cullen and me.[8]

Another undertaking which I thought necessary was the setting up of a periodical organ of the University, a *Catholic University Gazette*. This would contain a record of the University proceedings, would be a medium of intelligence between its governing body and members, would give a

[8] *Vide* also Note "The University Church," p. [305]. [WPN]

phantasia of life to it in the eyes of strangers, and would indoctrinate the Irish public in the idea of a University. I commenced it contemporaneously with my own installation in June, 1854, and inserted in it the papers on Universities which I had written with a view to it in the Spring of the year.[9] I could not continue it beyond a certain time, and I had from the first wished to get a good paid Editor for it. As early as 12th November, 1853, I settled with H. Wilberforce
[295] for him to take the Editorship of the *University Gazette* at £5 a number. As to the *Gazette* I bade him propose to Duffy to take copyright, responsibility, and profits, paying, when the *Gazette* answered, the £5 to the Editor, and allowing the Editor [that was myself] a veto on all the matter inserted, whether in advertisements or otherwise—size, octavo or quarto. Proposed to H. W. the first subject for it—history of

[9] Some of these articles, such as 'The Entrance Examination a Trial of Accuracy' (*CUG* 4) and 'Specimens of Youthful Inaccuracy of Mind' (*CUG* 6) were later incorporated into the second half of the *Idea.* Some were written to tackle the lack of educational training among Catholic youth, and were on what nowadays would be called study techniques and revision skills. In this way Newman attempted to provide guidance to the student who read the *Gazette* and to those who advised and taught him. Some of the articles touched on strategies for mastering particular subjects, such as 'On Latin Composition' (*CUG* 34) and 'The Study of Geometry' (*CUG* 43), while others were of a more general nature: two about techniques for improving one's memory, two on how to profit from reading, one on time management, and another on the purpose of lectures. There was even one on the wishful thinking and self-indulgence – such as the tendency to dabble—that students are prone to, and the need for them to follow a prescribed routine and avoid caprice. The fact that Newman was prepared to grapple with such matters illustrates his determination to meet the practical needs of the student who lacked basic training and orientation. These articles in the *Gazette* were anonymous, but their authorship has been attributed to Newman (V. F. Blehl, *John Henry Newman: A Bibliographical Catalogue of his Writings* (University of Virginia: University Press, 1978), pp. 87–92).

the rise of the University scheme.[10] The tone not controversial, but courteous to opponents and Queen's Colleges (Journal, pp. 1, 2). This scheme broke down, and so I record (p. 39) under date of 24th September, 1854: "I have offered Ornsby ... the Editorship of the *Gazette* at £50 [a year] and he has accepted it". This was after I had carried it on for some months. It fully answered my expectations while it was in my hands; afterwards, it fell off, and came to an end.[11] This was a misfortune. It was felt and expressed, after I had left, in the Report of a Committee of the Senate to the Bishops in July, 1859;[12] and the resumption of the publication, entitled, the *Catholic University Gazette* ... to "be exactly in the form, size, and type in which the first thirty-one numbers appeared from 1st of June, 1854, to 28th of December, 1854," was urged in a long note in the Appendix by Dr Dunne.

A third step I took in the summer of 1854 was not really mine, but Dr Ellis's, afterwards one of the Medical Professors; it was the purchase of the Medical School House in Cecilia Street. This was a great act, but only mine so far as I at once took up the idea and did my part in carrying it through. The purchase is noticed in my first [296] Annual Report—1854–55—p. 18. Catholics had up to that time no Medical School, and the consequences to Catholic practitioners and to the Catholic population are stated in my Second Report—1855–56—p. 10, etc. It was the great benefit that Dr Ellis did for us. The House was by a happy chance on sale, but would never have been sold to us if it had been known that we were trying for it. We kept our

---

[10] See the footnote on p. [lvi] about these university sketches, which were eventually published together as *The Rise and Progress of Universities*, the first and major part of *Historical Sketches*, vol. iii (1872, pp. 1–251).

[11] The last was no. 55, which appeared in August 1856.

[12] *Report on the Condition and Circumstances of the Catholic University of Ireland, Presented by a Committee of Senate* (1859), [special collection 34.G.2/2, UCD].

proceedings as quiet as we could; and Dr Ellis told me that for a fortnight he had not been able from nervousness to get a good night. At last it was secured, though not without the dissatisfaction of Dr MacHale, as he expressed in a letter to me which I have quoted above.[13] The House served another purpose besides that which was its direct service to us. It put our Medical Faculty in a bodily, visible shape before the Dublin public, and thus did for the University in regard to that important department what the Church was to do as regards theological and religious teaching. And it came into operation at once, for the Theatre, Dissecting Rooms, etc., etc., were all in order and recent use, whereas the Church was not built and opened till the Spring of 1856.

In my Journal I have the following notices of this transaction: "11th June. Dr Ellis has offered to get us the Medical School House in Cecilia Street for £1500. ... He let me mention the subject to the Archbishop, Dr Leahy, Surgeon O'Reilly, and Mr James O'Ferrall. Surgeon O'Reilly said it was better to buy than to build ... and the others were accordant. Dr Leahy thought the price an
[297] inferior question to that of whether we should get a House. ... Mr James O'Ferrall thought we might safely give £1500 ... so I am going to write to-day to Dr Cullen. ... 12th June. Surgeon O'Reilly has been down to the House in Cecilia Street, and is quite delighted with it. He recommends us to purchase very strongly. I told the Archbishop by letter I should proceed, unless I heard from him to the contrary."[14]

Another project at a very early date was the opening of the Medical Lodging House, for the protection of young medical students in a large city. This was the suggestion of Mr W. K. Sullivan, as I have noted in my Journal, p. 35.

---

[13] MacHale was unhappy that Newman had made the purchase without consulting the archbishops (MacHale to Newman, 6 October 1854, *LD* xvi, p. 273).

[14] The full journal entries can be found in *LD* xxxii, pp. 86–7.

"This," he said, "will be a popular measure, as lodgings and board in Dublin are bad and dear."[15] It was advertised in the columns of the *University Gazette*, 12th October, and following weeks, with a description of its circumstances, to hinder students from being deterred by any notion of its limiting their freedom. It was brought into effect in 1857.[16]

Mr Sullivan, whose advice I acted under, was all through my time of great assistance to me. His views were large and bold, and I cordially embraced them.[17] The old routine was to depend on external support, prestige, authority, etc., and of course such helps are not to be despised; but they are not all in all, nor are they imperative. It was a great point to gain the Medical House, but it was not everything. Dr Ellis did well in getting it for us, but he had little idea of making ventures. I have the following note in my Journal, under the date of 25th January, 1855: "I should have entered that at [298]

---

15 Journal entry, 27 June 1854, *LD* xxxii, p. 91.

16 A house was purchased in York Street, very close to the medical school, with the help of a grant of £200 from the bishops, and named St Luke's. This, the first licensed Hall, opened in late November 1857, a fortnight after term had begun, with fees of £30 p.a. By May 1858 its ten places were taken, and with an additional grant of £50 it was expanded to sixteen in time for the 1858/59 session, when it was oversubscribed (W. J. Rigney, 'Bartholomew Woodlock and the Catholic University of Ireland 1861–79', PhD i, University College Dublin, 1995, p. 356).

17 Sullivan was the academic who identified most closely with Newman's view on lay involvement and the need of the University for Ireland. By reputation a leading scientist and a man of wide interests and talents, he championed the lay cause after Newman's departure—and even hoped to take over the running of the University himself. He took a leading part in the negotiations to secure a charter for the Catholic University in 1859 and met with Disraeli. In 1866, when there was a spate of pamphlets about university education in Ireland, Sullivan published his own substantial contribution, entitled *University Education in Ireland. A letter to Sir John Dalberg Acton.* When he first considered resigning, Newman told him: 'It will be a great blow, if you leave the University, for I feel you are just the one person who could not be replaced. It would be perfect madness' if the University did not act to prevent his departure (Newman to Sullivan, 19 February 1859, *LD* xix, p. 44).

the end of last term. I have had a talk with Mr Sullivan about the Medical Professorships. He took, quite a different line from Mr O'Reilly (Surgeon), and Mr Ellis, etc., who had said, 'Who will you get to come until you get a whole *school*? for your certificate will not be taken.' But he took the line, 'Raise up something good, and people will come; the supply will create the demand.' And he said that there were three provinces unknown in the United Kingdom, except that something has been lately doing in Edinburgh, *viz*. Physiology, Pathology, Pharmacy. He was for employing German Professors (Catholics); he said they were good Catholics." He and Dr Lyons were the movement party among the Medical Professors afterwards, and Drs. Ellis, Hayden, and MacSwiney the conservative.

The establishment of a good School of Science was one of the foremost objects which I kept in view. I consulted the Observer (Manuel Johnson) at Oxford about an Astronomical Observatory; and he wished me rather to establish a Meteorological (*vide* Journal, p. 41). This I tried to do, with Mr Hennessy for Professor; but I never was able even to begin it.

A Chemical Laboratory I fitted up in the Medical House at a considerable expense in 1856.

Dr Moriarty, to whom I owed so many good suggestions, had early directed my attention to the formation of an institution for practical science, such as was to be found in Paris; but I never had the opportunity of becoming acquainted with the Paris institution so as to take the idea into consideration.

[299] The *Atlantis* magazine, which did not commence till 1858, originated in the same idea, *viz*. the object of encouraging our scientific labours, and forming the faculty, and making its members work together, and advertising the University. The literary portion of it was necessary as padding, because science does not deal in words, and the

results of a year's experiments may be contained in one or two pages;[18] but that literary portion ought to have been paid for, and was not, and so the publication dragged on its life with difficulty, and now, I suppose, may be considered to be defunct.

Another object which Dr Moriarty and others put before me, important in itself, and especially popular in Ireland, was the encouragement of Celtic Literature. Mr O'Curry, a man of unique knowledge in Celtic MSS, had no Catholic patrons, and was poorly countenanced, and partially supported by Trinity College. I was told he had unknown stores [*sic*] of Celtic learning which would die with him. My Journal, p. 21, notes as follows: "Had a very interesting conversation with Mr O'Curry, who is willing, or wishes, to be Professor or Lecturer of Irish Antiquities in the University. He showed me a mass of interesting ecclesiastical MSS which the Protestants will not print for him. I said the University *would.* He said it would be the most popular thing I could do in Ireland if I connected the University with such a work. He says he wants me to get the Irish MSS from St Isidore's in Rome. He has got a Mass, a Litany, etc., etc.[19] He is not a theologian. ... Mr O'Curry
seemed to enter into the matter *con amore* and, though he is [300]
engaged six hours a day for Government in Trinity College, I think he would prefer to be with us altogether." When I went to Rome at Christmas, 1855–6, I tried to get the MSS

[18] *Atlantis* was published biannually in 1858 and 1859, and single volumes appeared in 1860, 1862, 1863 and 1870. Each number was about 200 pages in length and included articles of a literary and scientific nature, largely the latter. Seven hundred and fifty of the first number were printed, and 290 were mailed to individuals or institutions in the British Isles or abroad.

[19] This appears to be a misreading for 'He has got a Map, a Library, etc., etc.' (Journal entry, 18 March 1854, *LD* xxxii, p. 81).

from St Isidore's, but of course in vain. I think I have heard they have been obtained since for the University.[20]

Mr Curry lectured for us and published one thick volume on the sources of Irish history; I think at the University's expense. I believe Mr Sullivan, since his lamentable and unexpected death, is engaged in publishing a second.[21] These are real works, and acquisitions which would to all appearance have been lost to the world but for the University. Also, in the course of a year or two, I went to the expense of having a font of Irish type cast for the use of the University; there being up to that time only the Trinity College type, and I think one other.

I was able to do nothing for the Faculty of Law, but it was not for not trying. The practical difficulty was the præmium there was on attending the Trinity College Lectures, in the shortening it gave of the course of years requisite for being called to the bar. As early as 16th February, 1854, I "offered to Mr T. O'Hagan," now Lord O'Hagan, "any Lectureship he would take, and asked him to recommend men from the bar" (Journal, p. 11). By 22nd March I had gained Bowyer's consent to helping me by delivering a course of Lectures (*ibid.* p. 21). About April or

[20] In March 1855 O'Curry spoke to Newman about the manuscripts, which were in the Irish Franciscan church in Rome. In June, when Newman heard that negotiations were under way for their purchase by Trinity College, Dublin, he contacted Cullen to ask if he could intervene. The manuscripts were transferred to the Friars Minor, Merchant's Quay, Dublin in 1872. See *LD* xvi, pp. 93n, 145, 272, 320.

[21] The lectures he gave in 1855/56 were published as *Lectures on the Manuscript Materials of Ancient Irish History* (1861). A later series of *Lectures on the Manners and Customs of the Ancient Irish* (3 vols, 1873), was posthumously published by W. K. Sullivan. During O'Curry's lifetime he also published in *Atlantis*. His joint work with John O'Donovan on Irish legal manuscripts was published posthumously as the *Ancient Laws and Institutes of Ireland* (6 vols, 1865–1901). O'Curry's industry and profound learning have ensured him a prominent place in the history of Irish studies. (*DIB*, *ODNB*)

May in the same year I had gained Myles O'Reilly's consent to undertake other Lectures (*ibid.* p. 26). By
November he had named his subject, "Natural Law, or the [301]
Philosophy of Law" (*ibid.* p. 54); and Mr Pigot had undertaken conditionally "The Law of Real Property".[22]

I ought to set down how I felt and acted on the question of conferring Degrees. The safe way seemed to be to gain the power from the State, or to obtain a Charter for the University as a University; and so felt the safe men. On the other hand, the go-ahead Irish party were for giving Degrees at all risks, and in spite of consequences. I liked the idea of the latter course myself, but did not think we were up to it. If Bishops and University authorities, as one man, adopted this policy without wavering, and with a stern determination to carry it out, I should have been for it, but this not only was not likely, but I knew they would not: the feeling of our English friends was so strong against it. And, moreover, I have no clear view what was the good of conferring Degrees till we have a name, though of course the two years which would be gained in preparation time for being called to the bar was no slight advantage. But on the whole Irish schools, etc., would take out testamurs and honours, whether they had legal value or not. What I most inclined to was the Louvain plan, which was the more to the purpose because our University was set up in one Brief after the pattern of Louvain. There Theological Degrees are given by power from Rome; and Degrees in other Faculties by passing examination before the State Board of Examiners. And, besides this, they confer their own Degrees (*i.e.*, Roman Degrees) in (at least) Arts, which are taken by the

[22] The greater part of this paragraph was used verbatim in the Advertisement (pp. [xxxv–xxxvi]), and it is there that the explanatory footnotes can be found. While acting as a Lecturer in Logic at the Catholic University, David Dunne trained as a barrister, and from 1864 he lectured in law as Professor of Law and Logic.

[302] Bishops for the Church schools, though they have no legal value. Accordingly I wished the State to charter us so far as to make us a corporation and to enable us to hold property; and then we should have power from Rome for Theology and for Arts for Church purposes, and then our youths might go to the Queen's University for their Degrees in Arts, Medicine, and Law. As early as March, 1854, this idea was suggested to me. In my Journal, under date of the 16th, I note down: "Yesterday at Allhallows. It was suggested, as it had struck me already, that the Belgian way was a precedent for our getting Degrees by passing examinations before the Queen's University. Only, since in Belgium there is a Concordat or the like, things must be very different from here, where Catholicism is ignored. Would the judges be fair to Catholics?" Of course such a plan involves some of the examiners being Catholics. I add: "*N.B.*—To get the real state of the case as regards the worth of Trinity Law and Medicine Degrees, and *what* is necessary for practising in either profession". I think it was in 1856 that I wrote a long letter to Monsell advocating the plan,[23] and I spoke of it to many others, but it met with acceptance in no quarter.[24]

---

[23] For Newman, affiliation to a non-Catholic establishment was only possible on condition that the University was given the right of having its own examiners in subjects such as history and metaphysics, since 'examinations and examiners every where determine the reading of the students and the grinding of the Tutors. These great subjects, to secure the real knowledge of which is one great reason for setting up a University, will either be taught and learned wrongly, or hurried over in generalities, unless we have Examiners of our own on them' (Newman to Monsell, 24 November 1856, *LD* xvii, p. 459).

[24] Newman was in favour of some form of affiliation, provided the necessary safeguards were in place, with the degree-conferring Queen's *University*, as opposed to becoming one of the Queen's *Colleges*. Although technically speaking it would place them in the position of a college, Newman argued that the situation was no different from Louvain, which was 'but a College in the eyes of the State' although it was 'bonâ fide a University' and 'recognised as such by all Catholics'.

As to the advice I received from political and legal authorities on the subject, first Monsell wrote to me 30th June, 1854, thus: "I think it would be unwise now to moot in any way the question of a Charter. Until the University exists it will not be recognized. To recognize it at any time will be unpopular, and therefore its recognition will be avoided even by our friends, as long as it can be so with [303]
decency. When it becomes a power, and shows sign of being a permanent one, it will be indecent to ignore it, but not till then. It would be unwise to commit the Government to hostility to it. It is difficult to get people to break pledges which it is their interest to keep. The time to ask for a Charter may come soon. If a large number of young men were in actual receipt of a high order of education there we might put great pressure on the Government. I do not see the advantage of creating a grievance at this moment. The Government are in advance of the country. They wish to do more for us than the country will allow them to do. It seems to me a great object to make Catholics feel this; to make them realize their actual position in relation to that public opinion which is, after all, the governor of this country. It

---

Newman thought they 'had a fair chance of getting Government to place us in the position of Louvain', but 'little chance in succeeding in gaining a State recognition of a Catholic University'; that they 'had more chance of gaining endowments from Parliament, if we came before it as claimants in the shape in which the Queen's Colleges were claimants, than if Parliament were called upon directly and distinctly to give [recognition] to a formal Catholic University' (Newman to Woodlock, 23 February 1868, *LD* xxiv, p. 40).

He felt that, 'if the present Government chartered and endowed us, without giving us the power of giving Degrees' they would have 'done a great deal — *you will have got the wedge in.* At a later time, you may get more.' Newman's 'only fear in this plan is that the Heads and the Professors of the University *will not* keep up the phantasia and claim of a University, which Louvain does successfully, should allow themselves to be triumphed over as if defeated, and should tamely submit to *be* a College' (Newman to Ornsby, 19 January 1859, *LD* xix, p. 23).

always seemed to me that Lord Aberdeen's goes as near to the wind as it can, and that any nearer approach to our wishes would infallibly upset it. The experience of the last two Sessions has shown this to be the case, and therefore it appears to me that we can gain nothing by any new grievance against them."[25]

In 1856, in consequence, I think, of the urgency of Dr Lyons and others in behalf of our creating Degrees, I took advice from different parties,[26] and had answers from Badeley and others. Just now I have mislaid Badeley's formal opinion, though I have his letter upon it. He was against our attempting to grant Degrees. He says: "What I have now written is pretty much in accordance with Hope's
[304] view; for, when I showed him your letter some time ago, he seemed to think that the conferring Degrees would be a source of danger, and that you had better confine yourself to Licences". I also wrote to Mr Pigot, on the purpose of getting the opinion of some Dublin lawyers on the subject, and have his answer upon it, addressed to Professor Hennessy.

N.B.—Vide for "the Charter," pp. [382–92], and in the Advertisement.

---

[25] This was a reply to a letter Newman wrote two days earlier, i.e. on 28 June 1854.

[26] Newman realised that a major problem with his proposal of affiliating with the Queen's University was that the nationalist press might raise an outcry against the plan, and scupper its chances by calling for subscriptions for the University to cease; the proposal was also unlikely to be supported by nationalist professors such as Robert Lyons and Eugene O'Curry.

NOTE

THE UNIVERSITY CHURCH[1]

ONE of the first proceedings of Pius IX after his return from exile was to take in hand a great project in Ireland for the promotion of learning, as a counterpoise to the evils of the Queen's Colleges. With this object he sent Dr Newman to Dublin to found there a Catholic University. In Dublin one of the first things urged upon him (though not officially) was that he should prepare to build a Church which would at once be the University Church, and a feature of that City. But other objects connected with the commencement of the University pressed too heavily upon his attention to allow his even entertaining the thought of such an undertaking. However, as time went on, when a building proper for the University sermons and functions was required, he went round the City to see which of its Churches would be most available for that purpose, as St Mary's at Oxford.

When he first came to Dublin, happening to say to Dr Cullen that he hoped his work in the University might lead to the establishment of an Oratory there, Dr Cullen at once replied: "I would give you St Audeon's for the purpose". But there the subject dropped. Naturally, however, when in want of a Church for his present need, his mind recurred to St Audeon's and he went to see it.

---

[1] Besides guidebooks for visitors to the University Church there are several scholarly publications about it, such as C. P. Curran, *Newman House and University Church* (1953); J. A. Gaughan, *Newman's University Church. A History and Guide* (1997); E. Kane, 'John Henry Newman's Catholic University Church in Dublin', *Studies: An Irish Quarterly Review* 119 (Summer/Autumn 1977), pp. 105–20 and 'John Henry Newman's Catholic University Church Revisited', *Artefact* 1 (Autumn 2007), pp. 6–27.

St Audeon's appeared to be suitable; its interior, though very bare, was handsome, church-like and spacious; and being newly built it was free from the characteristics of a secluded religious worship, which the then recent days of persecution had made necessary in the older Churches of the City.

But the locality of St Audeon's was an objection to its use as a University Church. Dr Newman felt the force of the objection, but being restricted in his choice, and regarding the use of St Audeon's as a temporary expedient, he was unwilling to consider
[306] it insuperable. The adoption of this Church might open up and improve the neighbourhood; reverence, too, for the Catholic religion among a Catholic population would itself be a protection, and justify a confidence that worship could be carried on with all decorum. There were also circumstances of the position which he thought greatly diminished the force of this objection of locality. The two famous Churches of Dublin, St Patrick's and Christ Church, were close at hand. To these Churches flocked the better class of Protestants, drawn to them by their fine choirs and the high ecclesiastical dignitaries attached to them. St Audeon's, therefore, would be accessible to the like class of Catholics. Moreover, he could not but expect, he said, that some of these same people when brought from a distance by the attractions of the two Protestant Churches, would from time to time be drawn to St. Audeon's, as being the University Church. These considerations had no little weight with him; they had an importance at that time which, perhaps, would be less recognized now.

St. Audeon's from its size and its large congregation of somewhat poor people, was a Church very different from what he would have chosen for himself, nevertheless he looked forward with a resolve to adapt himself to its exigencies, and with a half amusement at the prospect.

With Dr Cullen's permission, therefore, he entered into negotiations for the use of this Church, but when during their progress it became likely that it would be difficult to maintain the independence of the University under the dual management of University and Parochial Authorities, this risk forbade his giving further thought to St. Audeon's. And there was really no other Church available.

Could St. Audeon's have been used for the University pulpit, Dr Newman would have been spared great anxieties later on, and the University preaching would not have been delayed, as was the case, until the course of events was beginning to point towards the closing of his Rectorship.

From the first he had clearly seen the danger of the funds and the energy requisite for the nascent University being absorbed on fine buildings. In this Dr Cullen agreed with him. It was no [307]
imaginary danger, as was shown by the general excitement in Ireland a few years after his retirement, on the occasion of the laying of the first stone of a palatial building for the University; a design which never got beyond the foundations.[2] Moreover, he had come to Dublin for a limited time, and already three most valuable years for work had slipped away during the delays in bringing him into activity after his acceptance of the Rectorship. Seeing, therefore, the need of speedy action on both these

---

[2] Newman's successor, Bartholomew Woodlock, was appointed as Rector in 1861. After boosting the diocesan collections for the University to break-even point, Woodlock acquired ten acres of land at Drumcondra, on the north side of Dublin, as a new site for the University. The foundation stone was laid on 20 July 1862 amidst great ceremony; the procession from the pro-cathedral to the Drumcondra site took four hours and was watched by around 200,000. The ambitious building plans, which included two quadrangles, were drawn by the 'Irish Pugin' James J. McCarthy (1806–82), who was Professor of Architecture at the Catholic University.

But despite Woodlock's early successes and the optimism they generated, the symptoms of health were only temporary. The feeder schools he had set up failed to supply the University with many students —only thirty-four entered in six years (of whom just eighteen were Interns) and at a cost to the University of nearly £3,000—and the announcement of a rail-route across the Drumcondra site scotched the expansion plan and led to a crushing loss of £10,000. The two losses more than offset the gains in the collections, and the report of the University Finance Committee in September 1863 recommended slashing annual expenditure from £8,300 to £5,000. Once teaching staff were made redundant and buildings closed, the Catholic University effectively forfeited its claim to be a university-in-the-making, and reconciled itself to the status of a college, with the prospect of forging links with a degree-granting institution, either through affiliation or incorporation.

accounts, and determined that what was so essential to a University, the University preaching, should not be retarded, he proceeded to take measures to build at his own cost a chapel, which, though small, would have sufficed for his object. This chapel would have been attached to his own house in Harcourt Street.

Although there was nothing mean in what he contemplated building, a chapel such as the confraternity chapels which used to be so often met with in Rome and Italy, yet adverse criticism was not wanting. But to Dr Newman the very objections made to it showed its advantages. The fact that the site was small, shut in, and narrow, rendered large expenditure unnecessary, indeed, impossible, and its adjoining his own house would account for and excuse its deficiencies. Nor was a small building inconsistent with his idea of efficiency.[3] It made it unnecessary for him to divert his thoughts from his subject to consider the reach of his voice, and it enabled him to read from the countenances of his hearers whether he was making himself clear to their minds, an exceeding great help and encouragement to him. In addition to these advantages it could have been quickly constructed.

There was also another inducement to encourage him in this plan. The Mastership of the Temple Church[4] in London had always been regarded by Dr Newman as his beau ideal of a position for religious influence. Oxford, he said, with all its advantages, had the drawback of being a place of but temporary
[308] residence, its members coming and going within a very limited time. Upon those who remained there long, this gradual flowing away of those who had surrounded them, could not but have a most isolating effect, making them, as it were, more and more out of place; a disadvantage which, he said, must soon have applied to himself, had he remained there. At the Temple, however, was to be found an audience which for trained powers of mind was, perhaps, unique; an audience, moreover, that was unshifting, and

[3] *Vide* letter, 11th May, 1852, in the Advertisement. [WPN] This can be found on pp. [lxiii–lxiv].

[4] Temple Church was built by the Knights Templar and is now the church of Inner and Middle Temple, two of the four Inns of Court. The presiding clergyman is known as the Master of the Temple.

thus able to follow the "Master's" current of thought year after year. Now Dublin also was famous for the number and the standing of its Lawyers; the Medical Faculty, too, was in high repute; he felt that he could do a work among these that he had not had the opportunity of attempting elsewhere; and he had the hope that his intended little Chapel, with the Rectorship of the University, would afford him a sphere of influence, the best that in his circumstances he could have. On one occasion reminding those who stood by him discussing this plan, how much he had done at Oxford with the aid of a few others, he said: "Was it not a good work I began in Adam de Brome's Chapel[5] at Oxford? Why then should not just such another serve me here in Dublin, and I not do better work with the grace of being a Catholic?" He looked forward to happy work in this Chapel, but at the last moment the tenant occupying the premises needed refused to make way for him.

However, he did not spare himself; for very soon after the failure of his plan for a little Chapel, the prospects of the University justified a greater project. Bearing in mind the danger of injuring the great work he had in hand by the expense of magnificent buildings, he, at his own risk, brought about the erection of a Church which, in its interior, is dignified, even sumptuous. He did so in face of grave material difficulties with regard to the leasehold, and graver discouragements in the abandonment of his dislike of debt, and in the reflection that the building was not meant to be permanent. There are not many now alive who can have any idea of the anxiety which this Church brought upon him. It is in Stephen's Green in the rear of the [309]
University House.

Mention might be made of his care for all that pertained to the solemnity of the Services; the music, the ceremonies, the

---

[5] This was the chapel constructed next to the University Church in 1328 by its rector, Adam de Brome, who founded the House of the Blessed Virgin Mary, now Oriel College. In 1834, during the years when Newman was vicar of St Mary's (1828–43), he cleaned out the chapel, which had been neglected, and equipped it as a lecture room. The lectures he gave there on Wednesday evenings included his *Lectures on the Prophetical Office of the Church* (1837) and his *Lectures on Justification* (1838).

vestments, all had his attention, and he looked forward to the Church being perfect in these respects. Allusion, however, to such subjects may now seem superfluous, but, at the time spoken of, such matters had of necessity long been kept in the background and were then very much less regarded in Ireland than now.

The Church itself, in its style and decorations, was the outcome of his suggestions; the ancient Churches of Rome serving him as his model, both from his liking them, and from their historical associations.[6] It was opened on May 1st, 1856, by the Archbishop, Dr Cullen.[7] Greatly to the disappointment of Dr Newman he had failed to obtain the presence of Cardinal Wiseman to preach the opening sermon. He himself preached eight sermons in this Church; and it may be said, not without the consciousness of the prospect of a satisfactory result. [All were preached within the first year of the opening,—Vid. *Occasional Sermons*.][8] There are in it a bust of Dr Newman as Cardinal, made

---

[6] Defying the vogue for the Gothic style, Newman chose the form of a Byzantine basilica, which had the merits of functional beauty (being best for the acoustics and sight), lower cost (as most of the decoration was internal), suitability for the use of Irish marble, and relative harmony with the surrounding Georgian buildings. The basic design of the church and its decoration was decided on by Newman, and its execution and interpretation entrusted to John Hungerford Pollen, the Professor of Fine Arts. Newman worked closely with him on the plans and the construction, and used his stay in Rome at Christmas 1856 to commission copies of a set of tapestries designed for the Sistine Chapel by Raphael. Just ten months after Pollen had set to work, the University Church was opened. The church was so much to Newman's liking that he described it as 'the most beautiful one in the three kingdoms' (Newman to Pollen, 9 November 1856, *LD* xvii, p. 440). Measuring one hundred feet in length, thirty-six feet in breadth and forty high, it contained an ante-chapel and a spacious, aisle-less nave laid out on the plan of a plain basilica, and was decorated internally with coloured Irish marble columns; the ornate apse featured a scene depicting a vine rising from a field of birds and animals up to groups of saints, who surrounded Mary, *Sedes Sapientiae*, in their midst.

[7] The day was Ascension Thursday, and the Archbishop celebrated a pontifical High Mass.

[8] They were all pastoral sermons, having as a common theme the regeneration of the heart and the regaining of personal integrity. Three

since his death, and a tablet which he had placed there to secure masses for himself and certain other benefactors deceased.[9]

In his correspondence with Cardinal Wiseman about the opening of the Church, Dr Newman touches upon his desire that the Cardinal should be connected with the University as its first Chancellor.[10] His high position in the Church, his great reputation,

---

testimonies about them exist from those connected with the University. Thomas Arnold (1823–1900), second son of Dr Arnold of Rugby and Professor of English Literature at the Catholic University, found the Dublin sermons even more inspiring than those he had heard in Oxford; four decades later he could still remember one of them clearly. William Joseph Walsh, a student from St Laurence's House who later became Archbishop of Dublin, remembers that the sermons 'were read by Newman in a clear musical voice, unimpassioned, and well modulated, and that they were listened to with rapt attention by fashionable and cultured congregations' (P. J. Walsh, *William J. Walsh. Archbishop of Dublin* (Dublin: Talbot, 1928), p. 13). John Augustus O'Shea (1839–1905), a student at St Patrick's House, comments that the students were not generally carried away by his sermons. The language, of course, was polished, the thoughts elevated, the reasoning flawless, but the sermons suffered from one fatal drawback: they were read. Irish youths were accustomed to listening to priests who preached *ex tempore* and with passion; a discourse read from a manuscript might be more lucid and logical, but for them it lacked life. (J. A. O'Shea, *Roundabout Recollections* ii (London: Ward & Downey, 1892), p. 115)

As an Anglican, Newman had always written out his sermons beforehand and read them from the pulpit; on becoming a Catholic he began to preach from notes, writing them up in longer note form afterwards. See *Sermon Notes of John Henry Cardinal Newman, 1849–78*, ed. J. Tolhurst (1914; Leominster: Gracewing, 2000), pp. v–vi, xii–xiii. He did, however, revert to his former style on certain occasions – and the Dublin University sermons were among these. Nevertheless, the Dublin sermons are not at all like Newman's Oxford University sermons, but more like his parish sermons there: his thoughts are very direct and matter of fact, and expressed in simple, plain speech.

[9] The University Church still exists. A special commemorative stamp was issued for the 150th anniversary of its opening featuring a drawing of the apse. On the anniversary, modern reproductions of the original wall panels (painted by two French artists and paid for by Newman) were unveiled by the Taoiseach, Mr Bertie Ahern.

[10] See Newman to Wiseman, 9 April 1856, *LD* xvii, p. 208. Wiseman had previously told Newman that Pius IX had revealed to him in an audience

his facility of speech, and the ease with which he used his great and varied knowledge; his geniality, and the popularity he had acquired among the laity; the kindness with which his lectures before the Royal Society were received; the compliment to the English Bishops, moreover, of his selection, all seemed to Dr Newman to point out Cardinal Wiseman as the most natural person to be Chancellor. It was a subject, however, which Dr Newman could not do more than thus touch upon. Cardinal Wiseman never was Chancellor.

W. P. N.

---

that he intended to make Cardinal Cullen the Chancellor of the Catholic University (Wiseman to Newman, 20 January 1854, *AW*, p. 315). In 1855 Dunne told Ornsby (who passed on the information to Newman) that Cullen had been made 'Apostolic Visitor of the University' (3 September 1855, *LD* xvi, p. 537n), but he was probably confused; Cullen had been appointed Apostolic Delegate for Ireland.

EXTRACT FROM PROFESSOR O'CURRY'S PREFACE

Vid. *Lectures on the MS Materials of Ancient Irish History, by Eugene O'Curry* (Dec., 1860)[1]

WHEN the Catholic University of Ireland was established, and its staff of Professors from day to day announced in the public papers, I felt the deepest anxiety as to who the Professor of Irish History should be (if there should be one), well knowing that the only man living who could fill that important office with becoming efficiency as a scholar, was already engaged in one of the Queen's Colleges.[2] At this time, however, I can honestly declare that it never entered into my mind that *I* should or ought to be called to fill this important situation, simply because the course of my studies in Irish History and Antiquities had always been of a silent kind; I was engaged, if I may so speak, only in underground work, and the labours in which I had spent my life were such that their results were never intended to be brought separately before the public on my own individual responsibility. No person knows my bitterly felt deficiencies better than myself. Having been self-taught in all the little I know of general letters, and reared to mature years among an uneducated people, I always

---

[1] Eugene O'Curry gave six lectures in 1854/55, and a longer series in 1855/56; they were eventually published as *Lectures on the Manuscript Materials of Ancient Irish History* (1861). Newman arranged for this volume to be printed with a special font of Irish type cast for the purpose.

[2] Each of the Queen's Colleges had a chair of Celtic Languages: John O'Donovan at Belfast; Owen Connellan at Cork; and Cornelius Mahony at Galway. Such was the dearth of students that a Royal Commission reported: 'We cannot recommend that the chairs of the Celtic languages should be retained' (*Royal Commission Queen's Colleges* (1858), pp. 81–2). The scholar whom O'Curry refers to is John O'Donovan.

felt the want of early mental training.[3] . . . And it never occurred to me that I should have been deemed worthy of an honour which, for these reasons, I should not have presumed to seek. To say so much I feel due, not only to myself, but to the exalted and learned personages who, without any solicitation whatever on my part,
[311] overlooked my many deficiencies so far as to appoint me to the newly created Chair of Irish History and Archæology in this National University.

The definite idea of such a professorship is due to the distinguished scholar to whom the first organization of the University was committed. It was that idea which suggested the necessity for this first course of lectures "On the MS Materials of Ancient Irish History," as well as for that which immediately followed it, and in which I am still engaged, "On the Social Customs, Manners, and Life of the People of Ancient Erinn,"[4]—two preliminary or introductory courses, namely, on the two subjects to which this professorship is dedicated: on the existing remains of our History, and the existing monuments of our Archæology. . . . As to the work itself, its literary defects apart, I may claim for it at least the poor merit of being the first effort ever made to bring within the view of the student of Irish History and Archæology an honest, if not a complete, analysis of all the materials of that yet unwritten story which lies accessible, indeed, in our native language, but the great body of which, the flesh and blood of all the true History of Ireland, remains to this day unexamined and unknown to the world.

Under the existing circumstances of this poor dependent country, no work of this kind could well be undertaken at the

---

[3] O'Curry's father had spent some time as a wandering pedlar, and had acquired a deep interest in Irish folklore and music. It is likely that O'Curry was taught to read and write by his father, though he may have been helped by the Irish scholar Peter O'Connell, who compiled an unpublished Irish–English dictionary with the help of O'Curry's brother Malachy and used to visit the house. O'Curry worked on his father's farm and became a schoolmaster for a while. At the age of about thirty-three he got a post in the lunatic asylum at Limerick, where he worked for seven years. (*ODNB*)

[4] O'Curry's *Lectures on the Manners and Customs of the Ancient Irish* (3 vols, 1873) were published posthumously.

expense of the time and at the risk of a private individual. This difficulty, however, so far as concerns remuneration for labour, and expense of publication of its result, has been happily obviated in a way that even a few years ago could hardly have occurred to the mind of the most hopeful among us. It reflects, surely, no small credit on the infant Catholic University of Ireland, and conveys no light assurance of the national feeling which animated its founders from the beginning, not only that it was the first public establishment in the country spontaneously to erect a Chair of Irish History and Archæology,[5] but that it has provided with unhesitating liberality for the heavy expense of placing this [312]
volume—the first fruits of that Chair . . . before the public.

Little, indeed, did it occur to me on the occasion of my first timid appearance in that chair, that the efforts of my feeble pen would pass beyond the walls within which these lectures were delivered. There was, however, among my varying audience one constant attendant, whose presence was both embarrassing and encouraging to me—whose polite expressions at the conclusion of each lecture I scarcely dared to receive as those of approbation—but whose kindly sympathy practically exhibited itself not in mere words alone, but in the active encouragement he never ceased to afford me as I went along; often, for example, reminding me that I was not to be uneasy at the apparent shortness of a course of lectures, the preparation of which required so much of labour in a new field, and assuring me that in his eyes, and in the eyes of those who had committed the University to his charge, quantity was of far less importance than accuracy in careful examination of the wide range of subjects which it was my object to digest and arrange.[6] At the conclusion of the course, however, this great

---

[5] A chair of Irish was established at Trinity in 1840, but this was within the Divinity School and promoted and funded by Irish Evangelicals; in 1919 the appointment became a literary professorship (R. B. McDowell & D. A. Webb, *Trinity College Dublin 1592–1952: An Academic History* (Cambridge: CUP, 1952), pp. 190–1).

[6] Another striking instance of the way Newman dealt with the academic staff is the way he behaved towards John Hungerford Pollen, whom he had talent-spotted and launched into a career as an architect. At a turning-point in his life, when Pollen had resigned his Anglican curacy to become a Catholic, Newman boldly entrusted the gifted amateur artist not only

scholar and pious priest (for to whom can I allude but to our late illustrious Rector, the Rev. Dr Newman?),—whose warmly felt and oft-expressed sympathy with Erinn, her wrongs and her hopes, as well as her history, I am rejoiced to have an opportunity thus publicly to acknowledge—astonished me by announcing to me on the part of the University, that my poor lectures were deemed worthy to be published at its expense. Nor can I ever forget the warmth with which Dr Newman congratulated me on this termination of my first course, any more than the thoughtfulness of a dear friend with which he encouraged and advised me, during the progress of what was to me so difficult a task, that, left to myself, I believe I should soon have surrendered it in despair.[7]

---

with a chair in Fine Arts but also with the commission to build the University Church. Pollen's memoirs record that Newman was emphatic in his advice to the professors that they should focus on their special fields of research, whatever they might be: 'to cultivate them thoroughly; to make quite sure of the ground; to be in no hurry to put forward new conclusions, to keep them back perhaps for considerable intervals; to look at them all round, to reconsider them from time to time'. He had the knack of drawing out what each professor had to say on his own proper subject in easy conversation. 'He encouraged you to put your conclusions into terms; to see what they looked like from various sides; to reconsider, prune or develop as might be required.' Prompted by Newman, Pollen gave a series of lectures at the University which were published as *Lectures on the Basilicas* (1855). Besides working alongside Newman, Pollen found that relaxing with him in conversation, 'listening to talk that was never didactic and never dull', was refreshing after the day's toil (Pollen to Goldie, August 1890, *The Month* 507 (September 1906), pp. 317–18, 320).

[7] In his *Study of Celtic Literature* (London: Smith, Elder & Co., 1867), p. 28, Matthew Arnold refers to O'Curry as belonging 'to the race of giants in literary research and industry'. He went on to remark that his lectures, 'a splendid tribute of devotion to the Celtic cause, had no hearer more attentive, more sympathising, than a man, himself, too, the champion of a cause more interesting than prosperous,—one of those causes which please noble spirits, but do not please destiny, which have Cato's adherence but not Heaven's,—Dr Newman'.

SOME PORTIONS OF THE ADDRESS TO THE STUDENTS ON OPENING THE UNIVERSITY[1]

November, 1854

I DO not like to let you begin your studies, gentlemen, in the new and important institution which we are now commencing, without saying a few words to you which may serve as their introduction. Yet, to tell the truth, so many thoughts come into my mind connected with this subject, that my difficulty is lest by saying too much I should say little to the purpose. I want to put clearly before you, if I can, what is principally proposed by bringing you together here, and, unless I take care I shall give so many reasons that I shall fail in stating any one distinctly.

Of course it is obvious to say that you are brought here to make preparation for the prospective professions and pursuits for which you are intended—this is true. Some of you may be intended for the law, others for the medical profession, others for civil engineering—a pursuit which

---

[1] The setting for this address, on the evening before the first lectures were to take place, is described by Robert Ornsby in 'The Autumn Term, 1854', which should be read in conjunction with this piece. See pp. [319–24].

Newman wanted this welcome speech to freshers to be a solemn affair, as his intention was to set his stamp on the foundation from the very first moment, and to inspire the young men with his high ideal of what a university should be. He had already delivered lofty speeches and addresses to assembled clerics and dignitaries; now, for the first time, he would address those for whom the University was actually intended.

There are two autograph MSS of this address, both of which contain alterations (C.7.10, BOA).

has grown into great importance in late years—others for the ecclesiastical state, and it is quite certain that whatever you learn here will have a bearing on those professions; but I will not insist on this reason, both because it is so obvious,
[314] and also because there is another reason, more to the point of your coming here. You might learn your profession in other places besides this; but there is something else which you will learn here better than anywhere else, and though I may have some difficulty in bringing out all I have to say on the subject, yet I think I shall be able to do it sufficiently to proceed to several points on which I wish to give you some practical advice or information.

I will introduce what I have to say by something which I recollect passed many years ago between two persons—a mother and son—whom I knew well. The mother had been left a widow, and with small means, and she had several children to provide for; and one of them was offered a situation below that to which his birth and education entitled him. The young man was naturally unwilling to take it, and his mother tried to persuade him, and she made use of this argument: She said, "My dear Charles, I have always considered that it is not the place makes the man, but the man makes the place".

This was her saying, and see what she meant by it. She meant to say that if a man is well educated, of cultivated mind, well principled, and gentleman-like, whatever place he is in he will be valued for what he is, without a thought on the part of those who know him what his pursuit, or trade, or profession is, so that it is an honest one. A gentleman carries his own recommendation with him. He may be poor, he may be obliged to take a humble trade; but that matters not, he will adorn his place, he will render himself and his place respectable, if he has these personal
[315] recommendations. On the other hand, if he has them not, he may be higher in station, he may roll in wealth, he may have

a fine house and a grand establishment, and yet in a little while the world will find him out, and pass him by and think little of him, or even ridicule him—for after all it is the man makes the place, and not the place the man.

Now, you see what is implied in this sentiment, a great truth, *viz*., that there is an education necessary and desirable over and above that which may be called professional. Professions differ, and what is an education for one youth is not the education for another; but there is one kind of education which all should have in common, and which is distinct from the education which is given to fit each for his profession. It is the education which *made the man*; it does not make physicians, surgeons, or engineers, or soldiers, or bankers, or merchants, but it makes *men*. It is that education which enables the man to adorn the place, instead of the place adorning the man. And this is the education for which you especially come to the University—it is to be made *men*.[2]

Now, having said this, I am going to try to explain in detail *what* it is to be a *man*, as distinct from having a profession, and, to do this, I will continue the instance I have taken of the wise mother's speech to her son.

We will suppose this son of hers, who was a well-educated youth, in any situation whatever, high or low; well off in the world, or badly off. He will come across all sorts of persons; he meets some in the way of business, some in
times of recreation, some in the family circle, some in the [316]

[2] Alasdair MacIntyre draws on Newman in arguing that 'Liberal knowledge transforms us as human beings; it makes us into what we ought to be and need to be if we are to be good human beings' (from notes taken by Brian Boyd at the third of five lectures on Newman in a series 'God, Philosophy, Universities' at the University of Notre Dame on 6 November 2006). A liberal education schools the mind in how to make judgments—and this makes one better fitted to take any role. And this is why true liberal education is not impractical, though it looks askance at specialisation.

world at large. Except in the hours of business very few will care what his profession or trade is, it is nothing to them; but what they will see, and what they will be impressed with, is, what he is personally. They will say, perhaps, after first meeting him: "What a very well-behaved youth that is," or, again: "That seems a very intelligent young man". Then when they know him better, they will say: "He is so modest a person; he shows himself off so little, that at first I had not an idea how much there is in him; but really there is a very great deal in him. He has a very good judgment too for his years; he has thought and reflected, and has a great deal to say for himself." Then, as time goes on, whether in matters of business, or at other times, clever men will begin to take notice of him, and they will say: "A very clear-headed man that—he is a man whose opinion I should go by if I were in a difficulty. He has a great sobriety and soundness of understanding; he takes very sound views of things." And in consequence, when year goes after year, and the youth becomes of a mature age, thirty or thirty-five, or forty, he becomes gradually the centre of a great many people who make up to him for what is in him; or he is one of a number like himself who sway the current of affairs, public and private.

Now such a person is so far fulfilling the work for which he came on earth. I mean to say that such persons must be religious men or Catholics—of course they often are not; but I mean that, supposing they are religious men and good
[317] Catholics, they are in a position to do a great deal of good, which they never otherwise could do. Just as a strong man will make a better soldier than a weak one, so a man thus strong in intellect, thus cultivated and formed, will be able to do a great deal for God and the Church, for his Creator, his Lord and Saviour, and for his Christian brethren, which another man could not do, which he himself would not have

been able to do unless his mind had been thus cultivated and framed.

Now, on the other hand, take the case of a man who has grown up without learning to be a real man. Why, such a person is a boy all through his life, and there are a great many such. They have no opinion, no view, no resource; they are not fond of reading or thinking, they cannot amuse themselves; their only amusement is going out of doors for it; they have nothing to talk about; out of the abundance of the heart the mouth speaketh; they never have an opinion, and no one would think of asking for their opinion; when they are with friends they have nothing to converse about. When such a party get together, their conversation, so to call it, is of the most empty kind. Hence they get tired of themselves and of each other, and go out for amusements, and then, perhaps, get into bad amusements, because they have no resources.

Also,

Gentlemen, if I am called upon to state the difference
between a boy and a real man, I should say this—that a boy [318]
lives on what is without and around him; the one depends upon others for instruction and amusement, the other is able in great measure to depend upon himself. You come here to learn to pass from the state of boys to the state of men.

[319]

THE AUTUMN TERM, 1854

BY MR ORNSBY

From the *Catholic University Gazette*, of 1st February, 1855

PERHAPS it may interest the readers of the *Catholic University Gazette* to lay before them a brief account of the doings and progress of the University up to the close of the year 1854.

At the end of the preceding year, 1853, a great many persons whom we casually met in society and elsewhere, could be scarcely brought to believe that our University was a reality at all; that it was projected no one could deny, but many believed, in consequence of the long delay which had so often disappointed them of their expectations, that it was doomed never to take its place among the things of this world as a living and moving body. We are thankful to say our best hopes are now realized, and we have to congratulate the Catholic Church in these kingdoms upon what we dare to call a great fact; we have really a Catholic University. We wish to sketch the history of the actual events connected with it during its first Term.

The Classical and Mathematical schools of the University were opened on the Feast of St Malachy, 3rd November, 1854. There was no pomp and circumstance to set off the event; no crowds assembled to behold a spectacle; all this was rendered impossible, by the absence in Rome of our Archbishops,[1] and so quietly and peacefully, without noise or ceremony, our Institution commenced its career.

The examinations for entrance were conducted by the vice-Rector (Very Rev. Dr Leahy); the Professor of Classical

---

[1] Bishops and archbishops from all round the world were gathered in Rome prior to the proclamation, on 8 December 1854, of the dogma of the Immaculate Conception.

Literature (Mr Ornsby); and the Lecturer in Logic (Dr Dunne). [320]
The examinations consisted of Latin composition and of questions submitted to the candidates on paper; after which a further trial was given to each student separately, by questions asked and answered *viva voce*. Above twenty passed successfully, and immediately afterwards commenced the University course.

On Sunday, 5th November, the Rector (Very Rev. Dr Newman) gave a *soirée* at the University House, by way of introducing the students to their academical career. The Dean of Residence (Very Rev. Mr Flannery), the Professor of Classical Literature, the Lecturers in Logic and French Literature, and fifteen of the newly admitted students were present. They assembled in the Refectory, after which the list of names was read over by Dr Dunne, and the students were successively introduced to Dr Newman and to the Dean. This ceremony being concluded, Dr Newman, addressed the students to the following effect. He began by saying that the first question before them was: "What are they here *for*?" and the most obvious answer was, to prepare for their respective professions,—law, medicine, the ecclesiastical state, engineering, or mercantile pursuits. But that was not all that a University education was intended for.[2] He would explain his meaning by a story which he had heard many years ago, in early life. There was a widow lady who had suffered some reverses of fortune, and was left with a large family. One of them was obliged to accept a situation, which appeared beneath his rank, and expressed naturally some regret at this. The mother, who was a wise person, said: "My dear Charles, remember *the man makes the place, not the place the man*". They were here to receive, no matter what their intended profession was, an education which would alike fit them for all. Of course, the University was also

[2] What we need to learn from Newman, says the philosopher Alasdair MacIntyre, is 'that undergraduate education has its own distinctive ends, that it should never be regarded as a prologue to or a preparation for graduate or professional education, and that its ends must not be subordinated to the ends of the necessarily specialised activities of the researcher' ('The very idea of a university: Aristotle, Newman and us', *British Journal of Educational Studies* 57:4 (December 2009), p. 362). In other words, an undergraduate education should be regarded as an end in itself; it is about the 'making of men'—and of course today women.

intended to provide an education of special use in the professions, but it was more than that; it was something to fit them for every
[321] place and situation they might meet with in life. For instance, a man, as life goes on, suffers adversity; great changes befall him. If he has really a cultivated mind, he will act under these changed circumstances with grace and propriety. Or again, if sudden alterations the other way befall him, he will act in them too with calmness and as he ought to do. You often see people who cannot do this; who, if they come into a great fortune, don't know how to spend it properly, and throw their opportunities away. A well-trained mind will act under such circumstances with propriety. It will not be thrown off its balance by any of the changes of life, but will turn all to proper account, and conduct itself exactly as it should do throughout them all.

He went on to explain what a University was, and the nature of that University education from which hitherto, from the circumstances of the country, Catholics had been debarred. The Holy See had thought it was time this state of things should come to an end, and that the Catholics of this country, and all speaking the English language, should have the means afforded them of that higher education which hitherto the Protestants had monopolized. The idea of a University was, that it was a place of education to which people resorted from all quarters. They would here meet with men of various conditions, and from various places, and would add to each other's knowledge by that means. Again, a University ought to be in the Capital of a country, and that was the reason why the Catholic University was established in Dublin. Other places had their recommendations, but to the Capital, talent and distinction resorted. Hence it was that the Queen's Colleges, of the members of which he spoke with all kindness, never could be a University. He proceeded to speak of the discipline of a University, and reminded them that they were no longer boys but verging on manhood. Children must be governed to a great extent by fear. That was no longer the case with them. They were, to a certain extent, their own masters, the
[322] guardians of themselves. The authorities believed them to be intelligent youths, and would repose confidence in them, and believe their word, and they hoped to be met by a similar spirit of

confidence.[3] He alluded to the Romans putting on their *toga virilis*, and quoted the beautiful passage of St Paul about putting aside childish things.[4] In one sense, we were always children—children of our Heavenly Father, and we should be fools if we forgot that; but in a certain sense they should now feel that manhood had arrived, and they must endeavour to show a manliness of mind. They must begin well, and there would reign over the whole place a *genius loci*, a good general character and spirit.

The Rector then made some remarks on the time that had been selected for the opening, which was St Malachy's day, 3rd November. This was partly from devotion to the saint, whose name has always been held in much reverence in Ireland—he divided Ireland into the four archbishoprics which still remain—partly as the time when colleges in general open, and allowing for their long vacation, which would be from August to October inclusive.[5]

He went on to allude to the qualifications of those in whose charge they would be placed, the Vice-Rector, the Dean of Residence, and the Professors, and mentioned the hours of the academical day. There would be Mass at eight o'clock, breakfast at nine, lectures from ten till one or two, including French, which he thought necessary for all, and after that hour they would be their own masters till dinner at five, after which the hours would be settled by the Dean of Residence.[6] He ended by speaking of

---

[3] Here Newman signals his intent to establish a very different type of discipline from that which the students would have experienced at school. The student regime Newman hoped to establish laid stress on trust and the responsible use of freedom. He did not believe in smothering the young in rules or in mapping out their day with detailed timetables, as he meant to encourage them to take responsibility for their own actions and to learn from their mistakes.

[4] 1 Corinthians 13:11.

[5] St Malachi (1094–1148) was the greatest figure in the medieval Irish Church and the first native-born Irishman to be canonised.

[6] The earliest surviving lecture list comes from the second term and it shows that the young men would have been kept hard at it with lectures and classes. There were daily lectures in Classics and mathematics at 10 am, 11 am and 12 noon, and language classes in French between noon

their numbers, with which he was well pleased, though some of them might have expected more. They would look back with great pleasure, if they lived to be old, to St Malachy's day, 1854, on which they had taken part in the founding of the University, which would then be so great; and the fewness of the numbers with which they began would happily contrast with the magnitude
[320] to which in the course of years it will have arrived.[7] It reminded him of the scene of Shakespeare, in which Henry the Fifth, before the battle of Agincourt, when some of his attendants are discouraged by the fewness of his soldiers, bravely tells them that he would even have the numbers fewer rather than more. Westmoreland wishes but one ten thousand of those men who were that day idle in England were there to help them. The king replies:—

> What's he that wishes so?
> My cousin Westmoreland? No, my fair cousin;
> The fewer men, the greater share of honour.
> God's will! I pray thee, wish not one man more.
> . . . O do not wish one more.
> Rather proclaim it, Westmoreland, through our host,
> That he which hath no stomach to this fight,
> Let him depart; his passport shall be made,

---

and 2 pm; they were followed by an hour of Italian twice a week. Evening lectures took place every weekday at 8 pm, on French, Sacred Scripture, Spanish poetry, Irish literature or Classical literature, and occasionally these were followed at 9 pm by lectures in Italian or geography. During the summer term there were few evening lectures but, to compensate, lectures were introduced on Saturday mornings at 10 am, 11 am and noon.

[7] The young Catholics present no doubt shared Newman's dreams and dared to believe that the institution they were joining would one day challenge that long-established emblem of Protestant hegemony, Trinity College. Besides the vast difference in student numbers, they would have been conscious of the equally vast difference in buildings. The Catholic University was a small institution at the heart of Georgian Dublin, operating out of a central building which looked out across St Stephen's Green; just half a mile away from the bulk and splendour of Trinity College, the University would have appeared as a tiny, almost domestic, establishment, for all its ambitions.

And crowns for coming put into his purse.
This day is called the feast of Crispian:
He that outlives this day and comes safe home,
Will stand on tiptoe when this day is nam'd.
He that shall live this day, and see old age.
Will yearly on the Vigil feast his neighbours,
And say: To-morrow is Saint Crispian.
. . . Then shall our names,
Familiar in his mouth as household words,—
Harry the King, Bedford and Exeter,
Warwick and Talbot, Salisbury and Glo'ster,—
Be in their flowing cups freshly remember'd:
This story shall the good man teach his son;
And Crispin Crispian shall ne'er go by,
From this day to the ending of the world,
But we in it shall be remembered;
We few, we happy few, we band of brothers.

King Henry V, Act IV, Scene III

After this beautiful and animating discourse (of which we [324]
have only been able to give a most inadequate outline) the youthful academics separated, highly delighted with their first evening in college.[8]

[8] Though the number admitted at the Entrance Exams on 3 November was seventeen, it had risen to twenty by Monday, 6th November, when lectures began (Student register, 1854–79, CU6, UCDA).

[325]

UNIVERSITY AND KING'S COLLEGES IN LONDON

From the *Catholic University Gazette*, 3rd May, 1855[1]

ABOVE a quarter of a century has passed away, since the two London Institutions, whose names we have prefixed to this article, were founded; and an announcement lately made respecting them in the newspapers carries with it a moral for one who knows their history, which may be made intelligible, perhaps, even to those to whom their names are not so familiar. We think it was in the year 1827 that Mr Thomas Campbell, the poet, published a letter on the subject of a London University, which was followed up by the foundation of a great establishment in Gower Street. This undertaking was conceived and started with the special profession of excluding religion from its range of studies, being the first considerable embodiment of a principle

[1] This was one of a series of articles in the *Gazette* about existing universities; they were not only intended to inform students and the educated public about the various traditions that existed and to inspire them with such examples, but to highlight key features of the Catholic University and demonstrate that it aspired to match best practice elsewhere. In this article Newman dwells on the importance of a residential collegiate university and repeats his main educational objection to the newly-founded colleges of London University, that neither college nor university aimed at the 'philosophical idea of education, which was fulfilled in the old Universities'. He had already objected to arrangements at London University in the fifth Dublin discourse (pp. [243–70]).

which has since been extensively received among us.[2] Lord Brougham may be considered its real founder and master; and the powerful constitutional association, called the Whigs, were its chief patrons. The High Church party took the alarm at once; and, rightly jealous of the new institution, both on its own demerits and because of the precedent and pattern it furnished for similar establishments, founded in the next year a rival school on the basis of dogmatism. [326]
Under the circumstances nothing was more expedient than such a project; and thus King's College in the Strand commenced, under the shadow of the Protestant Episcopate, and with the warm support of the Duke of Wellington and the Tories.

Time went on, and a compromise was effected between the antagonists; a compromise, safe indeed in a country like Belgium, where the representative of dogmatism is no other than the Catholic Church herself; dangerous to it when London was the scene and Anglicanism its best champion. The elder institution relinquished its claim to be a University, and ranged itself, as "University College," under the supremacy of a Government University, which excluded religion quite as absolutely as that institution itself, and

[2] A major national grievance at the time came from the growing number of non-Anglicans who found themselves excluded from the two ancient universities by the religious test barriers there, which were originally devised to exclude Catholics. The needs of these Dissenters were partially met by the foundation in 1828 of London University, modelled not on Oxford or Cambridge but on Edinburgh and the German universities, and established as a secular institution. This entailed a double violation of Newman's principles: its professorial method of teaching and non-residential character emphasised the imparting of knowledge, rather than the forming of minds, while the non sectarian stance meant removing religious instruction, which for Newman lay at the heart of education. Only the second drawback was obviated when King's College was founded in 1829 by the Established Church, and then only partially, because its non-residential arrangements limited the scope of religious influence.

included King's College under its jurisdiction.[3] Since that time various establishments for education, in Ireland as well as England, some from indifference to all religions, others from a well-grounded confidence in their own, have followed the example of these two metropolitan bodies in placing themselves under the Government University.[4]

Next to the main objection to University College, which led to the Church of England foundation, none was more cogent at the time than the circumstance that neither that College, nor the University which rose out of it, aimed at the philosophical idea of education, which was fulfilled in the old Universities.[5] The latter were emphatically places of *residence* for those who came to them, the residence of many years: the University was an *Alma Mater* and College
[327] was a *Society*.[6] But a University which is scarcely more than a board of Examiners and an apparatus for Degrees, and a College which is but a collection of lecture-halls, open to young men who need never see each other or their professors elsewhere, in no way rise to the height of the ancient idea, of which they usurp the title. That ancient idea works well, even at the present day; and the *genius loci* and the traditions of Oxford have a powerful and peculiar effect

[3] The University of London received its Royal Charter in 1836, its two founding colleges being King's and University Colleges.

[4] In 1840 the University of London was granted the power to act as an examining body for teaching institutions that wished to affiliate. Seven Catholic colleges did so immediately, and others followed soon after. See Willson, *Our Minerva: The Men and Politics of the University of London*, pp. 178, 194, 319–20. The London University courses (and exams) supplied a stimulus for college studies, which were realigned to coincide with the Matriculation and BA syllabuses, and, after 1859, the Intermediate exam.

[5] In an English context, 'old or ancient universities' meant Oxford and Cambridge; in a British context, it also included Trinity College, Dublin, as well as the four pre-Reformation Scottish universities.

[6] For Newman's view on the differences between and the complementarity of 'college' and 'university', see pp. [6–8].

upon the national character. What did Gower Street offer, it was asked, more than the British Institution, or the Gresham Lectures?[7] In what sense was it a home? Of course they who made the objection did not wish it removed. Such a solution would have only made matters worse; for, if an institution representing the anti-dogmatic principle was dangerous to Christianity while under the disadvantages of Gower Street, much more was it likely to be formidable, if it could be brought into mediæval life and energy,—if it were able to show, in its own place and its own line of teaching, the raw material, and the specific type, the atmosphere, the sentiment, the *esprit de corps*, and the tradition of watch-words which characterize the University of Oxford.

With this introduction, we extract the following notice from the public prints:—

> A *new event* in the annals of the London University may be said to have taken place on Tuesday evening, when the members of the various Colleges affiliated to that Institution were, so to speak, *united for the first time*, at a social reunion. This event was celebrated by a great *soirée* at the University College in Gower Street North, given by the students of that College (acting quite independently of the authorities), to the [328]
> members of the University of London in general (*including especially the professors and students of King's College*), and the professors and students of the Independent New College, the Manchester New College, Stepney College, and Hackney College, all affiliated to the University.

We interrupt the narrative to observe, that only one of these Colleges (besides King's) is here described as connected with any particular religious body. We are

[7] The Gresham Lectures were established in 1597 by Sir Thomas Gresham, who endowed seven professorial chairs for the purpose. The lectures were to be given in London, though without enrolling students or awarding degrees.

informed that one is an "Independent" College; we may then be pretty sure, that the rest either profess Unitarianism, a persuasion which it is impolitic to name, or have as little to do with religion of any kind as University College itself. The account proceeds:—

> The laudable object of this *great gathering of the youthful intellect of the country* was to *promote kindly intercourse between the different Colleges*, and more particularly *to cultivate and cement the friendly feeling, or rather the* entente cordiale, *which now so happily subsists between the students of the two great Colleges in Gower Street and the Strand*. The re-union was held in the splendid Library of the College, which was especially fitted up for the occasion. The venerable founder of the Institution, Lord Brougham, arrived at about nine o'clock, and was received at the great entrance of the Library by etc., etc., who most ably officiated as *arbiter elegantiarum*. There were also present the following gentlemen, most of them more or less distinguished by their position in the literary, artistic, and scientific world; *viz. ... Special invitations had of course been sent to the Rev. Principal and the Divinity Professor of King's College; but none of them thought proper to attend*. The portrait of the late Mr Joseph Hume was also a conspicuous object. *A return* soirée *will probably be given next term by the students of King's College.*

[329] Another account, which correctly calls such a return of hospitalities, "King's following suit to University," adds:—

> Such re-unions cannot fail to be as useful in creating *good feeling and harmonious purpose*, as they are unquestionably pleasant in the play of conversation and the gathering of art.

It is plain from this account, that, as far as a commonwealth of letters and a traditionary teaching are the tokens of a great school, the London University is striving hard after them, and doubtless will do all that is possible to

energy and talent under the disadvantages of its structure. In the course of twenty-five years it has educated and brought around it a sufficient circle of able and active minds, though residence is not one of its provisions, to create to a certain extent an atmosphere of thought and a sympathetic feeling which makes it independent of patrons, or even of special professional talent. Its situation too in a great capital, which is naturally the haunt of the talent of the nation, and, as naturally, of scepticism in religion, allows of its being influential almost without substantive power, by placing it at the head of that talent, and enabling it to give to that scepticism form, development, and authority. It is plain too, that an institution of this kind, placed in London, enjoys not only the intellectual resources, but the national position of the metropolis.

Whether, then, we consider it as located in Gower Street, or represented by the chartered institution to which the name of University has been transferred, we must grant that [330] an academical body, in a certain sense, exists in the metropolis of England, a body which is something more than the buildings, and chairs, and benches, and regulations, of which it was originally to consist. It has taken form; and it at once proceeds to extend and perfect itself by drawing into its system, and assimilating to its principle, whatever is within its attraction; and it sets its eyes, with no unnatural ambition, upon the rival institution in the Strand, as affording matter at once of aggrandizement and triumph.

Not that we need have recourse to any sentiment of emulation, or any desire of a victory, to account for this invasion, on the part of the liberals of Gower Street, of the High Church College in the Strand. They are a living body, acting as living bodies act. To the present generation it is of little consequence with what particular views King's College was founded years ago; it matters to them as little, what the present authorities of that institution think of their interference. They have zeal, mind, the consciousness of power, a mission, a career before them; they have "young intellect," and the confidence that "young intellect" elsewhere will respond to their advances, and the reasonable expectation that there are no adverse principles in King's College, clear enough and strong enough to repress the spontaneous sympathy of its students in their behalf.

We cannot blame them, certainly, for acting according to their own views; who does not know the vigour of that rationalism which University College embodies? but what is
[331] really remarkable, and is brought out in these transactions for the contemplation of mankind, is the feebleness of King's in vindicating its special and fundamental doctrines. Twenty-five years ago, Lord Brougham was thought dangerous enough to require the establishment of a literary fortress to withstand his encroachments. The Tory nobility and the Protestant episcopate were urged by an imperative sense of duty to erect a representative of the dogmatism of the Establishment, and to provide a refuge for that religious earnestness which was proscribed in the lecture rooms of Gower Street. These statesmen and divines resolved to teach higher truths than were ever dreamed of in the project of Lord Brougham and the Whigs, and to arm the metropolitan student against the sophisms and delusions of latitudinarianism; and behold, at the end of the time, the "young intellect" of Gower Street signals to the "young intellect" of the Strand, and Lord Brougham is alive to be the witness of the success of that invitation, and of the impotence of the standing protest so gravely sustained against him. An *entente cordiale* is contemplated; and the recurrence of social meetings "cannot fail," in the words of the paragraph which we have extracted, "to be useful in creating good feeling and *harmonious* purpose" between two bodies, the latter of which was born and lives for no other purpose than to nullify the operations of the former.

Nor is this all: so strongly fortified, so confident is Gower Street, that it proceeds to animadvert on the authorities in the Strand, because, though forced to relinquish their students to an intercourse which they abominate, they do not take part in it themselves. "Special [332]
invitations," we are told, "had, *of course*, been sent to the Reverend Principal and the Divinity Professor of King's College, but none of them *thought proper* to attend." Thought proper! as if principle and conscience and honour had nothing to urge upon the unhappy men! for, what business would they have henceforth in London at all, the very moment after they had once set foot within Gower Street? Let them indignantly resign their position and its emoluments, rather than allow themselves to be thus prostituted to the exaltation of a principle, of which they are the avowed and pledged adversaries.

Nor is even this the full measure of that wantonness of triumph, in which, after the struggle of a quarter of a century, the liberal party is indulging over the professors of dogmatism. To say nothing of the well-known and life-long convictions of the respected ecclesiastic who presides over King's College, it must be borne in mind that he has lately taken part in discarding a professor whose theological views smacked more of Gower Street than of the Strand. Another is appointed in his place; we know not who; but it is not a great deal to assume that it is some one whose opinions are more in accordance with the received orthodoxy of the Church of England; yet, Principal and Professor, two clergymen, from their position emphatically dogmatic, are invited, *of course*, to a Gower Street *soirée* and create surprise and concern by not attending. There is, forsooth, no insult in the invitation, no affectation in the disappointment, no tyranny in the censure. And, by way of adding a [333]
finishing grace to this indelicate, ungentlemanlike proceeding, the students in Gower Street invite these

champions of the dogmatic principle to meet in his own domain the very patriarch of the liberalism they abhor; to present themselves before the majesty of the "venerable founder" of what some of themselves have in the language of invective called "godless" institutions, and that, in his capacity of founder, and in the very domicile and monument of his "godlessness".[8] These reverend divines are to recognize the apostle of young England, amid the very devices and trophies of his apostolate,—a man who has steadily devoted his great gifts to the advancement, of what he, of course, considers important truth, but which they know to be an awful falsehood, *viz.*, that man "has himself no control over his belief," and "can no more change it than he can the hue of his skin, or the height of his stature".

There is only one escape from this view of the matter; and, though it certainly shifts the criticism, it does not touch the main conclusion. We may conjecture, certainly, that King's College has already abandoned its religious professions, and does not move faster in its outward demonstration of liberalism, merely in order that it may do so more safely and successfully. And so much must be granted, that a Clergyman of the Established Church, one of the King's College Professors, is recorded as present at the "new event," and as taking his place in that memorable festivity by the side of the sceptic and the unbeliever. An
[334] explanation of this kind transfers the blame from Gower Street to the Strand, and substitutes hypocrisy at King's for mockery at University; but it increases instead of diminishes the force of the occurrence itself, as an evidence of the ascendancy of liberalism in the intellect of England. In that case, Lord Brougham does not anticipate merely, but he enjoys already, his triumph over the Church of England.

---

[8] The new university was nicknamed in the Tory press as 'the godless institution of Gower Street' and the 'radical infidel college' (R. Ashton, *Victorian Bloomsbury* (London: Yale, 2012), p. 21).

The Establishment has tried and failed to withstand English liberalism in London: will not the Catholic Church, by means of her own University, be more successful in Dublin?[9]

[9] As early as 1860 students at the Catholic University were being prepared for the London external exams, news of which drew from Newman the remark, 'What can be more disgraceful than its preparing men for the London University!' (Newman to Ornsby, 1 July 1860, *LD* xix, p. 380).

[335]

SENATE

N.B.—January 15, 1857. I opened the proceedings of the Senate by saying:—

That, while on the one hand, the Senate was the highest and ultimate authority, as regards legislation, in the University, and nothing was determined till the Senate had passed it, on the other hand, I should think it not respectful to its members that they should hear for the first time, by the formal notice summoning them, what the matters were for which they were summoned. And very inexpedient too, for it was very desirable that the views of its members on those matters should be generally ascertained before it was summoned, and that nothing should be brought forward that was repugnant to any great number of them, though that number were not a majority. I hope then that always, in any matter of consequence, the opinions not only of the Rector's Council, but of the Faculties, will be learned and their feelings consulted before the Senate is convoked to decide.

This, I trust, has been sufficiently done in the present instance, and, this being the case, I hope that in such words as I shall use in introducing the matters for which you are summoned, my Very Rev. and Rev. and Learned Professors and Learned Deans, you will not think me guilty of the
[336] impertinence of giving you advice or information, but rather I am repeating what you yourselves have said to me, whether in the way of objection or of counsel, and I am putting together in one what has been said to me at different times—stating the issue in which not my own deliberation only, but yours also have issued. If I leave anything unsaid,

or said wrongly, I shall have the satisfaction of your supplying it and correcting me.

SENATE

January 15, 1857

(i) Twelve present. Sitting according to rank.

(ii) "Constituatur, etc.," and sitting.

(iii) The subjects.

Five subjects from last time; for the Statutes were passed "on an understanding that certain Five Considerations, which had been submitted to the Senate by various Professors with reference to them, should be brought before it" again, *viz.*:—

1. The position of the Heads of Houses relative to the University.
2. The question of the time when the money for the Medical Burses ought to be paid.
3. The meaning of the words (p. 103) that the Professors "are bound to deliver by means of the Press, *expositions*".
4. The meaning of the Senate's jurisdiction over the University Press.
5. Reconsideration of the form of the Rule relative to the Affiliated Schools.[1] [337]

---

[1] *Vide* Report ii, App. iv, § 22. [WPN] See pp. [122–3].

Now I will take these points one by one.

1. "As to the time (2nd) when the money for the Medical Burses ought to be paid"—it is withdrawn; so I shall say no more about it, the point being already settled by Rule 26.
2. As to the meaning (3rd) of the words that "the Professors are bound to deliver by means of the Press, expositions". I will read the passage as it stands in the Rules and Regulations.[2] Now, I understand the word "and" to join together "lecture" and "the Press" *collectively*—meaning that those are the ways as one whole, by which they deliver expositions. Had "or" been used instead of "and," it might have been argued that Professors might only take the *choice which* of the two methods they should use.
3. As to the meaning (4th) of the Senate's jurisdiction over the University Press, the words are not used with any intention to exclude other and
[338] higher jurisdictions, as if we would exclude the jurisdiction of the Holy See to censure books or any other ecclesiastical jurisdiction, but merely to state the principle that as the University has jurisdiction over its members, so has it over its Press. It would be obviously preposterous if a printer could use the name of the University without being under the University's control.
4. As to the reconsideration (5th) of the form of the Rule, § 22, relative to Affiliated Schools, I have

[2] The Professors are put in trust of the particular science or department of learning which they undertake. They are bound to give themselves to the study of it, to extend its cultivation to the best of their powers, to be alive to its interests, and to deliver in their lectures, and by means of the Press, clear and adequate expositions of its principles and subject matter. Report ii, App. iv, § 3. [WPN] See p. [103].

reconsidered it, but I find nothing to alter. In saying this, I am not going by any judgment of my own; but, first, because I have heard no definite objection against it in detail (and principle does not come in, because it is the *form* which was questioned), and, on the other hand, five Bishops have expressed their approbation of it, by writing to affiliate their schools to us.

As then to these three points, I have nothing to propose. [It rests with the Deans of Faculty to propose any matter for discussion.]

5. As to the (1st) position of the Heads of Houses relative to the University, I have attempted to meet it in the new Statute about Residence which I am now to submit to the Senate. But there have been other reasons for it, and I will attempt to state them all.[3]

[3] In addressing the question of Heads of Houses, Newman used the opportunity to address the wider question of the residential nature of the University. Some background context is needed to understand the problem he was attempting to resolve.

The original intention was that the Catholic University should be residential, but by the end of the first term, the number of non-resident students had grown to the point that their status needed to be formalised. The *CUG* (7 December 1854) explained that 'externs' were of two descriptions. There were those paying for lectures, but without forming part of the University, 'that is, without being under the care of the Tutors, or being submitted to any of the examinations, or being eligible for its honours, or aiming at its degrees'; over such the University 'has no jurisdiction, and knows nothing of them out of lecture hours, and only requires that their conduct should not compromise or embarrass the authorities'. The other category were those 'who are really desirous of joining themselves to the academic body, and standing on a footing with residents'; they 'are required to unite themselves to some particular licensed establishment in the University', and doing so 'they will be altogether under the jurisdiction of the Dean of that particular establishment, and will be considered as simply members of it,

(1) As to the meaning of the consideration itself which
[339] primarily gives rise to the proposed statement, I conceive it to be this: That a Head of a House being established here (as the Rule says) with the approbation of the Archbishop and the permission of the Rector, and having students under his care, may, as time goes on, find the rule of the University

---

accidentally lodging out in such lodgings (*e.g.* their home) as the aforesaid Dean shall sanction'. The following April, Newman saw the wisdom of distinguishing the two categories, renaming the first group—those simply attending lectures—as 'auditors' (*CUG* 42 (5 April 1855), p. 409).

In this way Newman hoped that the externs would more or less be incorporated in the Collegiate Houses. The plan, however, met with only partial success, and Newman had to settle for the *modus vivendi* described in the Rules and Regulations, where it stated that the extern came under the Vice-Rector—not the Dean of his House—as regards discipline; that he should be indoors by 10 pm, attend lectures and High Mass on Sundays, and 'observe his religious duties' in the same way as an intern. The intended effect of the Rules and Regulations was to tidy up arrangements, but there remained aspects which were less than satisfactory: the absence of any collegiate life for the extern was one defect; the tenuous oversight by the (largely non-resident) Vice-Rector was another. In addition, the externs did not enjoy the benefit of tutorial teaching.

What was less than satisfactory for the externs was also problematic for the University. If the number of interns had been steadily increasing Newman might have left the question of the status of the extern to one side, but numbers were stagnant, and he was faced with the dilemma of how to attract more externs without compromising the residential character of the University.

It was with a view to increasing student numbers and improving the situation of the externs that Newman sought to re-define the constituent parts of the student body. In proposing the new statute, Newman had to juggle with a complex situation so as to satisfy opposing needs. On the one hand, he wanted to ensure that the principal features of his vision were preserved, and right at the core of this was his conception of residential living and its formative importance. On the other hand, he had to cater for other modes of student living as best he could.

By now he had been Rector for seven terms and was in a position to draw upon his experience and that of others in resolving what was partly a problem of supply and demand.

too stringent for him. He is under both the Rector and Vice-Rector. He reports the conduct of his inmates to them, as he cannot by his own act directly send them away. His advantages, on the other hand, are these: that he has a seat in the Senate, and at present a yearly grant in money towards his expenses.[4] But, on the whole, he may wish, without relinquishing his connexion with the University, to have more liberty, though at the sacrifice of the advantages at present enjoyed by him.

(2) It is to be expected, or at least it is not improbable, that in time to come young men, especially if they are youths of expectation, or foreigners, may find in time to come the Rector's and Vice-Rector's action upon the Collegiate Houses too strong for them, and in consequence refuse to come to us, except as Externs. That is, if we draw our rules too tight, they may simply break away; and I suppose any one will allow that for persons coming from a distance, especially if they have money at command, a town lodging, though in an approved house, is undesirable. Here then we need some connexion with the University less intimate than that of a Collegiate House.

(3) Again, it is desirable to induce the Medical Students to take up their abode in University Houses; but it cannot be [340]
expected that they will be willing to submit to the discipline of a Collegiate House, intended as it is for youths under twenty years of age.[5]

---

[4] According to the Rules and Regulations (p. [114]) each collegiate house received from the University an annual subsidy of £50; this was increased to £100 if it had more than five interns; to £150 when it more than twelve; and to £200 when it had more than twenty.

[5] With the number of medical students set to rise to eighty for the medical school's third academic session (1857/58) there was a growing demand for a residence for them. Taking advantage of the possibilities opened up by the statute, Dr Henry Tyrrell, one of the Demonstrators in Anatomy, took the initiative and approached Newman for advice about how to proceed. Newman advised Tyrrell to write to the University trustees for

Accordingly the Statute which I am introducing consults for the freedom both of Head and of Students, by introducing two new forms of Residence, in addition to that in Collegiate Houses.

---

aid, but meanwhile used the opportunity to encourage others to support him. Hope-Scott's offer of £150, on condition that Tyrrell was backed by the medical faculty, seems to have encouraged the archbishops to agree to set up the medical lodging (i.e. licensed) house under Tyrrell as dean.

What is noteworthy is the manner in which the medical faculty supported the initiative and shared Newman's concerns for the students. In a letter the faculty sent to Newman they explained they were unanimous in their desire for a special lodging house for medics and wanted to be the first to put the idea into practice, before other people in Dublin borrowed the idea from the *Gazette* and took the credit. They wrote of 'the lamentable consequences resulting from the exposure of inexperienced youth without guidance or restraint to the moral contagion of a large city at a time when temptation is strongest and a wholesome check most needed, namely after the business hours of the day when students come together and are left to determine for themselves how and where the night shall be spent'. They knew of several instances of upright students who had come to Dublin 'with a resolution to lead a regular and exemplary life' and had 'fallen within a year' and become a source of sadness to their families. The medical faculty believed that it was the special task of the Catholic University to remedy this great evil, and that upon it devolved 'the duty of demonstratively refuting the convenient but pernicious doctrine which unfortunately prevails to some extent amongst students, namely that the study of medicine necessitates and justifies a certain degree of moral laxity'. A related reason for providing a medical lodging house, they added, was that the University had the duty to provide 'a safe place of abode' for those who had finished the arts course and begun medicine, and were thereby disqualified from further residence at the Collegiate Houses. (Hayden & MacDermott (on behalf of the medical faculty) to Newman, [1857], Cullen Papers, 45/3/VIII(19), DDA).

The Trinity commissioners had suggested bringing the Trinity medical students within collegiate and religious discipline by introducing some form of tutorial control, such as by asking them to pay £2 for guardianship (*Royal Commission Trinity College* (1853), p. 63).

Of these, the first is being an inmate of what is called a Licensed House.[6] A Licensed House (as contemplated in the Statute I am introducing) is: (1) in the possession, as tenant, of a member of the University; (2) that member must be licensed by the Rector; (3) he and his House are under the general jurisdiction of the Rector. *Vide* Rule, p. 113; (4) he and it are not under the jurisdiction of the Vice-Rector; (5) he has not a seat in the Council; (6) he receives no University money; (7) nor can his youths hold University Exhibitions or Burses. If a Collegiate Head finds his position too confined for his purpose, he can turn his College into a Licensed House. If a young man shrinks from any future strictness of the Collegiate Houses, he need not become an extern, he may join a Licensed House.[7]

The second extension of the idea of residence is this: that youths, sleeping and taking their meals at home, are accounted residents so that they are *bonâ fide* present in some Collegiate House during the business hours of the day, say from 9 till 3. By home is understood, not only a father's room, but that of any one in *loco parentis*.

The second of these provisions answers an additional purpose; of which I now propose to speak. There is a difficulty in defining the local limit of residence and non- [341]
residence. Is Kingstown[8] residence? If not, why is Phibsborough? But if the boundaries of Dublin are not to be the limit, when will you get an intelligible one? It will be seen that, by the foregoing provision, youths living at home

[6] This was an unfortunately ambiguous term, given Dublin's reputation for drink!

[7] To some extent the draft statute formalised the existing situation, for lecturers such as Robert Ornsby and John Hungerford Pollen already took in student lodgers.

[8] Formerly a major port some seven miles south of Dublin, it was known as Dunleary until 1821, when it was renamed Kingstown in honour of King George VI's visit that year; in 1920 it was given its present name, Dún Laoghaire, the original Irish form of Dunleary.

at Kingstown are considered resident, provided they attend during the day a Collegiate House of the University.

Here we are brought to a last difficulty which required meeting. It has been asked whether the Students in ecclesiastical Seminaries, *e.g.* in England, could take their Theological Degrees at our University? The question involves several—whether passing through the Faculty of Philosophy and Letters could be dispensed with—whether standing could be dispensed with, and whether residence can be dispensed with. [*N.B.*—The *quantum* of residence another question not determined.] The present Statute only touches on the last of these—it decided that in no case is residence necessary for a degree. So far it approximates our University to the state of Trinity College in this city[9] and to the London University. In order, however, that there may

---

[9] It is worth noting the local situation in Dublin at the time. Despite similarities with the two ancient English universities and the claim that Trinity was a sister foundation, there were important differences, not least on account of their locations. As it was situated in the dominant Irish city, the majority of Trinity students did not live in college. In 1830 only 20% of the 1,800 students lived in, the rest living at home, with relations or in lodgings. In 1852, when the student population had shrunk to 1,217 undergraduates, just 118 resided in college and another 518 were domiciled in Dublin, of whom over 120 resided in lodgings and not with relatives. The commissioners investigating Trinity pointed out that no provision was made for this latter group and recommended that licensed halls or hostels be established for them with the same obligation to keep regular hours as those living in college (*Royal Commission Trinity College* (1853), p. 63). Nevertheless, about 80% of those who graduated lived in Dublin and attended lectures, because the majority of those living elsewhere failed to complete their degrees.

It was generally felt that the students living outside Dublin gave Trinity a bad name and they were referred to as 'back-stairs men'; most of them lived in England, paid their fees, and only crossed St George's Channel to sit their exams in order to gain what were known as 'steamboat' degrees (McDowell & Webb, *Trinity College Dublin*, pp. 115–17). The prevailing student conditions in Dublin were therefore quite unlike those at Oxford and Cambridge, and they strongly influenced the provision of residential arrangements at the Catholic University.

still be a bonus on residence and to prevent the administration of the University falling into the hands of persons who have never resided and are ignorant of its traditions, it is provided that Degrees taken by non-residents, though *bonâ fide* such and having all the advantages of a Degree outside the limits of the University, are little more than honorary within it; that is, that they do not carry with them such qualifications for holding office as go with a Degree gained after residence.

Summing up then what I have said, the Statute which I [342] am now going to propose for the acceptance of the Senate, will issue, if carried, in the following dispositions:—

(1) First, it abolishes the division of the members of the University into Interns and Externs, and substitutes for it that of Residents and Non-Residents—or rather it continues Interns to be synonymous with Residents; it makes Externs synonymous with Non-Residents.

(2) Both Residents and Non-Residents may, on passing the due Examinations, obtain Degrees. Whether or not time is an essential for Graduation it does not decide (though if place is not essential, one does not see why time need be), but it decides that place is not essential.

(3) Thirdly, it views Degrees in two aspects, in the original aspect historically and philosophically of a licence to teach and rule in the University, and in their popular and practical aspect of a testimonial externally addressed to the world. And it decides that the Degrees taken by "Residents" carry with them the former privilege as well as the latter, and that the Degrees taken by Non-Residents have the latter privilege only.

(4) Then, as to Non-Resident Degrees, they may be taken by persons residing not only at Kingstown, but in London or at Birmingham, and nothing is gained, over London, by residing in *lodgings* in Dublin (*i.e.*, in what used to be called the state of Extern); they require no attendance

at Lectures, nothing but examination (waiving the question of time).

(5) Lastly, as to Residence, it is defined to be one of
[343] three kinds: 1. Residents in Collegiate Houses. 2. In Houses kept by members of the University, and called Licensed Houses. 3. In parents' houses anywhere combined with daily presence in Collegiate Houses.[10]

[*N.B.*—Questions still to be settled.

I. Whether *time* necessary for Non-Resident Degrees (*i.e.* Degree without internal privileges).

---

[10] St Luke's, the first licensed hall, was opened for medics in late November 1857. See p. [297] for more details of its establishment. See Shrimpton, *MM*, p. 386 for the rules of St Luke's.

Originally Newman had envisaged St Mary's as a residence for English students, but in the event it became an international house. Unwilling to abandon his original idea and eager to use every means at his disposal to solve the ever-present recruitment problem, Newman approached Pollen to ask whether something could be done to persuade Catholic men of means in England to establish an English house at the University. He pointed out that the cause would help to increase numbers at the University, as well as advertise it, and he suggested the names of a few he thought might be willing to pay the rent of an imposing house nearby (29 December 1856, *LD* xvii, p. 488). A fortnight later, he had developed the idea further. 'I think the *only* way of giving the laity real power at the University, is by founding and supporting houses', because, by providing the funds, they would virtually have the presentation of the dean. He explained that he was about to pass through the Senate the statute about licensed houses, which 'would be αὐτόνομοι [autonomous], differing from Collegiate Houses in that they took no money from the University'. Their members would be considered, and have the privileges of, interns; their Heads would be Licensed, and the Rector would have only the veto, rather the appointment of the Dean. 'No thought is better than that of an English House', he told Pollen, and he suggested that the former Oriel tutor and convert Robert Wilberforce might be the one to head it (10 January 1857, *LD* xvii, pp. 490–1). When nothing came of this, Newman wrote to other convert friends in the hope that one of them might take up the idea of an English house.

2. Whether *standing* necessary for them.
3. Whether *passing through Philosophy and Letters* can be dispensed with in the case of Non-Resident Degrees (taking it for granted it never can in the case of Resident Degrees).
4. What is the *quantum* of residence in the case of Resident Degrees.
5. The *local limit* from the University Buildings, No. 86 Stephen's Green, of Collegiate and Licensed Houses.]

And now nothing is left but to propose the Statute in question for your acceptance.[11]

---

[11] The new statute was unanimously approved at an extraordinary meeting of the Arts faculty on 13 January 1857 and passed by the Senate two days later, but confusion over what it entailed as regards externs lasted for the remainder of the year or even longer. In a letter to the University Secretary written in December 1857, Newman makes reference to a document entitled 'Remarks on the Statute of January 1857', mentioning that they 'have passed the Council after a careful previous examination of some months' (Newman to Scratton, 1 December 1857, *LD* xviii, p. 191). This would suggest that the statute continued to be the subject of study, but, in the absence of this document, all that we have to go on are a few of Newman's letters to other members of the Council.

Writing to Dunne, Newman explained that, in order to 'enlist Dublin more in our favour', someone submitting himself to university discipline during 'the business hours' of the day, that is, from Mass onwards, should no longer be regarded as an extern (1 May 1857, *LD* xviii, p. 26). Later he asked Butler, the dean of the Arts faculty, 'Could we do any thing to call attention how we consider Externs as quasi interns, if they are in a Collegiate House during the business hours of day'? (15 November 1857, *LD* xviii, p. 172). He emphasised that he regarded it as a matter of principle that these 'quasi interns' paid their fees *and* tuition money. By way of justifying the new statute, Newman explained that, 'we were plagued with Externs coming and going, and our not knowing whether we had jurisdiction over them or not. The difficulty of an Extern is our having jurisdiction over a person who lives at home.' (19 November 1857, *LD* xviii, p. 180)

(iv) Now, we have to proceed to vote by ballot, first, for the selection of a Moderator of Studies; and, next, in confirmation of the appointment of Examiners.

First, then, for the selection of the Moderator of Studies, etc., with this end, let the Rule (10) concerning him first be read.

[344] Voting into the Ballot Box
Next the Examiners

I preface this vote, by saying that our arrangements for Examiners are not in that perfect state which is desirable, considering the supreme importance of the institution. Meanwhile, it must be observed that the vote we are about to give only relates to the Examiners for qualifications, that is *Degrees*, not to Examiners for Exhibitions, money presents, and the like, in the separate Houses, or the Lecture Rooms. First, then, I will read the Rule bearing on Examiners; and, next, I propose them: the Rev. Father O'Reilly, Professor of Dogmatic Theology; Dr MacDermott, Professor of Materia Medica; Mr Crofton,[12]

Thomas Scratton, the University Secretary, only grasped the implication of the new statute in November 1857, when he was in the process of charging non-residents who attended lectures as externs, and Newman pointed out that they should be treated as auditors instead. Scratton complained that 'not *one* Professor in the whole University was at all aware of the meaning of the New Statutes when they were passed – All (I think without exception) were taken by surprise at the particular sense afterwards attached to them by the Lord Rector' (30 November 1857, *LD* xviii, p. 192n).

[12] Morgan William Crofton (1826–1915) was educated at Trinity College Dublin where he was a gold medallist in mathematics and physics. From 1849 to 1852 he occupied the chair of natural philosophy (physics) at the newly founded Queen's College, Galway. He was received into the Catholic Church by Newman in 1851, and acted as examiner at the Catholic University in 1856/57, though he turned down Newman's

and Mr Scott,[13] both of whom have exercised the office before this.

Voting

(v) Stand—and say "Dissolvatur, etc."

---

invitation to become the University Observer (i.e. astronomer) and a Tutor in mathematics. For many years he taught at the Royal Military Academy, Woolwich, where he worked with J. J. Sylvester. He made significant contributions to mathematics in the areas of geometrical probability and integral calculus and was on the council of the London Mathematical Society. In 1882 he became one of the Catholic Fellows of the Royal University of Ireland. (*DIB*, *ODNB*)

[13] William Henry Scott (1819–59) was the son of a Staffordshire baronet. He was educated at Rugby School, became a scholar at Trinity College, Oxford and then a Fellow of Brasenose, 1844–50. He took Anglican orders, but became a Catholic in 1854. The following year he joined the Catholic University as a Tutor in Classics at St Mary's House, moving to St Patrick's in 1857. After acting as an examiner twice, Scott became the University's first Public Examiner in 1858/59.

[345]

THE CATHOLIC UNIVERSITY

ITS DEFENCE AND RECOMMENDATION[1]

I.

23rd JANUARY, 1858

WHEN we opened our columns to the letters of a correspondent, who assumed an almost hostile tone towards

[1] Towards the end of 1856 Newman urged the professors at the Catholic University to make use of the press to promote the University. A year later, Ornsby informed Newman that he had raised this matter among the professoriate and that they had appointed a committee (consisting of Butler, Dunne, Robertson and himself) to take action, though Ornsby was doubtful that it would achieve much (4 December 1857, *LD* xviii, p. 202n). Newman decided to take action himself and to do so by starting a controversy about the University. To this end he wrote a strong letter to the *Weekly Register* (12 December 1857), signed 'Q in the corner'; only the editor, Henry Wilberforce, knew that Newman was the author. The letter praised the Catholic University 'as an Irish institution', but argued 'it has nothing to do with England', while lamenting that 'it has got some of our best men from us, who ought to be devoting themselves to English objects' (*LD* xviii, pp. 200–1). After writing this 'very bitter letter', Newman encouraged Ornsby to answer it, but in the exchange of letters that followed, 'to my disgust, I [i.e. Newman] found I was beating him. But what it brought out clearly was the English sentiment. Not a word came in advocacy of the University from any English College or centre' ('Memorandum about my Connection with the Catholic University', *AW*, p. 330).

The six articles headed 'The Catholic University' appeared in the *Weekly Register* on 23 & 30 January, 6 & 13 February, 6 & 13 March 1858. The articles reproduced here in *MC* contain a few minor omissions; they appear in full in *LD* xviii, pp. 565–83.

the Catholic University of Ireland, we were perfectly aware that we exposed ourselves to the imputation of a disregard of great Catholic interests in the judgment of a large section of our readers, whose zeal in its behalf is more than enough to refute the charge of apathy urged against them generally by the writer in question. We published, however, his animadversions, for such they were in effect, because we really have greater confidence in the University than to imagine that it can be overset by a few rude words of an anonymous objector; because we are sure, on the contrary, that it will only gain by discussion; because we have the strong feeling that to smooth things over, and to hush them up, and to have a mortal dread of scandal—to be suspicious of light, and to speak by formulas, to give a hearing to one side only, and to garble or mutilate the evidence or arguments of the other—is not the way to recommend undertakings and to succeed in measures in this age and country, and in a matter such as the present. Above all, a [346]
newspaper is the very embodiment of the principle of free discussion in those things which are to be discussed at all. As to sacred things, these we accept as our fundamental principles, not as subjects for argument, and as little encumber them with our logic as we profane them with our scepticism; but when once a thing is acknowledged to be matter for discussion at all, it is matter for free discussion, and unless a given University be a point of faith or a trial of obedience, it affords a legitimate field for scrutiny and examination till the controversy is exhausted, or till public opinion is made up one way or the other. Authority and prescription are good in their place; and so private judgment, competition, and the voice of the community are good in their place too. The duty of a journalist is to be fair in admitting facts and arguments, and circumspect in coming to conclusions; and as we wish to set Protestants an example of honesty in our controversial dealings with

Protestants, so, in the case of Catholics, there is a call on us, and a still more urgent call, to be patient and tolerant of such sentiments and maxims as are open to Catholics to adopt, though different from our own.

If this view of our own position be correct as regards the varieties and conflicts of Catholic opinion in general, still more necessary is it in relation to matters which are still future, to experiments which are only in progress, and to results for which there is no parallel in the past. Now, together with an absolute confidence in the mission of the
[347] Catholic University, we candidly confess to great indistinctness ourselves as to the direction, the character, and the range of that mission; and if such ignorance is culpable, we must ascribe it to the teaching of the Rector himself, for he expressly tells us, in his University papers, that "each age has its own character and its own wants," and he trusts "that in each a loving Providence shapes the institutions of the Church as they may best subserve the objects for which she has been sent into the world". Then he continues: "*We cannot tell what* the Catholic University ought to be at this era; doubtless neither the University of Scotus nor that of Gerson, in matters of detail; but, if we keep great *principles* before us, and *feel our way* carefully, and ask guidance from above for *every step* we take, we may trust to be able to serve the cause of truth in our day and according to our measure, *and in that way which is most expedient and most profitable* as our betters did in ages past and gone".[2]

Fortified by these avowals on the part of a writer who, if any one, must be accounted true to the University, we are not ashamed to confess that we cannot predict the full work

---

[2] Quoted from 'Supply and Demand: The Schoolmen', *HS* iii, pp. 177–8. This chapter originally appeared as an article entitled 'The Communication of Knowledge, the Life of the Medieval Universities', *CUG* 8 (20 July 1854). The italics have been added by WPN.

which it will do, and the definite ground which it will cover, in the years which lie before it; though the very form of such a confession implies that a work and a territory it will have. And as to the particular question which has come into controversy in our columns, the connection of the new University with England, we frankly avow that we will not dogmatize upon it, nor reduce those to silence whose anticipations about it may be different from our own. We [348]
will not stop the mouths of Catholics who refuse to admit it. We will not pay the University the bad compliment of saying that England is necessary for its life. The University of Ireland is calculated, indeed, to do us English Catholics good service; but no one forces it upon us. It will have a great work, though . . . it is not seated on our soil, nor governed by our Bishops, nor supported by our money, nor filled by our youth. . . . It may consider, indeed, that an alliance with the Catholics of England would be an advantage both to itself and to them; but if, with a few noble exceptions, they do little or nothing for it, it can witness their reserve with equanimity, and hasten with candour to their explanations . . . we certainly do think that there are many Englishmen who keep silence, indeed, from kindness and delicacy, or from a nervous dislike to their opinion being known, or from thinking it no business of theirs, or that it would be injudicious to make a noise, or from having their own views about the future, but still who have a clear opinion that the University of Ireland is in no sense, and never can be, an institution for this country.

Moreover, there are many influential and excellent persons who find themselves bound up with the University of London by the ties of old recollections and perhaps attachments, and who have no wish, and feel it no duty, to break them. There are others, perhaps, who look hopefully to the future of Oxford, to the chance of rallying round them converts who have imbibed its academical traditions, and of

finding themselves in positions favourable to exerting an
[349] influence on the place; and who, in consequence, are indisposed to look across St George's Channel for an Alma Mater who cannot be reached without the penalty of sea sickness.[3] There are others, again, who think the very idea of a University premature, and the establishment of it unsound, until those peculiar methods and habits have been introduced into our primary and secondary education, which the Protestant public schools inherit, and of which a University should be the development.[4]

These various opinions need not be inconsistent with the conviction that the University inaugurated in Stephen's Green is a great Catholic work; that, at least, it must powerfully react upon our education in this country and indirectly subserve our general interests. They need not

---

[3] Newman crossed St George's Channel fifty-six times during the years he was connected with the Catholic University (*AW*, p. 333).

[4] A year before the University opened Newman had told Ornsby, 'One special idea I have (of course all this secret) is to try to get an influence over the principal schools and colleges in Ireland—we *depend* on them, and unless they send us well trained youths, we can do nothing' (24 December 1853, *LD* xxxi, pp. 41–2). Ornsby later remarked that the 'terrible deficiency of solid school education is an *ἀνήνυτον κακόν* [unending evil]' (19 November 1857, *LD* xviii, p. 203n). Newman addressed the problem of student supply in 1856 by appointing a committee consisting of Edward Butler, David Dunne and Michael Flannery to look into the matter; their proposal called for a system of affiliation of Irish schools to the University to increase its influence over them and to raise standards.

Officials at the Queen's Colleges blamed their low numbers on the difficulty of boys acquiring a Classical education, and when the *Report* on the Queen's Colleges appeared in 1858 it suggested that this was 'the most powerful cause of preventing the youth in Ireland availing themselves of the advantages held out by the Queen's Colleges' (*Royal Commission Queen's Colleges* (1858), p. 35). It was complaints from the Queen's Colleges about the deficiencies of the secondary schools which led to a commission being set up to inquire into the state of all the endowed schools of Ireland. The findings were published in the *Royal Commission Endowed Schools* (1858).

hinder us from giving it our attention, our sympathy, our intercessions, for its own sake, and from joyfully recognizing in its success the social advancement of a generous and oppressed people; . . . and the more so, that, as we said when we began, their free expression is for the advantage of the University itself, on the one hand by impressing its presence and its importance on men's minds, and on the other hand, by gaining for its authorities and friends the benefit of those various lights which the agitation of any practical question by a number of independent intellects cannot fail to throw upon its bearing and prospects. We intend to return to this subject.

[350]

II

30th JANUARY, 1858

WE confess to having a great jealousy of authority, prescription, prerogative, protection, so far as they are not based upon ecclesiastical principle and enjoined by a sacred sanction. Where religion speaks, social science is superseded; but in those matters which are left to ourselves, it is but an acquiescence in the custom of our country and the traditions of the day to adopt private judgment and free trade for our watchwords, and to denounce monopolies. We apply this broad statement to the case of the new University of Ireland. We do not wish to see it forced upon the Catholics of England. We should, in a particular case, obediently take what our spiritual governors, in their greater wisdom, felt it their duty to urge upon our acceptance; but, left to ourselves, we consider in this as in other matters, that a fair stage and no favour is the most congenial rule and the best policy for an Englishman to adopt. . . . We should be as sorry to hear that our Colleges were compelled to affiliate themselves to it, as to find that fathers of families were bound to send their sons to this or that College. The Colleges give a good preliminary education, and therefore fathers are only too glad to avail themselves of it for their
[351] children. Let the University in like manner gain a reputation for completing what the Colleges have begun, and the Colleges will find it their interest to connect themselves with the University, in preference to other rival institutions.

This being the state of the case, its business obviously is to show what it can do. Till it has time to show what it can do, we shall not be surprised if the Catholics of England delay to make up their minds in its favour; but so far forth as it is in a condition to give evidence of its capabilities we shall be surprised indeed if they do not make up for lost time by availing themselves of it without hesitation. It is true, another line of conduct was open to them, at least, in idea, *viz*., to have been co-founders of the University; but if the work is to be carried out by the hierarchy and money of Ireland, English Catholics cannot be called upon to use it till they find it worth using. Here, then, their only duty meanwhile is to be fair to it, under circumstances in which there are abundant opportunities for unfairness. So large a work as a University cannot be carried out all at once; there will be necessarily much of incompleteness—many a desideratum, many an hiatus, in its provisions for a long time to come. For a long time to come, therefore, it will be easy enough to find fault with it, and to ask a multitude of questions which it will be very difficult to answer. It will be easy to say: "Where is your recognition by the State? How do you mean to get it? Where are your degrees? Where are your theological students? Where are your lectures in law? Where are your collegiate buildings?" And this is what we [352]
mean by *unfairness*; for, on the other hand, it is just as easy, and far more amiable and more equitable, to inquire into what has actually been effected, or is in train to be effected, and to dwell upon the *positive* side of the subject. If bystanders will be content to put aside their own notions of what ought to be done first, what secondly, if they come to inquire about the University, willing to find what is in fact to be found, though they would rather have found something else, we think there would be much to tell them about it, and much to excite their Catholic sympathies; but it is too much the case with English Catholics to look with a

sort of incredulity and despair at every undertaking of which the Sister Isle is the scene.

This arises from their want of confidence, as they say, that Irishmen can persevere in any matter whatever.

They say that Repeal Agitations, anti-Establishment Leagues, and Defence Associations make an ephemeral noise and die away, and they anticipate the same fate for the Catholic University. We consider this to be a particularly unfair view of Ireland, as a few words will serve to explain. Because the phases of secular politics change with the moon, therefore among that people who have kept to this day the Faith which they possessed before the English were converted, great religious undertakings are to start and to come to nought; to begin with promises and end with disappointments! Now, are political measures and combinations much more variable and short-lived in Ireland than in England? It is the very nature of constitutional
[353] government and the rivalry of parties, to be ever in motion—now surging, now subsiding, now rolling in one direction, and now in the other. How few English statesmen have retained their consistency in the present day! What leader of Irish interests has changed as often as Lord Palmerston? Who has unsaid his first words, and renounced his old supporters so bravely as Lord John Russell? Was Sir Robert Peel a martyr to political principle? Have there been no late English coalitions which have suddenly been dissolved? Has not Mr Gladstone himself been accused of wavering between Lord Derby, Sir James Graham, and the Whigs? Have there been no formations and reformations of party, no vicissitudes in societies, unions, protests, and periodicals, in the High Church portion of the Establishment, or among the Tractarians? How are similar political changes in Irish politicians in point, when we speak of the solemn foundation of a University with the direct sanction and blessing of the Holy See?

To hear some persons talk, one would think that the foundation of a University was an every-day occurrence. Modifications of moment are, of course, conceivable in the Institution now commenced in Dublin, but we wish to be put into possession of the precedents on which is grounded the anticipation of its failure. It has a set of Professors superior, perhaps, in zeal and *esprit de corps*, and equal in ability, to the professorial staff anywhere; it has students as many as are found in German Universities of the first rank and name; it has a sufficiency of means, at present from the annual collections, and in prospect from the falling in of legacies; it has a Medical School in full operation; it has a [354]
periodical publication, as the register of its researches and experiments in the various departments of literature and science;[1] it has libraries accumulating on its hands faster than it can house them; it has a church of its own, handsome and large enough for all ecclesiastical and academical ceremonies. These are some of its positive achievements, to which it becomes English Catholics to have regard. What is to stop its course? What is to overset it? What does it lack? Well, it has one great want, certainly: the internal consolidation, the strength of traditional thought and usage, the definitiveness of duties, the prestige and renown, which time alone can give. It wants other things too; but those who have the proof that it has realized so much, need not scruple to accept its promise that it will accomplish in good time what remains to be done.

---

[1] The first number of *Atlantis* appeared a few days before this article was published.

[355]

III

6th FEBRUARY, 1858

DID the new Catholic University aim at nothing more than the establishment in the metropolis of Ireland of a School of Medicine, presided over by men who profess the Catholic religion and reverence its tenets, it would have proposed to itself an end sufficient to excite a powerful interest in its behalf among the Catholics of other lands; and were its only success, in consequence, that of stocking the country which has given it birth with Catholic practitioners, it would have received an adequate recompense for much greater labours and anxieties than those which have been involved in securing so valuable a result. We have no intention here of enlarging upon the importance of the Art of Medicine. Its services to mankind at large are as necessary as those of Religion itself, and far more widely and vividly recognized. It follows that while its professors occupy every part of a country and divide and subdivide its length and breadth among them, they everywhere come across the Parish Priest either as friends or as rivals, for neutrality is impossible where the territory is common to both. There cannot be a worse calamity to a Catholic people, than to have its medical attendants alien or hostile to Catholicity; there
[356] cannot be a greater blessing, than when they are intelligent Catholics, who acknowledge the claims of religious duty, and the subordination and limits of their own functions. No condition, no age of human life can dispense with the presence of the doctor and the surgeon; he is the

companion, for good or for evil, of the daily ministrations of religion, its most valuable support or its most grievous embarrassment, according as he professes or ignores its creed. And especially at those critical eras in the history of the individual, at birth and at death, he is often engaged in the solution of practical questions which come under the jurisdiction of a higher teaching, and is forced, whether he will or no, into cooperation or collision with Theology. Much, of course, might be said of Medicine regarded as a science, claiming to be one of the five departments of University knowledge, and connected with speculative philosophy generally. In this respect, too, it involves considerations of the highest moment; for it will be either the ally or the adversary of Revealed Truth, according to the hands which have the treatment of it; but we put aside this further view of it here. Looking at it merely as an art, and that one of the primary and most necessary arts of life, the difference which results to a Catholic population is incalculable between the presence of a body of practitioners who recognize the principles and laws of its religion, or of a body of men who are ignorant or make light of them.[1]

Such being the need of Catholic training for the Medical Faculty of a Catholic country, what, on the other hand, has hitherto been in matter of fact the state of the Medical [357]
Schools of Ireland before the establishment of the new University? Those who are made acquainted with it for the first time, those who know nothing of the tyrannous contempt with which Ireland has been in all matters habitually treated by the British Government, will not be able to credit the fact that a nation of many millions of Catholics is subjected to those disadvantageous circumstances which are disclosed by the authoritative statements which are now lying before us. From them we

[1] A similar passage to this had appeared in the *Report for the Year 1855–56*. See pp. [66–7].

gather too certainly that the medical establishments of Dublin are absolutely in the hands of the small Protestant minority of the country. At the date of the document which we use, and which is not much more than a year old, it appears that, out of all the Dublin hospitals, only three had any Catholic practitioner in them at all; and even in those three the Catholic officials did not exceed the number of Protestant. On the other hand, out of sixty-two medical officers altogether in the various hospitals, the Catholic portion did not exceed the number of ten. Again, out of five Medical Schools in Dublin (exclusive of the University) three had no Catholic lecturer at all, and the other two one apiece; so that out of forty-nine lecturers only two were Catholic. Putting the two lists together, we find that out of one hundred and eleven medical practitioners in situations of trust and authority, twelve were Catholic and ninety-nine Protestant; and this, we repeat, in the metropolis of a Catholic people. It is scarcely necessary to draw the conclusion, that the body of medical men to whom the care
[358] of the population is committed are either Protestants, or, at least, have in the whole course of their education imbibed a Protestant atmosphere, from the infection of which they could only be preserved by some happy prophylactic obtained from accidental and external sources. That there are those who have thus been preserved, and who are nothing else but an honour to Catholicity, we know well. How many we do not know; but for such alleviations of the evil we owe no thanks to the Dublin establishments themselves, and we have no sort of guarantee that those alleviations may not at any moment cease to exist or to operate.

Now, the Catholic University is reversing this unseemly state of things. Of course it does not grudge Protestants their rightful stations and their merited rewards; nor has it any intention of denying them the consideration due to their

virtues, their abilities, and their professional reputation; but it has set about, on the other hand, providing for Catholics also a position and an influence of their own. It has determined that monopoly shall cease, that free trade shall be the rule in medicine as well as in commercial transactions. It is providing for Catholic students an authoritative school and a safe home, where they may profess their religion without hesitation, practise it without shame, and carry its august decisions into the teaching of the lecture-room and the hospital. Already it has set up Professorships of Anatomy, Practice of Medicine, Surgery, Pathology, Chemistry, Materia Medica, and Medical Jurisprudence; and these departments of science are brought together in an establishment worthy of the distinguished [359]
persons who fill them. Its Medical House is one of the most complete in Ireland, or out of London, and contains under its roof two theatres, dissecting-rooms, rooms for anatomical preparations, and a chemical laboratory. This laboratory is especially deserving of notice. It is fitted up on the plan of those established in connection with certain German Universities, and, besides answering the purposes of the medical student, is designed to meet the wants both of those who pursue chemistry for purely scientific objects, and, again, of those who wish to apply it to manufactures. Moreover, it contains a very complete steam apparatus, to afford the student an opportunity of acquiring a knowledge of practical pharmacy. For his more enlarged literary inquiries, the University authorities have obtained from abroad a medical library well known to men of science in Germany. The library in question is the gradual aggregation of various collections, made ever since an early part of the eighteenth century by some eminent philosophers of that country. It has been recently enriched by the additions of Dr Von Ringseis, Rector of the University of Munich, from whose hands it has passed into the possession of the Irish

University. It comprises above 5000 volumes, including some of the richest and rarest works in medical literature from the earliest times of printing. Indeed, it may be said to represent the select works of the chief European schools, and includes treatises in the Greek, Latin, French, German, Dutch, Italian, as well as English language. This library was
[360] going to America, and its purchase by the University is a specimen of the zeal and vigilance which its Professors have shown, as far as the brief period has allowed during which it has been established, in making its establishments worthy of the metropolis of a great Catholic nation.[2]

Hitherto the influx of students into its Medical School has been most promising, amounting already, as we understand, to sixty young men, whose examinations have shown, that, to say the least, they are not inferior to the attendants in any other lecture-rooms. For the purposes of discipline, a medical lodging-house has been opened, which is presided over by a University official, and contains accommodation for such students as are willing to avail themselves of it.

Here, then, is what we consider one of those great *positive results* of the new Catholic University, to which we referred last week. Its ultimate benefit to the Irish people at large, to poor even more than to rich, is both momentous and inevitable; and we recommend this consideration to one of our correspondents, who insinuated that the Irish people will have no return for their contributions, unless the Faculty of Arts be given up to the purposes of a grammar and commercial school.

---

[2] See pp. [178–9] for more details about the acquisition of this medical library.

[361]

IV

13*th FEBRUARY*, 1858

IT is not easy for a visitor at first glance to determine whether, on a particular beach, the tide is on the ebb or on the flow. In both cases there is a great deal of tumult on the face of the water; billows rising and falling, curling, foaming, dashing against cliffs and falling back again, exhausting themselves and each other in a quarrel which has no meaning and no end. Yet wait a while in patience, and you will have infallible signs that the ocean is coming in, and is soon to submerge in one triumphant sweep the outlying rocks and the broad sand. So it is at this time with the Sister Island. The Englishman looks at the party contests, . . . and is impressed, at sight of them, with the one only thought that Irishmen have quarrelled and will quarrel. And yet all this while the commotion is not without a result; it is the return of the waters; it is the flowing in of Catholicity. Look back ten years, and you will see what has been gained, you will anticipate what will be gained in the ten years next to come.

We consider the Catholic University to be the event of the day in this gradual majestic resurrection of the nation and its religion. Careless spectators will confuse it with those ephemeral projects, which do but discourage patriotism by ensuring failure. They will pronounce it to be [362]
nothing else than one of those many political movements, not in Ireland only but (at least, in times past) in England, which rather express the sense of wrongs under which their

promoters labour, than guarantee the redress of them. And we will not deny that they have had some excuse for the mistake, in the circumstance that there are those who, having taken up the cause of the University as politicians, have, as politicians, proceeded to lay it down again. The warfare of politics is governed by the expediency of the moment; what is advisable at one time is not advisable at another. Statesmen have very different views of the posture of affairs, and of the measures which it demands, according as they are in office or in opposition. The battlefield is shifted, and a fresh arm of the service is necessary for victory. If such were the formal use of the Catholic University, we should not wonder at finding that it had done its work in three or four years, and, starting in 1854, was closing its gates and disposing of its premises in 1858. But there is a higher view, surely, which may be taken of its office and its destiny. It is possible for men to have thrown themselves into its cause, from a conviction of the social advantages which necessarily follow on the cultivation of literature and science. It is possible for them to have at heart the removal of the great civil penalty, under which, both here and in Ireland, Catholics for centuries had lain, from the unjust denial to them of facilities for the culture of the intellect. It is possible, without forgetting, nay, while deeply feeling, how much the last generation owes to political
[363] efforts, to hold at the same time that something besides efforts, even successful ones, is necessary for making the most of their results, *viz.* that high *status*, that commanding position in society, which an educated intellect and the reputation for mental attainments are the means of securing.

We have no intention here of dwelling on the grievances of Ireland. We do but take the fact as we find it, that, *quo jure quave injuria,*[1] the dominant class has hitherto been Protestant; that the standard of literature refinement and

[1] The phrase means ‘right or wrong’.

fashion has lain among Protestants, and has had to be sought for among Protestants; that Protestantism has been identified with every secular advantage, of whatever moral complexion, which men are accustomed to covet. In Dublin especially, whatever there has been of high society, of high education, of erudition, of literary fame, of wealth, of power, of rank, of splendour, has been, to say the least, in most intimate alliance with Protestantism. The old religion and the old pedigrees have been for three centuries out of date; new gods have reigned in Olympus. As in the Greek drama, old Cadmus and old Tiresias, if they were to have a chance of preferment, have been bound to adopt the new mode, to practise the new shuffle, and to shout the Dithyrambic.[2] The Castle[3] and Trinity College gave the tone to society and the law to thought.

We are intending no disrespect to the talent and learning of the celebrated foundation to which we have referred, nor to the persons of its authorities and officials. We doubt not, did we come into their neighbourhood, we should cheerfully take part in the good-will and echo the praises, which their [364]
social qualities elicit from those who have the honour of their acquaintance. Yet, looking at them from the point of view from which the impartial historian must regard them, we see in the magnificent institution of Elizabeth nothing more or less than an instrument of monopolizing literature and science for the uses of the State religion; of making the name of Protestant synonymous with mental illumination, and of Catholicity with bigotry and ignorance. And, as no Catholic can endure the very idea of the continuance of this tyrannical monopoly, so there is no Catholic but ought to

---

[2] This is a reference to the effect of the introduction of the Bacchic dithyrambic upon Greek drama.

[3] The reference is to Dublin Castle, the administrative seat of the British government in Ireland.

hail with thankfulness whatever opens upon Ireland the prospect of its overthrow.

Such a prospect, indeed, existed before the Catholic University commenced, and is rather realized than created by its establishment. We do not, indeed, pretend to have any intimate knowledge of Dublin society or its history;[4] but, if the testimony of those who have such knowledge is to be taken, a process has been going on for some years, tending towards the formation there, at length, of an upper class worthy of their country. The old names of the Irish race are mounting up into station and power; and the generation now entering upon the stage of life is in no slight measure free from dependence on Protestant patrons and the deterioration of Protestant influences. And, as year passes after year, doubtless the structure of society will be still further purified from ingredients which are foreign to the Irish faith and character, and will more faithfully represent the Catholic millions on which it is erected.

[365] Short as has been the career of the University hitherto, it has already given evidence of the part which it is to play in this peaceful revolution. It is perhaps invidious to select individual cases, when many might be given in illustration in all the three faculties which it has already set up; but as last week we dwelt upon the benefits to be anticipated from its School of Medicine, so now we wish to draw attention to one out of various instances which occur of such benefits in the School of Arts, or, as it is called, more intelligibly than tersely, of Philosophy and Letters. Considering the standing, as well as the history and special character of his reputation,

[4] Here Newman deliberately ignores the fact that five of the staff at the Catholic University had been educated at Dublin's Trinity College: Edward Butler, Terence Flanagan, Denis MacCarthy, Robert MacDermott and Aubrey de Vere. The latter, a convert to Catholicism, was the nephew of the first Lord Monteagle and younger brother of Sir Stephen de Vere, fourth baronet.

we shall not be considered disrespectful to others, who might be named, in singling out the Professor of Irish Archæology as a specimen of the great social change on which we have been dwelling. Here is a branch of learning recondite, rarely pursued, and from its title especially Irish, and moreover especially Catholic; and here is a scholar, *facile princeps* in his own department of it, who has been, during his hitherto career, cramped in his attempts, dwarfed in his designs, to give to the world the unrivalled treasures still extant of the antiquities of his country, for want of Catholic patronage. At Rome, at Paris, at Brussels, in London, in Oxford, all over Europe, as we are told, lie buried the most precious memorials of the national history, both before and since the Christian era. Few even know where they are; few know what they contain; few can decipher their contents; but Mr O'Curry, the gentleman in question, in spite of his singular qualifications for doing [366]
justice to this branch of antiquarian literature, has hitherto been determined in the direction of his researches by the caprice of a Parliamentary vote, or the accident of local Protestant cooperation; and, while in his investigations generally he has had to follow the paths of others rather than to strike out his own, he has been definitely debarred from such as were to terminate in illustrations of primitive Catholicism. He is said, before now, to have been instrumental in the conversion of a Protestant clergyman by showing to him MSS, ritual or devotional in their subject, which he could not get the means of giving to the Press; and had it not been for the Catholic University, the probability is that this eminent scholar would have carried to the grave with him, unvalued, unused, the keys which might unlock a world of curious and momentous knowledge. He would have shed lustre on Government commissions and on Trinity College publications; and there would have been the end of his biography. But a happier and more appropriate

destiny is in store, we may hope, both for him and for his favourite pursuit. Negotiations, we understand, have been opened for the possession, or, at least, for the use of the foreign MSS to which we have referred; and an advertisement has already appeared of an instalment of what is to be expected from him, in the shape of twenty-one lectures, delivered in the University Schools, in which he discusses the existing unpublished materials of ancient Irish history from its Pagan period down to the seventh century of Christianity.[5]

[5] Eugene O'Curry's *Lectures on the Manuscript Materials of Ancient Irish History* were published in 1861. See pp. [299–300] for more about the MSS referred to.

[367]

V

6th MARCH, 1858

THERE is a class of undertakings, not uncommon in the world, which are ushered in with noise; and wise men feel that where noise is there is seldom anything besides noise. The University lately set up in Dublin is, at least, safe from this criticism. Whatever be its faults, no one can accuse it of puffing itself too loudly, or of becoming a rallying point for party zeal. It is engaged in working, not for the present merely, but for the future; and accordingly it is not exposed to the temptation, which otherwise might beset it, of essaying brilliant displays, or of courting an ephemeral popularity. One cannot be surprised that it has not attained what it has never sought. Its sobriety and modesty certainly were not likely to commend it to those who think that work is got through by talk and profession, and have not shielded it from the importunate question, What has the University done? What is the University doing?

It is possible to be extreme in disregarding public opinion. A *quantum* of reputation is necessary for making progress in any great undertaking; it is the ready money, or rather the credit, which furnishes the exigencies of the day. It imparts to the parties engaged therein the strength of self- [368]
reliance and of sympathy. There is an impropriety in trying the strength of well-wishers too rudely, and in appealing simply to a future which they may never live to see. And there is an inconvenience in allowing the growth of a popular disrespect, which may be a provocation to acts of

insult or of injury. The authorities of the University seem to be aware of this danger, and of the duty under which they lie of meeting it. And this is the view we take—we shall presently say why—of their new scientific and literary periodical, the *Atlantis*: it is one of their ways of fulfilling a serious obligation.

This publication, though not many weeks old, has already made a considerable sensation; and we venture to affirm that, if its first number is to be a sample of what is to come, it cannot fail to continue to do so. It is an ambitious attempt, certainly; it aims at installing the University among our recognized oracles of intellectual activity, and it claims for it a European position. It will either be a great success, or a great failure. It implies that the University is already prepared for a trial of strength in the open field of literature and science. Its conductors, in their recent prospectus, inform us, that "In undertakings such as theirs, success, from the nature of the case, is another name for merit; and failure can only arise from causes traceable to themselves. If they are sanguine that they shall be able to answer to the profession which they make in the very fact of their commencing, it is because they trust they have the elementary qualifications of zeal, industry, and determination."[1]

[369] To any one who has followed the course of official and semi-official documents, with which the proceedings of the University have been accompanied, the motives for so bold a step will be easily understood. What the Professors are at present doing on the very scene of their labours, the schools they are bringing into shape, the students they are collecting, the minds they are forming, the plans of education they are systematizing, and the traditions they are establishing, cannot be seen or valued except on the spot.

---

[1] The passage quoted appears in both the first (pp. [429–30]) and second version (*LD* xviii, p. 150n) of the Prospectus.

Their friends are those who know them; beyond this personal range is the cold and dim region of uncertainty, ignorance, scepticism and ill-will, as regards their proceedings, of rumour, fiction, slander, and gossip. On this side of the water their cause is sometimes pronounced to be failing—a staff of Professors without academical heads, without students, without lectures, quarrelling among themselves, and quaking at the falling off of the funds. Such as this being the absurd representations which are made concerning them, they are reduced to the necessity of adopting the ancient disputant's method of refuting his sophistical opponent, *Solvitur ambulando,*[2] or the modern philosopher's dictum, *Cogito, ergo sum*. Their learned labours, recorded in the *Atlantis*, will be the summary sovereign demonstration that their University both is alive and is thriving, in spite of all that is conjectured to the contrary.

In taking this view of their proceedings, we are availing ourselves of statements made four years ago, before the University had commenced its operations. The present Rector, to whom the task of conducting them was [370] committed, laid it down as the historical idea and almost the essence of a University, that "demand and supply were all in all"; and (which is the particular principle in point here) that "the supply must be before the demand, though not before the need".[3] He clearly anticipated then, what indeed it was not hard to anticipate, that at first Professors would have to create the public interest, instead of merely satisfying it, and to draw students to their lecture-rooms,

[2] The phrase means, 'it is solved by walking', that is, the problem can be solved by a practical demonstration (referring to the response of Diogenes to the claim that motion is unreal by getting up and walking).

[3] This is a paraphrase of an extract from *HS* iii, p. 51. The chapter, 'Free Trade in Knowledge: The Sophists', first appeared in *CUG* 7 (7 July 1855) as 'What a University Does, and What It Does Not, Consist In'.

instead of finding them there ready to their hand. Nay, he thought it prudent to go beyond what was probable in his anticipations; for, in fact, their lecture-rooms have been fairly attended from the first. Starting, however, on this cautious assumption, he made it his great object, as far as possible, to set up the Professors in such advantageous circumstances, and in such an independent position, as would give full scope to their talents, even though they had no pupils at all, and would furnish the best opportunities, for their at least acting upon public opinion. In a word, since he could not at his will create lecture classes, he determined to create institutions.

This policy is laid down in a printed document of April, 1854, from which we proceed to quote a few sentences: "Considering," it said, "that we have the whole weight of Government, not only against us, but in favour of a rival system, it is imperative that the Professors appointed should be men of celebrity. Such celebrity is the only secular inducement to bring students to us in preference to the
[371] Government Colleges. Even able men, if they have not yet made a name, will be unequal to the special necessity of the moment." An important conclusion follows: "Since students, as has been said, are to be gained specially and pre-eminently by means of the celebrity of the Professors, it is plain that the Professors must be appointed independent of, and prior to, the presence of students. This has been the case in the history of Universities generally. This brings us to another practical conclusion: *we must commence by bringing into position and shape various large departments of knowledge*—by founding *institutions* which will have their value intrinsically, whether students are present or not. This, if we can manage to do it, will have a double advantage; such institutions, first, will attract students; next, they will have a sufficient object before students come." After giving instances of the institutions which might be

founded, it proceeds: "Not that such institutions are all of them possible all at once, but some of them are; and these, and such as these, might set to work, and would be producing results *before and during and until* the actual formation of classes of students in each department, for whose sake they are really set up. Astronomical observers, Professors of medical science, the decipherers and editors of ancient writings, chemists and geologists, would in various ways subserve the social interests of Ireland, even though their lecture-rooms at first were but partially filled."[4]

Some of these institutions, as the writer calls them, have already been called into existence; such are the Medical House, the Chemical Laboratory, the Irish Archæological [372] Department; the Libraries and Museums, which are in course of formation; and the University Church and its accompaniments. Now, the *Atlantis* is one of these, and, in some respects, the most important of all, because it is, in a certain sense, the organ and the record of their proceedings; and, again, because it is not of a local nature, but world-wide in the most emphatic way, increasing the "celebrity" of the Professors of the University, and making them useful to the literary and scientific world, even though they had no classes of students to instruct at home.

Our readers may now be interested to compare what we have been saying with the views professed in the original advertisement of the *Atlantis*, as it was published in the newspapers in the spring of last year: "The University," said the *pro tempore* Editor, "has already had a greater measure of success than even its most zealous friends, looking calmly at the difficulties under which it started, ventured to anticipate for it. It has at present in its lecture-rooms from a hundred and ten to a hundred and twenty students. It has,

---

[4] See Newman's memorandum, 29 April 1854, *LD* xvi, pp. 558–9, and the later version of 20 May 1854 on pp. [95–7]. The italics have been added by WPN.

moreover, done much to vanquish the most formidable of difficulties which can beset a public institution, struggling into existence and position; and that is, the apathy, the incredulity, the scorn, with which the very idea of its establishment was variously received, and that, even among those very classes for whose advantage it was specially designed. The fact of its being actually commenced, the number of able men whom it has enlisted in its service, the
[373] recognition and the prospects of its 'Medical School,' the popularity which has attended upon its new Church, the homage paid to it by the foreign youth who have sought it out from abroad in preference to their own schools,[5] have all combined to mitigate the prejudice and to overcome the disinclination of the Public mind towards it. But its success supplies a lesson as well as an encouragement. It teaches its members that they must, and may safely, *depend on themselves*. Up to this time, they have made their way, not by favour of external parties, patrons, influences, or contingencies, but *by means of their own reputation, courage, confidence, resources and energy*, under the blessing and protection of Heaven. If they are true to themselves, others will come over to them. They have but to proceed in the course which they have begun, and they are sure to make progress."

"It is in order, then, that the University may be taking another step in advance that a periodical is contemplated, as the repository and record of its intellectual proficiency. Such an undertaking naturally follows on the entrance of the Professors upon their respective provinces of labour. Nor

[5] Between 1854 and 1859, 106 students were entered in the books of the Catholic University, excluding the medical students and those attending the evening classes; of these, thirteen came from England or Scotland and fifteen from mainland Europe (Barr, *Paul Cullen*, pp. 221–3). Of the 191 students who registered between 1854 and 1861, 40, i.e. 21% of the total student population, came from outside Ireland (Rigney, 'Bartholomew Woodlock' i, p. 326).

will it only serve to tell the public what they are doing and what they can do; it will be their contribution to the science and literature of the day; it will be their advertisement, recommendation, and bond of connection, with the learned bodies of Great Britain and the Continent, and it will gain for them, in exchange for what they send, the various journals of a similar kind, many of them important and valuable, which issue periodically from those great centres of thought."[6]

Some excellent and true friends of the University have [374]
criticised the business-like tone and austere technicality of the number which has appeared, and have, in their kind interest for the fame of the University, wished somewhat of more indulgence to ordinary readers, by the introduction of matter less inexorably high and abstruse. But the very object of the publication is to record the successful diligence of the Professors in their respective studies—not to write eloquent reviews or essays, *currente calamo*, on curious or entertaining subjects. Ornamental writing is about as much out of place in the *Atlantis*, as *ormolu* clocks, Dresden china, and Axminster carpets in Pump Court or Copthall Buildings.[7] Scientific schools and circles abroad, where English is not vernacular, would not be impressed by fine periods, or edified by miscellaneous information. (*Vide* Appendix to the volume.)

---

[6] The full text can be found on pp. [429–30]. The italics have been added by WPN.

[7] These Dublin buildings housed law and business offices.

[375]

VI

13*th MARCH*, 1858

ONE of the main secrets of success is self-reliance.[1] This seems a strange sentiment for a Christian journalist to utter; but we speak of self in contrast, not with a higher power, but with our fellow-men. He who leans on others, instead of confiding in his own right arm, will do nothing great. Here, again, we must explain; for is not this the sentiment of every wild religionist who makes himself his own prophet and guide, and despises Holy Fathers and ecclesiastical rulers? Well, then, we are censuring dependence on others, when others are not representatives, in so far as they are relied on, of a higher and more sacred authority. We hope we have expressed ourselves without any paradox at last.

Now, there is a strong existing temptation, to which some men are more exposed than others, but all men under circumstances, of *not* relying on themselves. And this has been a special temptation of literary men and intellectual bodies, from the time of Pericles or Mæcenas down to that of Leo or Louis le Grand. And in the case of Universities in particular, as the schoolboy gets his themes done for him, as

[1] Exasperated by the lack of support for the Catholic University from, among others, schools in Ireland and England, Newman confided to the Dean of the Arts Faculty: 'I think we must depend on our own selves, and on none other, under Providence. Affiliated schools will not help us, that is their conductors will not. [. . .] Every school is for itself and no one else. We are our own best friends' (Newman to Butler, 19 November 1857, *LD* xviii, p. 179).

the undergraduate buys a *cram*,[2] so the venerable mother to whom he belongs may chance to have it firmly imprinted in [376] her academical intellect, that she cannot possibly prosper without the sanction of the State and the favour of great personages. This has never been the weakness, *exceptis excipiendis*,[3] of the English Universities. They have been dragooned, indeed, by tyrannical despotism; they have had theories, or have felt the passion of loyalty; they all but worship the law as the first of all authorities in heaven or upon earth; but when the question is that of submitting to the Government of the day, or to persons in power, it requires but little knowledge of the history, for instance, of Oxford, to be aware that it has been its rule to rely upon itself—upon its prejudices, if we will, but still on what was its own. Rather than consent to stultify its received principles and recorded professions by a sudden change in favour of Catholic emancipation, it rejected from its representation its favourite son, the Leader of the Commons, when he had deserted his own opinions and invited Alma Mater to follow him.[4] Nor could it honourably have taken another course; and, while we have no relish for political traditions which would have stood in the way of our having at this day any Catholic University at all, we hope that no Catholic University that is or that shall be, with its vantage-ground of higher principles, will ever show less

---

[2] During Newman's undergraduate days, besides the college lectures, a parallel, semi-official system had emerged, in which private coaches were engaged by serious students for individual or small-group tuition, or else engaged as 'cram coaches' by idle students in a last-minute attempt to salvage a degree. In student parlance, the private coach was either a 'class-coach' or a 'pass-coach'.

[3] That is, excepting what must be excepted, or, more loosely, with the necessary exceptions.

[4] Newman refers to Sir Robert Peel, one of the two MPs for Oxford University.

self-respect, consistency, and manliness,[5] than Protestant Oxford, in standing on its own sense of right and falling back upon its own resources.[6]

However, old Universities are but partially exposed to the temptation of courting the secular power, and of shifting
[377] with the times. It is when an academical body is struggling into position that the offers of the State are at once apposite and effectual; it is when it needs a principle of permanence, which the State can impart, whether in the form of legal recognition or of pecuniary aid. Under such circumstances, imagination is busy with those parties who are interested in its welfare, spreading out before them attractive pictures of the liberality and security of Government grants, and of the satisfactory *status* which is the result of a Charter and of the privilege of conferring degrees. And, on the other hand, memory is busy, too, holding out an over-true record of the anxious or the teasing warfare with a host of difficulties, great and little—the tedious and uncertain progress; the ups and downs, neither dignified nor pleasant; the wear and tear of mind, the discouragements from public opinion or popular rumour, amid which the private individual or body fights its way into station and prosperity. The temptation is strong to attempt a short cut to greatness; though, to tell the truth, a body which has been welded into one mass by the various strokes of fortune is likely to be less brittle, and to have more work in it, than if it had been cast in some external mould, and were subjected to conditions of size and shape which had been determined before its existence.

---

[5] For the mid-nineteenth century Victorian, the concept of 'manliness' encapsulated one of the essential ideals which a public-school and university education was supposed to foster. By early exposure to difficulties and hardships, self-reliance and character were cultivated—though not brains, for manliness coexisted happily with anti-intellectualism.

[6] Newman speaks in similar glowing terms about the Protestant schools of England. See, for example, *Idea*, pp. 7, 145, 377.

This, however, is a speculation, interesting indeed to pursue, but beside the purpose of these remarks; for we are contemplating, as is obvious, in what we have been saying, the new Catholic University; and, as regards this particular Institution, we are not called to the delicate task of adjusting [378]
the balance of advantages between State patronage and private enterprise in such great scientific and educational undertakings, for a very simple reason. It is true, indeed, that the new University has not the legal *status* and the Government favour, which have abstractedly so many recommendations; but it is certain also, as we consider, that, in matter of fact, in Ireland and at this time, its Professors, whatever else they might gain, would not gain much or anything towards the special objects for which it is instituted, by having those coveted distinctions. And though such an assertion may at first sight look like hazarding a second paradox, we are prepared to defend it.

What will be called, by enemies and timid supporters, the special hitch in the proceedings of the University at present, is, we suppose, not that its Professors are second-rate, nor that they idle away their time, nor that their salaries are insecure, nor that they are without a fair number of students; but that the students, though increasing, are not increasing in the exact ratio of the age of the University. If, then, State recognition can do anything at all for the University at this moment, here, and here only, is the one definite service which it is to render. The one *desideratum*, as hostile critics urge it, concerns, not the Professorial, but the Undergraduate body. Let there be no mistake on this point. Government need not be invoked to do for the Professors what the Professors can do for themselves, but what they cannot do without the Government. If Government does not do as much as this one thing, it does [379]
nothing at all. When these objectors cry out to them: "You will not get on without the Government; your talents, your

attainments, your honest diligence, your reputation, are worth nothing without Parliament and Law to back you"; what they really say, when brought to book, is this: "Your students, indeed, at present do not exceed those of one Oxford College; but with Government patronage, they will infallibly be as many as two, three, or four". If they do not mean this, it is hard to say what they mean which is to the purpose. Taking this, then, for granted, that the advocates for seeking Government aid put it forward as their strong point, that it will fill brimful the lecture-rooms of the Professors, we beg attention to the case of the Queen's University and Colleges in Ireland—institutions, of which the very name is suggestive of those high privileges which the Crown and Parliament can alone bestow; and let us ask whether the present condition of those Government bodies, composed, as they are, of Professors of first-rate ability and attainments, is such as to inspire us with any very sanguine hope that the Catholic University would gain much in that one respect in which it is supposed to need to gain by the circumstance of a legal recognition.

We shall not attempt any elaborate investigation into the state of the institutions in question, which we leave to the Blue-book, promised the world as long ago as August last, whenever it shall make its appearance.[7] In a matter so notorious, it will be enough to refresh the memory of any persons who have interested themselves in the subject by
[380] one or two documents which we happen to have at hand. It seems, then, that, as late as last year, the sum of £1625 was voted in Parliament for the Queen's University of Ireland, and £3200 for the Queen's Colleges.[8] It appears, too, that

[7] Newman refers to the *Report of Her Majesty's Commissioners Appointed to Inquire into the Progress and Condition of the Queen's Colleges at Belfast, Cork, and Galway* (1858), which was presented in Parliament on 20 April 1858.

[8] The sums for 1858 were £2,323 and £4,800 respectively.

the Cork College, in particular, has in its gift as many as fifty-five scholarships, for proficiency in literature, science, medicine, law, civil engineering, and agriculture; in all which departments of study it grants, by the medium of its University, diplomas and degrees. Of these scholarships, ten are of the value of £40 a year each, and forty-five of sums ranging between £24 and £15; making a total of £1400, as the educational encouragement given in one city and neighbourhood in the course of the year. Further, out of the whole number of students of the three Colleges, who presented themselves in Dublin in 1856 at the degree examination, as many as one-fourth were presented with a gold medal, and another fourth with a £12 prize. And yet, in spite of these inducements, the matter of fact is such that the College books do not fill, and even the students who come cannot be persuaded to present themselves for examination, but leave without taking a degree. Moreover, it appears that in 1856 there were only forty-eight examinees from all the three Colleges in the course of the year, or an average of sixteen per College, while the examiners amounted to as many as twenty-one. It appears also that, at the same date, there had only been one engineer's diploma gained in the course of six years, while the expense of the Professorship during that time had been £560. When the subject came before Parliament last session, statesmen of the most [381]
various shades of opinion—Whigs, Tories, Peelites, and Orangemen—seemed to acquiesce in these facts, and the only arguments by which Government carried the vote in behalf of the Colleges were such as these: That the scheme had certainly issued in disappointment, but that it was originally Sir Robert Peel's; that it was now established by Act of Parliament; that it was the expression of a principle of national policy; that it involved a theological question; that measures were in progress for its revision; that a Commission was to publish a report upon it in the course of

a few weeks; and that it was unbusiness-like to decide against it before having had the opportunity of reading what the Commissioners had to say.

Such is the result of a paper University, imposed *omnibus numeris*[9] on Ireland. Why should Government be thought able to secure a great accession of students for the Catholic University, when it is unable to collect them for its own favourite institution? Why should not our friends be content to work quietly, and to confide in themselves and in the future?[10]

---

[9] That is, in every detail.

[10] Having stirred up a controversy about the Catholic University in the *Weekly Register* with his letter signed 'Q in the corner', and then having tried 'to make up to the University by writing leading articles […] in its defence', Newman was disappointed with the response. He explained that, 'what came home to me clearly was, that I was spending my life in the service of those who had not the claim upon me which my own countrymen had: that, in the decline of my life, I was throwing myself out of that sphere of action and those connexions which I had been forming for myself so many years. All work is good, but what special claim had a University exclusively Irish upon my time?' ('Memorandum about my Connection with the Catholic University', *AW*, p. 330).

CONTEMPORARY EVENTS— HOME AFFAIRS

From *The Rambler*[1]

I

EDUCATION MOVEMENT IN IRELAND

1*st May*, 1859

WE just now alluded to the great education meeting at Cork;[2] but so much is doing in Ireland at the present moment in various ways in the cause of schools, seminaries, universities, and other educational establishments, or associations, that we have a difficulty in entering on a

[1] These three articles appeared in two consecutive numbers of this bi-monthly magazine, May and July 1859. Newman was editor of *The Rambler* for just these two issues.

[2] Above this article, in the 'Home affairs' section, Newman mentions 'the great meeting that was held in Cork', which took place in the cathedral on 2 March 1859 and was in favour of Catholic schools. It followed a meeting on 5 February called by Lord Fermoy, the Lord Lieutenant, to press for the establishment of intermediate schools for the middle classes. He was publicly supported by the Protestant Bishop of Cork and by Sir Robert Kane, the president of Queen's College, Cork. But the proposition was opposed on the ground that it would spread mixed education: neither the national schools nor the Queen's Colleges were acceptable; Ireland must have separate education systems; mixed education was being forced on the country in order to stamp out religion. These latter views were overwhelmingly endorsed at the February meeting (*The Tablet* 20:983 (11 February 1859), p. 109).

subject which will prove too great for the space we can afford to give it.

Before we draw attention to this meeting, it may be well to devote a few lines to a review of the state of the education question at this moment across St George's Channel. Though the English people cannot endure the thought of a compromise between religious parties on that vital subject in their own case, and the introduction of a system of mixed education, they think it good enough, or the very thing, for Ireland; and both Conservatives and Whigs have played a part in its establishment there. The Whigs began it, thirty years since, under Lord Grey, by setting up the national system of schools for the population
[383] at large;[3] Sir Robert Peel set up the three Queen's Colleges, at Cork, Belfast, and Galway, about fifteen years after; and Lord Clarendon, we believe, set up the Queen's University. Lately a commission has been appointed to inquire into the funds, and their application, of the endowed schools throughout the country, with a view of framing a large measure of intermediate education.[4] At the same time, the

[3] The System of National Education, which was introduced by the Whigs in 1831, depended on the principle of mixed or undenominational education, and so was only tolerated by Catholics as an uneasy compromise. Mixed education was unknown in Ireland until the foundation of the Society for Promoting the Education of the Poor in Ireland, devoted to the financial assistance of schools which did not promote any particular denomination. The *Report* (9 vols) of the Royal Commission of inquiry into Irish Education (1824–27) paved the way for Lord Derby's scheme of National Education. The hierarchy was divided over it, eighteen bishops siding with the Archbishop of Dublin in his willingness to accept the concessions offered Catholics, and ten with the Archbishop of Tuam in his refusal to accept the compromise. The divisions led to appeals to Rome from 1839 onwards. See D. H. Akenson, *The Irish Education Experiment: the National System of Education in Nineteenth-Century Ireland* (1970); also D. Kerr, *Peel, Priests and Politics* (Oxford: OUP, 1982), pp. 1–67.

[4] The *Royal Commission Endowed Schools* (1858) investigated mainly Protestant schools, as few Catholic ones had been endowed. It was

gates of Trinity College have been opened wider than before, and certain emoluments placed within the reach of persons of every denomination.[5] Such has been the gradual extension and advance of a scheme which, tending as it does, on the one hand, to educate all classes, on the other, to detach all whom it educates from the Catholic Church, cannot be considered a Whig or a Conservative scheme, for it belongs to one as much as to the other; nor a Tory scheme, for it has never been acceptable to the Orange party; but which, as being a deep design of English statesmen upon the faith of Ireland, and that on a basis of

---

complaints from the Queen's Colleges about the deficiencies of the secondary schools which led to a commission being set up to inquire into the state of all the endowed schools of Ireland. The problem was that the middle of the century had been a period of transition for secondary schools in Ireland, the National System having effectively destroyed the old Classical academies without providing any substitutes, while the new schools and colleges were only just beginning to appear. Officials at the Queen's Colleges blamed their low numbers on the difficulty of boys acquiring a Classical education, and when the *Report* on the Queen's Colleges appeared it suggested that this was 'the most powerful cause of preventing the youth in Ireland availing themselves of the advantages held out by the Queen's Colleges' (*Royal Commission Queen's Colleges* (1858), p. 35).

[5] By 1794 it had become politically expedient for the British government to open up degrees at Trinity to Catholics and Dissenters by removing the religious test barriers for undergraduates (although not for scholarships or fellowships). Relatively few Catholics took advantage of this relaxation, as the whole atmosphere at Trinity was permeated with Protestantism, and over time the arrangement was regarded with increasing disapproval in Catholic clerical circles. Nevertheless, some well-to-do Catholic families continued to patronise Trinity. During the mid-1850s the number of Catholics entering Trinity was approximately 20 a year, and this number rose to around 25 a year in the 1860s. Most of those doing so were studying for the Bar. Surprisingly, this included families with close ties to the Catholic University: Michael Errington, one of the members of the original Catholic University Committee, sent his eldest son George to the Catholic University in 1857, but in 1859 his younger son James went to Trinity; Richard More O'Ferrall, whose brother James was on the Committee, declined to send his only son to the Catholic University.

operation which would not for an instant be endured by their own countrymen, may, from its bold and over-bearing one-sidedness, be fitly called an English system.

However, even at the end of thirty years, the principle of mixed education has not taken root; and, in spite of its superficial progress, the establishments based on it seem falling to pieces. The system of poor-schools, commonly called the national system of education, we believe, was never approved at Rome; and, though for a time it worked well for Catholics, still, as time has gone on, it has become
[384] more and more distasteful both to the Church and to the Orange party. As to the Queen's University and Colleges, for the moneys they have consumed and the work they have done for it, we refer our readers to a recent Parliamentary return, of which we shall speak presently. The plan of intermediate education has not yet got so far as to be brought before the legislature.

Here we are concerned with the opposition directed against these measures by the Catholic body. As regards the national system of education for the humbler classes, it remains as yet untouched; though from the present aspect of things, it would not be surprising if the Protestant prelate, Dr Whately, who was the instrument of the Whigs in commencing it, was destined to see its termination.[6] The

---

[6] Richard Whately (1785–1863) was the only Church of Ireland episcopal supporter of the Whig government's national system of education. He chaired the board of commissioners when the Duke of Leinster was absent, and formed an alliance with his Catholic counterpart, Archbishop Daniel Murray. When, in 1852, he failed to ensure that his *Scripture Lessons* and *Lessons on the Truth of Christianity* were on the education board's list of approved books, he resigned. The board thus lost the last leading advocate of the Irish mixed system.

Whately and Newman had known each other well at Oriel. In fact, Whately had taken on the task of drawing the timid young graduate out of his shell, going for walks with him and conversing at length. When Whately was appointed Principal of Alban Hall, Oxford, Newman accepted the invitation to be his Vice-Principal; Whately also enlisted Newman's

scheme of higher or University education was disowned and resisted by the National Synod of Thurles, in 1850,[7] when a decree was passed for the erection of a Catholic University, which, as our readers know, has now been in operation for several years, and that with such promise, that a charter is in prospect, of which we shall speak before we conclude. The principal object, however, to which Catholic exertions have been directed during the last few months, has been to anticipate and act upon the projected Government measure of intermediate education, to which the labours of the late Commission necessarily tend. The great meeting of Cork was held with this purpose.[8]

---

assistance in rewriting his textbook, *Elements of Logic*, which became the standard work on logic for the next two decades. The two fell out over Catholic Emancipation and the re-election of Sir Robert Peel as MP for Oxford University and thereafter their paths diverged. When Newman arrived in Dublin, Whately declined to see him. (*ODNB*)

[7] At Thurles, the bishops voted by narrow margins—two and four votes respectively—to prohibit their clergy from holding office at the Queen's Colleges and to warn the laity strongly against attending them.

[8] The rest of this article was dedicated to the meeting in Cork. It was attended by four bishops, other ecclesiastical dignitaries, members of parliament, deputy-lieutenants, magistrates, three hundred priests, and around eight thousand of the Catholic laity. A unanimous resolution was passed, 'that no form of intermediate education is suited to a Catholic people unless it be granted to them in separate schools, and on terms always strictly in accordance with the teaching and discipline of the Catholic Church' (*The Rambler* (May 1859), p. 124).

[385]

II

A CHARTER TO THE CATHOLIC UNIVERSITY

1*st May*, 1859

THE same month which has witnessed the commencement of the movement in behalf of a Catholic system of intermediate schools, is also memorable for an important step in advance towards the secure establishment and legal confirmation of the Catholic University of Ireland. In a great undertaking such as this, to be simply *recognized* as existing is the whole of the battle; and the only protection which its enemies have against it, and their only weapon of attack, is to *ignore* it. This they have accordingly done as regards the University, as long as ever they could. The English newspapers either did not seem to know of its existence; or it was "Dr Cullen's College," "the Seminary in Stephen's Green," or "the Ultramontane Establishment".[1] But now a Cabinet Minister, the leader of the House of Commons, has received a deputation of members of Parliament, Protestant as well as Catholic, on the subject of conferring on it the legal power of granting

[1] These nicknames made fun of the fact that all major Catholic enterprises in Ireland were firmly under the control of the hierarchy and arranged along clerical lines. In fact the University was not in the least organised along seminary lines, and the hierarchy's control was remote. Amazingly for the time, Newman only employed two priests as lecturers at the University. Although Archbishop (later Cardinal) Cullen was the leading Ultramontane in the Irish hierarchy, his influence was limited during Newman's rectorate.

degrees. Here, then, the very fact of the deputation, and its admission to an audience, is the victory of the University. When they entered the Chancellor of the Exchequer's room, the battle was won: the present Government may refuse the request, there may be delay and trouble in [386] carrying the matter through, but it will be simply the University's fault and no one's else, if it does not now get a charter; it is but a matter of time. As a record to look back upon hereafter, we proceed to give some account of what passed at the interview of which we have been speaking.

The deputation consisted of every section of opinion among the Irish members of the House;[2] the speakers were Mr Maguire,[3] Mr Deasy,[4] and Mr Bowyer.[5] They represented to the Chancellor of the Exchequer that an application had been first made to him on the subject by the Rector and Professors of the University in the course of last July;[6] then in January of the present year, by all the

---

[2] Three lecturers from the Catholic University accompanied the MPs: David Dunne, Henry Hennessy and W. K. Sullivan.

[3] John Maguire (1801–65), MP for Dungarvan, was leader of the Irish Independent Party, then supporting the Tory government. He introduced the subject and spoke for 25 minutes.

[4] Rickard Deasy (1812–83) was MP for County Cork. He became Attorney-General for Ireland in 1860, then Baron of the Exchequer the following year, and in 1878 was appointed to the Irish Court of Appeal.

[5] Sir George Bowyer (1811–65) was MP for Dundalk and an expert on constitutional law. For more, see the relevant footnote on p. [xxxv].

[6] A memorial signed by the Rector and professoriate petitioning for a charter was delivered to Disraeli, then Chancellor of the Exchequer, by Audrey de Vere on 28 July 1858 (*LD* xviii, pp. 415–16). Having drafted the letter, Newman intended that 'the body of the Professors should have the *last* word upon it' (Newman to Butler, 20 July 1858, *LD* xviii, p. 418), Robert Ornsby liaising with the professors. At the same time a proposal drafted by Cullen was sent to Disraeli via Monsell from three of the archbishops. Not everyone at the Catholic University was in favour of gaining a charter; the priest, James Quinn, head of St Laurence's House, strongly opposed the petition, and thought that if a

Irish Catholic members of the House of Commons but one—that one, who otherwise would have taken part in it, being absent on the Continent; the deputation was now making a third application. No less a sum than £80,000 had been raised by voluntary subscriptions for the University; this had been done, not in opposition to the Queen's Colleges, but because of conscientious scruples which Irish Catholics felt in availing themselves of the advantages which those colleges furnished. Even the vice-president of Galway College had confessed to the late Royal Commissioners that "the objections to the colleges by the Roman Catholic prelates were not altogether unfounded"; for "there are certain chairs in which the professors have opportunities of throwing out innuendoes respecting the truth of revealed religion, and one of the text-books used in the colleges speaks slightingly of
[387] certain doctrines held by the Romanists". The Queen's Colleges had cost the country already an outlay of £375,000, whereas the deputation did not ask a shilling for the Catholic University. The University embraced five faculties, of which four were in active operation. The medical faculty was in possession of large buildings—theatres, laboratory, dissecting rooms; it had a library of 5000 well-selected and rare volumes, in seven languages. It had last year as many as eighty students, with the prospect of increase; and had commenced a system of lodging-houses. The faculties of philosophy and letters and of science had a periodical of their own for the advancement of the subjects they profess, which brought them into correspondence with learned bodies in Great Britain, the Continent, and the United States; and, in a word, last year there were as many as 249 students attending the University Lectures. This being the case,

---

charter was granted the University would 'become a mere state affair, and forfeit the support of the Irish people' (*LD* xviii, pp. 397–8n).

there was force in the words of the University memorial of last year: "We hope we may, without presumption, ask for that recognition from the State which we are continually obtaining from the great centres of learning and science of Europe and North America. In referring to the Charter lately granted by the Government to the Roman Catholic University of Quebec,[7] we both explain what we venture to anticipate, and our reason for anticipating it."[8]

It was also mentioned that as many as twenty-three Irish Bishops had written letters authorizing the deputation to make use of their names. Of these, for instance, the Archbishop of Cashel wished the Chancellor of the

---

[7] The University of Quebec developed out of the seminary at Quebec, which had been established in 1668 by François de Laval, the first Bishop of New France. The seminary received a Royal Charter on 8 December 1852, which granted it the right to confer degrees and created the Université Laval with 'the rights and privileges of a university' – a scheme approved by Pope Benedict XV. Its first Rector, the abbé Louis Casault, had visited Europe and studied the university systems there prior to the foundation. According to the terms of the charter, the Visitor was the (Catholic) Archbishop of Quebec, who had the right to veto appointments and regulations; the appointment of the Rector lay with the superior of the seminary; and the Council, together with the Rector, was to administer the University. The Council was composed of the directors of the seminary together with the three doyen professors of each of the four faculties (theology, law, medicine and the arts); and it was empowered to enact statutes and rules, on the sole condition that they contained nothing contrary to the laws of the United Kingdom or Canada (*Catholic Encyclopedia* (New York: Robert Appleton, 1910) ix, pp. 47–8).

Among Newman's collection of university charters can be found a copy of the charter granted to the University of Quebec, printed by The House of Commons, 15 April 1856 (C.6.1, BOA).

[8] Newman to Disraeli, 19 July 1858, *LD* xviii, p. 416. Monsell had advised Newman on 6 July to 'prepare and sign a document stating the early history, present position, and objects of the Catholic university and praying the government to grant it a charter after the form of that which has recently been granted to the University of Quebec' (*LD* xviii, p. 401).

[388] Exchequer to know his earnest desire, in conjunction with "all the Bishops of Munster and Dr Cullen," for the grant of a Charter; the Bishop of Kildare said, that "success in the application would be most gratifying to the Catholic people" of Ireland; the Bishop of Waterford, that "there was nothing which he desired more"; the Bishop of Cloyne, that he "felt the warmest interest in the success of the great undertaking"; and the Bishop of Kerry, that it was "the strong determination of the Catholic laity to keep intermediate or secondary education under purely Catholic tutelage," and that "a University was its necessary complement".

We quote these passages as a decisive answer to the rumour, which we know is even matter of gossip at Rome, that the Irish Bishops are lukewarm on the subject of an undertaking which they have themselves decreed in National Synod, and for which they have collected such large sums.

We give Mr Disraeli's answer at length.

Mr Disraeli said he hoped the deputation would now excuse him for bringing their conversation to a close; but a Cabinet had been suddenly called that day at two o'clock; such, however, was his anxiety to have the honour of receiving them, that he had had it delayed to three o'clock. He begged to assure them that, since his attention had been first called to the Catholic University of Ireland last year by Mr Monsell, the subject had engaged his earnest attention, and he had inquired into, and was quite aware of, all the circumstances of that institution. He had always felt that its existence was a memorable instance of the zeal
[389] and liberality of the Catholics of Ireland. In consequence of the weight to be attached to this deputation—of the importance of which he of course felt thoroughly aware—he should again bring the subject under the consideration of the Cabinet; and they might feel quite certain, that

whatever the decision of the Government might be, the subject would be considered with a full sense of the importance due to it. He distinctly held that the question ought not to be dealt with as one involving any rivalry between the Queen's Colleges and the Catholic University, but on its own merits. And he had again to repeat, that fully recognizing its importance, the Government would give the subject their most attentive consideration.[9]

We add the following information given by the *Nation* newspaper, which has an intrinsic probability:—

"There is in the hands of the four Archbishops one of the most remarkable and important rescripts upon the subject of education that has ever emanated from the Holy See. The Propaganda, in proof of its solicitude and anxiety regarding the education of the Catholics of Ireland, gives an historical *resumé* of the various Bulls, Rescripts, and other official documents, which it has forwarded upon this subject for the last century. It sets forth the unfavourable reports which have reached it respecting the working of the ordinary National Schools, of Model Schools, and of the Queen's Colleges, and refers to the projected scheme of intermediate schools. The Archbishops are called on to reply to a series of categorical propositions in relation to
those institutions; and, in so doing, to ascertain the opinion [390]
of their suffragan prelates, and inform the Holy See. Provincial Synods and a Council of the whole Irish Episcopacy are suggested; and we have reason to expect

[9] The deputation was received by Disraeli on 19 March 1859. Despite hopes to the contrary, on 6 June Lord Derby declared in the House of Lords that his government did not intend to grant the charter (*NU*, p. 485). Lord Derby's government, in which Disraeli was Chancellor of the Exchequer, fell on 11 June.

There are 62 items relating to this petition for a charter in C.6.15, BOA, and another 18 relating to charters and degrees in the period 1855–58 in C.6.14, BOA.

that a national meeting of the prelates will be held at the earliest possible moment."

III

THE CATHOLIC UNIVERSITY

1st July, 1859

IF Lord Derby has been embarrassed by the cry which has been raised against Cardinal Wiseman, Catholic interests have suffered from it also. Perhaps it was simply impossible for a Conservative Ministry to grant a charter to the new University, when once the attention of the Orange faction was drawn to the negotiation. However, we have gained that which in the *Rambler* for May was laid down as the main point, *recognition* of the University as existing. The charter now is but a matter of time, provided only that the University and its rulers are true to themselves. We then said, and we now repeat, "The very fact of the deputation, and its admission to an audience, is the victory of the University. The present Government may refuse the request, there may be delay and trouble in carrying the matter through, but it will be simply the University's fault and no one's else if it does not now get a charter."[1] We will add that we cannot complain though

[1] For fifteen years after Newman's departure, the Catholic University was kept alive by the prospect of government recognition and support. Negotiations began with Russell's Liberal government for a supplemental charter incorporating the Catholic University as a college into an enlarged Queen's University, but these came to an end in 1866; then hopes for an officially recognized Catholic University without government subsidy were extinguished when the scheme was withdrawn by Disraeli's Conservative government in 1868. Next,

that internal energy and life, which we know to exist in the University body, should be tried. Nothing is done well which is simply done from without. A present struggle is the token and warrant of future independence.[2]

[392] The other act of justice which the Conservative Ministry had shown a disposition to exercise towards us has, since the dissolution, been urged upon the public with great effect at the meeting to which we shall now refer.

Gladstone's Liberal government came near to clinching a solution in 1873, but the Bill for affiliation to a Dublin University, along with Trinity College and two of the Queen's Colleges, was defeated by a majority of three in Parliament (and precipitated the fall of the government). A second attempt at affiliation to a Dublin University, this time with the Disraeli government, failed in 1877; and a scheme to unite the Catholic University with Maynooth to form a new university called St Patrick's was also unsuccessful. Finally, in August 1879 Parliament passed the Royal University Act, which abolished the Queen's University (but not the three Colleges), and in its place established the Royal University of Ireland as an examining body entitled to grant degrees. In 1882, when it was close to extinction, the Arts faculty of the Catholic University was reconstituted as University College and made a constituent part of the Royal University of Ireland. In 1909 University College and the Catholic University Medical School were absorbed into University College Dublin, which became part of the newly formed National University of Ireland.

[2] The failure of the Catholic University to secure a charter can be attributed to the attitude of Paul Cullen and his determination to minimise lay influence in the governance and control of the University. See Shrimpton, *MM*, pp. 404–18.

SPEECH OF CARDINAL NEWMAN[1]

ON RECEIVING THE *BIGLIETTO* IN ROME[2]

May 12, 1879[3]

VI ringrazio, Monsignore, per la participazione che m'avete fatto, dell'alto onore che il Santo Padre si è degnato conferire sulla mia umile persona—[4]

[1] The autograph MS of this speech is eight pages long and contains many alterations (B.9.7, BOA).

[2] Pope Leo XIII was elected in February 1878, and among the first of those he raised to the cardinalate was Newman. This high honour meant for Newman the end of 'all those stories which have gone about of my being a half Catholic, a liberal Catholic, under a cloud, not to be trusted' (Newman to R. W. Church, 11 March 1879, *LD* xxix, p. 72). See Ker, *Newman: A Biography*, pp. 714–22.

[3] 'On Monday morning, May 12, Dr Newman went to the Palazzo della Pigna, the residence of Cardinal Howard, who had lent him his apartments to receive there the messenger from the Vatican bearing the *biglietto* from the Cardinal-Secretary of State, informing him that in a secret Consistory held that morning his Holiness had deigned to raise him to the rank of Cardinal. By eleven o'clock the rooms were crowded with English and American Catholics, ecclesiastics and laymen, as well as many members of the Roman nobility and dignitaries of the Church, assembled to witness the ceremony. Soon after midday the consistorial messenger was announced. He handed the *biglietto* to Dr Newman, who, having broken the seal, gave it to Dr Clifford, Bishop of Clifton, who read the contents. The messenger having then informed the newly-created Cardinal that his Holiness would receive him at the Vatican the next morning at ten o'clock to confer the *biretta* upon him, and having paid the customary compliments, his Eminence replied in what has become known as his "*Biglietto* Speech".' (Newman Reader website http://www.newmanreader.org/works/addresses/file2.html accessed 22 October 2018) The Palazzo della Pigna is more commonly known as Palazzo Maffei Marescotti.

[4] 'Thank you, Monsignor, for informing me of the high honour that the Holy Father has deigned to bestow on my humble person.' These opening

And, if I ask your permission to continue my address to you, not in your musical language, but in my own dear mother tongue, it is because in the latter I can better express my feelings on this most gracious announcement which you have brought to me than if I attempted what is above me.

First of all then, I am led to speak of the wonder and profound gratitude which came upon me, and which is upon me still, at the condescension and love towards me of the Holy Father in singling me out for so immense an honour. It was a great surprise. Such an elevation had never come into my thoughts, and seemed to be out of keeping with all my antecedents. I had passed through many trials, but they were
[394] over; and now the end of all things had almost come to me, and I was at peace. And was it possible that after all I had lived through so many years for this?

Nor is it easy to see how I *could* have borne so great a shock, had not the Holy Father resolved on a second act of condescension towards me, which tempered it, and was to all who heard of it a touching evidence of his kindly and generous nature.[5] He felt for me, and he told me the reasons why he raised me to this high position. Besides other words of encouragement, he said his act was a recognition of my zeal and good service for so many years in the Catholic cause; moreover, he judged it would give pleasure to English Catholics, and even to Protestant England, if I received some mark of his favour. After such gracious words from his Holiness, I should have been insensible and heartless if I had had scruples any longer.

---

words in Italian were written out for Newman on notepaper; in the margin Newman records, 'Words given my by Mgr Stonor to open my address with' (B.9.7, BOA).

[5] Newman had initially been reluctant to accept the honour as he presumed that he would have to leave the Birmingham Oratory and go and live in Rome, as was then the norm for cardinals who were not diocesan bishops. See Ker, *Newman: A Biography*, pp. 715–16.

This is what he had the kindness to say to me, and what could I want more? In a long course of years I have made many mistakes. I have nothing of that high perfection which belongs to the writings of Saints, *viz.*, that error cannot be found in them; but what I trust that I may claim all through what I have written, is this,—an honest intention, an absence of private ends, a temper of obedience, a willingness to be corrected, a dread of error, a desire to serve Holy Church, and, through Divine mercy, a fair measure of success. And, I rejoice to say, to one great [395]
mischief I have from the first opposed myself. For thirty, forty, fifty years I have resisted to the best of my powers the spirit of liberalism in religion. Never did Holy Church need champions against it more sorely than now, when, alas! it is an error overspreading, as a snare, the whole earth; and on this great occasion, when it is natural for one who is in my place to look out upon the world, and upon Holy Church as in it, and upon her future, it will not, I hope, be considered out of place, if I renew the protest against it which I have made so often.

Liberalism in religion is the doctrine that there is no positive truth in religion, but that one creed is as good as another, and this is the teaching which is gaining substance and force daily. It is inconsistent with any recognition of any religion, as *true*. It teaches that all are to be tolerated, for all are matters of opinion. Revealed religion is not a truth, but a sentiment and a taste; not an objective fact, not miraculous; and it is the right of each individual to make it say just what strikes his fancy. Devotion is not necessarily founded on faith. Men may go to Protestant Churches and to Catholic, may get good from both and belong to neither. They may fraternise together in spiritual thoughts and feelings, without having any views at all of doctrine in common, or seeing the need of them. Since, then, religion is so personal a peculiarity and so private a possession, we [396] must of necessity ignore it in the intercourse of man with man. If a man puts on a new religion every morning, what is that to you? It is as impertinent to think about a man's religion as about his sources of income or his management of his family. Religion is in no sense the bond of society.[6]

Hitherto the civil Power has been Christian. Even in countries separated from the Church, as in my own, the *dictum* was in force, when I was young, that: "Christianity was the law of the land". Now, everywhere that goodly framework of society, which is the creation of Christianity, is throwing off Christianity. The *dictum* to which I have referred, with a hundred others which followed upon it, is gone, or is going everywhere; and, by the end of the century, unless the Almighty interferes, it will be *forgotten*. Hitherto, it has been considered that religion alone, with its supernatural sanctions, was strong enough to secure submission of the masses of our population to law and order; now the Philosophers and Politicians are bent on satisfying this problem without the aid of Christianity. Instead of the Church's authority and teaching, they would substitute first of all a universal and a thoroughly secular education, calculated to bring home to every individual that to be orderly, industrious, and sober, is his personal interest.
[397] Then, for great working principles to take the place of religion, for the use of the masses thus carefully educated, it provides—the broad fundamental ethical truths, of justice, benevolence, veracity, and the like; proved experience; and those natural laws which exist and act spontaneously in society, and in social matters, whether physical or psychological; for instance, in government, trade, finance,

[6] Edward Short uses this paragraph to fine effect in his chapter 'Newman and the Liberals' in *Newman and History* (Leominster: Gracewing, 2017), pp. 133–202. In this he refutes one of the central tenets of Frank Turner in his *John Henry Newman: The Challenge to Evangelical Religion* (New Haven: Yale University Press, 2007).

sanitary experiments, and the intercourse of nations. As to Religion, it is a private luxury, which a man may have if he will; but which of course he must pay for, and which he must not obtrude upon others, or indulge in to their annoyance.

The general character of this great *apostasia* is one and the same everywhere; but in detail, and in character, it varies in different countries. For myself, I would rather speak of it in my own country, which I know. There, I think it threatens to have a formidable success; though it is not easy to see what will be its ultimate issue. At first sight it might be thought that Englishmen are too religious for a movement which, on the Continent, seems to be founded on infidelity; but the misfortune with us is, that, though it ends in infidelity as in other places, it does not necessarily arise out of infidelity. It must be recollected that the religious sects, which sprang up in England three centuries ago, and which are so powerful now, have ever been fiercely [398]
opposed to the Union of Church and State, and would advocate the un-Christianising of the monarchy and all that belongs to it, under the notion that such a catastrophe would make Christianity much more pure and much more powerful. Next the liberal principle is forced on us from the necessity of the case. Consider what follows from the very fact of these many sects. They constitute the religion, it is supposed, of half the population; and, recollect, our mode of government is popular. Every dozen men taken at random whom you meet in the streets has a share in political power,—when you inquire into their forms of belief, perhaps they represent one or other of as many as seven religions; how can they possibly act together in municipal or in national matters, if each insists on the recognition of his own religious denomination? All action would be at a deadlock unless the subject of religion was ignored. We cannot help ourselves. And, thirdly, it must be borne in

mind, that there is much in the liberalistic theory which is good and true; for example, not to say more, the precepts of justice, truthfulness, sobriety, self-command, benevolence, which, as I have already noted, are among its avowed principles, and the natural laws of society. It is not till we find that this array of principles is intended to supersede, to
[399] block out, religion, that we pronounce it to be evil. There never was a device of the Enemy so cleverly framed and with such promise of success. And already it has answered to the expectations which have been formed of it. It is sweeping into its own ranks great numbers of able, earnest, virtuous men, elderly men of approved antecedents, young men with a career before them.

Such is the state of things in England, and it is well that it should be realised by all of us; but it must not be supposed for a moment that I am afraid of it. I lament it deeply, because I foresee that it may be the ruin of many souls; but I have no fear at all that it really can do aught of serious harm to the Word of God, to Holy Church, to our Almighty King, the Lion of the tribe of Judah, Faithful and True, or to His Vicar on earth. Christianity has been too often in what seemed deadly peril, that we should fear for it any new trial now. So far is certain; on the other hand, what is uncertain, and in these great contests commonly *is* uncertain, and what is commonly a great surprise, when it is witnessed, is the particular mode by which, in the event, Providence rescues and saves His elect inheritance. Sometimes our enemy is turned into a friend; sometimes he is despoiled of that special virulence of evil which was so threatening; sometimes he falls to pieces of himself; sometimes he does just so much as is beneficial, and then is
[400] removed. Commonly the Church has nothing more to do

than to go on in her own proper duties, in confidence and peace; to stand still and to see the salvation of God.[7]

> *Mansueti hereditabunt terram,*
> *Et delectabuntur in multitudine pacis.*[8]

---

[7] The vicissitudes of the Church, its constant dying and rising again, is a favourite theme of Newman's. It fitted a pattern that was not man's, but of a higher order: 'It is the rule of God's Providence that we should succeed by failure' (Newman to Lord Braye, 29 October 1882, *LD* xxx, p. 142).

[8] 'His Eminence spoke in a strong, clear voice, and although he stood the whole time, he showed no signs of fatigue. After taking his seat, those present went up in turn to compliment him, Monsignor Stonor, at the request of Monsignor Cataldi, Master of the Ceremonies to His Holiness, presenting those with whom His Eminence was unacquainted. Among the many present were Dr Moran, Bishop of Ossory; Monsignor Lenti, Vice-Gerent of Rome; Dr O'Callaghan, Rector of the English College; Dr Giles, Vice-Rector of the English College; Monsignor Kirby, Rector of the Irish College; Dr Campbell, Rector of the Scotch College; Dr Smith, of the Propaganda; Dr O'Bryen; Dr Hostlot, Rector of the American College; F. Mullooly, Prior of St Clement's; Dr Mazière Brady, Lady Herbert of Lea, Marchioness Ricci, Baroness Keating, Prince and Princess Giustiniani Bandini, Commendatore de Rossi, Count de Redmond, General Kanzler, Professor Blackie, Sir Hungerford Pollen, Monsignors Folicaldi, Rinaldi, de Stacpoole and others, and nearly all the English residents now in Rome, both Catholic and Protestant.

'This Reply was telegraphed to London by the correspondent of *The Times* and appeared in full in that paper the next morning. Moreover, through the kindness of Fr Armellini, S.J., who during the night translated it into Italian, it was also given in full in the *Osservatore Romano* of the following day.' (Newman Reader website http://www.newmanreader.org/works/addresses/file2.html accessed 22 October 2018)

The day after the *Biglietto* speech, Newman went to the Vatican to receive the cardinal's biretta from the Pope, and two days later he was presented with the cardinal's hat at the English College.

The speech was published as *Speech of his Eminence Cardinal Newman on the Reception of the 'Biglietto' at Cardinal Howard's Palace in Rome on the 12th of May 1879* (Rome: Libreria Spithöver, 1879).

[401]

ADDRESSES TO CARDINAL NEWMAN FROM IRELAND

ON HIS ELEVATION TO THE SACRED COLLEGE,

WITH HIS REPLIES[1]

No. I

Address from the Irish Catholic Members of the House of Commons

(Presented on Friday, 4th April, 1879)

The Irish Catholic Members of Parliament met the Very Rev. Dr Newman on Friday afternoon at 22 Portman Square for the purpose of presenting an address of congratulation on his elevation to the Cardinalate.

The Members present were The O'Conor Don, Sir Joseph McKenna, Sir G. Bowyer, Bart., Right Hon. W. H. Cogan, Mr O'Clery, Colonel Colthurst, Major Nolan, Major O'Beirne, Serjeant Sherlock, Sir P. O'Brien, Bart., The O'Donoghue, Messrs Biggar, Callan, Collins, Dease, Delahunty, Ennis, Errington, A. Moore, O'Byrne, O'Connor Power, Tynan, Shell, etc.

Dr Newman, who came from Birmingham expressly for the occasion, entered the reception room shortly after one o'clock.

Sir J. McKenna, addressing Dr Newman, explained that the address about to be presented was purposely couched in the simplest terms.

---

[1] Five of the addresses and replies are reproduced here. The full collection can be found in *Addresses to Cardinal Newman with his Replies*.

To the Very Rev. Dr Newman

House of Commons, 25th March, 1879

VERY REV. AND DEAR SIR,

We, the undersigned Irish Catholic Members of Parliament, beg leave to offer you our heartfelt congratulations and to express to you with great respect the sincere satisfaction with which we hail your elevation to the Sacred College.

In conferring on you this signal mark of his favour, the Holy [402]
Father has met the wishes and rejoiced the hearts of all classes of your fellow-Catholics; for they see in it a recognition of the lofty genius you have devoted to the service of Religion, and the crowning of a life of self-sacrifice.

As Irishmen we specially welcome this high tribute to the merits of one whose sympathies have always been with our country, and who devoted many years of brilliant and devoted effort to her service in the still unfinished battle for educational liberty.

With profound respect,
We are,
Very Rev. and Dear Sir,
Your faithful Servants,

GEORGE E. BROWN,
LOUIS COLTHURST,
W. A. REDMOND,
EDWARD SHEIL,
RICHARD POWER,
CHARLES U. MELDON,
NICHOLAS ENNIS,
F. O'BEIRNE,
M. WARD,
J. TYNAN,
MYLES O'REILLY,
ARTHUR MOORE,
R. T. DIGBY,
O'CLERY,
A. M. SULLIVAN,
JOSEPH NEALE MCKENNA,
O'DONOGHUE,
JOHN BRADY,
JOSEPH BIGGAR,
J. G. MCCARTHY,
JOHN PHILIP NOLAN,
EDMUND DEASE,
W. R. O'BYRNE,
JAMES DELAHUNTY,
GEORGE BOWYER,
DENIS M. O'CONOR,
C. J. FAY,
PATRICK O'BRIEN,
EDWARD D. GRAY,
W. O'CONNOR POWER,

R. O'SHAUGHNESSY,
O'CONOR DON,
CHARLES FRENCH,
GEORGE MORRIS,
J. H. RICH,
H. A. LEWIS,
PHILIP CALLAN,
F. H. O'DONNELL,
DAVID SHERLOCK,
W. H. O'SULLIVAN,
N. D. MURPHY,
EUGENE COLLINS,
G. ERRINGTON,
W. H. COGAN.

[403] *To the Catholic Members of Parliament for Ireland*

April 4th, 1879

GENTLEMEN,

This is a great day for me, and it is a day which gives me great pleasure too. It is a pleasure to meet old friends, and it is a pleasure to meet new ones. But it is not merely as friends that I meet you, for you are representatives of an ancient and faithful Catholic people for whom I have a deep affection, and, therefore, in receiving your congratulations of course I feel very much touched by your address; but I hope you will not think it strange if I say that I have been surprised too, because while it is a great thing to please one's own people, it is still more wonderful to create an interest in a people which is not one's own. I do not think there is any other country which would have treated me so graciously as yours did. It is now nearly thirty years since, with a friend of mine, I first went over to Ireland with a view to the engagement which I afterwards formed there, and during the seven years through which that engagement lasted, I had continuous experience of kindness, and nothing but kindness, from all classes of people—from the hierarchy, from the seculars and regulars, and from the laity, whether in Dublin or in the country. Those who worked with me gave the most loyal support and loving help. As their first act they helped me in a great trouble in which I was involved. I had put my foot into an unusual legal

embarrassment, and it required many thousand pounds to draw me out of it. They took a great share in that work.[1] Nor did they show less kindness at the end of my time. I was [404]
obliged to leave from the necessities of my own congregation at Birmingham. Everybody can understand what a difficulty it is for a body to be without its head, and I only engaged for seven years, because I could not otherwise fulfil the charge which the Holy Father had put upon me in the Oratory.[2] When I left with reluctance and regret that sphere in which I found so many friends, not a word of disappointment or unkindness was uttered, when there might have been a feeling that I was relinquishing a work which I had begun, and now I repeat that, to my surprise, at the end of twenty years I find a silent memory cherished of a person who can only be said to have meant well though he did little;[3]—and now what return can I make to you to show my gratitude? None that is sufficient. But this I can say, that

---

[1] The collection in Ireland for the Achilli fund amounted to £2179, which was the third largest national contribution out of the total of £12,932 collected (*LD* xv, p. 389n).

[2] Newman had been ordained a priest in Rome on 30 May 1847 and in December had returned to England to set up the first English Oratory of St Philip Neri, in Birmingham, with Newman as its superior. To their Brief of Institution, the Pope had added on his own initiative that the Oratory should work especially 'among those in the higher ranks, the more learned and generally among the more educated' (*Newman the Oratorian: His Unpublished Oratorian Papers*, ed. P. Murray (Dublin: Gill & MacMillan, 1969), p. 426).

[3] Though Newman ceased to be Rector in November 1858, his connection with the Catholic University lasted one more academic year by virtue of his being the tenant of St Mary's House. The University Secretary took over the administration and financial responsibility of St Mary's and appointed a new Dean and Tutors, but the strict regime they tried to enforce alienated the students to the extent that by Easter 1859 all but one of them had been expelled or left voluntarily. Newman was kept informed of these developments and was drawn into the dispute as he had accepted most of the students and dealt with their parents. For more, see *MM*, pp. 345–55.

your address shall not die with me. I belong to a body which, with God's blessing, will live after me—the Oratory of St Philip. The paper which is the record of your generosity shall be committed to our archives, and shall testify to generations to come the enduring kindness of Irish Catholics towards the founder and first head of the English Oratory.

JOHN HENRY CARD. NEWMAN[4]

[4] 'This Reply to the Catholic Members of Parliament for Ireland, the first of Dr Newman's public Replies, was of necessity unprepared, for he did not receive the draft of the Address until after the reception was over; but it was written down by him and Mr Allies together at once after the gentlemen had left; and it contained, they believed, the very words he had used. He had not had any experience of proceedings such as this, and he was nervous and diffident about the result. However, on entering the room, he at once felt at ease, and his Reply, for its matter and delivery, and, indeed, in every respect, was considered a great success. He gained from this occasion a confidence in himself that he would be equal to similar and other calls upon him which his new position might bring.' (*Addresses to Cardinal Newman with his Replies*, p. 51n)

No. II

Address from the C. U. I. Bono Club[1] *of the Irish Catholic University*

(Presented Wednesday, 23rd July, 1879)

MAY IT PLEASE YOUR EMINENCE,

At a time when you are receiving the congratulations of Catholics from all parts of the world on your elevation to the dignity of Cardinal, we trust that you will not think it presumption in us to express the joy and pride with which we have heard of that elevation. The club on whose behalf we address you is formed mainly of ex-students of the Catholic University of Ireland over which you once presided, and it was founded with the object of discussing and taking action upon questions bearing on the welfare of that University. In the humble efforts which from time to time we have made for the advancement of the University education of Irish Catholics, we have found in your writings a never-failing counsel and guidance, and we therefore feel that we

---

[1] Besides standing for Catholic University of Ireland, the initials spell out the first word of the Latin legal adage *cui bono*, which means 'to whose benefit?'. The aim of the C.U.I. Bono Club was to lobby for the Catholic University. The earliest instance of their efforts appears to be a circular they issued in 1877 which criticised the bishops' policy on the future of the University (Circular dated 2 March 1877 signed by C. Dawson, G. Fottrell and J. Dillon on behalf of the C.U.I. Bono Club, Cullen papers, 45/6/VIII(4), DDA). Earlier, in 1873, past students had entered the debate about the future of the University by publishing in the *Freeman's Journal* the *Memorial Addressed by the Students and Ex-Students of the Catholic University of Ireland to the Episcopal Board of the University*. See Shrimpton, *MM*, pp. 412–14.

may with especial fitness avail ourselves of this opportunity to tender to you the expression of our gratitude, respect, and veneration.

As students of the Catholic University of Ireland, we can never forget that the "Lectures on the Scope and Nature of University Education" were delivered in our halls, and by our Rector. When you came to Ireland to undertake the Rectorship of the newly founded Catholic University, the Catholics of this
[406] country, owing to their having been for three centuries excluded from all share in the advantages of higher education, had no traditions to guide them in forming a correct estimate of what a University ought to be. Your great work, which we may justly call our Charter, has supplied the place of those traditions, and, thanks to it, the Irish people have now realised what a true University should be, and what inestimable benefits a National Catholic University could confer upon Ireland.

It is not as Irishmen only, but also as Catholics, that we owe you gratitude for your teaching in our University. You have shown that education is a field in which both clergy and laity can work together, harmoniously and without jealousy, for a common object, and in which both have duties, and both have rights, and in establishing this, you, as it appears to us, have rendered valuable assistance to the Catholic Church in her great struggle for freedom of education throughout the world.[2]

---

[2] It is likely George Fottrell drafted this address, and that he drew on a letter Newman had sent him after receiving a copy of the *Memorial*. This letter is worth quoting at length:

'One of the chief evils which I deplored in the management of the affairs of the University twenty years ago when I was in Ireland, was the absolute refusal with which my urgent representations were met, that the Catholic laity should be allowed to cooperate with the Archbishops in the work.

'As far as I can see, there are ecclesiastics all over Europe, whose policy it is to keep the laity at arms-length; and hence the laity have been disgusted and become infidel, and only two parties exist, both ultras in opposite directions. I came away from Ireland with the distressing fear that there was to be an antagonism, as time went on, between the hierarchy and the educated classes.

In one of the noblest passages in English literature you have proclaimed your sympathy with our country's past and your hope in the promise of her future. Seeking a fitting site for a University, you say of our country: "I look towards a land both old and young; old in its Christianity, young in the promise of its future; a nation which received grace before the Saxon came to Britain, and which has never quenched it; a Church which comprehends in its history the rise and fall of Canterbury and York, which Augustine and Paulinus found, and Pole and Fisher left behind them. I contemplate a people which has had a long night and which will have an inevitable day." And you proceed to prophesy for our University a glorious destiny to be attained in the future, "when its first founders and servants are dead and gone". It is our earnest [407]
hope that you, the most illustrious of our founders,[3] may yet live to see your prophecy at least in part fulfilled.

It was during your Rectorship that the Chair of Irish History and Archæology was founded in our University, and that a Professor of those subjects was first appointed in Ireland; and to your encouragement and practical sympathy, as warmly testified by Professor O'Curry, was due the preparation by him of those lectures on Irish History and Antiquities which are among the most honourable records of what the University has already done.

We venture to ask your acceptance of the *National Manuscripts of Ireland*, a work edited by a distinguished Irish scholar, in the hope that it may serve to remind you of the efforts which you made to foster Irish studies in our University, and that it may thus be to you a pleasing memento of your labours in an institution in which your name will ever be mentioned with veneration and love.

'You will be doing the greatest possible benefit to the Catholic cause all over the world, if you succeed in making the University a middle station at which clergy and laity can meet, so as to understand and to Yield to each other—and from which, as from a common ground, they may act in union upon an age, which is running headlong into infidelity' (Newman to Fottrell, 10 December 1873, *LD* xxvi, pp. 393–4).

[3] This is one of very few contemporary instances of Newman being described as a 'founder' of the Catholic University—and in this case, the 'most illustrious' of them.

In conclusion, we beg to tender to you our respectful congratulations upon the exalted dignity to which it has pleased the Holy Father to raise you, and to express our earnest hope that you may long be spared to serve the Church of which you are so illustrious an ornament.

Committee:—

GEORGE SIGERSON,
JOSEPH E. KENNY,
GERALD GRIFFIN,[5]
P. J. O'CONNOR,
MICHAEL BOYD,
GEORGE FOTTRELL, JUN.,[4]
CHARLES DAWSON,[6]
JOHN DILLON.[7]

Hon. Secs.:—

H. J. GILL, WILLIAM DILLON.

[4] (Sir) Charles Fottrell (1849–1925) was auditor of the L&H in 1871. His *Inaugural Address Delivered before the Literary and Historical Society of the Catholic University of Ireland* (1871) followed closely Newman's ideas about the university being a place for the formation of character. He was the moving force behind the *Memorial Addressed by the Students and Ex-Students of the Catholic University of Ireland to the Episcopal Board of the University* (1873); he was also heavily involved in the founding of C.U.I. Bono Club.

[5] Gerald Griffin, one of the founders of the C.U.I. Bono Club, looked after the University Medical College at 98 Leeson Street during 1863/64.

[6] Charles Dawson (1842–1917) entered the Catholic University in 1864 and was Auditor of the L&H for the session 1867/68. He became high sheriff of Limerick in 1876–77 and Lord Mayor of Dublin in 1882 and 1883, and later became MP for Carlow, 1880–85. (*DIB*)

[7] John Dillon (1851–1927) studied at the Catholic University 1865–70 and was Treasurer of the L&H in 1869/70 and Auditor in 1874/75. After an apprenticeship with a cotton broker in Manchester, he entered the Catholic University Medical School in 1878, obtaining his degree from the Royal College of Surgeons, but soon became a follower of Parnell and entered Parliament. He was imprisoned several times, and was eventually one of the leaders of the Irish Nationalist Party until its extinction in 1918. (*DIB, ODNB*)

To the Committee of the C. U. I. Bono Club [408]

23rd July, 1879

GENTLEMEN,

In thanking you for the Address of Congratulation which you have done me the honour to present me, I am led especially to express to you the pleasurable wonder I have felt on reviewing its separate portions, as they succeed one another, and on collecting my thoughts upon them; at the minute and most friendly diligence with which you have brought together and arranged before me whatever could be turned to my praise during the years in which I filled the distinguished and important post of Rector of your Catholic University.

I know well, or, if this is presumptuous to say, I sincerely believe, that a desire to serve Ireland was the ruling motive of my writings and doings while I was with you. How could I have any other? What right-minded Englishman can think of this country's conduct towards you in times past without indignation, shame, and remorse? How can any such man but earnestly desire, should his duty take him to Ireland, to be able to offer to her some small service in expiation of the crimes which his own people have in former times committed there?[8] This wish, I believe,

---

[8] Newman's comment to Gerard Manley Hopkins, then a lecturer at University College, that, 'If I were an Irishman, I should be (in heart) a rebel' (3 March 1887, *LD* xxxi, p. 195) reflected Newman's ability to enter into the hopes, dreams and anxieties of the young – but did not imply that he was wholly sympathetic to Irish revolutionaries. In 1881 he commented to the President of Maynooth, 'It is a probable opinion and therefore may be acted upon by an individual, that the Irish people has never recognized, rather have and continuously [...] protested against and rejected the sovereignty of England, and have seemingly admitted it only when they were too weak to resist; and therefore it is no sin to be what would be commonly called a rebel' (19 December 1881 (draft), *LD* xxx, pp. 32–3). See Ker, *Newman: a biography* (p. 729) for the context of this letter.

ruled me; but that in fact I had done any great thing during my seven years there, has never come home to me, nor have I had by me any tale of efforts made or of successes gained in your behalf, such as I might produce, supposing I was asked how I had spent my time, and what I had done, while Rector of the University.

[409] I cannot, then, deny, that, diffident as I have ever been, in retrospect of any outcome of my work in Ireland, it has been a great satisfaction to me and a great consolation to find from you and others that I have a right to think that those years were not wasted, and that the Sovereign Pontiff did not send me to Ireland for nothing.

There is another thought which your Address suggests to me, namely, that, as looking back to the years when I was in Ireland, I have, as it would seem, good hope after all that I had my share of success there, so now we must none of us be discouraged if during the twenty years which have elapsed since, we have had so many difficulties and a success not commensurate with them. The greater is a work, the longer it takes to accomplish it. *Tantæ molis erat Romanam condere gentem.*[9] You indeed, gentlemen, are not the persons to be accused of want of courage; but zealous men, though not discouraged, may be disappointed. Let us all then recollect that our cause is sure to succeed eventually, because it is manifestly just; and next, because it has the blessing on it of the Holy See. We must be contented with small successes when we cannot secure great ones, and we shall gain our object surely, if we resign ourselves to a progress which is gradual.

JOHN HENRY CARD. NEWMAN

---

[9] The phrase, which can be translated as 'so great a task it was to found the Roman nation', comes from Virgil's *Aeneid* 1.33.

No. III

Address from the City of Cork[1]

(Presented 10th May, 1879)

MOST EMINENT LORD,

The Bishop, Clergy, Mayor, and Catholic people of Cork, in accord with their fellow-countrymen generally, beg to approach you with sincere congratulations, on the auspicious occasion of your elevation to the high office and dignity of Cardinal of the Holy Roman Church.

Drawn by a singular grace of God from the darkness of error and schism into the light of Christ's true Church, you co-operated so faithfully with the heavenly gift as to become yourself a beacon-light to hundreds of others, who, moved by your example, and instructed by your writings, have followed you into the tranquil haven of the True Faith.

To the Church of your adoption you have proved yourself not only a devoted Son, but wherever battle was to be done for her cause a ready and irresistible Champion.

As Irishmen we owe you a special debt of gratitude, for that at the call of our Hierarchy, you left your home and detached yourself from your natural associations and devoted several years of your services to the interests of Catholic University Education amongst us, shedding by your name and literary labours a lustre on that Institution which you strove to establish in the face of nearly insurmountable difficulty.

---

[1] Newman had spent two nights in Cork during his tour of Ireland in February 1854.

[411] Wishing you years of honour and usefulness in your new and exalted position.

✠WILLIAM DELANY, Bishop of Cork.
PATRICK KENNEDY, Mayor of Cork.
JAMES DONEGAN J.P. MAJOR, Hon. Sec.
THOMAS LYONS, Hon. Treas.

Reply to the Address from the City of Cork

August 21*st*, 1879

MY LORD BISHOP, THE WORSHIPFUL THE MAYOR OF CORK, AND THE GENTLEMEN ASSOCIATED WITH YOU,

I well understand and feel deeply the honour done me in the Address on occasion of my recent elevation which I have received with your signatures attached, in the name of the Catholics, clergy and laity, forming the large and important population of Cork.

It is an additional mark of attention of which I am very sensible, that the Address is so beautifully illuminated, coming to me in a form as exquisite, considered as a work of art, as it is generous and kindly in the sentiments about me to which it gives expression.

You show a kindly sympathy for me, in what you say of my conversion to the Catholic Faith and the circumstances attendant on it; and I consider you to be very generous to me in the notice you take of my services so long ago in behalf of the Catholic University.

Certainly it is very gratifying to be told that my efforts then, such as they were, in the cause of University Education were not without effect; and, though I cannot
[412] myself estimate them as highly as you indulgently do, it is too pleasant to believe that in this matter you know better

than I, for me to make any violent attempt to prove that you speak too strongly in their commendation.

May I beg of you, my Lord Bishop, and of your associates in signing the Address, to convey to the Catholics of your city my most sincere thanks for it, and to assure them that I shall never lose the sense of pleasure which I derive from the friendliness with which they regard me, and for the warmth with which they have welcomed the gracious act towards me of the Holy Father.

JOHN HENRY CARD. NEWMAN

[413]

No. IV

Address from the Rector and Senate of the Catholic University of Ireland

(Presented 28th Oct., 1879)

The Bishop of Ardagh, the Right Rev. Dr Woodlock, waited on Cardinal Newman on Tuesday last at the Oratory, Birmingham, and presented to his Eminence the following address, which had been adopted by the Senate of the University presided over by Dr Woodlock as Rector.[1] Before reading it he reminded the Cardinal that he had graciously arranged to receive it last June, on the return of his Eminence and his own return from Rome; and expressed his great regret that his Eminence's protracted illness in Italy had rendered it impossible to carry out that arrangement; press of diocesan duties had subsequently placed it out of his (the Bishop's) power to come to Birmingham to perform this most agreeable duty, as his last official act in his capacity of Rector.

His Lordship then read the following:—

MAY IT PLEASE YOUR EMINENCE,

We, the Rector and Senate of the Catholic University of Ireland, beg to express to you our heartfelt and most respectful congratulations on the honour which you have received in being

---

[1] Bartholomew Woodlock (1819–1902) studied for the priesthood in Rome and on his return to Ireland, in 1842, was appointed Professor of Dogmatic Theology at the missionary seminary of All Hallows, later becoming president. In 1861 he became the Rector of the Catholic University, which had been without a head since Newman's departure in 1858. His rectorship began with great promise, but after only two years cuts had to be made and the fortunes of the University gradually dwindled. When he resigned in 1879, on being appointed Bishop of Armagh, the University was in a parlous state, despite his great personal abilities, energy and vision. (*DIB*)

raised by our Most Holy Father, Pope Leo XIII, to the dignity of Cardinal.

The great joy with which we, as an academical body, have welcomed this event, is a feeling which we share with the whole Catholic world. The name of Newman is indeed one which Christendom has learned to venerate on many grounds. In your earlier years, like St Augustine, an alien from Catholic communion, you were, like him, led, in your maturity, into the bosom of the Holy Catholic Church, by Divine Grace, using as its instrument learning and genius of the first order. Multitudes of [414]
disciples and friends followed your footsteps to the same refuge, and the blessed movement is not yet exhausted.[2] Through many years of labour you have placed at the service of the Church writings which, were it but for the consummate style that is their least praise, will always remain among the monuments of the English Language, whilst for the depth of thought and vast erudition they display, they will be treasured alike by the searcher after truth and by the learned in every age. You have established an important religious Congregation to aid in the reconstruction of Catholicism in your native land, under the invocation of a Saint whom you have taught England to venerate and cherish.

To these great services which you have rendered to the cause of learning and religion, we must add some that peculiarly interest ourselves. With another illustrious member of the Sacred College,

---

[2] W. G. Gorman's *Converts to Rome: A Biographical List of the More Notable Converts to the Catholic Church in the United Kingdom During the Last Sixty Years* (1910) provides a breakdown of the professions and status of about two thousand converts. They include 572 clergymen; 29 peers and 53 peeresses, 432 other members of the nobility and 42 baronets; 92 from the medical and 192 from the legal professions; 306 army and 64 naval officers; 39 from the diplomatic service; and 470 authors, poets and journalists. Some 586 were educated at Oxford and 346 at Cambridge. It is generally acknowledged that Newman's own conversion (in October 1845) had the greatest influence on that of others.

Patrick Allitt's *Catholic Converts: British and American Intellectuals turn to Rome* (1977) examines the collective impact of British and North-American converts on Catholic intellectual life.

whose loss you lately mourned with us,[3] you may in a great measure be regarded as Joint-founder of the Catholic University of Ireland, to which you devoted your best and most valued energies for many years. We have always looked back with gratitude and admiration to your labours, during the time you held office as first Rector of this University, and we feel assured that the plan for the higher education and the system of University government which you initiated and organized, will, centuries hence, be studied by all who may have to legislate for Catholic education, as among the most precious of the documents which they shall possess to inform and guide them.

In conclusion, we pray Almighty God that you may long be spared to adorn (like another great Oratorian, Cardinal Baronius) the Congregation which is so dear to your heart, and that many
[415] years of health and happiness may be in store for the noble life which is so worthily crowned by the Vicar of Christ.

We remain, my Lord Cardinal,
With profound respect,
Your Eminence's faithful friends,
✠BARTHOLOMEW WOODLOCK, Bp. of Ardagh,
Rector of the Catholic University of Ireland
THOMAS SCRATTON,[4] Secretary

Dublin, 12*th May*, 1879

---

[3] Paul Cullen was created the first cardinal of Ireland in 1866, and served on several Roman Congregations. He died in October 1878.

[4] Thomas Scratton (1821–95) studied at Christ Church, Oxford and took Anglican orders. He became a Catholic in 1850 and three months later tried his vocation at the Birmingham Oratory, but left within a year. Although unsure about how well he would get on with others, Newman appointed him Secretary of the Catholic University, where he remained until the reorganisation in 1879. Newman declined to support his application for the post of Secretary to the newly established Royal University, nor later for a professorship in Classics; Scratton sued the Irish bishops and obtained £300 in compensation for his dismissal. Newman found him a difficult character and regretted appointing him: he was unpopular, eager for a more prominent position within the University, gossiped, and tried to undermine Newman, whose educational ideas he did not grasp.

To the Rector and Senate of the Catholic University of Ireland

October 28th, 1879

MY DEAR FRIENDS,

This is not the first time that I have had the gratification of receiving from you a public expression of your attachment to me, and of your generous good opinion of my exertions in behalf of the University.[5] Many years have passed since then, and now I receive your welcome praise a second time, together with the additional gratification that is the second.

And I notice further with great gratitude, that, whereas in most cases the sentiments which lead to such an act of kindness become, as time goes on, less lively than they were at first, you, on the contrary, use even stronger and warmer language about me now, than that which cheered and gladdened me so much, and was so great a compensation of my anxieties, in 1858.

And there is still another pleasure which your Address has given me. Of course a lapse of time so considerable has [416] brought with it various changes in the constituent members, in the ruling and teaching body of the University. I consider it, then, to be a singular favour conferred upon me, that those whom I have not the advantage of knowing personally should join in this gracious act with those who are my old friends.

No earthly satisfaction is without its drawbacks, and my last remark naturally leads me on to one sad thought, which you yourselves, towards the end of your Address, have suggested. A great Prelate has been lately taken from us, to whose simple faith and noble constancy in the cause of the

[5] Newman probably refers to the letter from the professors and other officers of the Catholic University on his retirement from the rectorship in October 1858 (*LD* xviii, pp. 502–4).

University it is owing that the University maintains its place amid the many obstacles by which its progress has been beset. I ever had the greatest, the truest reverence for the good Cardinal Cullen. I used to say of him that his countenance had a light upon it which made me feel as if, during his many years at Rome, all the saints of the Holy City had been looking into it and he into theirs. And I have cause to know from the mouth of Pope Pius himself, that on a very critical occasion, he promptly, emphatically, and successfully, stood my friend. That was in the year 1867.[6] How sincere would have been his congratulations to me at this time! I am deprived of them; but by thus expressing my sense of my loss, I best relieve myself of the pain of it.

I cannot bring these acknowledgments to an end without tendering in turn my congratulations to you that the serious
[417] loss which you have lately sustained by the elevation to the Episcopate of my dear friend, your Rector, who has laboured for the University so long and with such devotion, has been so happily repaired by the appointment in his place of an Ecclesiastic whose antecedents are a guarantee for its prosperous advance in that enlarged field which is now open to its activity and its usefulness.[7]

And now, thanking you from a full heart for your indulgence and abundant kindness towards me, I will make no further claim upon your time, I subscribe myself, my dear friends, with much respect, your devoted servant,

JOHN HENRY CARD. NEWMAN

---

[6] After Newman's sermon 'The Pope and the Revolution' (preached on 7 October 1866 at the Birmingham Oratory) had been denounced to the Index of Prohibited Books, the Pope approached Cardinal Cullen for advice on how to proceed. See Memorandum: The Appeal to Cardinal Cullen, 16 June 1867, *LD* xxiii, pp. 251–2.

[7] Henry Neville (1822–89) acted as Rector from 1879 until 1883, when he resigned. He had been educated at St Patrick's, Maynooth, and later taught there as Professor of Philosophy then Professor of Theology.

No. V

Address from the Catholics of Ireland

(Presented Saturday, 10th April, 1880)

On Saturday afternoon an influential deputation from Ireland waited upon Cardinal Newman, at the Oratory, Birmingham, to present his Eminence with an Address of Congratulation on behalf of the Roman Catholic people of Ireland. Among the deputation were Lord O'Hagan, the Archbishop of Dublin, the Bishop of Galway, the Coadjutor-Archbishop of Tuam, the Bishop of Limerick, the Bishop of Clogher, Viscount Gormanston, Lord Emly, the Lord Chief Baron Palles, Lord Chief Justice Morris, Mr Justice Barry, Mr Justice Flanagan, Mr Errington, M.P., the Very Rev. N. Walsh, S.J., the Very Rev. Dr Molloy (Vice-president of the Roman Catholic University), Mr J. O'Hagan, Q.C., Mr J. H. Monahan, Q.C., Mr R. P. Carson, Q.C., Dr J. S. Hughes, Mr Ignatius Kennedy, Mr T. W. Flanagan, and others.

Lord O'Hagan read the following:—

MY LORD CARDINAL,

On behalf of the Catholics of Ireland, we approach your Eminence to congratulate you on your elevation to the Sacred Purple, and to express the sentiments of reverence and affection with which you have inspired them . . . To your high qualities and memorable acts eloquent testimony has been borne in the Addresses lately presented to your Eminence, and we are conscious that no words of ours can increase the universal estimation which they have commanded. But we remember with honest pride that our country has had peculiar relations with you; and as Catholic Irishmen we cannot refrain from the special utterance of our feelings towards one who has been so signally our friend and benefactor. In the prime of your years and the fulness of your fame you came to do us service. You left your

[419] home and those who were most dear to you, and the engagements and avocations in which you had found your happiness, to labour for our intellectual and moral well-being.[1] You dedicated yourself to the improvement of the higher education of our people—a work as noble in conception as it was difficult in execution; and whatever success that work has achieved, or may achieve hereafter, must be largely attributed to your Eminence. Of the wisdom of your administration as Rector of the Catholic University, the untiring toil you gave to all its details, and the enthusiastic attachment which bound to you its professors, its students, and all who came within the sphere of your influence, the memory has survived your departure, and is still fresh amongst us. And when you returned to England you left behind many precious and enduring memorials of your presence in the beautiful collegiate church, which we owe in great measure to you; the discourses you delivered within its walls, unsurpassed even among your own incomparable sermons; the excellent periodicals, the *Atlantis* and *Gazette*, which you brought into existence and enriched by some of the finest of your compositions; and above all those lectures and essays on University Education, abounding in ripe erudition, suggestive thought, perfect language, and sage counsel on matters affecting the highest human interest, which are a possession of incalculable worth to Ireland and the world. We cannot forget the words of cordial kindness in which you have proved so often your sympathy with the Irish race, and encouraged them to find in the remembrance of their faithfulness to their old religion the pledge and promise of a happier future. For these reasons we, who have watched your career with constant admiration and unwavering confidence, desire to offer you our homage, in union with that which has been tendered to you so abundantly on every side. You
[420] have not been altogether spared the dishonouring misconceptions

[1] At the top of the dedication page of the *Idea* Newman quotes the well-known phrase from the Gospel, *Hospes eram, et collegistis me* (Matthew 25:34), which is usually translated along the lines 'I was a stranger and you gave me shelter'. This refers to the manner in which his new co-religionists had rallied round him during the Achilli trial; but no doubt it also refers to the way in which his Irish hosts had welcomed him from England.

which have been the portion of the best and greatest of mankind. But they have ceased to trouble you. Your endowments of heart and intellect have compelled a recognition quite unexampled in its unanimity and earnestness; and we have come today, on the part of the Roman Catholic people of Ireland, to join in the applause with which the nations of Christendom have hailed your enrolment among the Princes of the Church, and to proclaim their reverential gratitude to the Sovereign Pontiff for the gracious act by which he has marked his appreciation of your labours, and crowned them with the highest earthly sanction.

Reply to the Address from the Catholics of Ireland

BIRMINGHAM, 10*th April*, 1880

MY LORD O'HAGAN,

I should be strangely constituted if I were not deeply moved by the Address which your Lordship has done me the honour of presenting to me, on occasion of my elevation by the grace of the Sovereign Pontiff to a seat in the Sacred College.

It almost bewilders me to receive an expression of approval, so warm, so special, so thorough, from men so high in station, ecclesiastical and civil, speaking, too, as they avow, in behalf of a whole Catholic people; and in order to this giving themselves the inconvenience and fatigue of a long journey in the midst of their serious occupations.[2] But while I reply to their commendation of me with somewhat of shame from the consciousness how much more I might have done, and how much better, still my reverence for them obliges me to submit myself to their [421]
praise as to a grave and emphatic judgment upon me, which

[2] Newman was well acquainted with the 'inconvenience and fatigue' of crossing St George's Channel, having done so fifty-six times in the service of the University.

it would be rude to question, and unthankful not to be proud of, and impossible ever to forget.

But their Address is not only an expression of their praise; it also conveys to me from Ireland a message of attachment. It is a renewal and enlargement of a singular kindness done to me a year ago, and even then not for the first time. I have long known what good friends I have in Ireland; they in their affection have taken care that I should know it, and the knowledge has been at times a great support to me. They have not been of those who trust a man one day and forget him the next; and, though I have not much to boast of in most points of view, I will dare to say, that, if, on my appointment to a high post in Ireland, I came there with the simple desire and aim to serve a noble people, who I felt had a great future, deeply sensible of the trust, but otherwise, I may say, without thought of myself—if this creates a claim upon your remembrance, I can with a good conscience accept it.

And here I am led on to refer to a special circumstance on which you touch with much delicacy and sympathy, and which I can hardly avoid, since you mention it, namely, the accident that in past years I have not always been understood, or had justice done to my real sentiments and intentions, in influential quarters at home and abroad. I will not deny that on several occasions this has been my trial,
[422] and I say this without assuming that I had no blame myself in its coming upon me. But then I reflected that, whatever pain that trial might cost me, it was the lightest that I could have, that a man was not worth much who could not bear it; that, if I had not had this, I might have had a greater; that I was conscious to myself of a firm faith in the Catholic Church, and of loyalty to the Holy See, that I was and had been blest with a fair measure of success in my work, and that prejudice and misconception did not last for ever. And my wonder is, as I feel it, that the sunshine has come out so

soon, and with so fair a promise of lasting through my evening.

My Lord and Gentlemen, in speaking so much of myself I feel I must be trying your patience; but you have led me on to be familiar with you. I will say no more than to offer a prayer to the Author of all good, that the best blessings may descend from Him on all those who have taken part in this gracious act, exercised towards one who has so faint a claim on their generosity.

JOHN HENRY CARD. NEWMAN

APPENDIX

THE FIRST STAFF OF PROFESSORS AND LECTURERS OF THE UNIVERSITY

From *The Catholic University Gazette*, 19th October, 1854

PERHAPS it may be interesting to the reader to be put in possession of a few particulars of the antecedents of some of the Gentlemen to whose care various departments of instruction are committed in the University. Of many of them indeed little need be said, as they are well known to Irishmen, either by their works or by their reputation. It is unnecessary, and would be officious, to use any commendatory words in behalf of Father O'Reilly, late Professor of Dogmatic Theology at Maynooth; of Dr Leahy, whose study of the Scriptures is only rivalled among Irish theologians by the Most Reverend Primate; of Mr Curry, whose original investigations into Irish Antiquities are appreciated by Protestants as well as by Catholics; of Mr MacCarthy, whose poems and other compositions, beautiful as they are, and emphatically popular, promise even more than they display; of Mr Butler, of Trinity College, many years head inspector of the National Board; of Mr John O'Hagan, and of Mr Allies. But there are others, who, from the accidents of their life, from their residence in foreign countries, or from the circumstance that their writings have been anonymous, or as being converts to the Catholic Church, seem to claim some sort of introduction, on entering the new field of exertion, to which they are devoting themselves. And though it is a claim which will be preferred by their friends, and not by themselves, yet even they at least must think it right to concede to the necessity of the case what personally they would be glad to decline.

Mr Flanagan has been employed in the profession of civil engineering many years in England and on the Continent. When a youth, at the instance of his uncle, Chief-Baron Woulfe, he was admitted for examination at the Royal Engineers; but, though his

answers in mathematics were so brilliant that he was called up before the senior officers to show his demonstrations of some of
[426] the problems put before him, he preferred ultimately, according to his original intention, to enter at Trinity College, where he gained the first honours in science at successive examinations over the heads of several gentlemen who have since earned a distinguished name and position in that seat of learning. A competent judge declared his conviction, that, had he been able to stand,[1] he would have had no difficulty in gaining the first fellowship for which he offered himself. Betaking himself to civil engineering, he studied his profession in Ireland and Belgium, and was employed in it for several years in the latter country. In England, he has successively held the offices of Resident Engineer of the Blackburn and Preston Railway, and Engineer-in-Chief, and afterwards General Manager, of the Blackburn and Bolton, and Blackburn and Clitheroe lines. Since, he has been the Engineer of the foreign lines, running from Antwerp to Rotterdam, and from Lisbon to Cintra. He was elected a member of the Institute of Civil Engineers, without being required first, as is usual, to become a graduate in it.

Dr Dunne was educated at the Irish College at Rome. In his first year's philosophy he made a *saggio*[2] in all the mathematical subjects of the year, and took the first premium in logic and metaphysics. He was afterwards selected by his Professor, in order to his degree, to defend as many as eight hundred conclusions in all philosophy, in metaphysics, psychology, and the philosophy of religion. In his second year of theology, he defended about eighty dogmatic propositions; and had prepared himself to defend propositions in *universâ theologiâ*, when circumstances made a change in his plans. The result of these successes was, that, by the early age of twenty-three, he had taken a Doctor's degree both in Theology and in Philosophy.[3]

---

[1] Degrees at Trinity were opened up to Catholics and Dissenters by the removal of the religious test barriers for undergraduates in 1794, but not for scholarships or fellowships. Scholarships and fellowships (except in the Divinity School) were opened up by Fawcett's Act in 1873.

[2] *Saggio* in this context means a display or performance.

[3] For more on Dunne, see the relevant footnote on p. [50].

Mr Robertson, though not Irish born, is of Irish descent. He has lived for some years in Germany, and is known to scholars as the translator into English of Mœhler's *Symbolique*, and Schlegel's *Philosophy of History*. His contributions to the *Dublin Review*, which are numerous, have for the most part turned upon questions involving historical research.[4]

Mr Healy Thompson is also closely connected with various Irish families of distinction. He is a Master of Arts of the University of Cambridge, having in the course of his residence there succeeded in becoming a Scholar and double prizeman at Emmanuel College, and in taking honours, both classical and [427] mathematical, at his University examination. Upon subsequent examinations in theology, he twice stood first in merit, and was selected for ecclesiastical preferment in consequence. He was also successively nominated Principal of several educational establishments, and held one of the most prominent positions, open to younger ecclesiastics in the Protestant Church, in the west end of London. After his conversion, he published two controversial works on the subject of the Papal Supremacy, the latter of which, on *The Unity of the Episcopate*, in answer to Mr Allies, at that time a Protestant, is strongly recommended by Dr Kenrick, Archbishop of Baltimore, in his work on the Primacy. Since then, besides other literary occupations, he has been one of the editors and writers of the series called "the Clifton Tracts," and is the compiler of the *Golden Manual*, a book of devotion much used in England.[5]

Mr Ornsby has been for the last five years a resident of Dublin, and, though pledged to no political party, has through that period taken a zealous and practical interest in every Catholic and Irish object. He is a Master of Arts of the University of Oxford, where he early distinguished himself by gaining one of Lord Crewe's exhibitions. On his examination for his Bachelor's degree, he gained the highest honours in classics, and was afterwards elected Fellow of Trinity College. Subsequently he

---

[4] For more on Robertson, see the relevant footnote on p. [49].

[5] Thompson originally accepted the offer of a tutorship but for reasons of health resigned shortly before the University was due to open. For more on Thompson, see the relevant footnote on p. [xxv].

served the College office of Lecturer in Rhetoric, and the University office of Master of the Schools; and was for four or five years actively engaged in private tuition. He has been, both before and since his conversion, a contributor to several periodical publications, a translator and editor of various historical and religious publications, and a constant writer of critical reviews. A life of St Francis de Sales, from his pen, is in the press.[6]

Signor Marani, a member of the University of Modena, has also resided some years in this place, and the high testimonials, which he has presented, show that he is too well known in its literary and domestic circles, to require more distinct notice here.[7]

Mr Stewart, who is a Master of Arts of Cambridge, began his career of academical success as a boy, by carrying off the first bursary for Latin prose composition from a hundred competitors. He gained also the first prize for Greek, three times; and, besides
[428] other successes, was gold medalist of his year. At Trinity College he was prizeman in his second year; and, in spite of severe illness, obtained, at his examination previous to his degree, both classical and mathematical honours. From that time to the date of his reception into the Catholic Church, he has been occupied in education, and in preparing young men for the Universities. The testimonials, which he has presented, contain letters in his favour from the Protestant Bishop of Durham, Dr Maltby, one of the first Greek scholars of his day, as well as from other graduates in Oxford and Cambridge.[8]

Mr P. le Page Renouf is a native of Guernsey, and has the advantage of being equally at home in the English and French language and literature. To these he has since added a knowledge of German. He had just commenced his course at Pembroke College, in the University of Oxford, when he submitted himself to the Catholic Church, and was in consequence obliged to leave the sphere of an honourable ambition. He soon distinguished himself, young as he was, by his writings in the *Dublin Review*

---

[6] For more on Ornsby, see the relevant footnote on p. [xxvi].
[7] For more on Marani, see the relevant footnote on p. [50].
[8] For more on Stewart, see the relevant footnote on p. [49].

and elsewhere, in answer to the views of Dr Newman and Mr Allies, both of them at that time members of the Establishment.[9]

[9] Mr Renouf left the Catholic University in 1864, in consequence of his appointment as one of Her Majesty's Inspectors of Schools. Shortly after the foundation of the University he had become Professor of Greek and Roman History, and when he left he retained the honorary title of Professor of Oriental Languages.

In 1886 he succeeded Dr S. Birch as Keeper of the Oriental Antiquities in the British Museum, and retired at the end of 1891. He also succeeded Dr Birch as president of the Society of Biblical Archæology, and most of his later literary work is to be found in the Translations and Proceedings of this Society.

He received the honour of knighthood on Her Majesty's birthday, May, 1896. [WPN]

For more on Renouf, see the relevant footnote on p. [50].

[429]

THE *ATLANTIS I*

A REGISTER OF LITERATURE AND SCIENCE[1]

From the Calendar of the Irish Cath. Univ. of the Session of 1856–57[2]

IT is proposed to commence a Literary and Scientific Periodical, to be published half-yearly, consisting mainly of the contributions of the Professors and others of the Catholic University.

The reasons for such an undertaking are as follows:—

The University is now completing its third session: in that time it has had a greater measure of success than even its most zealous friends, looking calmly at the difficulties under which it started, ventured to anticipate for it. It has at present in its lecture-rooms from a hundred and ten to a hundred and twenty students.

It has, moreover, done much to vanquish the most formidable of difficulties which can beset a public institution, struggling into existence and position; and that is, the apathy, the incredulity, the scorn, with which the very idea of its establishment was variously received, and that, even among those very classes, for whose advantage it was specially designed. The fact of its being actually commenced, the number of able men whom it has enlisted

[1] There are 95 items about the *Atlantis* at the BOA (C.6.35), including an undated printed sheet marked 'Private' and entitled 'Proposed Literary and Scientific Register'.

[2] A later version of the Prospectus for the *Atlantis*, dated 3 November 1857, can be found in *LD* xviii, p. 150n.

in its service, the recognition and the prospects of its Medical School, the popularity which has attended upon its New Church, the homage paid to it by the foreign youth who have sought it out from abroad in preference to their own schools, have all combined to mitigate the prejudice and to overcome the disinclination of the public mind towards it.

But its success supplies a lesson as well as an encouragement. It teaches its members that they must, and may safely, depend on themselves. Up to this time they have made their way, not by favour of external parties, patrons, influences, or contingencies, but by means of their own reputation, courage, confidence, resources, and energy, [430]
under the blessing and protection of heaven. If they are true to themselves, others will come over to them. They have but to proceed in the course which they have begun, and they are sure to make progress. On the other hand, under their particular circumstances, progress is necessary to success. They cannot afford to seem to the world to be doing nothing. In making their way against public opinion, the proverb *non progredi est regredi*[3] emphatically applies to them above others.

It is in order, then, that the University may be taking another step in advance, that a Periodical is contemplated as the repository and record of its intellectual proficiency. Such an undertaking naturally follows on the entrance of the Professors upon their respective provinces of labour. Nor will it only serve to tell the public what they are doing and what they can do; it will be their contribution to the science and literature of the day; it will be their advertisement, recommendation, and bond of connection, with the learned bodies of Great Britain and the Continent; and it will gain for them in exchange for what they send, the various journals of a similar kind, many of them important and

[3] Not to go forward is to go backward.

valuable, which issue periodically from those great centres of thought.

A publication of this nature cannot be set on foot without a considerable outlay. It is calculated that the expenses of each number, from first to last, will scarcely be less than £100. It is proposed to collect from friends and well-wishers of the University as much as will serve the purpose of carrying on the work for three years. Should it sustain itself during so considerable a period in a way adequate to the anticipations which may be fairly entertained of it, it is not unreasonable to expect that it will by that time have created sufficient interest among Catholics and Protestants to pay its way without any extraordinary effort.

J. H. N.

DUBLIN, *6th May*, 1857

REGISTER OF LITERATURE AND SCIENCE

Lists of subjects on which papers are promised by the Professors

1. Physiological Types, and the non-existence of Pathological Types.
2. Endemic constitutional status of present mixed Irish and Anglo-Irish races.

[431] 3. Physiological Œconomics of Armies in peace and war.
4. Growth, Nutrition, and elective Tissue-formation.
5. Generalization of elementary Histo-morphism.
6. On Histolysis.
7. The existence of peripheral neuro-dynamic Foci.
8. Physiological correlation as exemplified in the organ of vision; the value of this organ as a zoological test.
9. The existence of Butyric Acid among the products of the destructive distillation of Peat, and the formation of several other acids of the series (C H)n O_4 by the distillation of vegetable and animal substances.

10. Tri-methylamine, and some other products of the destructive distillation of Peat.
11. The resins obtained by the action of ammonia on Peat, and the changes which ammonia undergoes in peaty soils.
12. The chemical composition and products of oxidation by nitric acid, of the sporules *lycopodium clavatum*, and the general chemical constitution of the pollen of the phanerogamic plants.
13. The formation of the zeolites and other hydrated minerals, and the decomposing action of superheated steam as an agent in geological changes.
14. Contributions towards the nomenclature of the igneous rocks. —Composition of the intrusive, metamorphic, and ashy rocks of the Silurian and Cambrian periods in Ireland and North Wales.
15. The nature of the nitrogenous proximate principles of plants, and the influence of manures upon them; and the relation between the percentage of water and nitrogen in various parts of plants.
16. The chemical composition of the Ironstones, Limestones, and Coals of the Leitrim or Lough Allen coal field.
17. The influence which physical circumstances (physical geography, geology, and the fauna and flora of a region) exert upon the character of the language, mythology, and early literature of nations, as an element in the determination of the original areas occupied by races.—With some illustrations from the mythology of the Finnic and other branches of the Ugrian or Tschudic race.
18. Principles of meteorology.
19. The laws of the distribution of heat in islands. [432]
20. The influence of the distribution of land and water on terrestrial climate.

21. The general structure of the globe.
22. The mutual perturbations of the planets Jupiter, Saturn, Uranus, and Neptune.
23. Chronology of Trajan's reign.
24. The dates of our Lord's birth and crucifixion.
25. Studies on the monuments, language, and history of ancient Egypt.
26. Persian cuneiform Inscription at Behistun.
27. Philo and the Judæo-Alexandrian School.
28. The Book of Enoch.
29. The Ebionite heresy.
30. The respective tenets of Eutyches and of the Monophysites.
31. Glossary of theological terms found in the Fathers.
32. Recent researches into Waldensian Literature.
33. The popular tradition of the return of the Emperor Nero to life.
34. The moral and religious reaction of the sixteenth and seventeenth centuries in Italy, Spain, France, and Germany.
35. Historical contrast of the mission of the Dominicans with that of the Benedictines.
36. Life and character of Alcibiades.
37. Relations of English poetry to the Christian creed.
38. The principles of Basilican architecture.
39. The true principles of conventionalism in the use of natural forms in architecture.
40. The popular Irish tradition of St Patrick having banished all venomous reptiles out of Ireland, and of his having convinced King Laaghaire of the doctrine of the Holy Trinity by holding up a shamrock before him.

The Atlantis

Editors of the Register are the Very Rev. J. H. Newman,[4] *Rector, and W. K. Sullivan, Esq., D.Ph., Professor of Chemistry, etc., etc.*

[4] Newman contributed four articles: 'The Mission of the Benedictine Order', *Atlantis* 1 (January 1858), pp. 1–49; 'On the Formula, μία φύσις σεσαρκωμένη', *Atlantis* 2 (July 1858), pp. 330–61; 'The Benedictine Centuries', *Atlantis* 3 (January 1858), pp. 1–43; 'The Ordo de Tempore in the Roman Breviary', *Atlantis* 9 (February 1870), pp. 1–12.

[433]

THE *ATLANTIS* II

A Half-Yearly Register of Literature and Science Conducted by Members of the Catholic University of Ireland

Introduction to No. I, January, 1858, to the *Atlantis* magazine

THE object of the work, which these lines are intended to introduce to the public, is to serve principally as the repository and memorial of such investigations in Literature and Science, as are made by members of the new Catholic University of Ireland. It is natural that men, whose occupations are of an intellectual nature, should be led to record the speculations or the conclusions in which their labours have issued; and that, having taken this step, they should consider it even as a duty which we owe to society, to communicate to others what they have thought it worth while to record. A periodical publication is the obvious mode of fulfilling that duty.

The prospects of their work are to be determined by its object and character. They cannot hope to interest the general reader; but from this very circumstance they are happily precluded from the chance of competition with those various ably-conducted periodicals which already possess the popular favour. They do not aspire to include Theology, as such, among the subjects to which their pages are to be devoted; but here again they have the compensation, that they will not be running the risk, in anything they publish, of provoking that most serious of all rivalries, which is founded on a principle of duty. Thus they hope to take their place among such writers as are absolutely unable to stand in each other's way, because they are all employed upon a field where there is room for all, and supply a market which cannot be overstocked, in which no one's loss is another's gain, but the success of each is the benefit of all.

Accordingly, instead of fearing rivals in those who are engaged in similar pursuits, the Conductors of the *Atlantis* are secure of friends. In undertakings such as theirs, success, from the nature of the case, is another name for merit; and failure can only arise from causes traceable to themselves. If they are sanguine that they shall be able to answer to the profession which they make in the very fact of [434] their commencing, it is because they trust they have the elementary qualifications of zeal, industry, and determination.

The work will be published half-yearly, on the first of January and the first of July. Each number will be divided into three portions, devoted respectively to Literature, Science, and Notices, Literary or Scientific. . . .

The first number will appear on 1st January, 1858. . . .

CATHOLIC UNIVERSITY-HOUSE, DUBLIN,

3rd November, 1857

[435]

THE CATHOLIC UNIVERSITY OF IRELAND

ABSTRACT OF GROSS RECEIPTS AND EXPENDITURE FROM SEPT. 9, 1850, TO OCT. 4, 1855, BOTH INCLUSIVE

Dr.

To Amount contributed in Ireland, including sums not identified by dioceses and parishes		£27,616 0 10
Amount contributed by United States of America	£16,244 6 3	
Amount contributed b British America and Colonies	970 8 0	
Amount contributed by England, Scotland, etc.	4,166 15 0	
Amount contributed by sundry other places	55 13 4	
		21,437 2 7
Amount of interest received on stock	3,746 18 0	
Amount of anonymous donation, per Archbishop of Dublin	5,000 0 0	
Amount of anonymous, per ditto	271 0 0	9,017 18 0
		£58,071 1 5

Cr.

By Amount invested in Government stock	40,000 0 0
Deposits in Hibernian Bank bearing interest	6,547 6 1
Expenses establishing University, purchase of premises, and expenses of first year	8,384 1 2
Expenses of committee for collecting in	

Ireland, England, and America; printing, advertising, rent, salaries, furniture, books, postage, and parcels, for five years	2,823 1 9	
Ditto, ditto	20 7 6	
		2,843 9 3
Balance		296 4 11
		£58,071 1 5

[436]

THE CATHOLIC UNIVERSITY OF IRELAND COMMITTEE

1850

Most Rev. Paul Cullen, D.D., Archbishop of Armagh.
„ „ Daniel Murray, D.D., Archbishop of Dublin.
„ „ Michael Slattery, D.D., Archbishop of Cashel.
„ „ John MacHale, D.D., Archbishop of Tuam.
Right Rev. John Cantwell, D.D., Bishop of Meath.
„ „ Francis Haly, D.D., Bishop of Kildare.
„ „ Nicholas Foran, D.D., Bishop of Waterford.
„ „ John Derry, D.D., Bishop of Clonfert.

1851

Most Rev. Paul Cullen, D.D., Archbishop of Armagh.
„ „ Daniel Murray, D.D., Archbishop of Dublin.
„ „ Michael Slattery, D.D., Archbishop of Cashel.
„ „ John MacHale, D.D., Archbishop of Tuam.
Right Rev. John Cantwell, D.D., Bishop of Meath.
„ „ Francis Haly, D.D., Bishop of Kildare.
„ „ Nicholas Foran, D.D., Bishop of Waterford.
„ „ John Derry, D.D., Bishop of Clonfert.
Very Rev. Dean Meyler, V.G., Dublin.
„ „ Dominic O'Brien, D.D., Waterford.
„ „ Patrick Leahy, D.D., V.G., Cashel.
„ „ Peter Reynolds, D.D., Tuam.
Rev. John O'Hanlon, D.D., Maynooth.
Rev. Peter Cooper, D.D., Dublin.
Rev. James Maher, P.P., Carlow.
Rev. Patrick Brennan, P.P., Kildare.
Myles O'Reilly, Esq.
Charles Bianconi, Esq.

Sir Michael Dillon Bellew, Bart.
Thomas Boylan, Esq.
James O'Ferrall, Esq.
Thomas Meagher, Esq.
Michael Errington, Esq.
William Nugent Skelly, Esq.[1]

Honorary Secretaries	V. R. PATRICK LEAHY, D.D., V.G. REV PETER COOPER, D.D. W. NUGENT SKELLY, ESQ.

[1] The make-up of the Committee—four archbishops, four bishops, eight Priests and eight laymen—has been described in the footnote on p. [82]. C. G. Duffy's dismissal of the lay members as 'mere wooden figures set up for show' (*The League of North and South* (London: Chapman & Hall, 1886), p. 306) is inaccurate: O'Reilly and Bianconi were active and influential figures, and Errington played his part too.

[437]

APPENDIX

SPANISH UNIVERSITIES IN THE FIFTEENTH CENTURY

Put together and slightly abridged by Dr Newman from Prescott's *History of Ferdinand and Isabella*[1]

I HAVE already inserted a brief notice of the present number and pretensions of the Universities of Spain.[2] The reader

---

[1] Vide Catholic University Gazette, 7th December, 1854. [WPN]

One of Newman's aims for the *CUG* was to use it to reach out to a public which had practically no knowledge of what a university consisted of, no feel for higher education, and little exposure to university graduates. He sought to achieve this by presenting snapshots of the university in different historical eras.

Except for the few who could aspire to a career in medicine or law and undertake the extensive training this involved, Irish Catholics had little conception of why anyone should need—or want—to prolong their studies and postpone the start of gainful employment. In the minds of most Catholics, university education was associated with the ruling Protestant class; it was coloured by images of high-spirited exploits of privileged young men of means, for whom university was often a mere finishing school. W. M. Thackeray's novel *Pendennis* (1849) describes the lifestyle of a fashionable 'young buck' at Oxford and his extravagant spending habits and pastimes, which included horse-driving and hounds, as well as books, art, furniture and clothes. That this was not merely satirical fiction can be seen from the mention of the same habits in the *Royal Commission Oxford* (1852, p. 24).

Newman hoped that articles such as this one would give his readers a more uplifting vision of higher education, when conducted seriously and with a view to the common good.

perhaps will not be sorry to have his memory refreshed as to their condition, at the time of the revival of learning, four [438] centuries ago. Mr Prescott's *History of Ferdinand and Isabella*, is ready to our hand, and supplies us with the necessary information without our having the trouble of bringing together its various particulars for ourselves. Moreover, as it seems to confirm various points in the history of Universities, on which I have before now insisted, there is a reason for availing ourselves of his researches, over and above their intrinsic merit. I have ventured to put together passages from various parts of the work, and slightly to abridge them.

> "Previously to the introduction of printing," he says, "collections of books were necessarily very small and thinly scattered, owing to the extreme cost of manuscripts. The most copious library which the learned Saez could find any account of in the middle of the fifteenth century was owned by the Counts of Benavente, and contained not more than

---

[2] The Universities of Spain are at present (*i.e.*, since 1847) ten in number; Madrid, Barcelona, Granada, Oviedo, Salamanca, Seville, Santiago, Valentia, Valladolid, Saragossa.

1. The University of Madrid* is attended by 7000 students, and occupies the new building of St Isidore. It comprises five faculties.

2. The University of Barcelona, which has succeeded to those of Lerida, Palma, and Cervera, numbers about 1600 students. It has four faculties, but not theology.

3. The other eight Universities were founded at dates between A.D. 1222, which is the date of Salamanca, and A.D. 1580, the date of Oviedo.

These Universities have either three or four faculties. Oviedo, Seville, Valladolid, and Saragossa have the faculty of theology.

The annual expense to the Spanish government of these ten Universities, including the buildings, collections, and libraries, is more than two millions of francs (£80,000).

Vide the Louvain *Revue Catholique* for November, 1852.

*The University of Alcalá was transferred in 1837 to Madrid, *Vide Encyclopædia Brltannlca* (ed. 1888). [WPN]

120 volumes. Many of these were duplicates; of Livy alone there were eight copies. The cathedral churches in Spain rented their books every year by auction to the highest bidders, whence they derived a considerable revenue. It would appear from a copy of Gratian's Canons, preserved in the Celestine Monastery at Paris, that the copyist was engaged twenty-one months in transcribing that manuscript; at this rate, the production of four thousand copies by one hand would require seven thousand years, a work now easily performed in less than four months. Two thousand volumes may be procured now at a price which in those days would hardly have sufficed to purchase fifty.[3]

"Isabella inherited the taste of her father, John the Second, for the collecting of books. She endowed the Convent of San Juan de los Reyes, at the time of its foundation, 1477, with a library, consisting principally of manuscripts. The archives of Simancas contain catalogues of part of two separate collections belonging to her, whose broken remains have contributed to swell the magnificent library of the Escurial. Most of them are in manuscript, and the worn and battered
[439] condition of some of them proves that they were not merely kept for show. The larger collection comprised about two hundred and one articles, or distinct works; of these about a third was taken up with theology; one fifth, civil law and the municipal code of Spain; one fourth, ancient classics, modern literature, and romances of chivalry; one tenth, history; the residue is devoted to ethics, medicine, etc. Nothing could have been more opportune for the enlightened purpose of Isabella than the introduction of the art of printing into Spain, at the commencement of her reign. She saw, from the first moment, all the advantages which it promised for diffusing and perpetuating the discoveries of science. She encouraged its establishment by large privileges to those who exercised it, whether natives or foreigners, and by causing many of the works composed by her subjects to be printed at her own

---

[3] The above paragraph is contained in a Note, taken by Prescott from *Tratado de Monedas de Enrique III. Apud Moratin, Obras, ed. de la Acad.* (Madrid, 1830), tom. i, pp. 91, 92. [WPN]

charge. More printing presses were probably at work in Spain in the infancy of the art, than at the present day.

"She requested the learned Peter Martyr,[4] to repair to the Court, and open a school there for the instruction of the young nobility. In the month of September following, we have a letter dated from Saragossa, in which he thus speaks of his success: 'My house, all day long, swarms with noble youths, who, reclaimed from ignoble pursuits to those of letters, are now convinced that these, so far from being a hindrance, are rather a help in the profession of arms'. Another Italian scholar, Lucio Marineo Siculo, co-operated with Martyr in the introduction of a more liberal scholarship among the Castilian nobles. He was induced to visit Spain in 1486, and soon took his place among the professors of Salamanca, where he filled the chairs of poetry and grammar with great applause for twelve years. Under the auspices of these and other eminent scholars, both native and foreign, the young nobility of Castile applied with generous ardour to the cultivation of science; the large correspondence both of Martyr and Marineo includes the most considerable persons of the Castilian court; the numerous dedications to these persons of contemporary publications attest their munificent patronage of literary enterprise; and many of the highest rank entered on such severe literary labour

---

[4] The original article in the *CUG* had a long footnote on Peter Martyr: 'The author, whom I am using, speaks thus of this Peter Martyr in his *History of the Conquest of Mexico* ii., p. 85: "Pietro Martin de Angleria belonged to an ancient family of Arona in the north of Italy. In 1487 he was induced by the Count of Tendilla, the Spanish ambassador at Rome, to return with him to Castile. He was graciously received by Queen Isabella, always desirous to draw around her enlightened foreigners, who might exercise a salutary influence on the rough and warlike nobility of Castile. In 1525 he died, at the age of seventy. His character combined qualities not often found in the same individual; an ardent love of letters, with a practical sagacity which can only result from familiarity with men and affairs. Though passing his days in the gay and dazzling society of the capital, he preserved the simple tastes and dignified temper of a philosopher. Though deeply imbued with the learning of antiquity, and a scholar at heart, he had none of the feelings of the recluse, but took the most lively interest in the events that were passing around him".' (*CUG* 28 (7 December, 1854), p. 219)

as few, from the mere love of letters, are found willing to encounter.

"Don Gutierre de Toledo, son of the Duke of Alva, and a
[440] cousin of the king, taught in the University of Salamanca. At the same place, Don Pedro Fernandez de Velasco, son of the Count of Haro, who subsequently succeeded his father in the hereditary dignity of Grand Constable of Castile, read lectures on Pliny and Ovid. Don Alfonso de Manrique, son of the Count of Parades, was professor of Greek in the University of Alcalá. All ages seemed to catch the generous enthusiasm; and the Marquis of Denia, although turned of sixty, made amends for the sins of his youth by learning the elements of the Latin tongue at this late period. No Spaniard was accounted noble who held science in indifference. From a very early period, a courtly stamp was impressed on the poetic literature of Spain; a similar character was now imparted to its erudition, and men of the most illustrious birth seemed eager to lead the way in the difficult career of science, which was thrown open to the nation. In this brilliant exhibition, those of the other sex must not be omitted who contributed by their intellectual endowments to the general illumination of the period. The Queen's instructor in the Latin language was a lady named Dona Beatriz de Galindo, called, from her peculiar attainments, *la Latina*. Another lady, Dona Lucia de Meldrano, publicly lectured on the Latin classics in the University of Salamanca. And another, Dona Francisca de Lebrija, daughter of the historian of that name, filled the chair of rhetoric with applause at Alcalá.

"While the study of the ancient tongues came thus into fashion with persons of both sexes and of the highest rank, it was widely and most thoroughly cultivated by professed scholars. Men of letters, some of whom have been already noticed, were invited into Spain from Italy, the theatre at that time, on which, from obvious local advantages, classical discovery was pursued with greatest ardour and success. To this country it was usual also for Spanish students to repair, in order to complete their discipline in classical literature, especially the Greek, as first taught on sound principles of criticism by the learned exiles from Constantinople. The most

remarkable of the Spanish scholars, who made this literary pilgrimage to Italy, was Antonio de Lebrija. After ten years passed at Bologna and other seminaries of repute, he returned in 1473 to his native land, richly laden with the stores of various erudition. He was invited to fill the Latin chair at [441]
Seville, whence he was successively transferred to Salamanca and Alcalá, both of which places he long continued to enlighten by his oral instruction and publications. Another name, worthy of commemoration, is that of Arias Barbosa, a learned Portuguese, who, after passing some years, like Lebrija, in the schools of Italy, where he studied the ancient tongues under the guidance of Politiano, was induced to establish his residence in Spain. The scope of the present work precludes the possibility of a copious examination of the pioneers of ancient learning, to whom Spain owes so large a debt of gratitude. Among them, are particularly deserving of attention the brothers John and Francis Vergara, professors at Alcalá; Núnez de Guzman, professor for many years at Salamanca and Alcalá, and author of the Latin version of the famous Polyglot; Olivario; and Vives, whose fame rather belongs to Europe than his own country, who, when twenty-six years old, drew from Erasmus the encomium, that 'there was scarcely any one of the age whom he could venture to compare with him in philosophy, eloquence, and liberal learning'. But the most unequivocal testimony to the deep and various scholarship of the period is afforded by that stupendous literary work of Cardinal Ximenes, the Polyglot Bible, whose versions in the Greek, Latin, and Oriental tongues were collated, with a single exception, by Spanish scholars. Erasmus says that 'liberal studies were brought, in the course of a few years, in Spain to so flourishing a condition, as might not only excite the admiration, but serve as a model to the most cultivated nations of Europe'.

"The Spanish Universities were the theatre on which this classical erudition was more especially displayed. Previous to Isabella's reign, there were but few schools in the kingdom, not one, indeed, of any note, except in Salamanca; and this did not escape the blight which fell on every generous study. But, under the cheering patronage of the present government, they

were soon filled, and widely multiplied. Academies of repute were to be found in Seville, Toledo, Salamanca, Granada, and Alcalá; and learned teachers were drawn from abroad by the most liberal emoluments. At the head of these establishments stood 'the illustrious city of Salamanca,' as Marineo fondly terms it, 'mother of all liberal arts and virtues, alike renowned
[443] for noble cavaliers and learned men'. Such was its reputation, that foreigners, as well as natives, were attracted to its schools, and at one time, according to the authority of the same professor, seven thousand students were assembled within its walls. A letter from Peter Martyr to his patron the Count of Tendilla, gives a whimsical picture of the literary enthusiasm of this place. The throng was so great to hear his introductory lecture on one of the Satires of Juvenal, that every avenue to the hall was blockaded, and the professor was borne in on the shoulders of the students. He was escorted back in triumph to his lodgings, to use his own language, 'like a victor in the Olympic games,' after the conclusion of the exercise. Professorships in every department of science then studied, as well as of polite letters, were established at the new University, the 'New Athens,' as Martyr somewhere styles it. Before the close of Isabella's reign, however, its glories were rivalled, if not eclipsed, by those of Alcalá, which combined higher advantages for ecclesiastical with civil education, and which, under the splendid patronage of Cardinal Ximenes, executed the famous Polyglot version of the Scriptures, the most stupendous literary enterprise of that age.

"As far back as 1497, Ximenes had conceived the idea of establishing a University in the ancient town of Alcalá, where the salubrity of the air, and the sober, tranquil complexion of the scenery, on the beautiful borders of the Henares, seemed well suited to academic study and meditation. He even went so far as to obtain plans at this time for his buildings from a celebrated architect. Other engagements, however, postponed the commencement of the work till 1500, when the Cardinal himself laid the corner-stone of the principal college, with a solemn ceremonial and invocation of the blessing of Heaven on his designs. From that hour, amidst all the engrossing cares of church and state, he might be frequently seen on the ground, with the rule in his hand, taking the admeasurement of the buildings, and stimulating the industry of the workmen by seasonable rewards.

"The plans were too extensive, however, to admit of being speedily accomplished. Besides the principal college of San Ildephonso, named in honour of the patron saint of Toledo, there were nine others, together with an hospital for the reception of invalids at the University. These edifices were built in the most substantial manner; and such parts as admitted of it, as the libraries, refectories and chapels, were finished with elegance and even splendour. The city of Alcalá underwent many important and expensive alterations, in order to render it more worthy of being the seat of a great and flourishing University. The stagnant water was carried off by drains, the streets were paved, old buildings removed, and new and spacious avenues thrown open.

"At the expiration of eight years, the Cardinal had the satisfaction of seeing the whole of his vast design completed, and every apartment of the spacious pile carefully furnished with all that was requisite for the comfort and accommodation of the student. It was indeed a noble enterprise, more particularly when viewed as the work of a private individual. As such it raised the deepest admiration in Francis the First when he visited the spot a few years after the Cardinal's death. 'Your Ximenes,' said he, 'has executed more than I should have dared to conceive; he has done with his single hand what in France it has cost a line of kings to accomplish.'

"The erection of the buildings, however, did not terminate the labours of the Primate, who now assumed the task of digesting a scheme of instruction and discipline for his infant seminary. In doing this, he sought light wherever it was to be found, and borrowed many useful hints from the venerable University of Paris. His system was of the most enlightened kind, being directed to call all the powers of the student into action, and not to leave him a mere passive recipient in the hands of his teachers. Besides daily recitations and lectures he was required to take part in public examinations and discussions, so conducted as to prove effectually his talent and acquisition. In these gladiatorial displays Ximenes took the deepest interest, and often encouraged the generous emulation of the scholar by attending in person.

"Two provisions may be noticed as characteristic of the man. One, that the salary of a professor should be regulated by the number of his disciples; another, that every professor should be re-eligible at the expiration of every four years. It was impossible that any servant of Ximenes should sleep at his post.

"Liberal foundations were made for indigent students, especially in divinity. But the comprehensive mind of Ximenes embraced nearly the whole circle of sciences taught
[444] in other Universities. Indeed, out of the forty-two chairs, twelve only were dedicated to divinity and the canon law; whilst four were appropriated to medicine; one to anatomy; one to surgery; eight to the arts, as they were called, embracing logic, physics, and metaphysics; one to ethics; one to mathematics; four to the ancient languages; four to rhetoric; and six to grammar.

"Having completed his arrangements, the Cardinal sought the most competent agents for carrying his plans into execution; and this indifferently from abroad and at home. His mind was too lofty for narrow local prejudices; and the tree of knowledge, he knew, bore fruit in every clime. Lampillas, indeed, in his usual patriotic vein, stoutly maintains that the chairs of the University were all supplied by native Spaniards; but Alvaro Gomez, who flourished two centuries earlier, and personally knew the professors, is the better authority. The Cardinal took especial care that the emoluments should be sufficient to tempt talent from obscurity, and from quarters, however remote, where it was to be found. In this he was perfectly successful, and we find the University catalogue at this time inscribed with the names of the most distinguished scholars in their various departments, many of whom we are enabled to appreciate by the enduring memorials of erudition which they have bequeathed to us.

"In July, 1508, the Cardinal received the welcome intelligence that his academy was opened for the admission of pupils; and in the following month the first lecture, being on Aristotle's Ethics, was publicly delivered. Students soon flocked to the new University, attracted by the reputation of its professors, its ample apparatus, its thorough system of instruction, and, above all, its splendid patronage, and the high character of its founder. We have no information of their number in Ximenes's life-time; but it must have been very considerable, since no less than seven thousand came out to receive Francis the First on his visit to the University, within twenty years after it was opened.

"It was on occasion of Ferdinand's visit to Alcalá, that the rector of San Ildefonso, the head of the University, came out to receive the king, preceded by his usual train of attendants, with their maces, or wands of office. The royal guard, at this exhibition, called out to them to lay aside their insignia, as unbecoming any subject in the presence of his sovereign. 'Not so,' said Ferdinand who had the good sense to perceive that [445]
majesty could not be degraded by its homage to letters, 'not so; this is the seat of the Muses, and those who are initiated in their mysteries have the best right to reign here.'

"In the midst of his pressing duties, Ximenes found time for the execution of another work, which would alone have been sufficient to render his name immortal in the republic of letters. This was his famous Bible, or Complutensian Polyglot, as usually termed, from the place where it was printed, Alcalá or Complutum, so called, says Marineo, from the abundant fruitfulness of its soil. It was on the plan, first conceived by Origen, of exhibiting in one view the Scriptures in their various ancient languages. It was a work of surpassing difficulty, demanding an extensive and critical acquaintance with the most ancient, and consequently the rarest manuscripts. The character and station of the Cardinal afforded him, it is true, uncommon facilities. The precious collection of the Vatican was literally thrown open to him, especially under Leo the Tenth, whose munificent spirit delighted in the undertaking. He obtained copies, in like manner, of whatever was of value in the other libraries of Italy, and indeed of Europe generally; and Spain supplied him with editions of the Old Testament of great antiquity, which had been treasured up by the banished Israelites. Some idea may be formed of the lavish expenditure in this way, from the fact that four thousand crowns of gold were paid for seven foreign manuscripts, which, however, came too late to be of use in the compilation.

"The conduct of the work was entrusted to nine scholars, well skilled in the ancient tongues, as most of them had evinced by works of critical acuteness and erudition. After the labours of the day, these learned sages were accustomed to meet, in order to settle the doubts and difficulties which had arisen in the course of their researches, and, in short, to compare the results of their observations. Ximenes, who, however limited his attainments in general literature, was an excellent biblical critic, frequently presided, and took a prominent part in these deliberations. 'Lose no time, my friends,' he would say, 'in the prosecution of our glorious work; lest, in the casualties of life, you should lose your patron, or I have to lament the loss of those whose services are of more price in my eyes than wealth and worldly honours.'

[446] "The difficulties of the undertaking were sensibly increased by those of the printing. The art was then in its infancy, and there were no types in Spain, if indeed in any part of Europe, in the Oriental character. Ximenes, however, careful to have the whole executed under his own eye, imported artists from Germany, and had types cast in the various languages required, in his foundries at Alcalá.

"The work, when completed, occupied six volumes folio; it was not brought to an end till 1517, fifteen years after its commencement, and a few weeks only before the death of its illustrious projector. Alvaro Gomez relates that he had often heard John Broccario, the son of the printer, say that, when the last sheet was struck off, he, then a child, was dressed in his best attire, and sent with a copy to the Cardinal. The latter, as he took it, raised his eyes to heaven, and devoutly offered up his thanks for being spared to the completion of this good work. Then, turning to his friends who were present, he said that 'of all the acts which distinguished his administration, there was none, however arduous, better entitled to their congratulation than this.'

"Such were the gigantic projects which amused the leisure hours of this great prelate. Though gigantic, they were neither beyond his strength to execute, nor beyond the demands of his age and country. They were not like those works which, forced into being by whim or transitory impulse, perish with the breath that made them; but, taking deep root, were cherished and invigorated by the national sentiment, so as to bear rich fruit for posterity. This was particularly the case with the institution at Alcalá. It soon became the subject of royal and private benefaction. Its founder bequeathed it, at his death, a clear revenue of fourteen thousand ducats. By the middle of the seventeenth century, this had increased to forty-two, and the colleges had multiplied from ten to thirty-five.

"The rising reputation of the new academy, which attracted students from every quarter of the Peninsula to its halls, threatened to eclipse the glories of the ancient seminary at Salamanca, and occasioned bitter jealousies between them. The field of letters, however, was wide enough for both, especially as the one was more immediately devoted to theological preparation, to the exclusion of civil jurisprudence, [447]
which formed a prominent branch of instruction at the other. In this state of things, their rivalry, far from being productive of mischief, might be regarded as salutary, by quickening literary ardour, too prone to languish without the spur of competition. Side by side, the sister Universities went forward, dividing the public patronage and estimation. As long as the good era of letters lasted in Spain, the academy of Ximenes, under the influence of its admirable discipline, maintained a reputation inferior to none other in the Peninsula, and continued to send forth its sons to occupy the most exalted posts in church and state, and shed the light of genius and science over their own and future ages."

[Original title page]

NOTE

ON

CARDINAL NEWMAN'S

PREACHING AND INFLUENCE

AT OXFORD

PRINTED BY THE ABERDEEN UNIVERSITY PRESS

FOR PRIVATE CIRCULATION ONLY

FOR PRIVATE CIRCULATION

NOTE

ON

CARDINAL NEWMAN'S PREACHING AND INFLUENCE AT OXFORD[1]

It is mentioned in the advertisement to the volume of Cardinal Newman's *Catholic University Reports*, etc., that an extract about him from Principal Shairp's *Studies in Poetry and Philosophy*, which was to have been included in its first pages, had been withdrawn. The withdrawal is a great loss to the book, because the extract gives a very vivid idea of what Newman was found to be in Oxford, during the later years of his residence in that University; and, could it have been inserted as was intended, it would, while showing the fitness of his being selected to lay the foundation of the new University in Ireland, have served to link his old University life with his new. For these reasons, and because the time is now all but past to hear tell of him by contemporaries who had known him at Oxford, the same extract is given here for those who will welcome it as a sketch drawn from life by one so esteemed as Principal Shairp; and which, moreover, has the testimony of trustworthy contemporaries as to its correctness and truth. One such testimony shall precede it; it shall be followed by another which adds various details in the history of his Oxford preaching, and bears out what is said by

---

[1] From its title page and independent pagination this Note was obviously originally intended to be a separate pamphlet and had already been printed as such when Neville changed his mind and decided to have it bound in with the rest of *My Campaign in Ireland, Part I.*

Two reasons might have led Neville to change his mind; the fittingness of complementing the Note on the University Church with this Note, that is, Dublin with Oxford; and his desire to draw the reader's attention to Newman's earlier influence at Oxford.

Principal Shairp. Both are by the late Lord Coleridge, Lord Chief Justice of England.[2]

Similar records by other contemporaries of name could be given; a
[4*] portion of one such shall be used here; it is that of a third layman, Sir Francis Doyle, Principal Shairp's immediate predecessor in the Chair of Poetry at Oxford. Additional extracts, being remarks on Newman's Oxford Sermons themselves, taken from another of the Principal's volumes, *Aspects of Poetry*, will close the Note.

From Lord Coleridge

Heath's Court, Ottery St Mary,
24*th September*, 1866

MY DEAR SHAIRP,

On my return here I brought with me your article on Keble, which I read and then handed to my father who read it also. It is capital—quite the best thing I have seen about Keble; and the introduction about J. H. N. is delightful. To me, at least, there is not a syllable too much, and it says (much better) what I have been saying all my life as to his influence and the effect of its withdrawal on the University.[3]

Ever affectionately yours,

J. D. COLERIDGE

From Principal Shairp's Studies in Poetry, etc.; *vid. Essay on Keble*

"It was a strange experience for a young man trained anywhere, much more for one born and bred in Scotland, and brought up a Presbyterian, to enter Oxford when the religious movement was at its height. He found himself all at once in the
[5*] midst of a system of teaching which unchurched himself and all whom he had hitherto known. In his simplicity he had believed that spiritual religion was a thing of the heart, and that neither

[2] It was Lord Coleridge, at the time a scholar at Balliol, who first induced Shairp to go to hear Newman preach. [WPN] John Duke Coleridge (1820–94) was a lawyer and Liberal politician. His wife Jane was an artist who painted a well-known portrait of Newman.

[3] *Vid.* Knight's *Shairp and His Friends*, p. 226. [WPN]

Episcopacy nor Presbytery availeth anything. But here were men—able, learned, devout-minded men—maintaining that outward rites and ceremonies were of the very essence, and that where these were not, there was no true Christianity. How could men, such as these were reported to be, really go back themselves and try to lead others back to what were but the beggarly elements? It was all very perplexing, not to say irritating. However, there might be something more behind, which a young man could not understand. So he would wait and see what he should see.

"Soon he came to know that the only portions of Oxford society unaffected by the new influence, were the two extremes. The older dons, that is, the heads of houses and the senior tutors, were unmoved by it, except to opposition. The whole younger half of the undergraduates generally took no part in it. But the great body that lay between these extremes, that is, most of the younger fellows of colleges, and most of the scholars and elder undergraduates, at least those of them who read or thought at all, were in some way or other busy with the new questions. When in time the newcomer began to know some of the men who sympathised with the movement, his first impression was of something constrained and reserved in their manners and deportment. High character and ability many of these were said to have; but to a chance observer, it seemed that, in so far as their system had moulded them, it had made them the opposite of [6*]
natural in their views of things, and in their whole mental attitude. You longed for some free breath of mountain air to sweep away the stifling atmosphere that was about you. This might come partly, no doubt, from the feeling with which you knew that these men must from their system regard you, and all who had the misfortune to be born outside of their sacred pale. Not that they ever expressed such views in your hearing. Good manners, as well as their habitual reserve, forbade this. But, though they did not say it, you knew quite well that they felt it. And if at any time the "young barbarian" put a direct question, or made a remark which went straight at these opinions, they would only look at him, astonished at his rudeness and profanity, and shrink into themselves.

"Now and then, however, it would happen that some adherent, or even leading man of the movement, more frank and outspoken than the rest, would deign to speak out his principles, and even to discuss them with undergraduates and controversial Scots. To him, urging the necessity of Apostolical Succession, and the sacerdotal view of the Sacraments, some young man might venture to reply: 'Well! if all you say be true, then I never can have lived among people who were strangers to all these things, which, you tell me, are essentials of Christianity. And I am quite sure that, if I have never known a Christian till now, I shall never know one.' The answer to this would probably be: 'There is much in what you say. No doubt high virtues, very like the Christian graces, are to be found outside of the Christian Church. But it is a
[7*] remarkable thing, those best acquainted with Church history tell me, that outside of the pale of the Church the saintly character is never found.' This *naïf* reply was not likely to have much weight with the young listener. It would have taken something stronger to make him break faith with all that was most sacred in his early recollections. Beautiful examples of Presbyterian piety had stamped impressions on his memory not to be effaced by sacerdotal theories or subtleties of the schools. And the Church system which began by disowning these examples placed a barrier to its acceptance at the very outset.

"But however unbelievable their theory, further acquaintance with the younger men of the new school, whether junior fellows or undergraduate scholars, disclosed many traits of character that could not but awaken respect or something more. If there was about many of them a constraint and reserve which seemed unnatural, there was also in many an unworldliness and self-denial, a purity of life and elevation of aim, in some a generosity of purpose and depth of devotion, not to be gainsaid. Could the movement which produced these qualities, or even attracted them to itself, be wholly false and bad? This movement, however, when at its height, extended its influence far beyond the circle of those who directly adopted its views. There was not, in Oxford at least, a reading man who was not more or less directly influenced by it. Only the very idle or the very frivolous were wholly proof against it. On all others it impressed a sobriety of conduct and a seriousness not usually found among large bodies of young men.

It raised the tone of average morality in Oxford to a level which [8*]
perhaps it had never before reached. You may call it over-wrought and too highly strung. Perhaps it was. It was better, however, for young men to be so, than to be doubters or cynics.

"If such was the general aspect of Oxford society at that time, where was the centre and soul from which so mighty a power emanated? It lay, and had for some years lain, mainly in one man—a man in many ways the most remarkable that England had seen during this century, perhaps the most remarkable whom the English Church has produced in any century,—John Henry Newman.

"The influence he had gained, apparently without setting himself to seek it, was something altogether unlike anything else in our time. A mysterious veneration had by degrees gathered round him, till now it was almost as though some Ambrose or Augustine of elder ages had re-appeared. He himself tells how one day, when he was an undergraduate, a friend with whom he was walking in the Oxford street cried out eagerly, 'There's Keble!' and with what awe he looked at him!

A few years, and the same took place with regard to himself. In Oriel Lane light-hearted undergraduates would drop their voices and whisper, 'There's Newman!' when, head thrust forward, and gaze fixed as though on some vision seen only by himself, with swift, noiseless step he glided by. Awe fell on them for a moment, almost as if it had been some apparition that had passed. For his inner circle of friends, many of them younger
men, he was said to have a quite romantic affection, which they [9*]
returned with the most ardent devotion and the intensest faith in him. But to the outer world he was a mystery. What were the qualities that inspired these feelings? There was of course learning and refinement, there was genius, not indeed of a philosopher, but of a subtle and original thinker, an unequalled edge of dialectic, and these all glorified by the imagination of a poet. Then there was the utter unworldliness, the setting at naught of all things which men most prize, the tamelessness of soul, which was ready to essay the impossible. Men felt that here was

> One of that small transfigured band
> Which the world cannot tame.

"It was this mysteriousness which, beyond all his gifts of head and heart, so strangely fascinated and overawed,—that something about him which made it impossible to reckon his course and take his bearings, that soul-hunger and quenchless yearning which nothing short of the eternal could satisfy. This deep and resolute ardour, this tenderness yet severity of soul, were no doubt an offence not to be forgiven by older men, especially by the wary and worldly-wise; but in these lay the very spell which drew to him the hearts of all the younger and the more enthusiastic. Such was the impression he had made in Oxford just before he relinquished his hold on it. And if at that time it seemed to persons at a distance extravagant and absurd, they may since have learnt that there was in him who was the object of this reverence enough to justify it.

"But it may be asked, What actions or definite results were
[10*] there to account for so deep and widespread a veneration? There were, no doubt, the numerous products of his prolific pen, his works, controversial, theological, religious. But none of these were so deep in learning as some of Dr Pusey's writings, nor so widely popular as *The Christian Year*; yet both Dr Pusey[4] and Mr Keble were at that time quite second in importance to Mr Newman. The centre from which his power went forth was the pulpit of St Mary's, with those wonderful afternoon sermons. Sunday after Sunday, month by month, year by year, they went on, each continuing and deepening the impression the last had made. As the afternoon service at St Mary's interfered with the dinner-hour of the colleges, most men preferred a warm dinner without Newman's sermon to a cold one with it, so the audience was not crowded—the large church little more than half filled. The service was very simple,—no pomp, no ritualism; for it was characteristic of the leading men of the movement that they left these things to the weaker brethren. Their thoughts, at all events, were set on great questions which touched the heart of unseen things. About the service, the most remarkable thing was the beauty, the silver intonation, of Mr Newman's voice, as he read

[4] Edward Pusey (1800–82) was a Fellow at Oriel College and later Professor of Hebrew at Christ Church. He became the leader of the Tractarians after Newman's conversion.

the Lessons. It seemed to bring new meaning out of the familiar words. Still lingers in memory the tone with which he read: *But Jerusalem which is from above is free, which is the mother of us all.* When he began to preach, a stranger was not likely to be much struck, especially if he had been accustomed to pulpit-oratory of the Boanerges sort. Here was no vehemence, no declamation, no show of elaborated argument, so that one who [11*]
came prepared to hear a 'great intellectual effort' was almost sure to go away disappointed. Indeed, I believe that if he had preached one of his St Mary's sermons before a Scotch town congregation, they would have thought the preacher a 'silly body'. The delivery had a peculiarity which it took a new hearer some time to get over. Each separate sentence, or at least each short paragraph, was spoken rapidly, but with great clearness of intonation; and then at its close there was a pause, lasting for nearly half a minute; then another rapidly but clearly spoken sentence, followed by another pause. It took some time to get over this, but, that once done, the wonderful charm began to dawn on you. The look and bearing of the preacher were as of one who dwelt apart, who, though he knew his age well, did not live in it. From the seclusion of study, and abstinence, and prayer, from habitual dwelling in the unseen, he seemed to come forth that one day of the week to speak to others of the things he had seen and known. Those who never heard him might fancy that his sermons would generally be about apostolical succession or rights of the Church, or against Dissenters. Nothing of the kind. You might hear him preach for weeks without an allusion to these things. What there was of High Church teaching was implied rather than enforced. The local, the temporary, and the modern were ennobled by the presence of the catholic truth belonging to all ages that pervaded the whole. His power showed itself chiefly in the new and unlooked-for way in which he touched into life old truths, moral or spiritual, which all Christians acknowledge, but most have ceased to feel—when he spoke of 'Unreal Words,' of the 'Individuality of the Soul,' of [12*]
'The Invisible World,' of a 'Particular Providence'; or again, of 'The Ventures of Faith,' 'Warfare the Condition of Victory,' 'The Cross of Christ the Measure of the World,' 'The Church a Home for the Lonely'. As he spoke, how the old truth became new! how it came home with a meaning never felt before! He laid his finger

how gently, yet how powerfully!—on some inner place in the hearer's heart, and told him things about himself he had never known till then. Subtlest truths, which it would have taken philosophers pages of circumlocution and big words to state, were dropt out by the way in a sentence or two of the most transparent Saxon. What delicacy of style, yet what calm power! how gentle, yet how strong! how simple, yet how suggestive! how homely, yet how refined! how penetrating, yet how tender-hearted! If now and then there was a forlorn undertone which at the time seemed inexplicable, if he spoke of 'many a sad secret which a man dare not tell lest he find no sympathy,' of 'secrets lying like cold ice upon the heart,' of 'some solitary incommunicable grief,' you might be perplexed at the drift of what he spoke, but you felt all the more drawn to the speaker. To call these sermons eloquent would be no word for them; high poems they rather were, as of an inspired singer, or the outpourings as of a prophet, rapt yet self-possessed. And the tone of voice in which they were spoken, once you grew accustomed to it, sounded like a fine strain of unearthly music. Through the stillness of that high Gothic building the words fell on the ear like the measured drippings of water in some
[13*] vast dim cave. After hearing these sermons you might come away still not believing the tenets peculiar to the High Church system; but you would be harder than most men, if you did not feel more than ever ashamed of coarseness, selfishness, worldliness, if you did not feel the things of faith brought closer to the soul.

"There was one occasion of a different kind, when he spoke from St Mary's pulpit for the last time, not as Parish minister, but as University preacher. It was the crisis of the movement. On the 2nd of February, 1843, the Feast of the Purification, all Oxford assembled to hear what Newman had to say, and St Mary's was crowded to the door. The subject he spoke of was 'the theory of Development in Christian Doctrine,' a subject which since then has become common property, but which at that time was new even to the ablest men in Oxford. For an hour and a half he drew out the argument, and perhaps the acutest there did not quite follow the entire line of thought, or felt wearied by the length of it, lightened though it was by some startling illustrations. Such was the famous 'Protestantism has at various times developed into Polygamy,' or the still more famous 'Scripture says the sun moves round the earth, Science that the earth moves, and the sun is comparatively at rest. How can we determine which of these opposite statements is true, till we know what motion is?' Few probably who heard it have forgotten the tone of voice with which he uttered the beautiful passage about music as the audible embodiment of some unknown reality behind, itself sweeping like a strain of splendid music out of the heart of a subtle argument. [14*]

. . . . . .

"This was preached in the winter of 1843, the last time he appeared in the University pulpit. His parochial sermons had by this time assumed an uneasy tone which perplexed his followers with fear of change. That summer solved their doubt. In the quiet chapel of Littlemore which he himself had built, when all Oxford was absent during the long vacation, he preached his last Anglican sermon to the country people and only a few friends, and poured forth that mournful and thrilling farewell to the Church of England. The sermon is entitled 'The Parting of Friends'. . . . Then followed the resignation of his parish, the retirement to Littlemore, the withdrawal even from the intercourse of his friends, the unloosing of all the ties that bound him to Oxford, the two years' pondering of the step he was about to take. And at last, when in 1845 he went away to the Church of Rome, he did it by himself, making himself as much as possible responsible only for his own act, and followed by but one or two young friends who would not be kept back. Those who witnessed these things, and knew that, if a large following had been his object, he might, by leaving the Church of England three years earlier, in the plenitude of his power, have taken almost all the flower of young Oxford with him, needed no *Apologia* to convince them of his honesty of purpose.

"On these things, looking over an interval of five-and-twenty years, how vividly comes back the remembrance of the aching [15*]
blank, the awful pause, which fell on Oxford when that voice had ceased, and we knew that we should hear it no more. It was as when, to one kneeling by night, in the silence of some vast cathedral, the great bell tolling solemnly overhead has suddenly gone still. To many, no doubt, the pause was not of long continuance. Soon they began to look this way and that for new teachers, and to rush vehemently to the opposite extremes of

thought. But there were those who could not so lightly forget. All the more these withdrew into themselves. On Sunday forenoons and evenings, in the retirement of their rooms, the printed words of those marvellous sermons would thrill them till they wept, 'abundant and most sweet tears'. Since then many voices of powerful teachers they may have heard, but none that ever penetrated the soul like his.

"Such was the impression made by that eventful time on impartial but not uninterested spectators—on those who by early education and conviction were kept aloof from the peculiar tenets of High Churchmen, but who could not but acknowledge the moral quickening which resulted from the movement, and the marvellous character of him who was the soul of it.

"Dr Newman himself tells us that all the while the true and primary author of that movement was out of sight. The Reverend John Keble was at a distance from Oxford, in his vicarage at Hursley, there living in his own life, and carrying out in his daily services and parish Ministry those truths which he had first brought forward, and Newman had carried out, in Oxford."

[16*] *The following is by the late Lord Coleridge from his "In Memoriam" of Shairp in Knight's volume*, PRINCIPAL SHAIRP AND HIS FRIENDS.

. . . .

"No notice of Shairp—no notice of any Oxford man of that period who took life seriously and gave himself the trouble to think—can omit that great penetrating influence, that waking up of the soul, that revelation of hopes, desires, motives, duties not of this world, not ending here, even if they had here their beginning, which came to us week by week from the pulpit of St Mary's, and day by day from the writings and the silent presence amongst us of that great man who still survives at Birmingham, in venerable age but with undimmed mental eye, and unabated force of genius, a Roman cardinal in title, but the light and guide of multitudes of grateful hearts outside his own communion and beyond the limits of these small islands. No man has described better than Shairp that wonderful preaching, no one has done fuller justice to the prose-poetry of Cardinal Newman. I can recollect the beginnings;

I followed the gradual, half-reluctant, and doubtful, yet at last most hearty and generous growth of his admiration. Cardinal Newman's was at that time the only really religious teaching to which undergraduates were subject. A lecture on the Thirty-nine Articles and a terminal address before the terminal Communion were supposed to supply them abundantly with any religious guiding they might need. The tutors, many of them, were not only good men, but I believe very good men; they only followed the [17*] traditions of the place. But the authorities, as in the case of Wesley so in the case of Newman, altogether objected to any one else doing what they did not do themselves. In the rougher days of Wesley they encouraged the pelting of him, as he went to church, with mud and pebbles. In our day other means were used; four tutors protested, six doctors suspended, Hebdomadal Boards censured, deans of colleges changed the dinner hour, so as to make the hearing of Newman's sermon and a dinner in Hall incompatible transactions. This seemed then—it seems now—miserably small. It failed, of course; such proceedings always fail. The influence so fought with naturally widened and strengthened. There was imparted to an attendance at St Mary's that slight flavour of insubordination which rendered such attendance attractive to many, to some at any rate, who might otherwise have stayed away. In 1839 the afternoon congregation at St Mary's was, for a small Oxford parish, undoubtedly large—probably two or three times the whole population of the parish; but by 1842 it had become as remarkable a congregation as I should think was ever gathered together to hear regularly a single preacher. There was scarcely a man of note in the University, old or young, who did not, during the last two or three years of Newman's incumbency, habitually attend the service and listen to the sermons. One Dean certainly, who had changed the time of his College dinner to prevent others going, constantly went himself; and the outward interest in the teaching was but one symptom of [18*] the deep and abiding influence which Cardinal Newman exercised then, and exercises now, over the thoughts and lives of many men who perhaps never saw him, who certainly never heard him. Of this Shairp was a very striking instance. He came under the wand of the enchanter, and never threw off, or wished to throw off, the spell; to the end of his days there was no one with whose writings he was more familiar, no one who exerted a more poetical influence over his thoughts, his feelings, his whole nature. I do not mean that he ever became in doctrine what is commonly called a High Churchman; Newman taught principles of life and action rather than dogmas, though no doubt he drew his principles from what he believed to be dogmatic truths; and so it has happened in a hundred instances, of which Shairp is one, that men who have been unable to follow the Cardinal to his dogmatic conclusions have been penetrated and animated by his religious principles, and have lived their lives and striven to do their duty because of those principles which he was God's instrument to teach them. His loyalty to Cardinal Newman ended only with his life; what kindled it in him and in others I cannot describe without danger of seeming to exaggerate. How it was appreciated I hope the world will learn from your book in the Cardinal's own words."

From the Reminiscences of Sir Francis Doyle, Bart.

"That great man's extraordinary genius drew all those within
[19*] his sphere, like a magnet, to attach themselves to him and his doctrines. Nay, before he became a Romanist, what we may call his mesmeric influence acted not only on his Tractarian adherents, but even in some degree on outsiders like myself. Whenever I was at Oxford, I used to go regularly on Sunday afternoons to listen to his sermon at St Mary's, and I never heard such preaching since. I do not know whether it is a mere fancy of mine, or whether those who knew him better will accept and endorse my belief, that one element of his wonderful power showed itself after this fashion. He always began as if he had determined to set forth his idea of the truth in the plainest and simplest language—language, as men say, 'intelligible to the meanest understanding'. But his ardent zeal and fine poetical imagination were not thus to be controlled. As I hung upon his words, it seemed to me as if I could trace behind his will, and pressing, so to speak, against it, a rush of thought and feelings which he kept struggling to hold back, but in the end they were generally too strong for him, and poured themselves out in a torrent of eloquence all the more impetuous

from their having been so long repressed. The effect of these outbursts was irresistible, and carried his hearers beyond themselves at once. Even when his efforts of self-restraint were more successful, those very efforts gave a life and colour to his style which riveted the attention of all within the reach of his voice . . ." (p. 145).

Passages taken from Principal Shairp's ASPECTS OF POETRY, *being Lectures delivered as Professor of Poetry at Oxford.* [20*]

FROM LECTURE II
CRITICISM AND CREATION

"If poetry be the highest, most impassioned thoughts conveyed in the most perfect melody of words, we have many prose writers who, when at their best, are truly poets. Every one will recall passages of Jeremy Taylor's writings, which are, in the truest sense, not oratory, but poetry. Again, of how many in our time is this true? You can all lay your finger on splendid descriptions of nature by Ruskin, which leave all sober prose behind, and flood the soul with imagery and music like the finest poetry.

"As the highest instance of all I would name some of Dr Newman's Oxford sermons. Many of these, instinct as they are with high spiritual thought, quivering with suppressed but piercing emotion, and clothed in words so simple, so transparent, that the very soul shines through them, suggest, as only great poems do, the heart's deepest secrets, and in the perfect rhythm and melody of their words, seem to evoke new powers from our native language . . ." (p. 60).

FROM LECTURE XV
PROSE POETS—NEWMAN

"We saw how that which lay in the centre of Carlyle's great literary power, was the force of a vigorous personality, a unique character, an indomitable will. Not less marked and strong is the personality of Cardinal Newman, but the two personalities passed [21*]
through very different experiences. In the one the rough ore was

presented to the world, just as it had come direct from mother earth, with all the clay and mud about it. The other underwent in youth the most searching processes, intellectual and social; met, in rivalry or in friendship, many men of the highest order, his own equals, and came forth from the ordeal seven times refined. But this training no way impaired his native strength or damped his ardour. Only it taught him to know what is due to the feelings and convictions of others, as well as what became his own self-respect. He did not consider it any part of veracity to speak out at all hazards, every impulse and prejudice, every like and dislike which he felt. That a thing is true was, in his view, 'no reason why it should be said, but why it should be done, acted on, made our own inwardly'.[5] And as the firm fibre of his nature remained the same, all the training and refining it went through made it only more sure in aim, and more effective in operation . . ." (p. 440).

Then after speaking of Newman's poems in the *Lyra Apostolica*, Principal Shairp says:—

"Such short poems as these showed, long before 'The Dream of Gerontius' appeared, that Cardinal Newman possessed the true poet's gift, and could speak the poet's language, had he cared to cultivate it. But he was called to another duty and passed on. To an age which was set, as this age is, on material prosperity, easy living and all that gratifies the flesh, he felt called to speak a
[22*] language long unheard; to insist on the reality of the things of faith, and the necessity of obedience; to urge on men the necessity to crush self, and obey; to press home a severer, more girt-up way of living; to throw himself into strenuous conflict with the darling prejudices of his countrymen. It was in his *Parochial Sermons*, beyond all his other works, that he spoke out the truths which were within him—spoke them out with all the fervour of a prophet and the severe beauty of a poet. Modern English literature has nowhere any language to compare with the style of these Sermons, so simple and transparent, yet so subtle withal; so strong, yet so tender; the grasp of a strong man's hand, combined with the trembling tenderness of a woman's heart, expressing in a

[5] 'Unreal words', *Parochial and Plain Sermons* v (1840; 1869), p. 45.

few monosyllables truths which would have cost other men a page of philosophic verbiage, laying the most gentle yet penetrating finger on the very core of things, reading to men their most secret thoughts better than they knew them themselves . . ." (p. 443).

"Their style [shows] the assured self-possession of the finished athlete . . . with disciplined moderation, and delicate self-restraint [he] shrinks instinctively from over-statement, but penetrates . . . to the core by words of sober truth and 'vivid exactness' . . ." (p. 444).

"Cardinal Newman's mind," he goes on to say, "dwelt much in the remote past; but the objects it there held converse with were of a different order from those which attracted the gaze of Carlyle. . . . He could deal, as his Lectures on the Turks prove, with heroes and conquerors, with the great men and the famous in the world's affairs. But the one object which attracted his eye in all the past [23*]
was the stone hewn out of the side of the mountain which should crush to pieces all the kingdoms of the earth. The kingdom of Christ 'coming to us from the very time of the apostles, spreading out into all lands, triumphing over a thousand revolutions, exhibiting an awful unity, glorying in a mysterious vitality, so majestic, so imperturbable, so bold, so saintly, so sublime, so beautiful!' This was the one object which filled his heart and imagination. This was the vision which he had ever in his eye. . . . This was to him no sentimental dream, cherished in the closet, but unfit to face the world. It was a reality which moulded his own character and his destiny, and determined the work he set himself to do on earth. He saw, as he believed, a religion prevalent all around, which was secular and mundane, soft, and self-indulgent, taking in that part of the gospel which pleases the flesh, but shrinking from its sterner discipline and higher aspirations. He made it the aim of his life to introduce some iron into its blood, to import into the religion of his day something of the zeal, and devotion, and self-denying sanctity, which were the notes of the early Faith. The vision which he beheld in the primitive ages he laboured to bring home and make practical in these modern times. . . . But the world is so set on the genial, not to say jovial, it so loves the padding of material civilisation in which it enwraps itself, that it resents any crossing of the natural man, and will

always listen greedily to those teachers—and they are many—who persuade it that the flesh ought to have its own way. A teacher so to its mind the world has not found in Cardinal Newman.

[24*] "It is not, however, our part to estimate the need or the value of the work he has done. But it is easy to see how well his rare and peculiar genius fitted him for doing it. If, on the one side, he had the imaginative devotion which clung to a past ideal, he had, on the other side, that penetrating insight into human nature, which made him well understand his own age and its tendencies. He was intimately acquainted with his own heart, and he so read the hearts of his fellow-men, that he seemed to know their inmost secrets. In his own words he could tell them what they knew about themselves, and what they did not know, till they were startled by the truth of his revelations. His knowledge of human nature, underived from books and philosophy, was intuitive, first hand, practical. In this region he belonged to the prescientific era. He took what he found within him, as the first of all knowledge, as the thing he was most absolutely certain of. The feelings, desires, aspirations, needs, which he felt in his own heart, the intimations of conscience, sense of sin, longing for deliverance, these were his closest knowledge, to accept, not to explain away, or to analyse into nothing. They were his original outfit, they fixed his standard of judgment; they furnished the key by which he was to read the riddle of life, and to interpret the world; they were the 'something within him, which was to harmonise and adjust' all that was obscure and discordant without him. The nostrums by which these primal truths are attempted to be explained away now-a-days, heredity, antecedent conditions, these had not come much into vogue in his youth. But we know well enough how he would have
[25*] dealt with them. What I feel and know intimately at first hand, that I must accept and use as the condition of all other knowledge; I am not to explain this away by uncertain theories or doubtful analyses; I cannot unclothe myself of myself, at the bidding of any philosophical theory, however plausible. This is what he would have said.

"The sermons are full of such heart-knowledge, such reading to men of their own hidden half-realised selves" (pp. 448–452).

"Observe here," he says, p. 458, in speaking of the Sermon *Warfare the Condition of Victory*, "one very rare gift which Cardinal Newman has; he can in the midst of his most solemn and sacred thoughts introduce the homeliest illustrations, the most familiar images, and they produce no jar—you feel that all is in keeping."

And p. 459:—

"I might go on for a day quoting from the *Parochial Sermons* alone, passages in which the poet as well as the preacher speaks."

But of his own quotations from Newman, the Principal says, p. 454:—

"There is one thing which makes a difficulty in quoting passages in Dr Newman's writings which are most touching and most truly poetical. They do not come in at all as *purpurei panni*—as pieces of ornamental patchwork in the midst of his religious teaching, introduced for rhetorical effect. They are interwoven with his religious thought, are indeed essential parts of it, so that you cannot isolate without destroying them. And to quote here for the purpose of literary illustration, what were meant [26*]
for a more earnest purpose, would seem to be out of place if not irreverent. But there are touching passages of another kind, which are characteristic of Dr Newman's writings and give them a peculiar charm. They are those which yield momentary glimpses of a very tender heart that has a burden of its own, unrevealed to man. Nothing could be more alien to Dr Newman's whole nature, than to withdraw the veil, and indulge in those exhibitions of himself, which are now-a-days so common and so offensive. It is but a mere indirect hint he gives—a few indirect words, dropped as it were unawares, which many might read without notice, but which, rightly understood, seem breathed from some very inward experience. It is, as I have heard it described, as though he suddenly opened a book, and gave you a glimpse for a moment of wonderful secrets, and then as quickly closed it. But the glance you have had, the words you have caught, haunt you ever after with an interest in him who uttered them, which is indescribable.

The words, though in prose, become, what all high poetry is said to be, at once a revelation and a veil" (p. 254).

Two of the passages from the many which Principal Shairp has quoted in these Lectures shall be given.

> 1. Where Newman speaks of St John as having out-lived all his friends and having had to experience the dreariness of being solitary.
>
> "St John had to live in his own thoughts, without familiar friend, with those only about him who belonged to a younger generation. Of him were demanded by his gracious Lord, as pledge of his faith, all his eye loved and his heart held
> [27*] converse with. He was as a man moving his goods into a far country, who at intervals and by portions sends them before him, till his present abode is well-nigh unfurnished" (p. 258).[6]
>
> 2. Where Newman speaks of what is to be the ultimate end of the Christian life.
>
> "All God's providences, all God's dealings with us, all His judgments, mercies, warnings, deliverances, tend to peace and repose as their ultimate issue. All our troubles and pleasures here, all our anxieties, fears, doubts, difficulties, hopes, encouragements, afflictions, losses, attainments, tend one way. After Christmas, Easter, and Whitsuntide, comes Trinity Sunday, and the weeks that follow; and in like manner, after our soul's anxious travail, after the birth of the Spirit, after trial and temptation, after sorrow and pain, after daily dyings to the world, after daily risings unto holiness, at length comes that 'rest which remaineth unto the people of God'. After the fever of life, after wearinesses and sicknesses, fightings and despondings, languor and fretfulness, struggling and failing, struggling and succeeding, after all the changes and chances of this troubled and unhealthy state, at length comes death, at

---

[6] 'Ventures of faith', *Parochial and Plain sermons* iv (1839; 1869), p. 305.

length the White Throne of God, at length the Beatific Vision. After restlessness comes rest, peace, joy; our eternal portion, if we be worthy" (p. 459).[7]

"I know not," Principal Shairp says, in concluding his Lecture, "how this and other passages I have quoted, may strike those to whom they have not been long familiar. To me it seems, they [28*] have a sweetness and inner melody, which few other words have. They fall upon the heart like dew, and soothe it, as only the most exquisite music can. It may be that to the few who can still recall the tone of the voice which first uttered them, remembrance lends them a charm, which those cannot feel who only read them. These sermons were the first utterance of new thoughts in a new language, which have long since passed into the deeper heart of England. The presence and personality of the speaker, the clear pathetic tones of his voice, can only live in the memory of those who heard him in St Mary's, forty years ago."[8] But the thoughts, and the style in which they are conveyed, are so perfect that they preserve for future generations more of the man who spoke them than most discourses can. It is hardly too much to say that they have elevated the thought and purified the style of every able Oxford man who has written since, even of those who had least sympathy with the sentiments they express. But they, whose good fortune it was to hear them when they were first delivered, know that nothing they have heard in the long interval can compare with the pensive grace, the thrilling pathos of the sounds, as they then fell fresh from the lips of the great teacher" (pp. 459–460).

It might be wished that the account of Cardinal Newman as a preacher at Oxford were carried on into later times; but, as that would be going beyond what was originally intended, it is thought better to refrain from attempting it. WM. P. NEVILLE.

---

[7] 'Peace in Believing', *Parochial and Plain sermons* vi (1842; 1869), p. 369.

[8] The Lectures from which these passages are taken were delivered in the four years previous to September, 1881 (see Preface to the *Aspects of Poetry*). [WPN]

INDEX

The page numbers given below are those used for this critical edition.

The connection of individuals to the Catholic University is indicated in bold italics: adviser, catechist, chaplain, co-founder, committee member, dean (of collegiate house), examiner, financial auditor, professor (or lecturer), rector, secretary, student, tutor, vice-rector.

CPSIA information can be obtained
at www.ICGtesting.com
Printed in the USA
LVHW081626260821
696190LV00010B/130/J